Progress in Psychological Science around the World

Volume 1: Neural, Cognitive and Developmental Issues

Progress in Psychological Science around the World Volumes 1 and 2 present the main contributions from the 28th International Congress of Psychology, held in Beijing in 2004. These expert contributions include the Nobel Laureate presentation, the Presidential address, and the Keynote and State-of-the-Art lectures. They are written by international leaders in psychology from 25 countries and regions around the world. The authors present a variety of approaches and perspectives that reflect cutting-edge advances in psychological science.

This first volume addresses neural, cognitive, and developmental issues in contemporary psychology. It includes chapters on learning, memory, and motivation, cognitive neuroscience, and attention, emotion, and language, and covers life-span developmental psychology. Volume 2 goes on to discuss social and applied issues in modern psychology.

Progress in Psychological Science around the World, with its broad coverage of psychological research and practice, and its highly select group of world-renowned authors, will be invaluable for researchers, professionals, teachers, and students in the field of psychology.

Qicheng Jing is Professor of Psychology at the Institute of Psychology, Chinese Academy of Sciences.

Mark R. Rosenzweig is Professor of Graduate Studies at the Department of Psychology, University of California, Berkeley.

Géry d'Ydewalle is Director of the Laboratory of Experimental Psychology, University of Leuven.

Houcan Zhang is Professor of Psychology at the School of Psychology, Beijing Normal University.

Hsuan-Chih Chen is Professor of Psychology at the Department of Psychology, Chinese University of Hong Kong.

Kan Zhang is Professor of Psychology at the Institute of Psychology, Chinese Academy of Sciences.

Progress in Psychological Science around the World

Volume 1: Neural, Cognitive and Developmental Issues

Congress Proceedings: XVIII International Congress of Psychology, Beijing, 2004

edited by
Qicheng Jing, Mark R. Rosenzweig, Géry d'Ydewalle, Houcan Zhang, Hsuan-Chih Chen, and Kan Zhang

Psychology Press
Taylor & Francis Group
HOVE AND NEW YORK

First published 2006 by Psychology Press
27 Church Road, Hove, East Sussex, BN3 2FA

Simultaneously published in the USA and Canada
by Psychology Press
711 Third Avenue, New York NY 10017

First issued in paperback 2015

Psychology Press is an imprint of the Taylor & Francis Group, an informa business

Typeset in Times by
RefineCatch Limited, Bungay, Suffolk

Cover design by Jim Wilkie

British Library Cataloguing in Publication Data
A catalogue record for this book is available from the British Library

Library of Congress Cataloging-in-Publication Data
A catalogue record has been requested

ISBN 13: 978-1-138-88331-4 (pbk)
ISBN 13: 978-1-8416-9961-5 (hbk)

Contents

Contributors to Volume 1

Talis Bachmann, Institute of Law and Department of Psychology, University of Tartu, Kaarli Puiestee 3, Tallinn 10119, Estonia

Lars Bäckman, Aging Research Center, Box 6401, S-113 82 Stockholm, Sweden

Claus Bundesen, Center for Visual Cognition, Department of Psychology, University of Copenhagen, Njalsgade 90, DK-2300 Copenhagen S, Denmark

Hsuan-Chih Chen, Department of Psychology, The Chinese University of Hong Kong, Shatin, N.T., Hong Kong, China

Axel Cleeremans, Cognitive Science Research Unit, Université Libre de Bruxelles CP 191, Avenue F.-D. Roosevelt, 50, 1050 Bruxelles, Belgium

Michael C. Corballis, Department of Psychology, University of Auckland, Private Bag 92019, Auckland 1, New Zealand

Paul De Boeck, Department of Psychology, K.U. Leuven, Tiensestraat 102, B-3000 Leuven, Belgium

Cindy M. de Frias, Department of Psychology, Stockholm University, SE-10691 Stockholm, Sweden

Michel Denis, LIMSI-CNRS, Université de Paris-Sud, BP 133, 91403 Orsay Cedex, France

Michael Domjan, Department of Psychology, University of Texas at Austin, 1 University Place A8000, Austin, TX 78712, USA

Lars Farde, Department of Clinical Neuroscience, Section of Psychiatry, Karolinska Institute, Stockholm, Sweden

Charles R. Gallistel, Rutgers Center for Cognitive Science, Rutgers University, 152 Frelinghuysen Rd, Piscataway, NJ 08854–8020, USA

Giorgio Ganis, Harvard University, 830 William James Hall, 33 Kirkland Street, Cambridge, MA 02138, USA

Peter M. Gollwitzer, Psychology Department, New York University, New York, NY 10003, USA

Thomas Habekost, Center for Visual Cognition, Department of Psychology, University of Copenhagen, Njalsgade 90, DK-2300 Copenhagen S, Denmark

Glyn W. Humphreys, Behavioural Brain Sciences, School of Psychology, University of Birmingham, Birmingham B15 2TT, UK

Masako Jitsumori, Department of Cognitive and Information Sciences, Faculty of Letters, Chiba University, 1–33 Yayoi-cho, Inage-ku, Chiba 263–8522, Japan

Daniel Kahneman, Department of Psychology, Princeton University, Princeton, NJ 08544–1010, USA

Frank C. Keil, Department of Psychology, Yale University, 2 Hillhouse Avenue, New Haven, CT 06520, USA

Stephen M. Kosslyn, Harvard University, 830 William James Hall, 33 Kirkland Street, Cambridge, MA 02138, USA

Patrick Lemaire, LPC-CNRS & Université de Provence, 3 Place Victor Hugo, 13331 Marseille, France

Eric D. Leshikar, 405 Mathews St, Beckman Institute, The University of Illinois at Urbana-Champaign, Urbana, IL 61801, USA

K. C. Liang, Department of Psychology, National Taiwan University, 1 Roosevelt Road, Sect. 4, Taipei, Taiwan 106, China

Hans J. Markowitsch, Physiological Psychology, University of Bielefeld, P.O. Box 10 01 31, 33501 Bielefeld, Germany

Wolfgang H. R. Miltner, Friedrich-Schiller-Universität, Institut für Psychologie, Am Steiger 3/1, D-07743 Jena, Germany

Lars-Göran Nilsson, Department of Psychology, Stockholm University, SE-10691 Stockholm, Sweden

Lars Nyberg, Department of Psychology, Umeå University, S-901 87 Umeå, Sweden

Arne Öhman, Section of Psychology, Karolinska Institute and Hospital, SE 171 76 Stockholm, Sweden

Denise C. Park, 405 Mathews St, Beckman Institute, The University of Illinois at Urbana-Champaign, Urbana, IL 61801, USA

Jerker Rönnberg, Department of Behavioural Sciences, Linköping University, S-581 83 Linköping, Sweden

Tim Shallice, Institute of Cognitive Neuroscience, University College London, Alexandra House, 17 Queen Square, London, UK

Rainer K. Silbereisen, Institute of Psychology, Department of Developmental Psychology, Friedrich-Schiller-Universität Jena, Am Steiger 3/1, D-07743 Jena, Germany

Dirk Smits, K.U. Leuven, Belgium

Thomas Straube, Department of Biological and Clinical Psychology, Friedrich-Schiller University, Jena, Germany

Arlette Streri, Institut de Psychologie, Université René Descartes, 71 Avenue Edouard Vaillant, 92774 Boulogne-Billancourt Cedex, Paris, France

William L. Thompson, Harvard University, 830 William James Hall, 33 Kirkland Street, Cambridge, MA 02138, USA

Anne Treisman, Psychology Department, Princeton University, Princeton, NJ 08544–1010, USA

Thomas Weiss, Department of Biological and Clinical Psychology, Friedrich-Schiller University, Jena, Germany

Henry M. Wellman, Centre for Human Growth & Development, University of Michigan, 300 North Ingalls, Ann Arbor, MI 48109, USA

Editors

Hsuan-Chih Chen, Department of Psychology, Chinese University of Hong Kong, Shatin, N.T., Hong Kong (China)

Géry d'Ydewalle, Department of Psychology, University of Leuven, B-3000 Leuven, Belgium

Qicheng Jing, Institute of Psychology, Chinese Academy of Sciences, 10A Datun Road, Beijing 100101, China

Mark R. Rosenzweig, Department of Psychology, 3210 Tolman Hall, University of California, Berkeley, CA 94720–1650, USA

Houcan Zhang, School of Psychology, Beijing Normal University, Beijing 100875, China

Kan Zhang, Institute of Psychology, Chinese Academy of Sciences, 10A Datun Road, Beijing 100101, China

NOTE

On the opening page of Chapters 6, 16, 19, 20, 25, and 26 only the first-named author is pictured.

Committees

Executive Committee

Qicheng Jing (President), Kan Zhang (Secretary-General), Houcan Zhang (IUPsyS Vice-President), Géry d'Ydewalle (IUPsyS Liaison), Hsuan-Chih Chen, Yongming Chen, Chongde Lin, Zhongxian Lin, Deli Shen, Su Wang, Yufang Yang, Yutai Zhang

Scientific Committee

Yufang Yang (Chair), Yanjie Su (Deputy Chair), Weimin Mou (Deputy Chair), Jing Chen, Jinhong Ding, Su Li, Ye Liu, Binwu Qiu, Jiannong Shi, Yuming Xuan, Jianxin Zhang

Organising Committee

Kan Zhang (Chair), Xiaolan Fu (Deputy Chair), Hua Shu (Deputy Chair), Buxin Han (Deputy Secretary-General, EC), Xianghong Sun, Xiaomin Sun, Lili Wang, Shaoyuan Wu, Qingfang Zhang, Zhen Zhang, Liqi Zhu

International Advisory Committee

Kurt Pawlik (Chair), John Adair, Ruben Ardila, Hiroshi Azuma, A. V. Brushlinsky, Saths Cooper, Fergus Craik, Michel Denis, Raymond D. Fowler, Cigdem Kagitçibasi, Daniel Kahneman, Kevin McConkey, Jitendra Mohan, Elizabeth Nair, Lars-Göran Nilsson, Jose Prieto, Mark R. Rosenzweig, Herbert A. Simon, Harold W. Stevenson, Jan Strelau, Berhard Wilpert

IUPsyS Executive Committee (2000–2004)

Michel Denis (President), Géry d'Ydewalle (Past-President), Juan José Sanchez Sosa (Vice-President), Houcan Zhang (Vice-President), Michel Sabourin (Treasurer), Pierre Ritchie (Secretary-General), Merry Bullock (Deputy Secretary-General), John Adair, Ruben Ardila, Saths Cooper, Hiroshi Imada, Cigdem Kagitçibasi, Ingrid Lunt, Elizabeth Nair, Bruce Overmier, Ype Poortinga, Rainer Silbereisen

Preface

The two-volume *Progress in Psychological Science around the World, Proceedings of the 28th International Congress of Psychology* is a collection of invited papers presented at the Congress which was held in Beijing, 8–13 August 2004.

The first International Congress of Psychology was held in 1889 in Paris. Its closing banquet took place on the Eiffel Tower, which had been completed and inaugurated earlier that year. This was just 10 years after the founding of the first laboratory of psychology by Wilhelm Wundt. During the ensuing 115 years, International Congresses have taken place on four continents of the world. Eventually in 2004 the 28th International Congress of Psychology was held in Beijing, China, the first International Congress of Psychology held in an Asian developing country.

China is a country possessing both traditional cultural heritages and modern achievements. Beijing, which was the ancient capital of China through several dynasties, is now the capital of the People's Republic of China. It is a thriving center for political, scientific, and commercial endeavors, a place of global confluence and exchanges. Beijing is especially noted for its historical sites, such as the Great Wall, the Forbidden City, and the Temple of Heaven. The rich historical legacy of China reveals a long history of social changes and human interactions, providing a cultural environment especially suited for exchanges in the science of human behavior – psychology.

The Beijing Congress opened on the evening of 8 August 2004. At the opening ceremony, a welcome speech was made by the President of the Chinese Academy of Sciences, Vice-Chairman, National People's Congress of China, Professor Yongxiang Lu, followed by speeches by IUPsyS President Michel Denis and Congress President Qicheng Jing. It was highlighted by a Nobel Laureate address entitled "A perspective on cognitive illusions" by Dr Daniel Kahneman. Dr Kahneman was awarded the Nobel Prize in 2002. The opening addresses were followed by a Chinese acrobatic performance, a thrilling experience for all the participants. The Congress closed on the evening of 13 August. At the closing ceremony the organization of the next congress was handed to the German organizers, who will be hosting the 29th International Congress of Psychology in Berlin in 2008. It will be the fourth time that the International Congress has been held in Germany.

In addition to the Nobel Laureate presentation by Dr Daniel Kahneman and the Presidential address by Dr Michel Denis, the scientific programme of the Congress consisted of 32 Keynote and 35 State-of-the-Art addresses, 237 invited symposia, 432 thematic oral sessions, and 15 poster sessions. The program provided a current overview of the multifaceted nature of the science of psychology; highly distinguished scientists presented updated accounts of the various fields of research across 25 major areas in psychology. Altogether 5598 papers were presented at the Congress. The high quality of the scientific program can be attested by the often full house attendance in the meeting rooms; this happened even at the final sessions just before the closing of the Congress. The Congress in cooperation with IUPsyS organized nine workshops, the Young Psychologists Program and Advanced Research and Training Seminars. Other international organizations of psychology sponsored meetings of various kinds. The Beijing Congress had a total attendance of 6261 delegates from 78 countries, including countries and regions from which psychologists rarely participate in international congresses, such as Iran, Vietnam and Macau. This Congress was the largest both in attendance and in scope in the history of International Congresses of Psychology. An impressive scene at the Congress was the 200 Chinese psychology students, in yellow shirts with the Congress logo, who contributed excellent service during the meetings.

The two Proceedings volumes include the Nobel Laureate presentation, the Presidential address, the Keynote and the State-of-the-Art addresses of the Congress. Considering that the selection of chapters represents the current status of the accumulated knowledge from psychological research around the world, we felt it appropriate to give the volumes a common title: *Progress in Psychological Science around the World.* Altogether 69 invited speakers presented papers at the Congress; however, 11 speakers, for various reasons, were unable to provide manuscripts. Thus the Proceedings include 58 presentations. Care has been taken to divide the contributions into approximately equal-sized volumes: Volume I, Neural, Cognitive and Developmental Issues, comprising four subsections with 30 chapters; Volume II, Social and Applied Issues, comprising four subsections with 28 chapters. We have also tried for the first time to publish photographs of the authors together with their papers in the Proceedings. We appreciate the authors' cooperation with this request.

In preparation of the Congress, Dr Raymond Fowler was invited to participate in a Scientific Committee meeting in Beijing in January 2003 to discuss the nomination of invited speakers and the planning of the scientific program of the Congress. His experience was important to the formulation of the final scientific program. The manuscripts submitted to be published in the Proceedings were reviewed by the editors and received positive support from the authors. However, due to the large number of papers and expertise required in so many fields of psychology, the following colleagues were also invited to participate in the reviewing process: Drs Winton Au,

John Berry, Him Cheung, Chi-Yue Chiu, Fuxi Fang, Kwok Leung, Patrick Leung, and Xuchu Weng. Their hard work, along with the close cooperation of the authors, brought the editorial work of the Proceedings to a conclusion. We greatly appreciate their support.

We would like to express our sincere thanks to the editorial staff, Drs Guomei Zhou, Yuhao Sun, and Ye Liu who provided help in the earlier phase of the collection of the manuscripts. Particularly, we are indebted to Miss Hang Zhang; her skillful secretarial assistance and untiring dedication were indispensable to the production of the two volumes. Finally, we would like to express our gratitude to the staff of Psychology Press, who organized and oversaw the publication of the Proceedings, particularly to Managing Editor Ms Imogen Burch, and Senior Production Editor Ms Kathryn Russel, and to Ms Jenny Millington and Dr Lewis Derrick for copy-editing the two volumes. Their experience has greatly facilitated the completion of the Proceedings.

Qicheng Jing, Mark R. Rosenzweig,
Géry d'Ydewalle, Houcan Zhang,
Hsuan-Chih Chen, Kan Zhang (*Editors*)

1 A perspective on judgment and choice: Mapping bounded rationality

Daniel Kahneman
Nobel Laureate presentation, 28th International Congress of Psychology, Beijing, China, 8–13 August 2004

The work cited by the Nobel committee was done jointly with the late Amos Tversky (1937–1996) during a long and unusually close collaboration. Together, we explored a territory that Herbert A. Simon had defined and named – the psychology of bounded rationality (Simon, 1955, 1979). This article presents a current perspective on the three major topics of our joint work: heuristics of judgment, risky choice, and framing effects. In all three domains, we studied intuitions – thoughts and preferences that come to mind quickly and without much reflection. I review the older research and some recent developments in light of two ideas that have become central to social-cognitive psychology in the intervening decades: the notion that thoughts differ in accessibility – some come to mind much more easily than others – and the distinction between intuitive and deliberate thought processes.

The first section, Intuition and accessibility, distinguishes two generic modes of cognitive function: an intuitive mode in which judgments and decisions are made automatically and rapidly and a controlled mode, which is deliberate and slower. The section goes on to describe the factors that determine the relative accessibility of different judgments and responses. The second section, Framing effects, explains framing effects in terms of differential salience and accessibility. The third section, Changes or states: Prospect theory, relates prospect theory to the general proposition that changes and differences are more accessible than absolute values. The fourth section, Attribute substitution: A model of judgment by heuristic, presents an attribute substitution model of heuristic judgment. The fifth section, Prototype heuristics, describes that particular family of heuristics. A concluding section follows.

Note: Chapter 1 is reprinted from *American Psychologist*, *58*, Kahneman (2003). 'A Perspective on Judgment and Choice: Mapping Bounded Rationality.' pp. 697–720.

Intuition and accessibility

From its earliest days, the research that Tversky and I conducted was guided by the idea that intuitive judgments occupy a position – perhaps corresponding to evolutionary history – between the automatic operations of perception and the deliberate operations of reasoning. Our first joint article examined systematic errors in the casual statistical judgments of statistically sophisticated researchers (Tversky & Kahneman, 1971). Remarkably, the intuitive judgments of these experts did not conform to statistical principles with which they were thoroughly familiar. In particular, their intuitive statistical inferences and their estimates of statistical power showed a striking lack of sensitivity to the effects of sample size. We were impressed by the persistence of discrepancies between statistical intuition and statistical knowledge, which we observed both in ourselves and in our colleagues. We were also impressed by the fact that significant research decisions, such as the choice of sample size for an experiment, are routinely guided by the flawed intuitions of people who know better. In the terminology that became accepted much later, we held a two-system view, which distinguished intuition from reasoning. Our research focused on errors of intuition, which we studied both for their intrinsic interest and for their value as diagnostic indicators of cognitive mechanisms.

The two-system view

The distinction between intuition and reasoning has been a topic of considerable interest in the intervening decades (among many others, see Epstein, 1994; Hammond, 2000; Jacoby, 1991, 1996; and numerous models collected by Chaiken & Trope, 1999; for comprehensive reviews of intuition, see Hogarth, 2001; Myers, 2002). In particular, the differences between the two modes of thought have been invoked in attempts to organize seemingly contradictory results in studies of judgment under uncertainty (Kahneman & Frederick, 2002; Sloman, 1996, 2002; Stanovich, 1999; Stanovich & West, 2002). There is considerable agreement on the characteristics that distinguish the two types of cognitive processes, which Stanovich and West (2000) labeled *System 1* and *System 2*. The scheme shown in Figure 1.1 summarizes these characteristics: The operations of System 1 are typically fast, automatic, effortless, associative, implicit (not available to introspection), and often emotionally charged; they are also governed by habit and are therefore difficult to control or modify. The operations of System 2 are slower, serial, effortful, more likely to be consciously monitored and deliberately controlled; they are also relatively flexible and potentially rule governed. The effect of concurrent cognitive tasks provides the most useful indication of whether a given mental process belongs to System 1 or System 2. Because the overall capacity for mental effort is limited, effortful processes tend to disrupt each other, whereas effortless processes neither cause nor suffer much interference when combined with other tasks (Kahneman, 1973; Pashler, 1998).

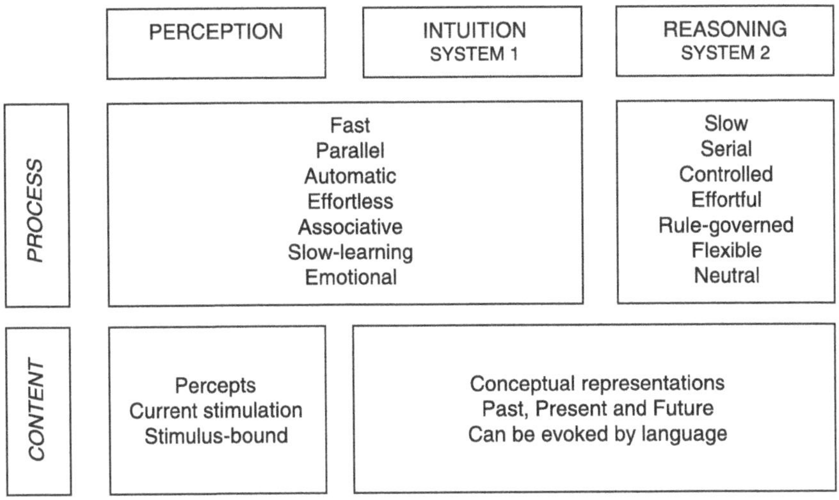

Figure 1.1 Process and content in two cognitive systems.

As indicated in Figure 1.1, the operating characteristics of System 1 are similar to thc fcatures of perceptual processes. On the other hand, as Figure 1.1 also shows, the operations of System 1, like those of System 2, are not restricted to the processing of current stimulation. Intuitive judgments deal with concepts as well as with percepts and can be evoked by language. In the model that is presented here, the perceptual system and the intuitive operations of System 1 generate *impressions* of the attributes of objects of perception and thought. These impressions are neither voluntary nor verbally explicit. In contrast, *judgments* are always intentional and explicit even when they are not overtly expressed. Thus, System 2 is involved in all judgments, whether they originate in impressions or in deliberate reasoning. The label *intuitive* is applied to judgments that directly reflect impressions – they are not modified by System 2.

As in several other dual-process models, one of the functions of System 2 is to monitor the quality of both mental operations and overt behavior (Gilbert, 2002; Stanovich & West, 2002). As expected for an effortful operation, the self-monitoring function is susceptible to dual-task interference. People who are occupied by a demanding mental activity (e.g., attempting to hold in mind several digits) are more likely to respond to another task by blurting out whatever comes to mind (Gilbert, 1989). The anthropomorphic phrase "System 2 monitors the activities of System 1" is used here as shorthand for a hypothesis about what would happen if the operations of System 2 were disrupted.

Kahneman and Frederick (2002) suggested that the monitoring is normally quite lax and allows many intuitive judgments to be expressed, including some that are erroneous. Shane Frederick (personal communication, April 29,

2003) has used simple puzzles to study cognitive self-monitoring, as in the following example: "A bat and a ball cost $1.10 in total. The bat costs $1 more than the ball. How much does the ball cost?" Almost everyone reports an initial tendency to answer "10 cents" because the sum $1.10 separates naturally into $1 and 10 cents and because 10 cents is about the right magnitude. Frederick found that many intelligent people yield to this immediate impulse: Fifty percent (47/93) of Princeton students and 56% (164/293) of students at the University of Michigan gave the wrong answer. Clearly, these respondents offered a response without checking it. The surprisingly high rate of errors in this easy problem illustrates how lightly the output of System 1 is monitored by System 2: People are not accustomed to thinking hard and are often content to trust a plausible judgment that quickly comes to mind. Remarkably, errors in this puzzle and in others of the same type were significant predictors of intolerance of delay and also of cheating behavior.

In the examples discussed so far, intuition was associated with poor performance, but intuitive thinking can also be powerful and accurate. High skill is acquired by prolonged practice, and the performance of skills is rapid and effortless. The proverbial master chess player who walks past a game and declares, "White mates in three," without slowing is performing intuitively (Simon & Chase, 1973), as is the experienced nurse who detects subtle signs of impending heart failure (Gawande, 2002; Klein, 1998). Klein (2003, chapter 4) has argued that skilled decision makers often do better when they trust their intuitions than when they engage in detailed analysis. In the same vein, Wilson and Schooler (1991) described an experiment in which participants who chose a poster for their own use were happier with it if their choice had been made intuitively than if it had been made analytically.

The accessibility dimension

A core property of many intuitive thoughts is that under appropriate circumstances, they come to mind spontaneously and effortlessly, like percepts. To understand intuition, then, one must understand why some thoughts come to mind more easily than others, why some ideas arise effortlessly and others demand work. The central concept of the present analysis of intuitive judgments and preferences is *accessibility* – the ease (or effort) with which particular mental contents come to mind. The accessibility of a thought is determined jointly by the characteristics of the cognitive mechanisms that produce it and by the characteristics of the stimuli and events that evoke it.

The question of why particular ideas come to mind at particular times has a long history in psychology. Indeed, this was the central question that the British empiricists sought to answer with laws of association. The behaviorists similarly viewed the explanation of "habit strength" or "response strength" as the main task of psychological theory, to be solved by a formulation integrating multiple determinants in the history and in the current circumstances of the organism. During the half century of the cognitive revolution, the measurement of reaction time became widely used as a general-purpose measure of response strength, and major advances were made in the study of why thoughts become accessible – notably, the distinctions between automatic and controlled processes and between implicit and explicit measures of memory. But no general concept was adopted, and research on the problem remained fragmented in multiple paradigms, variously focused on automaticity, Stroop interference, involuntary and voluntary attention, and priming.

Because the study of intuition requires a common concept, I adopt the term *accessibility*, which was proposed in the context of memory research (Tulving & Pearlstone, 1966) and of social cognition (Higgins, 1996) and is applied here more broadly than it was by these authors. In the present usage, the different aspects and elements of a situation, the different objects in a scene, and the different attributes of an object – all can be more or less accessible. Moreover, the determinants of accessibility subsume the notions of stimulus salience, selective attention, specific training, associative activation, and priming.

For an illustration of differential accessibility, consider Figures 1.2A and 1.2B. As one looks at the object in Figure 1.2A, one has immediate impressions of the height of the tower, the area of the top, and perhaps the volume of the tower. Translating these impressions into units of height or volume requires a deliberate operation, but the impressions themselves are highly accessible. For other attributes, no perceptual impression exists. For example, the total area that the blocks would cover if the tower were dismantled is not perceptually accessible, though it can be estimated by a deliberate procedure, such as multiplying the area of the side of a block by the number

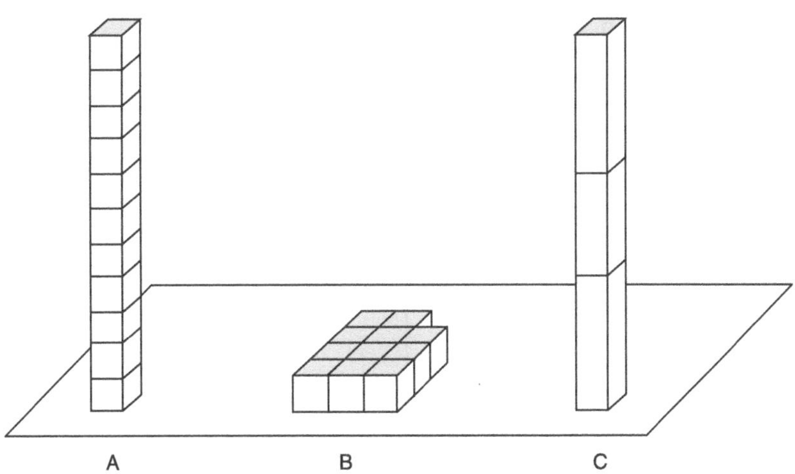

Figure 1.2 The selective accessibility of natural assessments.

of blocks. Of course, the situation is reversed with Figure 1.2B. Now, the blocks are laid out, and an impression of total area is immediately accessible, but the height of the tower that could be constructed with these blocks is not.

Some relational properties are accessible. Thus, it is obvious at a glance that Figures 1.2A and 1.2C are different but also that they are more similar to each other than either is to Figure 1.2B. Some statistical properties of ensembles are accessible, whereas others are not. For an example, consider the question "What is the average length of the lines in Figure 1.3?" This question is easily answered. When a set of objects of the same general kind is presented to an observer – whether simultaneously or successively – a representation of the set is computed automatically; this representation includes accurate impressions of the average (Ariely, 2001; Chong & Treisman, 2003). The representation of the prototype is highly accessible, and it has the character of a percept: One forms an impression of the typical line without choosing to do so. The only role for System 2 in this task is to map this impression of typical length onto the appropriate scale. In contrast, the answer to the question "What is the total length of the lines in the display?" does not come to mind without considerable effort.

These perceptual examples serve to establish the dimension of accessibility. At one end of this dimension are found operations that have the characteristics of perception and of the intuitive System 1: They are rapid, automatic, and effortless. At the other end are slow, serial, and effortful operations that people need a special reason to undertake. Accessibility is a continuum, not a dichotomy, and some effortful operations demand more effort than others. The acquisition of skill selectively increases the accessibility of useful responses and of productive ways to organize information. The master chess player does not see the same board as the novice, and the skill of visualizing the tower that could be built from an array of blocks could surely be improved by prolonged practice.

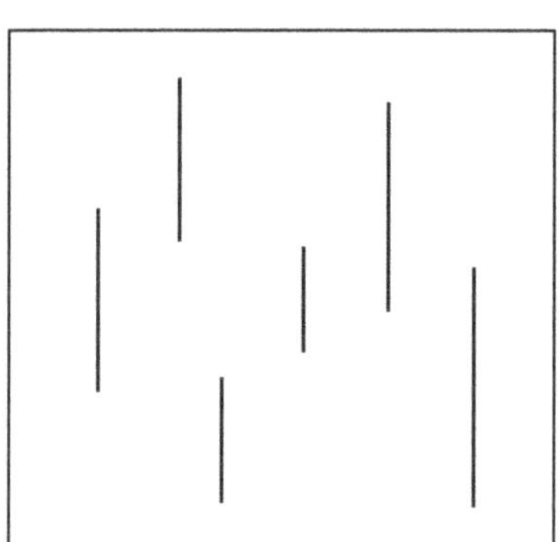

Figure 1.3 The selective accessibility of prototypical (average) features.

Determinants of accessibility

What becomes accessible in any particular situation is mainly determined, of course, by the actual properties of the object of judgment: It is easier to see a tower in Figure 1.2A than in Figure 1.2B because the tower in the latter is only virtual. Physical salience also determines accessibility: If a large green letter and a small blue letter are shown at the same time, green will come to mind first. However, salience can be overcome by deliberate attention: An instruction to look for the smaller letter will enhance the accessibility of all its features, including its color. Motivationally relevant and emotionally arousing stimuli spontaneously attract attention. All the features of an arousing stimulus become accessible, including those that have no motivational or emotional significance. This fact is known, of course, to the designers of billboards.

The perceptual effects of salience and of spontaneous and voluntary attention have counterparts in the processing of more abstract stimuli. For example, the statements "Team A beat Team B" and "Team B lost to Team A" convey the same information. Because each sentence draws attention to its subject, however, the two versions make different thoughts accessible. Accessibility also reflects temporary states of priming and associative activation, as well as enduring operating characteristics of the perceptual and cognitive systems. For example, the mention of a familiar social category temporarily increases the accessibility of the traits associated with the category stereotype, as indicated by a lowered threshold for recognizing manifestations of these traits (Higgins, 1996; for a review, see Fiske, 1998). Moreover, the "hot" states of high emotional and motivational arousal greatly increase the accessibility of thoughts that relate to the immediate emotion and current needs, as well as reducing the accessibility of other thoughts (Loewenstein, 1996).

Some attributes, which Tversky and Kahneman (1983) called *natural assessments*, are routinely and automatically registered by the perceptual system or by System 1 without intention or effort. Kahneman and Frederick (2002) compiled a list of natural assessments with no claim to completeness. In addition to physical properties such as size, distance, and loudness, the list includes more abstract properties such as similarity (see, e.g., Tversky & Kahneman, 1983), causal propensity (Heider, 1944; Kahneman & Varey, 1990; Michotte, 1963), surprisingness (Kahneman & Miller, 1986), affective valence (see, e.g., Bargh, 1997; Cacioppo, Priester, & Berntson, 1993; Kahneman, Ritov, & Schkade, 1999; Slovic, Finucane, Peters, & MacGregor, 2002; Zajonc, 1980), and mood (Schwarz & Clore, 1983). Accessibility itself is a natural assessment – the routine evaluation of cognitive fluency in perception and memory (see, e.g., Jacoby & Dallas, 1981; Johnston, Dark, & Jacoby, 1985; Schwarz & Vaughn, 2002; Tversky & Kahneman, 1973).[1]

The evaluation of stimuli as good or bad is a particularly important natural assessment. The evidence, both behavioral (Bargh, 1997; Zajonc, 1998) and neurophysiological (see, e.g., LeDoux, 2000), is consistent with the idea that the assessment of whether objects are good (and should be approached) or bad (and should be avoided) is carried out quickly and efficiently by specialized neural circuitry. Several authors have commented on the influence of this primordial evaluative system (here included in System 1) on the attitudes and preferences that people adopt consciously and deliberately (Epstein, 2003; Kahneman et al., 1999; Slovic et al., 2002; Wilson, 2000; Zajonc, 1998).

Figure 1.4 illustrates the effect of context on accessibility. An ambiguous stimulus that is perceived as a letter in a context of letters is seen as a number in a context of numbers. The figure also illustrates another point: The ambiguity is suppressed in perception. This aspect of the demonstration is spoiled for the reader who sees the two versions in close proximity, but when the two lines are shown separately, observers do not spontaneously become aware of the alternative interpretation. They "see" the interpretation that is the most likely in its context but have no subjective indication that it could be seen differently. Similarly, in bi-stable pictures such as the mother/daughter figure or the Necker cube, there is no perceptual representation of the instability. Almost no one (for a report of a tantalizing exception, see Wittreich, 1961) is able to see the Ames room as anything but rectangular, even when fully informed that the room is distorted and that the photograph does not provide enough information to specify its true shape. As the transactionalists who built the Ames room emphasized, perception is a choice of which people are not aware, and people perceive what has been chosen.

Uncertainty is poorly represented in intuition, as well as in perception. Indeed, the concept of judgment heuristics was invented to accommodate the observation that intuitive judgments of probability are mediated by attributes such as similarity and associative fluency, which are not intrinsically related to uncertainty. The central finding in studies of intuitive decisions, as described by Klein (1998), is that experienced decision makers working under pressure, such as captains of firefighting companies, rarely need to choose

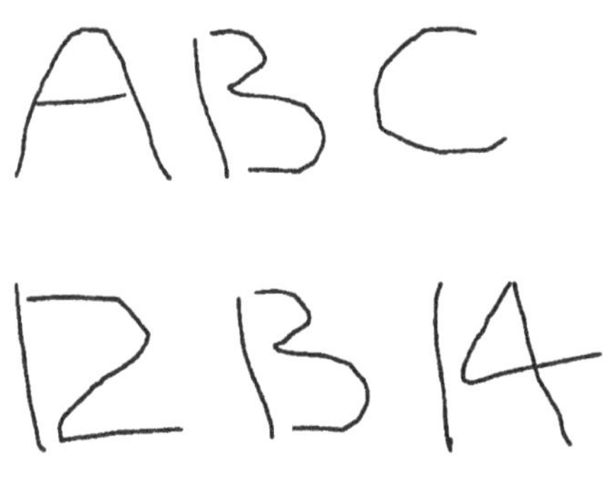

Figure 1.4 An effect of context on the accessibility of interpretations (after Bruner & Minturn, 1955).

between options because in most cases only a single option comes to their mind. The options that were rejected are not represented. Doubt is a phenomenon of System 2, a metacognitive appreciation of one's ability to think incompatible thoughts about the same thing.

Close counterfactual alternatives to what happened are perceived – one can see a horse that was catching up at the finish as almost winning the race (Kahneman & Varey, 1990). Norm theory (Kahneman & Miller, 1986) proposes that events evoke their own norms and that counterfactual alternatives to surprising occurrences are automatically accessible. In contrast to counterfactual alternatives to reality, competing interpretations of reality suppress each other: One does not see each horse in a close finish as both winning and losing.

As this discussion illustrates, much is known about the determinants of accessibility, but there is no general theoretical account of accessibility and no prospect of one emerging soon. In the context of research in judgment and decision making, however, the lack of a theory does little damage to the usefulness of the concept. In this respect, the conceptual status of the principles of accessibility resembles that of Gestalt principles of perceptual grouping, which are often invoked, both implicitly and explicitly, in the planning of research and in the interpretation of results. For these purposes, what matters is that empirical generalizations about the determinants of differential accessibility are widely accepted and that there are accepted procedures for testing the validity of particular hypotheses. For example, the claims about the differential accessibility of attributes in Figures 1.2 and 1.3 appeal to the consensual judgments of perceivers, but propositions about accessibility are also testable in other ways. In particular, judgments of relatively inaccessible properties are expected to be substantially slower and more susceptible to interference by concurrent mental activity, in comparison to judgments of accessible attributes.

Framing effects

In Figure 1.2, the same property (the total height of a set of blocks) is highly accessible in one display and not so in another, although both displays contain the same information. This observation is entirely unremarkable – it does not seem shocking that some attributes of a stimulus are automatically perceived while others must be computed or that the same attribute is perceived in one display of an object but must be computed in another. In the context of decision making, however, similar observations raise a significant challenge to the rational-agent model. The assumption that preferences are not affected by variations of irrelevant features of options or outcomes has been called *extensionality* (Arrow, 1982) and *invariance* (Tversky & Kahneman, 1986); it is an essential aspect of the concept of rationality held in economic theory. Invariance is violated in demonstrations of *framing effects* such as the Asian disease problem (Tversky & Kahneman, 1981).

Problem 1 – The Aslan Disease

Imagine that the United States is preparing for the outbreak of an unusual Asian disease, which is expected to kill 600 people. Two alternative programs to combat the disease have been proposed.

Assume that the exact scientific estimates of the consequences of the programs are as follows:

If Program A is adopted, 200 people will be saved.

If Program B is adopted, there is a one-third probability that 600 people will be saved and a two-thirds probability that no people will be saved.

Which one of the two programs would you favor?

In this version of the problem, a substantial majority of respondents favor Program A, indicating risk aversion. Other respondents, selected at random, receive a question in which the same cover story is followed by a different description of the options:

If Program A′ is adopted, 400 people will die.

If Program B′ is adopted, there is a one-third probability that nobody will die and a two-thirds probability that 600 people will die.

A clear majority of respondents now favor Program B′, the risk-seeking option. Although there is no substantive difference between the versions, they evidently evoke different associations and evaluations. This is easiest to see in the certain option because outcomes that are certain are overweighted relative to outcomes of high or intermediate probability (Kahneman & Tversky, 1979). Thus, the certainty of saving people is disproportionately attractive, and the certainty of deaths is disproportionately aversive. These immediate affective responses respectively favor Program A over Program B and Program B′ over Program A′. As in Figures 1.2A and 1.2B, the different representations of the outcomes highlight some features of the situation and mask others.

The question of how to determine whether two decision problems are the same or different does not have a general answer. To avoid this issue, Tversky and I restricted the definition of framing effects to discrepancies between choice problems that decision makers, upon reflection, consider effectively identical. The Asian disease problem passes this test: Respondents who are asked to compare the two versions almost always conclude that the same action should be taken in both. Observers agree that it would be frivolous to let a superficial detail of formulation determine a choice that has life-and-death consequences.

In another famous demonstration of an embarrassing framing effect, McNeil, Pauker, Sox, and Tversky (1982) induced different choices between surgery and radiation therapy by describing outcome statistics in terms of survival rates or mortality rates. Because 90% short-term survival is less threatening than 10% immediate mortality, the survival frame yielded a substantially higher preference for surgery. The framing effect was as pronounced among experienced physicians as it was among patients.

A different type of framing effect was demonstrated by Shafir (1993), who presented respondents with problems in which they played the role of a judge in adjudicating the custody of a child between divorcing parents. Each parent was described by a list of attributes. One of the descriptions was richer than the other. It contained more negative and more positive attributes. The framing of the instruction was varied. Some respondents were asked which custody request should be accepted; others decided which request should be rejected. The rich description was selected under both instructions, presumably because its numerous advantages were salient (accessible) when the task was to choose which custody request to accept and its numerous disadvantages were salient when the focus of the task was rejection.

A large-scale study by LeBoeuf and Shafir (2003) examined an earlier claim that framing effects are reduced, in a between-participants design, for participants with high scores on "need for cognition" (Smith & Levin, 1996). The original effect was not replicated in the more extensive study. However, LeBoeuf and Shafir showed that more thoughtful individuals do show greater consistency in a within-participants design, where each respondent encounters both versions of each problem. This result is in accord with the present analysis. Respondents characterized by an active System 2 are more likely than others to notice the relationship between the two versions and to ensure the consistency of the responses to them. Thoughtfulness confers no advantage in the absence of a usable cue and is therefore irrelevant to performance in the between-participants design. As was noted earlier, the accessibility of a thought depends both on the characteristics of the cognitive system and on the presence of an appropriate stimulus.

Framing effects are not restricted to decision making: Simon and Hayes (1976) documented an analogous observation in the domain of problem solving. They constructed a collection of transformation puzzles, all formally identical to the tower of Hanoi problem, and found that these "problem isomorphs" varied greatly in difficulty. For example, the initial state and the target state were described in two of the versions as three monsters holding balls of different colors. The state transitions were described in one version as changes in the color of the balls and in the other as balls being passed from one monster to another. The puzzle was solved much more easily when framed in terms of motion. The authors commented that "it would be possible for a subject to seek that representation which is simplest, according to some criterion, or to translate all such problems into the same, canonical, representation" but that "subjects will not employ such alternative strategies, even though they are available, but will adopt the representation that constitutes the most straightforward translation" (Simon & Hayes, 1976, p. 183).

The basic principle of framing is the passive acceptance of the formulation given. This general principle applies equally as well to puzzles, to the displays of Figure 1.2, and to the standard framing effects. People do not spontaneously compute the height of a tower that could be built from an array of blocks, and they do not spontaneously transform the representation of puzzles or decision problems. The brain mechanisms that support the comprehension of language have a substantial ability to strip the surface details and get to the gist of meaning in an utterance, but this ability is limited as well. Few people are able to recognize 137 × 24 and 3,288 as the same number without going through some elaborate computations. Invariance cannot be achieved by a finite mind.

The impossibility of invariance raises significant doubts about the descriptive realism of rational-choice models (Tversky & Kahneman, 1986). Absent a system that reliably generates appropriate canonical representations, intuitive decisions are shaped by the factors that determine the accessibility of different features of the situation. Highly accessible features influence decisions, whereas features of low accessibility are largely ignored. Unfortunately, there is no reason to believe that the most accessible features are also the most relevant to a good decision.

Changes or states: Prospect theory

A general property of perceptual systems is that they appear designed to enhance the accessibility of changes and differences (Palmer, 1999). Perception is *reference dependent*: The perceived attributes of a focal stimulus reflect the contrast between that stimulus and a context of prior and concurrent stimuli. Figure 1.5 illustrates reference dependence in vision. The two enclosed squares have the same luminance, but they do not appear equally bright. The point of the demonstration is that the brightness of an area is not a single-parameter function of the light energy that reaches the eye from that area. An account of perceived brightness also requires a parameter for a reference value (often called *adaptation level*), which is influenced by the luminance of neighboring areas.

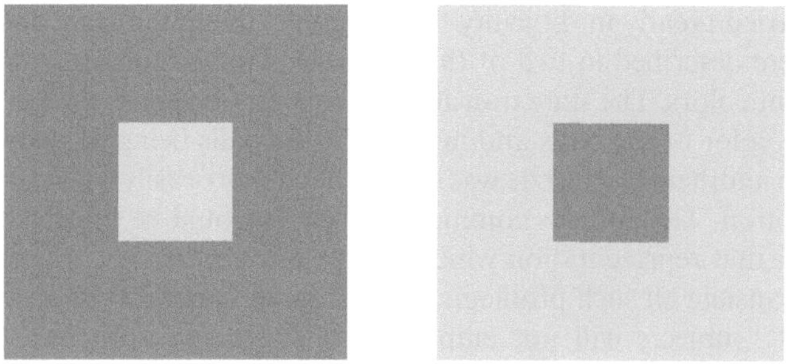

Figure 1.5 Simultaneous contrast and reference dependence.

The reference value to which current stimulation is compared also reflects the history of adaptation to prior stimulation. A familiar demonstration involves three buckets of water of different temperatures, arranged from cold on the left to hot on the right, with tepid in the middle. In the adapting phase, the left and right hands are immersed in cold and hot water, respectively. The initially intense sensations of cold and heat gradually wane. When both hands are then immersed in the middle bucket, the experience is heat in the left hand and cold in the right hand.

Reference dependence in choice

The facts of perceptual adaptation were in our minds when Tversky and I began our joint research on decision making under risk. Guided by the analogy of perception, we expected the evaluation of decision outcomes to be reference dependent. We noted, however, that reference dependence is incompatible with the standard interpretation of expected utility theory, the prevailing theoretical model of risky choice. This deficiency can be traced to the brilliant essay that introduced the first version of that theory (Bernoulli, 1738/1954). Bernoulli's great innovation was to abandon the standard way of evaluating gambles by their expected value – the weighted average of their outcomes (in ducats), each weighted by its probability. Instead, Bernoulli proposed that the value of a gamble is the probability-weighted average of the psychological values (utilities) of its outcomes, which he defined as states of wealth. Developing an argument that anticipated the psychophysics of Weber and Fechner by more than a century, Bernoulli concluded that the utility function of wealth is logarithmic. Economists discarded the logarithmic function long ago, but the idea that decision makers evaluate outcomes by the utility of wealth positions has been retained in economic analyses for almost 300 years. This is rather remarkable because the idea is easily shown to be wrong; I call it Bernoulli's error.

Bernoulli's (1738/1954) model of utility is flawed because it is *reference independent*: It assumes that the utility that is assigned to a given state of wealth does not vary with the decision maker's initial state of wealth. This assumption flies against a basic principle of perception, where the effective stimulus is not the new level of stimulation but the difference between it and the existing adaptation level. The analogy to perception suggests that the carriers of utility are likely to be gains and losses rather than states of wealth, and this suggestion is amply supported by the evidence of both experimental and observational studies of choice (see Kahneman & Tversky, 2000). The present discussion relies on two thought experiments of the kind that Tversky and I devised in the process of developing the model of risky choice that we called *prospect theory* (Kahneman & Tversky, 1979).

Problem 2

Would you accept this gamble?

50% chance to win $150

50% chance to lose $100

Would your choice change if your overall wealth were lower by $100?

There will be few takers of the gamble in Problem 2. The experimental evidence shows that most people reject a gamble with even chances to win and lose unless the possible win is at least twice the size of the possible loss (see, e.g., Tversky & Kahneman, 1992). The answer to the second question is, of course, negative.

Next, consider Problem 3.

Problem 3

Which would you choose?

Lose $100 with certainty

or

50% chance to win $50

50% chance to lose $200

Would your choice change if your overall wealth were higher by $100?

In Problem 3, the gamble appears much more attractive than the sure loss. Experimental results indicate that risk-seeking preferences are held by a large majority of respondents in choices of this kind (Kahneman & Tversky, 1979). Here again, the idea that a change of $100 in total wealth would affect preferences cannot be taken seriously.

Problems 2 and 3 evoke sharply different preferences, but from a Bernoullian perspective, the difference is a framing effect: When stated in terms of final wealth, the problems only differ in that all values are lower by $100 in Problem 3 – surely, an inconsequential variation. Tversky and I examined many choice pairs of this type early in our explorations of risky choice and concluded that the abrupt transition from risk aversion to risk seeking could not plausibly be explained by a utility function for wealth. Preferences appeared to be determined by attitudes to gains and losses, defined relative to a reference point, but Bernoulli's (1738/1954) theory and its successors did not incorporate a reference point. We therefore proposed an alternative theory of risk in which the carriers of utility are gains and losses – changes of wealth rather than states of wealth. Prospect theory (Kahneman & Tversky, 1979) embraces the idea that preferences are reference dependent and includes the extra parameter that is required by this assumption.

The distinctive predictions of prospect theory follow from the shape of the value function, which is shown in Figure 1.6. The value function is defined on gains and losses and is characterized by four features: (a) It is concave in the domain of gains, favoring risk aversion; (b) it is convex in the domain of losses, favoring risk seeking; (c) most important, the function is sharply kinked at the reference point and *loss averse* – steeper for losses than for gains by a factor of about 2–2.5 (Kahneman, Knetsch, & Thaler, 1991; Tversky & Kahneman, 1992); and (d) several studies suggest that the functions in the two domains are fairly well approximated by power functions with similar exponents, both less than unity (Swalm, 1966; Tversky & Kahneman, 1992). The power function is not surprising because the value function is a psychophysical mapping. However, the value function is not expected to describe preferences for losses that are large relative to total assets, where ruin or near ruin is a possible outcome.

Bernoulli's error – the assumption that the carriers of utility are final states – is not restricted to decision making under risk. Indeed, the error of reference independence is built into the standard representation of indifference maps, a basic tool of economic thinking. It is puzzling to a psychologist that these maps do not include a representation of the decision maker's current holdings of various goods – the counterpart of the reference point in prospect theory. The parameter is not included, of course, because economic theory assumes that it does not matter.

The core idea of prospect theory – that the value function is kinked at the reference point and loss averse – became useful to economics when Thaler (1980) used it to explain riskless choices. In particular, loss aversion explained a violation of consumer theory that Thaler identified and labeled the *endowment effect*: The maximum amount that people pay to acquire a good is commonly much less than the minimal amount they demand to part from it once they own it. The selling price often exceeds the buying price by a factor of 2 or more (Kahneman, Knetsch, & Thaler, 1990, 1991; Tversky & Kahneman, 1991). The interpretation is straightforward: A good is worth

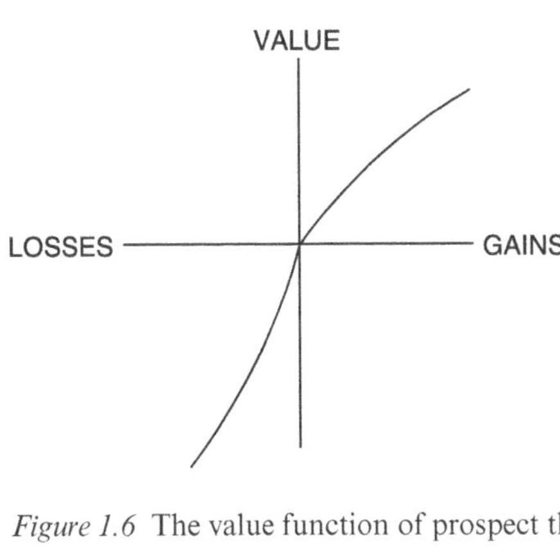

Figure 1.6 The value function of prospect theory.

more when it is considered as something that could be lost or given up than when it is evaluated as a potential gain.

Reference dependence and loss aversion help account for several phenomena of choice. The familiar observation that out-of-pocket losses are much more distressing than forgone gains is readily explained if these outcomes are evaluated on different limbs of the value function. The distinction between actual losses and lost opportunities is recognized in applications of the law (Cohen & Knetsch, 1992) and in lay intuitions about rules of fairness in the market (Kahneman, Knetsch, & Thaler, 1986). Loss aversion also contributes to the well-documented status-quo bias (Samuelson & Zeckhauser, 1988). Because the reference point is usually the status quo, the properties of alternative options are evaluated as advantages or disadvantages relative to the current situation, and the disadvantages of the alternatives loom larger than their advantages. Other applications of the concept of loss aversion are documented in several chapters in Kahneman and Tversky (2000).

Narrow framing

The idea that the carriers of utility are changes of wealth rather than asset positions was described as the cornerstone of prospect theory (Kahneman & Tversky, 1979, p. 273). This statement implies that choices are always made by considering gains and losses rather than final states, but there are exceptions to this claim. For an example, consider Problem 4.

Problem 4

Please estimate your total wealth, call it W.

Which of these situations is more attractive:

You own W

or

50% chance that you own W – $100

50% chance that you own W + $150

Informal experiments with problems of this type have consistently yielded a mild preference for the uncertain state of wealth and a strong impression that the stakes mentioned in the question are entirely negligible.

In terms of final states of wealth, Problem 4 is identical to Problem 2. Furthermore, most respondents agree, upon reflection, that the difference between the problems is inconsequential – too slight to justify different choices. Thus, the discrepant preferences observed in these two problems satisfy the definition of a framing effect. The manipulation of accessibility that produces this framing effect is straightforward. The gamble of Problem 2 is likely to evoke an evaluation of the emotions associated with the immediate outcomes, and the formulation does not bring to mind thoughts of overall wealth. In contrast, the formulation of Problem 4 favors a view of the uncertainty as trivially small in relation to W and does not evoke the emotional asymmetry of gains or losses. The two problems elicit different representations and, therefore, different preferences. Indeed, they are explained by different theories. Prospect theory (where value is attached to changes) is not applicable to Problem 4, and standard utility theory (where utility is attached to wealth) is not applicable to Problem 2.

Some real-world choices are made in the wealth frame. In particular, financial advisors and decision analysts often insist on formulating outcomes in terms of assets when eliciting their clients' preferences. These cases are rare, however. The effective outcomes in the overwhelming majority of decision problems are gains and losses, and Bernoulli's formulation is not useful to explain risky choices that are so framed. There is a genuine puzzle here: Why has a transparently incorrect model been retained for so long as the dominant theory of choice in economics and in other social sciences? The answer may well be that the assignment of utility to final states is compatible with the general assumption of rationality in economic theorizing.

Consider Problem 5.

Problem 5

Two persons get their monthly report from a broker:

A is told that her wealth went from 4M to 3M.

B is told that her wealth went from 1M to 1.1M.

(i) Who of the two individuals has more reason to be satisfied with her financial situation?

(ii) Who is happier today?

Problem 5 highlights the contrasting interpretations of utility in theories that define outcomes as states or as changes. In Bernoulli's analysis, only the first of the two questions is relevant, and only long-term consequences matter. Prospect theory, in contrast, is concerned with short-term outcomes, and the value function presumably reflects an anticipation of the valence and intensity of the emotions that are experienced at moments of transition from one state to another (Kahneman, 2000b, 2000c; Mellers, 2000). Which of these concepts of utility is more useful? For descriptive purposes, the more myopic notion is superior, but the prescriptive norms of reasonable decision making favor the long-term view. The Bernoullian definition of relevant outcomes is a good fit in a rational-agent model.

A particularly unrealistic implication of the rational-agent model is that agents make their choices in a comprehensively inclusive context, which incorporates all the relevant details of the present situation as well as expectations about all future opportunities and risks. Much evidence supports the contrasting claim that people's views of decisions and outcomes are normally characterized by *narrow framing* (Kahneman & Lovallo, 1993) and by the related notion of *mental accounting* (Thaler, 1985, 1999). The prevalence of the gains/losses frame illustrates narrow framing.

For another example, note that it has appeared natural to consider each of the preceding choice problems on its own, as a separate decision. However, this framing is unreasonable for decision makers who expect to live long enough to make many other decisions about accepting gambles. In the broader view, the choice of the moment is an occasion to apply a general policy, not an occasion for an isolated decision. Several experiments have shown that people are much more willing to accept gambles of positive expected value if they are assured of the opportunity to play several times (Benartzi & Thaler, 1999; Kahneman & Lovallo, 1993; Keren & Wagenaar 1987; Tversky & Redelmeier, 1992). In the broad view, of course, the distinction between single play and multiple play is largely irrelevant because life is likely to provide additional opportunities to gamble. Here again, however, people accept the frames that are suggested to them: They consider repeated plays when instructed to do so but focus on a single problem when it is presented on its own. A shared feature of these examples is that decisions made in narrow frames depart far more from risk neutrality than decisions made in a more inclusive context.

The prevalence of narrow frames is an effect of accessibility, which can be understood by referring to the displays of blocks in Figure 1.2. The same set of blocks is framed as a tower in Figure 1.2A and as a flat array in Figure 1.2B. Although it is possible to see a tower in Figure 1.2B, it is much easier to do so in Figure 1.2A. Narrow frames generally reflect the structure of the environment in which decisions are made. The choices that people face arise one at a time, and the principle of passive acceptance suggests that they are considered as they arise. The problem at hand and the immediate consequences of the choice are far more accessible than all other considerations, and as a result, decision problems are framed far more narrowly than the rational model assumes.

It is worth noting that an exclusive concern with the broad view and with the long term may be prescriptively sterile because the long term is not where life is lived. Utility cannot be divorced from emotion, and emotion is triggered by changes. A theory of choice that completely ignores feelings such as the pain of losses and the regret of mistakes is not just descriptively unrealistic. It also leads to prescriptions that do not maximize the utility of outcomes as they are actually experienced – that is, utility as Bentham conceived it (Kahneman, 1994, 2000a; Kahneman, Wakker, & Sarin, 1997).

Attribute substitution: A model of judgment by heuristic

The first joint research program that Tversky and I undertook was a study of various types of judgment about uncertain events, including numerical predictions and assessments of the probabilities of hypotheses. We reviewed this work in an integrative article (Tversky & Kahneman, 1974), which aimed to show

> that people rely on a limited number of heuristic principles which reduce the complex tasks of assessing probabilities and predicting values to simpler judgmental operations. In general, these heuristics are quite useful, but sometimes they lead to severe and systematic errors.
>
> (Tversky & Kahneman, 1974, p. 1124)

The second paragraph of that article introduced the idea that "the subjective assessment of probability resembles the subjective assessments of physical quantities such as distance or size. These judgments are all based on data of limited validity, which are processed according to heuristic rules" (Tversky & Kahneman, 1974, p. 1124). The concept of *heuristic* was illustrated by the role of the blur of contours as a potent determinant of the perceived distance of mountains. The observation that reliance on blur as a distance cue causes distances to be overestimated on foggy days and underestimated on clear days was the example of a heuristic-induced *bias*. As this example illustrates, heuristics of judgment were to be identified by the characteristic errors that they tend to cause.

Three heuristics of judgment, labeled *representativeness*, *availability*, and *anchoring*, were described in the 1974 review, along with a dozen systematic biases, including nonregressive prediction, neglect of base-rate information, overconfidence, and overestimates of the frequency of events that are easy to recall. Some of the biases were identified by systematic errors in estimates of known quantities and statistical facts. Other biases were identified by systematic discrepancies between the regularities of intuitive judgments and the principles of probability theory, Bayesian inference, or regression analysis. The article launched the so-called heuristics and biases approach to the study of intuitive judgment, which has been the topic of a substantial research literature (Gilovich, Griffin, & Kahneman, 2002; Kahneman, Slovic, & Tversky, 1982) and has also been the focus of substantial controversy.

Shane Frederick and I recently revisited the conception of heuristics and biases in the light of developments in the study of judgment and in the broader field of cognitive psychology in the intervening three decades (Kahneman & Frederick, 2002). The new model departs from the original formulation of heuristics in three significant ways: (a) It proposes a common process of attribute substitution to explain how judgment heuristics work, (b) it extends the concept of heuristic beyond the domain of judgments about uncertain events, and (c) it includes an explicit treatment of the conditions under which intuitive judgments are modified or overridden by the monitoring operations associated with System 2.

Attribute substitution

The 1974 article did not include a definition of judgmental heuristics. Heuristics were described at various times as principles, as processes, or as sources of cues for judgment. The vagueness did no damage because the research program focused on a total of three heuristics of judgment under uncertainty that were separately defined in adequate detail. In contrast, Kahneman and Frederick (2002) offered an explicit definition of a generic heuristic process of *attribute substitution:* A judgment is said to be mediated by a heuristic when the individual assesses a specified *target attribute* of a judgment object by substituting a related *heuristic attribute* that comes more readily to mind. This definition elaborates a theme of the early research, namely, that people who are confronted with a difficult question sometimes answer an easier one instead. The word *heuristic* is used in two senses in the new definition. The noun refers to the cognitive process, and the adjective in *heuristic attribute* specifies the attribute that is substituted in a particular judgment. For example, the representativeness heuristic is the use of representativeness as a heuristic attribute to judge probability. The definition of heuristics by attribute substitution does not coincide perfectly with the original conception offered by Tversky and Kahneman (1974). In particular, the new concept excludes anchoring effects, in which judgment is influenced by temporarily raising the accessibility of a particular value of the target attribute, relative to other values of the same attribute.

For a perceptual example of attribute substitution, consider the question "What are the sizes of the two horses in Figure 1.7, as they are shown on the page?" The images are in fact identical in size, but the figure produces a compelling illusion. The target attribute that the observer is instructed to report is two-dimensional size, but the responses actually map an impression of three-dimensional size onto units of length that are appropriate to the required judgment. In the terms of the model, three-dimensional size is the heuristic attribute. As in other cases of attribute substitution, the illusion is caused by differential accessibility. An impression of three-dimensional size is the only impression of size that comes to mind for naïve observers – painters and experienced photographers are able to do better – and it produces a perceptual illusion in the judgment of picture size. The cognitive illusions that are produced by attribute substitution have the same character: An impression of one attribute is mapped onto the scale of another, and the judge is normally unaware of the substitution.

The most direct evidence for attribute substitution was reported by Kahneman and Tversky (1973) in a task of categorical prediction. There were three experimental groups in the experiment. Participants in a base-rate group evaluated the relative frequencies of graduate students in nine

Figure 1.7 Attribute substitution in perception: A highly accessible heuristic attribute (three-dimensional size) substitutes for a less accessible target attribute (picture size).

Note. Photo by Lenore Shoham, 2003.

categories of specialization.[2] Mean estimates ranged from 20% for humanities and education to 3% for library science.

Two other groups of participants were shown the same list of areas of graduate specialization and the following description of a fictitious graduate student.

> Tom W. is of high intelligence, although lacking in true creativity. He has a need for order and clarity, and for neat and tidy systems in which every detail finds its appropriate place. His writing is rather dull and mechanical, occasionally enlivened by somewhat corny puns and by flashes of imagination of the sci-fi type. He has a strong drive for competence. He seems to have little feel and little sympathy for other people and does not enjoy interacting with others. Self-centered, he nonetheless has a deep moral sense.

Participants in a similarity group ranked the nine fields by the degree to which Tom W. "resembles a typical graduate student" (in that field). The description of Tom W. was deliberately constructed to make him more representative of the less populated fields, and this manipulation was successful: The correlation between the average representativeness rankings and the estimated base rates of fields of specialization was –0.62. Participants in the probability group ranked the nine fields according to the likelihood that Tom W. would have specialized in each. The respondents in the latter group were graduate students in psychology at major universities. They were told that the personality sketch had been written by a psychologist when Tom W. was in high school, on the basis of personality tests of dubious validity. This information was intended to discredit the description as a source of valid information.

The statistical logic is straightforward. A description based on unreliable information must be given little weight, and predictions made in the absence of valid evidence must revert to base rates. This reasoning implies that judgments of probability should be highly correlated with the corresponding base rates in this problem.

The psychology of the task is also straightforward. The similarity of Tom W. to various stereotypes is a highly accessible natural assessment, whereas judgments of probability are difficult. The respondents are therefore expected to substitute a judgment of similarity (representativeness) for the required judgment of probability. The two instructions – to rate similarity or probability – should therefore elicit similar judgments.

The scatter plot of the mean judgments of the two groups is presented in Figure 1.8A. As the figure shows, the correlation between judgments of probability and similarity is nearly perfect (0.98). The correlation between judgments of probability and base rates is –0.63. The results are in perfect accord with the hypothesis of attribute substitution. They also confirm a bias of *base-rate neglect* in this prediction task.

Figure 1.8B shows the results of another study in the same design, in which respondents were shown the description of a woman named Linda and a list of eight possible outcomes describing her present employment and activities.

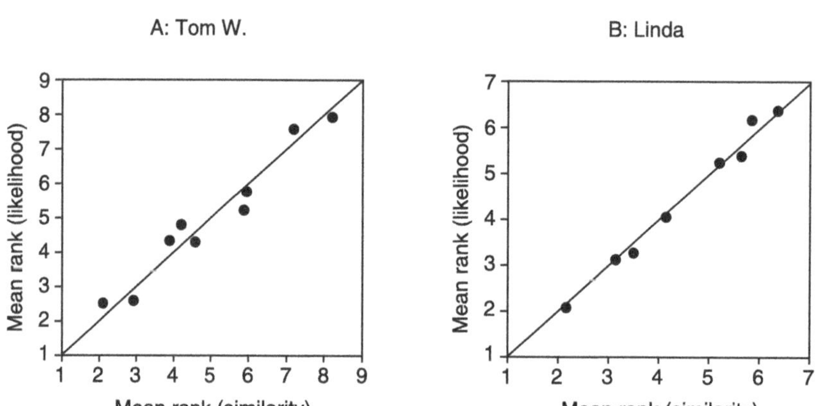

Figure 1.8 Mean judgments of probability are plotted against mean judgments of similarity (representativeness) for eight possible outcomes in the Linda problem.

The two critical items in the list were number 6 ("Linda is a bank teller") and the conjunction item, number 8 ("Linda is a bank teller and active in the feminist movement"). The other six possibilities were unrelated and miscellaneous (e.g., elementary school teacher, psychiatric social worker). As in the Tom W. problem, some respondents were required to rank the eight outcomes by the similarity of Linda to the category prototypes; others ranked the same outcomes by probability.

> Linda is 31 years old, single, outspoken and very bright. She majored in philosophy. As a student she was deeply concerned with issues of discrimination and social justice and also participated in antinuclear demonstrations.

As might be expected, 85% of respondents in the similarity group ranked the conjunction item (number 8) higher than its constituent, indicating that Linda resembles the image of a feminist bank teller more than she resembles a stereotypical bank teller. This ordering of the two items is quite reasonable for judgments of similarity. However, it is much more problematic that 89% of respondents in the probability group also ranked the conjunction higher than its constituent. This pattern of probability judgments violates monotonicity and has been called the *conjunction fallacy* (Tversky & Kahneman, 1983).

The results shown in Figure 1.8 are especially compelling because the responses were rankings. The large variability of the average rankings of both attributes indicates highly consensual responses and nearly total overlap in the systematic variance. Stronger support for attribute substitution could hardly be imagined. Other tests of representativeness in the heuristic elicitation design have been equally successful (Bar-Hillel & Neter, 2002; Tversky & Kahneman, 1982). The same design was also applied extensively in studies of support theory (Tversky & Koehler, 1994; for a review, see Brenner, Koehler, & Rottenstreich, 2002). In one of the studies reported by Tversky and Koehler (1994), participants rated the probability that the home team would win in each of 20 specified basketball games and later provided ratings of the relative strength of the two teams, using a scale in which the strongest team in the tournament was assigned a score of 100. The correlation between normalized strength ratings and judged probabilities was 0.99.

The essence of attribute substitution is that respondents offer a reasonable answer to a question that they have not been asked. An alternative interpretation that must be considered is that the respondents' judgments reflect their understanding of the question that was posed. This may be true in some situations: It is not unreasonable to interpret a question about the probable outcome of a basketball game as referring to the relative strength of the competing teams. In many other situations, however, attribute substitution occurs even when the target and heuristic attributes are clearly distinct. For example, it is highly unlikely that educated respondents have a concept of probability that coincides precisely with similarity or that they are unable to distinguish picture size from object size. A more plausible hypothesis is that an evaluation of the heuristic attribute comes immediately to mind and that its associative relationship with the target attribute is sufficiently close to pass the permissive monitoring of System 2. Respondents who substitute one attribute for another are not confused about the question that they are trying to answer – they simply fail to notice that they are answering a different one. When they do notice the discrepancy and suspect a bias, they either modify the intuitive judgment or abandon it altogether.

As illustrated by its use in the interpretation of the visual illusion of Figure 1.7, the definition of judgment heuristics by the mechanism of attribute substitution applies to many situations in which people make a judgment that is not the one they intended to make. There is no finite list of heuristic attributes. Kahneman and Frederick (2002) illustrated this conception by a study by Strack, Martin, and Schwarz (1988) in which college students answered a survey that included these two questions: "How happy are you with your life in general?" and "How many dates did you have last month?" The correlation between the two questions was negligible when they occurred in the order shown, but it rose to 0.66 when the dating question was asked first. The model of attribute substitution suggests that the dating question automatically evokes an affectively charged evaluation of one's satisfaction in that domain of life, which lingers to become the heuristic attribute when the happiness question is subsequently encountered. The underlying correlation between the judgment and the heuristic attribute is surely higher than the observed value of 0.66, which is attenuated by measurement error. The same experimental manipulation of question order was used in another study to induce the use of marital satisfaction as a heuristic attribute for well-being (Schwarz, Strack, & Mai, 1991). The success of these experiments suggests that ad hoc attribute substitution is a frequent occurrence. It is important to note that the present treatment does not make specific predictions about the heuristics that will be used in particular circumstances. It only provides (a) an approach that helps generate such predictions, based on the considerations of relative accessibility that were discussed earlier, and (b) two separate methods for testing heuristics, by examining predicted biases of judgment and by direct comparisons of the target and heuristic attributes.

The affect heuristic

The idea of an *affect heuristic* (Slovic et al., 2002) is probably the most important development in the study of judgment heuristics in the past few decades. There is compelling evidence for the proposition that every stimulus evokes an affective evaluation, which is not always conscious (see reviews by Bargh, 1997; Zajonc, 1980, 1998). Affective valence is a natural assessment and, therefore, a candidate for substitution in the numerous responses that express attitudes. Slovic and his colleagues (Slovic et al., 2002) discussed how a basic affective reaction can be used as the heuristic attribute for a wide variety of more complex evaluations, such as the cost–benefit ratio of technologies, the safe concentration of chemicals, and even the predicted economic performance of industries. Their treatment of the affect heuristic fits the present model of attribute substitution.

In the same vein, Kahneman and Ritov (1994) and Kahneman et al. (1999) proposed that an automatic affective valuation – the emotional core of an attitude – is the main determinant of many judgments and behaviors. In the study by Kahneman and Ritov, 37 public causes were ranked by average responses to questions about (a) the importance of the issues, (b) the size of the donation that respondents were willing to make, (c) political support for interventions, and (d) the moral satisfaction associated with a contribution. The rankings were all very similar. In the terms of the present analysis, the same heuristic attribute (affective valuation) was mapped onto the distinct scales of different target attributes. Similarly, Kahneman, Schkade, and Sunstein (1998) interpreted jurors' assessments of punitive awards as a mapping of outrage onto a dollar scale of punishments. In an article titled "Risk as Feelings," Loewenstein, Weber, Hsee, and Welch (2001) offered a closely related analysis in which emotional responses, such as the intensity of fear, govern diverse judgments (e.g., ratings of the probability of a disaster).

In terms of the scope of responses that it governs, the natural assessment of affect should join representativeness and availability in the list of general-purpose heuristic attributes. The failure to identify the affect heuristic much earlier and its enthusiastic acceptance in recent years reflect significant changes in the general climate of psychological opinion. It is worth noting that the idea of purely cognitive biases appeared novel and distinctive in the early 1970s because the prevalence of motivated and emotional biases of judgment was taken for granted by the social psychologists of the time. There followed a period of intense emphasis on cognitive processes in psychology generally and in the field of judgment in particular. It took another 30 years to achieve what now appears to be a more integrated view of the role of affect in intuitive judgment.

The accessibility of corrective thoughts

The present treatment assumes that System 2 continuously monitors the tentative judgments and intentions that System 1 produces. This assumption implies that errors of intuitive judgment involve failures of both systems: System 1, which generates the error, and System 2, which fails to detect and correct it (Kahneman & Tversky, 1982). To illustrate this point, Kahneman and Frederick (2002) revisited the visual example that Tversky and Kahneman (1974) had used to explain how heuristics generate biases: Blur is a good cue to the distance of mountains, but reliance on this cue causes predictable errors in estimates of distance on sunny or hazy days. The analogy was apt, but the analysis of the perceptual example neglected an important fact. Observers know, of course, whether the day is sunny or hazy. They could therefore apply this knowledge to counteract the bias – but unless they have been trained as sharp-shooters, they are unlikely to do so. Contrary to what the early treatment implied, the use of blur as a cue does not inevitably lead to bias in the judgment of distance – the error could just as well be described as a failure to assign adequate negative weight to ambient haze. The effect of haziness on impressions of distance is a failing of System 1: The perceptual system is not designed to correct for this variable. The effect of haziness on judgments of distance is a separate failure of System 2. The analysis extends readily to errors of intuitive judgment.

The observation that it is possible to design experiments in which cognitive illusions disappear has sometimes been used as an argument against the usefulness of the notions of heuristics and biases (see, e.g., Gigerenzer, 1991). In the present framework, however, there is no mystery about the conditions under which illusions appear or disappear: An intuitive judgment will be modified or overridden if System 2 identifies it as biased. This argument is not circular because a great deal is known about the conditions under which corrections will or will not be made and because hypotheses about the role of System 2 can be tested.

In the context of an analysis of accessibility, the question of when intuitive judgments will be corrected is naturally rephrased: When will corrective thoughts be sufficiently accessible to intervene in the judgment? There have been three lines of research on this issue. One explored the conditions that influence the general efficacy of System 2 and thereby the likelihood that potential errors will be detected and prevented. Other lines of research investigated the factors that determine the accessibility of relevant metacognitive knowledge and the accessibility of relevant statistical rules.

The corrective operations of System 2 are impaired by time pressure (Finucane, Alhakami, Slovic, & Johnson, 2000), by concurrent involvement in a different cognitive task (Gilbert, 1989, 1991, 2002), by performing the task in the evening for morning people and in the morning for evening people (Bodenhausen, 1990), and, surprisingly, by being in a good mood (Bless et al., 1996; Isen, Nygren, & Ashby, 1988). Conversely, the facility of System 2 is positively correlated with intelligence (Stanovich & West, 2002), with need for cognition (Shafir & LeBoeuf, 2002), and with exposure to statistical thinking (Agnoli, 1991; Agnoli & Krantz, 1989; Nisbett, Krantz, Jepson, & Kunda, 1983).

When people become aware of using a heuristic, they correct their judgment accordingly and may even overcorrect. For example, Schwarz and Clore (1983) showed that the normal effect of rainy weather on reports of general happiness is eliminated when respondents are first asked about the weather. The question about the weather has a metacognitive effect: It reminds respondents that they should not allow their judgments of well-being to be influenced by a transient weather-related mood. Schwarz, Bless, et al. (1991)

and Oppenheimer (in press) showed similar discounting effects in studies of the availability heuristic. In an elegant series of experiments, Oppenheimer showed that respondents who were asked to estimate the frequency of surnames in the U.S. population even tended to underestimate the frequency of famous surnames, such as Bush, as well as the population frequency of their own surname. He also reported that an availability effect (overestimating the frequency of words that contain letters of one's initials) was replaced by a significant effect in the opposite direction when people were first required to write down their initials. It may be significant that these demonstrations of metacognitive corrections were concerned with the availability heuristic and not with representativeness. The distinction between objective frequency and the availability of instances to memory is far more transparent than the distinction between probability and similarity, and it may be correspondingly easier to recognize availability biases in frequency judgments than to identify representativeness biases in statistical reasoning.

Nisbett, Krantz, and their colleagues mounted a substantial research program to investigate the factors that control the accessibility of *statistical heuristics* – rules of thumb that people can be trained to apply to relevant problems, such as "consider the size of the sample" (Nisbett et al., 1983). In one of their studies, Nisbett et al. (1983) compared formally identical problems that differed in content. They found that statistical reasoning was most likely to be evoked in the context of games of chance, was occasionally evoked in situations involving sports, but was relatively rare when the problems concerned the psychology of individuals. They also showed that the explicit mention of a sampling procedure facilitated statistical thinking (Nisbett et al., 1983; see also Gigerenzer, Hell, & Blank, 1988). Zukier and Pepitone (1984) found that respondents were more likely to use base-rate information when instructed to think as statisticians than when instructed to emulate psychologists. Agnoli and Krantz (1989) reported that brief training in the logic of sets improved performance in a simple version of the Linda problem. The findings indicate that the accessibility of statistical heuristics can be enhanced in at least three ways: by increasing the vigilance of the monitoring activities, by providing stronger cues to the relevant rules, and by extensive training in applied statistical reasoning.[3]

In the absence of primes and reminders, the accessibility of statistical heuristics is low. For an example, it is useful to consider how System 2 might have intervened in the problems of Tom W. and Linda that were described in an earlier section.

> Tom W does look like a library science person, but there are many more graduate students in humanities and social sciences. I should adjust my rankings accordingly.

> Linda cannot be more likely to be a feminist bank teller than to be a bank teller. I must rank these two outcomes accordingly.

Neither of these examples of reasoning exceeds the intellectual reach of the graduate students at major universities whose rankings were shown in Figure 1.8. However, the data indicate that very few respondents actually came up with these elementary corrections.

The present analysis of judgment implies that statistical training does not eradicate intuitive heuristics such as availability or representativeness but only enables people to avoid some biases under favorable circumstances. The results of Figure 1.8 support this prediction. In the absence of strong cues to remind them of their statistical knowledge, statistically knowledgeable graduate students made categorical predictions like everybody else – by representativeness. However, statistical sophistication made a difference in a more direct version of the Linda problem, which required respondents to compare the probabilities of Linda being "a bank teller" or "a bank teller who is active in the feminist movement" (Tversky & Kahneman, 1983). The incidence of errors remained high for the statistically naïve even in that transparent version, but the error rate dropped dramatically among the sophisticated.

Analogous corrections can be expected for other intuitive judgments: For example, reports of subjective well-being are strongly influenced by current mood and current preoccupations (Schwarz & Strack, 1999), but reminding respondents to think broadly about their lives would certainly cause them to bring other relevant considerations to bear on their responses. Similarly, the initial punitive decisions of jurors are likely to reflect an outrage heuristic (Kahneman, Schkade, & Sunstein, 1998), but jurors can also be instructed to consider other factors.

The analysis of corrective thoughts has a significant methodological implication; Different research designs are appropriate for the study of System 1 and of System 2. If the goal of the research is to study intuitive judgment, the design should minimize the role of deliberation and self-critical reflection. Intuitive judgments and preferences are therefore best studied in between-participants designs and in short experiments that provide little information about the experimenter's aims. Within-participant designs with multiple trials should be avoided because they encourage the participants to search for consistent strategies to deal with the task. Within-participant factorial designs are particularly undesirable because they provide an unmistakable cue that any factor that is varied systematically must be relevant to the target attribute (Kahneman & Frederick, 2002). The difficulties of these experimental designs were noted long ago by Kahneman and Tversky, who pointed out that "within-subject designs are associated with significant problems of interpretation in several areas of psychological research (Poulton, 1975). In studies of intuition, they are liable to induce the effect that they are intended to test" (Kahneman and Tversky, 1982, p. 500). Unfortunately, this methodological caution has been widely ignored.

A variety of research designs can be used to study different questions about System 2, such as the effects of training and intelligence or the efficacy of cues. Dual-task methods are most useful to test hypotheses about the existence of an underlying intuitive judgment that is modified by a corrective intervention of System 2. The test is not whether the judgment will be disrupted by a competing task – such a test would produce too many false positives. The specific prediction is that interference will cause judgments to become more similar to what they would be if System 2 had not had an opportunity to intervene.

The possible corrections in the Linda and Tom W. problems illustrate two possible outcomes of the intervention of System 2. In the case of the conjunction fallacy, the intuitive judgment would be rejected and replaced by another conclusion. In the case of base-rate neglect, the intuitive judgment could be adjusted to accommodate a new consideration. Because it is based on salient information and because it comes first, the intuitive impression is likely to serve as an anchor for subsequent adjustments, and the corrective adjustments are therefore likely to be small. Variations on this theme of anchoring on intuition are common in the literature (Epley & Gilovich, 2002; Epstein, 1994; Gilbert, 2002; Griffin & Tversky, 1992; Haidt, 2001; Hammond, 2000; Sloman, 2002; Wilson, 2000; Wilson, Centerbar, & Brekke, 2002). On the other hand, there are reports in which the correction just eliminates the bias of the heuristic judgment (see, e.g., Schwarz, Bless, et al., 1991), as well as occasional findings of overcorrection (Oppenheimer, in press). A plausible hypothesis is that adjustments that are based on the explicit identification of a bias are more likely to overcorrect, whereas adjustments based on the identification of an additional relevant considerations are generally insufficient.

Prototype heuristics

This section introduces a family of prototype heuristics, which share a common mechanism and a remarkably consistent pattern of cognitive illusions, analogous to the effects observed in the Tom W. and in the Linda problems (Kahneman & Frederick, 2002). Prototype heuristics can be roughly described as the substitution of an average for a sum – a process that has been extensively studied by Anderson in other contexts (e.g., Anderson, 1981, pp. 58–70, 1991a, 1991b, 1996). The study of prototype heuristics also illustrates the conditions under which System 2 prevents or reduces judgment biases.

Extensional and prototype attributes

The target assessments in several significant tasks of judgment and decision making are *extensional attributes* of categories or sets. The value of an extensional attribute in a set is an aggregate (not necessarily additive) of the values over its extension. Each of the following tasks is illustrated by an example of an extensional attribute and also by the relevant measure of extension. The argument of this section is that the target attributes in these tasks are low in accessibility and are therefore candidates for heuristic judgment.

1 Category prediction (e.g., *the probability that the set of bank tellers contains Linda/the number of bank tellers*);
2 Pricing a quantity of public or private goods (e.g., *the personal dollar value of saving a certain number of birds from drowning in oil ponds/the number of birds*);
3 Global evaluation of a past experience that extended over time (e.g., *the overall aversiveness of a painful medical procedure/the duration of the procedure*); and
4 Assessment of the support that a sample of observations provides for a hypothesis (e.g., *the probability that a specified sample of colored balls has been drawn from one urn rather than another/the number of balls*).

The logic of extensional attributes involves a general principle of conditional adding, which dictates that each element of the set adds to the overall value an amount that depends on the elements already included. In simple cases, the value is additive; The total length of the set of lines in Figure 1.3 is just the sum of their separate lengths. In other cases, each positive element of the set increases the aggregate value, but the combination rule is nonadditive (typically, subadditive).[4]

A category or set that is sufficiently homogeneous to have a prototype can also be described by its *prototype attributes*. Where extensional attributes are akin to a sum, prototype attributes are averages. As the display of lines in Figure 1.3 illustrates, prototype attributes are often highly accessible. This observation is well documented. Whenever people look at, or think about, an ensemble or category that has a prototype, information about the prototype becomes accessible. The classic discussion of basic-level categories included demonstrations of the ease with which features of the prototype come to mind (Rosch & Mervis, 1975). Even earlier, Posner and Keele (1968, 1970) had reported experiments in which observers were exposed on many trials to various distortions of a single shape. The prototype shape was never shown, but observers erroneously believed that it had been presented often. More recently, several studies in social psychology have shown that exposure to the name of a familiar social category increases the accessibility of the traits that are closely associated with its stereotype (see Fiske, 1998).

Because of their high accessibility, the prototype attributes are natural candidates for the role of heuristic attributes. A *prototype heuristic* is the label for the process of substituting an attribute of a prototype for an extensional attribute of its category (Kahneman & Frederick, 2002). The original instance of a prototype heuristic is the use of representativeness in category prediction. The probability of Linda being a bank teller is an extensional variable, but her resemblance to a typical bank teller is a prototype attribute.

Two tests of prototype heuristics

Because extensional and prototypical attributes are governed by characteristically different logical rules, the substitution of a prototype attribute for an extensional attribute entails two testable biases: extension neglect and violations of monotonicity. Tests of the two hypotheses are discussed in turn.

Tests of extension neglect

Doubling the frequencies of all values in a set does not affect prototype attributes because measures of central tendency depend only on relative frequencies. In contrast, the value of an extensional attribute increases monotonically with extension. The hypothesis that judgments of a target attribute are mediated by a prototype heuristic gains support if the judgments are insensitive to variations of extension.

The proposition that extension is neglected in a particular judgment has the character of a null hypothesis: It is strictly true only if all individuals in the sample are completely insensitive to variations of extension. The hypothesis must be rejected, in a sufficiently large study, if even a small proportion of participants show some sensitivity to extension. The chances of some individuals responding to extension are high a priori because educated respondents are generally aware of the relevance of this variable (Kahneman & Frederick, 2002). Everyone agrees that willingness to pay (WTP) for saving birds should increase with the number of birds saved, that extending a painful medical procedure by an extra period of pain makes it worse, and that evidence from larger samples is more reliable. Complete extension neglect is therefore an unreasonably strict test of prototype heuristics. Nevertheless, this extreme result can be obtained under favorable conditions, as the following examples show.

- The study of Tom W. (see Figure 1.8) illustrates a pattern of base-rate neglect in categorical prediction. This finding is robust when the task requires a ranking of multiple outcomes (Kahneman & Tversky, 1973). As noted in the preceding section, the sophisticated participants in this experiment were aware of the base rates and were capable of using this knowledge in their predictions – but the thought of doing so apparently occurred to almost none of them. Kahneman and Tversky also documented almost complete neglect of base rates in an experiment (the engineer/lawyer study) in which base rates were explicitly stated. However, the neglect of explicit base-rate information in this design is a fragile finding (see Evans, Handley, Over, & Perham, 2002; Kahneman & Frederick, 2002; Koehler, 1996).
- Participants in a study by Desvousges et al. (1993) indicated their willingness to contribute money to prevent the drowning of migratory birds. The number of birds that would be saved was varied for different

subsamples. The estimated amounts that households were willing to pay were $80, $78, and $88, to save 2,000, 20,000, or 200,000 birds, respectively. Frederick and Fischhoff (1998) reviewed numerous other demonstrations of *scope neglect* in studies of WTP for public goods. For example, Kahneman and Knetsch found that survey respondents in Toronto were willing to pay similar amounts to clean up the lakes in a small region of Ontario or to clean up all the lakes in that province (reported by Kahneman, 1986).

- In a study described by Redelmeier and Kahneman (1996), patients undergoing colonoscopy reported the intensity of pain every 60 seconds during the procedure (see Figure 1.9) and subsequently provided a global evaluation of the pain they had suffered. The correlation of global evaluations with the duration of the procedure (which ranged from 4 to 66 minutes in that study) was .03. On the other hand global evaluations were correlated (r = .67) with an average of the pain reported at two points of the procedure: when pain was at its peak and just before the procedure ended. For example, Patient A in Figure 1.9 reported a more negative evaluation of the procedure than Patient B. The same pattern of *duration neglect* and peak/end evaluations has been observed in other studies (Fredrickson & Kahneman, 1993; see Kahneman, 2000a, 2000b, for a discussion).

In light of the findings discussed in the preceding section, it is useful to consider situations in which people do not neglect extension completely. Extension effects are expected, in the present model, if the individual (a) has information about the extension of the relevant set, (b) is reminded of the relevance of extension, and (c) is able to detect that her intuitive judgment neglects extension. These conditions are least likely to hold – and complete neglect most likely to be observed – when the judge evaluates a single object and when the extension of the set is not explicitly mentioned. At the other

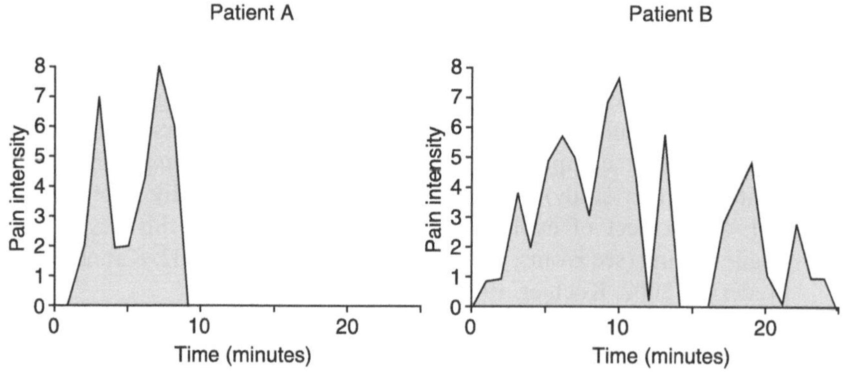

Figure 1.9 Pain intensity reported by two colonoscopy patients.

extreme, the conditions for a positive effect of extension are all satisfied in psychologists' favorite research design: the within-participant factorial experiment, in which values of extension are crossed with the values of other variables in the design. As noted earlier, this design provides an obvious cue that the experimenter considers every manipulated variable relevant, and it enables participants to ensure that their judgments exhibit sensitivity to all these variables. The factorial design is therefore especially inappropriate for testing hypotheses about biases of neglect (Kahneman & Frederick, 2002).

Tests of monotonicity

Extensional variables, like sums, obey monotonicity. The sum of a set of positive values is at least as high as the maximum of its subsets. In contrast, the average of a subset can be higher than the average of a set that includes it. Violations of monotonicity are therefore bound to occur when an extensional attribute is judged by a prototype attribute: It is always possible to find cases in which adding elements to a set causes the judgment of the target variable to decrease. This test of prototype heuristics is less demanding than the hypothesis of extension neglect, and violations of monotonicity are compatible with some degree of sensitivity to extension (Ariely & Loewenstein, 2000). Nevertheless, the systematic violation of monotonicity in important tasks of judgment and choice is the strongest source of support for the hypothesis that prototype attributes are being substituted for extensional attributes in these tasks.

- Conjunction errors, which violate monotonicity, have been demonstrated in the Linda problem and in other problems of the same type. The pattern is robust when the judgments are obtained in a between-participants design and when the critical outcomes are embedded in a longer list (Mellers, Hertwig, & Kahneman, 2001; Tversky & Kahneman, 1982, 1983). Tversky and Kahneman (1983) also found that statistically naïve respondents made conjunction errors even in a direct comparison of the critical outcomes. As in the case of extension neglect, however, conjunction errors are less robust in within-participant conditions, especially when the task involves a direct comparison (see Kahneman & Frederick, 2002, for a discussion).
- Hsee (1998) asked participants to price sets of dinnerware offered in a clearance sale. One of the sets consisted of 24 pieces, all in good condition. The other set included the same 24 pieces, plus 16 additional pieces, of which 7 were in a good condition and 9 were broken. Hsee drew an important distinction between two experimental conditions. When each respondent evaluated only one set of dinnerware (*separate evaluation*), mean WTP was $33 for the smaller set and $23 for the larger set ($p < .01$). In contrast, participants who evaluated both sets (*joint evaluation*) were

consistently willing to pay more for the larger set. List (2002) observed similar violations of dominance with a different good (sets of baseball cards) in a real market situation.

- Problems of the following kind have been used in several experiments (Griffin & Tversky, 1992; Kahneman & Tversky, 1972).

> A sample has been drawn from one of two urns. One urn contains 70% red balls and 30% white balls. The proportions are reversed in the other urn. What is the probability that each of these samples was drawn from the predominantly red urn?
>
> A sample of three red balls and zero white balls
> (3R, 0W)
> A sample of four red balls and three white balls
> (4R, 3W)
> A sample of seven red balls and three white balls
> (7R, 3W)

- The extensional target variable here is the degree of support for the "red" hypothesis relative to the "white" hypothesis. The normative solution is straightforward: Posterior probability (the target attribute) is determined by an additive combination over sample elements – the difference between the number of red and white balls in the sample. The psychological solution is equally straightforward: The prototype attribute (the heuristic) is an average of support, which corresponds to the proportion of red balls in the sample. Thus, the addition of 4R, 3W to 3R, 0W raises the value of the target attribute but reduces the value of the heuristic attribute. This particular example is fictitious, but the pattern of findings indicates that respondents would derive much more confidence from 3R, 0W than from 7R, 3W (Griffin & Tversky, 1992; Kahneman & Tversky, 1972).
- A randomized clinical experiment was conducted as a follow-up to the colonoscopy study described earlier. For half the patients, the instrument was not immediately removed when the clinical examination ended. Instead, the physician waited for about a minute, leaving the instrument stationary. The experience during the extra period was uncomfortable, but the procedure guaranteed that the colonoscopy never ended in severe pain. Patients reported significantly more favorable global evaluations in this experimental condition than in the control condition (Redelmeier, Katz, & Kahneman, 2003). Violations of dominance have also been confirmed in choices. Kahneman, Fredrickson, Schreiber, and Redelmeier (1993) exposed participants to two cold-pressor experiences, one with each hand: a short episode (immersion of one hand in 14 °C water for 60 seconds) and a long episode (the short episode plus an additional 30 seconds during which the water was gradually warmed to 15 °C). When participants were later asked which of the two experiences they

preferred to repeat, a substantial majority chose the long trial. This pattern of choices is predicted from the peak/end rule of evaluation, which was described earlier. The basic result was replicated with unpleasant sounds of variable loudness and duration (Schreiber & Kahneman, 2000).

The consistency of the results observed in diverse studies of prototype heuristics implies a need for a unified interpretation and challenges interpretations that apply to only a single domain. A number of authors have offered competing interpretations of base-rate neglect (Cosmides & Tooby, 1996; Koehler, 1996), insensitivity to scope in WTP (Kopp, 1992), and duration neglect (Ariely & Loewenstein, 2000). However, each of these interpretations is specific to a particular task and does not carry over to other demonstrations of extension neglect. Similarly, the attempts to describe the conjunction fallacy as a miscommunication between experimenter and respondent (Dulany & Hilton, 1991; Hilton & Slugoski, 2001) do not explain analogous violations of monotonicity in the cold-pressor experiment and in the pricing of private goods. In contrast, the account offered here (and developed in greater detail by Kahneman & Frederick, 2002) is equally applicable to diverse tasks that require an assessment of an extensional target attribute. Future discussions of the separate phenomena should take account of their generality across domains.

The findings obtained in choices and joint evaluations confirm the existence of two distinct ways of choosing, which were already identified in prospect theory (Kahneman & Tversky, 1979). In the nonanalytic procedure that I have called *choosing by liking* (Kahneman, 1994), the individual considers the global evaluation of the two options separately and selects the option that has the higher global value without detailed comparison of the alternatives. Choice by global value is the basic mechanism assumed in prospect theory. However, prospect theory also introduces the idea that if the decision maker detects that one option dominates the other, she will choose the dominant option without consulting their separate valuations. The same mechanisms apply to problems of judgment, such as the case of Linda, where some statistically sophisticated individuals detect that one of the sets includes the other and respond accordingly, ignoring representativeness. In Hsee's (1998) dinnerware study, respondents chose by liking in separate evaluation and chose by dominance in joint evaluation.

Joint evaluation is not sufficient to guarantee choice by dominance; it is also necessary for the decision makers to realize explicitly that one of the options is strictly better than the other. This requirement was not satisfied in the cold-pressor experiment. Although the participants were exposed to both experiences (joint evaluation), they did not notice that the long episode contained all the pain of the short one and then some extra pain. Most respondents would have made a different choice if they had understood the structure of the options.

The cases that have been discussed are only illustrations, not a comprehensive list of prototype heuristics. For example, the same form of nonextensional thinking explains why the median estimate of the annual number of murders in Detroit is twice as high as the estimate of the number of murders in Michigan (Kahneman & Frederick, 2002). It also explains why professional forecasters assigned a higher probability to "an earthquake in California causing a flood in which more than 1,000 people will drown" than to "a flood somewhere in the United States in which more than 1,000 people will drown" (Tversky & Kahneman, 1983).

The normative logic of belief and choice is extensional, and it requires appropriate valuation of extensional attributes, which include both probability and utility. The examples that were discussed in this section demonstrate pervasive violations of extensional logic in the intuitive evaluation of both evidence and outcomes. The substitution of prototype attributes for extensional attributes appears to be a general characteristic of System 1, which is incompatible with both Bayesian beliefs and utility maximization.

Conclusions

The starting point of the present analysis was the observation that complex judgments and preferences are called intuitive in everyday language if they come to mind quickly and effortlessly, like percepts. Other basic observations were that judgments and intentions are normally intuitive in this sense and that they can be modified or overridden in a more deliberate mode of operation. The labels *System 1* and *System 2* were associated with these two modes of cognitive functioning.

The preceding sections elaborated a single generic proposition: Highly accessible impressions produced by System 1 control judgments and preferences, unless modified or overridden by the deliberate operations of System 2. This template sets an agenda for research: To understand judgment and choice, we must study the determinants of high accessibility, the conditions under which System 2 overrides or corrects System 1, and the rules of these corrective operations. Much is known about each of the three questions.

First, consider the ways in which the concept of accessibility was used here. Framing effects were attributed to the fact that alternative formulations of the same situation make different aspects of it accessible. The core idea of prospect theory, that the normal carriers of utility are gains and losses, invoked the general principle that changes are relatively more accessible than absolute values. Judgment heuristics were explained as the substitution of a highly accessible heuristic attribute for a less accessible target attribute. The correction of intuitive judgments was attributed to the accessibility of competing considerations and to the accessibility of metacognitive awareness of bias. Finally, the proposition that averages are more accessible than sums unified the analysis of prototype heuristics. A recurrent theme was that different aspects of problems are made accessible in between-participants and in within-participant experiments and more specifically in separate and joint evaluations of stimuli. In all these contexts, the discussion appealed to rules of accessibility that are independently plausible and sometimes quite obvious.

As was noted earlier, the status of accessibility factors in psychological theorizing is, in principle, similar to the status of perceptual grouping factors. In both cases, there is no general theory, only a list of powerful empirical generalizations that provide an adequate basis for experimental predictions and for models of higher level phenomena. Unlike gestalt principles, which were catalogued a long time ago, a comprehensive list of the factors that influence accessibility is yet to be drawn. The list will be long, but many of its elements are already known. For example, it is safe to assume that similarity is more accessible than probability, that changes are more accessible than absolute values, that averages are more accessible than sums, and that the accessibility of a rule of logic or statistics can be temporarily increased by a reminder. Furthermore, each of these assumptions can be verified independently by multiple operations, including measurements of reaction time, susceptibility to interference by secondary tasks, and asymmetric priming effects. Assumptions about accessibility are incompletely theorized, but they need not be vague, and they can do genuine explanatory work. The claim "X came to mind because it was accessible under the circumstances of the moment" sounds circular, but it is not.

The discussion of judgment heuristics was restricted to the differential accessibility of attributes (dimensions) on which judgment objects vary, such as length or price, similarity and probability (Kahneman & Frederick, 2002). A similar analysis could be applied to the accessibility of particular values of attributes, such as "six feet" or "two dollars." Highly accessible values are generally overweighted, and when considered as possible answers to a question, they become potent anchors (Chapman & Johnson, 2002; Epley & Gilovich, 2002; Strack & Mussweiler, 1997). These effects of salience and anchoring play a central role in treatments of judgment and choice. Indeed, anchoring effects are among the most robust phenomena of judgment, and overweighting of salient values is likely to be the mechanism that explains why low-probability events sometimes loom large in decision making. The analysis of accessibility could readily be extended to deal with these observations.

The claim that cognitive illusions occur unless they are prevented by System 2 also sounds circular but is not. Circular inferences are avoidable because the role of System 2 can be independently verified in several ways. For example, the assumption that System 2 is vulnerable to interference by competing activities suggests that manifestations of intuitive thought that are normally inhibited will be expressed when people are placed under cognitive load. Another testable hypothesis is that intuitive judgments that are suppressed by System 2 still have detectable effects, for example, in priming subsequent responses.

Principles of accessibility determine the relative power of the cues to which the monitoring functions of System 2 respond. For example, it is known that differences between objects of choice or judgment are more salient in joint than in separate evaluation, and it is also known that any variable that is manipulated in a factorial design will attract some attention. Other cues can be found in the wording of problems and in the context of previous tasks. Many apparent inconsistencies in the literature on judgment heuristics are easily resolved within this framework (Kahneman & Frederick, 2002). The observation that a judgment bias appears in some situations but not in others usually provides information about the accessibility factors that trigger corrective operations. As already noted, the attribution of the variability of intuitive judgments to System 2 is a source of testable hypotheses. It suggests, for example, that intelligence will be correlated with susceptibility to biases only in problems that provide relatively weak cues to the correct solution. In the absence of cues, there is no opportunity for intelligence or sophistication to manifest itself. At the other extreme, when cues are abundant, even the moderately intelligent will find them (Kahneman, 2000c; Stanovich & West, 1999, 2002).

The model suggests five ways in which a judgment or choice may be made:

1 An intuitive judgment or intention is initiated, and

   (a) Endorsed by System 2;
   (b) Adjusted (insufficiently) for other features that are recognized as relevant;
   (c) Corrected (sometimes overcorrected) for an explicitly recognized bias; or
   (d) Identified as violating a subjectively valid rule and blocked from overt expression.

2 No intuitive response comes to mind, and the judgment is computed by System 2.

There is, of course, no way to ascertain precisely the relative frequencies of these outcomes, but casual observation suggests that Cases 1(a) and 1(b) are the most common and that Case 1(d) is very rare. This ordering reflects two major hypotheses about the role of intuition in judgment and choice. The first is that most behavior is intuitive, skilled, unproblematic, and successful (Klein, 1998). The second is that behavior is likely to be anchored in intuitive impressions and intentions even when it is not completely dominated by them. An essay with a related message (Haidt, 2001) suggested the image of the intuitive dog wagging the rational tail.

The analysis of intuitive thinking and choice that has been presented here provides a framework that highlights commonalities between lines of research that are usually studied separately. In particular, the psychology of judgment and the psychology of choice share their basic principles and differ mainly in content. At a more specific level, prototype heuristics solve structurally similar problems in diverse domains, where they yield closely similar patterns of results. Furthermore, the psychological principles that have been invoked are not specific to the domain of judgment/decision making. The analogy between intuition and perception has been especially fruitful in identifying the ways in which intuitive thought differs from deliberate reasoning, and the notions of accessibility and dual-process analyses play a fundamental role in other domains of social and cognitive psychology.

A general framework such as the one offered here is not a substitute for domain-specific concepts and theories. For one thing, general frameworks and specific models make different ideas accessible. Novel ideas and compelling examples are perhaps more likely to arise from thinking about problems at a lower level of abstraction and generality. However, broad concepts such as accessibility, attribute substitution, corrective operations, and prototype heuristics can be useful if they guide a principled search for analogies across domains, help identify common processes, and prevent overly narrow interpretations of findings.

Notes

1 The availability heuristic is based on an assessment of accessibility in which frequencies or probabilities are judged by the ease with which instances come to mind. Tversky and I were responsible for this terminological confusion (Tversky & Kahneman, 1973).
2 The categories were business administration, computer science, engineering, humanities and education, law, library science, medicine, physical and life sciences, and social sciences and social work.
3 The intervention of System 2 does not guarantee a correct response. The rules that people apply in deliberate reasoning are sometimes false.
4 If the judgment is monotonically related to an additive scale (such as the underlying count of the number of birds), the formal structure is known in the measurement literature as an *extensive structure* (Luce, Krantz, Suppes, & Tversky, 1990, chapter 3). There also may be attributes that lack any underlying additive scale, in which case the structure is known in the literature as a *positive concatenation structure* (Luce et al., 1990, chapter 19, Vol. III, p. 38).

Acknowledgments

This article is based on the author's Nobel Prize lecture, which was delivered at Stockholm University on December 8, 2002, and on the text and images to be published in *Les Prix Nobel 2002* (Frängsmyr, in press). The article was originally published in *American Psychologist*, No. 58, 2003, and I would like to thank the American Psychological Association, Inc. for giving permission to reprint the text in these Congress Proceedings.

Author's note. This article revisits problems that Amos Tversky and I studied together many years ago and continued to discuss in a conversation that spanned several decades. The article is based on the Nobel lecture, which my daughter Lenore Shoham helped put together. It draws extensively on an analysis of judgment heuristics that was developed in collaboration with Shane Frederick (Kahneman & Frederick, 2002). Shane Frederick, David Krantz, and Daniel Reisberg went well beyond the call of friendly duty in helping with this effort. Craig Fox, Peter McGraw, Daniel Oppenheimer, Daniel Read, David Schkade, Richard Thaler, and my wife, Anne Treisman, offered many insightful comments and suggestions. Kurt Schoppe provided valuable assistance, and Geoffrey Goodwin and Amir Goren helped with scholarly fact-checking. My research is supported by National Science Foundation Grant 285–6086 and by the Woodrow Wilson School for Public and International Affairs at Princeton University.

References

Agnoli, F. (1991). Development of judgmental heuristics and logical reasoning: Training counteracts the representativeness heuristic. *Cognitive Development*, *6*, 195–217.

Agnoli, F., & Krantz, D.H. (1989). Suppressing natural heuristics by formal instruction: The case of the conjunction fallacy. *Cognitive Psychology*, *21*, 515–550.

Anderson, N.H. (1981). *Foundations of information integration theory*. New York: Academic Press.

Anderson, N.H. (1991a). *Contributions to information integration theory: Vol. I. Cognition*. Hillsdale, NJ: Erlbaum.

Anderson, N.H. (1991b). *Contributions to information integration theory: Vol. II. Social*. Hillsdale, NJ: Erlbaum.

Anderson, N.H. (1996). *A functional theory of cognition*. Hillsdale, NJ: Erlbaum.

Ariely, D. (2001). Seeing sets: Representation by statistical properties. *Psychological Science*, *12*, 157–162.

Ariely, D., & Loewenstein, G. (2000). When does duration matter in judgment and decision making? *Journal of Experimental Psychology: General*, *129*, 524–529.

Arrow, K.J. (1982). Risk perception in psychology and economics. *Economic Inquiry*, *20*, 1–9.

Bargh, J.A. (1997). The automaticity of everyday life. In R. S. Wyer, Jr. (Ed.), *The automaticity of everyday life: Advances in social cognition* (Vol. 10, pp. 1–61). Mahwah, NJ: Erlbaum.

Bar-Hillel, M., & Neter, E. (2002). How alike is it versus how likely is it: A disjunction fallacy in probability judgments. In T. Gilovich, D. Griffin, & D. Kahneman (Eds.), *Heuristics and biases* (pp. 82–97). New York: Cambridge University Press.

Benartzi, S., & Thaler, R.H. (1999). Risk aversion or myopia? Choices in repeated gambles and retirement investments. *Management Science*, *47*, 364–381.

Bernoulli, D. (1954). Exposition of a new theory on the measurement of risk. *Econometrica*, *22*, 23–36. (Original work published 1738)

Bless, H., Clore, G.L., Schwarz, N., Golisano, V., Rabe, C., & Wolk, M. (1996). Mood and the use of scripts: Does a happy mood really lead to mindlessness? *Journal of Personality and Social Psychology*, *71*, 665–679.

Bodenhausen, G.V. (1990). Stereotypes as judgmental heuristics: Evidence of circadian variations in discrimination. *Psychological Science*, *1*, 319–322.

Brenner, L.A., Koehler, D.J., & Rottenstreich, Y. (2002). Remarks on support theory: Recent advances and future directions. In T. Gilovich, D. Griffin, & D. Kahneman

(Eds.), *Heuristics and biases* (pp. 489–509). New York: Cambridge University Press.

Bruner, J.S., & Minturn, A.L. (1955). Perceptual identification and perceptual organization. *Journal of General Psychology*, *53*, 21–28.

Cacioppo, J.T., Priester, J.R., & Berntson, G.G. (1993). Rudimentary determinants of attitudes: II. Arm flexion and extension have differential effects on attitudes. *Journal of Personality and Social Psychology*, *65*, 5–17.

Chaiken, S., & Trope, Y. (Eds.). (1999). *Dual-process theories in social psychology*. New York: Guilford Press.

Chapman, G.B., & Johnson, E.J. (2002). Incorporating the irrelevant: Anchors in judgments of belief and value. In T. Gilovich, D. Griffin, & D. Kahneman (Eds.), *Heuristics and biases* (pp. 120–138). New York: Cambridge University Press.

Chong, S.C., & Treisman, A. (2003). Representation of statistical properties. *Vision Research*, *43*, 393–404.

Cohen, D., & Knetsch, J.L. (1992). Judicial choice and disparities between measures of economic value. *Osgoode Hall Law Review*, *30*, 737–770.

Cosmides, L., & Tooby, J. (1996). Are humans good intuitive statisticians after all? Rethinking some conclusions from the literature on judgment and uncertainty. *Cognition*, *58*, 1–73.

Desvousges, W.H., Johnson, F., Dunford, R., Hudson, S., Wilson, K., & Boyle, K. (1993). Measuring natural resource damages with contingent valuation: Tests of validity and reliability. In J. A. Hausman (Ed.), *Contingent valuation: A critical assessment* (pp. 91–159). Amsterdam: North-Holland.

Dulany, D.E., & Hilton, D.J. (1991). Conversational implicature, conscious representation, and the conjunction fallacy. *Social Cognition*, *9*, 85–110.

Epley, N., & Gilovich, T. (2002). Putting adjustment back in the anchoring and adjustment heuristic. In T. Gilovich, D. Griffin, & D. Kahneman (Eds.), *Heuristics and biases* (pp. 139–149). New York: Cambridge University Press.

Epstein, S. (1994). Integration of the cognitive and psychodynamic unconscious. *American Psychologist*, *49*, 709–724.

Epstein, S. (2003). Cognitive-experiential self-theory of personality. In T. Millon & M. J. Lerner (Eds.), *Comprehensive handbook of psychology: Vol. 5. Personality and social psychology* (pp. 159–184). Hoboken, NJ: Wiley.

Evans, J.St.B.T., Handley, S.J., Over, D.E., & Perham, N. (2002). Background beliefs in Bayesian inference. *Memory and Cognition*, *30*, 179–190.

Finucane, M.L., Alhakami, A., Slovic, P., & Johnson, S.M. (2000). The affect heuristic in judgments of risks and benefits. *Journal of Behavioral Decision Making*, *13*, 1–17.

Fiske, S. (1998). Stereotyping, prejudice, and discrimination. In D.T. Gilbert & S.T. Fiske (Eds.), *The handbook of social psychology* (4th ed., Vol. 1, pp. 357–441). New York: McGraw-Hill.

Frängsmyr, T. (Ed.). (in press). *Les Prix Nobel 2002* [Nobel Prizes 2002]. Stockholm, Sweden: Almqvist & Wiksell International.

Frederick, S.W., & Fischhoff, B. (1998). Scope (in)sensitivity in elicited valuations. *Risk, Decision, and Policy*, *3*, 109–123.

Fredrickson, B.L., & Kahneman, D. (1993). Duration neglect in retrospective evaluations of affective episodes. *Journal of Personality and Social Psychology*, *65*, 45–55.

Gawande, A. (2002). *Complications: A surgeon's notes on an imperfect science*. New York: Metropolitan Books.

Gigerenzer, G. (1991). How to make cognitive illusions disappear: Beyond "heuristics and biases." In W. Stroebe & M. Hewstone (Eds.), *European review of social psychology* (Vol. 2, pp. 83–115). Chichester, UK: Wiley.

Gigerenzer, G., Hell, W., & Blank, H. (1988). Presentation and content – The use of base rates as a continuous variable. *Journal of Experimental Psychology: Human Perception and Performance*, *14*, 513–525.

Gilbert, D.T. (1989). Thinking lightly about others: Automatic components of the social inference process. In J. Uleman & J. A. Bargh (Eds.), *Unintended thought* (pp. 189–211). Englewood Cliffs, NJ: Prentice Hall.

Gilbert, D.T. (1991). How mental systems believe. *American Psychologist*, *46*, 107–119.

Gilbert, D.T. (2002). Inferential correction. In T. Gilovich, D. Griffin, & D. Kahneman (Eds.), *Heuristics and biases* (pp. 167–184). New York: Cambridge University Press.

Gilovich, T., Griffin, D., & Kahneman, D. (Eds.). (2002). *Heuristics and biases*. New York: Cambridge University Press.

Griffin, D.W., & Tversky, A. (1992). The weighing of evidence and the determinants of confidence. *Cognitive Psychology*, *24*, 411–435.

Haidt, J. (2001). The emotional dog and its rational tail: A social intuitionist approach to moral judgment. *Psychological Review*, *108*, 814–834.

Hammond, K.R. (2000). *Judgment under stress*. New York: Oxford University Press.

Heider, F. (1944). Social perception and phenomenal causality. *Psychological Review*, *51*, 358–374.

Higgins, E.T. (1996). Knowledge activation: Accessibility, applicability, and salience. In E.T. Higgins & A. Kruglanski (Eds.), *Social psychology: Handbook of basic principles* (pp. 133–168). New York: Guilford Press.

Hilton, D.J., & Slugoski, B.R. (2001). Conversational processes in reasoning and explanation. In A. Tesser & N. Schwartz (Eds.), *Blackwell handbook of social psychology: Vol. 1. Intraindividual processes* (pp. 181–206). Oxford, UK: Blackwell.

Hogarth, R.M. (2001). *Educating intuition*. Chicago: University of Chicago Press.

Hsee, C.K. (1998). Less is better: When low-value options are valued more highly than high-value options. *Journal of Behavioral Decision Making*, *11*, 107–121.

Isen, A.M., Nygren, T.E., & Ashby, F.G. (1988). Influence of positive affect on the subjective utility of gains and losses: It is just not worth the risk. *Journal of Personality and Social Psychology*, *55*, 710–717.

Jacoby, L.L. (1991). A process dissociation framework: Separating automatic from intentional uses of memory. *Journal of Memory and Language*, *30*, 513–541.

Jacoby, L.L. (1996). Dissociating automatic and consciously controlled effects of study/test compatibility. *Journal of Memory and Language*, *35*, 32–52.

Jacoby, L.L., & Dallas, M. (1981). On the relationship between autobiographical memory and perceptual learning. *Journal of Experimental Psychology: General*, *110*, 306–340.

Johnston, W.A., Dark, V.J., & Jacoby, L.L. (1985). Perceptual fluency and recognition judgments. *Journal of Experimental Psychology: Learning, Memory, and Cognition*, *11*, 3–11.

Kahneman, D. (1973). *Attention and effort*. Englewood Cliffs, NJ: Prentice Hall.

Kahneman, D. (1986). Comment. In R.G. Cummings, D.S. Brookshire, & W.D. Schultze (Eds.), *Valuing environmental goods* (pp. 185–193). Totowa, NJ: Rowman & Allenheld.

Kahneman, D. (1994). New challenges to the rationality assumption. *Journal of Institutional and Theoretical Economics, 150*, 18–36.

Kahneman, D. (2000a). Evaluation by moments: Past and future. In D. Kahneman & A. Tversky (Eds.), *Choices, values, and frames* (pp. 693–708). New York: Cambridge University Press.

Kahneman, D. (2000b). Experienced utility and objective happiness: A moment-based approach. In D. Kahneman & A. Tversky (Eds.), *Choices, values, and frames* (pp. 673–692). New York: Cambridge University Press.

Kahneman, D. (2000c). A psychological point of view: Violations of rational rules as a diagnostic of mental processes (Commentary on Stanovich and West). *Behavioral and Brain Sciences, 23*, 681–683.

Kahneman, D., & Frederick, S. (2002). Representativeness revisited: Attribute substitution in intuitive judgment. In T. Gilovich, D. Griffin, & D. Kahneman (Eds.), *Heuristics and biases* (pp. 49–81). New York: Cambridge University Press.

Kahneman, D., Fredrickson, D.L., Schreiber, C.A., & Redelmeier, D.A. (1993). When more pain is preferred to less: Adding a better end. *Psychological Science, 4*, 401–405.

Kahneman, D., Knetsch, J.L., & Thaler, R.H. (1986). Fairness as a constraint on profit seeking: Entitlements in the market. *American Economic Review, 76*, 728–741.

Kahneman, D., Knetsch, J.L., & Thaler, R.H. (1990). Experimental tests of the endowment effect and the Coase theorem. *Journal of Political Economy, 98*, 1325–1348.

Kahneman, D., Knetsch, J.L., & Thaler, R.H. (1991). The endowment effect, loss aversion, and status quo bias. *Journal of Economic Perspectives, 5*, 193–206.

Kahneman, D., & Lovallo, D. (1993). Timid choices and bold forecasts: A cognitive perspective on risk taking. *Management Science, 39*, 17–31.

Kahneman, D., & Miller, D.T. (1986). Norm theory: Comparing reality to its alternatives. *Psychological Review, 93*, 136–153.

Kahneman, D., & Ritov, I. (1994). Determinants of stated willingness to pay for public goods: A study in the headline method. *Journal of Risk and Uncertainty, 9*, 5–38.

Kahneman, D., Ritov, I., & Schkade, D. (1999). Economic preferences or attitude expressions? An analysis of dollar responses to public issues. *Journal of Risk and Uncertainty, 19*, 220–242.

Kahneman, D., Schkade, D.A., & Sunstein, C.R. (1998). Shared outrage and erratic awards: The psychology of punitive damages. *Journal of Risk and Uncertainty, 16*, 49–86.

Kahneman, D., Slovic, P., & Tversky, A. (Eds.). (1982). *Judgment under uncertainty: Heuristics and biases*. New York: Cambridge University Press.

Kahneman, D., & Tversky, A. (1972). Subjective probability: A judgment of representativeness. *Cognitive Psychology, 3*, 430–454.

Kahneman, D., & Tversky, A. (1973). On the psychology of prediction. *Psychological Review, 80*, 237–251.

Kahneman, D., & Tversky, A. (1979). Prospect theory: An analysis of decisions under risk. *Econometrica, 47*, 263–291.

Kahneman, D., & Tversky, A. (1982). On the study of statistical intuitions. In D. Kahneman, P. Slovic, & A. Tversky (Eds.), *Judgment under uncertainty: Heuristics and biases* (pp. 493–508). New York: Cambridge University Press.

Kahneman, D., & Tversky, A. (Eds.). (2000). *Choices, values, and frames*. New York: Cambridge University Press.

Kahneman, D., & Varey, C.A. (1990). Propensities and counterfactuals: The loser that almost won. *Journal of Personality and Social Psychology, 59*, 1101–1110.

Kahneman, D., & Wakker, P.P., & Sarin, R. (1997). Back to Bentham? Explorations of experienced utility. *Quarterly Journal of Economics, 112*, 375–405.

Keren, G., & Wagenaar, W.A. (1987). Violations of utility theory in unique and repeated gambles. *Journal of Experimental Psychology: Learning, Memory, and Cognition, 13*, 387–391.

Klein, G. (1998). *Sources of power: How people make decisions*. Cambridge, MA: MIT Press.

Klein, G. (2003). *Intuition at work: Why developing your gut instincts will make you better at what you do*. New York: Doubleday.

Koehler, D.J. (1996). A strength model of probability judgments for tournaments. *Organizational Behavior and Human Decision Processes, 66*, 16–21.

Kopp, R. (1992). Why existence value should be used in cost-benefit analysis. *Journal of Policy Analysis and Management, 11*, 123–130.

LeBoeuf, R.A., & Shafir, E. (2003). Deep thoughts and shallow frames: On the susceptibility to framing effects. *Journal of Behavioral Decision Making, 16*, 77–92.

LeDoux, J.E. (2000). Emotion circuits in the brain. *Annual Review of Neuroscience, 23*, 155–184.

List, J. (2002). Preference reversals of a different kind: The more is less phenomenon. *American Economic Review, 92*, 1636–1643.

Loewenstein, G. (1996). Out of control: Visceral influences on behavior. *Organizational Behavior and Human Decision Processes, 65*, 272–292.

Loewenstein, G., Weber, E.U., Hsee, C.K., & Welch, N. (2001). Risk as feelings. *Psychological Bulletin, 127*, 267–286.

Luce, R.D., Krantz, D.H., Suppes, P., & Tversky A. (1990). *Foundations of measurement: Vol. 3. Representation, axiomatization, and invariance*. San Diego, CA: Academic Press.

McNeil, B.J., Pauker, S.G., Sox, H.C., & Tversky, A. (1982). On the elicitation of preferences for alternative therapies. *New England Journal of Medicine, 306*, 1259–1262.

Mellers, B. (2000). Choice and the relative pleasure of consequences. *Psychological Bulletin, 126*, 910–924.

Mellers, B., Hertwig, R., & Kahneman, D. (2001). Do frequency representations eliminate conjunction effects? An exercise in adversarial collaboration. *Psychological Science, 12*, 269–275.

Michotte, A. (1963). *The perception of causality* (T.R. Miles & E. Miles, Trans.). New York: Basic Books.

Myers, D.G. (2002). *Intuition: Its powers and perils*. New Haven, CT: Yale University Press.

Nisbett, R.E., Krantz, D.H., Jepson, C., & Kunda, Z. (1983). The use of statistical heuristics in everyday inductive reasoning. *Psychological Review, 90*, 339–363.

Oppenheimer, D.M. (in press). Spontaneous discounting of availability in frequency estimations. *Psychological Science*.

Palmer, S.E. (1999). *Vision science: Photons to phenomenology*. Cambridge, MA: MIT Press.

Pashler, H.E. (1998). *The psychology of attention*. Cambridge, MA: MIT Press.

Posner, M.I., & Keele, S.W. (1968). On the genesis of abstract ideas. *Journal of Experimental Psychology, 77*, 353–363.

Posner, M.I., & Keele, S.W. (1970). Retention of abstract ideas. *Journal of Experimental Psychology*, *83*, 304–308.
Poulton, E.C. (1975). Range effects in experiments with people. *American Journal of Psychology*, *77*, 353–363.
Redelmeier, D., & Kahneman, D. (1996). Patients' memories of painful medical treatments: Real-time and retrospective evaluations of two minimally invasive procedures. *Pain*, *66*, 3–8.
Redelmeier, D.A., Katz, J., & Kahneman, D. (2003). Memories of colonoscopy: A randomized trial. *Pain*, *104*, 187–194.
Rosch, E., & Mervis, C.B. (1975). Family resemblances: Studies in the internal structure of categories. *Cognitive Psychology*, *7*, 573–605.
Samuelson, W., & Zeckhauser, R. (1988). Status quo bias in decision making. *Journal of Risk and Uncertainty*, *1*, 7–59.
Schreiber, C.A., & Kahneman, D. (2000). Determinants of the remembered utility of aversive sounds. *Journal of Experimental Psychology: General*, *129*, 27–42.
Schwarz, N., Bless, H., Strack, F., Klumpp, G., Rittenauer-Schatke, H., & Simons, A. (1991). Ease of retrieval as information: Another look at the availability heuristic. *Journal of Personality and Social Psychology*, *61*, 195–202.
Schwarz, N., & Clore, G.L. (1983). Mood, misattribution, and judgments of well-being: Informative and directive functions of affective states. *Journal of Personality and Social Psychology*, *45*, 513–523.
Schwarz, N., & Strack, F. (1999). Reports of subjective well-being: Judgmental processes and their methodological implications. In D. Kahneman, E. Diener, & N. Schwarz (Eds.), *Well-being: The foundations of hedonistic psychology* (pp. 61–84). New York: Russell Sage Foundation.
Schwarz, N., Strack, F., & Mai, H.P. (1991). Assimilation and contrast effects in part–whole question sequences: A conversational logic analysis. *Public Opinion Quarterly*, *55*, 3–23.
Schwarz, N., & Vaughn, L.A. (2002). The availability heuristic revisited: Ease of recall and content of recall as distinct sources of information. In T. Gilovich, D. Griffin, & D. Kahneman (Eds.), *Heuristics and biases* (pp. 103–119). New York: Cambridge University Press.
Shafir, E. (1993). Choosing versus rejecting: Why some options are both better and worse than others. *Memory and Cognition*, *21*, 546–556.
Shafir, E., & LeBoeuf, R.A. (2002). Rationality. *Annual Review of Psychology*, *53*, 419–517.
Simon, H.A. (1955). A behavioral model of rational choice. *Quarterly Journal of Economics*, *69*, 99–118.
Simon, H.A. (1979). Rational decision-making in business organizations. *American Economic Review*, *69*, 493–513.
Simon, H.A., & Chase, W.G. (1973). Skill in chess. *American Scientist*, *61*, 394–403.
Simon, H.A., & Hayes, J.R. (1976). Understanding process: Problem isomorphs. *Cognitive Psychology*, *8*, 165–190.
Sloman, S.A. (1996). The empirical case for two systems of reasoning. *Psychological Bulletin*, *119*, 3–22.
Sloman, S.A. (2002). Two systems of reasoning. In T. Gilovich, D. Griffin, & D. Kahneman (Eds.), *Heuristics and biases* (pp. 379–396). New York: Cambridge University Press.

Slovic, P., Finucane, M., Peters, E., & MacGregor, D.G. (2002). The affect heuristic. In T. Gilovich, D. Griffin, & D. Kahneman (Eds.), *Heuristics and biases* (pp. 397–420). New York: Cambridge University Press.

Smith, S.M., & Levin, I.P. (1996). Need for cognition and choice framing effects. *Journal of Behavioral Decision Making, 9*, 283–290.

Stanovich, K.E. (1999). *Who is rational? Studies of individual differences in reasoning.* Mahwah, NJ: Erlbaum.

Stanovich, K.E., & West, R.F. (1999). Discrepancies between normative and descriptive models of decision making and the understanding/acceptance principle. *Cognitive Psychology, 38*, 349–385.

Stanovich, K.E., & West, R.F. (2000). Individual differences in reasoning: Implications for the rationality debate. *Behavioral and Brain Sciences, 23*, 645–665.

Stanovich, K.E., & West, R.F. (2002). Individual differences in reasoning: Implications for the rationality debate. In T. Gilovich, D. Griffin, & D. Kahneman (Eds.), *Heuristics and biases* (pp. 421–440). New York: Cambridge University Press.

Strack, F., Martin, L.L., & Schwarz, N. (1988). Priming and communication: The social determinants of information use in judgments of life-satisfaction. *European Journal of Social Psychology, 18*, 429–442.

Strack, F., & Mussweiler, T. (1997). Explaining the enigmatic anchoring effect: Mechanisms of selective accessibility. *Journal of Personality and Social Psychology, 73*, 437–446.

Swalm, R.O. (1966). Utility theory: Insights into risk taking. *Harvard Business Review, 44*, 123–136.

Thaler, R.H. (1980). Toward a positive theory of consumer choice. *Journal of Economic Behavior and Organization, 1*, 39–60.

Thaler, R.H. (1985). Mental accounting and consumer choice. *Marketing Science, 4*, 199–214.

Thaler, R.H. (1999). Mental accounting matters. *Journal of Behavioral Decision Making, 12*, 241–268.

Tulving, E., & Pearlstone, Z. (1966). Availability versus accessibility of information in memory for words. *Journal of Verbal Learning and Verbal Behavior, 5*, 381–391.

Tversky, A., & Kahneman, D. (1971). Belief in the law of small numbers. *Psychological Bulletin, 76*, 105–110.

Tversky, A., & Kahneman, D. (1973). Availability: A heuristic for judging frequency and probability. *Cognitive Psychology, 5*, 207–232.

Tversky, A., & Kahneman, D. (1974, September 27). Judgment under uncertainty: Heuristics and biases. *Science, 185*, 1124–1131.

Tversky, A., & Kahneman, D. (1981, January 30). The framing of decisions and the psychology of choice. *Science, 211*, 453–458.

Tversky, A., & Kahneman, D. (1982). Evidential impact of base rates. In D. Kahneman, P. Slovic, & A. Tversky (Eds.), *Judgment under uncertainty: Heuristics and biases* (pp. 153–160). New York: Cambridge University Press.

Tversky, A., & Kahneman, D. (1983). Extensional vs. intuitive reasoning: The conjunction fallacy in probability judgment. *Psychological Review, 90*, 293–315.

Tversky, A., & Kahneman, D. (1986). Rational choice and the framing of decisions. *Journal of Business, 59*, S251–S278.

Tversky, A., & Kahneman, D. (1991). Loss aversion in riskless choice: A reference-dependent model. *Quarterly Journal of Economics, 106*, 1039–1061.

Tversky, A., & Kahneman, D. (1992). Advances in prospect theory: Cumulative representation of uncertainty, *Journal of Risk and Uncertainty*, *5*, 297–323.

Tversky, A., & Koehler, D.J. (1994). Support theory: A nonextensional representation of subjective probability. *Psychological Review*, *101*, 547–567.

Tversky, A., & Redelmeier, D.A. (1992). On the framing of multiple prospects. *Psychological Science*, *3*, 191–193.

Wilson, T.D. (2000). *Strangers to ourselves: Discovering the adaptive unconscious*. Cambridge, MA: Harvard University Press.

Wilson, T.D., Centerbar, D.B., & Brekke, N. (2002). Mental contamination and the debiasing problem. In T. Gilovich, D. Griffin, & D. Kahneman (Eds.), *Heuristics and biases* (pp. 185–200). New York: Cambridge University Press.

Wilson, T.D., & Schooler, J.W. (1991). Thinking too much: Introspection can reduce the quality of preferences and decisions. *Journal of Personality and Social Psychology*, *60*, 181–192.

Wittreich, W.J. (1961). The Honi phenomenon: A case of selective perceptual distortion. In F. P. Kilpatrick (Ed.), *Explorations in transactional psychology* (pp. 188–202). New York: New York University Press.

Zajonc, R.B. (1980). Feeling and thinking: Preferences need no inferences. *American Psychologist*, *35*, 151–175.

Zajonc, R.B. (1998). Emotions. In D.T. Gilbert, S.T. Fiske, & G. Lindzey (Eds.), *Handbook of social psychology* (4th ed., Vol. 1, pp. 591–632). New York: Oxford University Press.

Zukier, H., & Pepitone, A. (1984). Social roles and strategies in prediction: Some determinants in the use of base-rate information. *Journal of Personality and Social Psychology*, *47*, 349–360.

2 Psychological science in its multidisciplinary environment

Michel Denis

Presidential address, 28th International Congress of Psychology, Beijing, China, 8–13 August 2004

How is psychology prospering now as we attend the first International Congress of Psychology of this new millennium? This question is being asked at a time when the landscape of science is being reshaped, and similar questions apply not only to psychology, but to all the other sciences as well. Some scientists may be inclined to answer simply that psychology is still here, and is doing well. For others, the answer may be that something unusual is taking place, reflecting a deeper evolution, the sign of a transition towards a restructuring of the scientific domain. Between these two extremes, there are a number of other possible answers. Here, I will look at the current situation and the prospects for psychology as the science with the unique agenda of accounting for the human mind and human behavior. The agenda of psychology extends to forms of practice intended to assist the development of human mind and behavior, a practice based on rational knowledge and which has imposed on itself an evidence-based approach. Whether it is intended to contribute to general knowledge, or to address individual needs, psychological science is inspired by the same rational vision of human mental function.

"Psychological science" is the name by which the International Union sponsoring our Congress has defined its domain. Some criticize the fact that our Union sticks to what they perceive as an old-fashioned name. Why not simply refer to "psychology"? The designation of the Union as the International Union of Psychological Science (IUPsyS) dates back to its foundation in 1951. As is aptly recalled by the historians of the Union (Rosenzweig, Holtzman, Sabourin, & Bélanger, 2000), this designation was adopted to stress the methodological approach to mind and behavior to which the founders of the Union adhered, in contrast to the mentalistic approach to mind that was still prevalent at the turn of the 1950s. This terminology probably also reflected some sort of insecurity or lack of self-confidence. However, the value of this name was – and still is – that it reminds us that a scientific approach is the guiding thread linking all the activities in the Union's agenda.

Psychology, as a science, is dedicated to determining facts with a special status, in that they are obtained using rational methods, and the outputs gain their full value from this commitment to an empirical approach. Psychology reaches its goal by generating knowledge with a wide field of application – i.e., that is applicable to human beings in general. Sometimes, however, psychologists are invited to devote themselves to the investigation and treatment of individual cases. For instance, a psychologist may be invited to deal with the learning difficulties of a particular student, and to design a rehabilitation procedure for that particular case. Or he/she may be invited by the manager of an industrial plant to organize staff relationships. Or, again, he/she may be asked to advise about the most efficient way of delivering navigational assistance to visitors in a museum. In all such cases, the psychologist is expected to provide a diagnosis, and go on to recommend a practice that is based on documented and validated general scientific knowledge. In this context, we should not feel any embarrassment about retaining this reference to "psychological science".

Is psychology serving its goals adequately today?

Perhaps more than other sciences, psychology is rooted in society. We should probably say that it is rooted in a number of differing societies. The variety of social and economic contexts from country to country is such that different answers can be expected to the question of whether psychology is serving its goals adequately. This is a matter of priorities, as we shall see below.

No one disputes that a number of societal issues are directly connected to the goals of psychology as a science. This fact confronts psychologists with two possible approaches. Scientists who adopt the first approach justify their endeavors by the very fact that they are surrounded by questions posed by the society. They construct their research programs in response to the implicit or explicit needs of that society. The other approach is more demanding. Here, scientists not only generate knowledge, but they also try to make sure that society makes proper use of knowledge they have generated. This kind of involvement is hard for an individual scientist to achieve, and this task has to be entrusted to organizations, whether at the national, regional, or international level (the latter being the concern of the IUPsyS). Although psychology is doing well by having acquired a consultative status (for instance, in the United Nations system), more remains to be done. Another endeavor is to try to ensure that the voice of scientists is heard by the governing bodies of nations.

In this section, I will review some of the societal challenges to which psychologists are not only entitled to contribute, but in which they are expected to develop a proactive practice of their discipline.

Education

At least a third of the world's population is currently receiving (or ought to be receiving) education. Psychology deals with a number of educational issues which, at a first glance, may seem to be the same for all students worldwide, but in fact vary considerably from place to place. Consider the issue of school attendance in early childhood (say, from the age of 2), and the problems of psychological adaptation resulting from this social phenomenon. This concern is highly characteristic of developed countries. Next, consider the issue of teaching priorities for children whose school attendance is limited by the economic situation of the family. This is a priority for psychology in developing countries. Other issues have a more general scope, in that they are relevant in a wide range of societal contexts, such as the individuation of learning programs, the evaluation of the human capacities (and their adjustment to societal needs), life-long education, or failure at school. It is easy to understand why it is necessary to obtain a better understanding and description of these problems relating to learning in order to develop effective actions. In this domain, there are many signs indicating that psychology is doing well, even though it still has a lot more to do.

Health

Psychology is often assumed to be primarily concerned with mental health, a domain where scientists and professionals have been working hand in hand for a long time. Psychiatric problems are now being approached in new ways, and greater prominence is being given to the cognitive components involved. Communication disorders and autism are also important current topics. A rather new development for psychology is that of expressing an interest in health issues in general, and not only in mental health. Some of the problems encountered at the interface between mental and physical health have become more significant. Some of these concerns are relevant worldwide, such as HIV/AIDS, whereas others are primarily of concern in the more prosperous parts of the world, such as addictions, obesity, and aging-related disorders, which are all aspects of a problem revealing that the privileges of the developed world are rebounding on rich societies. Psychology also covers new health-related domains and can provide knowledge about them. For instance, one of the new features emerging from the domain is the fact that a number of disorders (and a number of remedies) depend not only on taking medication, but also on the individual's behavior. This is an obvious invitation to behavioral sciences, in particular psychology, to make their contribution.

Technology

Did psychological knowledge improve the situations that involve advanced technologies? In particular, did it improve the working conditions that involve such technologies? Rapid changes in the domain of work have created new situations, in which special cognitive resources are required. People now interact with machines and other sorts of artifacts in more and more settings, and this makes new demands on the users' cognition. Psychology is involved in designing these machines, both in order to adapt the machines to human capabilities and competences, and to ensure that people make the best use of the machines. In other words, a new perspective for psychology is to ensure that the "human factor" is taken into account properly in the communication loop involving artificial systems. An example of this need is the failure of many web sites to live up to the expectations of their users. Remember too that "smart" devices based on intelligent technologies are now found not only in the work place, but also in daily life, such as in GPS-based navigational devices in a world of generalized mobility. A genuine appeal is being addressed to psychology to help to enhance the value of these devices.

There is no reason to complain that industrialists do not pay enough attention to the quality of their products. Remember that these products (objects or services), in particular those used for communication purposes, whether they are computers, digital cameras, or mobile phones, are ultimately bought by the public in a competitive marketplace, which certainly motivates designers to make their products as functional and attractive as possible. It is in the interest of manufacturers to develop communication devices that provide their users with as much satisfaction and as little frustration as possible. To take just one example, mobile phone companies that want to provide user-friendly services know that it is crucial for them to involve psychologists in the process, in order to design systems and services that match both the expectations and the behavioral capabilities of their customers. They even have to consider how such services can be delivered to specific groups within the population, such as the visually handicapped, who have special needs when they come to interacting with devices such as mobile phones.

The critical point here is that companies have understood that psychologists can do a lot for them (or with them), not only because communication is a psychological issue in its own right, but because psychologists have the methodological skills required to measure performance and satisfaction. However, psychologists should be reminded that they must not just stand on the sidelines waiting to be contacted. They must be proactive in contacting the potential customers for psychology, including manufacturers. The goal is to use experimental methods to answer questions posed by manufacturers or service providers. Psychologists are becoming more aware of the value of practicing psychology within a society that has needs and expresses them. However, they must also be cautious. A company may decide to call in a psychologist as an expert in the production of a new object or service. However, many companies have a very vague notion of what a psychologist can actually do. Some of their needs may be better served by an expert in social relations or, as is being increasingly realized, by a philosopher. Companies need help in formulating their exact requirements, in order to find out whether a psychologist or a specialist in some other domain, such as the social sciences, will be most helpful.

Culture and social integration

Psychology has already demonstrated its ability to help to understand why and how people, and groups of people, do or do not integrate into their society (or into micro-societies). If an individual is not integrated, he/she is likely to become dysfunctional, and this may take a variety of forms, such as violence, exclusion, extreme behavior, or stigmatization. Psychologists should also keep in mind that people's ability to master language is a prerequisite for many forms of integration, particularly in multicultural, multilinguistic societies. This places new demands on educational and cultural policies, starting with the teaching of foreign languages.

From this overview of a few domains, it is easy to see that psychology lies at the core of many of the issues facing modern societies. Although this is not a new claim, it provides an opportunity to recall that the pervasiveness of psychological issues probably explains why psychology is taught in universities worldwide, and why it appeals so much both to students and to the general public. In this respect, one point on which psychologists do not always do very well is that of transmitting their scientific knowledge to the public (rather than reporting anecdotal or sensational data).

Is psychology serving cross-disciplinary research well?

A growing idea in the field of science is that even though the various disciplines derive their identity from a set of features that are specific to them, they also shape their prospects and design their agendas from the topics they share with other disciplines. This is true in particular of psychology, which has close links with neighboring disciplines, including biology and the life sciences as well as the human and social sciences, and which have recently been extended to include engineering and computer sciences (see Denis, 1998).

Several levels of these interactions between psychology and other disciplines can be distinguished (see Denis, 2000). The first level concerns the situations where one discipline contributes its expertise to the other, without this implying that the two disciplines are pursuing a truly common objective. For instance, in a medical survey of a population of workers, psychologists may be requested to provide ways of measuring the participants' mental capacities. In such a situation, the fact that one of the disciplines allows the other to benefit from a specific competence does not entail any notion of reciprocity. One discipline is helping the other to deal with a problem that is not primarily within its own sphere. However, the convergence of methods is a necessary step towards making an investigation a comprehensive one.

A further step may be taken when the disciplines engage in a project with a marked dimension of mutual involvement. The concept here is that more integrated cooperation is necessary to solve a common problem. For instance, how to design an interface or an intelligent computer system that can be used efficiently by its users? In such a project, not only do psychology and computer science pool their resources in a common endeavor, but the final outcome also depends essentially on their cooperation. While the first level mentioned above tends to be described as being "pluridisciplinary", the greater integration and convergence of the disciplines at the second level is better described as being "interdisciplinary".

In both these kinds of partnership, the identity of each discipline is preserved. However, a new question may emerge when the joint efforts of two disciplines reflect a broader approach, in which it would no longer seem to be relevant to maintain each discipline as a separate entity, but on the contrary seems to be necessary to make explicit the fact that the capacities have been integrated into a single perspective. This is a serious question, which has obvious implications, and this is what is driving the shift in the landscape of science. The concept of "transdisciplinary" research which is now emerging is a more ambitious one. The idea is that the scientific partners acknowledge the need to define a new domain that may encompass several existing disciplines (or parts of them). This is typically sanctioned by the creation of new labels to flag this integration. Examples that will be familiar to psychologists are those that have led to the concepts of "neuropsychology" or "psycholinguistics". More recently, the concept of "cognitive science" sounds more ambitious, since it involves a larger set of disciplines. Here, a common language has to be forged, which will integrate the original languages of each of the individual disciplines.

Should these various forms of cross-disciplinary interaction be encouraged in science as a goal in itself, in addition to the specific goals that each discipline properly pursues? In other words, should the interpenetration of disciplines be valued in itself? Conflicting opinions have been expressed about this issue. Some scientists are open to cross-disciplinary research, but still think that there is nevertheless no *a priori* value in this approach, and that the virtue of cross-disciplinary research is only guaranteed if there is a reason to think that the issue definitely cannot be solved by a single discipline. The cross-disciplinary perspective is just seen as a metamethod, which is therefore restricted to the areas of research that require this approach. As a matter of fact, many of the questions that psychologists are facing do not call for any input from other disciplines (for instance, designing a test to measure a cognitive capacity, or designing a method to describe a child's drawing behavior). However, consider the situation of a psychologist trying to model a cognitive function so that the model is compatible with current knowledge about brain function. This calls for cooperation with neuroscience, following an initial specification of the types of scientific data (cognitive and neuronal) that are involved in the research.

An alternative view is that the cross-disciplinary approach has intrinsic virtue. The concept here is that psychologists have to develop their thinking and practice as psychologists, but that precisely as psychologists, they must learn to think beyond psychology. This view is related to the fact that psychology perceives itself as having a special position among other disciplines, because it has a special capacity to integrate concepts and relate them to the human side of science. We should probably be cautious about claiming that we psychologists constitute the core of a family of sister sciences, and we must avoid "psychocentrism". However, it is interesting to note that this view of psychology as a core discipline is sometimes held by non-psychologists as well.

Actually, a number of core concepts of psychology, such as "mind", "cognition", "consciousness", "intelligence", are concepts of interest to other disciplines. I will consider in turn how relationships are developing between psychology and several sister disciplines, all of which use their own methods. Despite the methodological differences between the disciplines, many concepts are shared. Are the concepts that psychology shares with other disciplines responsible for the development of the cross-disciplinary potential of psychology, and its strengthened position at the interface of sciences?

Neuroscience

Psychology, as a study of mental processes, has always been motivated by the desire to achieve some insight into the substrate of mental processes. This is not its primary objective, but reflects the materialistic postulate that any process must be implemented by means of a physical infrastructure. Consequently, cognition, emotion, and the like are thought of as having neuronal substrates, and it is assumed that valuable information can be gained at the level of these substrates.

Before the label of "neuroscience" entered in the field, psychophysiology and psychology had worked hand in hand for decades. Psychophysiology dealt with measuring events generated in the central and peripheral nervous system, which were assumed to subserve mental events. What psychology learned was both the value and the limitations of the information provided by physiological indicators. To take a single example from a domain with which I am familiar, by the end of the 1960s, people researching imagery developed great enthusiasm for measuring pupil dilation as an indicator of the generation of visual images. In fact, the time pattern of this value was shown to vary depending on whether the words used as stimuli were high- or low-imagery nouns. However, there was some disappointment when it later turned out that these measurements did not in fact reflect a specific process (the creation of visual images), but the amount of cognitive effort associated with the creation of images.

Today, neuroscience and psychology have developed good relationships, especially since the upsurge of neuroimaging techniques. There was a true appeal to psychologists when it became obvious that the neuroimaging techniques were ready to provide answers, but that the questions had not yet been clearly posed. More importantly, it was clear that the experimental paradigms would have to be designed on the basis of the psychological knowledge available. Because psychology is a science both of mind and of behavior, it is irreplaceable for disciplines that at some point of their investigations have to rely on measures of behavior. The skills of psychologists in experimental design have been acknowledged, but beyond this, psychology can offer its theoretical models of mental functions. Simultaneously, psychology both helps neuroscience and is itself enriched by these interactions, by being forced to press forward and include the notion of the brain infrastructure of mental events when developing hypotheses about these mental events (see Henson, 2005).

Neuropsychology

Psychology provides models for neuropsychology, and helps in interpreting behavioral deficits resulting from cerebral lesions. An interesting development has taken place in this discipline – from clinical neuropsychology, the objective of which is to predict the site of a lesion from the behavioral dysfunctions observed, to cognitive neuropsychology, which attempts to make statements about normal cognitive function by studying impaired behavior. The object of these areas of study is the same – what changes is the focus. Close interactions with neuropsychology have enhanced the ability of psychology to formulate more articulated models of human cognition.

Similar processes are at work as regards the relationships that psychology entertains with psychiatry and neurology. With the latter, the cognitive aspect of degenerative illnesses has become an important challenge for psychology. To quote a recent study on Alzheimer patients (Denis, Ricalens, Baudouin, & Nespoulous, 2006), the spatial discourse of disoriented people is dramatically impoverished from the early stages of their illness, but some aspects are retained, i.e., they resist deterioration; one such aspect is the reference to visual landmarks. Although landmarks may be poorly or wrongly connected to one another in the patients' discourse, they nevertheless appear to be relatively unscathed. This is an interesting finding for the study of normal spatial cognition, and shows that landmarks are prominent items, connected to the procedural part of discourse. The latter is lost in Alzheimer patients, and the key elements of spatial discourse are those that are preserved in patients. This information is valuable for general psychology. It is also of potential value to inspire methods for behavioral remediation.

Sciences of language

Psychology has produced a variety of theoretical models of language production and language comprehension, as well as original data in these domains. These data are a primary source of inspiration for modern linguistics. Linguistic models, in particular, have attempted to account for the acquisition of the first language, as well as the second and further languages. They have accounted for the human cognitive architecture, as a prerequisite for the acquisition of reading and writing. They have helped us to understand the intimate mechanisms of speech production and speech comprehension. In exchange, theories and formal models in linguistics have contributed to developing the cognitive psychology of language and psycholinguistics, which have expanded to result in neuropsycholinguistics, a remarkable example of an interdisciplinary domain where three source disciplines are combined.

Informatics and computer science

An important shift in informatics occurred when the computer scientists started designing tools and algorithms to simulate human cognitive processing (including reading, speech recognition, categorization, and face recognition). Some took their inspiration from psychological theories, and their advances could probably have been made without any further input from psychologists. In fact, a significant subset of computer scientists thought that they should pursue their research in close partnership with psychologists, who had the background necessary to evaluate the cognitive validity of machine behavior. This contact has forced psychologists to become increasingly more explicit in formulating cognitive theories, and to describe in detail the processing steps that are necessary for a cognitive agent to perform a task.

Engineers devise technological devices, many of which are intended for use in the workplace, but also to an increasing extent, in daily life and by the general public. Psychologists have a role to play – and are playing this role – not because they have deliberately decided to impose themselves, but because it has been realized that these devices need to be designed with their future users in mind. This may seem to be self-evident, but people have been rather slow to take this idea on board. Note that this phenomenon is also true in other technological domains. The design of virtual environments is growing in importance, and psychology and ergonomics have a lot to say about the functional value and acceptability of these new devices.

The domain of computer science is of particular interest, in that it illustrates how people engaged in cross-disciplinary projects can be guided simultaneously by different sorts of motivation. Computer scientists are committed to designing artificial systems that work, without necessarily being interested in human cognition itself (or its limitations). The aim of psychologists is to provide accounts of cognitive functions; that is, to document a domain of the natural sciences. However, psychology can make its special contribution by going beyond the search for scientific knowledge. It can contribute to a concerted effort to improve the way human beings interact with the artificial devices they encounter in their environment.

Social sciences

Fruitful interactions are also occurring between psychology and social sciences, such as anthropology, ethnology, and sociology. Remarkable advances have been made in the domain of economics. It is significant that the two distinguished psychologists who have been awarded the Nobel Prize – Herbert Simon in 1978 and Daniel Kahneman in 2002 – were in fact recognized for the application of their work to the domain of economics. Several economists are currently turning to psychology and neuroscience. The domain of decision making (in game-play or in economic situations) is known to involve a number of cognitive and emotional factors, which are now accessible to cognitive and brain sciences (e.g., Camille, Coricelli, Sallet, Pradat-Diehl, Duhamel, & Sirigu, 2004).

What are psychology's new frontiers today?

A century after its birth, psychology appears to be firmly established as a discipline in the field of science. It has gained a genuine profile, and a clear conceptual and methodological identity. It is represented in top-level scientific organizations, the most eminent of which is the International Council for Science (ICSU). At the same time, over the past decade or so, psychology has shown a growing capacity to interact with other disciplines in investigating human cognition. Does this involve directing psychology towards new frontiers? I will consider this question by looking at the developing joint venture between psychology and neuroscience.

The starting point is the claim that in collaborative programs psychology can provide models that inspire research intended to identify the brain activity underlying mental processes. Neuroscience, and particularly cognitive neuroscience, takes the research findings of psychology into account, and vice versa. For many years, cognitive functions have been investigated without any reference to the physical brain that supports their operation. This is still an acceptable approach to understanding the algorithms underlying the functioning of cognitive agents, irrespective of whether the structure supporting this function is biological or artifactual in nature. However, in recent years there has been a marked shift to the position that models of cognitive processes must include the constraints imposed on processing by the physical substrate. It is the task of neuroscience to identify the cerebral infrastructure of these functions.

The progress of research in this domain results from a combination of two factors, namely the increased emphasis in neuroscience on model building, which was the result of closer interactions with psychology, and the development of sophisticated techniques, in particular those based on functional neuroimaging. The great value of these techniques, which were originally used to investigate regions of the brain involved in psychiatric syndromes, is that they can be applied to a wide range of people. These techniques have helped to identify the brain structures activated during the execution of cognitive tasks in every domain of cognition (including visual attention, mental imagery, language comprehension, motor activity, and decision making).

The rapid progress of scientific knowledge about the central nervous system and the high standing of "integrative neuroscience", which deals with the higher-order cognitive processes, has a negative impact, however. There is a certain trend towards marginalizing the part of psychological research that is exclusively focused on behavior. Although the extent of this trend varies from country to country, more and more psychologists apparently feel that it is essential to tackle psychological issues by simultaneously addressing the issue of their underlying neural structures. This trend has been amplified by a number of factors. One is that it is becoming easier and easier for psychologists to access neuroimaging facilities. Another factor is that in many places, psychologists who include the issue of the brain structures in their research programs are viewed as being scientifically more respectable by research agencies, by leading journals, and sometimes even by themselves!

This situation also has a positive aspect, since there is a permanent reminder that cognition is rooted in a neural substrate, and that the models developed must take these neural constraints into account. The unfortunate aspect is the risk that cognitive research could sooner or later be driven entirely by brain studies. Another risk is that the issue of brain infrastructure may be introduced into research programs too early, i.e., before articulated hypotheses about the cognitive processes have been developed and empirically tested.

Psychology today has good reasons to take pride in its role at the "crossroads" of cognitive science. To fulfill this role, it must promote cross-disciplinary projects by increasing its links with neuroscience and the other sciences. However, psychology is a discipline in its own right, and is not expected to dilute itself within other disciplines. To ensure this, it is essential for psychology to preserve a strong scientific and academic identity as a distinct discipline, and that psychologists should not feel ashamed to be doing purely behavioral research, provided that it is of good scientific quality. They should not behave as if they needed to cloak themselves in another discipline in order to gain scientific respectability.

Another way of looking at this situation is that we are perhaps witnessing a much deeper transformation that, at some point in the process, might involve a transdisciplinary perspective, with a more intimate merging of disciplines, and which will simultaneously account for both the mind (the process) and the brain (the substrate). If this is the case, the issue would no longer be to speculate whether psychology has a central role in the process or not. The frontiers would simply no longer be those that we have learned to recognize, and with which we are familiar. In this case, brain and cognitive sciences would involve the same scientists.

There is no doubt that the landscape is evolving towards a more biologically oriented psychology. It is important to see psychology as belonging to the field of biological sciences, but psychology should not forget that biological factors are only one facet of a more complex machinery that makes up the human entity – the human mind and the human brain – one of the most fascinating objects that science has ever had to investigate. For psychologists, keeping the links between their discipline and the human and social sciences is a way of being relevant to members of the public who are interested in psychology and make use of it.

References

Camille, N., Coricelli, G., Sallet, J., Pradat-Diehl, P., Duhamel, J.-R., & Sirigu, A. (2004). The involvement of the orbitofrontal cortex in the experience of regret. *Science, 304*, 1167–1170.

Denis, M. (1998). The place and role of psychology in cognitive science: An international survey. *International Journal of Psychology, 33*, 377–395.

Denis, M. (2000). Psychological science in cross-disciplinary contexts. In K. Pawlik & M.R. Rosenzweig (Eds.), *The international handbook of psychology* (pp. 585–597). London: Sage.

Denis, M., Ricalens, K., Baudouin, V., & Nespoulous, J.-L. (2006). Deficits in the spatial discourse of Alzheimer patients. In M. Hickmann & S. Robert (Eds.), *Space in languages: Linguistic systems and categories* (pp. 307–317). Amsterdam: John Benjamins.

Henson, R. (2005). What can functional neuroimaging tell the experimental psychologist? *Quarterly Journal of Experimental Psychology, 58*A, 193–233.

Rosenzweig, M.R., Holtzman, W.H., Sabourin, M., & Bélanger, D. (2000). *History of the International Union of Psychological Science (IUPsyS)*. Hove, UK: Psychology Press.

Section I

Learning, memory, and motivation

3 The nature of learning and the functional architecture of the brain

Charles R. Gallistel

Assumptions about the nature of learning and assumptions about the functional architecture of the brain are intimately intertwined in contemporary cognitive science and neuroscience. There are two radically different analytic frameworks for thinking about learning; for each, there is a corresponding functional architecture imputed to the brain.

On the first analysis, learning is the extraction from experience of information about the world, which is carried forward in memory to inform future behavior. On the second analysis, learning is the remolding of a plastic brain by experience so as to make the brain better adapted to the experienced world.

On the first analysis, the brain has the functional architecture of a Turing machine (Turing, 1936, see Figure 3.1A), that is, of an information-processing device, such as a conventional computer. The fundamental components of this architecture are a read/write memory (represented by the tape in Figure 3.1A) and compositional operators (represented by the addition register in Figure 3.1A).

The memory contains information about the world in the form of symbols. In a conventional computer, these are bit patterns, strings of 1s and 0s. They represent facts about the world, such as the width of a brick wall. Symbols representing facts about the world are the data on which a data-processing device like a computer operates. The essential function of the memory is the carrying of information forward in time. It is the repository where information resides when it is not in use.

Compositional operators compose new data structures or expand old data structures, by operating on data read from memory. Data structures are sets of related symbols, stored in memory in such a way as to encode the relations that obtain between them. An example would be a pair of symbols, representing the width and height of a wall. The pair is stored in such a way as to indicate which symbol represents the width, which the height, and which wall it is whose width and height they represent.

Composition means putting together. It is the essence of data processing. Multiplying two numerical symbols – for example, the symbols representing the width and height of the wall to obtain a symbol representing the area of the wall – is an example of a compositional operation. It puts together two

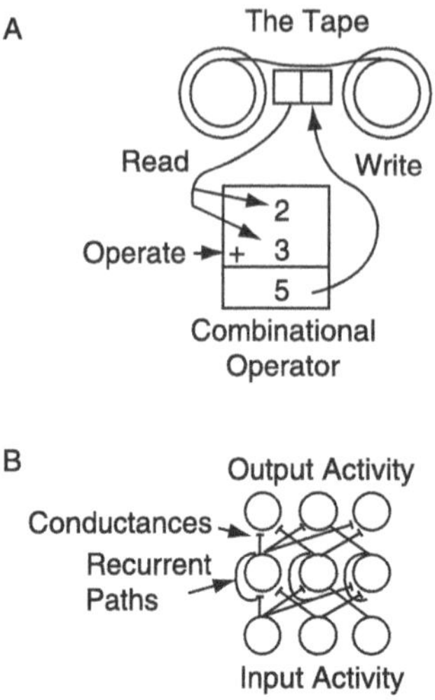

Figure 3.1 A. The functional architecture of an information-processing system. The tape is the read/write memory element with which Turing endowed his abstraction of the essential elements of a universal computing machine. The arithmetic summation is an example of the symbol-combining (compositional) operations that constitute the other essential element. B. The functional architecture of a recurrent switching net.

input symbols to generate a third symbol, their product. When this symbol is written into the right place in memory – taking its place among the other wall-related symbols – the data structure representing the wall is thereby expanded.

There is no memory in the conventional computer-science sense on the second analysis, the analysis inspired by current ideas about the structure and function of the nervous system. On this second analysis, the brain has the functional architecture of a recurrent switching network (Rumelhart & McClelland, 1986, see Figure 3.1B). The fundamental components of this architecture are nodes (pseudo-neurons) with variable activity levels. The nodes are connected to each other by graded and signed conductances, which determine the flow of activity between nodes. Critical components of this internodal connectivity are recurrent pathways, which conduct activity from a node back to itself. Without them there is no sustained activity in the network because, as Sherrington said of the nervous system: "[the function of a switching network] can be summed up in one word, *conduction*" (Sherrington, 1947).

What comes naturally

The two functional architectures differ strikingly in what they make it natural (easy, straightforward) for a brain to do. On the first analysis, what comes naturally is the composing of data structures: copying them, concatenating them, multiplying, dividing, adding, subtracting them, and so on, to create new data structures and new values for old ones. On this analysis, the brain represents the world by composing data structures that refer to selected aspects of it.

On the second analysis, what comes naturally is classification. A recurrent switching network settles into different stable patterns of activity (attractor states) depending on which input it gets. The number of distinct stable attractor states is, however, much less than the number of distinct inputs. Thus, many different inputs cause the system to settle into any given stable attractor state. This seems analogous to a category and its instances: instances (inputs) differ but they activate the same category (attractor state). The relation between inputs and the attractor states they activate is determined by the conductances in the switching network. The conductances are functions of a learning rule of some kind applied to the animal's experience. The conductance between a signal-sending node and a signal-receiving node determines the magnitude (and sign) of the effect that a signal from the sending node has on receiving node. Thus, what it is easy or natural for a recurrent switching network to do is to learn to categorize states of the world. A recurrent network represents the world by categorizing it.

The two frameworks also differ in their assumptions about how the brain's activity becomes manifest in behavior. On the first analysis, behavior-generating programs get control and decision variables from the information-processing system. They compare them to action-specific decision criteria (thresholds) to decide on actions, which are then parameterized by the control variables. The distinction between the information-processing component, which extracts information about the world from input, and the action-generating system, which makes use of the information, is generally readily apparent in this kind of architecture. On the second analysis, the distinction between these two roles is less clear. Often, the activity pattern on the output side of the network is taken, at least implicitly, to specify an action appropriate to the specified category.

Courts of last appeal

Partisans of the different frameworks differ in their courts of last appeal. For partisans of the first analysis, the court of last appeal is behavior: they argue, as I will argue, that the behavioral facts imply an information-processing architecture. There is no way to explain the behavioral facts except by assuming a read/write memory and the composition of data structures, both of which functionalities are absent in the second kind of architecture. Therefore, we must assume the existence of mechanisms in the nervous system that perform these functions, despite the fact that what we currently know about the nervous system does not support such an assumption. On this analysis, what we know about behavior is a guide to what we must look for in the nervous system.

For partisans of the second analysis, the court of last appeal is the nervous system. It manifestly has, they argue, the architecture they assume in modeling behavior. Open any textbook on the nervous system and what you find in the description of the system's observable structure and in the records of its electrical activity is the functional structure portrayed in Figure 3.1B. Nowhere do you find a description of a mechanism with the properties of a read/write memory. You find, it is true, descriptions of localized activity in anatomical spaces that map real-world spaces. For example, the location of activity in the deep layers of the superior colliculus (a two-dimensional anatomical space) maps the location of distal saccade targets in a two-dimensional directional space centered on the optic axis of the eye (Sparks & Groh, 1995). These localized activities look like candidate data structures; they look like vectors in the nervous system that refer to and may therefore represent vector variables in the world outside the brain. If, however, that is the appropriate interpretation of them, then something crucial is missing, namely a description of the mechanisms or processes that compose these data structures to create new data structures. How are they added, subtracted, multiplied, copied, concatenated, subordinated, and so on? If the nervous system is a system for composing data structures, what are its built-in compositional operations? On this question, the texts are also silent. Partisans of the second analysis take these silences as evidence of absence: what has not been described presumably does not exist and should not be assumed in making models meant to explain behavior.

The behavioral case

Many simple and robust behavioral phenomena seem inexplicable – or very awkwardly explicable – in the absence of a read/write memory and the composition of data structures. I briefly review three of them.

Dead reckoning

Experiment has shown that animals keep track of their position and heading relative to their nest and other points of interest in the world by integrating their velocity with respect to time, or, equivalently, by summing successive small displacement vectors to get the net displacement vector (Alyan & Jander, 1994; Alyan & McNaughton, 1999; Durier & Rivault, 1999; Etienne et al., 1991; Georgakopoulos & Etienne, 1994; Mittelstaedt & Mittelstaedt, 1980; Save et al., 1998; Schatz et al., 1999; Séguinot et al., 1993; Wehner & Wehner, 1986; Wohlgemuth et al., 2001).

Dead reckoning is dead easy in a device with the architecture shown in Figure 3.1A. A displacement vector is a simple data structure consisting of two symbols that together specify a small change in position, for example <0.9, 0.4>. The first of the two symbols represents the distance the animal has just moved in one of two perpendicular directions (e.g., north); the other represents the distance it has just moved in the other direction (e.g., east). Each small movement (change in position) generates a displacement vector. The running sum of these vectors – the sum of all the symbols in the first position together with the sum of all the symbols in the second position – is the net displacement, which represents where the animal is relative to where it started. (This running sum is often called the home vector.)

To implement dead reckoning in a system with the architecture of Figure 3.1B is awkward (Samsonovich & McNaughton, 1997). As Samuel Johnson said of a dog walking on its hind legs, "It is not done well, but you are surprised that it is done at all."[1]

The dance of the foraging bee

The foraging bee returning from a rich food source does a dance that specifies the direction and distance of the source (Frisch, 1967). The dance is in the form of a figure 8, with the "waggle" run constituting the common portion of the two loops. The angle of the waggle run with respect to vertical specifies the solar bearing of the source (its direction relative to the sun) and the number of waggles specifies the distance.

There are no implementational mysteries here, if we grant the bee's nervous system the functional architecture in Figure 3.1A. When the bee is at the source, its dead-reckoning vector specifies the source's location relative to the hive (a vector structure). As the bee ingests the nectar preparatory to carrying it back to the hive, it gets a sensory input specifying its richness (a scalar structure). It writes the location vector and the richness scalar to memory. When it reaches the hive, the dance program retrieves these data structures (reads the memory). It uses the scalar that represents the richness as a decision variable; only if its value exceeds a threshold (decision criterion) does the bee dance. If it does dance, the remembered location vector at the source parameterizes the behavior. Its angle specifies the direction of the waggle run, while its magnitude specifies the number of waggles.

How to implement this within the architecture in Figure 3.1B is another matter. Suppose we grant, as assumed in Samsonovich and McNaughton (1997), that several interconnected nets with purpose-specific structures give rise to activity patterns whose locations within the nets specify the bee's location when it is at the source. Now what? The net has no read/write memory, no way of preserving for future use the information about the world expressed in its current activity. If we shut off input to these nets to maintain the current activity patterns for future use, how does the bee find its way home? The activity patterns in these nets represent where the bee is at the moment in relation to the hive. That information is presumably crucial for the moment-to-moment control of the homeward flight, although how this control is effected is not specified in the model.

What neural nets have trouble accommodating is the fact that the information that informs behavior is not delivered to the brain all at once, nor at the time it is needed to inform behavior; it arrives piecemeal over time and often long before it is needed. This elementary truth about the character of experience is why the brain needs a read/write memory. Without it, there is no way to make the information gained from current experience accessible to future computation and behavioral control. Put another way, there is no way to compose the activity patterns in the output nodes of the architecture in Figure 3.1B, and that is a devastating shortcoming.

Temporal learning in conditioning experiments

In training phases of Pavlovian conditioning experiments, stimuli called conditioned stimuli (CSs for short), which are initially motivationally neutral (e.g., noises and lights), and unconditioned stimuli (USs for short), which are behaviorally motivating (e.g., foot shock), are repeatedly presented in one or more temporal relations to one another. After the training phases, the subject's reaction to the previously neutral stimuli is measured on test trials.

The temporal relations among the CSs and the US during the training phases determine the motivational valence of the subject's response to the CSs on the test trials. If, for example, a light regularly followed foot shock during one phase of training, the subject's reaction to the light on test trials involves the inhibition of the fear aroused by the anticipation of shock. This is usually explained by assuming that the conditioning experience has created an inhibitory connection (negatively signed conductance) between the node(s) activated by the light and the nodes whose activity constitutes the fear state, although what the learning rule is that creates a forward conductance (from the light node to the fear node) in response to the backward temporal pairing of the node-activating inputs (shock first, then noise) is not clear.

If in earlier phase of the training, the light was regularly preceded by a noise, and if the interval from noise to light in this phase was longer than the interval from shock to light in the latter phase of training, then when tested with the noise, the subject reacts fearfully to it (Barnet et al., 1997; Barnet & Miller, 1996; see Figure 3.2). This is harder to understand from the perspective of conductance changes within a switching network. The activity conducted from the node activated by light to the node whose activity constitutes fear is negatively signed. Activity in the light node reduces activity in the fear node. Because the excitation of the noise node regularly preceded the activation of the light node during the phase of training when they were paired, the sign of the conductance between them is presumably positive, which means that activity in the noise node increases activity in the light node. If activity in the noise node increases activity in the light node and activity in the light node decreases activity in the fear node, why does activating the noise node excite the fear node? It ought to inhibit it.

This latter result is much easier to understand if the brain has a compositional architecture with a read/write memory. From this perspective, the

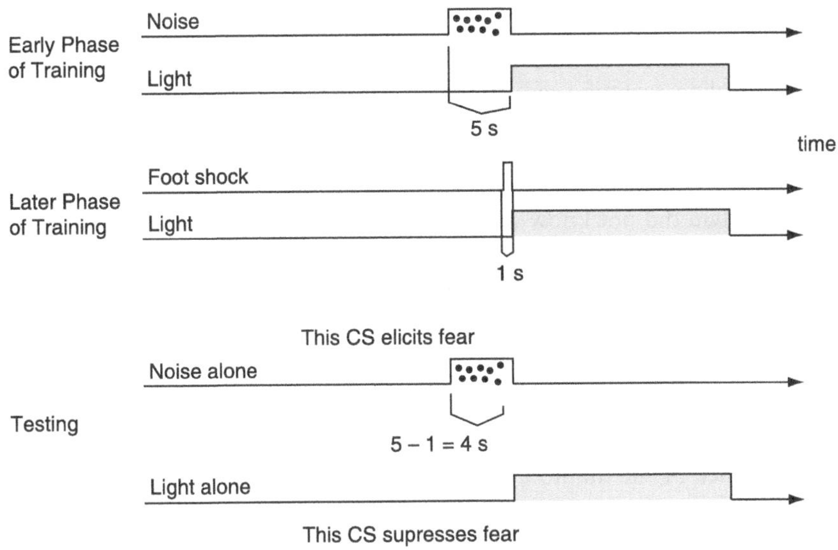

Figure 3.2 Simplified schematic of a Pavlovian conditioning experiment by Barnet and Miller (1996). During the first phase of training, the light (tint) followed the noise (dots) by 5 s. During the second phase of training, shock preceded the light by 1 s. When the two CSs (noise and light) were tested individually, following the second phase of training the light suppressed fear. The noise, which was paired only with the light during training, never with the shock, nonetheless elicited fear. The expected interval between the onset of noise and the onset of shock is 4 s, on the assumption that the brain can compose the remembered values of the noise–light interval (5 s) and the shock–light interval (–1 s).

training phase with the noise followed by the light created a data structure with three fields: one contained a vector specifying the properties of the noise, one a vector specifying the properties of the light, and one a scalar (single quantity) specifying the temporal interval between their onsets. We may represent this data structure as follows: {<noise>, interval, <light>}. The training phase with the shock followed by the noise created a second such data structure: {<shock>, interval, <light>}. The brain composed the two structures to generate a third such structure: {<noise>, interval, <shock>}. The scalar in the middle field of this third structure is the first interval minus the second interval. It represents the expected interval to shock onset following noise onset. This computed temporal expectation explains the subject's fearful reaction to the noise.

Here again, the compositional character of brain activity is evident in the behavior it generates. All of these examples are simple, and they are but a small sampling of the many well-established results from behavioral experiments that are unintelligible unless one assumes a read/write memory and a set of compositional operators (Gallistel, 1990; Gallistel & Gibbon, 2000,

2002). If behavior is the last court of appeal, then there are mechanisms in the nervous system not yet dreamed of in the philosophy of neuroscientists.

This is not the first time this state of affairs has arisen in the history of transdiscipline scientific reductionism. Lord Kelvin famously explained to Darwin that the enormous age for the earth implied by his theory of evolution was not consistent with what physicists knew about the conceivable duration of heat-generation processes in a body the size of the sun (Burchfield, 1990). Kelvin did not know what he did not know. In this case, what he did not know was radioactivity. Its discovery came many years later.

Before Watson and Crick's (1953) epoch-making deduction of the molecular structure of the gene, many biochemists doubted that there were genes (Judson, 1980). The geneticists' concept of a gene was biochemically unintelligible. The gene had two properties for which no plausible biochemical mechanism could be suggested. It was a (putatively) molecular structure that could somehow make a copy of itself. Second, it could somehow determine the sequence of the amino acids in the synthesis of an enzyme. Again, the doubters did not know what they did not know. When the revelation came, it created a new discipline, molecular biology, built on concepts foreign to the biochemistry that preceded this discovery.

These two examples urge caution on those who would disregard the seemingly clear neuroscientific implications of the behavioral data.

Note

1 Boswell, J. (1763). *Life of Johnson 1, Vol. ii, Ch. ix.*

References

Alyan, S., & Jander, R. (1994). Short-range homing in the house mouse, *Mus musculus:* Stages in the learning of directions. *Animal Behaviour*, *48*, 285–298.

Alyan, S., & McNaughton, B.L. (1999). Hippocampectomized rats are capable of homing by path integration. *Behavioral Neuroscience*, *113*(1), 19–31.

Barnet, R.C., Cole, R.P. et al. (1997). Temporal integration in second-order conditioning and sensory preconditioning. *Animal Learning and Behavior*, *25*(2), 221–233.

Barnet, R.C., & Miller, R.R. (1996). Second order excitation mediated by a backward conditioned inhibitor. *Journal of Experimental Psychology: Animal Behavior Processes*, *22*(3), 279–296.

Burchfield, J.D. (1990). *Lord Kelvin and the age of the Earth.* Chicago: University of Chicago Press.

Durier, V., & Rivault, C. (1999). Path integration in cockroach larvae, *Blattella germanica* (L.) (insect: Dictyoptera): Direction and distance estimation. *Animal Learning and Behavior*, *27*(1), 108–118.

Etienne, A.S., Hurni, C. et al. (1991). Twofold path integration during hoarding in the golden hamster. *Ethology, Ecology, and Evolution*, *3*, 1–11.

Frisch, K.V. (1967). *The dance-language and orientation of bees.* Cambridge, MA: Harvard University Press.

Gallistel, C.R. (1990). *The organization of learning*. Cambridge, MA: Bradford Books/ MIT Press.

Gallistel, C.R., & Gibbon, J. (2000). Time, rate and conditioning. *Psychological Review, 107*, 289–344.

Gallistel, C.R., & Gibbon, J. (2002). *The symbolic foundations of conditioned behavior*. Mahwah, NJ: Lawrence Erlbaum Associates Inc.

Georgakopoulos, J., & Etienne, A. (1994). Identifying location by dead reckoning and extenal cue. *Behavioural Processes, 31*, 57–74.

Judson, H. (1980). *The eighth day of creation*. New York: Simon & Schuster.

Mittelstaedt, M.L., & Mittelstaedt, H. (1980). Homing by path integration in a mammal. *Naturwissenschaft, 67*, 566–567.

Rumelhart, D.E., & McClelland, J.L. (Eds.). (1986). *Parallel distributed processing*. Cambridge, MA: MIT Press.

Samsonovich, A., & McNaughton, B.L. (1997). Path integration and cognitive mapping in a continuous attractor neural network model. *Journal of Neuroscience, 17*, 5900–5920.

Save, E., Cressant, A. et al. (1998). Spatial firing of hippocampal place cells in blind rats. *Journal of Neuroscience, 18*(5), 1818–1826.

Schatz, B., Chameron, S. et al. (1999). The use of path integration to guide route learning in ants. *Nature, 399*, 769–772.

Séguinot, V., Maurer, R. et al. (1993). Dead reckoning in a small mammal: The evaluation of distance. *Journal of Comparative Physiology, A, 173*, 103–113.

Sherrington, C.S. (1947). *The integrative action of the nervous system*. New Haven, CT: Yale University Press. (First published 1906)

Sparks, D.L., & Groh, J.F. (1995). The superior colliculus: A window for viewing issues in integrative neuroscience. In M.S. Gazzaniga (Ed.), *The cognitive neurosciences* (pp. 565–584). Cambridge, MA: MIT Press.

Turing, A.M. (1936). On computable numbers, with an application to the Entscheidungsproblem. *Proceedings of the London Mathematical Society 2nd series, 42*, 230–265.

Watson, J.D., & Crick, F.H.C. (1953). Molecular structure of nucleic acids. *Nature, 171*, 737–738.

Wehner, R., & Wehner, S. (1986). Path integration in desert ants: Approaching a long-standing puzzle in insect navigation. *Monitore Zoologica Italiana, 20*, 309–331.

Wohlgemuth, S., Ronacher, B. et al. (2001). Ant odometry in the third dimension. *Nature, 411*, 795–798.

4 Ecological and functional perspectives on Pavlovian conditioning

Michael Domjan

Pavlovian or classical conditioning has become one of the most extensively investigated learning paradigms. Because it can be conveniently conducted with either human or nonhuman subjects, it is a popular technique for the study of both the behavioral and neural mechanisms of associative learning.

Although it is common knowledge that the systematic study of classical conditioning originated with the work of Pavlov and his students, details of the first demonstrations of the phenomenon are less familiar. Pavlov was more responsible for discovering or establishing the theoretical significance of classical conditioning than for being the first one to observe the phenomenon (Rosenzweig, 1959). The first demonstration of classical conditioning in Pavlov's laboratory was conducted by Stephan Vol'fson, a student of Pavlov's who was studying how salivation was elicited by various substances (dry food, for example) (Boakes, 1984). Vol'fson repeatedly tested his dogs with these substances and observed that they salivated in response to the dry food the first time it was placed in the mouth. After several trials, the dogs also salivated to the *sight* of the dry food before it was placed in the mouth. Salivation in response to the sight of the dry food was a learned response.

The sensations of dry food in the mouth caused salivation unconditionally and hence these sensations were called the *unconditional* or *unconditioned stimulus* or *US*. In contrast, the effectiveness of the visual cues of the dry food at a distance was conditional upon pairing these cues with food in the mouth, and hence these visual cues came to be called the *conditioned stimulus* or *CS*. Salivation to the CS was called the *conditioned response* or *CR*.

Associationist vs functionalist perspectives

Because the CS had to be paired with the US a number of times before conditioned salivation occurred in Vol'fson's dogs, this type of learning was interpreted to reflect the formation of new associative linkages between the CS and the US or the CS and the CR. Thus, Pavlovian conditioning was soon considered to be a powerful technique for the study of associative learning and the neural mechanisms that were responsible for this type of learning. Pavlov assumed that associative learning occurs in the cerebral hemispheres and came to devote the latter part of his scientific career to the study of this type of learning as a means of uncovering the functions of the cerebral hemispheres (Pavlov, 1927). Others less concerned about neural mechanisms also latched onto the Pavlovian paradigm as a way to examine the behavioral mechanisms of associative learning. These developments were the foundations of the *associationist perspective* that has dominated the study of Pavlovian conditioning since its inception.

According to the associationist perspective, the primary goal of the study of Pavlovian conditioning is to examine the behavioral and neural mechanisms of the learning of associations between two events. Given this focus on new associations, associationists have been careful to select a conditioned stimulus that is unrelated to the unconditioned stimulus at the outset of training. This emphasis on the use of "arbitrary" or "neutral" conditioned stimuli has become so common that it has become part of the definition of Pavlovian conditioning offered by prominent authors (Anderson, 1995, p. 10; Bower & Hilgard, 1981, p. 49; Papini, 2002, p. 491; Shettleworth, 1998, p. 109; Staddon, 1983, p. 102). An arbitrary or neutral CS will (by definition) not elicit the conditioned response without the association. Therefore, one may assume that the development of the conditioned response provides a fairly direct measure of the strength of the CS–US association.

An arbitrary or neutral CS that is unrelated to the US is unlikely to occur with that US under natural circumstances. Therefore, CS–US pairings have to be arranged by the experimenter. This methodological necessity has encouraged associative investigations of Pavlovian conditioning to move further and further into the laboratory and away from the way the learning occurs in the natural environment of organisms. Studies are conducted in which the experimenter has full control of the presentation of the CS and the US and can schedule these to occur when they best suit the theoretical question being asked. Whether an association does (or does not) develop is then tracked by the occurrence of the conditioned response to the CS. (The key elements of the associationist perspective are presented in the left panel of Figure 4.1.)

Although the associationist perspective originated with Vol'fson's landmark experiment, its key features were not dictated by that study. Given an alternative theoretical orientation, Vol'fson's experiment could well have led to a more functionalist approach to the study of Pavlovian conditioning. Notice that in Vol'fson's experiment, the CS (the sight of dry food) was not arbitrary or unrelated to the US (dry food in the mouth). Rather, the CS and the US were features of the same object. Given this inherent relation between the CS and the US at the outset of training, one can imagine that the CS–US pairing could well have occurred in the natural environment, without experimenter intervention.

The basic assumption of the functionalist perspective is that Pavlovian conditioning is an adaptive form of learning that occurs in the natural environment of organisms and increases their reproductive fitness, either directly or indirectly. This assumption has important methodological

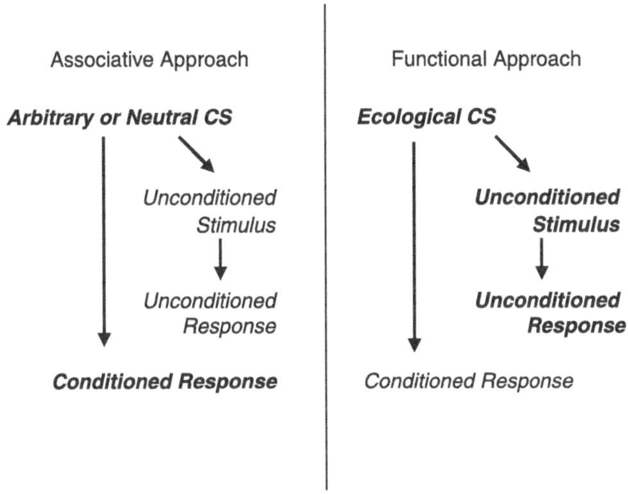

Figure 4.1 Contrasting emphases in the associationist and functionalist perspectives on Pavlovian conditioning. In the associationist perspective, the emphasis (indicated by the bold-faced terms) is on the use of an arbitrary or neutral CS, and conditioned responding that develops to this CS as a result of CS–US pairings. In the functionalist perspective, the emphasis is on the use of an ecological or naturalistic CS that is relevant to the US, and changes in how the unconditioned stimulus is perceived and responded to as a consequence of CS–US pairings.

consequences for the investigation of Pavlovian conditioning that contrast with the methodology dictated by the associationist perspective (see Figure 4.1, right panel). Because the functionalist approach focuses on Pavlovian conditioning as it might occur in the natural environment, it encourages the use of ecological rather than arbitrary or neutral conditioned stimuli. An ecological CS is a natural precursor of the US in the organism's natural environment. It is a stimulus that is encountered shortly before or in combination with the US as a natural consequence of the organization of the environment and the subject's interactions with that environment. Therefore, the intervention of an experimenter is not required for the pairing of an ecological CS with a US.

For CS–US pairings to occur under natural circumstances without experimenter intervention, the CS has to be related to the US at the outset of training. This was the case in Vol'fson's original experiment. The CS (sight of dry food) was a property of the object (dry food) that was also the source of the US (the oral sensations provided by dry food in the mouth). Having the CS and US be properties of the same object facilitates having the two stimuli encountered in combination with one another under natural circumstances. A CS can also occur in combination with a US if the CS is a natural precursor or a causal antecedent to the US in the organism's niche. The examples described below will illustrate cases in which the CS and the US are different attributes of the same object. Studies of conditioned stimuli that are causal antecedents of a US are not as readily available in the literature.

In addition to discouraging the use of arbitrary conditioned stimuli, the functionalist perspective encourages measurement of changes in the subject's response to the unconditioned stimulus as the critical behavioral change produced by Pavlovian conditioning. This is a consequence of the emphasis on the adaptive significance of Pavlovian conditioning. Adaptive significance implies that Pavlovian conditioning enables organisms to cope more effectively with events of great biological importance in their lives (Hollis, 1982, 1997). Conditioned stimuli are not of great biological importance. In fact, lack of biological significance is typically part of the definition of a conditioned stimulus (Gunther, Miller, & Matute, 1997; Pavlov, 1927). The important events in an organism's life are food, shelter, predatory defense, access to potential sexual partners, and the like. These are unconditioned stimuli, not conditioned stimuli. If Pavlovian conditioning increases reproductive fitness, it must achieve that end by enabling organisms to respond more effectively to unconditioned stimuli. Conditioned responses elicited by the CS do not reveal these changes. Rather, the changes should be evident in how an organism interacts with the US after exposure to the CS.

In the following discussion, I will describe some of the research that has been encouraged by, and is consistent with, the functionalist perspective. I will focus on research from my laboratory, since that is most familiar to me. However, I will also mention other relevant experiments. For a more complete discussion of these issues, see Domjan (2005) and Domjan, Cusato, and Krause (2004).

Learning with ecological vs arbitrary conditioned stimuli

Explicit examination of the effects of ecological vs arbitrary conditioned stimuli are not common in studies of Pavlovian conditioning. However, evidence of learning with ecological conditioned stimuli is available from a number of situations.

Poison-avoidance learning

Perhaps the most famous case of Pavlovian conditioning with an ecological conditioned stimulus is poison-avoidance learning. This form of learning helps animals avoid eating foods that make them sick (Rzoska, 1953). The conditioned stimulus is typically the taste of the poisonous food, and the unconditioned stimulus is provided by the post-ingestional distress that follows eating. This fits perfectly the characterization I provided above of a form of Pavlovian conditioning in which the CS is a natural precursor of the US. As in Vol'fson's experiment, the CS and the US are attributes of the same object, in this case the poisonous food. The subject cannot get exposure to the US without first ingesting the food and getting exposed to the flavor as a CS. The CS–US pairing is a natural feature of the environment, which does not require the intervention of an experimenter. Finally, the consequence of the learning, suppressed ingestion of the poisonous food and avoidance of the flavor, is clearly adaptive for the organism.

Learning about ecological conditioned stimuli would be of little theoretical consequence if such learning proceeded in the same way as learning about arbitrary cues. However, that is clearly not the case for poison-avoidance learning. In fact, poison-avoidance learning attracted a great deal of interest when it was first put to thorough experimental examination precisely because such learning had some unusual properties (Garcia, Hankins, & Rusiniak, 1974; Rozin & Kalat, 1971). In particular, taste aversions can be learned even if the aversive postingestional consequence is delayed for several hours after exposure to the novel flavor (Garcia, Ervin, & Koelling, 1966; Smith & Roll, 1967). Such long-delay learning does not occur if conditioned stimuli unrelated to ingestion are employed (Domjan & Wilson, 1972; Garcia & Koelling, 1966). Encouraged by these results, investigators sought to demonstrate instances of long-delay learning in other response systems (see Domjan, 1983, for a review). However, in those examples learning did not occur as rapidly and over as long CS–US intervals.

Taste is not the only possible attribute of a poisonous food. Consider a rat eating a rotten piece of meat that will make it sick. In addition to taste, the piece of meat also has a distinctive odor and a distinctive texture as the rat holds the food in its front paws. These odor and texture cues are ecological conditioned stimuli that have an inherent relation to the US, just as the taste does. Therefore, one might expect that rats will also learn aversions to the odor and texture of food. Consistent with this prediction, both odor and texture aversions have been demonstrated (e.g., Domjan, 1973; Domjan & Hanlon, 1982). In fact, the presence of a distinctive taste has been found to facilitate odor aversion learning (Bouton et al., 1986; Rusiniak, Palmerino, & Garcia, 1982).

Figures 4.2 and 4.3 provide an example (from Domjan & Hanlon, 1982) of poison avoidance learning to texture cues that are paired with toxicosis. Texture was provided by placing familiar food pellets into a metal sleeve whose surface was either stippled or smooth so that the rat would encounter the texture as it ate the food. One texture (the CS+) was paired with toxicosis and the other (the CS–) was not. Since the flavor of the CS+ and CS– was the same, the only basis for discrimination was the texture. Subjects learned an aversion to the texture that had been paired with the US. (For a similar study of aversion learning to the shape of food, see Domjan, Miller, & Gemberling, 1982.)

Although odor and texture cues can characterize poisonous foods, such cues can be also encountered in the absence of eating. Therefore, an important question is what makes odor and texture stimuli relevant to a toxicosis US. The primary difference between odors and textures encountered while

Figure 4.2 Rat eating a food pellet in a metal sleeve with a stippled texture.

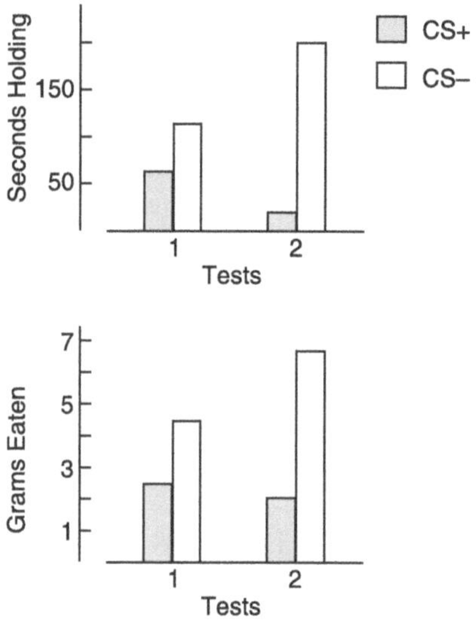

Figure 4.3 Seconds spent holding a food pellet in a metal sleeve with texture (smooth or stippled) that was paired with (CS+) or unpaired (CS–) with gastrointestinal distress. (From Domjan & Hanlon, 1982.)

walking around and odors and textures that characterize food is that food cues are encountered while eating. This suggests that the act of eating may serve to "gate" odor and texture cues into the feeding system and thereby make those cues more easily associated with poisoning. Consistent with this prediction, ingestive behavior facilitates odor aversion learning (Domjan, 1973). As it turns out, the act of ingestion also facilitates taste aversion learning (Domjan & Wilson, 1972). These findings illustrate how ecological factors related to what stimuli subjects encounter before a US and the circumstances under which they encounter these cues can have a major impact on the learning that results.

Sexual conditioning

Sexual conditioning has been conducted with a variety of different species including quail, rats, and a fish species, the blue gourami (see reviews by Domjan & Holloway, 1998; Krause, 2003; Pfaus, 1996; Woodson, 2002). The basic procedure involves presenting a conditioned stimulus paired with exposure to a sexual partner. In most of the experiments, the conditioned stimulus was an arbitrary cue (for example, a red light or an arbitrary odor), with little concern for how learning about such cues might compare with learning about ecologically relevant conditioned stimuli. However, studies with domesticated quail (*Coturnix japonica*) have explicitly examined how learning might be altered with the use of conditioned stimuli that are natural precursors of a sexual encounter in the quail's ecological niche.

Although some experiments with *Coturnix japonica* focused on the conditioning of females (Gutiérrez & Domjan, 1997), most of the research has been conducted with males as the target subject. If a male quail has been housed individually and is then provided with access to a sexually active female, copulation readily occurs, and the sexual reinforcement that is experienced is a highly effective US. Studies in which a localized stimulus (such as a small light or a block of wood) was used as the CS have shown that sexual conditioning results in the development of conditioned approach to the CS. In fact, the conditioned approach response develops even if the CS is located a couple of meters from the US and persists if the CS is moved after training (Burns & Domjan, 2000). Thus, the conditioned response is a form of sign tracking (Hearst & Jenkins, 1974).

Coturnix japonica are ground birds that rarely fly. They exist in the wild in the far East (e.g., Japan and Korea) and in Hawaii. Not much documentation is available about their natural habitat, but studies in Hawaii have indicated that they live in meadows with tall grass (Schwartz & Schwartz, 1949). In this type of environment when a male first sees a female he is likely to only see her head. Only as the two get closer together will they see each other's bodies (see Figure 4.4). In this sequence of events, the sight of the female's head serves as a reliable signal that she is nearby and thus functions as a naturalistic CS for social encounters. The naturalistic CS may be modeled in the laboratory by preparing a taxidermic model of a female's head, with limited neck feathers. One can then create an analogue of a natural social encounter by first presenting the head+neck model and then providing access to a live female. This sequence of events is illustrated in Figure 4.5.

A fundamental question that arises when a naturalistic CS is used is whether Pavlovian pairings are necessary to produce responding to the CS. Köksal, Domjan, and Weisman (1994) answered this question by comparing

Figure 4.4 Illustration of the natural sequence of events that occurs when a male and a female quail encounter each other before copulation. (Drawing by Susanna Douglas.)

Figure 4.5 Laboratory model of a natural encounter of a female by a male quail. Exposure to a taxidermic model of a female head and neck is followed by access to a live female.

the response of two groups of males. For the *paired* group, exposure to the head+neck model was immediately followed by copulatory opportunity. For the *unpaired* group, copulation occurred 25–35 minutes before exposure to the naturalistic CS. Every third day only the CS was presented as a test trial. The results, presented in Figure 4.6, indicated that paired subjects responded to the naturalistic CS significantly more than unpaired subjects. However, a modest level of responding also developed in the unpaired group. These results indicate that the naturalistic CS produced a modest level of responding, which was significantly enhanced by the Pavlovian conditioning procedure. Interestingly, a similar pattern of findings is typical in poison-avoidance learning. A novel taste elicits a modest degree of aversion (called

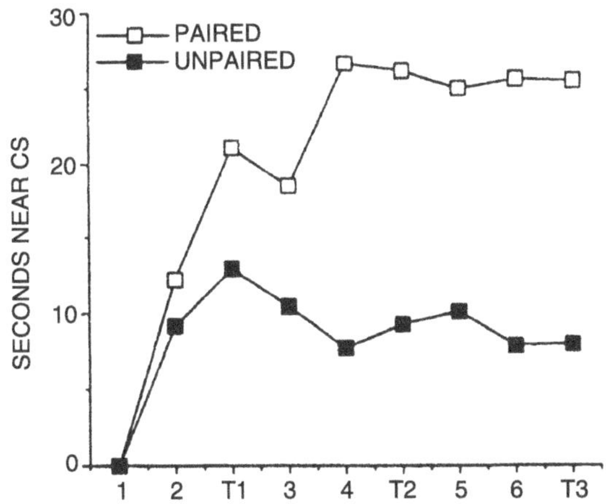

Figure 4.6 Approach to a head+neck CS that was paired or unpaired with copulatory opportunity. (From Köksal et al., 1994.)

flavor neophobia), which is enhanced by pairing the flavor with aversive postingestional consequences.

Given that Pavlovian conditioning is necessary for the development of substantial levels of responding to a head+neck CS, the next question is whether learning with such a CS proceeds in the same way as conditioning with arbitrary conditioned stimuli. This question has been addressed in a series of experiments (see Domjan et al., 2004, for a review) in which independent groups were conditioned with either the naturalistic CS or an arbitrary cue. The two stimulus objects used are shown in Figure 4.7. The arbitrary or neutral CS was made of terrycloth and had the same general size and shape as the naturalistic CS, but it did not include a taxidermic female head and neck.

The results of experiments comparing learning with the arbitrary and naturalistic CS indicated numerous significant differences. Responding to the naturalistic CS developed more rapidly and included a greater range of behaviors. Male quail not only approached and remained near the head+neck CS but also attempted to copulate with the CS object by making grab, mount, and cloacal contact responses directed at the CS (Cusato & Domjan, 1998). Such conditioned copulatory responses rarely developed with the arbitrary CS object.

In addition to showing more rapid learning and a broader range of conditioned responses, the naturalistic CS produced a variety of sexual learning effects that contrast with the typical findings that occur with arbitrary conditioned stimuli. For example, repeated exposure to a naturalistic CS in the absence of copulatory experience results in a slow recruitment or sensitization of approach behavior, rather than the habituation effect that is usually observed when an arbitrary CS is presented on the same schedule (Cusato &

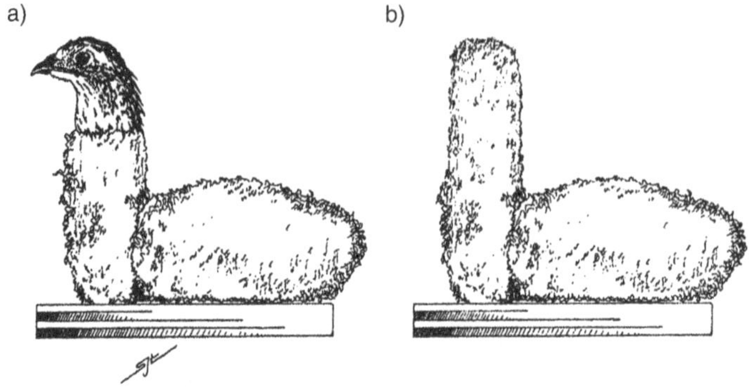

Figure 4.7 Two different objects used as conditioned stimuli in studies of sexual conditioning. The left panel shows an ecologically relevant CS that is made of terrycloth and includes a taxidermically prepared female head and neck feathers. The right panel shows an arbitrary CS that is made entirely of terrycloth. (Drawing by Stewart Hilliard.)

Domjan, 1998). Other experiments demonstrated that conditioning with the naturalistic CS was immune to the blocking effect: responding to the naturalistic CS was not disrupted by the presence of a different previously conditioned CS (Köksal et al., 1994). In addition, once responding developed to the naturalistic CS, it did not show the usual effects of extinction with repeated CS alone presentations (Krause, Cusato, & Domjan, 2003). Rather, responding persisted in extinction. Responding to the naturalistic CS also supported more second-order conditioning (Cusato & Domjan, 2001).

Another major difference was that responding to the naturalistic CS was not as readily disrupted by increases in the CS–US interval. Akins (2000) conditioned independent groups of subjects with either a 1-minute CS–US interval or a 20-minute delay between the start of the CS and the start of the US. Conditioned approach behavior readily developed with the 1-minute CS–US interval regardless of which CS was used. However, when the CS–US interval was 20 minutes, responding developed only with the CS that included cues of a female's head and neck. Thus, conditioned responding to the ecological CS was more persistent with increases in the CS–US interval than responding to the arbitrary CS. This finding is reminiscent of long-delay learning that occurs when poisoning follows exposure to a novel taste, a natural precursor of post-ingestional malaise.

The above findings indicate that learning with a natural precursor of the US proceeds in a markedly different fashion than learning with an arbitrary conditioned stimulus. These findings suggest that general conclusions about Pavlovian conditioning have to be tempered by considering the CS that is employed. In addition, the learning that we observed in the laboratory with arbitrary conditioned stimuli may not reflect how Pavlovian conditioning unfolds under natural circumstances. In particular, Pavlovian conditioning under natural circumstances may develop more rapidly, with longer CS–US interval, and may be resistant to blocking and extinction.

Other examples of learning with naturalistic conditioned stimuli

Most of the research on sexual conditioning conducted in my laboratory has been done with domesticated quail and visual cues as the CS. Sexual learning effects have been also documented with mammals, and one of these effects in particular involves naturalistic conditioned stimuli. In some mammalian species, the male's preference for an estrous female increases with sexual experience (e.g., Carr, Loeb, & Dissinger, 1965). This effect may be due to the Pavlovian association of the odor of an estrous female with subsequent copulatory reinforcement.

Evidence of learning with ecological conditioned stimuli is also available in several other response systems. In nursing an infant, for example, tactile and olfactory cues provided by the mother often precede attachment to the nipple. These cues can become conditioned to elicit orientation and suckling conditioned responses on the part of the infant (Blass, 1990). The process of nursing also results in conditioning of the mother. Tactile and olfactory cues provided by the infant precede the suckling stimulation provided by the infant and serve to condition oxytocin release and the milk let-down reflex on the part of the mother (Fuchs, Ayromlooi, & Rasmussen, 1987).

Naturalistic learning effects no doubt also occur in predator–prey interactions. Here the distal cues of the predator are followed by attack and potential injury to the prey. Studies with monkeys and humans have shown that ecologically relevant conditioned stimuli, such as the sight of a snake, become much more easily conditioned to elicit fear than irrelevant or arbitrary cues, such as the sight of a flower (Öhman & Mineka, 2001).

These examples illustrate that ecologically relevant Pavlovian conditioning may occur in a variety of response systems. However, in these other paradigms experiments have not been conducted to determine how unique learning is with ecological CSs. In many of these cases, we do not know whether learning with an ecological CS is resistant to blocking, extinction, and increases in the CS–US interval, as appears to be the case in the sexual conditioning of male quail.

Conditioned changes in responding to the unconditioned stimulus

In addition to encouraging a focus on ecologically relevant conditioned stimuli, a functional approach to Pavlovian conditioning assumes that this type of learning is adaptive. The adaptive significance of Pavlovian conditioning should be evident in improvements in how effectively an organism interacts with biologically significant events in its life. What are these biologically significant events? They are not conditioned stimuli. Conditioned stimuli are not important enough to warrant a response unless they have previously been associated with a US. By definition, biologically significant events are unconditioned stimuli that elicit a vigorous response without prior training (Gunther et al., 1997; Pavlov, 1927). Thus, a functional perspective suggests that Pavlovian conditioning should result in improvements in how effectively organisms interact with unconditioned stimuli. This requires detailed measurements of unconditioned behavior. Such measurements have been made in several response systems. I begin with examples from the sexual behavior system.

Conditioned changes in response to a sexual US

In the sexual behavior system, the presence of a sexual partner is the unconditioned stimulus, and copulation with the partner is the unconditioned response. One of the first hints that conditioning can alter unconditioned behavior was provided by measurements of the latency of copulation. Zamble et al. (1985) showed that male rats achieved ejaculation faster when copulating with a female if access to the female was provided after exposure to a sexually conditioned CS. In an analogous experiment, Domjan et al. (1986) showed that male quail were faster to grab a female in the back of the neck (initiating copulation) if that female appeared after exposure to a sexually conditioned CS.

If a Pavlovian CS enables a male to copulate more quickly, then Pavlovian conditioning might help determine the outcome when two males compete for access to a single female. Gutiérrez and Domjan (1996) tested this prediction in a large outdoor arena. Male quail were individually trained with one auditory cue (the CS+) serving as a signal for access to a female and another cue (the CS–) presented on noncopulation trials. Two males were then placed in the arena at the same time, and a female was introduced at one end following exposure to an auditory cue that was the CS+ for one of the males and the CS– for the other male. In this competition situation, the male that was able to predict access to the female copulated with her first.

The latency to copulate is but one measure of how subjects respond to a sexual US. In quail, another important measure is the efficiency of their copulatory behavior. Copulation in quail begins with the male grabbing the back of the female's neck in his beak, mounting on the back of the female with both feet, and then arching his body to bring his cloaca in contact with the female's. If the female is not cooperative, she will throw the male off her back, so he has to try again. Thus, depending on the female's cooperation, the male may have to make several grab and mount responses before achieving cloacal contact. We recently found that the efficiency of the male's copulatory behavior depends on the female, and this in turn determines whether the copulation is successful in fertilizing the female's eggs (Domjan, Mahometa, & Mills, 2003). More importantly, the efficiency of a male's copulatory behavior increases with repeated Pavlovian conditioning trials. This result is illustrated in Figure 4.8.

Increases in the efficiency of interacting with a biologically significant event are presumed to facilitate reproductive success. However, measures of how a subject interacts with a US do not provide direct evidence of adaptive significance. The ultimate measure of adaptation is the number of offspring that are produced. If Pavlovian conditioning increases copulatory efficiency and this is an adaptive change in behavior, then this change should be accompanied by increased reproductive success. Our first efforts to measure the reproductive consequence of Pavlovian conditioning involved measuring sperm output following exposure to a Pavlovian CS. Exposure to a distinctive context that was paired with copulation resulted in increased semen volume This result is illustrated in Figure 4.9. The increase in semen volume was in turn accompanied by increased numbers of spermatozoa in the ejaculate (Domjan, Blesbois, & Williams, 1998).

Increased sperm output stimulated by a Pavlovian CS should result in a greater number of fertilized eggs resulting from a copulation. This prediction was recently tested by Adkins-Regan and MacKillop (2003) and by Mahometa and Domjan (2005). In the experiment by Mahometa and Domjan, male–female pairs of quail received training in which a Pavlovian CS was presented to both subjects before they were permitted to copulate. During a single copulation test, the pairs of quail were assigned to four independent groups. In one group, both the male and the female received the Pavlovian CS before

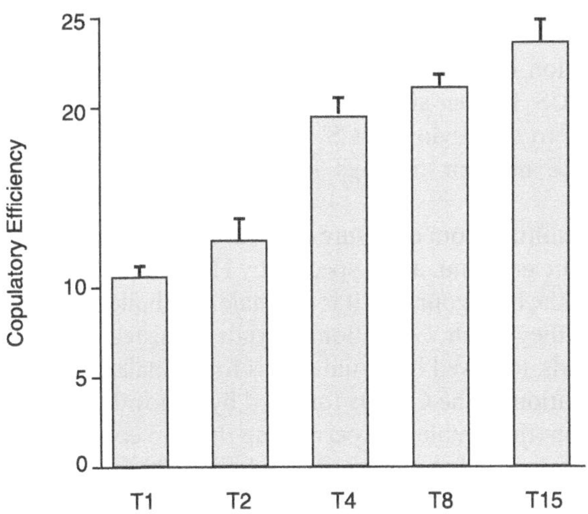

Figure 4.8 Copulatory efficiency on trials 1, 2, 4, 8, and 15 of Pavlovian conditioning. Copulatory efficiency was calculated as 100 times the ratio of the number of cloacal contacts divided by the sum of the number of grabs, mounts, and cloacal contacts. (Based on Mahometa & Domjan, 2005.)

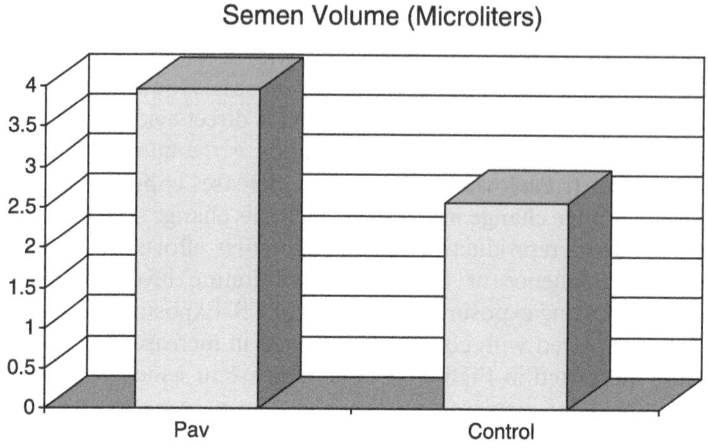

Figure 4.9 Effects of Pavlovian conditioning on semen volume in male quail. (Based on Domjan et al., 1998.)

being permitted to copulate. In other groups, only the male, only the female, or neither bird received the Pavlovian signal before copulation. The results, summarized in Figure 4.10, show that presenting the Pavlovian CS to both the male and the female resulted in significantly more fertilized eggs than in any of the other conditions. Furthermore, in this experiment, none of the other groups differed significantly from each other.

Adkins-Regan and MacKillop (2003) also found that presenting a Pavlovian CS increases fertilization success in quail. However, they reported that the increased fertilization occurs even if only the male or only the female receives the Pavlovian CS. In their study, it was not necessary for both sexual partners to be exposed to the Pavlovian CS. It is not clear what was responsible for the difference in their findings from those of Mahometa and Domjan.

Increased fertility resulting from exposure to a Pavlovian CS has been also demonstrated in the blue gourami, a fish species, by Hollis and her associates (Hollis et al., 1997). In the blue gourami, it is the male that builds the nest and cares for the eggs until they hatch. Conditioning trials consisted of presenting a CS light for 10 seconds, followed by visual access to a female for 5 minutes. After 18 trials, presentation of the CS was followed by removal of the barrier separating the male from the female and permitting them to court and reproduce during the next 6 days. Exposure to the Pavlovian CS facilitated these sexual interactions in a number of ways. The Pavlovian males showed significantly less biting, more nest building, shorter latencies to spawn, and greater numbers of offspring produced.

In another dramatic demonstration of the influence of Pavlovian conditioning on reproduction, Matthews, Ramsey, Domjan, and Crews (2004) examined which male sired more of the offspring when a female was permit-

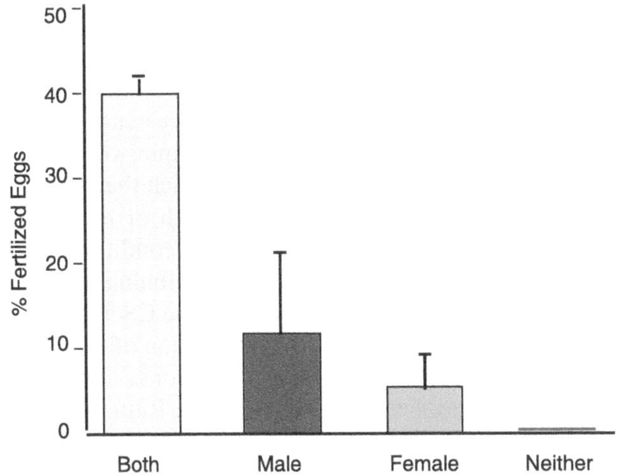

Figure 4.10 Percentage of fertilized eggs produced following a single copulatory episode in which either both the male and female were signaled, only the male was signaled, only the female was signaled, or neither quail was signaled. (After Mahometa & Domjan, 2005.)

ted to mate with two males in succession. One of the males received a Pavlovian CS prior to the copulation, and paternity was determined by genetic fingerprinting. The 11 females that participated in the experiment produced 38 offspring, 27 of which were sired by the Pavlovian male.

Other examples of conditioned changes in responding to the unconditioned stimulus

The research on sexual conditioning described above is unique in directly demonstrating that Pavlovian conditioning can increase reproductive success. However, numerous other lines of evidence are available indicating that Pavlovian conditioning changes how organisms interact with the unconditioned stimulus in a variety of response systems.

One of the first examples of conditioned changes in responding to the US was documented in eyeblink conditioning, where Kimble and Ost (1961) found that the magnitude of the eyeblink response to a puff of air was smaller if the US was preceded by a Pavlovian CS. Subsequent investigators found that this effect only occurs if the US is of high intensity. The opposite outcome is observed if the US is of low intensity (Donegan & Wagner, 1987).

Another early demonstration of Pavlovian modification of responding to an unconditioned stimulus is the fear-potentiated startle procedure. In this procedure, the magnitude of the startle response to a brief loud auditory cue is measured as the unconditioned response. If the startle-eliciting stimulus occurs during the presentation of a fear-conditioned CS, the magnitude of the startle response is substantially increased (Brown, Kalish, & Farber, 1951; Walker & Davis, 2002).

Another area in which investigators have been keenly interested in conditioned changes in responding to an unconditioned stimulus is drug tolerance and sensitization. Drug tolerance refers to a decrease in response to a drug US that frequently occurs with repeated administrations of the drug. In contrast, drug sensitization refers to cases in which the response to a drug US increases with repeated drug experiences. Both of these types of changes have been discussed in the context of Pavlovian conditioning. These analyses assume that each drug administration is a conditioning trial in which cues related to the administration of the drug serve as the CS and interoceptive cues produced by the drug serve as the US. Presentation of the CS is then assumed to activate processes that alter the subject's response to the drug US (Robinson & Berridge, 2000; Siegel et al., 2000; Woods & Ramsay, 2000).

Conditioned changes in responding to an unconditioned stimulus have also been documented in the defensive behavior system. Pavlovian conditioning increases territorial defensive behavior in blue gouramis (Hollis, 1990) and reduces the pain that is elicited by a potential source of injury (Fanselow, 1991). This latter phenomenon is called conditioned hypoalgesia.

The above conditioned modifications in unconditioned behavior are consistent with the functionalist claim that for Pavlovian conditioning to be adaptive it has to involve changes in how the organism interacts with the unconditioned stimulus. If these changes are indeed adaptive, then they should also increase reproductive fitness. Unlike the studies of sexual conditioning which included direct measurements of fertilization success, the adaptive significance of these other conditioned changes in unconditioned behavior is open to speculation. In some of these cases, plausible arguments are not difficult to make. Increased territorial defense, for example, no doubt facilitates securing resources needed for successful reproduction (e.g., a potential nest site). Conditioned hypoalgesia probably serves to promote successful defensive behavior by suppressing recuperative responses to pain that might interfere with escape from a predator (Bolles & Fanselow, 1980). It is more difficult to see how changes in responses to a US may be adaptive when those changes involve attenuated responses to the US under certain parametric conditions and augmented reactions under other circumstances (e.g., Donegan & Wagner, 1987). The functionalist approach does not claim to have a ready explanation for such enigmas. However, it directs our attention to inquire how such changes in responses to a US might be adaptive.

Conclusion

The functionalist approach assumes that Pavlovian conditioning readily occurs in nature and is of adaptive significance. This claim has frequently been made. However, its implications have not been fully appreciated. In this presentation I explored two important implications of the functionalist approach. The first is that for Pavlovian conditioning to occur in nature, the CS cannot be an arbitrary or neutral stimulus because without experimental intervention an arbitrary cue does not occur sufficiently often with a US to become conditioned. Rather, an ecological conditioned stimulus has to have a pre-existing or inherent relation to the US to become a reliable signal for that US. The CS may be a stimulus early in the causal chain that leads to the US or it might be a portion of the US encountered at distance that is not intense or big enough to produce a strong unconditioned response without learning.

I reviewed a number of prominent examples of Pavlovian conditioning with ecological CSs. Some of these examples have not been examined in great detail. However, among those that have been studied extensively (taste aversion learning, sexual conditioning, and fear conditioning), the results with ecological CSs have been at variance with what is usually found with arbitrary cues. Ecological CSs led to more rapid learning, a greater range of conditioned responses, and resistance to blocking, extinction, and increases in the CS–US interval. Whether similar effects occur with all ecological conditioned stimuli remains to be seen. However, the research to date suggests that in extrapolating from the laboratory to natural ecosystems, one has to carefully consider the nature of the CS that is used. I do not mean to cast doubt on the occurrence of Pavlovian conditioning in nature. Rather, I want to emphasize that Pavlovian conditioning outside the laboratory requires special kinds of conditioned stimuli.

The second major implication of a functionalist perspective that has not been fully appreciated is that to be adaptive, Pavlovian conditioning has to improve how an organism reacts to the US. Therefore, a functionalist approach encourages the search for conditioning effects not in the development on new responses to the CS, but in modifications of how the organism responds to the US. A corollary to this claim is that these changes in response to the US will be of adaptive significance. The first component of this claim has been demonstrated in numerous response systems. In a variety of situations, including drug conditioning, fear conditioning, and sexual conditioning, investigators have found that organisms react to a US differently following exposure to a Pavlovian CS than in the absence of such a cue. In general, the presentation of a Pavlovian CS recruits processes that enable the organism to respond to the US more quickly, more efficiently, and more effectively. If the US is a drug or a cutaneous aversive stimulus, the conditioned change in the response to the US may involve a reduced reaction to the US. In other cases, the conditioned change in the UR is an increase in reactivity.

The adaptive significance of conditioned changes in responding to the US has been directly demonstrated only in sexual conditioning. Subjects respond to a sexual partner with shorter latencies, less aggression, and more courtship and cooperation if the sexual partner is encountered following a Pavlovian CS. In addition, studies with domesticated quail and the blue gourami have shown that such interactions result in greater quantities of sperm released and greater numbers of offspring produced. These findings underscore the basic claims of a functionalist approach to Pavlovian conditioning and encourage its further exploration in other response systems.

References

Adkins-Regan, E., & MacKillop, E.A. (2003). Japanese quail (*Coturnix japonica*) inseminations are more likely to fertilize eggs in a context predicting mating opportunities. *Proceedings of the Royal Society of London (B)*, *270*, 1685–1689.

Akins, C.K. (2000). Effects of species-specific cues and the CS–US interval on the topography of the sexually conditioned response. *Learning & Motivation*, *31*, 211–235.

Anderson, J.R. (1995). *Learning and memory*. New York: John Wiley.

Blass, E.M. (1990). Suckling: Determinants, changes, mechanisms, and lasting impressions. *Developmental Psychology*, *26*, 520–533.

Boakes, R.A. (1984). *From Darwin to behaviorism*. Cambridge: Cambridge University Press.

Bolles, R.C., & Fanselow, M. S. (1980). A perceptual-defensive-recuperative model of fear and pain. *Behavioral Brain Science*, *3*, 291–323.

Bouton, M.E., Jones, D.L., McPhillips, S.A., & Swartzentruber, D. (1986). Potentiation and overshadowing in odor-aversion learning: Role of method of odor presentation, the distal–proximal distinction, and the conditionability of odor. *Learning and Motivation*, *17*, 115–138.

Bower, G.H., & Hilgard, E.R. (1981). *Theories of learning* (5th ed.). Englewood Cliffs, NJ: Prentice Hall.

Brown, J.S., Kalish, H.I., & Farber, I.E. (1951). Conditioned fear as revealed by magnitude of startle response to an auditory stimulus. *Journal of Experimental Psychology*, *41*, 317–328.

Burns, M., & Domjan, M. (2000). Sign tracking in domesticated quail with one trial a day. Generality across CS and US parameters. *Animal Learning & Behavior*, *28*, 109–119.

Carr, W.J., Loeb, L.S., & Dissinger, M.E. (1965). Responses of rats to sex odors. *Journal of Comparative and Physiological Psychology*, *59*, 370–377.

Cusato, B., & Domjan, M. (1998). Special efficacy of sexual conditioned stimuli that include species typical cues: Tests with a CS preexposure design. *Learning and Motivation*, *29*, 152–167.

Cusato, B., & Domjan, M. (2001, April). *Second-order sexual conditioning in male domesticated quail*. Paper presented at meetings of the Southwest Psychological Association, Houston, TX.

Domjan, M. (1973). Role of ingestion in odor-toxicosis learning in the rat. *Journal of Comparative and Physiological Psychology*, *84*, 507–521.

Domjan, M. (1983). Biological constraints on instrumental and classical conditioning: Implications for general process theory. In G.H. Bower (Ed.), *The psychology of learning and motivation* (Vol. 17, pp. 215–277). New York: Academic Press.

Domjan, M. (2005). Pavlovian conditioning: A functional perspective. *Annual Review of Psychology*, *56*, 179–206.

Domjan, M., Blesbois E., & Williams, J. (1998). The adaptive significance of sexual conditioning: Pavlovian control of sperm release. *Psychological Science*, *9*, 411–415.

Domjan, M., Cusato, B., & Krause, M. (2004). Learning with arbitrary versus ecological conditioned stimuli: Evidence from sexual conditioning. *Psychonomic Bulletin & Review*, *11*, 232–246.

Domjan, M., & Hanlon, M.J. (1982). Poison-avoidance learning to food-related tactile stimuli: Avoidance of texture cues by rats. *Animal Learning & Behavior*, *10*, 293–300.

Domjan, M., & Holloway, K.S. (1998). Sexual learning. In G. Greenberg & M.M. Haraway (Eds.), *Comparative psychology: A handbook* (pp. 602–613). New York: Garland.

Domjan, M., Lyons, R., North, N.C., & Bruell, J. (1986). Sexual Pavlovian conditioned approach behavior in male Japanese quail (*Coturnix coturnix japonica*). *Journal of Comparative Psychology*, *100*, 413–421.

Domjan, M., Mahometa, M., & Mills, A.D. (2003). Relative contributions of the male and female to sexual behavior and reproductive success in the Japanese quail (*Coturnix japonica*). *Journal of Comparative Psychology*, *117*, 391–399.

Domjan, M., Miller, V., & Gemberling, G.A. (1982). Note on aversion learning to the shape of food by monkeys. *Journal of the Experimental Analysis of Behavior*, *38*, 87–91.

Domjan, M., & Wilson, N.E. (1972). Specificity of cue to consequency in aversion learning in the rat. *Psychonomic Science*, *26*, 143–145.

Donegan, N.H., & Wagner A.R. (1987). Conditioned diminution and facilitation of the UR: A sometimes-opponent-process interpretation. In I. Gormezano, W.F. Prokasy, & R.F. Thompson (Eds.), *Classical conditioning* (3rd ed., pp. 339–369). Hillsdale, NJ: Lawrence Erlbaum Associates Inc.

Fanselow, M.S. (1991). Analgesia as a response to aversive Pavlovian conditioned stimuli: Cognitive and emotional mediators. In M.R. Denny (Ed.), *Fear, avoidance, and phobias* (pp. 61–86). Hillsdale, NJ: Lawrence Erbaum Associates Inc.

Fuchs, A.-R., Ayromlooi, J., & Rasmussen, A.B. (1987). Oxytocin response to conditioned and nonconditioned stimuli in lactating ewes. *Biology of Reproduction*, *37*, 301–305.

Garcia, J., Ervin, E.R., & Koelling, R.A. (1966). Learning with prolonged delay of reinforcement. *Psychonomic Science*, *5*, 121–122.

Garcia, J., Hankins, W.G., & Rusiniak, K.W. (1974). Behavioral regulation of the milieu interne in man and rat. *Science*, *185*, 824–831.

Garcia, J., & Koelling, R.A. (1966). Relation of cue to consequence in aversion learning. *Psychonomic Science*, *4*, 123–124.

Gunther, L.M., Miller, R.R., & Matute, H. (1997). CSs and USs: What's the difference? *Journal of Experimental Psychology: Animal Behavior Processes*, *23*, 15–30.

Gutiérrez, G., & Domjan, M. (1996). Learning and male–male sexual competition in Japanese quail (*Coturnix japonica*). *Journal of Comparative Psychology*, *110*, 170–175.

Gutiérrez, G., & Domjan, M. (1997). Differences in the sexual conditioned behavior of male and female Japanese quail (*Coturnix japonica*). *Journal of Comparative Psychology*, *111*, 135–142.

Hearst, E., & Jenkins, H.M. (1974). *Sign-tracking: The stimulus–reinforcer relation and directed action*. Austin, TX: Psychonomic Society.

Hollis, K.L. (1982). Pavlovian conditioning of signal-centered action patterns and autonomic behavior: A biological analysis of function. *Advances in the Study of Behavior*, *12*, 1–64.

Hollis, K.L. (1990). The role of Pavlovian conditioning in territorial aggression and reproduction. In D.A. Dewsbury (Ed.), *Contemporary issues in comparative psychology* (pp. 197–219). Sunderland, MA: Sinauer.

Hollis, K.L. (1997). Contemporary research on Pavlovian conditioning: A "new" functional analysis. *American Psychologist, 52*, 956–965.

Hollis, K.L., Pharr, V.L., Dumas, M.J., Britton, G.B., & Field, J. (1997). Classical conditioning provides paternity advantage for territorial male blue gouramis (*Trichogaster trichopterus*). *Journal of Comparative Psychology, 111*, 219–225.

Kimble, G.A., & Ost, J.W.P. (1961). A conditioned inhibitory process in eyelid conditioning. *Journal of Experimental Psychology, 61*, 150–156.

Köksal, F., Domjan, M., & Weisman, G. (1994). Blocking of the sexual conditioning of differentially effective conditioned stimulus objects. *Animal Learning Behavior, 22*, 103–111.

Krause, M. (2003). Behavioral mechanisms and the neurobiology of conditioned sexual responding. *International Review of Neurobiology, 56*, 1–34.

Krause, M.A., Cusato, B., & Domjan, M. (2003). Extinction of conditioned sexual responses in male Japanese quail (*Coturnix japonica*): Role of species typical cues. *Journal of Comparative Psychology, 117*, 76–86.

Mahometa, M.J., & Domjan, M. (2005). Classical conditioning increases reproductive success in Japanese quail (*Coturnix japonica*). *Animal Behaviour, 69*, 983–989.

Matthews, R.N., Ramsey, M., Domjan, M., & Crews, D. (2004, April). *Microsatellite markers increase reliability in paternity testing of Japanese quail.* Paper presented at meetings of the Southwest Psychological Association, San Antonio, TX, USA.

Öhman, A., & Mineka, S. (2001). Fear, phobias and preparedness: Toward an evolved module of fear and fear learning. *Psychological Review, 108*, 483–522.

Papini, M.R. (2002). *Comparative psychology*. Upper Saddle River, NJ: Prentice Hall.

Pavlov, I.P. (1927). *Conditioned reflexes* (G.V. Anrep, Trans.). Oxford: Oxford University Press. (Reprinted by Dover Publications, New York, 1960)

Pfaus, J.G. (1996). Homologies of animal and human sexual behaviors. *Hormones and Behavior, 30*, 187–200.

Robinson, T.E., & Berridge, K.C. (2000). The psychology and neurobiology of addiction: An incentive-sensitization view. *Addiction, 95* (Suppl. 2: Animal models of craving research), S91–S117.

Rosenzweig, M.R. (1959). Salivary conditioning before Pavlov. *American Journal of Psychology, 72*, 628–633.

Rozin, P., & Kalat, J.W. (1971). Specific hungers and poison avoidance as adaptive specializations of learning. *Psychological Review, 78*, 459–486.

Rusiniak, K.W., Palmerino, C.C., & Garcia, J. (1982). Potentiation of odor by taste in rats: Tests of some nonassociative factors. *Journal of Comparative and Physiological Psychology, 96*, 775–780.

Rzoska, J. (1953). Bait shyness, a study in rat behaviour. *British Journal of Animal Behaviour, 1*, 128–135.

Schwartz, C.W., & Schwartz, E.R. (1949). *A reconnaissance of the game birds in Hawaii.* Hilo, HI: Hawaii Board of Commissioners of Agriculture & Forestry.

Shettleworth, S.J. (1998). *Cognition, evolution, and behavior*. New York: Oxford University Press.

Siegel, S., Baptista, M.A.S., Kim, J.A., McDonald, R.V., & Weise-Kelly, L. (2000). Pavlovian psychopharmacology: The associative basis of tolerance. *Experimental Clinical Psychopharmacology, 8*, 276–293.

Smith, J.C., & Roll, D.L. (1967). Trace conditioning with X-rays as an aversive stimulus. *Psychonomic Science*, *9*, 11–12.
Staddon, J.E.R. (1983). *Adaptive behavior and learning*. Cambridge: Cambridge University Press.
Walker, D.L., & Davis, M. (2002). Quantifying fear potentiated startle using absolute versus proportional increase scoring methods: Implications for neurocircuitry of fear and anxiety. *Psychopharmacology*, *164*, 318–328.
Woods, S.C., & Ramsay, D.S. (2000). Pavlovian influences over food and drug intake. *Behavioral Brain Research*, *110*, 175–182.
Woodson, J.C. (2002). Including "learned sexuality" in the organization of sexual behavior. *Neuroscience & Biobehavioral Reviews*, *26*, 69–80.
Zamble, E., Hadad, G.M., Mitchell, J.B., & Cutmore, T.R. (1985). Pavlovian conditioning of sexual arousal: First- and second-order effects. *Journal of Experimental Psychology: Animal Behavior Processes*, *11*, 598–610.

5 Categorization and concept formation in pigeons: A perspective on comparative cognition

Masako Jitsumori

In the research field of comparative cognition, cognitive processes of animals have been studied by comparisons among diverse animal species, such as pigeons, rats, monkeys, and apes, including humans. The studies have shown generality and the limits of generality among different animal species, and also species-specific adaptive behaviors and their ecological determinants. Comparative cognition provides a unique opportunity to investigate functional and evolutionary significance of cognition and the underlying mechanisms that have evolved for dealing with cognitive problems. One of the most fundamental cognitive abilities of diverse animal species, including humans, is to categorize objects existing in the world around them. The ability of organisms to categorize objects enables them to learn about their environment economically, with a decrease in the amount of information that they would otherwise have to acquire. Categorization is of great relevance for most living animals, to cope with the stimulus variability and complexity in their environments. It is plausible to infer that the competencies of categorization have evolved to cope with the continuities and discontinuities existing in the external world. If this is true, the cognitive systems of diverse animal species, including humans, should be tied to (and constrained by) the basic structure of the real world. Otherwise, their ancestors might not have survived.

Recent relevant studies in animals fall into two general groups. In one, the formation of stimulus classes on the basis of perceptual similarity among various stimuli has been investigated. Investigators use visual stimuli that are not defined by a simple few features, such as photographs of natural objects (e.g., Herrnstein & Loveland, 1964) and artificial stimuli that are constructed by mimicking the properties of natural categories (e.g., Jitsumori, 1993, 1994; Lea & Harrison, 1978). Studies in the second group investigate the formation of stimulus classes based on shared function among stimuli that bear no obvious similarity to one another. Such nonsimilarity-based functional classes have been examined using physical stimuli, such as colors, tilted lines, and geometric shapes, that are associated with a common response (e.g., Wasserman, Devolder, & Coppage, 1992), a common stimulus (e.g., Urcuioli & Zentall, 1993), or a common response outcome (e.g.,

Edwards, Jagielo, Zentall, & Hogan, 1982). These two lines of research differ theoretically and methodologically, and have been conducted separately in this research field. A series of experiments reported in this chapter were designed to bridge between the formation of perceptually defined stimulus classes and the formation of nonsimilarity-based stimulus classes, using pigeons as experimental subjects. The advantage of using pigeons, the species that is visually sophisticated but phylogenetically distantly related to humans, is to provide insights about the underlying nonverbal cognitive processes.

Categorization of pictures of natural objects

Following the pioneering work by Herrnstein and Loveland (1964), it has been repeatedly documented that animals, particularly pigeons, can classify photographs that are not defined by a few simple features but contain a particular type of natural object (for a review, see Jitsumori & Delius, 2001). In most of the categorization experiments, pigeons are first trained to classify a certain number of different stimuli. Half of the stimuli, defined as the positive set, depict objects of a particular stimulus class, for example, *tree*. The other half of the stimuli, defined as the negative set, depict other objects but not *tree*. Pigeons are rewarded for responding to the positive stimuli and not rewarded for responding to the negative stimuli (go/no-go discrimination). After they have learned to discriminate between these stimuli, they are tested for transfer to new exemplars. A high degree of transfer to novel exemplars of the stimulus sets is said to indicate that they have learned to categorize the stimuli (e.g., Keller & Schoenfeld, 1950). By using pictures depicting a variety of natural objects, such as trees, people, a specific person, bodies of water, and so forth, it has been repeatedly documented that animals, particularly pigeons, are capable of classifying photographs of natural objects, in accord with the human taxonomies of real-world objects (see also Jitsumori, 2004).

For humans, pictures depicting objects in the same natural categories are more perceptually similar to one another than those depicting objects from different categories. This may also be true for pigeons, as it has been shown that pigeons trained to classify pictures into natural categories learn far faster than pigeons trained to sort the same pictures into pseudo-categories (Bhatt, Wasserman, Reynolds, & Knauss, 1988). Given the many other findings suggesting that human and pigeon categorizations share more similarities than differences (e.g., Jitsumori, 1996; Jitsumori & Matsuzawa, 1991; Jitsumori & Ohkubo, 1996; Jitsumori & Yoshihara, 1997), we may claim that such categorical coherence is an essential property of natural objects and is exploited by the visual systems of diverse animal species including humans and pigeons, although perceived features and the salience of the features undoubtedly differ from species to species.

If the competencies of categorization have evolved to cope with the existing continuities and discontinuities in the external world, the basic cognitive systems of humans and animals like pigeons may share general properties that mirror the structure of the external world (broken lines in Figure 5.1). Categorical coherence or correlational structure of category features may enable pigeons to classify photographs of natural objects, i.e., two-dimensional reflections of real-world objects, in accord with the human taxonomies (solid lines in Figure 5.1). Note, however, that this does not necessarily mean that pigeons recognize three-dimensional objects in the two-dimensional pictures. Regardless of the presence or absence of picture–object equivalence (e.g., Jitsumori & Makino, 2004; Jitsumori, Natori, & Okuyama, 1999), real objects and their two-dimensional pictures may possess some perceptual features in common.

Categorization of objects structured by family resemblance

Empirical studies in the last several decades, specifically those pursued by Eleanor Rosch (e.g., Rosch, 1978; Rosch & Mervis, 1975), revealed that some natural categories are internally structured into prototypical and nonprototypical members, with nonprototypical members tending toward an ordering from better to poorer exemplars. Categories of highly variable members are structured by so-called *family resemblance* (Wittgenstein, 1953) or criss-crossing similarities. For example, ostriches and penguins do not have attributes shared by many other birds, and they themselves are not very similar to each other, but we place them into the same category due to the existence of many other kinds of bird that differ in degree of prototypicality. From the perspective of comparative cognition, a question of interest is whether animals perceive a correlational feature structure of diverse objects structured by family resemblance.

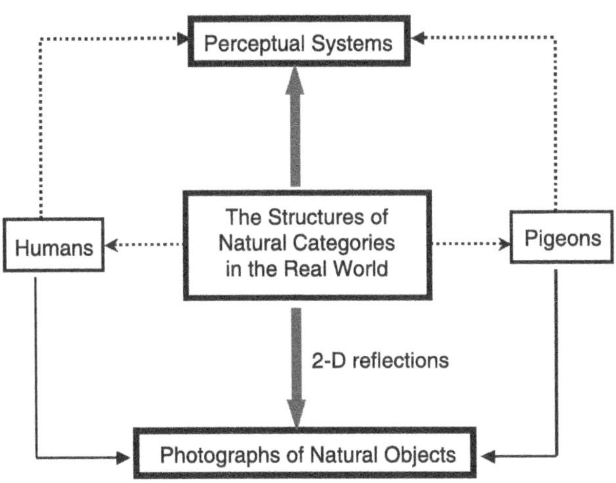

Figure 5.1 Why do pigeons classify photographs of natural objects, in accord with the human taxonomies of real-world objects? See text for details.

A simple form of the category that bears family resemblance consists of the exemplars AB, BC, CD, and DE. The centrally located exemplars, BC and CD, are good exemplars, in the sense that they possess the features shared by other exemplars. The peripherally located exemplars, AB and DE, are poor exemplars. The poor exemplars do not share features, but the category as a whole is structured by family resemblance. Makino and Jitsumori (2000) examined whether pigeons are capable of learning the categories structured by family resemblances (see also Jitsumori, 2004). Human faces were used as stimuli, simply because it is easy to create visual categories structured by family resemblances, by means of morphing. Morphing is a technique of computer graphics that combines two or more images. Two categories were prepared, each of which consisted of four arbitrarily assigned original faces (A, B, C, and D), six 50% averages of the possible pairs of these faces (AB, AC, AD, BC, BD, and CD), and an average face created by 25% morphing of the original faces (ABCD). Figure 5.2 shows black-and-white reproductions of the faces belonging to the same category (AD and BC are not shown). In this category, the original faces are poor exemplars, the 50% morphings are good exemplars, and the average is a prototype of the category. In a go/no-go

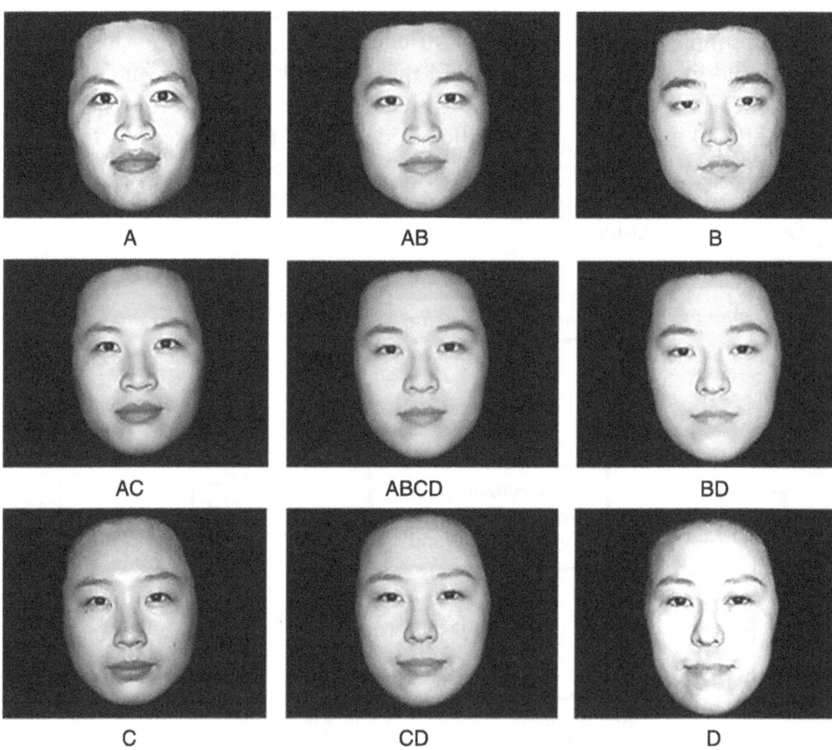

Figure 5.2 Black-and-white reproductions of the faces belonging to the same category structured by family resemblance (Makino & Jitsumori, 2000).

discrimination procedure, pigeons were trained to discriminate between the good exemplars (the 50% morphed images) of the two categories. Note that AB and CD, AC and BD, and AD and BC in each set are not particularly similar to one another, but they are structured by a network of criss-crossing similarities.

The pigeons were then tested in extinction with the stimuli including the 50% morphed images used for training, the original faces, and the averages. The mean discrimination ratios for the average faces, the 50% morphings, and the original faces were 0.87, 0.84, and 0.76, respectively. An important finding is that a high level of transfer occurred not only to the prototypes but also to the poor exemplars (the original faces A, B, C, and D). Because the original faces were arbitrarily assigned as members of the two categories, there was no way of knowing which original face belonged to which category before categorization learning with the 50% morphed images (AB, AC, AD, BC, BD, and CD) took place. Thus, the discrimination training with the good exemplars enabled the pigeons to correctly classify not only the prototypes but also the poor exemplars that were not particularly similar to one another within the categories. We may conclude that pigeons are capable of learning the categories consisting of a wide variety of exemplars that are structured by family resemblance.

Although there was no statistical difference in performance between the good exemplars used for training and the novel prototypes, the pigeons showed the most pronounced discrimination to the prototypes. Thus, a prototype effect was obtained. According to prototype models (e.g., Reed, 1972), categories are represented by a central tendency that summarizes the instances used for categorization training. New stimuli are classified on the basis of how similar they are to the abstracted prototypes. In contrast, exemplar models (e.g., Medin & Schaffer, 1978) assume that categories are represented by individual exemplars that are stored as separate memory traces, and new stimuli are classified based on their similarity to the stored exemplars. The likelihood of classifying a new stimulus into the category increases with the similarity of the stimulus to the stored exemplars in that category and decreases with the similarity to the alternative category exemplars.

According to an exemplar model, the probability that an old positive stimulus, for example AB, will be classified into the positive category is

$$
\begin{aligned}
&[(1) + (\mathrm{ac}) + (\mathrm{ad}) + (\mathrm{bc}) + (\mathrm{bd}) + (\mathrm{cd})] \\
&\div [(1) + (\mathrm{ac}) + (\mathrm{ad}) + (\mathrm{bc}) + (\mathrm{bd}) + (\mathrm{cd}) \\
&+ (ab) + (ac) + (ad) + (bc) + (bd) + (cd)],
\end{aligned}
$$

where ac, ad, bc, bd, and cd are the respective similarity parameters of the positive training stimuli and *ab*, *ac*, *ad*, *bc*, *bd*, and *cd* are those of the negative training stimuli. The similarity parameter is set at 1 when the two stimuli are identical. When the parameters of the stimuli that contain 50% A or 50% B (ac, ad, bc, and bd) are equal to the value 0.8, and those of the stimuli that contain 0% A and 0% B (cd, *ab*, *ac*, *ad*, *bc*, *bd*, and *cd*) are equal to the value 0.2, the probability of the old positive stimulus AB being classified into the positive category is .78. The probability that the positive prototype ABCD will be classified into the positive category is

$$[(ab) + (ac) + (ad) + (bc) + (bd) + (cd)]$$
$$\div [(ab) + (ac) + (ad) + (bc) + (bd) + (cd)$$
$$+ (\mathit{ab}) + (\mathit{ac}) + (\mathit{ad}) + (\mathit{bc}) + (\mathit{bd}) + (\mathit{cd})].$$

When all six parameters of the positive stimuli are equal to the value 0.8 and those of the negative stimuli are equal to the value 0.2, the probability of the positive prototype being classified into the positive category is .80. Similarly, the probability of a positive original face, for example A, being classified into the positive category will be .71, with the parameters of the stimuli that contain 50% A being equal to 0.8 and those of the stimuli that contain 0% A being equal to 0.2. The present exemplar model is based on a simple additive-similarity calculation and the similarity parameters are not obtained through a best-fitting procedure but simply determined on the basis of the morphed proportion of the component face(s) shared by the two faces. Nevertheless, it well describes the observed tendency of the pigeons' transfer performance on both the prototypes and the poor exemplars.

The present category structure does not allow us to provide qualitative contrasts between the predictions from the prototype-based and exemplar-based similarity models. One may therefore argue that the prototype effect shown by the pigeons could be explained without the need to posit a prototype-abstraction process. An important implication of the present finding is that learning with good exemplars enables pigeons to easily and correctly classify highly variable category members, including those that are not particularly similar to one another. This result represents the very nature of the categories structured by family resemblances.

Functional equivalence

The above-noted findings suggest that exemplar learning and similarity-based generalization may enable pigeons to form stimulus classes that comprise highly variable stimuli structured by family resemblance. Then, a question of interest is whether pigeons treat the highly variable exemplars as "functionally equivalent" as members of the same class. The concept of "functional equivalence" arose from the "generic" property of the discriminative stimulus (S^D) defined by Skinner (1935). That is, a number of distinct stimuli, say A, B, and C, come to constitute a stimulus class under certain conditions. If observed behaviors can be described consistently by the three-term contingency of Equation (5.1), where R represents a given response and Rft represents reinforcement that occurs contingent to the response, then it is said that A, B, and C are functionally equivalent members of the class. This relation should be differentiated from a set of multiple contingencies shown in Equation (5.2).

$$S^D(A, B, C) - R - Rft. \tag{5.1}$$

$$\begin{aligned} &S^D(A) - R - Rft, \\ &S^D(B) - R - Rft, \\ &S^D(C) - R - Rft. \end{aligned} \tag{5.2}$$

In both cases, the discriminative stimuli, A, B, and C, have the same effects on the observed response R. How can one differentiate the former functional equivalence class from the latter multiple contingencies?

Lea (1984) argued that only if the members of a stimulus set subsequently attract the same response in other situations should we say that the set constitutes a concept, or a functional equivalence class. It is often said that animals learn a "concept" when they form a nonsimilarity-based equivalence class. A similar argument can be seen in Herrnstein's (1990) discussion of levels of stimulus control. Herrnstein (1990) argued that, in a true conceptualization rather than mere generalization within classes, the effects of contingencies applied to members of the same set propagate to other members more than can be accounted for by the similarities among members of the set.

Vaughan's (1988) study was the first one to demonstrate the formation of equivalence classes in pigeons. He randomly divided 40 slides of trees into two sets and trained pigeons to respond to the 20 slides in the positive set and not to respond to the 20 slides in the negative set, in a go/no-go discrimination procedure. Because the randomly divided positive and negative pictures depicted trees, there was no basis for a grouping or dividing of the stimuli on the basis of their physical similarities and dissimilarities. Thus, the pigeons had to learn to respond or not to respond to each individual picture. After completion of the discrimination training, the reinforcement contingencies for the two sets of stimuli were reversed. The pigeons required many sessions to reverse their responding to the individual pictures. After they had learned the reversal, reversals were repeated many times. Eventually, the pigeons could come to reverse their responding to all the pictures soon after they experienced the reversal with just a few pictures. This rapid reversal suggested that the pigeons had learned the functional equivalence classes of the stimuli randomly divided into the two sets.

The pigeons in Vaughan's study learned to reverse their responding only slowly and required a large number of reversals to learn the equivalence classes. In the natural environment, most animals may not be required to learn equivalences among the stimuli that cannot be grouped or divided on the basis of their similarities and dissimilarities. Equivalence is critical for animals to behave adaptively to a number of distinct stimuli existing in the environment, and this ability is expected to be linked to the animals' necessity to identify diverse items as edible, mateable, threatening, water-offering, home-directing, and so forth. It is quite likely that the natural objects having the same functional properties are more perceptually similar to one another than those having different functional properties, which may possibly promote animals to learn functional equivalences of objects in their natural environment.

Perceptual transitivity

From a naturalistic point of view, it is likely that the cognitive systems of animals, including humans and pigeons, are designed to take advantage of resemblance within categories. For example, it may be easy to learn equivalence between perceptually similar exemplars AB and BC, and also between BC and CD. The equivalences learned between the perceptually similar exemplars may promote the emergence of untrained equivalence between the perceptually dissimilar exemplars AB and CD. Because AB and CD are to be related through BC, which is perceptually similar to each of these exemplars, this emergent relation will be called "perceptual transitivity" in this chapter. Emergence of the untrained equivalence may indicate that the exemplars AB, BC, and CD have been learned as the members of the same functional equivalence class. Perceptual transitivity may effectively expand the equivalence class by including new stimuli in the class. Suppose that a new exemplar DE is introduced into the class. The new exemplar will be learned equivalent to the perceptually similar exemplar CD with ease. This relation may propagate to the other exemplars of the class, forming an equivalence network among the exemplars structured by family resemblance.

Jitsumori, Shimada, and Inoue (in press) examined whether pigeons would be able to interrelate perceptually dissimilar exemplars as functionally equivalent through perceptual transitivity. The method was a modification of Vaughan's that was developed by Delius and colleagues to analyze the associations among a small number of artificial stimuli in a two-alternative forced-choice task (e.g., Jitsumori, Siemann, Lehr, & Delius, 2002). In our study, two categories were created by morphing of human faces (Figure 5.3). In Category 1, the centrally located stimulus, the prototype (M1), was a male student from Europe and the peripherally located poor exemplars (A1, B1, and C1) were female Japanese students. So, the poor exemplars were somehow similar to one another. This was done in an attempt to increase family resemblance within the category. Good exemplars were created by means of 50% morphing of the prototype and one of the poor exemplars. The good exemplars (AM1, BM1, CM1) were thus substantially similar to the prototype and also to the corresponding poor exemplar, and they themselves were quite similar to one another. Thus the highly variable exemplars of the category were structured by family resemblance. Similarly, Category 2 was created

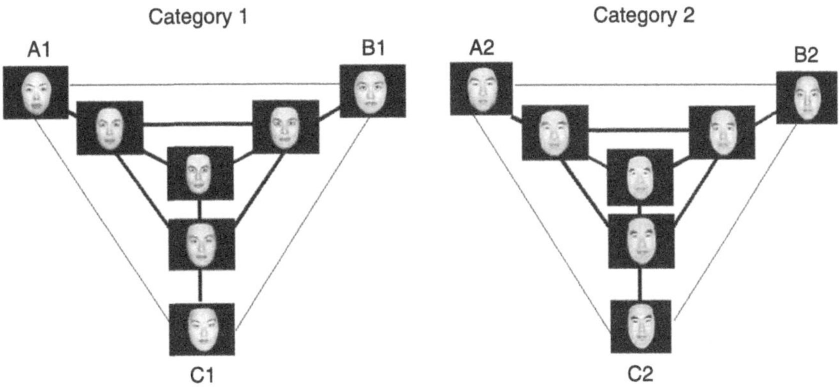

Figure 5.3 Black-and-white reproductions of the categories used by Jitsumori et al. (in press).

using a male professor as the prototype and male students as the poor exemplars.

In the first phase of the experiment, we trained four experimentally naive pigeons to learn equivalences among the good exemplars AM, BM, and CM in each category. The pigeons were first trained to learn AM↔BM equivalence by means of repeated reversals of two-alternative forced-choice discrimination. In this task, a face from Category 1 and a face from Category 2 were presented side by side on the two horizontally aligned keys. With the stimulus pairs AM1+AM2–, BM1+BM2–, AM1+BM2–, and BM1+AM2–, the pigeons were trained to choose AM1 and BM1 in Category 1 over AM2 and BM2 in Category 2. Choice of the positive stimulus was rewarded by foods and choice of the negative stimulus produced a 3-s timeout, during which the keys were illuminated red. After completion of the training, the pigeons were then trained with the reversed AM1–AM2+, BM1–BM2+, AM1–BM2+, and BM1–AM2+ pairs, and then again with the re-reversed AM1+AM2–, BM1+BM2–, AM1+BM2–, and BM1+AM2– pairs, and so forth. Across repeated reversal sessions, whenever AM1 signaled reward, BM1 did so too, and vice versa. Similarly, whenever AM2 signaled reward, MB2 did so too, and vice versa. Thus, the repeated reversal training could have established the AM↔BM equivalence relations (i.e., AM1↔BM1 and AM2↔BM2). Reversals were repeated until the pigeons could come to reverse their choices soon after reversals. One pigeon, Bird 2, showed difficulty with reversal and this bird was discarded from the experiment. The remaining three pigeons were then trained to learn the BM↔CM equivalences.

Testing sessions were designed to determine whether the pigeons would show emergence of the untrained AM↔CM equivalence. As in Jitsumori et al. (2002), probe trials were inserted among training trials to determine whether and to what extent the contingencies of reinforcement that were applied to training stimuli would control pigeons' choice of test stimuli when they were included within the same sessions. Although responding was not reinforced on probe trials, the choices were scored as correct or incorrect according to the contingencies that were in effect for the training stimuli.

The test for AM↔CM equivalence consisted of the AM→CM test and CM→AM test, between which the training and test roles of the stimulus pairs were exchanged symmetrically. For the AM→CM test, the AM1 AM2 pair served in training trials and the CM1 CM2 pair served in probe trials. The reinforcement allocation of the training pair was reversed between two successive testing sessions. Therefore, if the pigeons chose test stimuli according to the contingencies that were in effect for the training stimuli in each testing session, the mean test performance over the two testing sessions would be near 100% correct. Similarly, the test for CM→AM was carried out using CM1 CM2 as the training pair and AM1 AM2 as the probe pair. The mean performance accuracy on probe trials averaged across the three pigeons was 91% correct in the AM→CM test and 90% correct in the CM→AM test, respectively. Because the pigeons passed the AM→CM and CM→AM tests, we considered that they had formed the equivalence classes consisting of the good exemplars (AM, BM, and CM). Because the good exemplars in each class might be perceptually similar to one another for pigeons, the formation of the equivalence classes could be based on perceptual similarities or generalization within the classes

We then examined whether untrained M→(A, B, C) and (A, B, C)→M relations would emerge without additional training. For the M→(A, B, C) test, the pair of prototypes served in training trials and all the possible pairs of the poor exemplars served in probe trials. For the (A, B, C)→M test, the pairs of the poor exemplars served in training trials and the prototypes served in probe trials. As in Figure 5.4 (left), one of the three pigeons passed the tests for M↔(A, B, C) equivalence, despite the fact that these stimuli had never appeared during the preceding training sessions. This means that the acquired equivalences among the good exemplars enabled the pigeon to form the untrained equivalence between the prototype and poor exemplars. The remaining two pigeons were then given repeated reversal training to establish M↔(AM, BM, CM) and (AM, BM, CM)↔(A, B, C) equivalences. As in Figure 5.4 (right), subsequent testing revealed that the pigeons passed the M↔(A, B, C) equivalence tests. It was thus shown that the untrained M↔(A, B, C) equivalence did emerge transitively based on explicitly trained M↔(AM, BM, CM) and (AM, BM, CM)↔(A, B, C) equivalences. We may conclude that the pigeons incorporated separately trained multiple equivalences into a larger functional equivalence class consisting of stimuli that bear family resemblance.

To evaluate this finding, we measured perceptual similarity between the prototype and poor exemplars. One control group of pigeons was trained to discriminate between the poor exemplars of the categories and they were

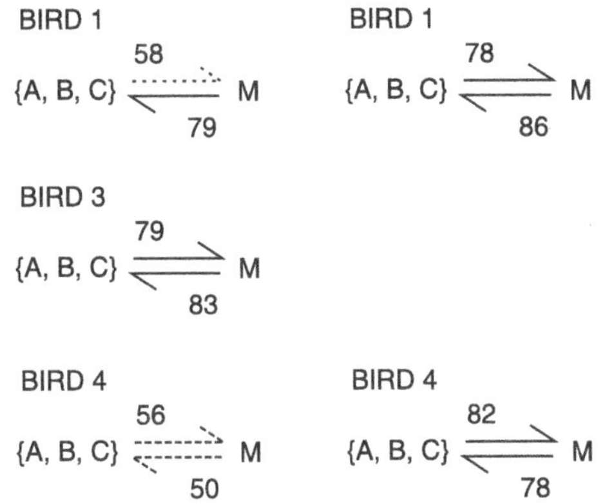

Figure 5.4 Percentage correct scores on probe trials during M→(A, B, C) and (A, B, C)→M testing sessions, conducted before (left) and after (right) training of the M↔(AM, BM CM) and (AM, BM CM)↔(A, B, C) equivalences. Solid arrows represent the stimulus relations that tested as having been learned. Broken arrows represent the stimulus relations that tested as not having been learned. (Reproduced from Jitsumori et al., in press.)

then tested for transfer to the prototypes on probe trials. Another control group was trained to discriminate the prototypes and they were then tested for transfer to the poor exemplars. Thus, training and testing stimuli were exchanged symmetrically between the control groups. Testing accuracies were 53% correct and 59% correct, respectively (average = 56%), a finding in accord with the fact that the poor exemplars and the prototype of the same categories were designed to be physically dissimilar.

The findings from the control groups suggested that the experimental group pigeons formed the untrained equivalence between the perceptually dissimilar stimuli through perceptual transitivity. In other words, the pigeons' behavior was in accord with the rule "if the prototype and good exemplars are equivalent and if the good exemplars and poor exemplars are equivalent, then the poor exemplars and prototype are equivalent".

Equivalence network

In Jitsumori et al. (in press), the same pigeons, including Bird 2, were then explicitly trained to learn equivalence classes consisted of the prototype (M), good exemplars (AM, BM, CM), and poor exemplars (A, B, and C). Repeated reversal training was conducted by using all possible pairs of the stimuli. Subsequent testing confirmed that the pigeons had learned the M↔(A, B, C) equivalence, but none of them fully passed the tests for the A↔B, B↔C, and A↔C equivalences. We then continued the repeated reversal training by adding the 50% morphings of the poor exemplars, AB, BC, and CA, which allowed the pigeons to pass all the tests for the A↔B, B↔C, and A↔C equivalences. Again, the dissimilar original faces were learned as equivalent through perceptual transitivity. Figure 5.5 compares the testing performances obtained before (left) and after (right) the repeated reversal training conducted by using the prototypes, good exemplars, poor exemplars, and the 50% morphed images of the poor exemplars.

Furthermore, subsequent testing revealed that the newly introduced poor exemplars, AB, BC, and CA, were learned as equivalent to the prototype and even to the most distantly related poor exemplars. That is, the pigeons passed the tests for the M↔AB, M↔BC, and M↔CA equivalences as well as the AB↔C, BC↔A, and CA↔B equivalences. Figure 5.6 illustrates the equivalence network eventually learned by the pigeons in the study by Jitsumori et al. (in press).

Levels of equivalence

It is worth summarizing the above-noted findings in terms of the levels of equivalence.

Level 1: Equivalence based on perceptual similarity

Among the possible factors in the formation of equivalence classes, the most obvious would be based on perceptual similarities, or generalization within classes. Equivalence classes at this level involve stimuli that are distinguishable

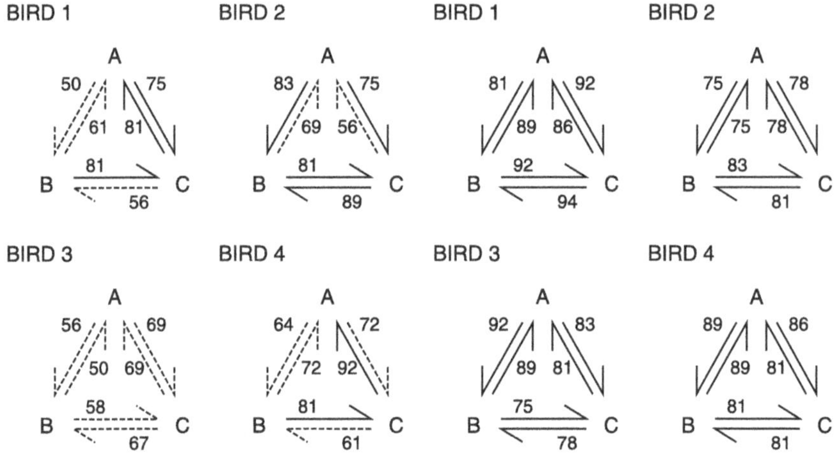

Figure 5.5 Percentage correct scores on probe trials during A→B, B→A, B→C, C→B, C→A, and A→C testing sessions, conducted before (left) and after (right) the repeated reversal training with the prototypes (M), good exemplars (AM, BM, CM), poor exemplars (A, B, C) and the 50% morphed images of the poor exemplars (AB, BC, CA). (Reproduced from Jitsumori et al., in press.)

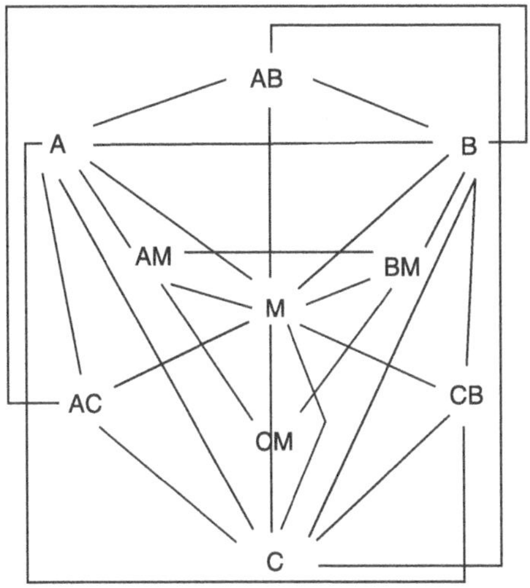

Figure 5.6 A schematic representation of the equivalence network learned by pigeons (Jitsumori et al., in press).

but still subjected to a spontaneous perceptual generalization between the stimuli. The emergence of untrained AM↔CM equivalence from the trained AM↔BM and BM↔CM equivalences indicates that pigeons are capable of forming equivalence classes at this level. Importantly, the pigeons performed accurately on probe trials, independently of the contingencies of reinforcement most recently applied to the probe pairs when they had appeared as training pairs. As such, any of the exemplars would contribute in causing pigeons to change their behaviors to all other exemplars of the class. Undoubtedly, the competence to learn perceptually defined equivalence classes is essential for animals to survive and to reproduce in their natural environments.

Level 2: Perceptual transitivity

The emergence of untrained M↔(A, B, C) equivalence based on the trained M↔(AM, BM, CM) and (AM, BM, CM)↔(A, B, C) equivalences indicates that pigeons are capable of relating perceptually dissimilar stimuli transitively through the exemplar that is perceptually similar to each of these stimuli. Note that, because M↔(AM, BM, CM) and (AM, BM, CM)↔(A, B, C) equivalences were learned in the separate training stages, M↔(A, B, C) equivalence could never be learned by common response functions but could be derived by integrating the separately learned multiple equivalences. Perceptual transitivity undoubtedly accelerates expansion of the perceptually defined equivalence class at Level 1. Perceptual transitivity may be of great relevance for most animals to cope with variability of natural objects existing in the world around them.

Level 3: Equivalence network

In an equivalence network, even poor exemplars that are dissimilar in various ways can be bound together. Our pigeons successfully learned equivalences between distantly related poor exemplars, for example, AB and C, BC and A, and AC and B. Because 50% morphed images of these exemplars were not presented as stimuli for the pigeons, the equivalences could not be established by simple perceptual transitivity at Level 2. What is still unclear is whether the exemplars were internally related by nodal functions or if they were processed as the category as a whole. It is clear, however, that pigeons are capable of learning equivalence networks consisting of a wide variety of exemplars structured by family resemblance.

Level 4: Equivalences among physically similar and disparate stimuli

Equivalence classes consisting of physically similar and disparate stimuli are often referred to as generalized equivalence classes. Suppose that a physically disparate stimulus X, for example a color or a geometric figure, is learned as equivalent to a given member of the category. If this relation will propagate to other members of the category, we may say that the category members and the physically disparate stimuli X have been learned as equivalent. In the case where the equivalence relation propagates spontaneously to all the members, independently of the nodal distances, we may conclude that the various exemplars have been processed as the category as a whole, in the sense that they are all equally associated to the stimulus X.

Level 5: Nonsimilarity-based transitivity

Suppose that an additional stimulus Y that is dissimilar to X and also to the members of the category has been learned as equivalent to any of the category members. Then X and Y will be equivalent transitively. Obviously, the formation of an equivalence class consisting of perceptually dissimilar stimuli (the category members, X, and Y, in this case) is a more complicated problem than those at the preceding levels. However, Jitsumori et al. (2002) suggested that this might be within the competencies of pigeons. In this study, dot-matrix patterns were randomly assigned as members of two stimulus classes, with the patterns being denoted as A, B, C, and D in each class. In sequential training phases, the birds were trained to form A↔B, C↔D, A↔C, and B↔D equivalences through repeated reversals of the reinforcement contingencies. The birds were then tested for the formation of the trained equivalences and the untrained A↔D and B↔C equivalences to assess whether the untrained equivalences had emerged by transitive extension of the trained equivalences. Only two of four pigeons exhibited emergence of one of these untrained equivalences, by interrelating the separately trained equivalences, thus forming three-member functional equivalence classes consisting of perceptually dissimilar stimuli. Although an equivalence class consisting of dissimilar stimuli is difficult for pigeons to learn, this is still within the competencies of pigeons.

A more sophisticated equivalence at this level is symbolic equivalence. Suppose that an additional stimulus Z is trained to be equivalent to X. If the untrained equivalence between Z and Y will be derived, and furthermore Z will be equivalent to any members of the conceptual category, then it may be said that the symbolic stimuli X, Y, and Z have been learned as equivalent.

Level 6: Equivalences among categories

Most objects can be classified into several different categories that differ in inclusiveness. For example, we classify a chair into the categories *kitchen chair*, *chair*, *furniture*, *artifact*, and even *entity*, each of which is more inclusive than the preceding one. Under some conditions, two or more categories may be learned as equivalent as the members of a more abstract category. It is plausible to infer that the equivalence at this level is an extension of the equivalences at the preceding levels. However, no one has yet even attempted to train animals to learn a hierarchical structure of categories.

Concluding remarks

The experiments reported in this article were designed to investigate nonverbal cognitive abilities of categorization and concept formation, using pigeons as experimental subjects. The study took a kind of synthetic approach and used artificial stimuli that were designed to form the categories structured by family resemblances. The findings demonstrated that pigeons are capable of forming equivalence classes among highly variable category members. Pigeons readily learn equivalences up to Level 3 (equivalence network). With difficulty, they would be induced to rise to Level 4 (generalized equivalence class) or Level 5 (nonsimilarity-based equivalence).

The findings reported in this article may effectively bridge between the studies of equivalence classes and the studies of categorization in the field of comparative cognition. As I have discussed, the former group uses physical stimuli, such as colors, tilted lines, and geometric shapes, to investigate acquired equivalence relations among physically different stimuli. The latter group investigates learning of open-ended categories by animals, using photographs of natural objects and artificial stimuli that are constructed by mimicking the properties of natural categories. The studies reported in this chapter demonstrated that these different lines of research could effectively converge to provide insights into functional and evolutionary significance of cognitive abilities of animals to categorize stimuli structured by family resemblance. The findings suggested the convergent evolution of the pigeon and human cognitive systems, both of which are designed to cope with the continuities and discontinuities existing in the external world.

References

Bhatt, R.S., Wasserman, E.A., Reynolds, W.F., & Knauss, K.S. (1988). Conceptual behavior in pigeons: Categorization of both familiar and novel examples from four classes of natural and artificial stimuli. *Journal of Experimental Psychology: Animal Behavior Processes*, *14*, 219–234.

Edwards, C.A., Jagielo, J.A., Zentall, T.R., & Hogan, D.E. (1982). Acquired equivalence and distinctiveness in matching-to-sample by pigeons: Mediation by reinforcer-specific expectancies. *Journal of Experimental Psychology: Animal Behavior Processes*, *8*, 244–259.

Herrnstein, R.J. (1990). Levels of stimulus control: A functional approach. *Cognition*, *37*, 133–166.

Herrnstein, R.J., & Loveland, D.H. (1964). Complex visual concept in the pigeon. *Science*, *146*, 549–551.

Jitsumori, M. (1993). Category discrimination of artificial polymorphous stimuli based on feature learning. *Journal of Experimental Psychology: Animal Behavior Processes*, *19*, 244–254.

Jitsumori, M. (1994). Discrimination of artificial polymorphous stimuli by rhesus monkeys (*Macaca mulatta*). *The Quarterly Journal of Experimental Psychology*, *47*B, 371–386.

Jitsumori, M. (1996). A prototype effect and categorization of artificial polymorphous stimuli in pigeons. *Journal of Experimental Psychology: Animal Behavior Processes*, *22*, 405–419.

Jitsumori, M. (2004). Categorization and formation of equivalence classes in animals: Studies in Japan on the background of contemporary developments. *Japanese Psychological Research*, *46*, 182–194.

Jitsumori, M., & Delius, J.D. (2001). Object recognition and object categorization in animals. In T. Matsuzawa (Ed.), *Primate origins of human cognition and behavior* (pp. 269–292). Tokyo: Springer-Verlag.

Jitsumori, M., & Makino, H. (2004). Recognition of static and dynamic images of depth-rotated human faces by pigeons. *Learning & Behavior*, *32*, 145–156.

Jitsumori, M., & Matsuzawa, T. (1991). Picture perception in monkeys and pigeons: Transfer of rightside-up versus upside-down discrimination of photographic objects across conceptual categories. *Primates*, *32*, 473–482.

Jitsumori, M., Natori, M., & Okuyama, K. (1999). Recognition of moving video images of conspecifics by pigeons: Effects of individuals, static and dynamic motion cues, and movement. *Animal Learning & Behavior*, *27*, 303–315.

Jitsumori, M., & Ohkubo, O. (1996). Orientation discrimination and categorization of photographs of natural objects by pigeons. *Behavioural Processes*, *38*, 205–226.

Jitsumori, M., Shimada, N., & Inoue, S. (in press). Family resemblances facilitate pigeons to form and to expand functional equivalence classes. *Learning and Behavior*.

Jitsumori, M., Siemann, M., Lehr, M., & Delius, J.D. (2002). A new approach to the formation of equivalence classes in pigeons. *Journal of the Experimental Analysis of Behavior*, *78*, 397–408.

Jitsumori, M., & Yoshihara, M. (1997). Categorical discrimination of human facial expressions by pigeons: A test of the linear feature model. *The Quarterly Journal of Experimental Psychology*, *50*B, 253–268.

Keller, F.S., & Schoenfeld, W.N. (1950). *Principles of psychology*. New York: Appleton-Century-Crofts.
Lea, S.E.G. (1984). In what sense do pigeons learn concepts? In H.L. Roitblat, T.G. Bever, & H.S. Terrace (Eds.), *Animal cognition* (pp. 263–276). Hillsdale, NJ: Lawrence Erlbaum Associates Inc.
Lea, S.E.G., & Harrison, S.N. (1978). Discrimination of polymorphous stimulus sets by pigeons. *Quarterly Journal of Experimental Psychology*, *30*B, 521–537.
Makino, H., & Jitsumori, M. (2000). Category learning and prototype effect in pigeons: A study by using morphed images of human faces. *Japanese Journal of Psychology*, *71*, 477–485 [in Japanese with English abstract].
Medin, D.L., & Schaffer, M.M. (1978). Context theory of classification learning. *Psychological Review*, *85*, 207–238.
Reed, S.K. (1972). Pattern recognition and categorization. *Cognitive Psychology*, *3*, 382–407.
Rosch, E. (1978). Principles of categorization. In E. Rosch & B.B. Lloyd (Eds.), *Cognition and categorization* (pp. 27–48). Hillsdale, NJ: Lawrence Erlbaum Associates Inc.
Rosch, E., & Mervis, C.B. (1975). Family resemblances: Studies in the internal structure of categories. *Cognitive Psychology*, *7*, 573–605.
Skinner, B.F. (1935). The generic nature of the concepts of stimulus and response. *Journal of General Psychology*, *6*, 32–48.
Urcuioli, P.J., & Zentall, T.R. (1993). A test of comparison-stimulus substitutability following one-to-many matching by pigeons. *The Psychological Record*, *43*, 725–744.
Vaughan, W. (1988). Formation of equivalence sets in pigeons. *Journal of Experimental Psychology: Animal Behavior Processes*, *14*, 36–42.
Wasserman, E.A., Devolder, C.L., & Coppage, D.J. (1992). Nonsimilarity-based conceptualization in pigeons. *Psychological Science*, *3*, 374–379.
Wittgenstein, L. (1953). *Philosophical investigations*. New York: Macmillan.

6 The effect of genetics and vascular health on memory functioning: The Betula Study

Lars-Göran Nilsson and Cindy M. de Frias

The understanding of complex cognitive functions like memory requires understanding of a series of steps along a continuum from the molecular/genetic level, to the cellular level, to the synaptic level, to the network level, and to behavior. At present, there is no research covering all these stages. Important progress is being made in many laboratories all over the world. One important step in the development of memory research was the recent inclusion of genetics. In fact the history of genetics is relatively brief.

As described by Plomin (2003), the 20th century has been called the century of the gene. The word genetics was coined in 1903; deoxyribonucleic acid (DNA) was suggested as the molecule for genetics in 1944; Watson and Crick published their article about the double helix of DNA in 1953; and the Human Genome Project ended just a few years ago with the identification of some 30,000 genes, many fewer than previously thought. Although the identification of the genes is an important initial step, discoveries of their functions are the ultimate goal in this development. In this chapter, we will describe one approach to relating genes to memory function.

For various reasons, it is a rather arduous task to find those genes that are related to memory function. For one thing, where should one begin searching among those 30,000 genes identified? Another reason why this research task is difficult is that very large databases are required in order to establish an association between a particular gene and memory. We have access to a large database that makes such studies possible; the Betula Study (Nilsson et al., 1997). The name Betula is derived from the Latin word for birch tree, which is the symbol for Umeå – a city in northern Sweden where the study is being conducted. Although genetics provides the most recent input to research on memory, the brain-imaging techniques of positron emission tomography (PET) and functional magnetic resonance imaging (fMRI), developed in recent years as valuable tools for understanding memory, have also added a new dimension to research in this field. In the Betula Study we have combined genetics and brain imaging to gain access to new secrets of memory. A brief description of Betula follows.

The Betula Study

The Betula Study was originally motivated by the wish to explore various aspects of the development of memory functioning and health in adulthood and late life, particularly in light of the fact that an increasingly large portion of the population consists of elderly people. In addition to studying the development of memory and health in general, two more specific purposes were (a) to explore early, pre-clinical signs and potential risk factors of dementia, and (b) to obtain premorbid measures of memory and health in people who will suffer accidents or acquire various diseases during the course of the study. Since the inception of the study, two related purposes have been added, namely to examine what the characteristics of successful aging are, and to determine the prerequisites for early diagnosis of neurodegenerative diseases.

The measures taken to accomplish these goals require an interdisciplinary approach involving scientists from several medical, social, and psychological fields. Specifically, the aims of the study require the planning, conducting and analyzing of data from medical examinations, blood sample testing, DNA extraction and genotyping, health status enquiries, explorations of daily living and leisure activities, critical life events, examination of social and economic factors, and an extensive examination of a wide variety of memory functions.

Several unique features of the Betula Study include its research design, the large number of participants throughout the adult lifespan (35 to 95 years of age), a large number of health-related and social variables, and a large number of well-defined and theoretically motivated cognitive tests with a sharp focus on memory function.

The design employed for this study was modeled after Schaie (1965, 1977). Schaie proposed the longitudinal cohort-sequential design, to be able to separate the effects of the three major sources of variation in developmental research: age, cohort, and time of measurement. The general design of the study, described in detail elsewhere (see Nilsson et al., 1997), is outlined in Table 6.1. There are five independent samples (S1, S2, S3, S4, and S5), and four waves of completed data collection (T1, T2, T3, and T4), and a fifth wave is planned.

The research design for the Betula Study presents clear advantages when

Table 6.1 The Betula design. Return rates are given in parentheses

T1 (1998–90)	S1					
T2 (1993–95)	S1 (86%)	S2	S3			
T3 (1998–00)	S1 (85%)	S2 (83%)	S3 (86%)	S4		
T4 (2003–05)	S1	S2	S3	S4	S5	
T5 (2008–10)*	*S1*	*S2*	*S3*	*S4*	*S5*	*S6*

* planned

compared to traditional cross-sectional or single-cohort longitudinal designs, because it is possible to examine multiple forms of sequential designs to disentangle age, cohort, and period effects. To our knowledge, no previous study focusing on memory and health has employed this type of extensive design.

At T1, S1 participants were 35, 40, 45, 50, 55, 60, 65, 70, 75, and 80 years of age. There were 100 persons in each of the 10 age cohorts. At T2, two new samples were added to the Betula Study. The participants of S2 were 35, 40, 45, . . ., 80 years of age in 5-year intervals, whereas the participants of S3 were 40, 45, 50, . . ., 85 years of age. At T3, another new sample (S4) was included to control for practice effects in S1–S3. A total of 600 persons were included in this sample, with 50 individuals in each of 12 different age cohorts (35, 40, 45, . . ., 90 years of age). A new sample (S5) was included to control for the size of the practice effects that will have emerged up to T4. It should be observed that the proportion of returnees is high and stable (83–86%). Averaged across S1–S3, the reasons for non return were as follows: 7% died before T3, 4% refused further participation, and 4% had moved or were unavailable for other reasons.

Recruitment of each new sample of participants started by randomly obtaining names from the population registry in Umeå, Sweden, in each of the cohorts. The number of males and females selected for inclusion reflected the proportion of males and females in each age cohort of the population, for an overall ratio of 47/53 (males to females). As described in Nilsson et al. (1997), participants and drop-outs did not differ and participants did not differ from the population as a whole on a series of background variables, except for education and income, which was higher among participants.

The general aim was to devise a battery of memory tasks that would cover a wide range of memory processes and systems for evaluating normal memory change (primary aging) and also disease-related decline (secondary aging). The memory tests employed in the Betula Study are listed in Table 6.2. These tests were extensively described in Nilsson et al. (1997) and will not be reiterated here. Necessary changes were made in the test battery over measurement occasions. These modifications reflect the refinement of theory and methods in memory research.

The basic rationale used for investigating the development of health in adulthood and old age was to cover a wide range of potentially important physical and mental health factors and to relate these indexes of health status to memory performance. The methods used to collect these data were questionnaires, interviews, and a regular health examination including blood sampling. In addition to questions aimed at disclosing the participants' subjective health by asking for self-descriptions of diseases (i.e., diabetes mellitus, angina pectoris, etc.), assessments of vision, hearing, nutrition, and blood pressure were collected.

The social variables of Betula include socio-economic variables, marital status, type of dwelling, education, leisure activities, current daily activities, profession, profession and activities of spouse, number of children, age of

Table 6.2 Memory tasks and other cognitive tasks used in the Betula Study. The test occasions at which each test was administered are given in parentheses

Episodic memory
Face recognition (T1–T4), *yes/no, 16 items at study, 32 items at test*
Name recognition(T1–T4), *four-alternative forced choice, 16 items at study*
Sentence learning with encoding enactment(T1–T4), *free recall, two cued recall tests, yes/no recognition, source recall, 16 items at study*
Sentence learning without encoding enactment(T1–T4), *free recall, two cued recall tests, yes/no recognition, source recall, 16 items at study*
Word recall (T1–T4) with or without concurrent card sorting at study or test, *free recall, 12 items*
Learning of facts (T1–T2), *cued recall, source recall, 10 items*
Prospective memory (T1–T4), *recall without and with reminding cue*
Memory for activities (T1–T4), *free recall*

Semantic memory
Knowledge recall, (T1–T2, T4)
Word fluency (T1–T4), *initial letter A*
Word fluency (T1–T4), *initial letter M, five-letter words*
Word fluency (T1–T4), *initial letter B, names of professions*
Word fluency (T1–T4), *initial letter S, five-letter names of animals*
Word comprehension (T1–T4), *30 items*

Priming
Name-stem completion (T1–T4)
Word fragment completion (T2–T4)

Other tasks
Block design (T1–T4)
Tower of Hanoi (T2–T3)
Mini-Mental State Examination (T1–T4)
Draw-a-man-test (T1–T2)
Letter–digit substitution (T3–T4)
Odor identification (T3–T4)

parents at birth of participant, place of living at childhood and adolescence, and number of friends. A detailed description of these variables was presented in Nilsson et al. (1997).

When the project started, a relatively small group of scientists, primarily in psychology, was involved. Gradually, and in relation to the research directions undertaken, the project, the number of persons, and the number of disciplines involved have increased. By involving geneticists in Betula we have been able to extract DNA for more than 3000 individuals. So far we have focused the genotyping on only a few genes. Apolipoprotein E (APOE) is one such gene. The ε4 allele of the Apolipoprotein E gene (APOE-ε4) is a well-established risk factor for cardiovascular disorders in middle age and for Alzheimer's disease (AD) in old age (e.g., Corder et al., 1993; Dupuy et al., 2001). Onset age of AD occurs earlier in individuals having at least one ε4 allele, relative to the carriers of the ε2 and ε3 alleles (e.g., Flory et al., 2000). The three alleles of APOE, ε2, ε3, and ε4, differ in their relative frequency, with ε3 being the most common allele occurring in about 72%, whereas ε2, and ε4 occur in about 8% and 20% of the population, respectively (Eggertsen et al., 1993).

Catechol O-methyltransferase (COMT) is another gene of recent focus. The metabolism of dopamine is catalyzed by the enzyme catechol O-methyltransferase (COMT). The coding region of the COMT gene comprises a single nucleotide polymorphism (SNP), leading to a Val to Met substitution ($Val^{158}Met$). This SNP has been shown to influence the activity and thermal stability of the enzyme (Lachman et al., 1996; Lotta et al., 1995) in vitro. The Met allele has one quarter of the enzyme activity of the Val allele at body temperature (Lachman et al., 1996). Carriers of the Met/Met genotype are expected to experience slower inactivation of dopamine as compared to carriers of the Val/Val genotype (Weinberger et al., 2001).

Major findings in the Betula Study

The research conducted to date falls into three broad categories: (1) longitudinal assessment of memory and health, (2) gene associations with dementia, neurodegeneration and cognitive function, and (3) brain imaging in relation to memory and genes. These areas are described below.

Memory systems

In an early paper, Nyberg (1994) used the Betula data from S1 at T1 to test two models of declarative memory by means of confirmatory factor analysis. A unitary model was compared with the two-factor episodic–semantic model proposed by Tulving (1972, 1983). The results supported a division of declarative memory into memory for personal events and memory for facts. Nyberg et al. (2003) recently tested competing models (e.g., two factors vs four factors) of declarative memory and its age invariance. The results support the view that episodic memory is more age sensitive than semantic memory, but also that aging has differential effects within these two forms of memory.

Memory assessment: Cross-sectional vs longitudinal findings

In two recent papers we have described findings not previously known in the research literature. In a recently completed longitudinal analysis of changes in memory performance from T1 to T3, it was observed that the decline in episodic memory may appear at a later stage than has been indicated in cross-sectional analyses (Rönnlund et al., 2005). Whereas the cross-sectional data suggest that episodic memory declines in a linear fashion from age 35, the longitudinal data indicate stability up to age 60. Rönnlund and Nilsson (2006) demonstrated differences in cognitive profiles between cross-sectional and longitudinal analyses. When proper control was made for cohort differences and practice effects the two curves overlapped. The difference between cross-sectional and longitudinal assessment is a new finding that has gained considerable attention and interest in the international research community. The planned research will examine whether there are systematic and interpretable differences between various cognitive functions, and the potential overlap between cross-sectional and longitudinal data.

Successful aging

In most studies of aging and cognition, older non-demented adults are treated as one, single homogeneous group. However, in a highly influential paper published in *Science* in 1987, Rowe and Kahn introduced a distinction between "usual" (often termed normal) and "successful" aging. Most non-demented elderly can be characterized as showing normal aging in the presence of cognitive impairment. In contrast, a minority of older adults seem to age successfully and show no cognitive decline. Since this distinction was introduced, successful aging has been examined in several large-scale population-based studies around the world. These studies have generated some knowledge about what characterizes successful aging, but they suffer from a major limitation in light of the original proposal by Rowe and Kahn (1987, 1997). Specifically, a sample of younger adults was not included in these previous investigations. This is a noteworthy omission, as Rowe and Kahn argued that whether or not an older individual can be labelled as a "successful ager" is determined (at least in part) by the performance of younger individuals. If younger individuals are omitted from the sample, and successful aging is defined by the upper third of the age distribution, it is possible to miscalculate (i.e., overestimate) the number of individuals in this category. In a recently completed study (Habib, Nyberg, & Nilsson, in press) we have contrasted various ways of defining successful aging, notably in relation to older adults only or in relation to younger adults. The results show conclusively that when successful aging is defined in relation to younger individuals, only about *5–10%* of the elderly can be said to have aged successfully.

The extensive set of variables that are included in the Betula battery has made it possible to identify a set of non-cognitive variables on which the successfully aged differ from the usual group. These variables include education, living conditions, objective and subjective health, and lifestyle factors (e.g., having close friends). An additional example is dental status, a variable that has not received much attention in the context of aging and cognition. In collaboration with dentists, we have conducted more thorough examinations of the relation between dental health and memory (Bergdahl et al., 2006).

Our results indicate that some older individuals show no cognitive decline over the years. Importantly, however, this conclusion rests on cross-sectional data analyses. Currently, we are examining whether longitudinal patterns of change in cognition can differentiate between successful and normal aging. Information on non-cognitive variables (e.g., social relationships) can be used as additional indicators of successful aging. There are data to suggest that an individual can, at least in part, exercise an influence on her or his cognitive functions by participating in mentally and physically stimulating activities. Our studies have the potential to single out the most critical (and measured) factors and some of these will hopefully be ones that can be affected through self-initiated efforts.

Sex differences in memory

Sex differences in memory are well documented. However, explanations are as yet unknown. In a cross-sectional study, Herlitz, Nilsson, and Bäckman (1997) examined potential sex differences in episodic memory, semantic memory, primary memory, and priming. There were no differences between men and women on age, education, or on a global test of intellectual functioning. Men outperformed women on a visuo-spatial task and women outperformed men on tests of episodic memory and verbal fluency. There were no differences between men and women on tasks assessing semantic memory, primary memory, or priming. In a follow-up study, de Frias, Nilsson, and Herlitz (in press) reported that these sex differences were stable over a 10-year period. Relatedly, research has indicated that episodic recognition memory entails at least two distinct states of awareness (Tulving, 1985). Recognition can occur when a stimulus evokes conscious recollection or, alternatively, when a stimulus gives rise to feelings of familiarity, without any recollective experience. Larsson, Lövdén, and Nilsson (2003) reported that recollection was higher among women than men, although familiarity-based recognition was equally large across sex.

Yonker, Eriksson, Nilsson, and Herlitz (2003) examined the role of estrogen in several cognitive tasks on the basis of cross-sectional Betula data. A total of 18 men and 18 women were matched on age and estradiol level, which is the active form of estrogen. The correlation between estradiol level and cognitive performance was significant for face recognition in women, but not men. Because sex differences remained in verbal episodic memory tasks and face recognition despite matched levels of estradiol, circulating estradiol does not seem to be of critical importance for explaining sex differences in episodic memory. Further studies on sex differences in cognitive function are in progress.

Memory dysfunction as an early sign of dementia

Lövdén et al. (2005) demonstrated that, when applying cluster analysis to memory data obtained at T1 for S1, one of the six clusters that emerged contained data from only those individuals who, at T3, had become diagnosed as demented. This is an important new finding in that it implies that memory data might be used as one component in detecting early signs of dementia. Future research will include attempts to (1) make a more refined description of what the characteristic features are that are connected with later development of dementia, using both cognitive and non-cognitive variables, (2) to extend the time window from 10 to 15 years for this retrospective clustering of individual data, and (3) to combine data on memory function with genetic markers and brain imaging to increase both selectivity and specificity of predictions regarding who will later become demented.

During the past decade, a number of studies have highlighted that the neuropathological changes associated with Alzheimer's disease affect regions of the brain involved in olfaction. For example, both the hippocampus and the entorhinal cortex receive direct input from the olfactory bulb and represent structures that show an early involvement in the disease (e.g., Braak & Braak, 1992, 1997). Research focusing on olfactory dysfunction as a preclinical marker for cognitive decline and impending dementia has yielded some interesting findings. For example, a longitudinal study demonstrated that ε4 positive anosmics (smell blind) showed a five-fold greater risk of cognitive decline compared to that of ε4 negative normosmics (normal sense of smell; Graves et al., 1999). Also, Devanand et al. (2000) reported that deficits in identifying olfactory information were a reliable marker for follow-up diagnosis of Alzheimer's disease, although global cognitive status was controlled for. This finding suggests that olfactory testing may serve as a clinical tool in identifying persons in a pre-clinical stage of a neurodegenerative disease. From T3, the Betula project also comprises a test assessing odor identification. Thus, Betula offers a unique possibility to further explore the relationships between olfactory functioning, genetic variation, and neurodegenerative disorder.

Blood pressure as a predictor of cognitive decline

The Betula Study is part of a European collaborative study on vascular determinants of brain lesion. The CASCADE Study (Cardiovascular Determinants of Dementia) was designed to examine long-term (10–20-year) and short-term (5-year) cardiovascular risk factors for, and the cognitive consequences of, brain abnormalities. In each of the 10 participating national studies, a random sample of at least 100 subjects aged 65–75 years participated. White matter lesions and atrophy were measured with structural magnetic resonance imaging (Launer et al., 2000). Cognitive function was measured with nine tests of memory and executive function from the Betula test battery (Nilsson et al., 2005b). The studies included in CASCADE are ongoing and geographically spread throughout Europe to capture the cardiovascular risk gradient. One study on diabetes has been completed (Schmidt et al., 2004) and several others on a variety of other factors are in progress.

In two studies by Söderlund et al. (2003, 2004), the occurrence of cerebral white matter hyperintensities (lesions), and their associations with blood pressure and cognitive function, were examined in a population-based sample of 123 Betula participants between 64 and 74 years old. Magnetic resonance imaging (MRI) detected subcortical and periventricular changes in 90% and 67% of the cases, respectively. Damage in both locations was related to elevated diastolic blood pressure measured 5 and 10 years earlier. Subcortical hyperintensities were only weakly associated with impaired motor speed. Periventricular changes showed a negative relation to episodic memory, which was still significant after adjusting for blood pressure. Collectively, these findings suggest that white matter hyperintensities are associated with impaired cognitive functioning. Blood pressure is one factor that might increase the risk for clinically significant white matter hyperintensities.

Recently, we examined whether dementia was associated with high levels of systolic blood pressure, diastolic blood pressure, and pulse pressure (systolic minus diastolic blood pressure) 10 years prior to clinical diagnosis (Nilsson et al., 2004). This is the first study to examine this issue in a sample of middle-aged and older men and women using a long (10-year) pre-clinical period. Using logistic regression, blood pressure at T1 was used to predict dementia status at T3. Systolic and diastolic blood pressures and pulse pressure were entered as continuous variables. Evidence was observed for the long-term effect of elevated levels of systolic blood pressure and pulse pressure on the risk for developing dementia. Persons who were to be diagnosed with dementia 10 years later had higher systolic pressure and greater pulse pressure at baseline assessment. Further research on this topic is planned when a 15-year frame has elapsed at T4.

A recent normative paper by Wahlin et al. (2002) serves as an excellent basis for future studies of cognitive aging as influenced by vitamin deficiencies of B12 and folic acid, including the long-term effects of hypertension and cardiovascular disease on white-matter hyperintensities and brain atrophy, and the effects these lesions may have on cognitive function many years later (Söderlund et al., 2004). Another area of current research on the topic of diseases in old age affecting cognitive function is the study of diabetes in relation to cognition. E. Nilsson et al. (2004) found that diabetics and persons with elevated HbA_{1C} performed at a lower level than age-matched controls on tasks assessing episodic memory. Elevated levels of HbA_{1C} are indicative of lack of glycemic control, which may be indicative of diabetes. The results obtained in this study suggest that it is not the presence of diabetes in itself, at least not type II diabetes, but rather glycemic derangement that causes cognitive deficits. This finding is in the process of being examined further in ongoing research. The fact that diabetics can also benefit from cognitive support (enacted encoding and cueing at retrieval) similar to nondiabetics could indicate that cognitive performance is impacted in a similar way by diabetes as by normal aging.

Dementia, neurodegeneration and cognitive function in relation to genes

Within the Betula Study we have demonstrated strong associations between episodic memory in non-demented individuals and immune-response related markers Complement C3 and Haptoglobin (Nilsson et al., 1996). In a recent study (Nilsson et al., 2005a), we examined the effect of the ε4 allele of APOE in non-demented individuals aged 35 to 85 years. We found a more pronounced ε4-related deficit for participants aged 65 years and older in tasks assessing episodic recall. Relatively smaller ε4-related deficits for these same individuals were found in episodic recognition and verbal fluency. No deficits were found in tasks assessing vocabulary, primary memory, and priming. We also demonstrated that carriers of the ε4 allele between the ages of 50 and 60 years performed at a higher level than non-carriers of ε4 allele in episodic recall tasks. But no allele effect for this age group was noted for episodic recognition tasks, or semantic memory, primary memory, and priming tasks. Furthermore, we found a dose effect, such that homozygotes for the ε4 alleles had a more pronounced deficit in acquiring and recollecting episodic information than carriers of one ε4 allele, who in turn were more impaired than non-ε4 carriers. The pattern of findings observed for older ε4 carriers suggests that these individuals have particular difficulty when the executive task demands are high. Several factors (e.g., smaller hippocampal volumes, less effective neural repair mechanisms, pre-clinical dementia) may account for these findings. On the basis of the data obtained, we argued that analyses of the effect of specific genes on memory function should be accompanied by assessment of performance at a specific level (e.g., recall), with due attention to the age of the individual.

In two recent papers we have examined the role of the COMT gene on memory, executive functions, and fluid intelligence, in a 5-year study of nondemented adult men (de Frias et al., 2004, 2005). In one study, de Frias et al. (2004) reported that carriers of the Met/Met genotype (with low enzyme activity) performed better on episodic and semantic memory, as compared to carriers of the Val allele (with higher enzyme activity). Division of episodic memory into its recall and recognition components showed that the difference was specific to episodic recall, not recognition tasks. In a second study, de Frias et al. (2005) assessed executive functioning (letter fluency, working memory, and Tower of Hanoi tasks) and fluid intelligence (using block design) in relation to variation in the COMT gene polymorphism. Carriers of the Met/Met genotype performed better on block design and executive function (measured by a single factor), as compared to carriers of the Val allele. An age by COMT interaction for block design located the effect for middle-aged men only. Individuals with the Val/Val genotype declined in executive functioning over the 5-year period, whereas carriers of the Met allele remained stable in performance. The mediating mechanism responsible for the effect of COMT on cognitive performance is possibly dopamine.

In future research we aim to study both functional single-nucleotide polymorphisms (SNPs) and to determine haplotypes in candidate genes or chromosomal regions. The haplotype diversity will then be exploited in both genetic linkage and direct association studies. We will continue to study associations between genes and both cognitive function and mental health. We will be able to evaluate changes in cognitive function and genetic variations. The prion protein and very low-density lipoprotein genes have already been associated with cognitive impairment. Genes could have the effect of either increasing the susceptibility to a disease or protecting an individual from developing a disease. We will assess gene and environment effects on longevity, cognition, and health of individuals.

Based on gene function we have divided all available cognitive function and dementia related genes into three groups: The first group is Aβ and lipid metabolism related genes. Several of these genes, such as APP (amyloid precursor protein), APOE, PS1, and PS2 (presenilin 1 and 2) have been associated in earlier studies with dementia and Alzheimer's disease. Disease-predisposing mutations have been identified and they will be interesting to study in the Betula cohort. Other polymorphisms in these genes, such as promoter mutations in APOE and PS1, are also interesting since they affect gene activity. Other genes in this group are secretases involved in APP cleavage, lipid receptors and related proteins, and proteins detected in neurofibrillary tangles and senile plaques.

The second group of genes are those involved in oxidative stress. This group includes nitric oxide synthases (NOS), iron metabolizing enzymes and oxygen radical scavengers. NO production in the brain is enhanced in patients with AD, and there is growing evidence that NO is involved in neuronal death. The oxidative stress caused by NO in the brain could be genetically regulated, and NOS genes could modulate the disease susceptibility. Iron metabolizing enzymes are attractive candidates for AD and dementia in general, since iron is present in amyloid plaques and facilitates the aggregation of Aβ peptide. Oxygen radical scavengers have previously been associated with several neurological disorders.

The third group of genes are those involved in inflammation/apoptosis. Apoptosis is a fundamental cellular process responsible for neuronal death. Therefore genes regulating this process have been attractive candidates for a number of neurological conditions. In our study we are planning to include several apoptosis and inflammation related genes, which in previous studies have been associated with dementia.

Brain imaging, genes, and memory

A sub-discipline that has received extensive current interest is labelled cognitive neuroscience of aging (see Cabeza, Nyberg, & Park, 2004). At the core of this field is the issue of whether it can be established how biologically determined factors that induce structural brain-changes can be countered by various experience-based factors. Examples of issues that have received much interest include functional brain-imaging findings that whereas younger adults typically activate unilateral brain regions, older adults tend to activate bilateral regions (Cabeza et al., 2002). Changes in activation patterns as a function of genetic status have also been noted (Bookheimer et al., 2000).

Previous studies in the field have largely been based on relatively small samples and there are several inconsistent findings in the literature. We have recently completed a large-scale fMRI data collection involving 60 individuals from the Betula Study for whom we have genetic data and longitudinal cognitive data. In one project (Persson et al., 2005) we have analyzed brain activity as a function of 10-year longitudinal data. The results show that bilateral activity accompanies cognitive decline over the years. Thus, the bilateral response seen for older adults in age-comparative brain-imaging studies seems to be a response to cognitive difficulties in the older group. This is an important conclusion that we are planning to follow up by doing longitudinal fMRI studies.

In another project (Lind et al., 2006) we have analyzed fMRI data in relation to genetic data. In particular, we have classified the 60 individuals as carriers or non-carriers of the genetic risk factor for Alzheimer's dementia (APOEε4). Our fMRI results show that functional brain activity differs systematically as a function of genetic risk, with at-risk individuals showing reduced brain activity in parietal and frontal areas. The effect is modulated by whether an individual carries one or two APOEε4 alleles in a dose-related manner. These findings provide strong evidence for brain–gene interactions prior to disease onset (see Reiman et al., 2004).

In the context of brain, cognition, and genetic factors, it can be mentioned that the Betula Study offers a unique possibility to assess how head injury affects neuropsychological and cognitive performance. Specifically, since hundreds of individuals are followed over time, some will likely suffer injuries during the course of the study yet still continue to participate. We have identified a sub-population of individuals who have suffered mild head injury and for whom we have both pre- and post-injury cognitive data. Sundström et al. (2004) found that head injury predicted the development of cognitive impairment – but only for APOEε4 carriers. Notably, this effect was so subtle that within-person comparisons (before vs after injury performance) were necessary to detect the effect. In future studies we will relate head injury to the risk for developing dementia.

In future linked projects we also plan to examine how age-related cognitive change and genetic factors relate to structural brain changes. Specifically, we will do manual tracings of hippocampal volume for all individuals and also whole brain voxel-based morphometry. This technique will provide information on how the size of grey matter is related to various subject-related factors. A similar approach will be used for brain white matter on the basis of diffusion tensor imaging. Finally, a formidable challenge will be to integrate functional and structural brain data with different background factors to assess higher-order interactions among variables.

Acknowledgements

The Betula Study is funded by the Bank of Sweden Tercentenary Foundation (1988-0082:17), the Swedish Council for Planning and Coordination of Research (D1988-0092, D1989-0115, D1990-0074, D1991-0258, D1992-0143, D1997-0756, D1997-1841, D1999-0739, B1999-474), the Swedish Council for Research in the Humanities and Social Sciences (F377/1988–2000), and the Swedish Council for Social Research (1988–1990: 88-0082, and 311/1991–2000). Cindy de Frias is supported by a postdoctoral fellowship from the Canadian Institutes of Health Research – Institute of Aging.

References

Bergdahl, M., Habib, R., Bergdahl, J., Nyberg, L., & Nilsson, L.-G. (2006). *Natural teeth and preserved cognitive function in humans*. Manuscript submitted for publication.

Bookheimer, S.Y., Strojwas, M.H., Cohen, M.S., Saunders, A.M., Pericak-Vance, M.A., Mazziotta, J.C. et al. (2000). Patterns of brain activation in people at risk for Alzheimer's disease. *New England Journal of Medicine*, *343*, 450–456.

Braak, H., & Braak, E. (1992). The human entorhinal cortex: Normal morphology and lamina-specific pathology in various diseases. *Neuroscience Research*, *15*, 6–31.

Braak, H., & Braak, E. (1997). Frequency of stages of Alzheimer's-related lesion in different age categories. *Neurobiology of Aging*, *18*, 351–357.

Cabeza, R., Anderson, N.D., Kester, J., & McIntosh, A.R. (2002). Aging gracefully: Compensatory brain activity in high-performing older adults. *Neuroimage*, *17*, 1394–1402.

Cabeza, R., Nyberg, L., & Park, D. (2004). *Cognitive neuroscience of aging*. Oxford: Oxford University Press.

Corder, E.H., Saunders, A.M., Strittmatter, W.J., Schmwchel, D.E., Gaskell, P.C., Small, G.W. et al. (1993). Gene dose of apolipoprotein E type 4 allele and the risk of Alzheimer's disease in late onset families. *Science*, *261*, 921–923.

de Frias, C.M., Annerbrink, K., Eriksson, E., Adolfsson, R., & Nilsson, L.-G. (2004). COMT gene polymorphism is associated with memory in adulthood and old age. *Behavior Genetics*, *34*, 533–539.

de Frias, C.M., Annerbrink, K., Westberg, L., Eriksson, E., Adolfsson, R., & Nilsson, L.-G. (2005). Catechol O-Methyltransferase Val^{158}Met polymorphism is associated with executive functioning and fluid intelligence in nondemented adults. *Journal of Cognitive Neuroscience*, *17*, 1018–1025.

de Frias, C.M., Herlitz, A., & Nilsson, L.-G. (in press). Sex differences in cognition are stable over a 10-year period in adulthood and old age. *Aging, Neuropsychology, and Cognition.*

Devanand, D.P., Michaels-Marston, K.S., Liu, X.H., Pelton, G.H., Padilla, M., Marder, K. et al. (2000). Olfactory deficits in patients with mild cognitive impairment predict Alzheimer's disease at follow-up. *American Journal of Psychiatry, 157*, 1399–1405.

Dupuy, A.M., Mas, E., Ritchie, K., Descomps, B., Badiou, S., Cristol, J.P. et al. (2001). The relationship between apolipoprotein E4 and lipid metabolism is impaired in Alzheimer's disease. *Gerontology, 47*, 213–218.

Eggertsen, G., Tegelman, R., Ericsson, S., Angelin, B., & Berglund, L. (1993). Apolipoprotein-E polymorphism in a healthy Swedish population – variation of allele frequency with age and relation to serum-lipid concentrations. *Clinical Chemistry, 39*, 2125–2129.

Flory, J.D., Manuck, S.B., Ferrell, R.E., Ryan, C.M., & Muldoon, M.F. (2000). Memory performance and the apolipoprotein E polymorphism in a community sample of middle-aged adults. *American Journal of Medical Genetics, 96*, 707–711.

Graves, A.B., Bowen, J.D., Rajaram, L., McCormick, W.C., McCurry, S.M., Schellenberg, G.D. et al. (1999). Impaired olfaction as a marker for cognitive decline. *Neurology, 53*, 1480–1487.

Habib, R., Nyberg, L., & Nilsson, L.-G. (in press). Characterizing high-performing older adults in a population-based study: Level of education predicts success over time. *Aging, Neuropsychology, and Cognition.*

Herlitz, A., Nilsson, L.-G., & Bäckman, L. (1997). Gender differences in episodic memory. *Memory & Cognition, 25*, 801–811.

Lachman, H.M., Papolos, D.F., Saito, T., Yu, Y.M., Szumlanski, C.L., & Weinshilboum, R.M. (1996). Human catechol-O-methyltransferase pharmacogenetics: Description of a functional polymorphism and its potential application to neuropsychiatric disorders. *Pharmacogenetics, 6*, 243–250.

Larsson, M., Lövdén, M., & Nilsson, L.-G. (2003). Sex differences in recollective experience for olfactory and verbal information. *Acta Psychologica, 112*, 89–103.

Launer, L., Oudkerk, M., Nilsson, L.-G., Alperovitch, A., Berger, K., Breteler, M.M.B. et al. (2000). CASCADE: A European collaborative study on vascular determinants of brain lesion: Study design and objectives. *Neuroepidemiology, 19*, 113–120.

Lind, J., Persson, J., Ingvar, M., Larsson, A., Cruts, M., Van Broeckhoven, C. et al. (2006). Reduced functional brain activity response in cognitively intact Apolipoprotein ε4 carriers. *Brain*, 0314.

Lotta, T., Vidgren, J., Tilgmann, C., Ulmanen, I., Melén, K., Julkunen, I. et al. (1995). Kinetics of human soluble and membrane-bound catechol O-methyltransferase: A revised mechanism and description of the thermolabile variant of the enzyme. *Biochemistry, 34*, 4202–4210.

Lövdén, M., Bergman, L., Adolfsson, R., Lindenberger, U., & Nilsson, L.-G. (2005). Studying individual aging in an interindividual context: Typical paths of age-related, dementia-related, and mortality-related cognitive development in old age. *Psychologing and Aging, 20*, 303–316.

Nilsson, E., Wahlin, Å., Fastbom, J., & Nilsson, L.-G. (2004). *Diagnosed and undiagnosed diabetes mellitus in the Betula project: Effects on episodic memory and utilization of cognitive support.* Poster presented at the Cognitive Aging Conference, Atlanta, GA, USA.

Nilsson, L.-G., Adolfsson, R., Bäckman, L., Cruts, M., Nyberg, L., Small, B.J. et al.

(2005a). The influence of APOE status on episodic and semantic memory: Data from a population-based study. Manuscript submitted for publication.
Nilsson, L.-G., Adolfsson, R., Bäckman, L., de Frias, C.M., Molander, B., & Nyberg, L. (2004). Betula: A prospective cohort study on memory, health and aging. *Aging, Neuropsychology and Cognition*, *11*, 134–148.
Nilsson, L.-G., Bäckman, L., Erngrund, K., Nyberg, L., Adolfsson, R., Bucht, G. et al. (1997). The Betula prospective cohort study: Memory, health, and aging. *Aging, Neuropsychology & Cognition*, *4*, 1–32.
Nilsson, L.-G., Sikström, C., Adolfsson, R., Erngrund, K., Nylander, P-O., & Beckman, L. (1996). Genetic markers with high versus low scoring on episodic memory tasks. *Behavior Genetics*, *26*, 555–562.
Nilsson, L.-G., Söderlund, H., Berger, K., Breteler, M., de Ridder, M., Dufoil, C. et al. (2005b). Cognitive test battery of CASCADE: Tasks and data. *Aging, Neuropsychology, and Cognition*, *12*, 32–56.
Nyberg, L. (1994). A structural equation modeling approach to the multiple memory systems question. *Journal of Experimental Psychology: Learning, Memory and Cognition*, *20*, 485–491.
Nyberg, L., Maitland, S.B., Rönnlund, M., Bäckman, L., Dixon, R.A., Wahlin, Å. et al. (2003). Selective adult age differences in an age-invariant multi-factor model of declarative memory. *Psychology & Aging*, *18*, 149–160.
Persson, J., Nyberg, L., Lind, J., Larsson, A., Nilsson, L.-G., Ingvar, M. et al. (2005). Structure–function correlates of cognitive decline in aging. *Cerebral Cortex*, 0914.
Plomin, R. (2003). 50 years of DNA. *APS Observer*, *16*, 7–8.
Reiman, E.M., Chen, K., Alexander, G.E., Caselli, R.J., Bandy, D., Osborne, D. et al. (2004). Functional brain abnormalities in young adults at genetic risk for late-onset Alzheimer's dementia. *Proceedings of the National Academy of Science USA*, *101*, 284–289.
Rönnlund, M., & Nilsson, L.-G. (2006). Adult life-span patterns in WAIS block design performance: Cross-sectional versus longitudinal age gradients and relations to demographic predictors. *Intelligence*, *34*, 63–78.
Rönnlund, M., Nyberg, L., Bäckman, L., & Nilsson, L.-G. (2005). Stability, growth, and decline in adult life span development of declarative memory: Cross-sectional and longitudinal data from a population-based sample. *Psychology and Aging*, *20*, 3–18.
Rowe, J.W., & Kahn, R.L. (1987). Human aging: usual and successful. *Science*, *237*, 143–149.
Rowe, J.W., & Kahn, R.L. (1997). Successful aging. *Gerontologist*, *37*, 433–440.
Schaie, K.W. (1965). A general model for the study of developmental problems. *Psychological Bulletin*, *64*, 92–107.
Schaie, K.W. (1977). Quasi-experimental research designs in the psychology of aging. In J.E. Birren & K.W. Schaie (Eds.), *Handbook of the psychology of aging* (pp. 39–58). New York: Van Nostrand.
Schmidt, R., Launer, L.J., Nilsson, L.-G., Pajak, A., Sans, S., Berger, K. et al. (2004). MRI of the brain in diabetes mellitus: The cardiovascular determinants of dementia (CASCADE) study. *Diabetes*, *53*, 687–692.
Söderlund, H., Nyberg, L., Adolfsson, R., Nilsson, L.-G., & Launer, L.J. (2003). High prevalence of white matter hyperintensities in normal aging: Relation to blood pressure and cognition. *Cortex*, *39*, 1093–1105.

Söderlund, H., Nyberg, L., & Nilsson, L.-G. (2004). Cerebral atrophy as predictor of cognitive performance in healthy Swedish adults from the Betula prospective cohort study of aging, memory and health. *Acta Neurologica Scandinavica*, *109*, 398–406.

Sundström, A., Marklund, P., Nilsson, L.-G., Cruts, M., Adolfsson, R., Van Broeckhoven, C. et al. (2004). ApoE influences on neuropsychological function after mild head injury: Within-person comparisons. *Neurology*, *62*, 1963–1966.

Tulving, E. (1972). Episodic and semantic memory. In E. Tulving & W. Donaldson (Eds.), *Organization of memory* (pp. 381–403). New York: Academic Press.

Tulving, E. (1983). *Elements of episodic memory*. Oxford: Clarendon Press.

Tulving, E. (1985). Memory and consciousness. *Canadian Psychologist*, *26*, 1–12.

Wahlin, Å., Bäckman, L., Hultdin, J., Adolfsson, R., & Nilsson, L.-G. (2002). Reference values of serum levels of vitamin B12 and folic acid in a poulation-based sample of adults between 35 and 80 years of age. *Journal of Public Health Nutrition*, *5*, 505–511.

Weinberger, D.R., Egan, M.F., Bertolino, A., Callicott, J.H., Mattay, V.S., Lipska, B.K. et al. (2001). Neurobiology of schizophrenia and the role of atypical antipsychotics: Prefrontal neurons and the genetics of schizophrenia. *Biological Psychiatry*, *50*, 825–844.

Yonker, J., Eriksson, E., Nilsson, L.-G. & Herlitz, A. (2003). Sex differences in episodic memory: Minimal influence of estradiol. *Brain and Cognition*, *52*, 231–238.

7 Memory and memory disorders: Neuroimaging correlates of organic brain damage and psychic disturbances

Hans J. Markowitsch

Memory is the glue that holds our personality together. More than 130 years ago, Ewald Hering (1870), a physiologist known for his opponent-color theory or the Hering-Breuer reflex, stated that memory unites the countless single phenomena into a whole, and that without its binding power our consciousness would disintegrate into as many fragments as there are moments. While at that time memory was considered to be a unity, soon afterwards a time-based distinction into short-term ("on-line") and long-term memory followed (reviewed in Markowitsch, 1992) (Figure 7.1), to which much more recently Baddeley (2001) added several versions of his "working memory". Working memory refers to the active processing of short-term acquired information and also includes the process of making long-term stored information available again during retrieval.

Support for the existence of distinct short-term and long-term memory systems stems largely from findings in focally brain-damaged patients who have an intact capacity to remember information within the timeframe of seconds to minutes (about 4 bits; Cowan, 2000), but who are unable to remember information long term. Patient HM, a subject lacking his medial temporal lobes bilaterally due to brain surgery, is the most well-known example (Corkin, 2002; Scoville & Milner, 1957). Richards (1973) performed an interesting experiment on HM which has implications for the distinction between short-term and long-term memory: He asked him to reproduce time intervals in a range from 1 to 300 seconds. HM was quite accurate until 20 seconds, but showed a clear underestimation thereafter, so that Richards concluded that 1 hour equals about 3 minutes to HM (or 1 year 3 hours).

A further distinction – based on material and content – resulted from the work of Endel Tulving (1972, 1983, 2002; Tulving & Markowitsch, 1998) on the human level, and of Mishkin and Petri (1984) and Squire and Zola-Morgan (1988) based on work with animals, although some preliminary attempts had been made earlier (reviewed in Markowitsch, 1992).

We presently distinguish five long-term memory systems which are

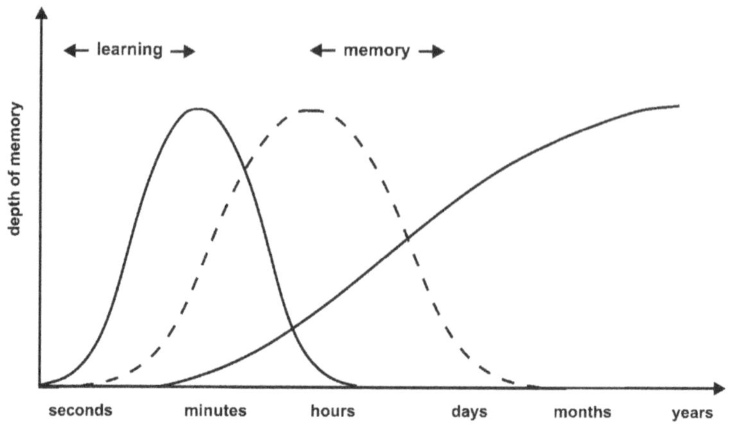

Figure 7.1 Sketch of the relations between memory strength and duration for the two principal time-related memory systems, short-term and long-term memory. The left-most ("Gaussian") solid line refers to short-term memory, the right solid line to long-term memory. Some authors propose an intermediate memory system, which is sketched by the dotted line.

depicted in Figure 7.2. These memory systems are considered to be hierarchically ordered, starting with *procedural memory* as the lowest and ending with *episodic* (or *episodic-autobiographical*) memory as the highest system. *Procedural memory* stands for motor-related skills (e.g., driving a car, riding a bike, swimming, playing cards or piano), *priming* stands for a higher likeliness to re-identify stimuli that one had perceived (non-consciously or sub-consciously) at a previous time point. *Perceptual memory* refers to being familiar with a stimulus on the basis of pre-semantic features. Fact-like, context-free information is represented in the *semantic memory system*. Tulving (2002) sees the *episodic memory system* as the conjunction of subjective time, autonoetic consciousness, and the experiencing self; frequently it is affect related. Tulving (personal communication, 2003) defines episodic memory in the following words:

> Episodic memory is a recently evolved, late-developing, and early-deteriorating brain/mind ("neurocognitive") memory system. It is oriented to the past, more vulnerable than other memory systems to neuronal dysfunction, and probably unique to humans. It makes possible mental time travel through subjective time – past, present, and future. This mental time travel allows the "owner" of episodic memory ("self"), through the medium of autonoetic awareness, to remember one's own previous "thought-about" experiences, as well as to "think about" one's own possible future experiences. The operations of episodic memory require, but go beyond, the semantic memory system. Retrieving information from episodic memory ("remembering") requires the establishment and

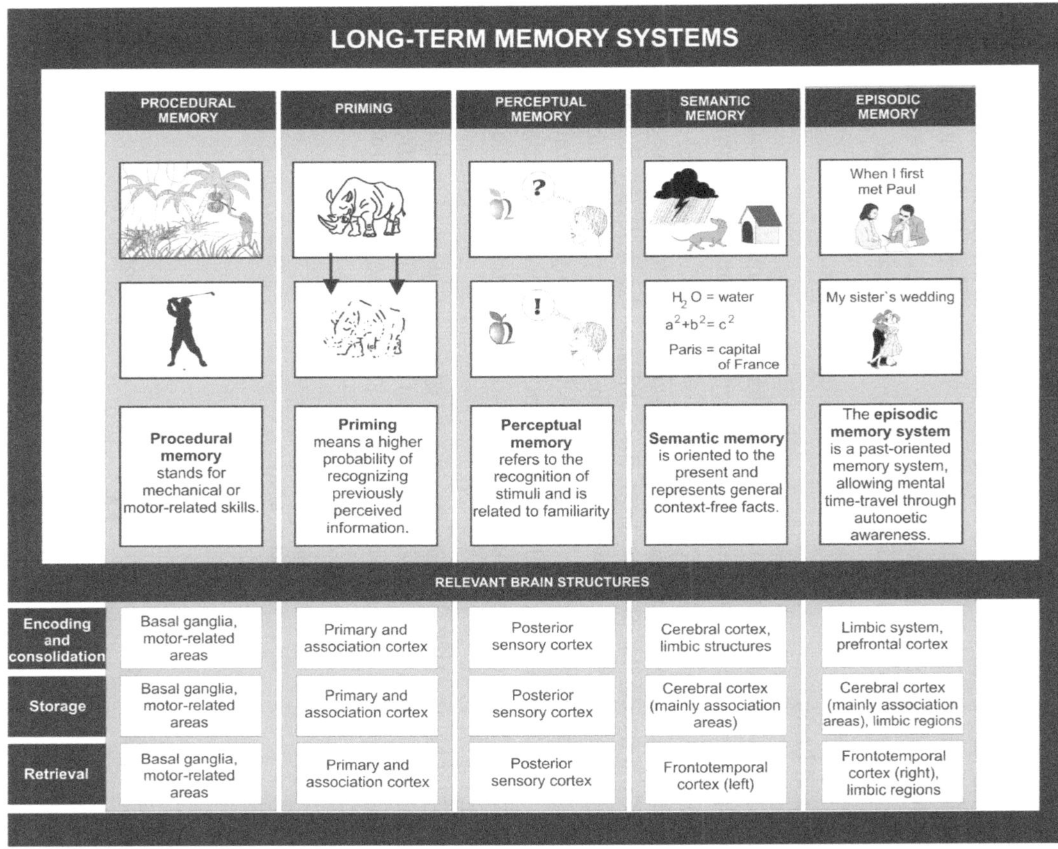

Figure 7.2 The five principal memory systems important for human information processing. Procedural memory is largely motor-based, but also includes sensory and cognitive skills ("routines"). Priming refers to a higher likeliness of re-identifying previously perceived stimuli. Perceptual memory allows an object, item, or person to be distinguished on the basis of distinct features. Declarative memory is context-free and refers to general facts. It is also termed semantic memory or the knowledge systems. The episodic memory system is context specific with respect to time and place. It allows mental time travel. Examples are events such as the last vacation or the dinner of the previous night.

maintenance of a special mental set, dubbed episodic "retrieval mode". The neural components of episodic memory comprise a widely distributed network of cortical and subcortical brain regions that overlap with and extend beyond the networks subserving other memory systems. The essence of episodic memory lies in the conjunction of three concepts – self, autonoetic awareness, and subjective time.

Principally, procedural memory and priming act on the subconscious or semi-conscious level, while the other three memory systems require conscious processing of information. With reference to individuals with brain damage or to subjects having been exposed to major stress or trauma situations, portions of memory may be impaired in two time directions – forward ("anterograde amnesia") and backward ("retrograde amnesia") (Figure 7.3).

Memory and brain

Since the Greek and Roman times attempts have been made to establish distinct relations between brain regions and specific functions, culminating at the beginning of the nineteenth century with Gall's (1825) phrenology. The phrenologists thought that specific "faculties" were related to specific regions ("modules") in the cerebrum. Even from the outside of the skull, the abilities should be visible and correlated with size. Again, scientific progress changed the view towards a mixture of serial and parallel processing in the brain. A somewhat coarse view on possible interdependencies between memory – starting with information encoding and ending with information retrieval – is sketched in Figure 7.4.

In general, I assume that short-term memory engages regions of (primarily the left) lateral parietal and possibly portions of the dorsolateral prefrontal cortex. This argument is based on patient data (Markowitsch et al., 1999a),

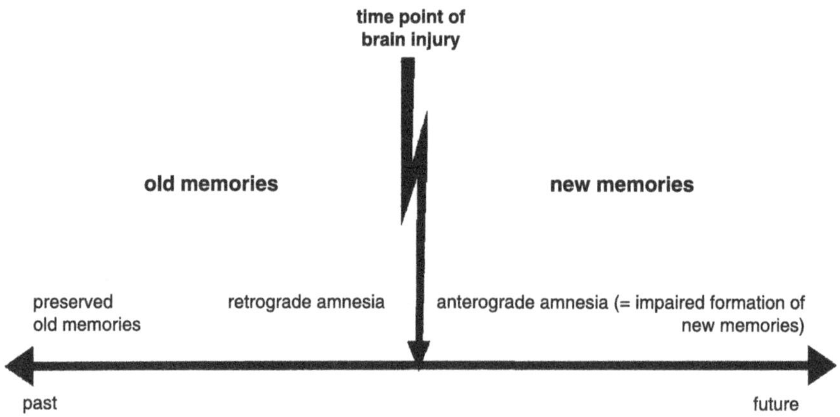

Figure 7.3 Possible consequences of brain injury on old and new memories.

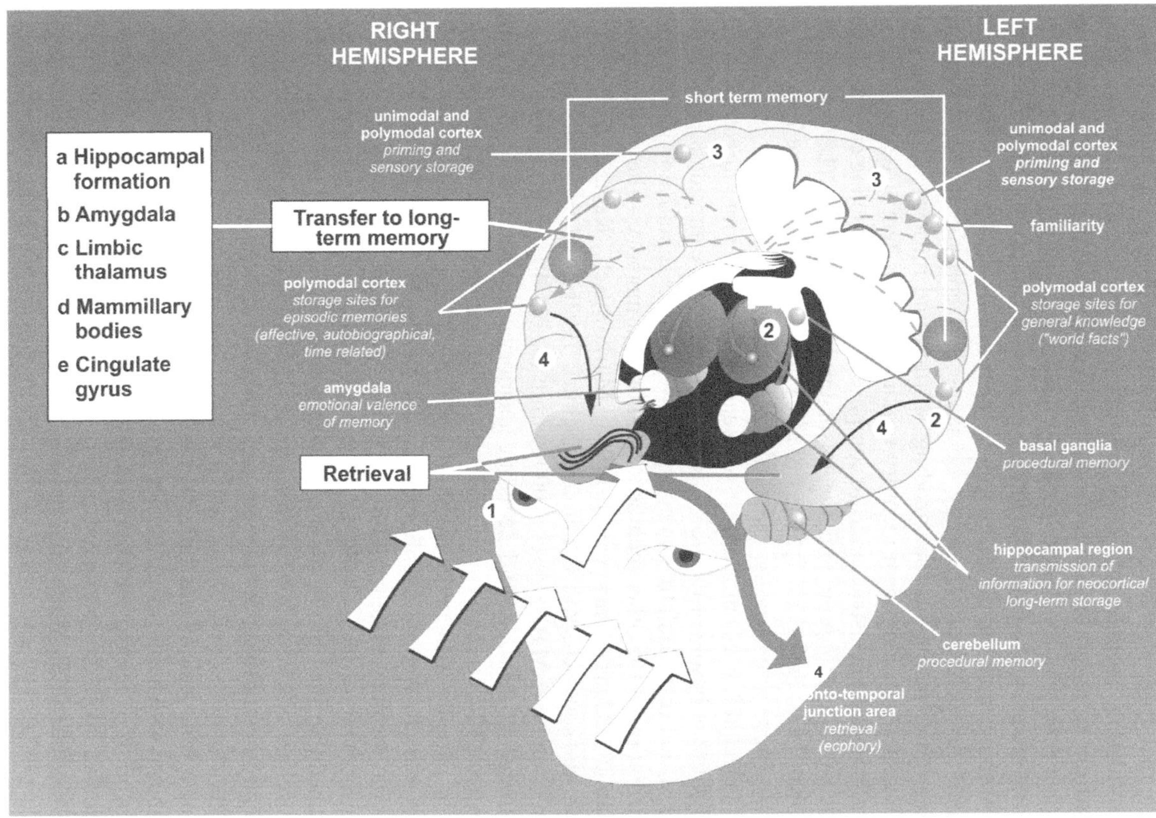

Figure 7.4 Sketch of memory processing by the brain.

functional imaging results (Todd & Marois, 2004), electrophysiological studies in normal human subjects (Babiloni et al., 2004; Vogel & Machizawa, 2004), and animal work (Fuster, 1997; Goldman-Rakic & Friedman, 1991). For the more "simple" memory systems – procedural memory, priming, perceptual memory – the brain regions active during encoding, further consolidation, storage, and retrieval appear to be largely the same. They constitute large motor-system associated regions (basal ganglia, premotor, supplementary motor cortex, probably portions of the cerebellum) for procedural memory, the unimodal and association regions of the cerebral cortex for priming, and unimodal as well as polymodal sensory and association cortices for perceptual memory. Semantic and episodic memory systems engage different regions for encoding, storage, and retrieval. Encoding and the transfer into long-term memory require limbic-system structures. These so-called bottleneck structures are composed of two interacting circuits – the medial or Papez circuit and the basolateral limbic circuit (Livingston & Escobar, 1971; Papez, 1937; Sarter & Markowitsch, 1985) (Figure 7.5).

The Papez circuit is the classical one, which originally was introduced as a "mechanism of emotions". Nowadays this role is more directly associated with the basolateral limbic circuit. Within this the amygdala is the classical structure modulating memory. However, one should not neglect the contribution of the other members to emotional memory – the mediodorsal thalamic nucleus (Markowitsch, 1988; Markowitsch, Kessler, & Denzler 1986; Markowitsch, von Cramon & Schuri, 1993b) and the septal nucleus (Von Cramon & Markowitsch, 2000) within the basal forebrain.

Storage of episodic and semantic memory is considered to be largely a matter of the cerebral cortex. Evidence for this statement comes from studies on patients with major cerebral cortical damage (Kessler et al., 1999; Markowitsch, Weber-Luxenburger, Ewald, Kessler, & Heiss, 1997b). For the episodic memory system additional limbic structures are considered to be relevant (Markowitsch, 2005). In accordance with Figure 7.4 it is furthermore assumed that the right hemisphere – which is also considered the "emotional hemisphere" (Schore, 2002; Van Lancker, 1991) – is predominantly relevant for episodic-autobiographic memories, and the left hemisphere for semantic memories.

For a long time it was thought that impairments in retrieval are always combined with impairments in encoding. This view had to be given up after the description of several patients with selective (episodic) retrograde amnesia, combined with a preserved ability for long-term encoding of new information (Kroll, Markowitsch, Knight, & von Cramon, 1997; Markowitsch et al., 1993a). The uniformity of their brain damage led to the proposal that structures of the inferolateral prefrontal cortex and the temporo*lateral* cortex are necessary for triggering the retrieval of old memories (Markowitsch, 1995). From the results of patients with major brain damage to these structures within one hemisphere it was furthermore postulated that this regional combination of the right hemisphere is relevant for retrieving

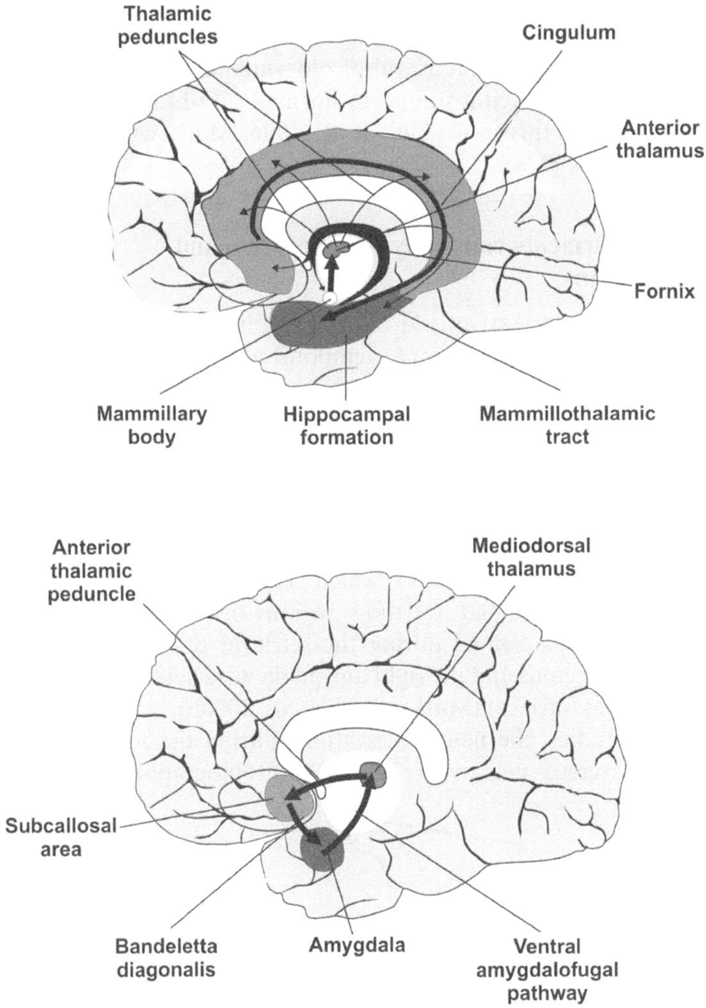

Figure 7.5 The medial (or Papez) circuit and the basolateral limbic circuit. The medial circuit is probably more relevant for the cognitive acts of memory processing, the basolateral one for the affective evaluation of information. Both circuits interact with each other. The Papez circuit interconnects the hippocampal formation via the (postcommissural) fornix to the mammillary bodies, these via the mammillothalamic tract (or tractus Vicq d'Azyr) to the anterior thalamus, the anterior thalamus with its cortical projection targets reaches the cingulate gyrus, and the subicular part of the hippocampal formation and the cingulum fibres in addition project back from the cingulate gyrus into the hippocampal formation. (The precommissural fornix in addition provides a bidirectional connection between the hippocampal formation and the basal forebrain.) The basolateral limbic circuit links the amygdala, mediodorsal thalamic nucleus, and area subcallosa with each other by distinct fibre projections, namely the ventral amygdalofugal pathway, the inferior thalamic peduncle, and the bandeletta diagonalis.

episodic-autobiographical episodes, while the same regions of the left hemisphere are relevant for the retrieval of old semantic memories (Figure 7.6). Results from neuroimaging studies in normal, non-brain-damaged subjects strongly supported this view (Fink et al., 1996; Markowitsch, Fink, Thöne, Kessler, & Heiss, 1997a).

Memory impairments caused by psychic stress and trauma situations

The finding that retrieval of old autobiographical memories resulted in a primarily right hemispheric fronto-temporal activation pattern encouraged us to study several modifications of this paradigm. First we looked at what happened when normal subjects invented episodic-like memories and retrieved them together with true, autobiographical ones. The invented memories were – at least for a non-informed listener – indistinguishable from the true ones; they were also considerably affect-laden and complex. Nevertheless, fictitious memory retrieval activated only the precuneus – that is, that region of the human cortex which has been termed the mind's eye (Fletcher et al., 1995) – but not those regions of the right temporo-frontal cortex which were activated during the retrieval of true autobiographical episodes. These regions and the right amygdala were activated during true old autobiographical retrieval (Markowitsch et al., 2000b).

In further studies, the neural activations during the retrieval of positive (e.g., happy) versus negative (e.g., sad) autobiographical episodes were

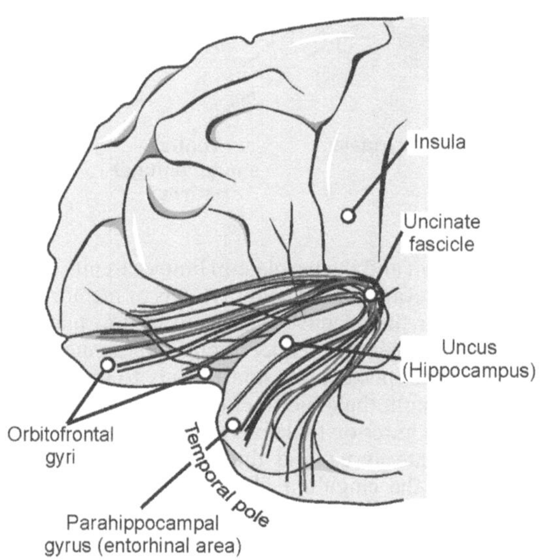

Figure 7.6 Schematic view of the anterior lateral half of the human cerebral cortex showing the temporofrontal region implicated in the retrieval of episodes (right hemisphere) and facts (left hemisphere).

studied with fMRI (Markowitsch, Vandekerckhove, Lanfermann, & Russ, 2003; Piefke, Weiss, Zilles, Markowitsch, & Fink, 2003). Normal subjects were asked to retrieve episodes from their past and to rate them with respect to their affective valence. Two comparisons were of particular interest: positive versus negative and negative versus positive ones. Results revealed two distinct frontal foci for the two kinds of emotional retrograde memories: Negatively (as opposed to positively) rated emotional episodes from the past resulted in symmetrical lateral orbitofrontal activations, while positively (as opposed to negatively) rated ones correlated with medial orbitofrontal/subgenual activations. Furthermore, the left hippocampal region was activated during the retrieval of positive episodes. These findings point to distinct basal frontal foci which work as hubs to wider and primarily cortical nets engaged in ecphorizing old autobiographic episodes of a positive or negative character.

Patients with dissociative memory disorders – formerly termed psychogenic amnesia or psychogenic fugue condition – similarly demonstrated neural correlates of their altered cognitive conditions. Dissociative amnesia is considered to be a condition where unprocessed or imperfectly processed memories are retained from consciousness ('hysterical neuroses') and may lead to depersonalization and other identity disturbances. In addition psychogenic fugue conditions meet the requirement of leaving the home town ("fleeing" – therefore "fugue") and having the urge to travel away from the usual center of living.

In some of such patients, studies with functional imaging methods found hypometabolic brain activity in the right temporo-frontal region – therefore closely resembling that of a patient with similar amnesia for old personal memories, but an organic background of brain damage (Markowitsch, 1999a, b) (Figure 7.7).

An especially interesting patient was a 23-year-old man who had major anterograde amnesia and 6 years of retrograde amnesia after a traumatic experience (Markowitsch, Kessler, Van der Ven, Weber-Luxenburger, & Heiss, 1998; Markowitsch, Kessler, Weber-Luxenburger, Van der Ven, & Heiss, 2000a). The patient saw the outbreak of an open fire in the cellar of his house and the next morning he was severely disturbed and amnesic. This condition remained unchanged for about 8 months and manifested as severe verbal and nonverbal amnesia in both anterograde and retrograde directions. Some time after the trauma condition he could report that at the age of 4 years he had seen a man burning to death in his car. Since then fire had meant a life-threatening situation to him. Apparently, the new fire situation had resulted in a sudden and major release of glucocorticoids (stress hormones) leading to a block of the normal mnestic information flow. After about 8 months – and with medical and psychotherapeutic treatment – the patient improved cognitively, but even after 12 months he had not fully recovered, with problems remaining especially with respect to his verbal long-term memory. Two fluoro-deoxy-D-glucose-positron-emission-tomographic

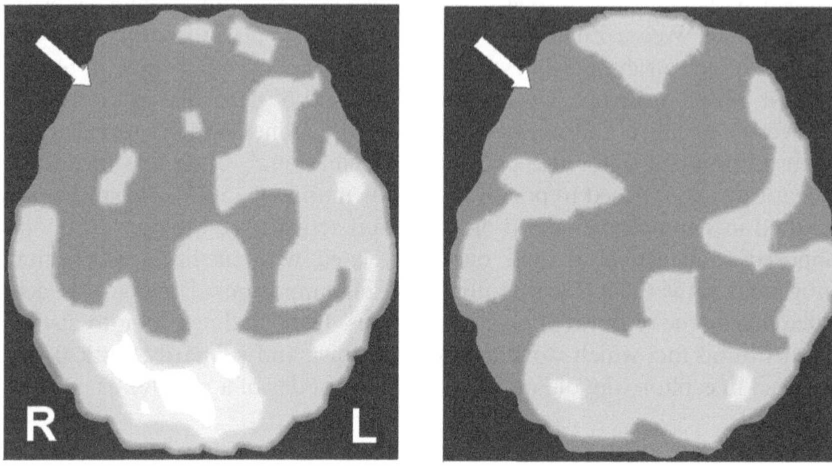

Figure 7.7 Sketches of horizontal views of the brains of a patient with organic brain damage (left), and of another one in whom any evidence for "organicity" was lacking. Hypometabolic zones (dark) are nevertheless seen in the right temporo-frontal zone of both patients.

(FDG-PET) investigations were done, the first several weeks after the psychic trauma and the second after 12 months. The first one revealed a general reduction in his brain metabolism together with a further decrease in the memory-processing regions of the temporal lobes and the medial diencephalon. At the time point of the second FDG-PET, glucose scores had returned to a normal level.

This case demonstrates first that environmental stress conditions may result in major behavioral consequences. Second, it indicates that psychic stress may alter brain metabolism significantly and lastingly, probably due to a major and persistent release of stress hormones (glucocorticoids) in the brain (O'Brien, 1997). (Glucocorticoids have most of their receptors in the regions of the hippocampal formation and the amygdala.) Third, it demonstrates that recovery of cognitive functions is possible for such patients and may depend on a particular combination of psychotherapy and anti-depressive treatment (Markowitsch et al., 2000a).

From these and related patients we conclude that a phenomenon termed "mnestic block syndrome" can be described as resulting from major stress and trauma conditions (Markowitsch, 1999b; Markowitsch et al., 1999c). Patients with mnestic block syndrome – and consequently a functional (psychic, psychosomatic) form of amnesia – demonstrate cognitive similarities to patients with organic amnesia: They are able to act socially appropriately, have a normal short-term memory capacity, the ability to store new information long term (although more on the semantic than on the episodic level), but a severe retrograde amnesia on the autobiographical level. More exceptionally, however, patients with selective anterograde amnesia on the autobiographical level have been described (Markowitsch, Kessler, Kalbe, & Herholz, 1999b). From the above descriptions it becomes obvious that similar kinds of amnesia – largely centered towards the individual's biography – can occur with and without concomitant brain damage. It can be concluded that major and prolonged stress can indeed be detrimental to brain function and may even lead to neuronal deterioration. Consequently, it can be proposed that psychiatric and neurological disease conditions, leading to amnesia, have similar bases in the brain and that learning to cope with stress situations is of major importance.

Acknowledgement

Research for studies reported in this chapter was supported by the German Research Council (DFG; grants Ma 795 and by the VolkswagenStiftung).

References

Babiloni, C., Babiloni, F., Carducci, F., Cincotti, F., Vecchio, F., Cola, B. et al. (2004). Functional frontoparietal connectivity during short-term memory as revealed by high-resolution EEG coherence analysis. *Behavioral Neuroscience*, *118*, 687–697.

Baddeley, A.D. (2001). Is working memory still working? *American Psychologist*, *56*, 851–864.

Corkin, S. (2002). What's new with the amnesic patient H.M.? *Neuroscience*, *3*, 153–160.

Cowan, N. (2000). The magical number 4 in short-term memory: A reconsideration of mental storage capacity. *Behavioral and Brain Sciences*, *24*, 87–185.

Fink, G.R., Markowitsch, H.J., Reinkemeier, M., Bruckbauer, T., Kessler, J., & Heiss, W.-D. (1996). Cerebral representation of one's own past: Neural networks involved in autobiographical memory. *Journal of Neuroscience*, *16*, 4275–4282.

Fletcher, P.C., Frith, C.D., Baker, S.C., Shallice, T., Frackowiak, R.S.J., & Dolan, R.J. (1995). The mind's eye – precuneus activation in memory related imagery. *NeuroImage*, *2*, 195–200.

Fuster, J.M. (1997). *The prefrontal cortex* (3rd ed.). Philadelphia, PA: Lippincott-Raven.

Gall, F.J. (1825). *Sur les fonctions du cerveau et sur celles de chacune de ses parties* (6 vols.). Paris: Baillière.

Goldman-Rakic, P.S., & Friedman, H.R. (1991). The circuitry of working memory revealed by anatomy and metabolic imaging. In H.S. Levin, H.M. Eisenberg, & A.L. Benton (Eds.), *Frontal lobe function and dysfunction* (pp. 72–91). New York: Oxford University Press.

Hering, E. (1870). *Ueber das Gedächtnis als eine allgemeine Funktion der organisierten Materie. Vortrag gehalten in der feierlichen Sitzung der Kaiserlichen Akademie der Wissenschaften in Wien am XXX. Mai MDCCCLXX.* Leipzig: Akademische Verlagsgesellschaft. [Transl. as: Hering, E. (1895). *Memory as a general function of organized matter*. Chicago: Open Court.]

Kessler, J., Markowitsch, H.J., Ghaemi, M., Rudolf, J., Weniger, G.H., & Heiss, W.-D.

(1999). Degenerative prefrontal damage in a young adult: Static and dynamic imaging and neuropsychological correlates. *Neurocase*, *5*, 173–179.

Kroll, N., Markowitsch, H.J., Knight, R., & von Cramon, D.Y. (1997). Retrieval of old memories – the temporo-frontal hypothesis. *Brain*, *120*, 1377–1399.

Livingston, K.E., & Escobar, A. (1971). The anatomical bias of the limbic system concepts: A proposed reorientation. *Archives of Neurology*, *24*, 90.

Markowitsch, H.J. (1988). Diencephalic amnesia: A reorientation towards tracts? *Brain Research Reviews*, *13*, 351–370.

Markowitsch, H.J. (1992). *Intellectual functions and the brain. An historical perspective*. Toronto: Hogrefe & Huber Publs.

Markowitsch, H.J. (1995). Which brain regions are critically involved in the retrieval of old episodic memory? *Brain Research Reviews*, *21*, 117–127.

Markowitsch, H.J. (1999a). Functional neuroimaging correlates of functional amnesia. *Memory*, *7*, 561–583.

Markowitsch, H.J. (1999b). Neuroimaging and mechanisms of brain function in psychiatric disorders. *Current Opinion in Psychiatry*, *12*, 331–337.

Markowitsch, H.J. (2005). The neuroanatomy of memory. In P. Halligan & P. Wade (Eds.), *The effectiveness of rehabilitation for cognitive deficits* (pp. 105–114). Oxford: Oxford University Press.

Markowitsch, H.J., Calabrese, P., Liess, J., Haupts, M., Durwen, H.F., & Gehlen, W. (1993a). Retrograde amnesia after traumatic injury of the temporo-frontal cortex. *Journal of Neurology, Neurosurgery and Psychiatry*, *56*, 988–992.

Markowitsch, H.J., Fink, G.R., Thöne, A.I.M., Kessler, J., & Heiss, W.-D. (1997a). Persistent psychogenic amnesia with a PET-proven organic basis. *Cognitive Neuropsychiatry*, *2*, 135–158.

Markowitsch, H.J., Kalbe, E., Kessler, J., von Stockhausen H-M., Ghaemi, M., & Heiss, W.-D. (1999a). Short-term memory deficit after focal parietal damage. *Journal of Clinical and Experimental Neuropsychology*, *21*, 784–796.

Markowitsch, H.J., Kessler, J., & Denzler, P. (1986). Recognition memory and psychophysiological responses towards stimuli with neutral and emotional content. A study of Korsakoff patients and recently detoxified and longterm abstinent alcoholics. *International Journal of Neuroscience*, *29*, 1–35.

Markowitsch, H.J., Kessler, J., Kalbe, E., & Herholz, K. (1999b). Functional amnesia and memory consolidation. A case of persistent anterograde amnesia with rapid forgetting following whiplash injury. *Neurocase*, *5*, 189–200.

Markowitsch, H.J., Kessler, J., Russ, M.O., Frölich, L., Schneider, B., & Maurer, K. (1999c). Mnestic block syndrome. *Cortex*, *35*, 219–230.

Markowitsch, H.J., Kessler, J., Van der Ven, C., Weber-Luxenburger, G., & Heiss, W.-D. (1998). Psychic trauma causing grossly reduced brain metabolism and cognitive deterioration. *Neuropsychologia*, *36*, 77–82.

Markowitsch, H.J., Kessler, J., Weber-Luxenburger, G., Van der Ven, C., & Heiss, W.-D. (2000a). Neuroimaging and behavioral correlates of recovery from "mnestic block syndrome" and other cognitive deteriorations. *Neuropsychiatry, Neuropsychology, and Behavioral Neurology*, *13*, 60–66.

Markowitsch, H.J., Thiel, A., Reinkemeier, M., Kessler, J., Koyuncu, A., & Heiss, W.-D. (2000b). Right amygdalar and temporofrontal activation during autobiographic, but not during fictitious memory retrieval. *Behavioural Neurology*, *12*, 181–190.

Markowitsch, H.J., Vandekerckhove, M.M.P., Lanfermann, H., & Russ, M.O. (2003).

Engagement of lateral and medial prefrontal areas in the ecphory of sad and happy autobiographical memories. *Cortex*, *39*, 643–665.

Markowitsch, H.J., von Cramon, D.Y., & Schuri, U. (1993b). Mnestic performance profile of a bilateral diencephalic infarct patient with preserved intelligence and severe amnesic disturbances. *Journal of Clinical and Experimental Neuropsychology*, *15*, 627–652.

Markowitsch, H.J., Weber-Luxenburger, G., Ewald, K., Kessler, J., & Heiss, W.-D. (1997b). Patients with heart attacks are not valid models for medial temporal lobe amnesia. A neuropsychological and FDG-PET study with consequences for memory research. *European Journal of Neurology*, *4*, 178–184.

Mishkin, M., & Petri, H.L. (1984). Memories and habits: Some implications for the analysis of learning and retention. In L.R. Squire & N. Butters (Eds.), *Neuropsychology of memory* (pp. 287–296). New York: Guilford Press.

O'Brien, J.T. (1997). The "glucocorticoid cascade" hypothesis in man. *British Journal of Psychiatry*, *170*, 199–201.

Papez, J.W. (1937). A proposed mechanism of emotion. *Archives of Neurology and Psychiatry*, *38*, 725–743.

Piefke, M., Weiss, P.H., Zilles, K., Markowitsch, H.J., & Fink, G.R. (2003). Differential remoteness and emotional tone modulate the neural correlates of autobiographical memory. *Brain*, *126*, 850–868.

Richards, W. (1973). Time reproductions by H.M. *Acta Psychologica*, *37*, 279–282.

Sarter, M., & Markowitsch, H.J. (1985). The amygdala's role in human mnemonic processing. *Cortex*, *21*, 7–24.

Schore, A.N. (2002). Dysregulation of the right brain: A fundamental mechanism of traumatic attachment and the psychopathogenesis of posttraumatic stress disorder. *Australian and New Zealand Journal of Psychiatry*, *36*, 9–30.

Scoville, W.B., & Milner, B. (1957). Loss of recent memory after bilateral hippocampal lesions. *Journal of Neurology, Neurosurgery, and Psychiatry*, *20*, 11–21.

Squire, L.R., & Zola-Morgan, S. (1988). Memory: Brain systems and behavior. *Trends in Neurosciences*, *11*, 170–175.

Todd, J.J., & Marois, R. (2004). Capacity limit of visual short-term memory in human posterior parietal cortex. *Nature*, *428*, 751–754.

Tulving, E. (1972). Episodic and semantic memory. In E. Tulving & W. Donaldson (Eds.), *Organization of memory* (pp. 381–403). New York: Academic Press.

Tulving, E. (1983). *Elements of episodic memory*. Oxford: Clarendon Press.

Tulving, E. (2002). Episodic memory: From mind to brain. *Annual Review of Psychology*, *53*, 1–25.

Tulving, E., & Markowitsch, H.J. (1998). Episodic and declarative memory: Role of the hippocampus. *Hippocampus*, *8*, 198–204.

Van Lancker, D. (1991). Personal relevance and the human right hemisphere. *Brain and Cognition*, *17*, 64–92.

Vogel, E.K., & Machizawa, M.G. (2004). Neural activity predicts individual differences in visual working memory capacity. *Nature*, *428*, 748–751.

Von Cramon, D.Y., & Markowitsch, H.J. (2000). The septum and human memory. In R. Numan (Ed.), *The behavioral neuroscience of the septal region* (pp. 380–413). Berlin: Springer.

8 Successful goal pursuit

Peter M. Gollwitzer

What can today's psychology of motivation reply to the layman's question of "How do I attain my goals?" Most importantly, nowadays, research on the psychology of goals suggests that this question needs to be broken down by differentiating between successful goal setting and successful goal implementation. The distinction between goal setting and goal striving was originally emphasized by the German psychologist Kurt Lewin (1926). It turns out to be very useful for understanding the many new findings produced by the renaissance of research on goals (Gollwitzer & Moskowitz, 1996; Oettingen & Gollwitzer, 2001), and thus we will use it to organize our answer to the question of what people can do to increase their chances of meeting their goals.

Selecting appropriate goals

If people want to increase the chances of meeting their goals they need to first select appropriate goals. It seems wise to select goals to which one can commit strongly, as strong goals (intentions) have a better chance of being attained (Ajzen, 1991). Strong goal commitments are commonly based on the belief that a given goal is both desirable and feasible. The person should thus consult their needs and motives to determine the desirability of a goal (Brunstein, Schultheiss, & Grassmann, 1998) and to determine its feasibility. On the other hand, it is necessary to reflect on one's skills, talents, and competencies, as well as the likelihood that goal-related outcomes will lead to desired consequences (Bandura, 1997; Heckhausen, 1977). It is important to recognize, however, that perceiving a goal as highly feasible and attractive does not yet make for strong goal commitments. Recent research suggests that a certain mode of thinking about the desired future (i.e., mentally contrasting the desired future with the obstacles of present reality) is needed first. If people simply dream about a positive future, or only dwell on the negative reality, it is not guaranteed that high-feasibility beliefs are indeed translated into strong goal commitments (Oettingen, Pak, & Schnetter, 2001).

It also matters how the desired goal state is framed. Researchers have discovered that conceptualizing one's goals in terms of promoting positive outcomes vs preventing negative outcomes (promotion vs prevention goals;

Higgins, 1997), acquiring competence vs demonstrating the possession of competence (learning vs mastery goals; Dweck, 1999), and attaining external vs internal rewards (extrinsic vs intrinsic goals; Ryan & Deci, 2000) affects goal attainment, whereby promotion, learning, and intrinsic conceptualizations are commonly associated with better outcomes than prevention, mastery, and extrinsic conceptualizations. Even the degree of precision with which the desired outcome is spelled out, in terms of when (time frame) and at what level of achievement (standards of quantity and quality) it is to be completed, affects a person's chances of reaching the desired goal. It is commonly observed that goals with a proximal vs a distal time frame (or deadline) are more likely to be achieved, and it is the goals with specific rather than "do your best" standards that lead to better performances.

Implementing chosen goals

But Kurt Lewin's distinction between goal setting and goal striving reminds us that goal attainment may not be secured solely by forming strong goal commitments and framing the goals at hand in an appropriate manner. There is the second issue of implementing a chosen goal (i.e., goal striving), and one wonders what people can do to enhance their chances of being successful at this phase of goal pursuit. The answer boils down to the following: We need to prepare ourselves so that our chances to overcome the major difficulties of goal implementation are kept high. But what are these difficulties or problems? There are at least four problems that stand out. These problems include getting started with goal pursuit, staying on track, calling a halt, and not overextending oneself. Getting started with goal pursuit is often difficult, because we are busy with other things and thus fail to detect, attend to, and remember to use good opportunities to act towards the chosen goal. But even if we notice the presence of a good opportunity we are often too slow to seize it in time (Gollwitzer, 1993). Once we get started with goal-directed actions, we face the problem of staying on track. This becomes difficult when distractions mount, in particular very tempting distractions (Mischel, Shoda, & Rodriguez, 1989). But forced disruptions that demand the resumption of goal-directed activity also threaten staying on track (Gollwitzer & Liu, 1995; Mahler, 1933) as do increases in task difficulty that demand more effort expenditure (Wright, 1996). Moreover, successful goal implementation requires that we call a halt to using a chosen means or route to goal attainment if this means (or route) lacks instrumentality (Kruglanski, 1996), and it demands disengagement from goal pursuit altogether if the originally desired goal turns into something unattractive or unfeasible (Carver & Scheier, 1998). Finally, goals cannot be implemented successfully if we over-extend our striving for the goal at hand. People commonly hold more than one goal, and overextending oneself in the pursuit of the goal at hand puts people at a disadvantage with respect to the successful implementation of the other goals one is also holding (i.e., ego-depletion effect; Muraven &

Baumeister, 2000). In the present chapter, I will argue that a person can best prepare for these problems of goal implementation by making if–then plans (i.e., form implementation intentions) that specify these critical situations in the if-part and an appropriate goal-directed response in the then-part.

Implementation intentions: Planning out goal implementation in advance

Implementation intentions are if–then plans that connect anticipated critical situations with responses that will be effective in accomplishing one's goals. Whereas goal intentions or goals specify what one wants to do/achieve (i.e., "I intend to perform behaviour *X*!, or "I intend to achieve outcome *X*!"), implementation intentions specify the behaviour that one will perform in the service of goal achievement if the anticipated critical situation is actually encountered (i.e., "If situation *Y* occurs, then I will initiate goal-directed behaviour *Z*!"). Implementation intentions are subordinate to goal intentions because, whereas a goal intention only states *what* one will do or achieve, an implementation intention spells out the *when*, *where*, and *how* of what one will do or achieve.

To form an implementation intention, the person must first anticipate critical situations and then think of possible responses to that situation that are instrumental for goal attainment. For example, the person with the goal intention to eat healthily might anticipate the critical situation of "when the waiter describes the various daily specials at the restaurant tomorrow evening" and then think of a possible goal-instrumental response, such as "then I'll just order a salad!" Implementation intention formation is thus the mental act of linking an anticipated critical situation to an effective goal-directed response in an if–then format. This link is reinforced by an act of will in the sense that the person intends to perform the specified behavior when the critical situation is encountered (i.e., If _______, then I will _______!).

The mental links created by implementation intentions are expected to facilitate goal attainment on the basis of psychological processes that relate to both the anticipated critical situation (the if-component of the plan) and the intended behaviour (the then-component of the plan). Because forming implementation intentions implies the selection of a critical future situation, it is assumed that the mental representation of this situation becomes highly activated, and hence more accessible (Gollwitzer, 1993, 1999). This heightened accessibility should benefit information processing in relation to the specified situation. In particular, people should be in a good position to identify and take notice of the critical cue when they encounter it later.

Processes related to the if-component

Several studies have tested the idea that the mental representation of the situation specified in the if-part of the implementation intention becomes highly accessible by examining how well participants holding implementation intentions detected, attended to, and recalled the critical situation compared to participants who had only formed goal intentions (Gollwitzer, Bayer, Steller, & Bargh, 2002; Webb & Sheeran, 2004). Evidence that implementation intentions improve detection of the critical situation was obtained in a study using the embedded figures test (Gottschaldt, 1926), where smaller a-figures were hidden within larger b-figures (Gollwitzer et al., 2002). Enhanced detection of the hidden a-figures was observed when participants had specified the a-figure in the if-part of an implementation intention (i.e., had made plans on how to create a traffic sign from the a-figure). Equivalent findings were obtained in a study that used a classic illusion from the psychology of language (Webb & Sheeran, 2004, Study 1). Participants who formed if–then plans in relation to the critical letter F showed superior letter detection compared to a variety of control conditions – even though detection was extremely difficult.

In a study using a dichotic-listening paradigm, Gollwitzer et al. (2002) observed that words describing the anticipated critical situation attracted attention among implementation intention participants. Participants who formed if–then plans seemed to find it difficult to ignore information about the critical situation presented in the unattended channel; the consequence was that their shadowing performance for the attended material decreased relative to goal intention participants. This finding implies that opportunities to act that are specified in implementation intentions will not easily escape people's attention, even when people are busy with other ongoing tasks.

Processes related to the then-component

The mental act of linking a critical situation and an intended goal-directed behavior in the form of an if–then plan parallels the formation of associations between situations and actions during the development of *habits*. Habits and if–then plans are both characterized by strong links between (mental representations of) particular cues and responses. Most important, in the same way that the operation of habits is automatic, in the sense that action control becomes immediate, efficient, and needless of conscious intent (Aarts & Dijksterhuis, 2000; Sheeran, Aarts, Custers, Rivis, Webb, & Cooke, 2005; Verplanken & Faes, 1999; Wood, Quinn, & Kashy, 2002), so responses specified in implementation intentions should also be initiated immediately, efficiently, and without the need of a conscious intent. There is evidence that action control by implementation intentions also exhibits these features of automaticity.

Gollwitzer and Brandstätter (1997, Study 3) showed the immediacy of action initiation by implementation intentions in a study where participants were asked to form plans that specified viable opportunities for presenting counter-arguments to a series of racist remarks made by a confederate. Participants who formed implementation intentions initiated the relevant counter-argument more quickly (i.e., closer to the intended time) than did participants who had only formed goal intentions to counter-argue (for similar findings see Orbell & Sheeran, 2000; Webb & Sheeran, 2004). The efficiency of action initiation was tested by Brandtstätter, Lengfelder, and Gollwitzer (2001, Studies 3 and 4) using a Go/No-Go task. Participants formed the goal intention to press a button as quickly as possible if numbers appeared on the computer screen but not if letters appeared. Participants in the implementation intention condition also planned to press the button particularly fast if the number 3 was presented. This Go/No-Go task was then embedded as a secondary task in a dual task paradigm. Findings showed that implementation intention participants showed a substantial increase in speed of responding to the number 3 compared to the control group, regardless of whether the primary task that had to be performed simultaneously was easy or difficult. These findings support the idea that implementation intention effects are efficient; the operation of if–then plans cannot require much in the way of cognitive resources, because they facilitated performance even when two tasks were undertaken at the same time.

The redundancy of conscious intent for implementation intention effects has also been demonstrated in several experiments. Bayer, Moskowitz, and Gollwitzer (2002) tested whether implementation intentions lead to action initiation without conscious intent once the critical situation is encountered. In these experiments, the critical situation was presented subliminally and its impact on preparing to perform (Study 1) or performing (Study 2) respective goal-directed behaviours was assessed. For instance, participants in Study 2 were asked to classify a series of geometrical figures (e.g., circles, eclipses, triangles, squares) into rounded vs angular objects using left vs right button-press responses. All participants formed the goal intention to classify the figures as quickly and accurately as possible. Implementation intention participants also made the following plan: "And if I see a triangle, then I will press the respective button particularly fast!" Participants worked on a set of 240 figures, presented in succession on a computer screen. Some of the figures were preceded by the subliminal presentation of the critical figure (i.e., a triangle), whereas others were preceded by a control prime (i.e., the % symbol). Findings indicated that participants in the implementation intention condition had faster classification responses for angular figures when the triangle instead of the % symbol was presented as a subliminal prime; no such speed-up effect was observed among goal intention participants.

In another study, Sheeran, Webb, and Gollwitzer (2005, Study 2) gave participants the conscious goal to solve a series of puzzles as accurately as possible. One half of the participants also formed an implementation intention in relation to another dimension of performance, namely to answer the puzzles as quickly as possible. This implementation intention manipulation was then crossed with a situational priming manipulation that was designed to activate the goal of responding quickly. Speed and accuracy of responses to the puzzles were measured subsequently. Even though participants indicated no awareness that the puzzle task activated a task-relevant goal (during debriefing all participants reported that their only goal was to solve the puzzles accurately), the results showed that the puzzles were solved fastest when participants were primed with the goal of responding quickly and had formed an if–then plan. These findings indicate that people's conscious intent is not required for implementation intentions to affect performance – people need not be aware that they have encountered the critical cue specified in their plan (Bayer et al., 2002) or even be aware of the goal driving their behavior (Sheeran et al., 2005).

Both implementation intentions and habits engender swift, effortless responses that do not require conscious instigation or guidance. In addition, these effects of if–then plans and habits are both underpinned by strong associations between cues and responses. However, there is an important difference between implementation intentions and habits, which accrues from the fact that the respective cue–response links have different origins. In the case of habits, frequent and consistent execution of a response in the presence of a particular stimulus leads to the development of the relevant associations. In the case of implementation intentions, the same linkage can be fashioned *in situ* by an act of will. Implementation intention effects thus represent an important sub-type of automaticity that differs from the automaticity in habits (Gollwitzer & Schaal, 1998; Sheeran et al., 2005). Implementation intentions allow people to choose – consciously and in advance – what goal-directed responses will be elicited automatically, and what situational cues will elicit them. By making an if–then plan, people decide to delegate control of their behavior to pre-selected situational features with the express purpose of reaching their goals. This is what is meant by the idea that forming an implementation intention entails *strategic automation of goal pursuit* (Gollwitzer, 1993, 1999).

Implementation intentions and overcoming problems of goal implementation

Given these special features of action control by implementation intentions, one wonders whether people benefit from forming implementation intentions when they are confronted with the four central problems of goal implementation: getting started, staying on track, calling a halt, and not overextending oneself. In the following, I will present implementation intention research on these four issues.

Getting started

There are at least three reasons why getting started can be difficult. The first has to do with remembering one's goal intention (Einstein & McDaniel, 1996). When acting on a given goal is not part of one's routine, or when one has to postpone acting on it, one can easily forget to do so. Dealing with many things at once or becoming preoccupied by a particular task can make this even more likely, especially when the given goal is new or unfamiliar. Empirical support for this reason for people's difficulties in getting started on their goals comes from retrospective reports by inclined abstainers. For example, 70% of participants who had intended to perform a breast self-examination but failed to do so, offered forgetting as their reason for non-performance (Milne, Orbell, & Sheeran, 2002; Orbell, Hodgkins, & Sheeran, 1997). Also, meta-analysis has shown that the longer the time interval between measures of goal intentions and goal achievement, the less likely it is that intentions are realized (Sheeran & Orbell, 1998). These findings suggest that remembering one's goal intentions does not come easily to people.

But even if one remembers what one is supposed to do, there is a second problem that needs to be solved: responding to the critical situation in time. This problem is especially acute when the critical situation presents itself only briefly. In these circumstances, people may fail to initiate goal-directed responses either because they fail to notice that the critical situation is present, or because they are unsure how they should act when this moment presents itself, or they simply procrastinate in acting on it. Oettingen, Hönig, and Gollwitzer (2000, Study 3) showed that considerable slippage can occur even when people have formed strong goal intentions to perform a behavior at a particular time. Participants were provided with diskettes containing four concentration tasks and formed goal intentions to perform these tasks on their computers at a particular time each Wednesday morning for the next 4 weeks. The program on the diskette recorded the time that participants started to work on the task from the clock on participants' computers. Findings indicated that the mean deviation from the intended start time was 8 hours, that is, a discrepancy of 2 hours on average for each specified opportunity. Similar findings were obtained by Dholakia and Bagozzi (2003, Study 2) when participants' task was to evaluate a website that could be accessed only during a short time window. Here, only 37% of participants who formed a respective goal intention were successful at accomplishing the task. In sum, people may not get started with goal pursuit because they fail to seize good opportunities to act.

There are also many instances where people remember their goal intentions (e.g., to order a low-fat meal) and recognize that the critical situation is present (e.g., the waiter describing the specials of today), but nonetheless fail to initiate goal-directed behaviors, because they start to reflect anew on the desirability of the goal intention (i.e., start to have second thoughts about eating healthily). This problem has to do with overcoming an initial reluctance to act that is likely to arise when people have decided to pursue a goal that involves a trade-off between attractive long-term consequences versus less attractive short-term consequences (Mischel, 1996). For example, a strong goal intention to order low-fat meals is commonly formed on the basis of long-term deliberative thinking according to which eating low-fat food is perceived as highly desirable; however, once the critical situation is confronted, short-term desirability considerations are triggered that occupy cognitive resources at the moment of action (e.g., the low-fat meal is perceived as tasteless at the critical juncture).

Numerous studies suggest that the problem of getting started on one's goals can be solved effectively by forming implementation intentions. For instance, Gollwitzer and Brandstätter (1997, Study 2) analyzed a goal intention (i.e., writing a report about how one spent Christmas Eve) that had to be performed at a time (i.e., during the subsequent Christmas holiday) where people are commonly busy with other things. Still, research participants who had furnished their goal intention with an implementation intention that specified when, where, and how one wanted to get started on this project were about three times as successful in writing the report as mere goal intention participants. Similarly, Oettingen et al. (2000, Study 3) observed that implementation intentions helped people to act on their task goals (i.e., taking a concentration test) on time (e.g., at 10 am in the morning of every Wednesday over the next 4 weeks). Other studies have examined the effects of implementation intentions with goal intentions that are somewhat unpleasant to perform. For instance, the goal intentions to perform regular breast examinations (Orbell et al., 1997), cervical cancer screenings (Sheeran & Orbell, 2000), resumption of functional activity after joint replacement surgery (Orbell & Sheeran, 2000), and engaging in physical exercise (Milne et al., 2002), were all more readily acted upon when people had furnished these goals with implementation intentions. Moreover, implementation intentions were found to help in meeting goal intentions where it is easy to forget to act (e.g., regular intake of vitamin pills, see Sheeran & Orbell, 1999; the signing of work sheets with the elderly, see Chasteen, Park, & Schwarz, 2001).

The results of the sum of these studies clearly indicate that acting on a goal is facilitated by forming implementation intentions that plan out in advance how one intends to get started. Apparently, the various cognitive mechanisms triggered by if–then plans automate action initiation, thus facilitating it. This conclusion is supported by the finding that the beneficial effects of implementation intentions are commonly more apparent with difficult to implement goals as compared to easy goals. For instance, implementation intentions were more effective in helping people to act on difficult as compared to easy personal projects during the Christmas break (Gollwitzer & Brandstätter, 1997, Study 1), and forming implementation intentions were more beneficial to frontal lobe patients, who typically have severe problems with executive control, than to college students (Lengfelder & Gollwitzer, 2001, Study 2).

Straying on track

Many goals cannot be accomplished by simple discrete one-shot actions but require continuous striving and repeated complex behavioral performances to be attained. Once a person has initiated these more complex goal pursuits, bringing them to a successful ending may get very difficult when certain internal (e.g., being anxious, tired, overburdened) or external (e.g., temptations, distractions) stimuli are not conducive to goal realization but instead generate interferences that could potentially derail the ongoing goal pursuit. Thus, one wonders whether implementation intentions can facilitate the shielding of such goal pursuits from the negative influences of interferences from inside and outside the person.

There are two major strategies in which implementation intentions can be used to shield an ongoing goal pursuit: (a) directing one's implementation intentions towards the suppression of negative influences, and (b) directing one's implementation intentions towards spelling out the ongoing goal pursuit so that it becomes sheltered from these negative influences. For instance, if a person wants to avoid being unfriendly to a friend who is known to make outrageous requests, she can protect herself from showing the unwanted unfriendly response by forming suppression-oriented implementation intentions. Suppression-oriented implementation intentions can take different formats. They may focus on reducing the intensity of the unwanted response by intending not to show the unwanted response: "And if my friend approaches me with an outrageous request, then I will not respond in an unfriendly manner!" But they may also try to reduce the intensity of the unwanted response by specifying the initiation of the respective antagonistic response: "And if my friend approaches me with an outrageous request, then I will respond in a friendly manner!" Finally, suppression-oriented implementation intentions may even focus a person away from the critical stimulus: "And if my friend approaches me with an outrageous request, then I'll ignore it!"

Two lines of experiments analyzed the effects of suppression-oriented implementation intentions. The first line looked at the control of unwanted spontaneous attending to tempting distractions (Gollwitzer & Schaal, 1998, Studies 1 and 2). Participants had to perform a boring task (a series of simple arithmetic tasks) while being bombarded with attractive distracting stimuli (e.g., video clips of award-winning commercials). Whereas control participants were asked to form a mere goal intention ("I will not let myself get distracted!"), experimental participants in addition formed one of two implementation intentions: "And if a distraction arises, then I'll ignore it!" or "And if a distraction arises, then I will increase my effort at the task at hand!" The ignore-implementation intention always helped participants to ward off the distractions (as assessed by their task performance), regardless of whether the motivation to perform the tedious task (assessed at the beginning of the task) was low or high. In contrast, the effort-increase implementation-intention was effective only when motivation to perform the tedious task was low. Apparently, when motivation is high to begin with, effort-increase implementation intentions may create over-motivation that hampers task performance. It seems appropriate therefore to advise motivated individuals who suffer from being distracted (e.g., ambitious students doing their homework) to resort to ignore-implementation intentions, rather than to adhere to implementation intentions that focus on the strengthening of effort.

The second line of experiments analyzing suppression-oriented implementation intentions studied the control of the automatic activation of stereotypical beliefs and prejudicial evaluations (Gollwitzer & Schaal, 1998, Studies 3 and 4). In various priming studies with short stimulus-onset asynchronies of less than 300 ms between primes (presentations of members of stigmatized groups) and targets (adjectives describing relevant stereotypical attributes or neutral positive/negative adjectives), implementation intentions helped to inhibit both the automatic activation of stereotypical beliefs about and prejudicial evaluations of women, the elderly, and the homeless. These implementation intentions (i.e., if–then plans) specified being confronted with a member of the critical group in the if-part, and either "then I won't stereotype" (respectively: "then I won't evaluate negatively") or "then I will ignore the group membership" in the then-part. Regardless of which then-parts were used, both types of suppression-oriented implementation intentions were effective.

The research presented in the last two paragraphs used implementation intentions that specified a potential interference in the if-part. The specified interference was linked to a then-part that described an attempt at suppressing the unwanted negative influence of this interference on one's goal pursuit. Self-regulation by this type of implementation intentions implies that one has to be in a position to anticipate these potential interferences on the way to the goal; one even needs to know what kind of unwanted responses these interferences elicit, if one prefers to specify not showing this response in the then-part of the implementation intention (rather than showing a goal-directed response or simply ignoring the interfering event). Fortunately, a simpler way of using implementation intentions to protect an ongoing goal pursuit from getting derailed is also available. Instead of gearing one's implementation intentions toward anticipated potential interferences and the disruptive responses triggered thereby, one may form implementation intentions geared at stabilizing the ongoing goal pursuit at hand. Using again the example of a tired person who is approached by her friend with an outrageous request, and who will likely respond in an unfriendly manner: If this person has stipulated in advance in an implementation intention what she will converse about with her friend, the critical interaction may simply run off as planned, and being tired should thus fail to affect the person's relating to her friend. As is evident from this example, the present self-regulatory strategy should be of special value whenever the influence of detrimental self-states (e.g., being tired, irritated, anxious) on derailing one's goal-directed behavior has to be controlled. This should be true no matter whether such self-states and/or their negative influences on one's goal-directed behavior reside in consciousness or not.

Gollwitzer and Bayer (2000; Gollwitzer, Bayer, & McCulloch, 2005) tested this hypothesis in a series of experiments in which participants were asked (or not) to make if–then plans regarding the implementation of an assigned task goal. Prior to beginning work on the task, participants' self-states were manipulated so that the task at hand became more difficult (e.g., a state of self-definitional incompleteness prior to a task that required perspective taking, see Gollwitzer & Wicklund, 1985; a good mood prior to a task that required evaluation of others nonstereotypically, see Bless & Fiedler, 1995; a state of ego-depletion prior to solving difficult anagrams, see Baumeister, 2000; Muraven, Tice, & Baumeister, 1998). The induced critical self-states negatively affected task performance only for those participants who had not planned out in advance how they wanted to perform the task at hand (i.e., had only set themselves the goal to come up with a great performance). Implementation-intention participants were effectively protected from the negative influences associated with the induced detrimental self-states.

People's goal pursuits, however, are not only threatened by detrimental self-states but also by adverse situational conditions. There are many situations that have negative effects on goal attainment unbeknown to the person who is striving for the goal. A prime example is the social loafing phenomenon where people show reduced effort in the face of work settings that produce a reduction of accountability (i.e., performance outcomes can no longer be checked at an individual level). As people are commonly not aware of this phenomenon, they cannot form implementation intentions that specify a social loafing situation as a critical situation, thereby rendering an implementation intention that focuses on suppressing the social loafing response an unviable self-regulatory strategy. As an alternative, people may again resort to forming implementation intentions that stipulate how the intended task is to be performed, and thus effectively block any negative situational influences.

Supporting this contention, when Endress (2001) performed a social loafing experiment that used a brain-storming task (participants had to find as many different uses for a common knife as possible), she observed that implementation intentions ("And if I have found one solution, then I will immediately try to find a different solution!") but not goal intentions ("I will try to find as many different solutions as possible!") protected participants from social loafing effects. Findings reported by Trötschel and Gollwitzer (2004) also support the notion that goal pursuits planned by forming implementation intentions become invulnerable to adverse situational influences. In their experiments on the self-regulation of negotiation behavior, loss-framed negotiation settings failed to unfold their negative effects on fair and cooperative negotiation outcomes when the negotiators had planned out their goal intentions in advance to be fair and cooperative with if–then plans. Finally, in further experiments (Gollwitzer, 1998), it was observed that competing goal intentions activated outside of a person's awareness (by using goal-priming procedures described in the first part of this chapter) failed to affect a person's ongoing goal pursuit, if this goal pursuit was planned out in advance via implementation intentions.

It appears, then, that the self-regulatory strategy of planning out goal pursuits in advance via implementation intentions allows the person to reap the desired positive outcomes without having to change the environment from an adverse to a facilitative one. This is very convenient, as such environmental change is often very cumbersome (e.g., it takes the costly interventions of mediators to change the loss frames adopted by conflicting parties into gain frames) or not under the person's control. Moreover, people are often not aware of the adverse influences of the current environment (e.g., a de-individuated work setting or a loss-framed negotiation setting), or they do not know what alternative kind of environmental setting is actually facilitative (e.g., an individualized work setting or a gain-framed negotiation setting).

Callling a halt

There is a further self-regulatory problem with successful goal implementation: switching to better means when the chosen means turn out to be unproductive, or disengaging from a failing goal pursuit altogether so that other pressing goals can finally be served (Carver & Scheier, 1999; Gollwitzer, 1990). People often fail to readily disengage from chosen means and goals because of a strong self-justification motive (Brockner, 1992). However, such escalation effects should be reduced effectively by the use of implementation intentions that specify exactly when to switch to a different means or when to stop a failing goal pursuit, as action control is then delegated to this specified cue. The self-regulatory strategy, of setting goals (e.g., to avoid the escalation of commitment by always pursuing the best strategy, or never to pursue failing goals) should be comparatively less effective, as it demands effortful deliberation of the instrumentality of the faulty means or the feasibility or desirability of the failing goal, which will – to make things worse – likely be biased by self-defensiveness.

Henderson, Gollwitzer, and Oettingen (2004, Study 1) tested the hypothesis that furnishing disengagement goals with implementation intentions should help people to more effectively relinquish a failing strategy of goal pursuit. For this purpose, a classic paradigm was used that creates a strong escalation tendency (Bobocel & Meyer, 1994): Participants had to choose and subsequently justify their choice between four different strategies of performing an assigned test measuring an important aptitude (i.e., general academic knowledge). Prior to working on the test with the chosen strategy, participants in the mere goal-intention condition repeated the statement "I will always pursue the best strategy!" Participants in the implementation-intention condition repeated the above goal intention to themselves along with the respective plan "And if I receive disappointing feedback, then I'll switch to a different strategy!" Implementation intentions did indeed facilitate switching to a different strategy: 66% in the goal-intention group, but 93% in the implementation-intention group disengaged from their initial strategy when false failure feedback was given on participants' quality of test performance. In Experiment 2, Hendersen et al. (2004) explored whether disengagement from a failing course of goal-directed action is still furthered by implementation intentions even if a substitute course of goal-directed action (i.e., an alternative strategy or means) is absent: that is, the person needs to disengage from a failing goal pursuit altogether. Again, implementation-intention participants were more successful in doing so than mere goal participants who only had set themselves the goal to stop a failing goal pursuit.

Not overextending oneself

Given the many benefits of forming implementation intentions, one wonders whether goal implementation based on if–then plans means overextending oneself, so that subsequent goal striving suffers. Two such cost issues have been analyzed empirically so far: First, it was analyzed whether action control via implementation intentions produced a high degree of ego-depletion (Muraven et al., 1998) that consequently handicaped needed self-regulatory resources. Second, even though implementation intentions can successfully suppress unwanted thoughts, feelings, and actions in a given context, these very thoughts, feelings, and actions may rebound in a temporally subsequent, different context (Wegner, 1994).

The assumption that implementation intentions subject behavior to the direct control of situational cues (Gollwitzer, 1993) implies that the self is not implicated when behavior is controlled via implementation intentions. As a consequence, the self should not become depleted when task performance is regulated by implementation intentions. Indeed, using different ego-depletion paradigms, research participants who used implementation intentions to self-regulate in one task do not show reduced self-regulatory capacity in a subsequent task. Whether the initial self-regulation task was controlling emotions while watching a humorous movie (Gollwitzer & Bayer, 2000), or performing a Stroop task (Webb & Sheeran, 2003, Study 1), implementation intentions successfully preserved self-regulatory resources as demonstrated by greater persistence on subsequent difficult tasks.

To test whether striving for fairness goals by using suppression-oriented implementation intentions produces rebound effects, Gollwitzer, Trötschel, and Sumner (2004) ran two experiments using research paradigms developed by Macrae, Bodenhausen, Milne, and Jetten (1994). In both studies, participants first had to suppress the expression of stereotypes in a first-impression formation task that focused on a particular member of a stereotyped group (i.e., homeless people). Rebound was measured either in terms of subsequent expression of stereotypes in a task that demanded the evaluation of the group of homeless people in general (Study 1), or a lexical decision task that assessed the accessibility of homeless stereotypes (Study 2). Participants who had been assigned the mere goal of controlling stereotypic thoughts while forming an impression of the given homeless person were more stereotypical in their judgments of homeless people in general (Study 1) and showed a higher accessibility of homeless stereotypes (Study 2) than participants who had been asked to furnish this lofty goal with relevant if–then plans. Rather than causing rebound effects, implementation intentions appear to be effective in preventing them.

Summary and conclusion

People can do a lot to make their goal pursuits more successful. First, they need to strongly commit to their goals, and this is facilitated when both high-desirability and high-feasibility beliefs are respected, and when goal contents are framed appropriately. Second, as research on implementation intentions has observed, planning out in advance how one wants to act on a chosen goal increases the likelihood that one will successfully traverse the major problems of goal implementation: getting started, staying on track, calling a halt, and not overextending oneself.

References

Aarts, H., & Dijksterhuis, A. (2000). The automatic activation of goal-directed behaviour: The case of travel habit. *Journal of Environmental Psychology*, *20*, 75–82.

Ajzen, I. (1991). The theory of planned behavior. *Organizational Behavior and Human Decision Processes*, *50*, 179–211.

Bandura, A. (1997). *Self-efficacy: The exercise of control*. New York: Freeman.

Baumeister, R. (2000). Ego depletion and the self's executive function. In A. Tesser & R. Felson (Eds.), *Psychological perspectives on self and identity* (pp. 9–33). Washington, DC: American Psychological Association.

Bayer, U.C., Moskowitz, G.B., & Gollwitzer, P.M. (2002). *Implementation intentions and action initiation without conscious intent*. Unpublished manuscript, University of Konstanz, Germany.

Bless, H., & Fiedler, K. (1995). Affective states and the influence of activated general knowledge. *Personality and Social Psychology Bulletin*, *21*, 766–778.

Bobocel, R.D., & Meyer, J.P. (1994). Escalating commitment to a failing course of action: Separating the roles of choice and justification. *Journal of Applied Psychology*, *79*, 360–363.

Brandstätter, V., Lengfelder, A., & Gollwitzer, P.M. (2001). Implementation intentions and efficient action initiation. *Journal of Personality and Social Psychology*, *81*, 946–960.

Brockner, J. (1992). The escalation of commitment to a failing course of action: Toward theoretical progress. *Academy of Management Review*, *17*, 39–61.

Brunstein, J.C., Schultheiss, O.C., & Grassman, R. (1998). Personal goals and emotional well-being: The moderating role of motive dispositions. *Journal of Personality and Social Psychology*, *75*, 494–508.

Carver, C.S., & Scheier, M.F. (1998). *On the self-regulation of behavior*. New York: Cambridge University Press.

Carver, C.S., & Scheier, M.F. (1999). Themes and issues in the self-regulation of behavior. In R.S. Wyer Jr. (Ed.), *Advances in social cognition* (Vol. 12). Mahwah, NJ: Lawrence Erlbaum Associates Inc.

Chasteen, A.L., Park, D.C., & Schwarz, N. (2001). Implementation intentions and the facilitation of prospective memory. *Psychological Science, 12*, 457–461.

Dholakia, U.M., & Bagozzi, R.P. (2003). As time goes by: How goal and implementation intentions influence enactment of short-fuse behaviors. *Journal of Applied Social Psychology, 33*, 889–922.

Dweck, C.S. (1999). *Self-theories: Their role in motivation, personality, and development*. Philadelphia, PA: Psychology Press.

Einstein, G.O., & McDaniel, M.A. (1996). Retrieval processes in prospective memory: Theoretical approaches and some new empirical findings. In M. Bradimonte, G.O. Einstein, & M.A. McDaniel (Eds.), *Prospective memory: Theory and applications* (pp. 115–141). Mahwah, NJ: Lawrence Erlbaum Associates Inc.

Endress, H. (2001). *Die Wirksamkeit von Vorsätzen auf Gruppenleistungen: Eine empirische Untersuchung anhand von brainstorming* [Implementation intentions and the reduction of social loafing in a brain storming task]. Unpublished MA thesis. University of Konstanz, Germany.

Gollwitzer, P.M. (1990). Action phases and mind-sets. In T. Higgins & R. Sorrentino (Eds.), *Handbook of motivation and cognition: Foundations of social behavior* (Vol. 2, pp. 53–92). New York: Guilford Press.

Gollwitzer, P.M. (1993). Goal achievement: The role of intentions. *European Review of Social Psychology, 4*, 141–185.

Gollwitzer, P.M. (1998). *Implicit and explicit processes in goal pursuit*. Paper presented at the Symposium "Implicit vs Explicit Processes" at the Annual Meeting of the Society of Experimental Social Psychology, Lexington, Kentucky.

Gollwitzer, P.M. (1999). Implementation intentions: Strong effects of simple plans. *American Psychologist, 54*, 493–503.

Gollwitzer, P.M., & Bayer, U.C. (2000). *Becoming a better person without changing the self*. Paper presented at the Self and Identity Pre-conference of the Annual Meeting of the Society of Experimental Social Psychology, Atlanta, Georgia.

Gollwitzer, P.M., Bayer, U., & McCulloch, K. (2005). The control of the unwanted. In R. Hassin, J. Uleman, & J.A. Bargh (Eds.), *The new unconscious* (pp. 485–515). Oxford: Oxford University Press.

Gollwitzer, P.M., Bayer, U.C., Steller, B., & Bargh, J.A. (2002). *Delegating control to the environment: Perception, attention, and memory for pre-selected behavioral cues*. Unpublished manuscript, University of Konstanz, Germany.

Gollwitzer, P.M., & Brandstätter, V. (1997). Implementation intentions and effective goal pursuit. *Journal of Personality and Social Psychology, 73*, 186–199.

Gollwitzer, P.M., & Liu, C. (1995). Wiederaufnahme [Resumption]. In J. Kuhl & H. Heckhausen (Eds.), *Enzyklopaedie der Psychologie. Teilband C/IV/4: Motivation, Volition und Handlung* (pp. 209–240). Goettingen: Hogrefe.

Gollwitzer, P.M., & Moskowitz, G.B. (1996). Goal effects on action and cognition. In E.T. Higgins & A.W. Kruglanski (Eds.), *Social psychology: Handbook of basic principles* (pp. 361–399). New York: Guilford Press.

Gollwitzer, P.M., & Schaal, B. (1998). Metacognition in action: The importance of implementation intentions. *Personality and Social Psychology Review, 2*, 124–136.

Gollwitzer, P.M., Trötschel, R., & Sumner, M. (2004). *Mental control via implementation intentions is void of rebound effects*. Unpublished manuscript, University of Konstanz, Germany.

Gollwitzer, P.M., & Wicklund, R.A. (1985). Self-symbolizing and the neglect of others' perspectives. *Journal of Personality and Social Psychology, 56*, 531–715.

Gottschaldt, K. (1926). Über den Einfluß der Erfahrung auf die Wahrnehmung von Figuren [On the effects of familiarity on the perception of figures]. *Psychologische Forschung*, *8*, 261–317.

Heckhausen, H. (1977). Achievement motivation and its constructs: A cognitive model. *Motivation and Emotion*, *4*, 283–329.

Henderson, M.D., Gollwitzer, P.M., & Oettingen, G. (2004). *Using implementation intentions to disengage from a failing course of action: The effects of planning on escalation of commitment*. Manuscript submitted for publication.

Higgins, E.T. (1997). Beyond pleasure and pain. *American Psychologist*, *52*, 1280–1300.

Kruglanski, A.W. (1996). Goals as knowledge structures. In P.M. Gollwitzer & J.A. Bargh (Eds.), *The psychology of action* (pp. 599–618). New York: Guildford Press.

Lengfelder, A., & Gollwitzer, P.M. (2001). Reflective and reflexive action control in patients with frontal brain lesions. *Neuropsychology*, *15*, 80–100.

Lewin, K. (1926). Vorsatz, Wille und Bedürfnis [Intention, will, and need]. *Psychologische Forschung*, *7*, 330–385.

Macrae, C.N., Bodenhausen, G.V., Milne, A.B., & Jetten, J. (1994). Out of mind but back in sight: Stereotypes on the rebound. *Journal of Personality and Social Psychology*, *67*, 808–817.

Mahler, W. (1933). Ersatzhandlungen verschiedenen Realitätsgrades [Substitute activities at different levels of reality]. *Psychologische Forschung*, *18*, 27–89.

Milne, S., Orbell, S., & Sheeran, P. (2002). Combining motivational and volitional interventions to promote exercise participation: Protection motivation theory and implementation intentions. *British Journal of Health Psychology*, *7*, 163–184.

Mischel, W. (1996). From good intentions to willpower. In P.M. Gollwitzer & J.A. Bargh (Eds.), *The psychology of action: Linking cognition and motivation to behavior* (pp. 197–218). New York: Guilford Press.

Mischel, W., Shoda, Y., & Rodriguez, M.L. (1989). Delay of gratification in children. *Science*, *244*, 933–938.

Muraven, M., & Baumeister, R.F. (2000). Self-regulation and depletion of limited resources: Does self-control resemble a muscle? *Psychological Bulletin*, *126*, 247–259.

Muraven, M., Tice, D.M., & Baumeister, R.F. (1998). Self-control as a limited resource: Regulatory depletion pattern. *Journal of Personality and Social Psychology*, *74*, 774–789.

Oettingen, G., & Gollwitzer, P.M. (2001). Goal setting and goal striving. In A. Tesser N. Schwarz (Vol. Eds.), M. Hewstone & M. Brewer (Series Eds.), *Intraindividual processes. Volume 1 of the Blackwell handbook in social psychology* (pp. 329–347). Oxford: Blackwell.

Oettingen, G., Hönig, G., & Gollwitzer, P.M. (2000). Effective self-regulation of goal attainment. *International Journal of Educational Research*, *33*, 705–732.

Oettingen, G., Pak. H., & Schnetter, K. (2001). Self-regulation of goal setting: Turning free fantasies about the future into binding goals. *Journal of Personality and Social Psychology*, *80*, 736–753.

Orbell, S., Hodgkins, S., & Sheeran, P. (1997). Implementation intentions and the theory of planned behavior. *Personality and Social Psychology Bulletin*, *23*, 945–954.

Orbell, S., & Sheeran, P. (2000). Motivational and volitional processes in action initiation: A field study of the role of implementation intentions. *Journal of Applied Social Psychology*, *30*, 780–797.

Ryan, R.M., & Deci, E.L. (2000). When rewards compete with nature: The undermining of intrinsic motivation and self-regulation. In C. Sansone & J. Harackiewicz

(Eds.), *Intrinsic and extrinsic motivation: The search for optimal motivation and performance* (pp. 13–54). San Diego, CA: Academic Press.

Sheeran, P., Aarts, H., Custers, R., Rivis, A., Webb, T.L., & Cooke, R. (2005). The goal-dependent automaticity of drinking habits. *British Journal of Social Psychology*, *44*, 47–64.

Sheeran, P., & Orbell, S. (1998). Do intentions predict condom use? A meta-analysis and examination of six moderator variables. *British Journal of Social Psychology*, *37*, 231–250.

Sheeran, P., & Orbell, S. (1999). Implementation intentions and repeated behavior: Augmenting the predictive validity of the theory of planned behavior. *European Journal of Social Psychology*, *29*, 349–369.

Sheeran, P., & Orbell, S. (2000). Using implementation intentions to increase attendance for cervical cancer screening. *Health Psychology*, *19*, 283–289.

Sheeran, P., Webb, T.L., & Gollwitzer, P.M. (2005). The interplay between goal intentions and implementation intentions. *Personality and Social Psychology Bulletin*, *31*, 87–98.

Trötschel, R., & Gollwitzer, P.M. (2004). *Implementation intentions and the control of framing effects in negotiations*. Manuscript submitted for publication.

Verplanken, B., & Faes, S. (1999). Good intentions, bad habits, and effects of forming implementation intentions on healthy eating. *European Journal of Social Psychology*, *29*, 591–604.

Webb, T.L., & Sheeran, P. (2003). Can implementation intentions help to overcome ego-depletion? *Journal of Experimental Social Psychology*, *39*, 279–286.

Webb, T.L., & Sheeran, P. (2004). Identifying good opportunities to act: Implementation intentions and cue discrimination. *European Journal of Psychology*, *34*, 407–419.

Wegner, D.M. (1994). Ironic processes in mental control. *Psychological Review*, *101*, 34–52.

Wood, W., Quinn, J.M., & Kashy, D.A. (2002). Habits in everyday life: Thought, emotion, and action. *Journal of Personality and Social Psychology*, *83*, 1281–1297.

Wright, R.A. (1996). Brehm's theory of motivation as a model of effort and cardiovascular response. In P.M. Gollwitzer & J.A. Bargh (Eds.), *The psychology of action: Linking cognition and motivation to behavior* (pp. 424–453). New York: Guilford Press.

Section II

Cognitive neuroscience

9 Imaging cognition: Recent developments and a tentative hierarchical cognitive model

Lars Nyberg

Functional magnetic resonance imaging (fMRI) is today one of the most widely used brain-mapping techniques (Logothetis et al., 2001). However, it has a rather brief history (see Raichle, 2001). Around the time of the 1992 ICP meeting in Brussels, a landmark fMRI paper was presented (Ogawa & Lee, 1990). Four years later, at the time of the ICP meeting in Montreal, a few fMRI papers were to be found in the Medline database (Figure 9.1). During the subsequent 10-year period, spanning the ICP meeting in Stockholm in 2000 and the latest ICP meeting in Beijing in 2004, a dramatic increase in the number of published papers is evident (Figure 9.1). A number of factors may account for this "fMRI explosion", including accessibility (fMRI scanners can be found in numerous sites around the world), cost (compared to positron emission tomography, PET, fMRI studies are less expensive), and non-invasiveness (the commonly studied Blood-Oxygen-Level-Dependent

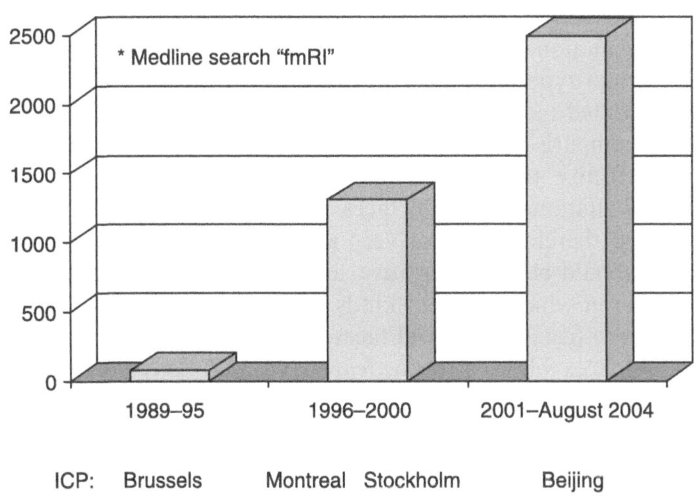

Figure 9.1 Rapid expansion of publications of fMRI papers according to a Medline search of "fMRI". The time axis indicates the approximate time of organization of various ICP meetings during the relevant time period.

signal, BOLD, relies on functionally induced inter-regional differences in blood oxygenation).

In the present chapter some recent developments in fMRI research will be discussed. These include methodological developments (new fMRI designs) as well as theoretical developments (new study domains and cross-domain comparisons). In the final section of the chapter, possible implications of results from fMRI studies for cognitive theories are discussed and a hierarchical cognitive model is tentatively proposed.

New fMRI designs

The traditional and most frequently used fMRI design is the *blocked* or *on/off* design. Basically, this design involves repeated alternation between two or more experimental conditions. For example, in a study of regions that become more active during visual stimulation, one might alternate between 30-s blocks of visual stimulation and equally long baseline blocks. The visual blocks may include presentation of a checkerboard pattern every 3 s, and the baseline blocks may include presentation of a fixation cross at the same rate. The statistical analysis would aim at finding brain regions in which the activity systematically changes in relation to the alternation between visual and baseline blocks. Most likely, regions in occipital cortex would show greater activity, as indexed by the BOLD signal, during the visual blocks.

The blocked design is a very useful and powerful design. However, it has certain limitations that are critical from a psychological point of view. For example, the presentation of many events in a blocked fashion may lead to shifts in the strategy the participants are using. Such shifts would go unnoticed and only serve to increase the error variance in the data. Also, a blocked presentation format prevents analysis of how the brain is activated during a certain type of event. If a block of events, say pictures of fearful faces, is presented in a study of how the brain responds to fear, one would hope that a comparison of blocks of fearful faces with blocks of neutral faces would be sensitive to the fear manipulation. However, it might be that blocked presentation of fearful faces has the effect that the participants habituate and therefore are not very affected by the facial expressions. A design that should be more sensitive, and not contaminated by habituation effects, is one in which different kinds of events are presented in an intermixed sequence (e.g., five neutral faces followed by one fearful followed by three neutral faces followed by one fearful, etc.). This type of design, known as an *event-related design*, would permit separate analysis of the neutral and emotional events. The event-related design is very useful for addressing many psychological research questions, as it permits stimuli to be presented in a similar fashion to psychological experiments.

In the above example of an event-related design, the presentation of a face was defined as the event of interest. A novel extension of the event-related design can be termed *within-event design*. In this design the goal is to decompose an event into multiple components. For example, if a piece of music is presented and the participant is asked to identify the name of the piece, the "global event" of listening to the piece might be broken down into sub-event components such as auditory perception, recognition, and decision making. With the within-event design, the goal is to isolate brain activity that relates to each component or sub-event. In the section on new study domains, this design will be exemplified in the context of a study of visual awareness.

A further example of a relatively recent fMRI design is the *mixed blocked/event-related design*. As the name indicates, the goal of this design is to identify activity changes that have different time courses. The event-related design can identify brain regions in which transient stimulus-locked activity changes occur. Such activity changes may also be the source of regional effects that are identified in blocked designs. An additional source of regional activity changes detected in blocked designs can be signals that are sustained over time and not locked to the processing of individual stimuli. Processes that may correlate with a sustained BOLD signal include remembering the specific instructions (maintaining task context) and upholding a certain strategy. In the typical blocked design the transient and sustained signals cannot be resolved, but in the mixed design this is made possible by presenting the events within task blocks in a certain manner. Specifically, the events are presented at irregular intervals (in a so-called jittered fashion), and the intervals can vary from only 1 or a few seconds up to more than 20 s. The specific presentation rate of events in a given mixed design must be adapted to fit the research question, but in general it is important to include some long inter-stimulus intervals in order to be able to resolve sustained and transient signals. In the section on cross-domain studies, the mixed design will be exemplified in the context of a study of transient and sustained effects during attention and memory tasks. For a more in-depth discussion of various fMRI designs, the interested reader is recommended to consult Donaldson and Buckner (2001).

New study domains

In the early days of functional brain imaging, the number of study topics was quite limited. In a published review of PET studies until December 1995 (Cabeza & Nyberg, 1997), we classified studies into eight different categories (attention, perception, language, etc.). In a subsequent review (Cabeza & Nyberg, 2000) that covered PET and fMRI studies published up to December 1998, two new main categories (imagery and episodic memory encoding) and several sub-categories (e.g., problem solving under working memory) were added.

This trend, that fMRI is being used to study a greater diversity of topics, has continued. One salient example is work on emotion. In his introduction to the section on emotion in Gazzaniga's 1995 volume *The Cognitive*

Neurosciences, Ledoux noted that emotion had not been a much studied topic in research on the relation between brain and mind. This state of affairs had changed radically by the time of the publication of the second edition of the volume (Gazzaniga, 2000). At this time, Ledoux commented on the large increase in researchers working in the area of emotion and the greater range of topics.

Another example of the application of fMRI to new study domains is consciousness. Schacter introduced the section on consciousness in *The New Cognitive Neurosciences* (Gazzaniga, 2000), and in this introduction he wrote: "Although the use of neuroimaging to understand problems related to consciousness is just beginning, we can expect many more such studies in the future" (p. 1274). This prediction has already come true. Since the year 2000, a number of studies related to consciousness have been published (e.g., Bar et al., 2001; Beck et al., 2001; Dehaene et al., 2001; Feinstein et al., 2004; Kjaer et al., 2001; Portas et al., 2000; Sterzer et al., 2002). Many of the studies have been concerned with visual awareness. That is, they have attempted to identify changes in brain activity that relate to conscious awareness of a visual stimulus. One such study, which employed a within-cvent design, will be described in more detail below (Eriksson et al., 2004).

In the study by Eriksson et al. (2004), the within-event design was used to identify changes in brain activity that were related to subjective awareness of a visual object, and to differentiate this activity from activity related to a subsequent period of sustained perception. For this purpose, special visual displays were constructed (Figure 9.2a). Each display included a concrete object, for example an animal, and the task of the subject was to detect this object. When an object "popped out", the participants pressed a button and this elicited a sound. They were instructed to actively hold the percept in mind over a period after stimulus identification. During this period, a sound was presented and they were then supposed to again press a button. By including these sub-events within each trial, it was possible to specify three independent effects of interest that isolated perceptual awareness, sustained perception, and sensori-motor processes (Figure 9.2b).

Some previous studies on visual perceptual awareness had focused on activity changes in visual regions (e.g., Tong et al., 1998). While such changes are clearly of importance, it had been suggested that additional involvement of fronto-parietal regions is necessary for conscious awareness (Rees et al., 2002). The results of the Eriksson et al. (2004) study provided support for this position. Each of the three effects of interest was associated with a distinct pattern of brain activity. This speaks to the effectiveness of the within-event design to differentiate between sub-events. As expected, the sensori-motor effect involved increased activity in auditory cortex and in motor cortex. Perceptual awareness involved increased activity in visual regions and also in fronto-parietal cortex (Figure 9.3). Fronto-parietal activity was also seen during the period of sustained perception. Thus, this study showed that transient activation changes in fronto-parietal regions relate to the sudden conscious

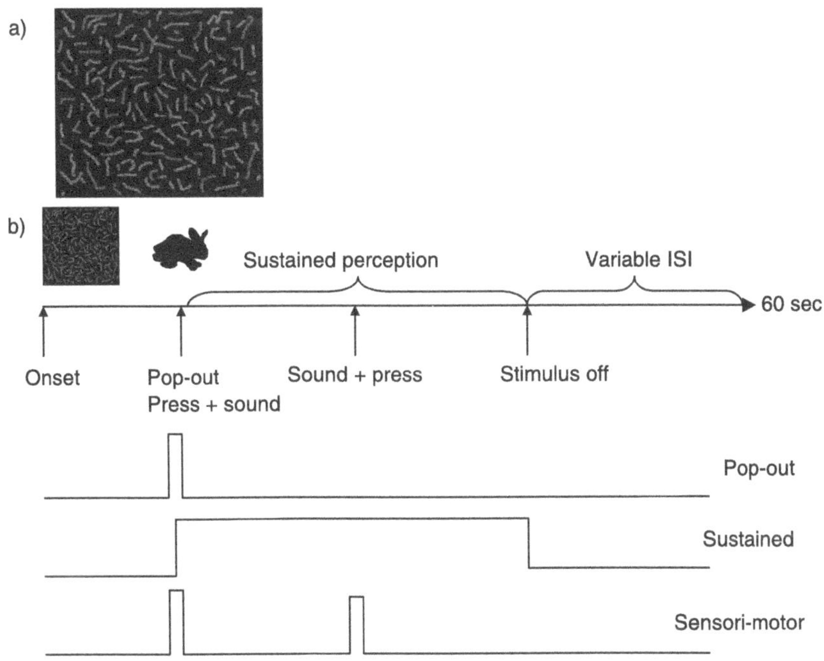

Figure 9.2 (a) Example of a visual stimulus (a rabbit); (b) effects of interests in the within-event fMRI design [adapted after Eriksson, J., Larsson, A., Riklund Åhlström, K., & Nyberg, L. (2004). Visual consciousness: Dissociating the neural correlates of perceptual transitions from sustained perception with fMRI. *Consciousness and Cognition, 13*, 61–72].

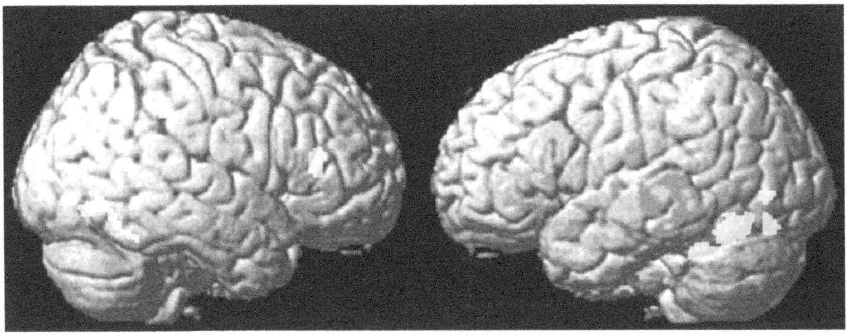

Figure 9.3 Visual and fronto-parietal brain activity associated with visual consciousness awareness [adapted after Eriksson, J., Larsson, A., Riklund Åhlström, K., & Nyberg, L. (2004). Visual consciousness: Dissociating the neural correlates of perceptual transitions from sustained perception with fMRI. *Consciousness and Cognition, 13*, 61–72].

experience of seeing an object, and sustained fronto-parietal activity relates to the process of holding this perceptual object active over time. As it turns out, similar activation profiles have been seen in other functional domains, and we will return to the functional meaning of fronto-parietal activation changes later on.

Cross-domain studies

Typically, functional brain-imaging studies are designed to study certain processes within specific functional domains (e.g., object recognition within visual perception, covert reading within language, post-retrieval monitoring within episodic retrieval). However, as more and more studies accumulate, it becomes evident that some activity patterns generalize across functional domains. In our review of PET and fMRI studies (Cabeza & Nyberg, 2000), we put a focus on cross-domain similarities by including a section entitled "review by region" in addition to "review by function". In a subsequent chapter (Cabeza & Nyberg, 2003), we presented a more quantitative analysis of 136 studies of perception, attention, working memory, semantic memory/episodic encoding, and episodic memory retrieval. We also summarized several fMRI studies that have examined more than one functional domain within one and the same study (Braver et al., 2001; Cabeza et al., 2002, 2003; LaBar et al., 1999; Nyberg et al., 2002, 2003; Ranganath et al., 2003). The results converged on several cross-domain similarities. In particular, similarities in fronto-parietal activity were pronounced in studies of attention, working memory, and episodic memory retrieval.

A recent empirical review supported and extended our previous conclusion (Naghavi & Nyberg, 2005). The purpose of this review was to assess the degree of anatomical overlap among the activation patterns associated with attention, working memory, episodic memory retrieval, and also conscious visual perception. As was noted in the above discussion of consciousness, fronto-parietal activation is a common finding in studies of visual consciousness and the review revealed a high degree of anatomical overlap across the four functional domains (Figure 9.4).

In another recent study, we used the mixed fMRI design to better characterize overlapping regions in terms of sustained or transient activation changes (Marklund et al., 2003). The study included tests of sustained attention, declarative long-term memory, and working memory. The basic design involved presentation of a specific test instruction followed by 90-s task blocks during which eight events were presented in a jittered fashion. Analysis of brain regions that showed a sustained activation profile revealed that two regions in right ventral and medial frontal cortex were activated throughout the task block across all tests (Figure 9.5a). That is, activity in these regions increased after the test instruction and remained increased during the entire 90-s block (i.e., also during fairly long interstimulus intervals). Given this pattern of activation profile it was suggested that these activation increases

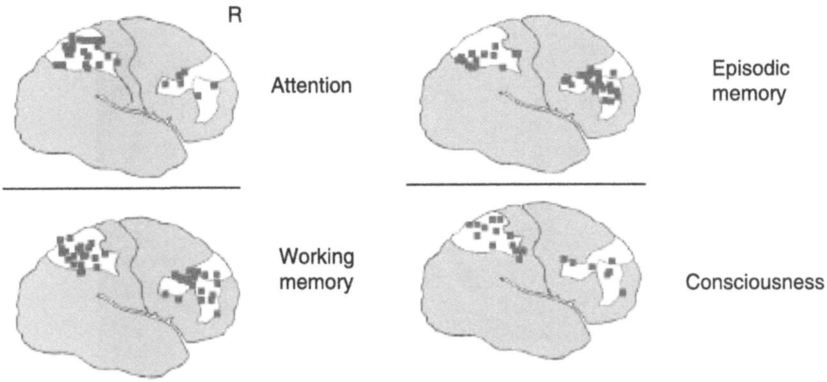

Figure 9.4 Common fronto-parietal activity in studies of attention, working memory, episodic memory retrieval, and visual consciousness [adapted after Naghavi, H.R., & Nyberg, L. (2005). Common fronto-parietal activity in attention, memory, and consciousness: Shared demands on integration? *Consciousness and Cognition*, *14*, 390–425].

reflected attention and the apprehension of upcoming events. Activity in other brain regions, such as the anterior prefrontal cortex, was sustained during the memory tasks but not the attention task. This activity was related to maintaining the appropriate task set or mode while awaiting the next test stimulus (see Sakai & Passingham, 2003).

Analysis of brain regions that showed transient activity increases during the presentation of test items in the memory tasks identified a region in dorsolateral frontal cortex (Figure 9.5b) and in superior parietal cortex. Transient activation of these regions during diverse retrieval tasks indicates that they mediate general processes such as holding an active representation in memory. A similar view was proposed by Courtney et al. (1997, p. 611): "Activation of the same (frontal) areas by both long-term retrieval and working memory is consistent with the idea that retrieval produces an active representation of the recalled material much like the active representation of material held during a working memory delay."

Finally, all memory tasks were associated with selective transient activity increases. The working memory task was an *n*-back task and this task selectively activated the premotor area. The *n*-back task requires updating the contents of working memory when new items are presented, and the premotor area has been associated with this process (Collette & Van der Linden, 2002).

Taken together, there is considerable overlap in activation patterns across cognitive domains, notably in frontal and parietal regions. As will be discussed in some more detail below, such overlap may reflect the operation of shared processes across functional domains.

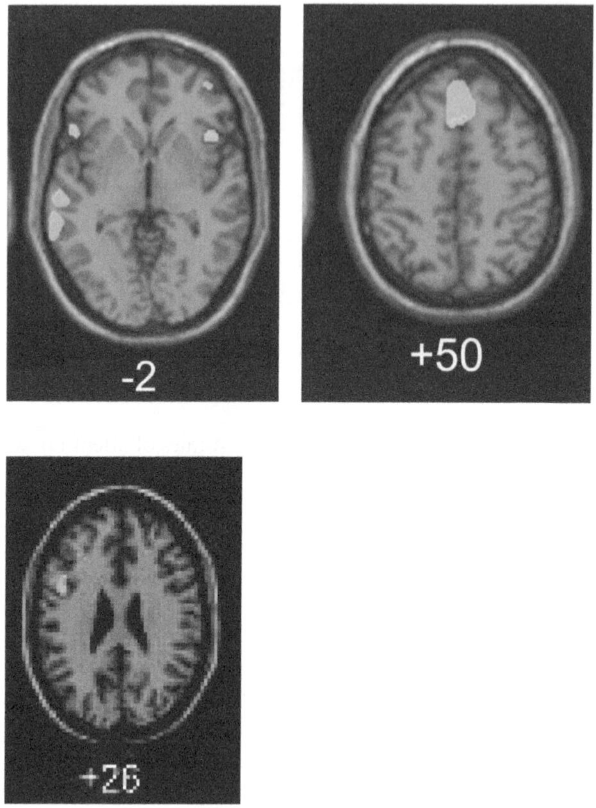

Figure 9.5 (a) Common sustained brain activity in ventrolateral and medial frontal cortex during tests of attention, working memory, and declarative long-term memory (light areas); (b) transient brain activity in dorsolateral prefrontal cortex during tests of working memory and declarative long-term memory [adapted after Marklund, P., Nyberg, L., Fransson, P., Ingvar, M., Petersson, K.M., & Cabeza, R. (2003). *Similarities and differences in state- and item-related BOLD signal changes during long-term memory tasks: A test of the working-memory hypothesis.* Poster presented at the First NorFA Meeting: Functional Neuroimaging Network, Södergarn, Sweden, 28–31 August 2003].

A hierarchical cognitive model

Observations of consistent activation of brain regions across a number of functional domains have implications for the understanding of their functional role (see Cabeza & Nyberg, 2000). Such findings may point to a more general role of certain brain regions in cognitive processes than what was originally conceived (e.g., Ranganath & D'Esposito, 2001), and/or to a heterogeneous functional architecture of certain brain regions (e.g., Bush et al.,

2002). Here I will focus on the potential implications of such findings for cognitive theories.

From the day of the publication of the famous volumes of William James (1890) onwards, textbooks in cognitive psychology have discussed various cognitive functions in separate chapters. In the same spirit, most cognitive theories to date are restricted to certain functional domains (e.g., perception, attention, memory, etc.). A notable exception is the theory of cognition proposed by Anderson and his colleagues (e.g., Anderson & Lebiere, 1998). According to this theory, the cognitive architecture can be described in terms of a set of modules (e.g., intentional module, declarative module). Each module is associated with a buffer that holds a limited amount of information from its module. In addition, a central production system coordinates the behavior of the various modules. More recently, the theory has been extended to the neural domain through fMRI experiments. Neural correlates of some of the buffers have been identified, and their temporal activation profile was found to be well predicted by the theory (see Anderson et al., 2004).

Here I would like to close by tentatively proposing a "*hierarchical cognitive model*". The model is sketched in Figure 9.6. As can be seen, the model assumes several different levels. At the first level (I), basic attentional processes are included (vigilance). It is assumed that most if not all cognitive tasks will require that the participant maintains an alert, attentive state throughout the task (e.g., memory tasks, problem-solving tasks, mathematical tasks, etc.). There are data to associate such basic attentional processes with ventrolateral prefrontal cortex and the anterior cingulate cortex (see Cabeza & Nyberg, 2000). Similarly, as discussed in the empirical section above, we have associated these regions with basic attention and provided evidence that their temporal activation profile is sustained (i.e., the activity in these regions is maintained throughout a task – also in-between the presentation of specific test items).

The second level also includes a basic process: maintenance of task set. Maintaining the appropriate task set is necessary in most cognitive tasks to ensure that task-relevant processing is conducted once a test stimulus is presented ("remember what to do"). This process is intimately related to "intention". The demands on the task-set process are lower in tasks that involve continuous on-line processing (e.g., vigilance tests), and this is illustrated in Figure 9.6 by the dotted line that bypasses the task-set process. As was noted above, we have obtained evidence that a sustained activity increase in regions in anterior prefrontal cortex is related to maintaining task set, and similar findings have been reported by others (e.g., Sakai & Passingham, 2003). Importantly, it is assumed that this process and the associated regions are engaged regardless of the type of task set (e.g., memory tasks, problem-solving tasks, mathematical tasks, etc.).

The third level might be conceptualized as the "executive level". When the appropriate task set is maintained, specific processes must then be activated

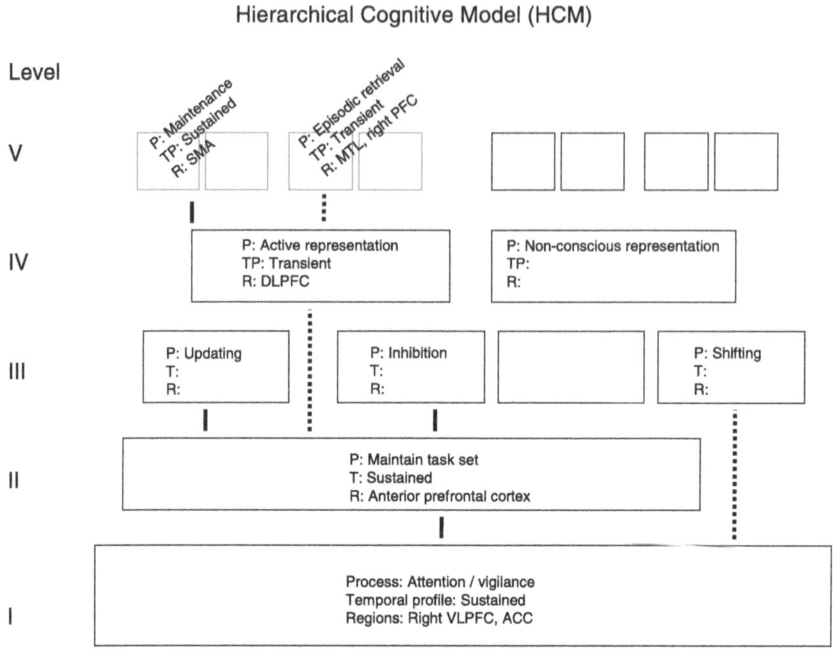

Figure 9.6 Hierarchical cognitive model. The model differentiates between various levels, where each level is associated with certain processes (P). When possible, associated brain regions (R) along with their temporal profiles (T) are suggested. Interactions between levels are indicated by filled and dotted vertical lines. Empty boxes are included to highlight that additional processes most likely remain to be specified at certain levels.

to carry out the specified task ("the goal"). So-called executive processes are associated with this "implementation stage" of cognitive processing. No consensus has been reached concerning the taxonomy of executive processes. Figure 9.6 includes three executive processes that were identified in an analysis by Miyake and colleagues (Miyake et al., 2000), but additional ones likely exist. As these kinds of processes were not explicitly discussed in the empirical section of this chapter, possible neural correlates and temporal activation profiles are not specified in the figure (various frontal regions are strong candidates). Some tasks, such as overt reading or naming, may pose minimal executive demands. This is illustrated in the figure by the dotted line that bypasses the third level.

The fourth level is the representational level. Many cognitive tasks are done on the basis of some kind of stimulus representation. Above, this was exemplified by becoming aware of the content/meaning of an ambiguous picture, holding information in working memory, and successful retrieval of information from explicit long-term memory. All these different tasks involve an active conscious representation in mind, as do many other tasks as well.

The available evidence links the process of active/aware stimulus representation to transient activation of regions in dorsolateral prefrontal cortex. Under certain conditions, such as visual masking, the same processes are presumably at work at Levels I–III but pronounced differences in Level IV frontal activity can be seen depending on whether an active conscious representation is elicited or not (e.g., Dehaene et al., 2001).

At the fifth level, more task-specific processes are included. In Figure 9.6, one such process is maintenance. This process is critical for tests of working memory. We and others have obtained evidence that temporary maintenance of information relates to sustained activation of the supplementary motor area (e.g., Petit et al., 1998). The vertical lines that connect the left-most units in Figure 9.6, across Levels I–IV, illustrate the idea that successful performance on, say, a 2-back test of working memory will depend on all these processes along with synchronized activity in the relevant regions. The dotted line between Levels IV and V implies that if the task-set process at Level II specifies a different task to be performed, in this case episodic memory retrieval instead of working memory maintenance, different processes will be included. Differences might happen at the third executive level (as indicated by the right-most vertical lines that connect task set at Level II with inhibition at Level III). Different processes will also be engaged at Level V as different task-specific process(es) will be added depending on the test demands. In the present example, the process of episodic retrieval is added at Level V. This process has been associated with activity in medial-temporal lobe regions (e.g., Nyberg, McIntosh et al., 1996; Squire, 1992) and also in right frontal cortex (Nyberg, Cabeza, & Tulving, 1996). Examples of other task-specific processes include spatial shifts of attention, semantic categorization, and many more.

Clearly, the proposed model is tentative and many details remain to be worked out and tested. It is quite likely that additional levels should be included in the model. For example, there is much evidence that a process such as episodic retrieval at Level V can be further decomposed into various component processes that have unique neural signatures (e.g., Henson et al., 1999; Nyberg et al., 1995). Interactions among levels, vertically as well as horizontally, must be worked out. Also, in the present formulation of the model, interactions of cognitive processes with sensori-motor processes are left out. With these limitations in mind, I conclude by submitting that models of this kind, which focus on interrelations among various cognitive (and neural) processes, will be essential for furthering our understanding of the organization of cognitive processes in the brain.

Acknowledgements

The work discussed in the present chapter was supported by grants from the Swedish Science Council (*VR*) and Umeå University (*UFBI*). I like to thank my graduate students, in particular Johan Eriksson and Petter Marklund, and my colleagues for their contributions. Special thanks to Roberto Cabeza with whom I have had many exciting discussions of these topics.

References

Anderson, J.R. et al. (2004). An integrated theory of the mind. *Psychological Review*, *111*, 1036–1060.

Anderson, J.R., & Lebiere, C. (1998). *The atomic components of thought*. Mahwah, NJ: Lawrence Erlbaum Associates Inc.

Bar, M., Tootell, R.B.H., Schacter, D.L., Greve, D.N., Fischl, B., Mendola, J.D. et al. (2001). Cortical mechanisms specific to explicit visual object recognition. *Neuron*, *29*, 529–535.

Beck, D.M., Rees, G., Frith, C.D., & Lavie, N. (2001). Neural correlates of change detection and change blindness. *Nature Neuroscience*, *4*, 645–650.

Braver, T.S., Barch, D.M., Kelley, W.M., Buckner, R.L., Cohen, N.J., Miezin, F.M. et al. (2001). Direct comparison of prefrontal cortex regions engaged by working and long-term memory tasks. *NeuroImage*, *14*, 48–59.

Bush, G. et al. (2002). Dorsal anterior cingulate cortex: A role in reward-based decision making. *PNAS*, *99*, 523–528.

Cabeza, R., Dolcos, F., Graham, R., & Nyberg, L. (2002). Similarities and differences in the neural correlates of episodic memory retrieval and working memory. *NeuroImage*, *16*, 317–330.

Cabeza, R., Dolcos, F., Prince, S.A., Rice, H.J., Weissman, D.H., & Nyberg, L. (2003). Attention-related activity during episodic memory retrieval: A cross-function fMRI study. *Neuropsychologia*, *41*, 390–399.

Cabeza, R., & Nyberg, L. (1997). Imaging cognition: An empirical review of PET studies with normal subjects. *Journal of Cognitive Neuroscience*, *9*, 1–26.

Cabeza, R., & Nyberg, L. (2000). Imaging cognition II: An empirical review of 275 PET and fMRI studies. *Journal of Cognitive Neuroscience*, *12*, 1–47.

Cabeza, R., & Nyberg, L. (2003). Seeing the forest through the trees: The cross-function approach to imaging cognition. In A. Zani & A.M. Proverbio (Eds.), *The cognitive electrophysiology of mind and brain* (pp. 41–68). Oxford: Elsevier Science.

Collette, F., & Van der Linden, M. (2002). Brain imaging of the central executive component of working memory. *Neuroscience & Biobehavioral Reviews*, *26*, 105–125.

Courtney, S.M., Ungerleider, L.G., Keil, K., & Haxby, J.V. (1997). Tranisent and sustained neural activity in a distributed neural system for human working memory. *Nature*, *386*, 608–611.

Dehaene, S., Naccache, L., Cohen, L., Le Bihan, D., Mangin, J.-F., Poline, J.-B. et al. (2001). Cerebral mechanisms of word masking and unconscious repetition priming. *Nature Neuroscience*, *4*, 752–758.

Donaldson, D.I., & Buckner, R.L. (2001). Effective paradigm design. In P. Jezzard, P.M. Matthews, & S. Smith (Eds.), *Functional MRI: An introduction to methods* (pp. 177–195). New York: Oxford University Press.

Eriksson, J., Larsson, A., Riklund Åhlström, K., & Nyberg, L. (2004). Visual consciousness: Dissociating the neural correlates of perceptual transitions from sustained perception with fMRI. *Consciousness and Cognition*, *13*, 61–72.

Feinstein, J.S., Stein, M.B., Castillo, G.N., & Paulus, M.P. (2004). From sensory processes to conscious perception. *Consciousness and Cognition, 13*, 323–335.

Gazzaniga, M.S. (2000). *The new cognitive neurosciences* (2nd ed.). Cambridge, MA: MIT Press.

Henson, R.N.A. et al. (1999). Recollection and familiarity in recognition memory: An event-related functional magnetic resonance imaging study. *Journal of Neuroscience, 19*, 3962–3972.

James, W. (1890). *The principles of psychology* (Vols. 1 & 2). New York: Dover Publications, Inc.

Kjaer, T.W., Nowak, M., Kjaer, K.W., Lou, A.R., & Lou, H.C. (2001). Precuneus–prefrontal activity during awareness of visual verbal stimuli. *Consciousness and Cognition, 10*, 356–365.

LaBar, K.S., Gitelman, D.R., Parrish, T.B., & Mesulam, M-M. (1999). Neuroanatomic overlap of working memory and spatial attention networks: A functional MRI comparison within subjects. *NeuroImage, 10*, 695–704.

Logothetis, N.K., Pauls, J., Augath, M., Trinath, T., & Oeltermann, A. (2001). Neurophysiological investigation of the fMRI signal. *Nature, 412*, 150–157.

Marklund, P., Nyberg, L., Fransson, P., Ingvar, M., Petersson, K.M., & Cabeza, R. (2003). *Similarities and differences in state- and item-related BOLD signal changes during long-term memory tasks: A test of the working-memory hypothesis.* Poster presented at the First NorFA Meeting: Functional Neuroimaging Network, Södergarn, Sweden, 28–31 August 2003.

Miyake, A., Friedman, N.P., Emerson, M.J., Witzki, A.H., Howerter, A., & Wager, T.D. (2000). The unity and diversity of executive functions and their contributions to complex "frontal lobe" tasks: A latent variable analysis. *Cognitive Psychology, 41*, 49–100.

Naghavi, H.R., & Nyberg, L. (2005). Common fronto-parietal activity in attention, memory, and consciousness: Shared demands on integration? *Consciousness and Cognition, 14*, 390–425.

Nyberg, L., Cabeza, R., & Tulving, E. (1996). PET studies of encoding and retrieval: The HERA model. *Psychonomic Bulletin & Review, 3*, 135–148.

Nyberg, L., Marklund, P., Persson, J., Cabeza, R., Forkstam, C., Petersson, K.M. et al. (2003). Common prefrontal activations during working memory, episodic memory, and semantic memory. *Neuropsychologia, 41*, 371–377.

Nyberg, L., McIntosh, A.R., Houle, S., Nilsson, L.-G., & Tulving, E. (1996). Activation of medial temporal structures during episodic memory retrieval. *Nature, 380*, 715–717.

Nyberg, L., Petersson K.M., Cabeza, R., Forkstam, C., & Ingvar, M. (2002). Brain imaging of human memory systems: Between-systems similarities and within-system differences. *Cognitive Brain Research, 13*, 281–292.

Nyberg, L., Tulving, E., Habib, R., Nilsson, L.-G., Kapur, S., Houle, S. et al. (1995). Functional brain maps of retrieval mode and recovery of episodic information. *NeuroReport, 7*, 249–252.

Ogawa, S., & Lee, T.M. (1990). Magnetic resonance imaging of blood vessels at high fields: In vivo and in vitro measurements and image simulation. *Magnetic. Resonance Medicine, 16*, 9–18.

Petit, L., Courtney, S.M., Ungerleider, L.G., & Haxby, J.V. (1998). Sustained activity in the medial wall during working memory delays. *Journal of Neuroscience, 18*, 9429–9437.

Portas, C.M., Strange, B.A., Friston, K.J., Dolan, R.J., & Frith, C.D. (2000). How does the brain sustain a visual percept? *Proceedings of the Royal Society of London: Biological Sciences*, *267*, 845–850.

Raichle, M.E. (2001). Functional neuroimaging: A historical and physiological perspective. In R. Cabeza & A. Kingstone (Eds.), *Handbook of functional neuroimaging of cognition* (pp. 3–26). Cambridge, MA: MIT Press.

Ranganath, C., & D'Esposito, M. (2001). Medial temporal lobe activity associated with active maintenance of novel information. *Neuron*, *31*, 865–873.

Ranganath, C., Johnson, M.K., & D'Esposito, M. (2003). Prefrontal activity associated with working memory and episodic long-term memory. *Neuropsychologia*, *41*, 378–390.

Rees, G., Kreiman, G., & Koch, C. (2002). Neural correlates of consciousness in humans. *Nature Reviews Neuroscience*, *3*, 261–270.

Sakai, K., & Passingham, R.E. (2003). Prefrontal interactions reflect future task operations. *Nature Neuroscience*, *6*, 75–81.

Squire, L.R. (1992) Memory and the hippocampus: A synthesis from findings with rats, monkeys, and humans. *Psychological Review*, *99*, 195–231.

Sterzer, P., Russ, M.O., Preibisch, C., & Kleinschmidt, A. (2002). Neural correlates of spontaneous direction reversals in ambiguous apparent visual motion. *NeuroImage*, *15*, 908–916.

Tong, F., Nakayama, K., Vaughan, J.T., & Kanwisher N. (1998). Binocular rivalry and visual awareness in human extrastriate cortex. *Neuron*, *21*, 753–759.

10 The divided brain

Michael C. Corballis

Our bodies and brains are largely bilaterally symmetrical, an arrangement that goes back at least to the Bilateria, a lineage dating from some 600 million years ago (Chen et al., 2004) which includes over 1.5 million present-day animal species, including humans. Its emergence marks the transition from stationary or drifting planktonic animals to active swimmers and burrowers. Bilateral asymmetry was probably an adaptation to directional movement, which defines an anterior–posterior axis in addition to the dorsal–ventral one. The third axis, orthogonal to these two, is the left–right axis, and organs of movement are then arranged symmetrically to either side of this axis, presumably to ensure linear movement. With very few exceptions, legs, wings, swimming muscles (in fish), and flippers are bilaterally symmetrical.

The bilateral symmetry of the organs of movement then creates pressure to ensure bilateral symmetry of the sense organs. The eyes, ears, and skin senses are evenly placed on either side, since any asymmetry could leave the organism exposed to attack, or impervious to prey, on the weaker flank. It follows from the symmetry of the motor and sensory organs that the neural machinery for both action and perception is also for the most part symmetrical. For most animals, behavior is dominated by sensorimotor activity, involving reactions to an environment that is without overall left–right bias. Symmetry is much less apparent in parts of the body not involved in locomotion or sensorimotor behavior. The internal organs, including the heart, lungs, and stomach, are arranged asymmetrically, presumably for more efficient packaging. But the brain, with its origins in sensorimotor activity, remains for the most part built on a bilaterally symmetrical plan.

The brain is not only symmetrical; it is also *double*. In treating intractable epilepsy, surgeons sometimes resort to commissurotomy, splitting the brain through the midsagittal plane to disconnect the left and right halves. Roger W. Sperry, who pioneered the psychological investigation of the split brain, wrote that split-brained patients behave as if they had "two separate conscious entities or minds running in parallel in the same cranium, each with its own sensations, perceptions, cognitive processes, learning experiences, memories and so on" (Sperry, 1966–67, p. 318). People can also function remarkably well following the removal of an entire cerebral cortex (e.g.,

Hertz-Pannier et al., 2002). These observations suggest limitations on the popular notion that the two sides of the brain serve complementary functions.

Brain evolution suggests rather a trade-off between symmetry and lateralization. With respect to basic perceptual and motor functions, there are clear benefits to bilateral symmetry, given that we live in a world that is mostly without systematic left–right biases. We have nevertheless created left–right asymmetries in the manufactured world, such as the direction of script, traffic conventions, and so forth. Some of these are disadvantageous to left-handers – such as scissors, corkscrews, or the placement of door handles. Generally, the advantages of symmetry apply more to behaviors that are reactions to the environment than operations on the environment. There may be advantages to having one hand or its controlling cerebral hemisphere specialized for intricate activities involving tools, as in writing, for example. One advantage of unilateral control is that it is not constrained by the relatively slow conduction time between hemispheres, so that computations can be carried out with greater speed (Ringo, Doty, Demeter, & Simard, 1994). Another advantage of hemispheric specialization is that it avoids duplication, which is a waste of neural space, and may lead to interhemispheric conflict (Corballis, 1991).

It is often claimed that cerebral asymmetry is exclusive to humans, perhaps even a defining characteristic (e.g., Corballis, 1991). Most people are right-handed, and most are also left-cerebrally dominant for language. Genetic theories of these asymmetries typically postulate that they arose from a genetic mutation in the hominid lineage (e.g., Annett, 1995, 2002; Corballis, 1997; McManus, 1999). It has even been proposed that this mutation not only resulted in cerebral asymmetry, but also gave birth to language, theory of mind, a vulnerability to psychosis, and the speciation of *Homo sapiens* (Crow, 2002).

Humans are cognitive specialists, with large brains even by primate standards (Passingham, 1982), so there may be some truth to the idea that cerebral asymmetry makes us special. The evolution of cognition and the relative independence from stimulus control may well have favored hemispheric specialization at the expense of bilateral symmetry. But it is increasingly clear that cerebral and behavioral asymmetries are widespread in nature, and that at least some of the asymmetries observed in other species operate according to principles similar to those documented in humans. Consequently, any sense that humans are special may derive, not from cerebral asymmetry per se, but from the nature of the functions that are lateralized.

The following section reviews evidence for animal asymmetries, emphasizing those that may provide insight into the nature and origins of our own lopsidedness. I focus on population-level asymmetries – that is, asymmetries that go in the same direction in the majority of the population – which may be contrasted with fluctuation asymmetries, in which the direction varies at random. Population-level asymmetries, such as handedness and cerebral dominance for language, imply some degree of genetic programming, and are probably dependent on evolutionary contingencies.

Lateral asymmetries in nonhumans and humans

Visual asymmetries

Lateral asymmetries in vision have been widely documented in birds. For example, New Caledonian crows appear to favor the right eye, and therefore the left hemisphere, when constructing digging tools from pandanus leaves (Hunt, Corballis, & Gray, 2001). Not only does this parallel the human preference for the right hand (left hemisphere) in tool making and tool use, but it also suggests that manufacture itself – and its cultural transmission – may not be unique to humans (Hunt & Gray, 2003).

Chicks show a right-eye advantage in fine visual discrimination, suggesting a left-hemispheric advantage. This arises because the right eye is exposed to light in the egg, prior to hatching, whereas the left eye is not (Rogers, 1990). Nevertheless it appears to have adaptive significance. Chicks raised without this pre-hatching asymmetry do not show the bias, and are disadvantaged relative to lateralized birds in monitoring a hovering predator while discriminating grain from non-edible grit (Rogers, 2002a). This suggests that the lateralized brain is better able to carry out two tasks at once. The avian right hemisphere is also better able to make use of the large-scale geometry of the environment when re-orienting in space (Vallortigara, Pagni, & Sovrano, 2004). A left-hemispheric advantage for fine-grained analysis and a right-hemisphere advantage for more global vision have also been well documented in humans (Ivry & Robertson, 1998).

Vocalization

Vocalization is largely under the control of the left hemisphere in many species, even the frog (Bauer, 1993), suggesting an ancestry going back to the very origins of the vocal cords 170 million years ago. In passerine birds, too, vocalization seems to be controlled by the left hemisphere (Nottebohm, 1977 – but see Goller & Suthers, 1995). Marmosets open the right side of the mouth wider when making social contact calls, implying left cerebral dominance, but the left side wider when expressing fear, implying right cerebral dominance for emotion (Hook-Costigan & Rogers, 1998). This pattern mimics that found in humans, with the right side of the mouth dominant for speech (e.g., Graves & Potter, 1988) and the left for emotional expression (Davidson, 1995). These asymmetries are also evident in 5- to 12-month-old human babies, who open the right side wider when babbling, and the left side wider when smiling (Holowka & Petitto, 2002). In adults, the asymmetry even influences the McGurk effect, in which the perception of spoken syllables depends as much on movements of the mouth as on the actual sounds emitted (McGurk & MacDonald, 1976). This effect is present when viewers see only the right side of the mouth, not when they see the left side (Nicholls, Searle, & Bradshaw, 2004).

Asymmetries for vocalization apply to perception as well as production. A left-hemispheric advantage for the perception of species-specific vocalizations has been demonstrated in mice (Ehert, 1987), rhesus monkeys (Hauser & Anderson, 1994), and Japanese macaques (Heffner & Heffner, 1984). In chimpanzees, the left temporal planum is larger on the left than on the right (Gannon, Holloway, Broadfield, & Braun, 1998; Hopkins, Marino, Rilling, & MacGregor, 1998), an asymmetry that is well documented in humans (e.g., Foundas, Leonard, Gilmore, Fennell, & Heilman, 1996). This too may reflect an asymmetry in the perception of species-specific vocal communication.

Behavioral asymmetries

Many species show consistent biases in overt behavior, such as turning to escape predators or to attack prey. Faced with a barrier through which a predator is visible, some fish species show population-level biases to turn left or right, while others do not (Bisazza, Cantalupo, Capocchiano, & Vallortigara, 2000). These biases were correlated with the gregariousness of the species, suggesting a social influence – species that swim together turn together, presumably to avoid collisions. Tadpoles are biased to turn left when escaping a predator, but to turn right when surfacing for air (Rogers, 2002b). A right-hemisphere bias for social responses is apparent in fish (Sovrano, Bisazza, & Vallortigara, 2001), chicks (Vallortigara & Andrew, 1994), sheep (Peirce, Leigh, & Kendrick, 2000), and monkeys (Vermeire, Hamilton, & Erdmann 1998), and may relate to the right-hemispheric involvement in social understanding in humans (e.g., Sperry, Zaidel, & Zaidel, 1979). The right hemisphere is also the more specialized for aggression in toads (e.g., Rogers, 2002b), lizards (Deckel, 1995), chicks (Howard, Rogers, & Boura, 1980), baboons (Casperd & Dunbar, 1996), and humans (Devinsky et al., 1994).

The left hemisphere, though, is dominant for feeding. Chicks (Deng & Rogers, 1997), pigeons (Güntürkun, 1985), zebra finches (Alonso, 1998), and toads (Vallortigara, Rogers, Bisazza, Lippolis, & Robins, 1998) respond to prey or feeding matter preferentially with the right eye. This may be related to left-hemispheric control of the mouth, an asymmetry that may be widespread in vertebrates and may also relate to the left-hemispheric control of vocalization (Andrew, Tommasi, & Ford, 2000).

Handedness

The clearest case of limb asymmetry in nonhumans comes, not from primates, but from parrots. Some 90% of parrots show a strong preference for the left foot in picking up objects, a bias comparable to that of human right-handedness (Rogers, 1980). Second place may go to the walrus, since some 77% of them prefer the right flipper when feeding, and several bones are longer in the right than in the left flipper (Levermann, Galatius, Ehlme,

Rysgaard, & Born, 2003). There have been claims that monkeys show a preference for the left hand (MacNeilage, Studdert-Kennedy, & Lindblom, 1987), but the evidence has been mixed. If true, this asymmetry may reflect a right-hemispheric bias for spatial perception.

McGrew and Marchant (1997) sound a caution, concluding that, among nonhuman primates, "only chimpanzees show signs of a population bias . . . to the right, but only in captivity and only incompletely" (p. 201). The evidence for a right-hand preference in chimpanzees comes from Hopkins and his colleagues, but appears to be restricted to certain activities, such as extracting peanut butter from a glass tube (Hopkins, 1996) or gestural communication (Hopkins & Leavens, 1998), and the ratio of right- to left-handers is only about 2:1, whereas in humans it is about 8:1. This bias in captive chimpanzees may be a consequence of human contact (Marchant & McGrew, 2001), although this is disputed (Hopkins, Wesley, Izard, Hook, & Schapiro, 2004).

Summary

The above review is by no means exhaustive. It should serve, however, to illustrate that humans are not unique in displaying asymmetries. Moreover, some of the principles underlying these asymmetries seem to apply to both human and nonhuman species. The right hemispheric is the more specialized for emotion, aggression, social behavior, and holistic perception, the left for detailed visual analysis, feeding behavior, and species-specific communication. These asymmetries probably vary between species, depending on ecological or social factors.

Rarely are the asymmetries absolute – each hemisphere, for example, appears to have some capacity to undertake the specialty of the other. Further, not all members of the species show the same directional asymmetry, despite the overall population bias. The percentage of individuals who reverse the dominant asymmetry ranges from some 10% to 35% (Ghirlanda & Vallortigara, 2004). This suggests a trade-off between symmetry and asymmetry, and one or other may dominate depending on survival contingencies.

Cerebral and manual asymmetries in humans

The false idea that cerebral asymmetry is uniquely human may reflect an age-old desire to place humans above other species, closer to angels than to apes. Nevertheless, part of the reason our lopsidedness seems so salient is that it applies to activities that are themselves characteristically human, if not uniquely so. Handedness is most obvious in tool use, as in writing, hammering, or throwing. Such activities are themselves characteristically human, although whether they place us close to angels may be debated. Moreover, it is generally agreed that true language is uniquely human (e.g., Chomsky, 1966; Pinker, 1994). Hence any sense of human uniqueness may apply to the activities that are lateralized, rather than to the lateralization itself.

Left-cerebral dominance for language nevertheless remains a distinctive feature of the human brain, and may well be more pronounced than asymmetries associated with communication in other species. Speech production has been identified with Broca's area in the left frontal cortex, but the left precentral area of the insula may actually be more critical (Dronkers, 1996). The distinguishing characteristic of language relative to other forms of communication is grammar, which, although associated with Broca's area, probably involves widespread and diffuse regions of the left hemisphere (Dick et al., 2001). Cerebral asymmetry for language was corroborated by work on the split brain, which again revealed only the left side to be capable of articulate speech (Sperry, 1966–67, 1974, 1982). This work also rather surprisingly showed that the right hemispheres of at least some split-brained patients were capable of comprehension, albeit at a less sophisticated level than the left hemisphere (Zaidel, 1976). Gazzaniga (1983) maintained that right-hemisphere comprehension is the exception rather than the rule, but Zaidel (1983) in turn disputed this. This issue remains unresolved.

Brain imaging has further demonstrated the dominance of the left hemisphere in language. Broca's area is larger on the left than on the right in most people (Foundas et al., 1996), as is the temporal planum. Functional imaging shows that areas of the left hemisphere are activated during both the production (e.g., Heim & Friederici, 2003) and comprehension (e.g., Springer et al., 1999) of speech. Left-hemisphere dominance for speech perception is evident from fMRI recordings even in 3-month-old infants (Dehaene-Lambertz, Dehaene, & Hertz-Pannier, 2002).

Although the right hemisphere has some involvement in language processing (e.g., Gernsbacher & Kaschak, 2003), it is clear that in most people language is largely left-hemispheric, occupying widespread circuits in that hemisphere. This may also explain a striking *right*-hemisphere dominance for spatial attention. Right-hemisphere damage often produces a neglect of the left side of space, whereas comparable damage to the left hemisphere seldom produces the reverse asymmetry. Although the parietal lobe is usually implicated in neglect, Karnath, Ferber, and Himmelbach (2001) have argued that the critical area is actually the right-hemispheric homologous to Wernicke's area, suggesting that the asymmetry may have been a secondary consequence of language representation in the left hemisphere (see Corballis, 1991). There is no evidence for any asymmetry in spatial attention in animals comparable to that demonstrated by left hemineglect in humans (Driver & Vuilleumier, 2001).

Right-handedness in humans may also be a consequence of cerebral asymmetry for speech. Along with others, I have argued that language itself may derive from manual gestures, rather than from primate calls (Armstrong, Stokoe, & Wilcox, 1995; Corballis, 2001b; Hewes, 1973; Rizzolatti & Arbib, 1998). If this is so, the shift from gestural to vocal language was presumably gradual, so that language for much of our recent evolutionary history was a combination of the two. As we saw earlier, left-hemispheric control of vocalization may go back far in evolution, so the gradual assimilation of vocalization into the language system may have lateralized the neural circuits involved (Corballis, 2003). Indeed, people habitually gesture with their hands while they speak, and in right-handers the right hand predominates (Kimura, 1973). This account might explain why the extreme right-handedness observed in the human population is not evident in nonhuman primates. It may have had a spin-off in recent human evolution. As vocalization gradually took over, so the hands were released for other activities, such as tool making, resulting in the manual specialization and sophisticated manufacture evident in modern human society. The release of the hands may explain what has come to be termed the "human revolution" that took place some 40,000 years ago in Europe, and probably earlier in Africa (Corballis, 2004).

Genetic models

Despite our predominant right-handedness, a minority remains stubbornly left-handed or ambidextrous. Similarly, language in a minority is right-hemispheric, and sometimes bilateral. The asymmetry in language representation, moreover, is loosely correlated with handedness (Knecht et al., 2000). There is at least a weak parental influence on handedness, as revealed in data summarized by McManus and Bryden (1992) – see Table 10.1. Although it is clear that handedness does not "breed true", a single-gene model can accommodate the data reasonably well.

In 1972, Annett published the remarkable insight that the true dichotomy may not be between left- and right-handers, but rather between right-handers and those without any genetic predisposition to be either left- or right-handed. A similar principle underlies other genetically determined asymmetries, such as that of the heart and other visceral organs (Layton, 1976). In the most recent formulation of her theory, Annett (2002) proposed a single locus for what she calls the right shift (RS) gene. One allele, designated RS+, shifts the distribution of differences in manual performance from one with a

Table 10.1 Percentage of left-handed offspring by parental combination, and prediction from McManus's model

	Parental handedness		
	R–R	*R–L*	*L–L*
% left-handed offspring	9.5	19.5	26.1
Predicted by McManus's model with $p(D) = .76$	9.45	20.24	28.87

Reproduced with the author's permission from part of Table 1 of the article "The genetics and evolution of handedness" by M.C. Corballis, and published in *Psychological Review*, Volume 104, pp. 714–727, 1997. Copyright is held by the American Psychological Association.

mean difference of zero to one with a mean difference favoring the right hand. The other, designated RS–, has no directional influence.

Since individuals inherit two alleles, this gives rise to three genotypes. In those carrying two RS+ alleles, designated RS++, the distribution is strongly shifted to the right. In heterozygotes, RS+–, the distribution is less strongly shifted to the right, while in those carrying two RS– alleles, RS– –, the distribution is centered on zero. The two alleles may therefore be considered to underlie the trade-off between symmetry and asymmetry, and they are maintained in balance in the population by a heterozygote advantage in fitness. Annett makes it clear that the RS gene influences cerebral dominance rather than handedness per se.

McManus (1999) has proposed a similar theory but, unlike Annett, argues that handedness is better defined in terms of a binary preference rather than a performance difference: We are either right-handed or left-handed. He too postulates a single gene with a dextral (D) allele coding for right-handedness and left cerebral dominance for speech, and a chance (C) allele leaving these asymmetries to chance. DD homozygotes are assumed to be right-handed and left-cerebrally dominant for speech, while CC homozygotes are equally divided among the four combinations of handedness and speech dominance. Among DC heterozygotes, 75% are right-handed and, independently of that, 75% are left-cerebrally dominant for speech.

Both models provide good fits to the data on the inheritance of handedness. Table 10.1 shows how McManus's model fits, with the proportion *p*(D) of D alleles in the population estimated at .76. This might seem high, but perhaps reflects a society in which dextrality, or left-cerebral dominance, has greater adaptive fitness than the lack of consistent handedness or cerebral dominance. Variations in this parameter might explain cultural differences in handedness, although the heterozygotic advantage ensures that both alleles are maintained in the population. Figure 10.1 shows how the asymptotic value of *p*(D) varies depending on the relative fitness of CC and DD genotypes.

The models can also account for the relations between handedness and language dominance. Studies based on the Wada test (Rasmussen & Milner, 1977), electroconvulsive therapy (ECT) (Warrington & Pratt, 1973), and brain imaging (Knecht et al., 2000; Pujol, Deus, Losilla, & Capdevila, 1999) are reasonably consistent in showing that over 90% of right-handers are left-cerebrally dominant for language, as are some 70% of left-handers. McManus's model, on the assumption that *p*(D) = .76, predicts that 90.6% of right-handers and 69% of left-handers will be left-cerebrally dominant for language – figures reasonably close to empirically determined values.

Both Annett and McManus assume that the mutation that gave rise to the RS+ or D allele occurred in hominid evolution. McManus (1999) has speculated that it may have occurred in one of the genes creating the leftward asymmetry of the heart, allowing the asymmetry to affect neural tissue as well as the heart rudiment. It seems entirely possible, though, that similar

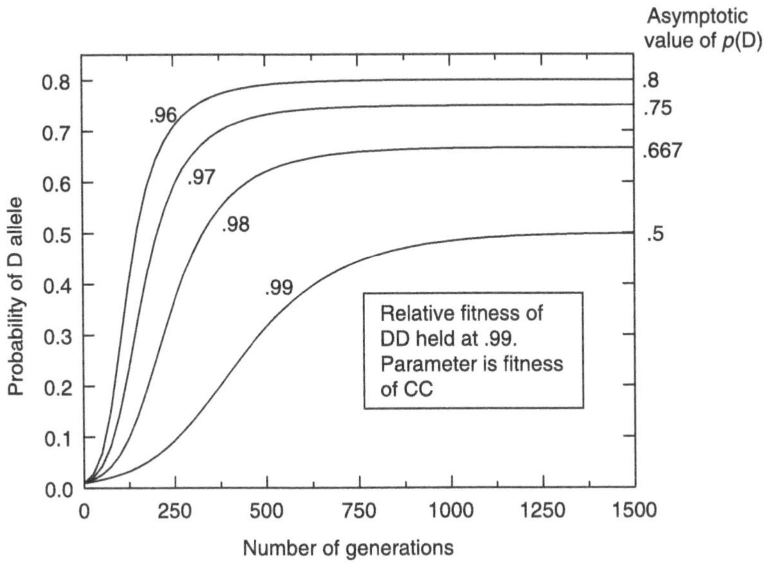

Figure 10.1 Suppose a mutation creates a dextral allele D in 1% of a population. The figure shows the increase in the probability of the D allele, *p*(D), over successive generations. In this example, the relative fitness of the CD genotype is held at 1.0 and that of the DD genotype at 0.99. The rise of the D allele is shown for four different fitnesses: 0.99, 0.98, 0.97, and 0.96, yielding different asymptotic values of *p*(D). The asymptote would be less than 0.5 if the fitness of the CC genotype were to exceed that of the DD genotype. At asymptote, the ratio of *p*(D): *p*(C) is given by $(1–f_{CC})$:$(1–f_{DD})$, where f_{DD} and f_{CC} are the fitnesses of DD and CC genotypes relative to that of the CD genotype.

genetic influences may explain the cerebral asymmetries in other species. Across many species, the proportion of individuals reversing the population-level bias ranges from about 10% to about 35% (Ghirlanda & Vallortigara, 2004), and both extremes are evident in humans. Some asymmetries, such as a right-ear advantage in dichotic listening, right-eye dominance, and a host of postural asymmetries including a right head-turning tendency in newborns, favor one side over the other in the ratio of 2:1 (Previc, 1991). This ratio also matches that favoring right-handedness in captive chimpanzees (Hopkins, 1996).

The D (or RS+) allele may operate against a prior asymmetry of 67% right-handedness; in this formulation, the proportion of left-handers in the CC (or RS– –) genotype should be 33%, not 50% (Corballis, 1997). In fitting her model to the data, Annett (1995) obtained almost exactly this value. Perhaps, then, there are (at least) two genetic influences, one creating a two-thirds majority with the same directional asymmetry, and the other increasing it to about 90%. These influences may operate in many different species, perhaps explaining why the modal values seem to be around 67% and 90%.

The gene or genes that create these biases remain hypothetical, although there have been some leads. Crow (2002) argued that the laterality gene is located in the Xq21.3/Yp11.2 region of homology on the X and Y chromosomes, and suggested protocadherinXY as a likely candidate. An argument against this is that polymorphisms are unstable on the Y chromosome, although it is possible that the gene is on the X chromosome alone (Corballis, 2001a). However, a genome-wide search has since offered little support for X-linkage, and suggests the region 2p11.2–12 on chromosome 2 as a better bet (Francks et al., 2002). Further analysis revealed significant paternal linkage within this site (Francks et al., 2003), suggesting that imprinting may play a role. But it is perhaps unlikely that single-gene models will provide the whole answer, although they provide a useful starting point.

The trade-off between symmetry and asymmetry

What, then, are the relative advantages of D and C alleles (to use, without prejudice, McManus's terminology)? In so far as the D allele stands for asymmetry and the C allele for symmetry, they capture something of the trade-off alluded to earlier. Part of the trade-off may have to do with the relative advantages of language and spatial ability. Annett (2002) proposed that left-cerebral dominance for language is achieved through the "pruning" of the right hemisphere, with some loss of spatial function. Thus DD individuals may benefit from left-hemispheric dominance for language and manual function, but at the expense of spatial abilities. CC individuals may be at risk of divided hemispheric control over speech, with increased risk of stuttering (Foundas et al., 2003) and reading disability (Annett, 2002), but may benefit from greater spatial awareness and more balanced motor skill. Heterozygotic DC individuals may be less prone to either deficiency, and so have the better of both worlds.

A study of 12,770 11-year-olds in the UK suggests that the deficits shown by CC individuals may extend beyond language abilities. The children's handedness was assessed in a test of skill (checking squares). Their scores on verbal ability, nonverbal ability, reading comprehension, and mathematical ability all showed a dip at the point of equality between the hands (Crow, Crow, Done, & Leask, 1998). Assuming CC individuals were more likely to be represented at the point of equality than either DC or DD individuals, this result suggests that they are at greater risk of poor academic performance. Crow et al. (1998) refer to ambidexterity as "the point of hemispheric indecision" – the symmetrical brain is unable to make up its mind. The risk of impediment in CC individuals is still relatively small, since many will display asymmetry in one or other direction by chance.

What, then, are the compensatory advantages of a more symmetrical brain? Many prominent athletes and sportspeople have mixed dominance, such as batting right-handed and bowling left-handed in cricket, perhaps deriving their benefit from an extra measure of perceptual and motor balance.

Left-handers may also benefit precisely from being in a minority, providing an element of surprise in fighting, or in sports such as tennis or baseball (Raymond, Pontier, Dufour, & Moller, 1996). A more subtle argument has to do with escape from predation. If most members of a group turn left to escape a predator, individuals among the left-turning mob are less likely to be caught than are those who turn right. However a predator may well chase the left-turners since there is a better chance of capturing at least one victim. There may therefore be an advantage in being among a right-turning minority, but only so long as it *is* a minority (Ghirlanda & Vallortigara, 2004).

Variation in cerebral asymmetry may also lead to different cognitive styles. Barnett and Corballis (2002) found that the relation between magical ideation and handedness was the reverse of that between intellectual achievements and handedness: Mixed-handers were the most prone to magical ideation, characterized by mild paranoia and superstition, and scores on magical ideation decreased as handedness became more extreme in either direction. Mixed handedness – or perhaps "hemispheric indecision" – is also associated with a greater sensitivity to sensory illusions (Niebauer, Aselage, & Schutte, 2002) and schizophrenia (e.g., Claridge, Clark, Davis, & Mason, 1998), and belief in the paranormal seems to be associated with symmetrical brain activity (Pizzagalli et al., 2000).

Jaynes (1976) speculated that cerebral asymmetry emerged in the second millennium BCE in response to various catastrophes, such as floods, invasions, and eruptions. Prior to this, people were governed by hallucinations, invoking the gods, but cerebral asymmetry allowed the left hemisphere to create a sense of self, with people taking responsibility for their own actions. Jaynes's theory makes little evolutionary sense, since human handedness and cerebral asymmetry almost certainly go back at least 2 million years (Corballis, 1997). Nevertheless there may well be some truth to the idea that cerebral asymmetry underlies rational thought, and that a lack of asymmetry leads to more delusional and perhaps hallucinatory thinking.

At least some of these thought processes may be linked to religion. Although religious activities may seem irrational and sometimes counterproductive, they may have been selected because they promote inter-group alliances (Hayden, 1987). Others have argued that religion is a system used by elites to maintain social control (e.g., Cronk, 1994). While this implies a social rather than an evolutionary origin, there may well have been selection of those predisposed to accept arbitrary leadership. Obedience is a common religious virtue. Religion is undoubtedly a complex phenomenon, but still a universal one, and is in many respects at odds with scientific rationalism. The trade-off between symmetry and asymmetry, or the C and D alleles, may therefore have a bearing on the age-old struggle between religion and science, exemplified in religious opposition to such scientific luminaries as Charles Darwin and Galileo, or indeed in scientific opposition to religion.

Magical thinking may also be related to creativity. Leonhard and Brugger (1988) note a link between paranormal thought, delusional thought, and creativity, and relate this to right-hemispheric activation, but it may have to do with lack of cerebral dominance rather than with right-hemisphere function itself. The evidence of Crow et al. (1998) notwithstanding, Singh and O'Boyle (2004) report that mathematically gifted adolescents show no hemispheric asymmetry on tasks involving global–local judgments and matching letters, whereas average-ability adolescents and college students show a left-hemispheric advantage, suggesting that the mathematically gifted may lack cerebral asymmetry.

Two individuals who may serve as CC icons are Leonardo da Vinci and Albert Einstein. Leonardo was the prototypical "Renaissance Man", artist, scientist, and inventor. He was left-handed, and habitually wrote backwards. Einstein was probably right-handed, but was said to be slow to develop speech and a slow learner, and post-mortem analysis of his brain revealed "an unusual symmetry between the hemispheres" (Witelson, Kigar, & Harvey, 1999, p. 2151), especially in the occipital and parietal lobes. He is also reported to have said "I want to know how God created this world."

Conclusions

The brain and nervous system are built on a bilaterally symmetrical plan. Yet symmetry is readily broken if there are advantages in lateralization of function. Handedness and cerebral asymmetry are examples, but there are countless other examples in the animal world, some of which are precursors to our own lopsidedness. However, these asymmetries are not absolute, and there are individual differences both within and between species, implying a degree of genetic control. The simplest genetic theories postulate a single laterality gene with one allele specifying a directional asymmetry and another leaving the direction of asymmetry to chance. If there is indeed a genetic component to cerebral asymmetry, it may well provide an important basis for individual differences, perhaps creating a balance between the complementary advantages and disadvantages of bilateral symmetry and lateralization.

Cerebral asymmetry is not uniquely human, but some lateralized functions may well be unique to our species. This applies especially to language, which requires widespread neural circuitry, and occupies a good proportion of the left hemisphere, which may in turn have created a complementary asymmetry in the right hemisphere for spatial attention. Right-handedness is also exceptionally developed in humans. Yet not all humans show these high degrees of asymmetry, and there may be some advantages to an unlateralized brain that offset the advantages of lateralization. Some of these advantages may come about precisely because those who possess them are in a minority. If nearly all tennis players were left-handed, the advantage of surprise would be transferred to the right-handed.

Is there an ultimate source of biological asymmetries? Ivan Beale and I once wrote:

> Could there be a link between the asymmetry of nuclear decay, the asymmetry of living molecules, and the left–right gradient which seems to underlie the morphological asymmetries of animals and men, including cerebral asymmetries in the human brain? We have no idea.
>
> (Corballis & Beale, 1976, p. 197)

McManus (2002) has bravely tried to find that cosmic link. But that's another story.

Acknowledgments

The ideas in this chapter have benefited from personal contact with a number of people, including Ivan Beale, Tim Crow, Russell Gray, Bill Hopkins, Gavin Hunt, Chris McManus, Lesley Rogers, Giorgio Vallortigara, and Faraneh Vargha-Khadem. They do not necessarily agree with me.

References

Alonso, V. (1998). Lateralization of visual guided behaviour during feeding in zebra finches (*Taeniopygia guttata*). *Behavioral Processes*, *43*, 257–263.

Andrew, R.J., Tommasi, L., & Ford, N. (2000). Motor control by vision and the evolution of cerebral lateralization. *Brain and Language*, *73*, 330–335.

Annett, M. (1972). The distribution of manual asymmetry. *British Journal of Psychology*, *63*, 343–358.

Annett, M. (1995). The right shift theory of a genetically balanced polymorphism for cerebral dominance and cognitive processing. *Current Psychology of Cognition*, *14*, 427–80.

Annett, M. (2002). *Handedness and brain asymmetry: The right shift theory*. Hove, UK: Psychology Press.

Armstrong, D.F., Stokoe, W.C., & Wilcox, S.E. (1995). *Gesture and the nature of language*. Cambridge: Cambridge University Press.

Barnett, K.J., & Corballis, M.C. (2002). Ambidexterity and magical ideation. *Laterality*, *7*, 75–84.

Bauer, R.H. (1993). Lateralization of neural control for vocalization by the frog (*Rana pipiens*). *Psychobiology*, *21*, 243–248.

Bisazza, A., Cantalupo, C., Capocchiano, M., & Vallortigara, G. (2000). Population lateralization and social behaviour: A study with 16 species of fish. *Laterality*, *5*, 269–284.

Casperd, J.M., & Dunbar, R.I.M. (1996). Asymmetries in the visual processing emotional cues during agonistic interactions in gelada baboons. *Behavioral Process*, *37*, 57–65.

Chen, J.-Y., Bottjer, D.J., Oliveri, P., Dornbos, S.Q., Gao, F. et al. (2004). Small Bilaterian fossils from 40 to 55 million years before the Cambrian. *Science*, *305*, 218–222.

Chomsky, N. (1966). *Cartesian linguistics: A chapter in the history of rationalist thought*. New York: Harper & Row.

Claridge, G., Clark, K., Davis, C., & Mason, O. (1998). Schizophrenia risk and handedness: A mixed picture. *Laterality*, *3*, 209, 220.

Corballis, M.C. (1991). *The lopsided ape*. New York: Oxford University Press.
Corballis, M.C. (1997). The genetics and evolution of handedness. *Psychological Review*, *104*, 714–727.
Corballis, M.C. (2001a). Is the handedness gene on the X chromosome? *Psychological Review*, *108*, 805–810.
Corballis, M.C. (2001b). *From hand to mouth: The origins of language*. Princeton, NJ: Princeton University Press.
Corballis, M.C. (2003). From mouth to hand: Gesture, speech, and the evolution of right-handedness. *Behavioral and Brain Sciences*, *26*, 198–208.
Corballis, M.C. (2004). The origins of modernity: Was autonomous speech the critical factor? *Psychological Review*, *111*, 543–552.
Corballis, M.C., & Beale, I.L. (1976). *The psychology of left and right*. Hillsdale, NJ: Lawrence Erlbaum Associates Inc.
Cronk, L. (1994). Evolutionary theories of morality and the manipulative use of signals. *Zygon*, *29*, 81–101.
Crow, T.J. (2002). Sexual selection, timing, and an X-Y homologous gene: Did Homo Sapiens speciate on the Y chromosome? In T.J. Crow (Ed.), *The speciation of modern* Homo Sapiens (pp. 197–216). Oxford: Oxford University Press.
Crow, T.J., Crow, L.R., Done, D.J., & Leask, S. (1998). Relative hand skill predicts academic ability: Global deficits at the point of hemispheric indecision. *Neuropsychologia*, *36*, 1275–1282.
Davidson, R.J. (1995). Cerebral asymmetry, emotion, and affective style. In R.J. Davidson & K. Hugdahl (Ed.), *Brain asymmetry* (pp. 361–389). Cambridge, MA: MIT Press.
Deckel, A.W. (1995). Laterality of aggressive responses in *Anolis*. *Journal of Experimental Zoology*, *272*, 194–200.
Dehaene-Lambertz, G., Dehaene, S., & Hertz-Pannier, L. (2002). Functional neuroimaging of speech perception in infants. *Science*, *298*, 2013–2015.
Deng, C., & Rogers, L.J. (1997). Differential contributions of the two visual pathways to functional lateralization in chicks. *Behavioural Brain Research*, *87*, 173–182.
Devinsky, O., Ronsaville, D., Cox, C., Witt, E., Fedio, P., & Theodore, W.H. (1994). Interictal aggression in epilepsy: The Buss-Durkee hostility inventory. *Epilepsia*, *35*, 585–590.
Dick, F., Bates, E., Wulfeck, B., Utman, J.A., Dronkers, N.F., & Gernsbacher, M.A. (2001). Language deficits, localization, and grammar: Evidence for a distributed model of language breakdown in aphasic patients and neurologically intact individuals. *Psychological Review*, *108*, 759–788.
Driver, J., & Vuilleumier, P. (2001). Perceptual awareness and its loss in unilateral neglect and extinction. In S. Dehaene (Ed.), *The cognitive neuroscience of consciousness* (pp. 39–88). Cambridge, MA: MIT Press.
Dronkers, N.F. (1996). A new brain region for coordinating speech articulation. *Nature*, *384*, 159–161.
Ehert, G. (1987). Left hemisphere advantage in the mouse brain for recognizing ultrasonic communication calls. *Nature*, *325*, 249–51.
Foundas, A.L., Corey, D.M., Angelis, V., Bollich, A.M., Crabtree-Hartman, E., & Heilman, K.M. (2003). Atypical cerebral laterality in adults with persistent developmental stuttering. *Neurology*, *61*, 1378–1385.
Foundas, A.L., Leonard, C.M., Gilmore, R.L., Fennell, E.B., & Heilman, K.M.

(1996). Pars triangularis asymmetry and language dominance. *Proceedings of the National Academy of Sciences, USA*, *93*, 719–722.
Francks, C., DeLisi, L.E., Shaw, S.H., Fisher, S.E., Richardson, A.J., Stein, J.F. et al. (2003). Parent of origin effects on handedness and schizophrenia susceptibility on chromosome 2p12-q11. *Human Molecular Genetics*, *12*, 3225–3230.
Francks, C., Fisher, S.E., McPhie, I.L., Richardson, A.J., Marlow, A.J., Stein, J.F. et al. (2002). A genome-wide linkage screen for relative hand skill in sibling pairs. *American Journal of Human Genetics*, *70*, 800–805.
Gannon, P.J., Holloway, R.L., Broadfield, D.C., & Braun, A.R. (1998). Asymmetry of chimpanzee planum temporale: Human-like brain pattern of Wernicke's area homolog. *Science*, *279*, 220–221.
Gazzaniga, M.S. (1983). Right hemisphere language following bisection: A 20-year perspective. *American Psychologist*, *38*, 525–537.
Gernsbacher, M.A., & Kaschak, M.P. (2003). Neuroimaging studies of language production and comprehension. *Annual Review of Psychology*, *54*, 91–114.
Ghirlanda, S., & Vallortigara, G. (2004). The evolution of brain lateralization: A game-theoretical analysis of population structure. *Proceedings of the Royal Society of London*, *271*, 853–857.
Goller, F., & Suthers, R.A. (1995). Implications for lateralization of bird song from unilateral gating of bilateral motor patterns. *Nature*, *373*, 63–63.
Graves, R.E., & Potter, S.M. (1988). Speaking from two sides of the mouth. *Visible Language*, *22*, 129–137.
Güntürkun, O. (1985). Lateralization of visually controlled behavior in pigeons. *Physiology and Behavior*, *34*, 575–577.
Hauser, M.D., & Anderson, K. (1994). Functional lateralization for auditory temporal processing in adult, but not infant rhesus monkeys: Field experiments. *Proceedings of the National Academy of Sciences, USA*, *91*, 3946–3948.
Hayden, B. (1987). Alliances and religious ecstasy: Human responses to resource stress. *Journal of the Scientific Study of Religion*, *26*, 81–91.
Heffner, H.E., & Heffner, R.S. (1984). Temporal lobe lesions and perception of species-specific vocalizations by Japanese macaques. *Science*, *226*, 75–76.
Heim, S., & Friederici, A.D. (2003). Phonological processing in language production: Time course of brain activity. *Neuroreport*, *14*, 2031–2033.
Hertz-Pannier, L., Chiron, C., Jambaqué, I., Renaux-Kieffer, V., Van de Moortele, P.-F., Delalande, O. et al. (2002). Late plasticity for language in a child's non-dominant hemisphere. *Brain*, *125*, 361–372.
Hewes, G.W. (1973). Primate communication and the gestural origins of language. *Current Anthropology*, *14*, 5–24.
Holowka, S., & Petitto, L.A. (2002). Left hemisphere cerebral specialization for babies while babbling. *Science*, *297*, 1515.
Hook-Costigan, M.A., & Rogers, L.J. (1998). Lateralized use of the mouth in production of vocalizations by marmosets. *Neuropsychologia*, *36*, 1265–1273.
Hopkins, W.D. (1996). Chimpanzee handedness revisited: 55 years since Finch (1941). *Psychonomic Bulletin and Review*, *3*, 449–457.
Hopkins, W.D., & Leavens, D.A. (1998). Hand use and gestural communication in chimpanzees (*Pan troglodytes*). *Journal of Comparative Psychology*, *112*, 95–99.
Hopkins, W.D., Marino, L., Rilling, J.K., & MacGregor, L.A. (1998). Planum temporale asymmetries in great apes as revealed by magnetic resonance imaging (MRI). *Neuroreport*, *9*, 2913–2918.

Hopkins, W.D., Wesley, M.J., Izard, M.K., Hook, M., & Schapiro, S.J. (2004). Chimpanzees (*Pan troglodytes*) are predominantly right-handed: Replication in three populations of apes. *Behavioural Neuroscience*, *118*, 659–663.

Howard, K.J., Rogers, L.J., & Boura, A.L.A. (1980). Functional lateralisation of the chicken forebrain revealed by use of intracranial glutamate. *Brain Research*, *188*, 369–382.

Hunt, G.R., Corballis, M.C., & Gray, R.D. (2001). Laterality in tool manufacture by crows. *Nature*, *414*, 707.

Hunt, G.R., & Gray, R.D. (2003). Diversification and cumulative evolution in New Caledonian crow tool manufacture. *Proceedings of the Royal Society of London B*, *270*, 867–874.

Ivry, R.B., & Robertson, L.C. (1998). *The two sides of perception*. Cambridge, MA: MIT Press.

Jaynes, J. (1976). *The origins of consciousness in the breakdown of the bicameral mind*. Boston, MA: Houghton Mifflin.

Karnath, H.-O., Ferber, S., & Himmelbach, M. (2001). Spatial awareness is a function of the temporal not the posterior parietal lobe. *Nature*, *411*, 950–953.

Kimura, D. (1973). Manual activity while speaking: I. Right-handers. *Neuropsychologia*, *11*, 45–50.

Knecht, S., Dräger, B., Deppe, M., Bobe, L., Lohmann, H., Flöel, A. et al. (2000). Handedness and hemispheric language dominance in healthy humans. *Brain*, *123*, 2512–2518.

Layton, W.M. Jr. (1976). Random determination of a developmental process. *Journal of Heredity*, *67*, 336–338.

Leonhard, D., & Brugger, P. (1988). Creative, paranormal, and delusional thought: A consequence of right hemisphere semantic activation? *Neuropsychiatry, Neuropsychology and Behavioral Neurology*, *11*, 177–183.

Levermann, N., Galatius, A., Ehlme, G., Rysgaard, S., & Born, E.W. (2003). Feeding behaviour of free-ranging walruses with notes on apparent dextrality of flipper use. *BMC Ecology*, *3*, 9.

MacNeilage, P.F., Studdert-Kennedy, M.G., & Lindblom, B. (1987). Primate handedness reconsidered. *Behavioral and Brain Sciences*, *10*, 247–303.

Marchant, L.F., & McGrew, W.C. (2001). Wild chimpanzees are manually unlateralized: Replicative data from the Mahale Mountains, Tanzania. *American Journal of Physical Anthropology*, *Supplement 32*, 102.

McGrew, W.C., & Marchant, L.F. (1997). On the other hand: Current issues in a meta-analysis of the behavioural laterality of hand function in nonhuman primates. *Yearbook of Physical Anthropology*, *40*, 201–232.

McGurk, H., & MacDonald, J. (1976). Hearing lips and seeing voices. *Nature*, *264*, 746–748.

McManus, I.C. (1999). Handedness, cerebral lateralization, and the evolution of handedness. In M.C. Corballis & S.E.G. Lea (Eds.), *The descent of mind* (pp. 194–217). Oxford: Oxford University Press.

McManus, I.C. (2002). *Right hand, left hand*. London: Weidenfeld & Nicolson.

McManus, I.C., & Bryden, M.P. (1992). The genetics of handedness, cerebral dominance and lateralization. In I. Rapin & S.J. Segalowitz (Eds.), *Handbook of neuropsychology, Vol. 6: Developmental neuropsychology, Part 1* (pp. 115–144). Amsterdam: Elsevier.

Nicholls, M.E.R., Searle, D.A., & Bradshaw, J.L. (2004). Read my lips: Asymmetries in the visual expression and perception of speech revealed through the McGurk effect. *Psychological Science*, *15*, 138–141.

Niebauer, C.L., Aselage, J., & Schutte, C. (2002). Hemispheric interaction and consciousness: Degree of handedness predicts the intensity of a sensory illusion. *Laterality*, *7*, 85–96.

Nottebohm, F. (1977). Asymmetries for neural control of vocalization in the canary. In S. Harnad, R.W. Doty, L. Goldstein, J. Jaynes, & G. Krauthamer (Eds.), *Lateralization in the nervous system* (pp. 23–44). New York: Academic Press.

Passingham, R.E. (1982). *The human primate*. San Francisco: W.H. Freeman.

Peirce, J.W., Leigh, A.E., & Kendrick, K.M. (2000). Configurational coding, familiarity and the right hemisphere advantage for facial recognition in sheep. *Neuropsychologia*, *38*, 475–483.

Pinker, S. (1994). *The language instinct*. New York: Morrow.

Pizzagalli, D., Lehmann, D., Gianotti, L., Koenig, T., Tanaka, H., Wackermann, J. et al. (2000). Brain electric correlates of strong belief in paranormal phenomena. *Psychiatry Research: Neuroimaging Section*, *100*, 139–54.

Previc, F. (1991). A general theory concerning the prenatal origins of cerebral lateralization in humans. *Psychological Review*, *98*, 299–334.

Pujol, J., Deus, J., Losilla, J.M., & Capdevila, A. (1999). Cerebral lateralization of language in normal left-handed people studied by functional MRI. *Neurology*, *52*, 1038–1043.

Rasmussen, T., & Milner, B. (1977). The role of early left-brain injury in determining lateralization of cerebral speech functions. *Annals of the New York Academy of Sciences*, *299*, 355–369.

Raymond, M., Pontier, D., Dufour, A., & Moller, A.P. (1996). Frequency-dependent maintenance of left handedness in humans. *Proceedings of the Royal Society of London B*, *263*, 1627–1633.

Ringo, J.L., Doty, R.W., Demeter, S., & Simard, P.Y. (1994). Time is of the essence: A conjecture that hemispheric specialization arises from interhemispheric conduction delay. *Cerebral Cortex*, *4*, 331–343.

Rizzolatti, G., & Arbib, M.A. (1998). Language within our grasp. *Trends in Neuroscience*, *21*, 188–194.

Rogers, L.J. (1980). Lateralization in the avian brain. *Bird Behavior*, *2*, 1–12.

Rogers, L.J. (1990). Light input and the reversal of functional lateralization in the chicken brain. *Behavioural Brain Research*, *38*, 211–221.

Rogers, L.J. (2002a). Evolution of hemispheric specialization: Advantages and disadvantages. *Brain and Language*, *73*, 236–253.

Rogers, L.J. (2002b). Lateralized brain function in anurans: Comparison to lateralization in other vertebrates. *Laterality*, *7*, 219–240.

Singh, H., & O'Boyle, M.W. (2004). Hemispheric interactions during global–local processing in mathematically gifted adolescents, average-ability youth, and college students. *Neuropsychology*, *18*, 371–377.

Sovrano, V.A., Bisazza, A., & Vallortigara, G. (2001). Lateralization of responses to social stimuli in fishes: A comparison between different methods and species. *Physiology and Behavior*, *74*, 237–244.

Sperry, R.W. (1966–1967). Mental unity following surgical section of the cerebral hemispheres. *Harvey Lectures*, *62*, 293–323.

Sperry, R.W. (1974). Lateral specialization in the surgically separated hemispheres.

In F.O. Schmitt & F.G. Worden (Eds.), *The neurosciences: Third study program* (pp. 5–19). Cambridge, MA: MIT Press.

Sperry, R.W. (1982). Some effects of disconnecting the cerebral hemispheres. *Science, 217*, 1223–1227.

Sperry, R.W., Zaidel, E., & Zaidel, D. (1979). Self recognition and social awareness in the disconnected right hemisphere. *Neuropsychologia, 17*, 153–166.

Springer, J.A., Binder, J.R., Hammeke, T.A., Swanson, S.J., Frost, J.A., Bellgowan, P.S.F. et al. (1999). Language dominance in neurologically normal and epilepsy subjects. *Brain, 122*, 2033–2045.

Vallortigara, G., & Andrew, R.J. (1994). Differential involvement of right and left hemisphere in individual recognition in the domestic chick. *Behavioural Processes, 33*, 41–58.

Vallortigara, G., Pagni, P., & Sovrano, V.A. (2004). Separate geometric and non-geometric modules for spatial reorientation: Evidence from a lopsided animal brain. *Journal of Cognitive Neuroscience, 16*, 390–400.

Vallortigara, G., Rogers, L.J., Bisazza, A., Lippolis, G., & Robins, A. (1998). Complementary right and left hemifield use for predatory and agonistic behavior. *Neuroreport, 9*, 3341–3344.

Vermeire, B.A., Hamilton, C.R., & Erdmann, A.L. (1998). Right-hemispheric superiority in split-brain monkeys for learning and remembering facial discriminations. *Behavioral Neuroscience, 112*, 1048–1061.

Warrington, E.K., & Pratt, R.T.C. (1973). Language laterality in left handers assessed by unilateral ECT. *Neuropsychologia, 11*, 423–428.

Witelson, S.F., Kigar, D.L., & Harvey, T. (1999). The exceptional brain of Einstein. *The Lancet, 353*, 2149–2153.

Zaidel, E. (1976). Auditory vocabulary of the right hemisphere following brain bisection or hemidecortication. *Cortex, 12*, 191–211.

Zaidel, E. (1983). A response to Gazzaniga: Language in the right hemisphere. *American Psychologist, 38*, 542–546.

11 Mental imagery and the human brain

Stephen M. Kosslyn, Giorgio Ganis, and William L. Thompson

Mental imagery occurs when perceptual information is accessed from memory, giving rise to the experience of "seeing with the mind's eye", "hearing with the mind's ear", and so on. In contrast, perception occurs when information is registered directly from the senses. Mental images need not be simply the recall of previously perceived objects or events; they can also be created by combining and modifying stored perceptual information in novel ways. Imagery has played a central role in theories of mental function at least since the time of Plato. It has fallen in and out of fashion, in large part because it is inherently a private affair – by definition restricted to the confines of one's mind. Thus, imagery has been difficult to study. In fact, in 1913 the founder of Behaviorism (the school of psychology that focused solely on observable stimuli, responses, and the consequences of responses), John B. Watson, denied that mental images even existed. Instead, he suggested, thinking consists of subtle movements of the vocal apparatus (Watson, 1913). In spite of the fact that Alan Paivio and his colleagues were able to show that the use of imagery dramatically improves memory (Paivio, 1971), many researchers were not convinced that imagery is a distinct form of thought. Indeed, Watson's position was echoed 60 years later by Zenon Pylyshyn, who championed the view that mental images are not "images" at all, but rather rely on mental descriptions no different in kind from those that underlie language. According to Pylyshyn (1973), the pictorial aspects of imagery that are evident to conscious experience are entirely epiphenomenal, like the heat thrown off by a lightbulb when you read (which plays no role in the reading process; see also Pylyshyn, 2002, 2003).

The emergence of cognitive neuroscience has opened a new chapter in the study of imagery. An enormous amount has been learned about the neural underpinnings of visual perception, memory, emotion, and motor control. Much of this information has come from the study of animal models. Unlike language and reasoning, these more basic functions have many common features among higher mammals – including humans. In addition, neuroimaging technologies developed in recent years, especially positron emission tomography (PET) and functional magnetic resonance imaging (fMRI), allow theories of imagery to be tested objectively in humans. Researchers have taken advantage of these developments to show that mental imagery draws on much of the same neural machinery as perception in the same modality, and can engage mechanisms used in memory, emotion, and motor control.

In this chapter we draw on results from a variety of methods, including studies of the effects of selective brain damage on behavior, neuroimaging, and studies examining the effects of transcranial magnetic stimulation (TMS). Each method has its strengths and weaknesses, but they are complementary. Thus, for example, neuroimaging provides only correlational data (when engaged in a particular task, a particular set of brain areas is activated) but can monitor the entire brain; TMS can be used to establish causal roles of distinct areas (e.g., by showing that performance in a task that draws on a specific brain area is impaired following TMS to that area), but must be targeted to a specific location. To the extent that the same conclusions are reached using different methods, these conclusions can be taken increasingly seriously.

We briefly review three main classes of research: evidence that imagery engages brain mechanisms that are used in perception and action; evidence that visual mental imagery engages even the earliest visual cortex (Areas 17 and 18); and evidence that imagery engages mechanisms that control physiological processes such as heart rate and breathing, having effects much like those that occur with the corresponding perceptual stimuli.

Imagery, perception, and action

We begin with visual imagery, which is by far the most intensively studied modality, and then turn to auditory and motor imagery.

Visual mental imagery

Well over 100 years ago, researchers described brain-damaged patients who had lost the ability to form visual mental images after they became blind (for a review, see Farah, 1984; however, see also Chatterjee & Southwood, 1995). Methods from cognitive psychology have allowed researchers to characterize such deficits with increasing precision. For example, some patients have perceptual deficits in only one of the two major cortical visual functions. One major visual pathway runs from the occipital lobe down to the inferior temporal lobes (the so-called "object properties processing" pathway; see Ungerleider & Mishkin, 1982); when damaged, the animal or person cannot easily recognize shape. The other major visual pathway runs from the occipital lobe to the posterior parietal lobes (the so-called "spatial properties processing" pathway); when damaged, the animal or person cannot easily register location. The parallel deficits appear in imagery: Damage to the occipital–temporal pathway disrupts the ability to visualize shape (as used, for example, to determine from memory whether George Washington had a beard), whereas damage to the occipital–parietal pathway disrupts the ability to visualize locations (as used, for example, to indicate the locations of furniture in a room when your eyes are closed; see Levine, Warach, & Farah, 1985). Indeed, very subtle deficits can occur in imagery that parallel the deficits found in perception. For example, some brain-damaged patients can no longer distinguish colors perceptually or in imagery (De Vreese, 1991) and others can no longer distinguish faces perceptually or in imagery (Young et al., 1994).

However, although the deficits in imagery and perception often parallel each other, this is not always the case. In a seminal literature review and analysis, Farah (1984) showed that some patients have selective problems in generating images even though they are able to recognize and identify perceptual stimuli. In addition, patients have been reported who could visualize but had impaired perception (e.g., Behrmann, Winocur, & Moscovitch, 1992; Jankowiak et al., 1992). In short, the results from research with brain-damaged patients suggest that visual mental imagery and visual perception share many common mechanisms, but do not draw on identical processes. Although shape, location, and surface characteristics are represented and interpreted in comparable ways during both functions, the two differ in key ways: Imagery, unlike perception, does not require low-level organizational processing. And perception, unlike imagery, does not require us to activate information in memory when the stimulus is not present (for recent reviews see Behrmann, 2000; Ganis, Thompson, Mast, & Kosslyn, 2003; Kosslyn, Thompson, & Ganis, 2006).

The results of neuroimaging studies that compare imagery and perception have dovetailed nicely with those from studies of brain-damaged patients. One study, for example, found that of all the brain areas activated during perception and during imagery, approximately two-thirds were activated in common (Kosslyn, Thompson, & Alpert, 1997). A recent study, using matched perception and imagery tasks, found an even higher overlap: over 90% of the brain was activated in common (Ganis, Thompson, & Kosslyn, 2004), with many brain regions attaining near 100% overlap. Presumably, lesions in the areas not activated in common produce the dissociations, where imagery or perception is disrupted independently, whereas lesions in the areas activated in common produce the more frequently reported parallel deficits in imagery and perception.

Finally, studies of deficits following brain damage have underscored the fact that "imagery" – like all other cognitive functions – is not a single, undifferentiated ability. Rather, it is a collection of abilities, which can be disrupted independently. For example, some patients can make imagery judgments about the shape or color of objects but have difficulty imagining an object rotating (for example, when trying to decide whether the letter "p" would be another letter when rotated 180 degrees, or whether "Z" would be another letter when rotated 90 degrees clockwise). Other patients have the reverse pattern of deficits. Indeed, when subjects perform different imagery tasks while their brain activity is monitored, different patterns of activation are observed. For example, when subjects mentally rotate patterns, their parietal lobes (often bilaterally) and right frontal lobes typically are strongly activated (e.g., Cohen et al., 1996; Jordan et al., 2001; Kosslyn et al., 1998; Richter et al., 2000). In contrast, if they are asked to visualize previously memorized patterns of stripes and judge which are longer, wider and so on (all on the basis of their mental images, with eyes closed), these areas are not activated, but other areas in the occipital lobe and left association cortex are activated (Kosslyn et al., 1999).

Depending on the precise task, different sets of processes are activated (O'Craven & Kanwisher, 2000). Indeed, brain activation during mental imagery may vary according to the type of object that is visualized. Using fMRI, O'Craven and Kanwisher (2000) found activation in the "FFA" (fusiform face area) when subjects visualized faces. Conversely, when subjects visualized indoor or outdoor scenes depicting a spatial layout, these researchers found activation in the "PPA" (parahippocampal place area). There was no hint of activation of the PPA during face imagery nor of the FFA during place imagery. These results are similar to what was observed when subjects actually perceived faces and places. The findings underscore that imagery and perception share very specific, specialized mechanisms.

Auditory imagery

Do the first three notes of the children's song "Three blind mice" ascend or descend? Most people report that they "hear" the song in the process of deciding the notes descend. Remarkably little research has addressed auditory imagery per se. Zatorre and Halpern (1993) studied brain-damaged patients to discover whether specific brain areas are critical for auditory imagery. They studied a group of patients who had had the left or right temporal lobe removed (for the treatment of otherwise intractable epilepsy) and compared them to otherwise similar control subjects. In one condition, the subjects heard a familiar song while also reading the lyrics, and judged which of two particular words had the higher pitch. In another condition, the subjects saw the lyrics and made the same judgments, but did not actually hear the song – and thus had to rely on their mental imagery. The patients with right-temporal lesions were impaired in both conditions, compared to both other groups. These findings demonstrate that at least some of the neural structures that play a key role in pitch discrimination in perception also play a comparable role in imagery.

Most research on auditory imagery has focused on imagery for music. Zatorre et al. (1996) asked whether auditory imagery draws on the same mechanisms used in auditory perception. Their subjects either listened to songs and judged the relative pitch of pairs of words, or imagined hearing songs and made the same judgments. No auditory stimulation was present during the baseline condition, which required the subjects to judge the relative length of visually presented words. PET revealed that many of the same areas were in fact activated in common in these tasks, including bilateral associative auditory cortex (BA 21/22, in spite of the fact that the left temporal lobe has often been identified with the perception of language and the right with music or environmental sounds), bilateral frontal cortex (BA45/9 and 10/47), left parietal cortex (BA 40/7), and supplementary motor cortex (BA 6). The bilateral activation in associative auditory cortex observed in the previous study, in apparent contrast with the patient studies, may reflect the fact that these researchers used verbal melodies.

Indeed, in a subsequent study, Halpern and Zatorre (1999) asked musically trained subjects to listen to the opening notes of familiar (nonverbal) melodies and then continue "hearing the melody with the mind's ear". Again using PET, they found activation in two regions of the right temporal lobe (the superior and inferior temporal cortex), which is consistent with their earlier study of brain-damaged patients; both of these areas are involved in storing and interpreting nonverbal sounds. Moreover, auditory imagery of a melody that required retrieval from memory also activated two right-hemisphere regions, in the frontal lobe and superior temporal gyrus (which is critical for auditory perception). Finally, the supplementary motor area (SMA) was also activated by auditory imagery, regardless of whether the melody was retrieved or simply rehearsed on-line. This is interesting because no overt behavior was required. Halpern and Zatorre believe that stored movements are used in this sort of imagery – which makes sense for melodies, where one can subvocalize the tune as part of the process of retrieving the information.

Finally, Griffiths (2000) reports a novel study of patients who became deaf and then hallucinated hearing music. These patients were neither psychotic nor beset with an obvious neurological problem, such as epilepsy. Griffiths was able to perform PET while the patients had such hallucinations, and reports that the posterior temporal lobes, in auditory cortex, were activated as well as several other areas (specifically, the right basal ganglia, the cerebellum and the inferior frontal cortices).

In short, auditory imagery appears to draw on most of the neural structures used in auditory perception. However, unlike visual imagery (as discussed shortly), there is no evidence that the first auditory cortical area to receive input from the ears, Area A1, is activated during auditory imagery.

Motor imagery

When people are asked to imagine walking to a specific goal placed in front of them and to indicate when they would have arrived, their estimates of transit time are remarkably similar to the actual time they subsequently require to walk that distance (Decety & Jeannerod, 1995). In such tasks, people report that they imagine moving. Many studies have now been carried out to investigate the neural bases of such motor imagery, and to distinguish motor imagery from purely visual imagery. Although visual imagery may often accompany motor imagery, researchers have documented that motor imagery relies on distinct mechanisms. Specifically, many researchers have shown that cortex used in movement control also plays a role in motor imagery. Indeed, in a classic study, Georgopoulos, Lurito, Petrides, Schwartz and Massey (1989) recorded activity in individual neurons in the motor strip of monkeys while the animals were planning to move a lever along a specific arc. They found that these neurons fired in a systematic sequence, depending on their orientation tuning. Specifically, at first, only neurons tuned for orientations near the starting position of the lever fired, followed by those tuned for orientations slightly farther along the trajectory, and so on. All of this occurred before the animal actually began moving. However, these findings do not show that mental rotation occurs in the motor strip itself; it is possible that the computation takes place elsewhere in the brain (e.g., the posterior parietal lobes), and that the results of such computation are simply being executed in the motor strip.

Indeed, a host of neuroimaging studies of "mental rotation" have now been reported, all of which have shown that multiple brain areas are activated during mental rotation. For example, Richter et al. (2000) measured brain activation with fMRI while subjects mentally rotated the three-dimensional multi-armed angular stimuli invented by Shepard and Metzler (1971), which look as if they had been constructed by gluing small cubes together to form the arms. Subjects were shown pairs of such shapes and asked to report whether the figures in each pair were the same or mirror-reversed. Richter et al. report that the superior parietal lobules (in both hemispheres) were activated during this task, as well as premotor cortex (in both hemispheres), supplementary motor cortex, and also the left primary motor cortex.

Other neuroimaging studies have provided strong support for the role of motor processes in mental transformations. For example, Parsons et al. (1995) showed subjects a picture of a hand, which could be rotated to various degrees; each picture was presented in the left visual field (so the image was registered first by the right hemisphere) or in the right visual field (so the image was registered first by the left hemisphere). The subjects were to decide whether each picture was a left or a right hand. Parsons et al. expected motor cortices to be activated in this task if subjects imagined rotating their own hand into congruence with the stimulus. And in fact, not only was supplementary motor cortex activated bilaterally, but prefrontal and insular premotor areas were also activated in the hemisphere contralateral to the stimulus handedness – suggesting that subjects did in fact imagine the appropriate movements. Many other areas, including in the frontal and parietal lobes, and basal ganglia and cerebellum, were active, as was Area 17.

Is motor imagery used only to rotate parts of one's body? Some researchers (e.g., Decety, 1996; Jeannerod, 1994; Jeannerod & Decety, 1995) have suggested that people often transform images by imagining what they would see if the objects were manipulated in a specific way. One PET study directly compared rotation of hands versus inanimate objects (Kosslyn et al., 1998), again using the three-dimensional multi-armed angular stimuli invented by

Shepard and Metzler (1971). The subjects compared pairs of drawings and decided whether they were identical or mirror-images (using the task and stimuli from the original Shepard & Metzler study). In the experimental condition, the figures were presented at different relative orientations, and one had to be "mentally rotated" into congruence with the other; in the baseline condition, the figures were presented at the same orientation, and thus no mental rotation was necessary. The comparison of the two conditions revealed which areas were activated specifically by mental rotation. The corresponding design was used for drawings of hands, but now the subjects decided whether the two hands in a pair were both left or both right or whether one was a left hand and one a right hand. In this study, several motor areas were activated when subjects mentally rotated hands, including primary motor cortex (Area M1), premotor cortex, and the posterior parietal lobe. None of the frontal motor areas was activated when objects were mentally rotated. However, Cohen et al. (1996) used fMRI to study mental rotation of exactly the same inanimate objects and found that premotor cortex was activated in this task, but only in half the subjects.

The fact that only some subjects had activation in a motor area during mental rotation of inanimate objects suggests that there may be two strategies for performing such rotations. One strategy involves imagining what you would see if you manipulated an object; the other involves imagining what you would see if someone else (or an external force, such as a motor) manipulated an object. To test this idea, Kosslyn, Thompson, Wraga, and Alpert (2001) asked subjects to perform the same mental rotation task used by Cohen et al., but with a twist: Immediately prior to the task, the subjects saw a wooden model of that type of stimulus (one not actually used in the task) either being rotated by an electric motor or they themselves physically turned the stimulus. They were told that during the task they should imagine the stimuli being rotated just as they had seen the model rotate at the outset. In this experiment, Area M1 was activated when subjects mentally rotated stimuli after having themselves physically rotated the stimulus (and then imagined themselves doing so), and not when they saw the electric motor rotating the stimulus at the outset. The motor strategy can apparently transfer implicitly as well: After completing a task where participants mentally rotated drawings of human hands, motor areas of the brain became active even when participants mentally rotated objects not related to the human body (Shepard–Metzler figures; Wraga et al., 2003).

These results show that imagining oneself manipulating an object is one way in which mental transformation of objects in general (not just body parts) can take place – and they also show that humans can voluntarily adopt this strategy or use a strategy in which they imagine what they would see if an external force transformed an object. Finally, one can ask whether primary motor cortex plays a functional role in allowing subjects to manipulate objects in images. It is possible that the actual computation is taking place in another area that incidentally sends activation to primary motor cortex.

To test this hypothesis, Ganis, Keenan, Kosslyn, and Pascual-Leone (2000) disrupted function in the left primary motor cortex by administering TMS while subjects mentally rotated pictures of hands and feet (with the to-be-rotated stimulus appearing in the right visual field). The TMS was time-locked so that it disrupted neural processing only a specific amount of time after the stimulus appeared. Subjects required more time to perform this task if a single magnetic pulse was delivered to the motor strip (roughly over the "hand area") 650 ms after the stimuli were presented (but not at the other temporal delays tested); moreover, rotation of hands was impaired more than rotation of feet, as expected if this area is specialized for controlling the hand per se. Within the limits of the spatial resolution afforded by the TMS technique, these results suggest that activation in this area reflects processing used to perform the task. However, we cannot say whether this area is the site of processing or merely relays information computed elsewhere in the brain.

In short, mental imagery can engage the motor system. This finding may help to explain why "mental practice" can improve actual performance (e.g., Driskell, Cooper, & Moran, 1994; Maring, 1990; Weiss et al., 1994). In this case, imagining making movements may not only exercise the relevant brain areas, but may build associations among processes implemented in different areas – which in turn facilitate complex performance.

Imagery and early visual cortex

A large portion of research on the neural bases of imagery focuses on whether early visual cortex is activated during imagery. Early visual cortex comprises Areas 17 and 18, the first two cortical areas to receive input from the eyes. Researchers have wanted to know whether visual imagery activates these early areas for three main reasons. First, these areas are known to be topographically organized; that is, they preserve (roughly) the local spatial geometry of the retina – and thus patterns of activation in them serve to depict shape. If these areas are activated during imagery, and such activation plays a functional role, this would be evidence that imagery relies on representations that depict information, not describe it. (In other words, this would be evidence that mental imagery relies on actual images which use space on the cortex to depict space in the world.) Second, such findings cannot be explained by appeal to "tacit knowledge", which Pylyshyn (1981) used to explain away the findings from earlier behavioral experiments that attempted to demonstrate that imagery relies on depictive representations. According to this view, subjects in imagery experiments may have unconsciously tried to imitate what they thought they would have done in the corresponding perceptual situation (such as by taking more time to scan farther distances across an imaged scene). But such tacit knowledge, stored as descriptions, would not explain why early visual cortex would be activated when subjects had their eyes closed during imagery. Third, if imagery can alter the activation of early visual cortex, this suggests that one's beliefs and expectations can (at least under some circumstances) modulate what one actually sees during perception. And this finding would have clear-cut implications for the reliability of eyewitness testimony and the veracity of visual memory more generally.

More than 50 neuroimaging studies have examined activation in early visual cortex (for reviews, see Kosslyn & Thompson, 2003; Thompson & Kosslyn, 2000). The studies used, in decreasing order of sensitivity, fMRI, PET, and single photon emission computer tomography (SPECT).

The following studies seem to provide the strongest support for activation in early visual cortex during visual mental imagery. The subjects had their eyes closed during all of the neuroimaging tasks, and thus activation of early visual cortex could not have been caused by seeing patterns. First, in one study, subjects were asked to visualize line drawings of objects at different sizes (as if they fitted into boxes that were memorized before the PET scan; Kosslyn et al., 1995). Not only was Area 17 activated, compared to a control condition in which identical auditory cues were provided but no imagery was used, but also the specific locus of activation depended on the size of the imaged object. Even though subjects' eyes were closed, the mere fact of visualizing an object at a larger size shifted the activation to more anterior parts of the calcarine sulcus (the major anatomical landmark of Area 17) – just as is found in perception proper (e.g., Sereno et al., 1995). This result was replicated by Tootell, Hadjikani, Mendola, Marrett, and Dale (1998), using fMRI and using a precise method to localize Area 17; there is no doubt that varying the size of objects in mental images shifts the locus of activation along Area 17 comparably to what occurs in perception.

Second, Klein, Paradis, Poline, Kosslyn, and LeBihan (2000) used event-related fMRI to chart activation in Area 17 when visual mental images were formed. They found clear activation in every subject, with a clearcut temporal pattern; activation began about 2 s after an auditory cue, and peaked around 4–6 s later, before dropping off during the next 8 s or so. But is such activation playing a functional role in imagery? In another study, subjects memorized four quadrants, each with black-and-white stripes (which varied in length, width, orientation, and separation), and later had to visualize them and make subtle shape comparisons, such as which set had longer or wider stripes (Kosslyn et al., 1999). PET scanning revealed that Area 17 was activated during this task. Moreover, when TMS was applied to Area 17 prior to the task, every subject subsequently required more time to make these judgments than when TMS was applied so that it did not affect Area 17. Indeed, the magnitude of the decrement in performance was the same when subjects had their eyes closed and visualized the stripes as when they had their eyes open and made judgments based on visible stripes. This makes sense if Area 17 is critical in both the imagery and perceptual versions of the task. Indeed, Farah, Soso, and Dasheiff (1992) found that after one occipital lobe was surgically removed from a patient (as part of a medical treatment), the apparent size of images decreased by approximately half – as expected if each occipital lobe represents the contralateral part of space.

Finally, in another PET study, subjects closed their eyes and visualized named letters of the alphabet, in uppercase form (Kosslyn et al., 1996b). Four seconds after forming the image, they were asked to judge whether the letter had a specific characteristic (such as any curved lines); the response times and error rates were recorded at the same time that subjects' brains were scanned. Not only were variations in the level of activation in Area 17 significantly correlated with the time subjects required to make the judgments, but this correlation was present even after all other correlations between variations in regional cerebral blood flow and response time were statistically removed.

These results indicate that: (1) activation in Area 17 is systematically related to spatial properties of the imaged object; (2) if Area 17 is impaired, via TMS or brain damage, so is the use of visual imagery; and (3) the activation in Area 17 is not likely to be an artifact of activation in other areas, which is merely incidentally sent (via neural connections) to Area 17.

Given these positive results, why have so many studies failed to find activation in Area 17? Thompson and Kosslyn (2000) report a meta-analysis which suggests that the sensitivity of the technique is important (note the proportion of fMRI studies that detected such activation versus those that did not, 21:3, compared to the corresponding proportion for the much less sensitive SPECT technique, 2:7). In addition, the meta-analysis revealed that if a task requires subjects to find a high-resolution detail in an image (such as by evaluating the shape of an animal's ears or comparing two similar sets of stripes), activation in early visual cortex is likely. Furthermore, if a task requires a spatial judgment (which may be mediated by the parietal lobe), activation is less likely. Indeed, many of the studies that did not report activation in early visual cortex used spatial tasks (Mellet et al., 1995, 1996, 2000). These results were confirmed by a more extensive meta-analysis that examined 59 neuroimaging studies of visual mental imagery (Kosslyn & Thompson, 2003).

A second puzzle is why some brain-damaged patients continue to have some use of imagery in spite of the fact that early visual cortex has been severely damaged (Chatterjee & Southwood, 1995). Probably the most straightforward account for this finding is that early visual cortex is not necessary for all forms of visual imagery. Indeed, Crick and Koch (1995) make a good case that the experience of visual perception does not arise from early visual cortex, but rather from later areas that receive input from the earlier ones. The same is probably true in imagery: If later areas are activated in the absence of the appropriate immediate sensory input, one may experience visual imagery. However, such later areas do not make fine spatial variations accessible to later processes, and hence one apparently needs to reconstruct the local geometry in earlier areas (which have much smaller receptive fields, and hence higher resolution) if one must extract fine-grained details from the imaged object.

Imagery: The world within

The great Behaviorist B.F. Skinner (1977, p. 6) wrote, "There is no evidence of the mental construction of images to be looked at or maps to be followed. The body responds to the world, at the point of contact; making copies would be a waste of time." We hope that we have convinced the reader that the first part of this claim is incorrect; images are in fact internal representations. We now briefly consider the second part, whether having such representations is a "waste of time".

Specifically, there is much evidence that imagery of emotional events activates the autonomic nervous system and (as also evident in single-cell recordings in humans) the amygdala. That is, visualizing an object has many of the same effects on the body as actually seeing the object. For example, Lang et al. (1993) showed that skin conductance increases, as do heart rate and breathing rate, when subjects view pictures of threatening objects. And the same result occurs when they merely visualize the objects. Indeed, Kosslyn et al. (1996a) found that mental images of aversive stimuli activate the anterior insula, the major cortical site of feedback from the autonomic nervous system. In addition, Kreiman, Koch, and Fried (2000) recorded from single cells in the human brain (hippocampus, amygdala, entorhinal cortex, and parahippocampal gyrus) while subjects were shown pictures or formed mental images of those same pictures. Some of the cells that responded selectively when subjects viewed specific visual stimuli (e.g., faces) also responded selectively when those same stimuli were visualized. Of particular interest, this pattern was seen in the amygdala, which is known to play a key role in certain emotions, especially fear and anger (LeDoux, 1995, 1996). Thus, imagery can engage neural structures also engaged in perception, and those neural structures in turn can affect events in the body itself.

Conclusions

Imagery is no longer seen as an awkward holdover from a previous, less rigorous age, a topic unfit for polite company. Rather, researchers agree that most of the neural processes underlying like-modality perception are also used in imagery, and imagery in many ways can "stand in" for a perceptual stimulus or situation. Imagery can not only engage the motor system, but can also affect the body much as can actual perceptual experience.

Nevertheless, many questions remain. For example: Under what circumstances is early sensory cortex recruited during imagery? Why is early sensory cortex often recruited during visual mental imagery, but not during auditory imagery? Why do people differ so much in their imagery abilities? Do genetics affect some aspects of imagery more than others? How does semantic content in images engage specific mechanisms?

Unlike even 20 years ago, we can now seek answers to such questions. Indeed, advances in fMRI technology, as well as the advent of additional technologies such as diffuse optical tomography (DOT; e.g., Obrig et al., 2000), promise to facilitate studies of the neural bases of imagery. Of particular importance, these brain-imaging technologies will allow large-scale individual differences studies to be conducted. Such studies can relate differences in patterns of brain activation to differences in performance, which in turn should tell us not only about what the brain is doing, but also about how and why people differ in their modes of thinking.

Acknowledgements

This chapter is based on an article published by Kosslyn, S.M., Ganis, G., and Thompson, W. L. (2001). Neural foundations of imagery. *Nature Reviews Neuroscience*, *2*, 635–642. It is adapted with permission of the publisher. This work was supported in part by grants Grant R01 MH060734-05A1 from the National Institute of Mental Health and ROLE Grant REC-0411725 from the National Science Foundation.

References

Behrmann, M. (2000). The mind's eye mapped onto the brain's matter. *Current Directions in Psychological Science*, *9*, 50–54.

Behrmann, M., Winocur, G., & Moscovitch, M. (1992). Dissociation between mental imagery and object recognition in a brain-damaged patient. *Nature*, *359*, 636–637.

Chatterjee, A., & Southwood, M.H. (1995). Cortical blindness and visual imagery. *Neurology*, *45*, 2189–2195.

Cohen, M.S. et al. (1996). Changes in cortical activity during mental rotation: A mapping study using functional MRI. *Brain*, *119*, 89–100.

Crick, F., & Koch, C. (1995). Are we aware of neural activity in primary visual cortex? *Nature*, *375*(6527), 121–123.

De Vreese, L.P. (1991). Two systems for colour-naming defects: Verbal disconnection vs colour imagery disorder. *Neuropsychologia*, *29*, 1–18.

Decety, J. (1996). Neural representation for action. *Reviews in the Neurosciences*, *7*, 285–297.

Decety, J., & Jeannerod, M. (1995). Mentally simulated movements in virtual reality: Does Fitts's law hold in motor imagery? *Behavioral and Brain Research*, *72*, 127–134.

Driskell, J., Copper, C., & Moran, A. (1994). Does mental practice enhance performance? *Journal of Applied Psychology*, *79*, 481–492.

Farah, M.J. (1984). The neurological basis of mental imagery: A componential analysis. *Cognition*, *18*, 245–272.

Farah, M.J., Soso, M.J., & Dasheiff, R.M. (1992). Visual angle of the mind's eye before and after unilateral occipital lobectomy. *Journal of Experimental Psychology: Human Perception & Performance*, *18*, 241–246.

Ganis, G., Keenan, J.P., Kosslyn, S.M., & Pascual-Leone, A. (2000). Transcranial magnetic stimulation of primary motor cortex affects mental rotation. *Cerebral Cortex*, *10*, 175–180.

Ganis, G., Thompson, W.L., & Kosslyn, S.M. (2004). Brain areas underlying visual mental imagery and visual perception: An fMRI study. *Cognitive Brain Research, 20*, 226–241.

Ganis, G., Thompson, W.L., Mast, F.W., & Kosslyn, S.M. (2003). Visual imagery in cerebral visual dysfunction. *Neurologic Clinics, 21*, 631–646.

Georgopoulos, A.P., Lurito, J.T., Petrides, M., Schwartz, A.B., & Massey, J.T. (1989). Mental rotation of the neuronal population vector. *Science, 243*, 234–236.

Griffiths, T.D. (2000). Musical hallucinosis in acquired deafness: Phenomenology and brain substrate. *Brain, 123*, 2065–2076.

Halpern, A.R., & Zatorre, R.J. (1999). When that tune runs through your head: A PET investigation of auditory imagery for familiar melodies. *Cerebral Cortex, 9*, 697–704.

Jankowiak, J., Kinsbourne, M., Shalev, R.S., & Bachman, D.L. (1992). Preserved visual imagery and categorization in a case of associative visual agnosia. *Journal of Cognitive Neuroscience, 4*, 119–131.

Jeannerod, M. (1994). The representing brain: Neural correlates of motor intention and imagery. *Behavioral and Brain Sciences, 17*, 187–245.

Jeannerod, M., & Decety, J. (1995). Mental motor imagery: A window into the representational stages of action. *Current Opinion in Neurobiology, 5*, 727–32.

Jordan, K., Heinze, H.J., Lutz, K., Kanowski, M., & Jancke, L. (2001). Cortical activations during the mental rotation of different visual objects. *Neuroimage, 13*, 143–152.

Klein, I., Paradis, A.-L., Poline, J.-B., Kosslyn, S.M., & Le Bihan, D. (2000). Transient activity in human calcarine cortex during visual imagery. *Journal of Cognitive Neuroscience, 12*, 15–23.

Kosslyn, S.M. et al. (1996a). Neural effects of visualizing and perceiving aversive stimuli: A PET investigation. *NeuroReport, 7*, 1569–1576.

Kosslyn, S.M. et al. (1999). The role of area 17 in visual imagery: Convergent evidence from PET and rTMS. *Science, 284*, 167–170.

Kosslyn, S.M., DiGirolamo, G., Thompson, W.L., & Alpert, N.M. (1998). Mental rotation of objects versus hands: Neural mechanisms revealed by positron emission tomography. *Psychophysiology, 35*, 151–161.

Kosslyn, S.M., & Thompson, W.L. (2003). When is early visual cortex activated during visual mental imagery? *Psychological Bulletin, 129*, 723–746.

Kosslyn, S.M., Thompson, W.L., & Alpert, N.M. (1997). Neural systems shared by visual imagery and visual perception: A positron emission tomography study. *NeuroImage, 6*, 320–334.

Kosslyn, S.M., Thompson, W.L., & Ganis, G. (2006). *The case for mental imagery*. New York: Oxford University Press.

Kosslyn, S.M., Thompson, W.L., Kim, I.J., & Alpert, N.M. (1995). Topographical representations of mental images in primary visual cortex. *Nature, 378*, 496–498.

Kosslyn, S.M., Thompson, W.L., Kim, I.J., Rauch, S.L., & Alpert, N.M. (1996b). Individual differences in cerebral blood flow in area 17 predict the time to evaluate visualized letters. *Journal of Cognitive Neuroscience, 8*, 78–82.

Kosslyn, S.M., Thompson, W.L., Wraga, M., & Alpert, N.M. (2001). Imagining rotation by endogenous versus exogenous forces: Distinct neural mechanisms. *NeuroReport, 12*, 2519–2525.

Kreiman, G., Koch, C., & Fried, I. (2000). Imagery neurons in the human brain. *Nature, 408*(6810), 357–361.

Lang, P.J., Greenwald, M.K., Bradley, M.M., & Hamm, A.O. (1993). Looking at pictures: Affective, facial, visceral, and behavioral reactions. *Psychophysiology, 30*, 261–273.

LeDoux, J.E. (1995). Emotion: Clues from the brain. *Annual Review of Psychology, 46*, 209–235.

LeDoux, J.E. (1996). *The emotional brain: The mysterious underpinnings of emotional life*. New York: Simon & Schuster.

Levine, D.N., Warach, J., & Farah, M.J. (1985). Two visual systems in mental imagery: Dissociation of "what" and "where" in imagery disorders due to bilateral posterior cerebral lesions. *Neurology, 35*, 1010–1018.

Maring, J.R. (1990). Effects of mental practice on rate of skill acquisition. *Physical Therapy, 70*, 165–172.

Mellet, E. et al. (1996). Functional anatomy of spatial mental imagery generated from verbal instructions. *Journal of Neuroscience, 16*, 6504–6512.

Mellet, E. et al. (2000). Neural correlates of topographic mental exploration: The impact of route versus survey perspective learning. *NeuroImage, 12*, 588–600.

Mellet, E., Tzourio N., Denis, M., & Mazoyer, B. (1995). A positron emission tomography study of visual and mental spatial exploration. *Journal of Cognitive Neuroscience, 4*, 433–445.

Obrig, H. et al. (2000). Near-infrared spectroscopy: Does it function in functional activation studies of the adult brain? *International Journal of Psychophysiology, 35*, 125–142.

O'Craven, K.M., & Kanwisher, N. (2000). Mental imagery of faces and places activates corresponding stimulus-specific brain regions. *Journal of Cognitive Neuroscience, 12*, 1013–1023.

Paivio, A. (1971). *Imagery and verbal processes*. New York: Holt, Rinehart & Winston.

Parsons, L.M. et al. (1995). Use of implicit motor imagery for visual shape discrimination as revealed by PET. *Nature, 375*, 54–58.

Pylyshyn, Z.W. (1973). What the mind's eye tells the mind's brain: A critique of mental imagery. *Psychological Bulletin, 80*, 1–24.

Pylyshyn, Z.W. (1981). Psychological explanations and knowledge-dependent processes. *Cognition, 10*, 267–274.

Pylyshyn, Z.W. (2002). Mental imagery: In search of a theory. *Behavioral and Brain Sciences, 25*, 157–238.

Pylyshyn, Z.W. (2003). Return of the mental image: Are there pictures in the brain? *Trends in Cognitive Sciences, 7*, 113–118.

Richter, W. et al. (2000). Motor area activity during mental rotation studied by time-resolved single-trial fMRI. *Journal of Cognitive Neuroscience, 12*, 310–320.

Sereno, M.I. et al. (1995). Borders of multiple visual areas in humans revealed by functional magnetic resonance imaging. *Science, 268*(5212), 889–893.

Shepard, R.N., & Metzler, J. (1971). Mental rotation of three-dimensional objects. *Science, 171*, 701–703.

Skinner, B.F. (1977). Why I am not a cognitive psychologist. *Behaviorism, 5*, 1–10.

Thompson, W.L., & Kosslyn, S.M. (2000). Neural systems activated during visual mental imagery: A review and meta-analyses. In A.W. Toga & J.C. Mazziotta (Eds.), *Brain mapping II: The systems* (pp. 535–560). San Diego, CA: Academic Press.

Tootell, R.B.H., Hadjikani, N.K., Mendola, J.D., Marrett, S., & Dale, A.M. (1998). From retinotopy to recognition: fMRI in human visual cortex. *Trends in Cognitive Science, 2*, 174–183.

Ungerleider, L.G., & Mishkin, M. (1982). Two cortical visual systems. In D.J. Ingle, M.A. Goodale & R.J.W. Mansfield (Eds.), *Analysis of visual behavior* (pp. 549–586). Cambridge, MA: MIT Press.

Watson, J.B. (1913). Psychology as the behaviorist views it. *Psychological Review*, *20*, 158–177.

Weiss, T., Hansen, E., Rost, R., & Beyer, L. (1994). Mental practice of motor skills used in poststroke rehabilitation has own effects on central nervous activation. *International Journal of Neuroscience*, *78*, 157–166.

Wraga, M.J., Thompson, W.L., Alpert, N.M., & Kosslyn, S.M. (2003). Implicit transfer of motor strategies in mental rotation. *Brain and Cognition*, *52*, 135–143.

Young, A.W., Humphreys, G.W., Riddoch, M.J., Hellawell, D.J., & de Haan, E.H. (1994). Recognition impairments and face imagery. *Neuropsychologia*, *32*, 693–702.

Zatorre, R.J., & Halpern, A.R. (1993). Effect of unilateral temporal-lobe excision on perception and imagery of songs. *Neuropsychologia*, *31*, 221–232.

Zatorre, R.J., Halpern, A.R., Perry, D.W., Meyer, E., & Evans, A.C. (1996). Hearing in the mind's ear: A PET investigation of musical imagery and perception. *Journal of Cognitive Neuroscience*, *8*, 29–46.

12 Objects, actions, and affordances: The cognitive neuroscience of action selection

Glyn W. Humphreys

I discuss converging evidence from experimental psychology, cognitive neuropsychology and functional brain imaging on the question of how actions are retrieved from visually presented objects. I argue that structural information from objects is coded in terms of the actions that can be performed on object parts, and this structural information can be linked directly to 'afford' associated actions. These affordances modulate action retrieval independently of semantic information about inter-object associations and contextual knowledge. I show how the findings on action retrieval can be captured by a 'dual route' model combining affordance- and semantic-based routes to action. I discuss the implications for understanding a variety of neuropsychological disorders and normal cognitive development.

In everyday life we carry out many hundreds of visually guided actions on the objects that surround us. We may reach and grasp a kettle and pour boiling water from it into a teapot; we may pour from a jug of milk and from a teapot into a cup; and we may raise the cup to our lips to drink. Although each of these actions seems simple enough, the processes involved are complex. We need to use visual information to guide the reach and grasp actions. Moreover, having grasped an object, we must effect the appropriate category of action – pouring from a jug but drinking from a cup. Over the past 20 years a considerable amount of research has been carried out into understanding how visual information is used in prehensile reach and grasp actions (see Milner & Goodale, 1995, for one review). However, much less work has been conducted into the factors that determine the categories of action we perform with objects, once the objects have been grasped. In this chapter I discuss research within my laboratory that has focused on this last question – how categories of action are selected from visually presented objects. The research uses converging evidence to reveal both the underlying cognitive architecture and the neural substrate of action selection, and it uses computational modelling to provide an explicit account of both normal performance and its breakdown following brain damage. The work suggests that, in addition to action selection based on contextual and associative knowledge about objects, action selection is influenced by 'affordances' derived from the visual properties of objects. There are important implications of this idea for understanding how behaviour must be controlled when performing everyday actions, which I discuss in relation to work in both cognitive neuropsychology and developmental psychology.

Neuropsychological evidence for affordances

The term 'affordance' was introduced into the literature by the ecological psychologist J.J. Gibson (1979), to describe the possibilities for action offered by objects. Gibson pointed out that, depending our current behavioural goal, the same object could 'afford' different actions – a cup may be used for drinking but also it could also be used to catch a spider if that was what was needed. Gibson claimed that objects were perceived in terms of these affordances for action. Although the idea has had its advocates (e.g., Bruce, Green, & Georgeson, 1996), there has been remarkably little supportive evidence that affordances mediate action. Part of the problem has been in defining what is meant by the term 'affordance'. What I mean by the term is some direct link between the perceived visual properties of an object and an action that may be performed with it. This link may, but does not need to, be based on a stored representation of the particular object. Crucial to the idea of affordances is that particular categories of action may be cued directly by the visual properties of an object even if the object has never been encountered before. An example is shown in Figure 12.1. Although many people will never have seen an object such as that illustrated in the figure, there is nevertheless high consistency in judgements of how it might be used ('push the top left part down!').

I first entertained the idea that affordances can play a role in action selection when conducting neuropsychological research with patients who seemed to have impaired recognition but who could nevertheless still use objects appropriately. Jane Riddoch and I (Riddoch & Humphreys, 1987) worked with a patient JB, who was often unable to name objects correctly but who could nevertheless gesture how the objects should be used. The gestures could

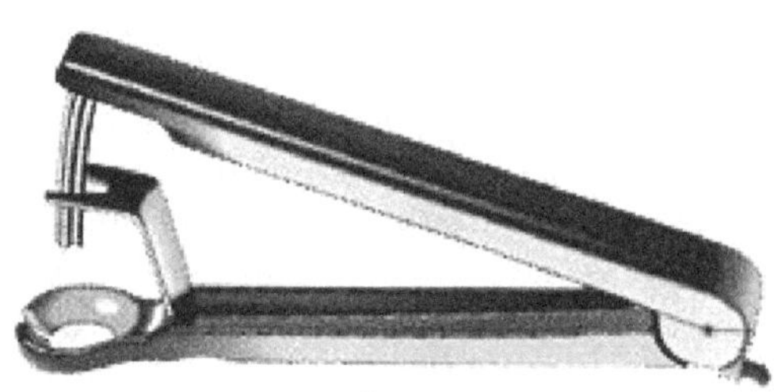

Figure 12.1 An instrument to remove a stone from an olive. Although this object is very unfamiliar to many observers, there is nevertheless high agreement about how it might be used.

be highly specific, such as making a jabbing gesture with his left hand to a fork but a cutting gesture with his right hand to a knife. Yet despite this, JB was impaired at judging which objects might be used together (e.g., matching together a knife and fork and rejecting a teaspoon), indicating a problem in accessing what might standardly be termed 'semantic' memory (i.e., associative and/or contextual knowledge). To account for the results, we argued that JB could make gestures using direct, learned associations between objects and action. These gestures could be effected even when he could not gain access to detailed semantic knowledge. This suggests that there may be a direct 'route' to action not mediated by semantic knowledge; an 'affordance' route to action.

Jane Riddoch, Cathy Price, and I (Riddoch, Humphreys, & Price, 1989) also observed what in many respects appeared to be the opposite pattern of deficit, in the syndrome of 'visual apraxia' (see also DeRenzi, Faglioni, & Sorgato, 1982). The term apraxia is applied to patients who fail to use objects correctly even when they have no motor or recognition deficit. In visual apraxia, this problem is most pronounced when objects are presented visually, although the same patients may make appropriate gestures when given the object's name and they may even be able to name the object in front of them! Here recognition is intact but visually driven actions are impaired. The impairment could occur if damage to the visual route to action 'blocks' action selection from other modalities. For instance, correct gesturing to an object name may involve retrieving semantic information about the object's function and using this information to select the appropriate action. In visual apraxia, the damaged visual route seems to prevent the apparently intact semantic route from operating normally, perhaps because there is competition when multiple affordances are offered through the visual route. It is difficult to understand this pattern of behaviour unless a visual route could modulate semantic retrieval processes.

More recently, Jane Riddoch and I (Humphreys & Riddoch, 2001) have provided other evidence for affordances directing action from the syndrome of unilateral neglect. This syndrome is characterised by patients failing to respond to stimuli presented on the side of space contralateral to their lesion. In one interesting case we found that a neglect patient could detect targets in multi-object displays when cued with an action ('find the object to drink from') but not when cued with the object's name ('find the cup'). This cueing-by-action was successful when the objects were oriented with their handles pointing towards the patient, but not otherwise. We suggested that a visual route to action was left relatively intact in this case and that the lesion disrupted the ability of the patient to use semantic cues to direct action. The fact that the 'action benefit' was found only when objects were placed in an appropriate orientation for a grasp response further suggests that the affordance of the object for action was important, rather than semantic cues (which would be the same irrespective of the orientation of the objects; indeed object orientation had no effect when the patient was cued by the target's name).

Evidence from experimental psychology

Neuropsychological cases can provide striking evidence for either the selective preservation or disruption of a visual route to action. Evidence from normal subjects, however, is somewhat more scanty. Some anecdotal findings come from diary studies of errors made in everyday action. For example, Reason (1984) noted that participants sometimes reported making visual errors in which they mistakenly used one object as another visually similar neighbour (e.g., using hair spray as a deodorant). Such errors could arise because subjects make actions directly linked to use the visual properties of objects, which overlap between the neighbour and the object for the intended action.

Raffaella Rumiati and I (Rumiati & Humphreys, 1998) provided evidence that similar errors could be elicited under laboratory conditions when participants are forced to act to a fast response deadline. We had subjects make gestures to pictures of objects, and asked them to try to complete the gestures before a tone was presented. The error rate for actions was increased under these conditions, with a relatively high proportion of the errors being to objects that were visually related to the target (e.g., making a hammering gesture to the picture of a razor). Proportionately fewer errors were semantically related to targets (e.g., making a lathering gesture to the face when a razor was presented). In contrast to these results with pictures, when the stimuli were presented as words then only semantic errors arose. The semantic errors presumably reflect activation when semantic access to action is incomplete. Similarly, the visual errors to objects may reflect activation when a visual route to action is not completed before the deadline. Since visual errors predominated with objects, it appears that there is early activation of actions based on partial visual cues, so that errors under deadline conditions reflect these actions rather than actions cued by semantic properties of the stimuli.

Evidence for action biasing search, similar to the neuropsychological evidence reported by Humphreys and Riddoch (2001) comes from Bekkering and Neggers (2002). They showed that people are more sensitive to the orientation of stimuli when they are asked to make a grasp response to a target compared to when they make a pointing response. It appears that action can prime the perceptual system to be responsive to action-related properties of the environment.

The nature of the direct route to action

Evidence from normal participants, then, converges with neuropsychological data in suggesting that categories of action can be cued directly by the visual properties of objects. Other neuropsychological research helps to reveal the nature of this direct visual route – and in particular, the nature of the visual information that supports responses through this route. Marie Pierre Vernier,

Jane Riddoch, and I have worked with one patient, JP, who suffered a stroke affecting the left inferior frontal cortex. Following this, JP was selectively impaired at responding to tools and body parts. When given a name she was unable to point to a tool or body part shown amongst other items from the same category, and she was also poor at matching these objects with associates (e.g., match a hammer with a nail, either presented as an object alongside the target object or as a name). This suggests that there was a problem in retrieving semantic information about these items. We then presented JP with an 'object decision' task, in which she was shown pictures and had to decide if they depicted real objects or nonsense objects ('nonobjects'). She performed object decisions at a high level when the nonobjects were created by altering the spatial relations between the parts of objects so that the objects could not easily be used (Figure 12.2). However, she was quite impaired when the nonobjects had plausible parts in the correct spatial relations (see Figure 12.3). The ability to carry out some types of object decision, in the face of very impaired semantic matching, suggests that JP could access some form of pre-semantic stored knowledge about objects. This process was sensitive to whether the parts of objects were positioned to enable the objects to be easily used, but it was not particularly sensitive to whether the stimulus as a whole was visually familiar. Hence JP was impaired at discriminating nonobjects that were visually unfamiliar as a whole, but whose parts were in the correct position for object use. It seems that, in vision, pre-semantic structural representations are encoded on the basis of whether the parts are in the correct relative locations for action.

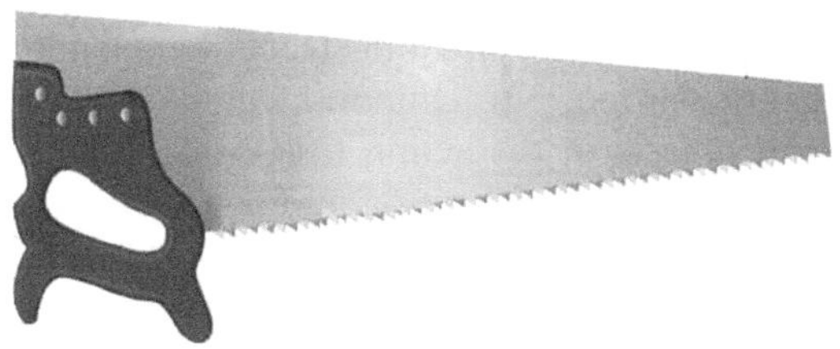

Figure 12.2 Example of a nonobject created by interchanging the locations of its parts, so that it can no longer be used in a plausible manner.

Figure 12.3 Example of nonobjects created with parts placed in positions where they can easily be used.

Interestingly, JP was sometimes able to gesture to objects, despite her semantic impairment. However, such gestures seemed very often to be plausible attempts at object use rather than indicating access to stored object–action associations. For instance, she used a razor to scrape along a table rather than to shave. This is just what we would expect if her actions were dependent on affordances, derived from the pre-semantic structural representations of objects, instead of being constrained by semantic knowledge.

Neural substrates of affordances?

A number of studies, using functional brain imaging, have demonstrated that, even in tasks such as object naming, there is activation of areas of the cortex associated with object use and movement (e.g., Chao, Haxby, & Martin, 1999; Grabowski, Damasio, & Damasio, 1998; Grafton, Fadiga, Arbib, & Rizzolatti, 1997; Martin et al., 1995). These studies suggest that knowledge of object use may be contacted to facilitate the name retrieval process, for instance by enabling functionally different objects to be differentiated (see Humphreys, Riddoch, & Forde, 2002). However, the studies are not informative about how this knowledge of object use is accessed – does access operate from semantic or visual representations? To address this last question, Jackie Phillips, Cathy Price, Uta Nopenney, and I (Phillips et al., 2002) conducted a study using PET methodology to image areas of cortex specifically activated in the retrieval of action information from objects relative to words. Participants saw pictures of objects, nonobjects or words, and they had to decide whether a 'twist' or 'pour' action would normally be made to each target item. The brain activity involved in each of these tasks was then compared with that involved in a control task, where size judgements were made to the same stimuli. We found that the left occipito-temporal region was selectively activated by nonobjects and objects in the action task compared with the control task, and the difference between the action and control tasks in this region was larger for nonobjects and objects than for words. Occipito-temporal regions of the brain have been associated with high-level processing of the structural properties of objects (e.g., Ungerleider & Haxby, 1994). The imaging data suggest that, when actions are made to objects, there is enhanced processing of the structural properties of the stimuli that might support these actions (with nonobjects and objects, relative to words). Consequently, increased activation is found in areas of cortex associated with processing of the structural properties of objects (in occipito-temporal cortex). This fits with our argument from patient JP, that structural processing may be sensitive to how parts are coded for action.

A computational account

The experimental and neuropsychological research I have outlined has highlighted that visual information can directly cue categories of action. This process can be preserved even when access to semantic knowledge breaks down (e.g., in the syndrome of 'optic aphasia'), and, when visual links to action are damaged, retrieval of actions through a semantic route can be impaired (in 'visual apraxia'). This last result indicates that the visual route to action can modulate semantic retrieval processes. To provide a more detailed account of such interactions, it can be useful to develop explicit, computational models of performance, where interactions between processing routes have to be spelled out. One attempt to do this here was made by Eun Young Yoon, Dietmar Heinke, and myself (Yoon, Heinke, & Humphreys, 2002). The model, known as NAM (for Naming and Action Model), uses the architecture shown in Figure 12.4. NAM adopts an 'energy minimisation' approach, in which responses are effected once activation within the network enters a stable state (a so-called 'basin of attraction'). In NAM, the visual route provides a first 'push' within the network towards an appropriate basin of attraction for a given object, a process that is then supplemented by activation along the semantic pathway. However, since the visual route provides the first push, the network can continue to operate to generate action from an object even when the semantic route is damaged. This simulates the syndrome optic aphasia. The converse of this, however, is that damage to the visual route can push activation away from the appropriate basin of attraction, even when the semantic route is preserved. Then, performance can be worse when

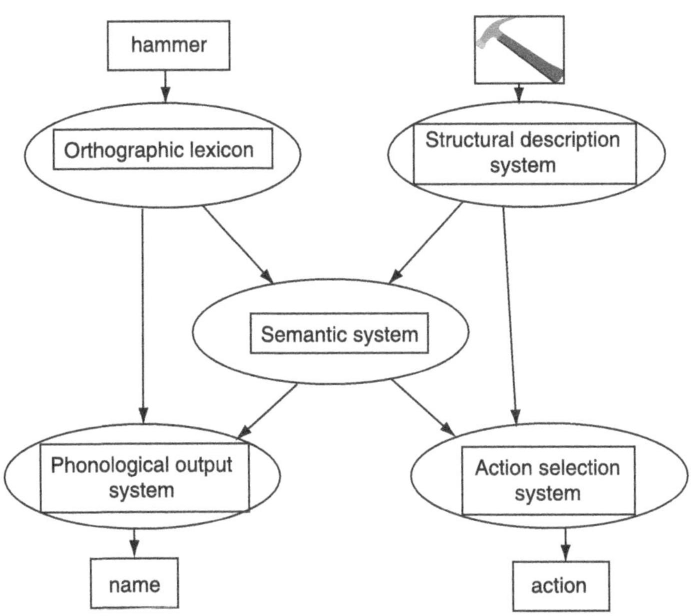

Figure 12.4 The functional architecture of NAM (Naming and Action Model), used to account for both normal and pathological patterns of action selection by Yoon et al. (2002).

visual input is given than when there is no visual input and actions are derived solely from semantic/contextual knowledge. This simulates visual apraxia. It may be noted that, in more traditional cognitive models with independent 'dual route' architectures (e.g., see Coltheart, 1985, for this approach to word recognition), it is difficult to understand visual apraxia. This is because, in traditional dual route architectures, an intact semantic route to action should operate in isolation from the visual route, and the semantic route appears intact in visual apraxia. In NAM, though, the visual route modulates semantic retrieval of action, even though the architecture of the routes enables each to be damaged selectively. It seems that interactions of the kind simulated by NAM are necessary to account for human neuropsychological data.

Implications of having a direct visual route to action

The approach I have outlined to the question of how categories of action are selected has emphasised the importance of drawing on converging evidence, in order to provide as full a picture as possible of the cognitive architecture underlying performance. Thus I have argued that experimental studies with normal participants, neuropsychological studies, studies using functional brain imaging, and studies using explicit computational models can complement one another, demonstrating not only the existence of particular 'routes to action' but also something of their nature and how the routes interact. The functional imaging and neuropsychological research also speaks to issues of where these different routes may be localised within the brain.

If the argument for a direct, affordance-based route to action is correct, then there are important implications for understanding how actions are controlled – particularly when we enter environments containing multiple objects rather than the single objects used in many of the studies. Take an everyday life task like making a cup of tea. Here we must use each individual object appropriately, and efficient task performance also depends on carrying out the steps in the task in an optimal order, without repeating an action or omitting early actions in the sequence (e.g., not putting water in the kettle). We must also ignore irrelevant objects that happen to be in the room. Now if some objects have stronger affordances than others, then actions may be strongly activated by those objects even when the objects should not be used at that particular time. Thus there will need to be some form of control process that itself modulates the effects of affordances on action selection. A neuropsychological disorder, known as 'action disorganisation syndrome', has been identified in which patients fail to perform everyday life tasks in an organised manner at least in part because they are strongly cued by the environment to act on objects rather than acting within the constraints of the task (e.g., Humphreys & Forde, 1998; Schwartz, 1995). In some developmental pathologies, such as autism, there may also be strong propensities to act to 'pre-potent' environmental cues (Hughes, Russell & Robbins, 1994).

The idea of a direct, 'afforded' route to action provides one way to conceptualise aspects of these disorders. It is for future work to link models that specify how actions are activated from single objects to models that specify how we carry out tasks with multiple steps, where the appropriate objects have to be selected for action as well as the appropriate actions selected from objects (see Riddoch, Humphreys, & Edwards, 2000a, 2000b). These latter models will have important implications for understanding many aspects of everyday behaviour and for understanding a variety of pathologies.

Acknowledgements

The work reported in this article has been supported by grants from the Medical Research Council and the Wellcome Trust. The research has benefited from interactions from many friends and colleagues whom I thank: Jane Riddoch, Martin Edwards, Emer Forde, Dietmar Heinke, Jackie Phillips, Cathy Price, Raffaella Rumiati, Marie Pierre Vernier, and Eun Young Yoon. I also thank the patients who have contributed much to our understanding through their kind participation in the research.

References

Bekkering, H., & Neggers, S.F.W. (2002). Visual search is modulated by action intentions. *Psychological Science*, *13*, 370–374.

Bruce, V., Green, P.R., & Georgeson, M.A. (1996). *Visual perception: Physiology, psychology and ecology* (3rd ed.). London: Psychology Press.

Chao, L.L., Haxby, J.V., & Martin, A. (1999). Attribute-based neural substrates in temporal cortex for perceiving and knowing about objects. *Nature Neuroscience*, *2*, 913–919.

Coltheart, M. (1985). The cognitive neuropsychology of reading. In M.I. Posner & O.S.M. Marin (Eds.), *Attention & performance XI*. Hillsdale, NJ: Lawrence Erlbaum Associates Inc.

DeRenzi, E., Faglioni, P., & Sorgato, P. (1982). Modality-specific and supramodal mechanisms of apraxia. *Brain*, *105*, 301–312.

Gibson, J.J. (1979). *The ecological approach to visual perception*. Boston, MA: Houghton-Mifflin.

Grabowski, T.J., Damasio, H., & Damasio, A.R. (1998). Premotor and prefrontal correlates of category-related lexical retrieval. *Neuroimage*, *7*, 232–243.

Grafton, S.T., Fadiga, L., Arbib, M.A., & Rizzolatti, G. (1997). Premotor cortex activation during observation and naming of familiar tools. *Neuroimage*, *6*, 231–236.

Hughes, C., Russell, J., & Robbins, T. (1994). Specific planning deficit in autism: Evidence of a central executive dysfunction. *Neuropsychologia*, *32*, 477–492.

Humphreys, G.W., & Forde, E.M.E. (1998). Disorder action schema and action dysorganization syndrome. *Cognitive Neuropsychology*, *15*, 771–811.

Humphreys, G.W., & Riddoch, M.J. (2001). Detection by action: Evidence for affordances in search in neglect. *Nature Neuroscience*, *4*, 84–88.

Humphreys, G.W., Riddoch, M.J., & Forde, E.M.E. (2002). The principle of target–competitor differentiation in object recognition and naming (and its role in category

effects in normality and pathology). In E.M.E. Forde & G.W. Humphreys (Eds.), *Category specificity in mind and brain*. London: Psychology Press.
Martin, A., Haxby, J.V., Lalonde, F.M., Wiggs, C.L., & Ungerleider, L.G. (1995). Discrete cortical regions associated with knowledge of color and knowledge of action. *Science*, *270*, 102–105.
Milner, A.D., & Goodale, M.A. (1995). *The visual brain in action*. London: Academic Press.
Phillips, J.A., Humphreys, G.W., Nopenney, U., & Price, C.J. (2002). The neural substrates of action retrieval: An examination of semantic and visual routes to action. *Visual Cognition*, *9*, 662–684.
Reason, J.T. (1984). Lapses of attention in everyday life. In W. Parasuraman & R. Davies (Eds.), *Varieties of attention*. Orlando, FL: Academic Press.
Riddoch, M.J., & Humphreys, G.W. (1987). Visual object processing in a case of optic aphasia: A case of semantic access agnosia. *Cognitive Neuropsychology*, *4*, 131–185.
Riddoch, M.J., Humphreys, G.W., & Edwards, M. (2000a). Visual affordances and object selection. In S. Monsell & J. Driver (Eds.), *Attention & performance XVIII*. Cambridge, MA: MIT Press.
Riddoch, M.J., Humphreys, G.W., & Edwards, M.G. (2000b). Neuropsychological evidence distinguishing object selection from action (effector) selection. *Cognitive Neuropsychology*, *17*, 547–562.
Riddoch, M.J., Humphreys, G.W., & Price, C.J. (1989). Routes to action: Evidence from apraxia. *Cognitive Neuropsychology*, *6*, 437–454.
Rumiati, R.I., & Humphreys, G.W. (1998). Recognition by action: Dissociating visual and semantic routes to action in normal observers. *Journal of Experimental Psychology: Human Perception and Performance*, *24*, 631–647.
Schwartz, M.F. (1995). Re-examining the role of executive functions in routine action production. *Annals of the New York Academy of Sciences*, *769*, 321–335.
Ungerleider, L.G., & Haxby, J.V. (1994). "What" and "where" in the human brain? *Current Opinion in Biology*, *4*, 157–164.
Yoon, E.Y., Heinke, D., & Humphreys, G.W. (2002). Modelling direct perceptual constraints on action selection: The Naming and Action Model (NAM). *Visual Cognition*, *9*, 615–661.

13 The fractionation of executive functions

Tim Shallice

Two frequently encountered ideas in cognitive neuroscience are that there is a hierarchical organisation in the control of action with its culmination in prefrontal cortex, and that there are two domains in the control of action, one automatic and the other controlled. The Norman and Shallice model (1986) was where these ideas were first combined. The model essentially has three levels. The lowest level is of a set of separable functionally specific computational systems, a standard neuropsychological perspective. The second level – contention scheduling – contains units (schemas) which represent well-learned individual motor and cognitive skills, organised, as skills are, in hierarchical structures. The schema units are activated by environmental trigger units and are in mutually inhibitory interaction. The highest level – that of the Supervisory System – comes into play in non-routine situations.

This chapter considers two aspects of the model. The first is whether the behaviour that results from lesions to the prefrontal cortex, where the Supervisory System is held to be situated, corresponds to what would be expected given the properties of contention scheduling. The second is whether Dennett's harsh critique of the postulation of the Supervisory System concept, namely of 'an ominously wise overseer – homunculus that handles the hard cases in the workshop of consciousness' can be confronted by showing how the system can be fractionated into subcomponents.

Contention scheduling is based on a production system architecture in which the individual productions (schemas) receive activation and the most activated schema is selected to control the lower-level computationally specific systems by means of lateral inhibition, given that its activation level is above threshold. As this is essentially an associationist framework, variables like frequency, familiarity, age-of-acquisition are relevant. Such variables work well in accounting for behaviour following prefrontal lesions. Thus one situation has been described where prefrontal patients find acquisition of a rule easier than controls. This is a delayed alternation procedure in which subjects must select between two alternative responses once every 15 seconds (Verin et al., 1993). This is also a situation that 6-year-old children found very easy (Houdé et al., 2001). This suggests that the task is controlled by a very basic and early-acquired schema in contention scheduling. Other experiments show similar effects with respect to frequency and familiarity. For instance, Jahanshahi et al. (1998) used TMS (transcranial magnetic stimulation) to investigate random generation of digits, a task that Baddeley (1986) had argued relied on the Supervisory System because whatever schema was controlling the production of a digit, a different schema would be needed for the production of the next digit, or the overall output would be grossly non-random. What was found was that rTMS to the left dorsolateral prefrontal cortex led to a large increase in responding with the next digit up or down. In other words, a temporary lesion to the Supervisory System led to the use of the highest-frequency schema, as would be predicted on the current theory. So lesions to the prefrontal cortex seem to give rise to behaviour that fits with the characteristics of contention scheduling.

A standard criticism of the Supervisory System model is that the Supervisory System is a homunculus. More recently, we have argued that the Supervisory System can be internally fractionated. Take as an analogy the medical expert decision-making model of Fox and Das (2000). This is a model that takes as an empirical starting point the patient presenting with a particular symptom. Its ultimate goal is the operation of an appropriate care package. Overall the model has six different computational domains. It is argued that the computations in each of the six different domains need to be underpinned by a different logic. If one employs the principle that sufficiently different types of computation, which are in a sense part of the human phenotype, are carried out in different regions of cortex, then this would provide an in-principle argument that different parts of prefrontal cortex might be used for different Supervisory System subprocesses. This is proposed in the Mark II Supervisory System model of Shallice and Burgess (1996; see also Shallice, 2004).

In confronting a non-routine situation, a key process is the selection of a strategy to apply. Prefrontal patients are impaired at selecting an appropriate strategy in such a situation, when compared with normal subjects, or even with patients with lesions of posterior cortex (e.g., Burgess & Shallice, 1996a; Owen et al., 1990). Producing a strategy in a non-routine situation can involve one of three processes. Explicit problem solving can occur. Also a possible strategy could have been worked out in advance, and stored in the form of an intention to be realised when the appropriate situation occurred. However the simplest process is the spontaneous generation of strategy. For instance, Burgess and Shallice (1996a) required subjects to complete a sentence frame – that is, a sentence without its single-word natural conclusion – with a word unrelated to any word in the sentence or to its natural conclusion. This test was used to try to isolate the problem of the inhibition of a prepotent response that is often thought of as being the core difficulty frontal patients have in tackling the Wisconsin card-sorting task. However, when presented with a series of sentence frame problems of this type, normal subjects abstract or induce that the difficulty will arise of trying to remove from their mind the prepotent response itself. They therefore use a procedure of attempting to think of a word before they hear the sentence frame. For instance, they look round the room and select an object. When the sentence frame is presented, they rapidly check that their candidate word is unrelated to any word in the sentence frame or its natural conclusion, and if so, give it as the response. Prefrontal patients report the use of this strategy much less frequently than do normal subjects or patients with posterior lesions.

The abstract processes underlying production of a strategy appear to be located in the left prefrontal cortex. The Jahanshahi et al. (1998) study just discussed provides supporting evidence, as does a functional imaging study using the same paradigm carried out by Jahanshahi et al. (2000) which showed a parallel degree of activation in left dorsolateral prefrontal cortex with the degree of randomness of the response, as the rate of production of responses increased. No other area of the cortex showed a similar relationship. A second study which shows a similar relation is that of Fletcher, Shallice, and Dolan (1998a). They used the situation of having to encode for later retention a list of words. It has been known since the seminal work of Mandler (1967) that retention is far superior if the words are organised into an overarching semantic structure. Subjects in our experiment had to encode 16 words from four related subcategories on a single trial, such as four types of bread, four of meat, four of fish, and four drinks. They were in three memory conditions. In one condition words were presented in blocks of four, one block to each subcategory. In a second condition they were randomly presented, but the four subcategories were prespecified before the list was presented. Finally, in the third condition words were randomly presented without any prior knowledge of the list structure. At the same time, subjects had to carry out a sensory-motor task involving moving a joystick from a central position to one of four other positions. Movement to the other four positions can occur in a regular sequence, the easy sensory-motor condition, or be randomly ordered, much the more difficult sensory-motor condition. Behavioural measures of retrieval performance outside the scanner showed that one condition was much worse than the others. This was when the difficult sensory-motor task was combined with a random word list without prespecified organisation. In this condition subjects recalled fewer words and their recall was much less well organised in terms of subcategories. If one looked at the PET activations, then one structure showed a significant interaction between memory and sensory-motor task. Again this was the left dorsolateral prefrontal cortex, which was much more strongly activated in the difficult memory condition when that was combined with the easy sensory-motor task. In other words when the selection of a specific appropriate strategy for organising the words was demanding, but the subjects succeeded in carrying it out, there was large extra activation in the left dorsolateral prefrontal cortex. This fits with the left dorsolateral prefrontal cortex being a structure that is critical in generation and or execution of a strategy.

Of course, it might be argued that the lateralisation shown in the studies was just a question of the material being used. However a complementary study of Fletcher et al. (1998b) showed that this is unlikely to be the case. When subjects in the scanner had to retrieve a list of words that had been presented outside the scanner beforehand, and this was compared with retrieving comparable paired associates, then it was the right frontal cortex that was critical. Free recall of a list of words activated the right dorsolateral prefrontal cortex significantly more than did retrieving a set of paired associates. Why might this be? A neuropsychological study of Stuss et al. (1994) gives an idea. Stuss et al. compared a group of patients with left frontal lesions, one with right frontal lesions, and a group of normal controls in a task of free recall of 16 words similar to the one used in the Fletcher et al. studies. An interesting effect was found with the right frontal group. They retrieved more words than the patients with left frontal lesions. However, they tended to repeat words in their output protocols at roughly 250% of the rate of the normal control group. It appeared that they had not adequately checked their output.

Checking of one's behaviour in non-routine situations is a pervasive human trait. It involves far more complex processing than 'mere monitoring' (Karmiloff-Smith, 1986). First, checking can involve quite complex inferences, which may even be unconscious (Burgess & Shallice, 1996b). Second, checking may be against criteria that relate to high-level task goals, as examples given by some authors indicate. Third, checking can be against a context-dependent level of aspiration rather than an absolute standard (De Groot, 1965). Then, as examples given by Rizzo et al. demonstrate, the comparison can concern efficiency rather than correctness, and can involve a number of different criteria simultaneously. It is the claim of this chapter that such checking processes are controlled by a predominantly right prefrontally localised subsystem of the Supervisory System.

A system that controls checking should have a number of characteristics. First, it should come into play in conditions of uncertainty. Second, it should be involved particularly after a putative solution has been obtained. Third, it will be required when a decision is needed between two competing alternatives. An impairment of such a system should result in the application of inappropriately lax criteria, the fourth property, and excessive capture errors, the fifth. Finally, its function should not be reducible simply to the control of cognitive effort.

All these characteristics apply if such a system were localised in dorsolateral prefrontal cortex, particularly predominantly right dorsolateral prefrontal cortex (see Shallice, 2004). The evidence is based on fMRI studies (e.g., Henson et al., 1999, concerning the first property discussed in the previous paragraph; Henson et al., 2002, concerning property three), EEG studies (e.g., property two, Wilding & Rugg, 1996), rTMS (e.g., property four, Rossi et al., 2001), and neuropsychological studies (e.g., properties five and six, Reverberi et al., 2005; Stuss et al., 2005).

Consider two examples. Rossi et al. presented subjects with 96 magazine pictures for 2 s each. An hour later they were presented with 48 of these for recognition together with 48 distractors. They were given rTMS over the left or right frontal cortex or sham TMS. rTMS over the right frontal cortex at encoding or over the left frontal cortex at retrieval led to performance no different from that with sham TMS. However if it was presented to the left frontal cortex at encoding or the right frontal cortex at retrieval, rTMS led to greatly reduced performance. In particular, if it was presented to the right frontal cortex at retrieval, subjects made over 40% false positive responses. In other words their criteria were excessively lax.

A second neuropsychological example comes from Reverberi et al. (2005). In this study we used the Brixton Spatial Rule Attainment task of Burgess and Shallice (1996c). In this task subjects are presented with cards on each of which there are two rows of five circles. On each card one of the circles is coloured blue. The blue circle moves from card to card according to a simple rule, with each rule operating for between five and nine cards. The task of the subject is to guess where the blue circle will be on the next card. Patients with prefrontal lesions have a special problem with this task. They have much greater difficulty in abstracting the rule. The present study added an extra factor. In the second half of the study, in addition to the cards with the blue circle on them, there were cards with red circles on them. There were sequences of four such cards following, say, seven blue cards obeying a rule. The subject's task was to touch each red card but to otherwise ignore them. Following red cards there were two blue cards and the subject's task was to continue to follow the rule that had been operative before the red cards were presented. It was found that the group of subjects with left frontal lesions were very poor at abstracting rules. By contrast, the group with right frontal lesions were as good as normal subjects at abstracting rules. However, they were very much subject to being captured by the rule represented by the irrelevant red cards, by continuing to follow this rule when the blue cards returned. They did this three times as often as normal subjects. In other words they were particularly susceptible to capture errors.

There is thus considerable evidence that the right prefrontal cortex, and presumably its dorsolateral regions, is the seat of the processes involved in checking. This fits surprising well with work from a quite different tradition that of 'psychological well-being'. Richard Davidson and his colleagues have shown, using a variety of paradigms and samples (e.g., Urry et al., 2004), that people with higher 'psychological well-being' tend to have higher power in the alpha band over right frontal electrodes than over left, compared to those with lower psychological well-being. As alpha power is held to be inversely correlated with activation (Davidson et al., 1990), this corresponds to positive well-being being positively correlated with the degree of left frontal activation. This finding and related ones of Davidson's group fit with the following hypothesis. To operate effectively in the world requires that one makes extensive use of the strategy-generation systems for confronting novelty. Operating effectively in the world in turn should tend to produce a state of positive well-being. However, if one is frequently in a state of uncertainty, doubt, or worry, which will tend to correspond to a state of low well-being, then one will be using checking or monitoring systems extensively. Therefore, overall the higher the state of well-being the more the former systems would tend to be active compared with the latter. This corresponds to greater well-being being found with greater left compared to right prefrontal activation.

Returning to the general argument of this chapter, there is also evidence that another critical supervisory subprocess, namely that of setting up, holding, and realising intentions, involves the frontal polar regions (Burgess et al., 2000, 2001; Shallice & Burgess, 1991). Thus the idea that a Supervisory System exists in prefrontal cortex and can be fractionated into subsystems that are anatomically at least partially distinct and which carry out complementary supervisory subfunctions is receiving increasing support.

References

Baddeley, A.D. (1986). *Working memory*. Oxford: Oxford University Press.

Burgess, P., Quayle, A., & Frith, C.D. (2001). Brain regions involved in prospective memory as determined by positron emission tomography. *Neuropsychologia*, *39*, 545–555.

Burgess, P., & Shallice, T. (1996a). Response suppression, initiation and strategy following frontal lobe lesions. *Neuropsychologia*, *34*, 263–273.

Burgess, P., & Shallice, T. (1996b). Confabulation and the control of recollection. *Memory*, *4*, 359–412.

Burgess, P., & Shallice, T. (1996c). Bizarre responses, rule detection and frontal lobe lesions. *Cortex*, *32*, 241–260.

Burgess, P., Veitch, E., Costello, A., & Shallice, T. (2000). The cognitive and neuro-anatomical correlates of multitasking. *Neuropsychologia*, *38*, 848–863.

Davidson, R.J., Chapman, J.P., Chapman, L.J., & Henriques, J.B. (1990). Asymmetrical brain actively discriminates between psychometrically matched verbal and spatial cognitive tasks. *Psychophysiology*, *27*, 528–543.

De Groot, A.D. (1965). *Thought and choice in chess*. The Hague: Mouton.

Fletcher, P.C., Shallice, T., & Dolan, R.J. (1998a). The functional roles of prefrontal cortex in episodic memory. I Encoding. *Brain*, *121*, 1239–1248.

Fletcher, P.C., Shallice, T., Frith, C.D., Frackowiak, R.S.J., & Dolan, R.J. (1998b). The functional roles of prefrontal cortex in episodic memory. II Retrieval. *Brain*, *121*, 1249–1256.

Fox, J., & Das, S.K. (2000). *Safe and sound: Artificial Intelligence in hazardous applications*. Menlo Park, CA: AAAI Press.

Henson, R.N.A., Rugg, M.D., Shallice, T., Josephs, O., & Dolan, R.J. (1999). Recollection and familiarity in recognition memory: An event-related fMRI study. *Journal of Neuroscience*, *19*, 3962–3972.

Henson, R.N.A., Shallice, T., Josephs, O., & Dolan, R.J. (2002). Functional magnetic resonance imaging of proactive interference during spoken recall. *NeuroImage*, *17*, 543–558.

Houdé, O., Angard, B., Pillon, B., & Dubois, B. (2001). A new window on child prefrontal functions: Inhibition of a non-strategic alternation-pointing scheme. *Current Psychology Letters, 5.*

Jahanshahi, M., Dirnberger, G., Fuller, R., & Frith, C.D. (2000). The role of the dorsolateral prefrontal cortex in random number generation: A study with positron emission tomography. *NeuroImage, 12*, 713–725.

Jahanshahi, M., Profice, P., Brown, R.G., Ridding, M.C., Dirnberger, G., & Rothwell, J.C. (1998). The effects of transcranial magnetic stimulation over the dorsolateral prefrontal cortex on suppression of habitual counting during random number generation. *Brain, 121*, 1533–1544.

Karmiloff-Smith, A. (1986). From metaprocesses to conscious access: Evidence from children's metalinguistic and repair data. *Cognition, 23*, 95–147.

Mandler, G. (1967). Organizational memory. In K.Spence & J.T. Spence (Eds.), *The psychology of learning and motivation* (pp. 327–372). New York: Academic Press.

Norman, D.A., & Shallice, T. (1986). Attention to action: Willed and automatic control of behaviour. In R.J. Davidson, G.E. Schwartz, & D. Shapiro (Eds.), *Consciousness and self regulation: Advances in research* (Vol. IV, pp. 1–18). New York: Plenum.

Owen, A.M., Downes, J.D., Sahakian, B.J., Polkey, C.E., & Robbins, T.W. (1990). Planning and spatial working memory following frontal lobe lesions in man. *Neuropsychologia, 28*, 1021–1034.

Reverberi, C., Lavaroni, A., Gigli, G.L., Skrap, M., & Shallice, T. (2005). Specific impairments of rule induction in different frontal lobe subgroups. *Neuropsychologia, 43*(3), 460–472.

Shallice, T. (2004). The fractionation of supervisory control. In M.S. Gazzaniga (Ed.), *The cognitive neurosciences III.* Cambridge, MA: MIT Press.

Shallice, T., & Burgess, P. (1991). Deficits in strategy application following frontal lobe damage in man. *Brain, 114*, 727–741.

Shallice, T., & Burgess, P.W. (1996). Domains of supervisory control and the temporal organisation of behaviour. *Philosophical Transactions of the Royal Society of London, B, 351*, 1405–1412.

Stuss, D., Alexander, M.P., Palumbo, C., Buckle, L., Sayer, L., & Pogue, J. (1994). Organisational strategies of patients with unilateral or bilateral frontal lobe injury in word list learning tasks. *Neuropsychology, 8*, 355–373.

Stuss, D.T., Alexander, M.P., Shallice, T., Picton, T.W., Binns, M.A., Macdonald, R. et al. (2005). Multiple frontal systems controlling response speed. *Neuropsychologia, 43*(3), 396–417.

Urry, H.L., Nitschke, J.B., Dolski, I. et al. (2004). Making a life worth living: Neural correlates of well-being. *Psychological Science, 15*, 367–372.

Verin, M., Partiot, A., Pillon, C., Malapani, C., Agid, Y., & Dubois, B. (1993). Delayed response tasks and prefrontal lesions in man – Evidence for self-generated patterns of behaviour with poor environmental modulation. *Neuropsychologia, 31*, 1379–1396.

Wilding, E.L., & Rugg, M.D. (1996). An event-related potential study of recognition memory with and without retrieval of source. *Brain, 119*, 889–906.

14 A single metatheoretical framework for a number of conscious-vision phenomena

Talis Bachmann

A considerable part of information processing in the human mind is carried out at the preconscious level. For sensing and perceiving we do not need to be in a state that will by default explicate the contents of sensed and perceived information in explicit representations of which we become aware. Experimental evidence supporting this conjecture includes data on masked priming of perceptual form or conceptual representations, preconscious processing of subdominant information in binocular rivalry, preconscious processing of sensory objects made indiscriminable by crowding, subthreshold sensory discrimination of weak or isoluminant stimuli, subthreshold affective processing, etc. (e.g., de Gelder, de Haan, & Heywood, 2001; Dehaene & Naccache, 2001; Dixon, 1981; He, Cavanagh, & Intriligator, 1996; Jaśkowski, van der Lubbe, Schlotterbeck, & Verleger, 2002; Kinoshita & Lupker, 2003; Marcel, 1983; Morris, Öhman, & Dolan, 1998; Moutoussis & Zeki, 2002; VanRullen & Koch, 2003).

Quite often it is assumed that attention is the psychological process that does the trick and guarantees an explicit (conscious) format for preconsciously perceived sensoria. However, this assumption has encountered strong objections. It has been convincingly argued that attention cannot be equated with consciousness (Baars, 1997; Crick & Koch, 2003; Kentridge, Heywood, & Weiskrantz, 2004; Lamme, 2003; Naccache, Blandin, & Dehaene, 2002). First, maximum concentration of undistracted attending does not guarantee awareness of information that is in the focus of attending, such as in backward masking or in crowding effects. ("Crowding" refers to the effect where a stimulus that can be well perceived if presented in isolation becomes indiscriminable in awareness when adjacent additional stimuli are added to the display.) Second, selective attention also improves processing of preconscious and subconscious information. Third, attention can select between different objects or stimuli that are already consciously perceived. Fourth, neurobiological structures that control attention are different from neurobiological structures that are necessary for phenomenal consciousness, although there is some overlap of course (e.g., see works of Arnold Scheibel or David LaBerge). Attention is defined as selective activity and presetting priorities irrespective of whether or not the *result* of this activity also implies clear and enhanced conscious apprehension of the actual sensoriae.

In this chapter I argue that there is one important principal psychological process in addition to sensation, perception, and attention (and memory that is the *sine qua non* of any cognitive processes anyway) without which it is difficult to understand the regularities of a multitude of sensory-perceptual phenomena that can be explicitly experienced and reported by the human observers of the pertinent stimulation. I will argue that we should posit the existence of (and accept within our basic theoretical thinking) an autonomous cognitive process, the dedicated function of which is to upgrade or modulate preconscious perceptual activities so that the results of these activities become explicit, conscious representations. In doing this I (1) describe a modern understanding of the basic underlying neurobiological mechanisms for conscious perception; (2) list a set of experimental phenomena from visual cognition research, where awareness of the actual sensory stimulation appears as a dependent experimental variable, and provide a psychobiological explanation of these phenomena based on the construct of *pertention*; (3) present some arguments supporting the need for a special pertentional mechanism for transforming preconscious representations into conscious ones.

Basic neurobiology of perceptual processes

Recently, Crick and Koch (2003) suggested for visual consciousness the function to provide a subject with the best current interpretation of the stimuli. Environmental conditions are not the "stimulus", but just the constraints within which an organism has to carry out its exploratory and adaptive activity. To accomplish this, the visual system has to rely on a set of different types of specialized and hierarchically organized neurons: (1) the drivers located mostly in the back of the cortex that signal the presence of specific features of stimulation and thus carry the basic content of stimulation; (2) the modulators located in the front of the cortex and in the subcortical structures that increase or decrease the activity of drivers according to situational or contextual pertinence and importance; (3) enabling neurons that function so as to provide necessary background activity for explicit representation (consciousness) to be possible at all; (4) penumbra that themselves do not participate directly in encoding, enabling, or modulating functions but which are necessary as a support and maintenance system. To understand the neurobiological meaning of explicit ("conscious") perception, we have to understand the computational functions and processing algorithms of the basic types of neurons in dealing with sensory data.

When an organism is actively searching his/her environment, reacting to the impinging stimulation and building up or reactivating an informational model of the surroundings and the situation (i.e., its representation), several functions of information processing have to be carried out. They are as follows.

(1) *Sensing*, where specialized modular systems in the back of cortex (e.g., V1, V2, V3, V4, MT, inferotemporal and temporal cortices), including selectively tuned driver neurons with small receptive fields become activated so as to extract and encode (reactivate) specific features inherent in the actual sensory input. This system provides the elementary featural contents ("what it is" type of information) of what is coming to be perceived, such as location, colour, brightness, size, edges, orientation, spatial frequency, motion. It also provides some physical integrated (complex and hypercomplex) characteristics combined on the basis of simple features – e.g., visual forms, patterns. This system receives input from receptors, conveys the signals via the relay nuclei (e.g., lateral geniculate) up to the back of cortex, and activates the drivers that are selectively tuned to their particular features. Two main streams, ventral and dorsal, originate from this up-flow (Milner & Goodale, 1995). The contact with the designated drivers can be effected very fast, for instance, within 10–40 ms. The activity of this specific system (SP) is necessary for providing the elementary constituents of the contents of perceptual images; however, it is insufficient for the explicit status ("conscious quality") of these content-specific data. Sensing means a find-a-code type of operation for featural information executed by computations that are implemented mainly by the activity of drivers and their penumbra.

(2) *Perceiving*, where feature-level drivers send their signals upstream to the advanced temporal, parietal, and prefrontal modules of SP, specifying the gist of the sensory content (e.g., image of a scene or object), and activate higher-level nodes. Generalized visual categories, proto-object level of input specification, and meaning of the stimulation are specified ("suggested" and "hypothesized"); however the initial stages of this process are characterized by ambiguity, instability, and lack of invariant integration at first. Computational pluralism, with less probable interim outcomes of computation remaining uninhibited and available for further operations at par with the most-probable computational variants, characterizes this state. It takes about 50–100 ms to fulfill neural computations up to this stage. The next stage in perceiving requires that re-entrant (backpropagating, reverse-hierarchical) input from the generalized, gist-related nodes arrives back to the early levels in the back of cortex, providing necessary modulations that help to disambiguate and individuate the perceived objects and scenes (Crick & Koch, 2003; Hochstein & Ahissar, 2002; Kanwisher, 2001; Lamme, 2003). This means integrating the gist-representation (proto-object representation) related activity in the more advanced cortical sites with the activity in the back of the cortex that stands for the local detailed features. Top-down signals from the front of the cortex to the back of the cortex act as modulators of the early activity that help to shape the structuring of the neuronal pool which stands for the invariant, active, detailed representation of the actual input. This process takes about 100–150 ms at least.

For Lamme (2003), Hochstein and Ahissar (2002), Kanwisher (2001), and Crick and Koch (2003), the re-entrant modulation within SP (i.e., within the cortical tissue) seems sufficient for awareness of stimulation. For me (and probably for Bogen, 1995; Edelman & Tononi, 2000; Llinás, 2001), top-down modulation from the front of the cortex remains insufficient for explicit representation to be created. It is necessary to synchronize the activity within SP with the subcortical activity from the non-specific thalamic nuclei (the NSP). The NSP include among other structures intralaminar nuclei, *nucleus reticularis thalami* and pulvinar, and possibly brainstem reticular activating afferents. Perceiving means integration of multifeatured data carried by a multitude of drivers under supervision from the category-specific nodes higher up in the hierarchy, and possibly by coordinated bottom-up and top-down activity involving re-entrant signaling.

(3) *Attending*, where a subset of designated drivers, specified according to receptive field location, sensory features, conceptual categories, or other pre-selected characteristics, becomes singled out and selectively facilitated (or filtered out of the inhibited competitors). Attending happens under the control of higher-level nodes in parietal and/or frontal parts of the cortex and means preselecting a domain or place and concentrating processing resources on the selected representations. Cortical modulators fulfill the control functions. As stated before, attention cannot be equated with consciousness (Baars, 1997; Crick & Koch, 2003; He et al., 1996; Kentridge et al., 2004; Lamme, 2003; Naccache et al., 2002). It takes from 150 ms up to 400 ms to preset and effect attentional focusing (Posner, 1975; van der Heijden, 1992). The fast delay of the SP responses in cortex that stand for preconscious sensing and preconscious perceiving amounts to about 20–80 ms and top-down controlled attention takes no less than about 150–250 ms. We also know that in a sequence of two consecutive and spatially overlapping stimulus objects that are presented with stimulus onset asynchrony (SOA) of about 50–100 ms, the subsequent object becomes explicitly perceived and the preceding object does not reach awareness. Taken together, this seems to mean that the spontaneous process of generation of perceptual consciousness is slower than the specific process of representation; however, it is faster than the time it takes to effect the preset process of selective attention. Something is missing here in the list of necessary cognitive operations that allow us to describe the stages and constituent processes of explicit perception. The missing item in the list is what I deal with next.

(4) *Generating conscious status* for the perceptual processed data, where (a) enabling neurons in the ascending reticular activating system and non-specific thalamus set cortical neurons at the activity level that is necessary for wakefulness, (b) modulating neurons in the NSP thalamus (and possibly in the front of cortex) modulate the activity of drivers so that preconscious sensory and perceptual information encoded and represented by these drivers becomes explicitly experienced (conscious). Earlier, I used the concept of perceptual retouch for this purpose (Bachmann, 1984, 1994). More recently, I have suggested a special term for the psychophysiological process that has the function of transforming preconscious perceptual (representational)

information into explicitly sensed/perceived information (Bachmann, 1999): *pertention*. In terms of meaning it serves the same function as "perceptual retouch". It is my firm belief that considerable controversies and disagreements in neuroscience and psychology originate from the absence of a special concept for the operation of transforming preconscious information into consciously experienced information. Using terms like attention and perception instead just creates confusion, not least because perception can be preconscious and attention does not guarantee consciousness for the objects in attended locations. While attention is under the subject's direct control, pertention is a spontaneous operation.

The basic neural mechanism that works as the basis of pertention involves efferent fibers from subcortical thalamic (featurally non-specific!) neurons that project onto apical dendrites of cortical driver neurons, the respective synapses, and local circuitry that carries out increase in the gain of driver responses and coincidence detection (and thus synchronization) between the activity of driver neurons in SP and the activity of modulating neurons in NSP. Crick and Koch (2003) interpret cortical frontal neurons as the main mechanism of modulation that works in a top-down manner, and render intralaminar and other NSP-thalamic neurons the role of the enabling factor. I believe that NSP thalamus sends its modulating efferent impulses upstream to the cortical drivers and thus fulfills the function of pertention (see Bachmann, 1994, 1999, for the arguments in favor of considering NSP as the modulator that is necessary for perceptual consciousness). Importantly, it is known that signals within SP that travel from receptors to cortical drivers and signal the presence of specific features (i.e., the stimulation content) are insufficient for the conscious awareness of this content. Modulation from NSP thalamus is a necessary addition in order to guarantee that the SP contents become explicitly perceived.

Afferent shipment of impulses that carry specific content is much faster (cortical latencies about 20–50 ms) than the thalamic non-specific modulation which is evoked by actual stimulation via collaterals that bypass classical sensory relays. The latter process takes about 80–150 ms to be shipped to cortical levels where the content-specific drivers reside. Also, receptive fields of the NSP modulator neurons are much larger than receptive fields of the drivers in SP. Among other things, non-specific efferents from the thalamus branch widely in cortical areas containing SP neurons.

The standard local effect of the afferents from NSP thalamus is to quantally increase the EPSPs of the driver neurons. This leads to (1) increase in the cumulative and/or epoch frequency of firing of the driver neurons that carry the specific contents of stimulation (and, consequently, increase in the signal-to-noise ratio of respective information) and higher probability of inclusion in the widespread global activity; (2) decrease in the latency with which a driver begins to fire; (3) increase in the flow of synaptic mediator substances associated with activation and alertness. The more global effect, based on local presynaptic gain effects and coincidence detection, involves (re)setting the global coherence of activity in the neurons that represent the current most important input; this process is under the NSP control which is capable of synchronizing the activity of mutually distant pools of neurons (Edelman & Tononi, 2000; Llinás, 2001; Ward, 2003). This process takes a relatively long time if compared with the fast action of specific encoding within SP.

The activity of the mechanisms of "conscious" perception is usually described exclusively from within the domain of cortical SP processes and respective cortical levels of representation. I would like to insist that we supplement this picture with the contribution of the so-called non-specific thalamic modulation systems, considered to be necessary for conscious perceptual experience (Bachmann, 1984, 1994; Bogen, 1995; Crick, 1984; Crick & Koch, 2003; Llinás, 2001; Magoun, 1958; Rees, Kreiman, & Koch, 2002; Schiff & Purpura, 2002). If not for anything else, then because of the simple truth that most of the data in the scientific psychology of perception and attention are based on explicit experience of stimulation used as independent variables in the experiments we do. The concept of pertention is used as the necessary psychological concept for specifying the spontaneous neurobiological process that bears the function of upgrading preconscious perceptual representations to consciously experienced ones that can be explicitly described and reported.

Experimental phenomena of visual perceptual consciousness: Pertentional interpretations

Successive form recognition (mutual masking) and metacontrast

Two successive and spatially overlapping targets (small well-contrasted geometric forms F1 and F2) are presented with varying SOAs; both targets have to be recognized. Typical experimental results can be found in Bachmann and Allik (1976). With very short SOAs, forms blend into one noisy entity and both of them cannot be perfectly identified. With intermediate SOAs around 40–80 ms, perceptibility of F1 drops essentially to chance level of recognition while F2 becomes almost perfectly perceived. With SOA reaching about 150 ms, F1 also becomes perfectly recognizable and both targets are clearly and successively perceived. It is important to note that even though the contrast and intensity of F1 considerably exceeded those of F2 in some follow-up studies (Bachmann, 1989, 1994), at intermediate SOAs F2 nevertheless dominates and F1 is deprived of the explicit, conscious status. If F1 consists in a single letter and F2 in a pair of mutually identical letters (but different from F1), then the result of mutual masking depends on the relative spatial position of the letters, but only if SOA is short or intermediate (Bachmann, Luiga, & Põder, 2005). With shorter time intervals a pair of F2 letters masks the F1 letter more strongly if F1 is flanked by F2 letters, as in a typical crowding display and similarly to metacontrast masking, compared to the conditions where F1 itself is one of the flanking stimulus letters. With long

SOAs at 100 ms, there is no difference in the masking level between the flanking and flanked conditions for F1, although masking is still very strong at about 30% correct. Thus with longer SOAs object competition for consciousness is what matters instead of early-vision sensory characteristics of the stimulus objects.

The dominance of F2 over F1 at intermediate SOAs is explained as a result of association of the delayed process of pertention (i.e., slow NSP modulation that was evoked by F1) with the arrival of the maximized, initial sensing activity from F2 at the respective cortical drivers. As a result, the gain and spiking frequency for the carriers of F2 information exceed respective values of the carriers of F1 information and pertention makes F2 salient in awareness, which makes F2 the prime matter of attention. The fact that an even more intense F1 can be effectively masked by a weaker F2 is due to the importance of the NSP process that was evoked by F1 in explicating F2.

In metacontrast, F1 and F2 are spatially adjacent and do not overlap. Nevertheless, observers consciously perceive F2 instead of the target F1, which remains out of awareness, provided that optimal SOA intervals of about 40–80 ms are used. The explanation is basically the same as for mutual masking. Because NSP neurons have larger receptive fields than SP drivers, the spatially adjacent preceding stimulus can cause NSP modulation that spatially also covers receptive fields of drivers that stand for sensory input originating from the neighbouring *specific* receptive field. The neighboring specific receptive fields are located within a common *non-specific* receptive field. The relatively slow process of pertention that was initiated by F1 becomes effective with a delay that leads F2 specific features to dominate conscious perception.

Proactive facilitation between successive forms

In this paradigm, two successive spatially overlapping or closely adjacent visual forms (F1 and F2) are presented. The delay with which F2 becomes visible is measured by temporal order judgment (TOJ) or other techniques and compared to the delay in the control condition where F2 is presented alone or preceded by some different stimulus than F1. It appears that F2 subjective contrast is increased (Bachmann, 1988) and its perceptual latency decreased (Aschersleben & Bachmann, 2005; Bachmann, 1989; Scharlau, 2004; Scharlau & Neumann, 2003; Vorberg et al., 2003) if a prime (F1) precedes F2. Importantly, the proactive facilitation effect occurs even though F1 is backward-masked to invisibility. The above-described economy in time of microgenesis of perceptual awareness is explained as originating from an NSP source of facilitatory modulation (e.g., pertentional retouch from the thalamus): without F1, the sense information in SP for F2 has to persist long before the slow-latency pertentional activity from NSP arrives at the critical drivers in SP. Respective drivers that stand for F2 begin spiking late. On the other hand, if F1 has already set the NSP modulation in motion, F2-specific signals become upgraded by presynaptic NSP impulses earlier and visual latency for F2 decreases. Pertention evoked by F1 presentation facilitates pertentional effects for F2. (Nothing changes much if F1 itself remains preconscious.)

Perception of targets presented within RSVP streams of invariant items and the flash-lag effect

It appears that target objects (e.g., letter *Z*) within streams of unchanging items (e.g., letter *I*) tend to be perceived before the replicas of the same targets that are simultaneously presented out of stream, in isolation (Bachmann & Põder, 2001; Bachmann, Luiga, Põder, & Kalev, 2003). The perceptual speeding-up of microgenesis of the samples of in-stream stimulation accumulates and sampling obtains its maximum perceptual speed within the first 150 ms from the stream onset (the temporal advantage of the in-stream target perception over the isolated target perception amounting to 60–80 ms). At the subsequent epochs of stream, in-stream temporal facilitation somewhat subsides; however, it persists with the value of about 30 ms up to and above the stream epochs that are characteristic for attentional blink (Chun & Potter, 1995; Raymond, Shapiro, & Arnell, 1992). The time values and the essence of the in-stream facilitation effect permit us to consider the effect as a variety of the well-known flash-lag effect (FLE; see Eagleman, 2001; Krekelberg & Lappe, 2001; Nijhawan, 1994; Whitney, 2002). In both cases the isolated presentation of the target is juxtaposed experimentally with the continuously changing stimulus (a moving object that changes its spatial position or an object that continuously changes its color or spatial frequency). And in both cases perception of the "flashed" (i.e., isolated, out-stream) object lags behind the perception of the object that is undergoing continuous change or is presented within the continuously presented stream of sensory input.

We can conclude that (1) microgenesis of in-stream objects is facilitated; (2) the most conspicuous temporal facilitation takes place between 100 and 150 ms after stream onset; (3) in-stream facilitation is sustained at the epochs of stream presentation that are typically associated with attentional blink (200–400 ms); (4) temporal values of in-stream microgenetic acceleration are compatible in static and dynamic displays of streamed input.

What about explanation of in-stream facilitation and FLE as based on the concept of pertention? Again, at the onset of stream, it takes some time until NSP modulation becomes optimized, and sampling of information from the first items in stream for phenomenal representation is slow. With ever more advanced epochs of stream (up to about 100–200 ms post-onset), the NSP modulation has been better and better prepared and the sensory SP information about the items in stream becomes explicated by pertention faster than the items that appear as the first ones in stream or that are presented in isolation ("flashed").

What about attentional blink and pertention? When pertentional activity becomes associated with setting or holding the F1-related information in working memory (e.g., 200–300 ms after F1 onset), which requires extra afference from NSP, there will be too few pertentional resources left for the SP information of F2 to be sufficiently upgraded in order to capture attention. Here, attention and pertention interact almost in parallel but serve different functions.

Line-motion effect

If F1 that represents a small visual object such as a dot is briefly flashed and followed by an F2 which is a solid line that at one of its ends is contiguous with the preceding dot (F1), observers experience a filling-in-like illusion, that something in the line begins to "grow" or move from the location of F2 that is closest to the former F1 position and expands towards the other end of F2 (e.g., Hikosaka, Miyauchi, & Shimojo, 1993). Visible expansion of the line that is presented as F2, with expansion starting from the locus of preliminarily presented F1, could well exemplify the visible spatiotemporal gradient of pertention as it unfolds on-line with NSP modulation. The sense data about F2 that were encoded preconsciously by drivers, becomes continuously upgraded to explicit format by spatially spreading presynaptic activation first instigated at the receptive field centered on F1, but gradually spreading to more advanced locations specified by SP content of F2. Unfolding of the effect of pertention can be observed on-line!

The Fröhlich effect

If an object in motion is occluded by a solid occluding surface and appears from behind this occluder, then observers do not perceive the locus where the object first appeared where it actually appeared, but at a position advanced in the direction of motion (Fröhlich, 1923). According to the pertentional explanation it takes time to apply NSP modulation to the sensory data about the moving object in SP. When the first afferent shipments of NSP modulation arrive in visual sensory cortex to upgrade respective SP data for awareness, the locational feature of the moving object has changed already and the first location that can be supported by pertentional reference has a spatially advanced value. This creates the Fröhlich illusion.

Precuing of visuospatial attention

If spatial attention is cued to a location in space, the processing of perceptual objects from that location is facilitated (both in terms of decreasing RT and enhancing sensory/perceptual discrimination), compared to the control conditions without precuing or with nonselective precuing (Posner, 1975; van der Heijden, 1992). While top-down controlled central precuing clearly refers to the effect of attentional mechanisms on the perceptual processing, there is a component in precuing that takes its effect automatically and spontaneously and is based on the effect of physical precues that occupy the same or spatially adjacent location as the target stimulus that will be facilitated. This component works even if the attentional control settings do not require responding from the locally precued spatial position (Bachmann et al., 1999; Wright & Richard, 2003). My hypothesis is that in this case we rather should speak about pertention than about attention: a precue initiates the slow and spatially coarse NSP modulation that will be optimized and upgrades the following target for salient awareness after a critical time interval, say 80–150 ms. Part of the effects of attentional precues have truly attentional origins; however, some of the effects of precues are mediated by the spontaneous process of pertention based on the effects of NSP on the specific sensory processing.

A sample of perceptual multistability phenomena

I would also like to hypothesize that several intriguing phenomena, where consciousness (awareness) of the invariant actual sensory-perceptual stimulation is a variable, appear as the results of variation in the level and/or direction of the effects of pertention. They are: binocular rivalry (e.g., Wilson, Blake, & Lee, 2001), motion-induced blindness (Bonneh, Cooperman, & Sagi, 2001), and reversal of ambiguous figures. SP representations are continually activated within cortical SP modules, but the alternating application of the NSP modulation from the non-specific thalamus is what varies. It therefore generates alternation in the contents of subjects' awareness. Because deliberate attention does not help much in order to change these contents at will, we should seek an explanation in the spontaneous process of pertention.

Justification for the necessity of the NSP-based pertention process as a special psychological concept

Why cannot consciousness functions be fulfilled exclusively or primarily by the SP subsystems of perceptual processing in cortex, and why should we need an extra mechanism, the NSP, in order to process visual information for explicit perception? Would it not be more parsimonious that just SP systems would suffice? Is pertention not a redundant concept? It seems to me that there are several adaptively useful properties in the pertentional system. The existence of a special, dedicated mechanism for consciousness (i.e., for explicating implicit perception) is justified for several reasons.

1 In the course of perception microgenesis (see Bachmann, 2000, for a review), the representational state supported by the active driver neurons is initially noisy, ambigous, nonstabilized. A subject should not *see* this, as long as we stick to the conceptualization of consciousness as

the best current interpretation of the environmental stimulation (Crick & Koch, 2003). Only as soon as the disambiguated and stabilized preconscious perceptual representations have emerged, does pertention become effective. If the consciousness-property of perception were proper for all SP processes (interim neural computations included), noisy and inexplicable states would be experienced. We have not evolved for seeing noise.

2 In order to carry out SP computations regarding features and objects fast enough and with minimum occurrence of errors, it would be desirable to avoid burdening the system of specific data processing with an additional capacious task – for instance, the task of generating consciousness. For this purpose, a special (however "non-specific" in terms of computing the contents – this function is left for SP) process termed pertention is used.

3 Consciousness-property per se as a characteristic of mental information-processing systems has to be unspecific, invariant to specific contents, if it is expected to keep the function of providing subjective unity and consistency to conscious cognition from the first-person perspective. The neurobiological means that brings together a variety of qualitatively different sensory contents as the experiences of the same person, has to be itself universal and to lack any sensory specificity. To put it in comparison – a mirror that is expected to reflect equally well everything that is patterned and qualia-laden, and to do this irrespective of how this patterning and quality-communicating is instantiated, should itself carry no patterning. For this, a special, general-purpose system of pertention is needed.

4 It is parsimonious to carry out some processing without concomitant consciousness being associated with the processed data. Some tasks are better left for preconscious activities. The SP system should and can do this, being specific to informational contents. But this also means that there should be some additional mode of activity reserved for processing up to the consciously explicated level.

5 If what Gregory (1998) suggests is correct, and if one of the prime functions of consciousness is to define the present moment (as different from past and future), then almost by definition there should be some process that is specialized for consciousness. This is because computation of the sensory-perceptual content of the stimulation within SP is heavily dependent on information stored in memory, the effects of dispositional, needs-related factors included. As taken exclusively from within SP processing, it may happen that the sense of past, present, and future appears as hopelessly confused. However the pertentional process that has a privileged position to associate the highest explicit saliency of the processed perceptual information with what is actually out there stimulating the receptors, is just for the function of flagging the present. Adaptively sensible reacting very much depends on distinguishing between past information and the present information. We

remember well the difficulties that Luria's patient S. encountered when his imagination, remembering, and perception were compatible in terms of sensory salience (Luria, 1969).

Based on the considerations presented in this chapter and its references, it seems that pertention as an autonomous process has evolved as a neurobiological, adaptively meaningful inevitability. As viewed from the pertentional perspective, the many hitherto apparently unrelated visual phenomena become meaningfully interrelated. On the other hand, psychophysical experiments show that pertention, if properly characterized by its spatiotemporal and neurobiological properties, is an empirically falsifiable concept.

Acknowledgments

The preparation of this article was partly supported by the Estonian Science Foundation grants # 4967 and # 5778.

References

Aschersleben, G., & Bachmann, T. (2005). *Synchronisation and metacontrast stimulation: Evidence for the dual-process attentional theory*. Manuscript submitted for publication.

Baars, B.J. (1997). *In the theater of consciousness: The workspace of the mind*. Oxford: Oxford University Press.

Bachmann, T. (1984). The process of perceptual retouch: Nonspecific afferent activation dynamics in explaining visual masking. *Perception & Psychophysics*, *35*, 69–84.

Bachmann, T. (1988). Time course of the subjective contrast enhancement for a second stimulus in successively paired above-threshold transient forms: Perceptual retouch instead of forward masking. *Vision Research*, *28*, 1255–1261.

Bachmann, T. (1989). Microgenesis as traced by the transient paired-forms paradigm. *Acta Psychologica*, *70*, 3–17.

Bachmann, T. (1994). *Psychophysiology of visual masking: The fine structure of conscious experience*. Commack, NY: Nova Science Publishers.

Bachmann, T. (1999). Twelve spatiotemporal phenomena, and one explanation. In G. Aschersleben, T. Bachmann, & J. Müsseler (Eds.), *Cognitive contributions to the perception of spatial and temporal events* (pp. 173–206). Amsterdam: Elsevier.

Bachmann, T. (2000). *Microgenetic approach to the conscious mind*. Amsterdam/Philadelphia: John Benjamins.

Bachmann, T., & Allik, J. (1976). Integration and interruption in the masking of form by form. *Perception*, *5*, 79–97.

Bachmann, T., Luiga, I., & Põder, E. (2005). Variations in backward masking with different masking stimuli: I. Local interaction vs attentional switch. *Perception*, *34*, 131–137.

Bachmann, T., Luiga, I., Põder, E., & Kalev, K. (2003). Perceptual acceleration of objects in stream: Evidence from flash-lag displays. *Consciousness and Cognition*, *12*, 279–297.

Bachmann, T., Mäger, K., Sarv, M., Kahusk, N., & Turner, J. (1999). Time-course of spatial-attentional focusing in the case of high processing demand on the peripheral precue. *European Journal of Cognitive Psychology*, *11*, 167–198.

Bachmann, T., & Põder, E. (2001). Change in feature space is not necessary for the flash-lag effect. *Vision* Research, *41*, 1103–1106.

Bogen, J.E. (1995). On the neurophysiology of consciousness: I. An overview. *Consciousness and Cognition*, *4*, 52–62.

Bonneh, Y., Cooperman, A., & Sagi, D. (2001). Motion-induced blindness in normal observers. *Nature*, *411*, 798–801.

Chun, M.M., & Potter, M.C. (1995). A two-stage model for multiple target detection in rapid serial visual presentation. *Journal of Experimental Psychology: Human Perception and Performance*, *21*, 109–127.

Crick, F. (1984). Function of the thalamic reticular complex: The searchlight hypothesis. *Proceedings of the National Academy of Sciences USA*, *81*, 4586–4590.

Crick, F., & Koch, C. (2003). A framework for consciousness. *Nature Neuroscience*, *6*, 119–126.

de Gelder, B., de Haan, E., & Heywood, C. (Eds.). (2001). *Out of mind: Varieties of unconscious processes*. Oxford: Oxford University Press.

Dehaene, S., & Naccache, L. (2001). Towards a cognitive neuroscience of consciousness: Basic evidence and a workspace framework. *Cognition*, *79*, 1–37.

Dixon, N.F. (1981). *Preconscious processing*. Chichester, UK: Wiley.

Eagleman, D.M. (2001). Visual illusions and neurobiology. *Nature Reviews Neuroscience*, *2*, 920–926.

Edelman, G.M., & Tononi, G. (2000). *A universe of consciousness: How matter becomes imagination*. New York: Basic Books.

Fröhlich, F.W. (1923). Über die Messung der Empfindungszeit. *Zeitschrift für Sinnesphysiologie*, *54*, 58–78.

Gregory, R. (1998). Flagging the present with qualia. In S. Rose (Ed.), *From brains to consciousness? Essays on the new sciences of the mind* (pp. 200–209). Harmondsworth, UK: The Penguin Press.

He, S., Cavanagh, P., & Intriligator, J. (1996). Attentional resolution and the locus of visual awareness. *Nature*, *383*, 334–337.

Hikosaka, O., Miyauchi, S., & Shimojo, S. (1993). Voluntary and stimulus-induced attention detected as motion sensation. *Perception*, *22*, 517–526.

Hochstein, S., & Ahissar, M. (2002). View from the top: Hierarchies and reverse hierarchies in the visual system. *Neuron*, *36*, 791–804.

Jaśkowski, P., van der Lubbe, R., Schlotterbeck, E., & Verleger, R. (2002). Traces left on visual selective attention by stimuli that are not consciously identified. *Psychological Science*, *13*, 48–54.

Kanwisher, N. (2001). Neural events and perceptual awareness. *Cognition*, *79*, 89–113.

Kentridge, R.W., Heywood, C.A., & Weiskrantz, L. (2004). Spatial attention speeds discrimination without awareness in blindsight. *Neuropsychologia*, *42*, 831–835.

Kinoshita, S., & Lupker, S.J. (Eds.). (2003). *Masked priming: The state of the art*. New York: Psychology Press.

Krekelberg, B., & Lappe, M. (2001). Neuronal latencies and the position of moving objects. *Trends in Neurosciences*, *24*, 335–339.

Lamme, V.A.F. (2003). Why visual attention and awareness are different. *Trends in Cognitive Sciences*, *7*, 12–18.

Llinás, R.R. (2001). *I of the vortex: From neurons to self.* Cambridge, MA: MIT Press.
Luria, A.R. (1969). *The mind of a mnemonist.* London: Jonathan Cape.
Magoun, H.W. (1958). *The waking brain.* Springfield, IL: C.C. Thomas.
Marcel, A.J. (1983). Conscious and unconscious perception: Experiments on visual masking and word recognition. *Cognitive Psychology, 15,* 197–237.
Milner, A.D., & Goodale, M.A. (1995). *The visual brain in action.* Oxford: Oxford University Press.
Morris, J.S., Öhman, A., & Dolan, R.J. (1998). Conscious and unconscious emotional learning in the human amygdala. *Nature, 393,* 467–470.
Moutoussis, K., & Zeki, S. (2002). The relationship between cortical activation and perception investigated with invisible stimuli. *Proceedings of the National Academy of Sciences USA, 99,* 9527–9532.
Naccache, L., Blandin, E., & Dehaene, S. (2002). Unconscious masked priming depends on temporal attention. *Psychological Science, 13,* 416–424.
Nijhawan, R. (1994). Motion extrapolation in catching. *Nature, 370,* 256–257.
Posner, M.I. (1975). *Chronometric explorations of mind.* Hillsdale, NJ: Lawrence Erlbaum Associates Inc.
Raymond, J.E., Shapiro, K.L., & Arnell, K.M. (1992). Temporary suppression of visual processing in an RSVP task: An attentional blink? *Journal of Experimental Psychology: Human Perception and Performance, 18,* 849–860.
Rees, G., Kreiman, G., & Koch, C. (2002). Neural correlates of consciousness in humans. *Nature Reviews Neuroscience, 3,* 261–270.
Scharlau, I. (2004). Evidence against response bias in temporal order tasks with attention manipulation by masked primes. *Psychological Research/Psychologische Forschung, 68,* 224–236.
Scharlau, I., & Neumann, O. (2003). Temporal parameters and time course of perceptual latency priming. *Acta Psychologica, 113,* 185–203.
Schiff, N.D., & Purpura, K.P. (2002). Towards a neurophysiological foundation for cognitive neuromodulation through deep brain stimulation. *Thalamus & Related Systems, 2,* 55–69.
van der Heijden, A.H.C. (1992). *Selective attention in vision.* London: Routledge.
VanRullen, R., & Koch, C. (2003). Competition and selection during visual processing of natural scenes and objects. *Journal of Vision, 3,* 75–85.
Vorberg, D., Mattler, U., Heinecke, A., Schmidt, T., & Schwarzbach, J. (2003). Different time courses for visual perception and action priming. *Proceedings of the National Academy of Sciences USA, 100,* 6275–6280.
Ward, L.M. (2003). Synchronous neural oscillations and cognitive processes. *Trends in Cognitive Sciences, 7,* 553–559.
Whitney, D. (2002). The influence of visual motion on spatial position. *Trends in Cognitive Sciences, 6,* 211–216.
Wilson, H.R., Blake, R., & Lee, S.-H. (2001). Dynamics of travelling waves in visual perception. *Nature, 412,* 907–910.
Wright, R.D., & Richard, D.M. (2003). Sensory mediation of stimulus-driven attentional capture in multiple-cue displays. *Perception & Psychophysics, 65,* 925–938.

Section III

Attention, emotion, and language

15 How the deployment of attention determines what we see

Anne Treisman

Perception comprises a range of different ways of informing ourselves about the environment for a variety of different purposes including understanding, recognition and prediction, aesthetic appreciation, and the control of action. One important tool adapting the visual system to different perceptual tasks is the set of control systems that we call attention. Attention can be allocated to different aspects of the environment and in different ways, ranging from the focused analysis of local conjunctions of features to the global registration of scene properties. I will describe the theoretical framework that I use and some research exploring the effects of these different ways of allocating attention to displays with multiple stimuli.

General framework

Figure 15.1 shows a first rapid pass through the visual system before attention is brought to bear, or when attention is focused elsewhere. Visual stimuli are initially registered as implicit conjunctions of features by local units in V1 that respond to many of their properties. At this level they function as filled locations in a detailed map of discontinuities, although of course the information about their properties is implicitly present to be extracted by further processing. Contingent adaptation effects (McCollough, 1965) are probably determined at this early level. They are retinotopically determined, and independent of attention (Houck & Hoffman, 1986).

Specialized units then respond selectively to different "features", and form feature maps in various extra-striate areas. A "red" unit, for example, would pick up from any V1 detectors that respond to red stimuli in their receptive fields, regardless of the other properties to which they are tuned. The feature maps retain implicit information about the spatial origins through their links back to V1 but they do not otherwise make the locations explicitly available.

At a higher level in the ventral pathway, nodes in a recognition network representing object types for familiar entities are activated to different degrees,

Note: Reprinted with modifications from *Visual Cognition* (2006, in press).

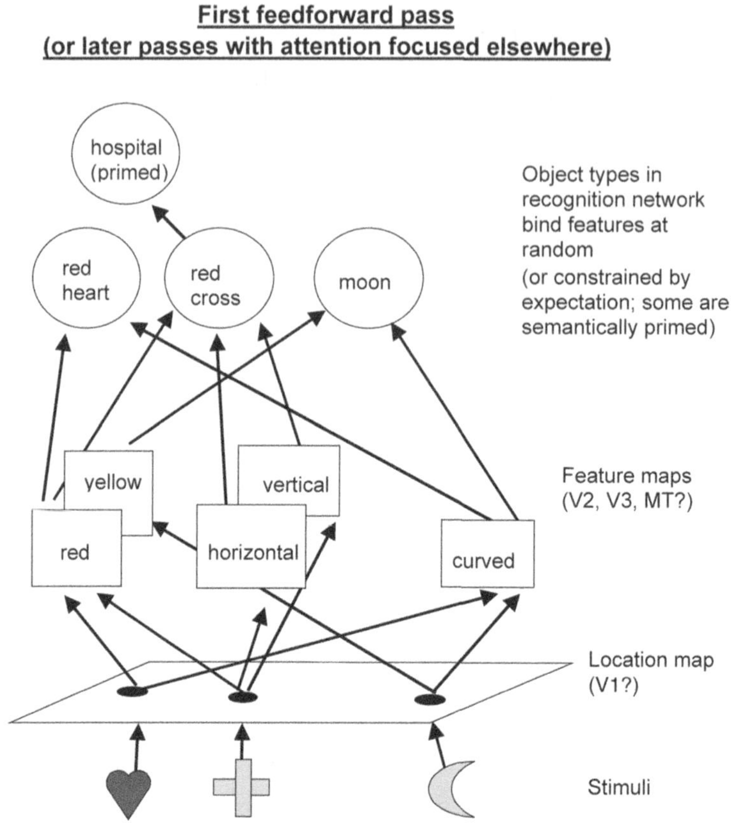

Figure 15.1 Sketch of model before attention acts (preattentive processing) or when attention is focused elsewhere (inattention).

depending on how many of their features are present but regardless of how these are conjoined.[1] In this preattentive or inattentive phase, features activate any object types with which they are individually consistent, and may inhibit those with which they conflict, activating particular recognition nodes to differing degrees depending on the level of feature support. Topdown expectations may also prime predicted objects. Because the feature access is nonselective, illusory conjunctions will be activated as well as correct conjunctions. Figure 15.1 shows the nodes for a red cross and, through associative priming, for hospital, being activated by what is actually a yellow cross and a red heart. The initial access to identities on the first pass is very fast, taking only 150 ms or so (Thorpe, Fize, & Marlot, 1996), although not all are later confirmed and consciously seen. So far the information is mostly unconscious and not explicitly available, although it may trigger responses based on the semantic categories activated (see below).

Our hypothesis (Treisman & Gelade, 1980) was that incorrect conjunctions

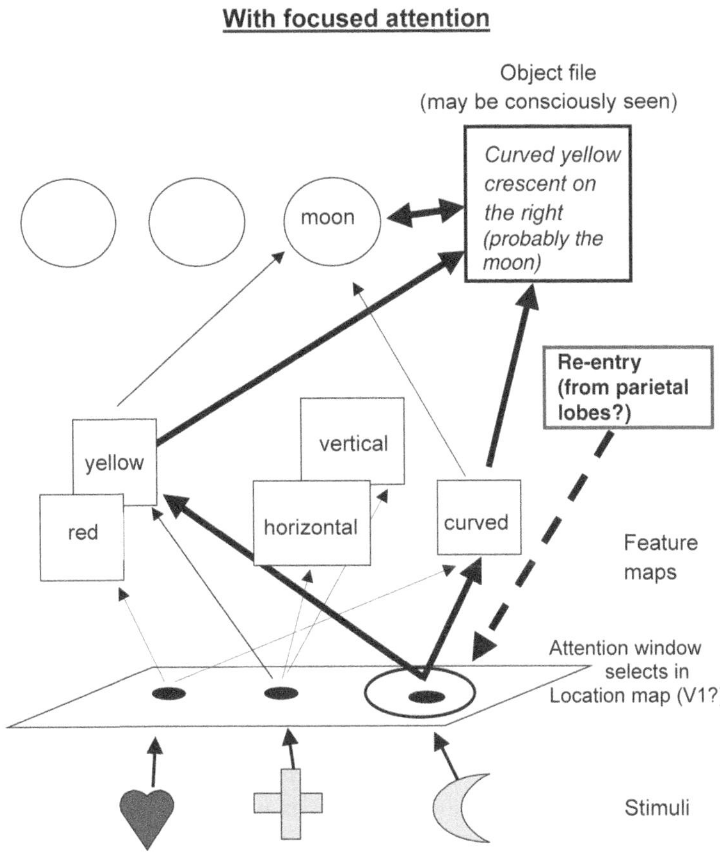

Figure 15.2 Sketch of model with attention focused on one object. The features in the selected location are collected in an object file where they are bound. Non-selected features are excluded from the object file but may still prime object nodes in recognition network.

are weeded out by focused attention. Figure 15.2 shows the attention window narrowly focused onto one object location and suppressing any features outside the currently selected area. One way this might be implemented is through a re-entry process, controlled by parietal areas, acting back on the map of locations, perhaps in V1, to serially select the contents of different locations (Treisman, 1996). An "object file", addressed by its location at a particular time, is formed to represent the attended object (Kahneman, Treisman, & Gibbs, 1992). Within it, the selected features are bound and then compared to the set of currently active representations in the recognition network to retrieve the identity of the object – in this case the moon. Conscious perception depends on these object files.[2] The recognition network is a long-term store of knowledge used to identify objects but not to represent the current scene.

This account provides a dual representation of object identities, one implicit and unconscious and the other explicit and conscious: On the one hand, there is a continuum of activation in the recognition network of object types, modulated both by expectations and by the amount of feature support allowed through at any time by the window of attention. In addition, the attended features are assembled to form a few explicit object tokens or "object files" that encode information from particular objects in their particular current instantiation, specifying the spatial relations and conjunctions of features, and mediating conscious experience. The number of object files that can be set up and maintained in working memory is very limited – only two to four bound objects (Luck & Vogel, 1997). However, the semantic knowledge primed in the recognition network may be much richer (see discussion below).

The window of attention set by the parietal scan can take on different apertures, to encompass anything from a finely localized object to a global view of the surrounding scene. The resulting object file may represent the scene as a whole (e.g., an ocean beach), a pair of objects within the scene (e.g., a woman walking her dog), or even a single part of one object (e.g., the handle of a cup). In combination, these samples at differing scales build up a representation both of a background setting and of some objects within it.

Evidence for feature integration theory (FIT)

The evidence that led to this theory includes the following findings:

1 Search for a conjunction target requires focused attention whereas search for targets coded by separate features is parallel. This early claim was supported by several experiments (Treisman & Gelade, 1980), but its generality was soon challenged. When the features of the conjunction are defined by separate dimensions and are highly discriminable, a strategy for guiding the search can bypass the need to bind every distractor (Treisman, 1988; Treisman & Sato, 1990; Wolfe, Cave, & Franzel, 1989). Because the strategy also depends on spatial selection (controlled from the relevant feature maps), this strategy fails for conjunctions of parts within objects, for example a rotated T among rotated Ls, where both parts are present in every item and only their arrangement changes. It also cannot be used when the target is unknown and defined as the odd one out in a background of known conjunctions (Treisman & Sato, 1990).

2 Participants make binding errors if attention is diverted or overloaded. When we flashed displays of three colored letters and asked observers to attend primarily to two flanking digits, they reported many illusory conjunctions such as a red E or a green T when the stimuli were actually a red O, a blue T, and a green E (Treisman & Schmidt, 1982).

3 A spatial cue in advance of the display helps the identification of a conjunction target much more than identification of a feature target (Treisman, 1988).

4 Boundaries or shapes defined only by conjunctions are difficult to see, whereas feature-defined boundaries give easy segregation and shape recognition (Treisman & Gelade, 1980, Wolfe & Bennett, 1997). It seems that we cannot "hold onto" more than one conjunction at a time.
5 Priming can be object specific. For example, a letter primes report of a matching letter when it reappears in the same frame, even after moving to a new location (Kahneman et al., 1992). This suggests that temporary episodic object tokens are set up to represent objects in their current specific instantiations, and to bind their features across space and time.
6 Search for conjunctions activates the same parietal areas as shifting attention spatially (Corbetta, Shulman, Miezin, & Petersen, 1995).
7 Patients with bilateral parietal lesions lose their ability to localize objects spatially. Since this rules out spatial attention, FIT predicts that they should experience problems with binding and with individuating objects. This prediction is confirmed (Humphreys, Cinel, Wolfe, Olson, & Klempen, 2000; Robertson, Treisman, Friedman-Hill, & Grabowecky, 1997). The patient we studied saw illusory conjunctions even with displays of only two objects. He was unable to find conjunction targets in visual search tasks but had no problem searching for targets defined by a single feature. If the deficit reflects a perceptual space that has collapsed down to a single functional location, it could also explain their simultanagnosia. Our account of these deficits is depicted in Figure 15.3. The model gives a way of integrating the two symptoms described by Balint (1909) – localization failures and simultanagnosia – while adding the third prediction, that these patients should have major problems with binding.

Binding, perceptual organization, and visual search

The first new experiment that I will describe, done in collaboration with my students, Evans and Hu, explored the effect of perceptual organization on search for conjunction targets; specifically, what determines the units that are entered into object files. A debate over whether attention selects locations or objects has been going on for years. Debates that last that long usually get the answer "both". It is certainly the case that one can attend to a particular currently empty location and that this causes a faster response to whatever appears in that location. But it is also true that object characteristics can mould attention to fit them, and that responses are triggered faster to two parts of the same object than to equidistant parts of two different objects (Egly, Driver, & Rafal, 1994).

But what defines an object before it has been selected and attended? In feature integration theory, preattentive grouping must take place either in the separate feature maps, where it will be defined by separate colors, orientations, directions of movement and so on, but not by conjunctions of those features, or in the map of filled locations where properties such as connectedness, proximity, and colinearity could play a role in defining the candidate objects

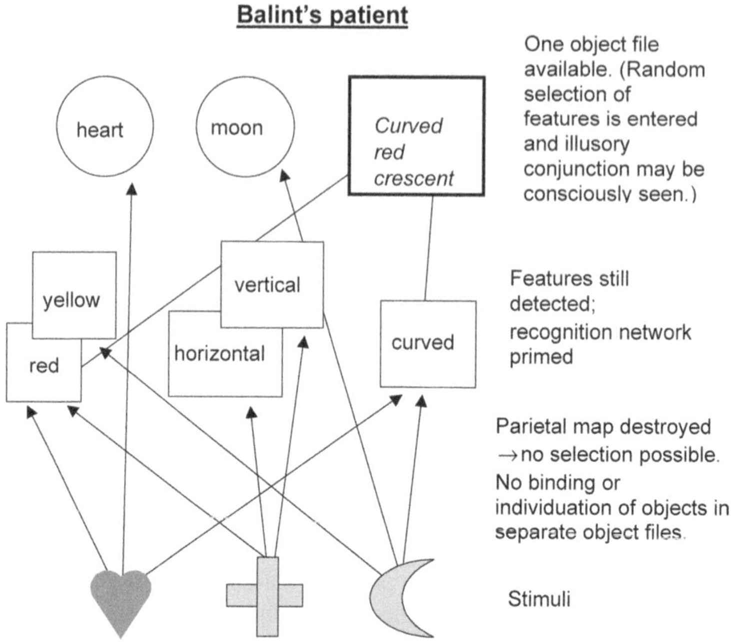

Figure 15.3 Sketch of model for Balint's patient with bilateral parietal damage. The location map has been destroyed, preventing feature binding and the individuation of different simultaneously presented objects through spatial attention. As a result, binding errors are frequent and only one object file is available at any given time.

for focused attention. Grouping can also be influenced by top-down control, in a recursive interaction.

Balint's patients may provide some useful empirical evidence on what counts as a perceptual unit. Their simultanagnosia allows them to perceive only a single object, so an object may be whatever they can see at any given time. The circularity can be broken by seeing how well their responses predict attentional performance in normal participants. Humphreys and Riddoch (1993) showed a Balint's patient an array of dots in either one or two colors. He was unable to tell whether the array contained two colors or not, since he saw only one dot of the many presented. However when heterogenous pairs of dots were joined with connecting lines he was suddenly able to do the task. The lines made each pair into a unitary object so that two dots of different colors were now consciously accessible instead of one. However, when the lines connected matching pairs he failed. Robertson and I tried replicating this experiment with our Balint's patient. Unfortunately he did not show the effect. However he did make an intriguing remark that is also relevant to our question. He said, "You know I can only see one or two of the whole bunch of them." Now where was that "bunch" that he knew about but allegedly could not see? Our guess is that he occasionally opened a larger object file, letting in a patch of dots as a single object. I will return to that observation later in the chapter.

Inspired by Humphrey's patient, Evans, Hu, and I explored a prediction about perceptual units and binding in normal participants. The target in our visual search task was a conjunction of shape and color – a blue circle among green circles and blue triangles. We used displays with lines that either connected the elements or left them unconnected. The lines connected either mixed or matching pairs (see Figure 15.4). The Balint's data suggest that connecting lines make perceptual units out of the pairs. If so, the linking might help when the pairs match, since there would be fewer items to search. But it should hinder when they are mixed because each object would contain both target features – circle and blue. Attention would have to narrow down to the separate shapes within the pairs, breaking the natural units. Search should be slower, and the risk of illusory conjunctions should increase.

The four conditions, Mixed Linked, Mixed Separate, Matching Linked, and Matching Separate, were randomly mixed within blocks. There were three display sizes: for each condition: 4 pairs in a 4 × 3 matrix; 9 pairs in a 5 × 5 matrix and 16 pairs in a 7 × 7 matrix. The 3 × 4 and 5 × 5 matrixes were randomly located in the 7 × 7 matrix, which was centered on the screen, so the densities and the average distances of elements from the initial fixation point were approximately matched. A target was present on half the trials. The displays remained visible until participants responded. There were 12 participants, all students at Princeton University.

Participants missed far more targets in some conditions than in others, implying that they sometimes stopped the search without completing it, making it difficult to compare the search times across conditions. To correct for the different rates of missed targets, we reasoned as follows: If participants

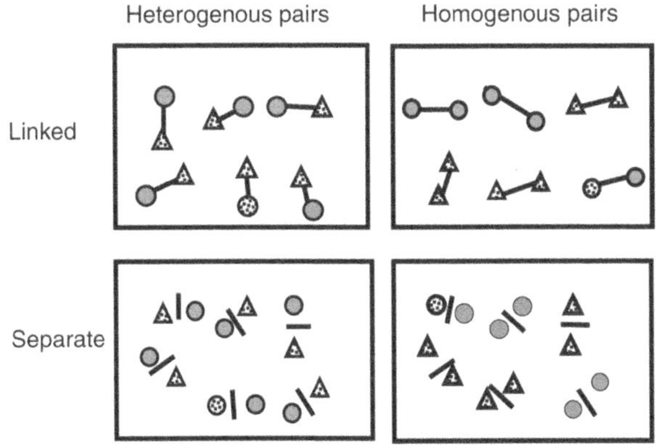

Figure 15.4 Stimuli used in visual search and grouping experiment (Evans, Hu, & Treisman, unpublished). The target was a blue circle (shown as speckled) among blue triangles and green circles (shown as gray).

Table 15.1 Search functions for the four conditions shown in Figure 15.5

	Mixed pairs			*Matching pairs*		
	Slope estimate	*Intercept*	*Mean % missed targets*	*Slope estimate*	*Intercept*	*Mean % missed targets*
Linked	187	359	21	108	470	12
Separate	130	452	8	98	480	5

The numbers are the means of 2 (Target Present) and (Target Absent) slopes, calculated after correcting the display sizes for the proportion of targets missed on Target Present trials at each display size.

missed targets with probability p in displays of n items, they presumably searched only $(1 - p)$ of the n items. We calculated the search rates replacing the objective display sizes with these estimates of the number of items searched. Since the functions appeared to increase linearly with the number of items and the slope ratios of target absent to target present were close to 2 to 1 (averaging 2.1), we assumed that they reflected serial self-terminating search. To get a concise summary of performance in the four conditions, we took the mean of the slopes for target absent and twice the slopes for target present (since only half the items would be checked in a self-terminating search). These are shown in Table 15.1.

The Mixed Linked condition, as predicted, gave by far the worst performance – search times per item nearly double those for the Matching Linked, and much worse than those for the Mixed Separate. The object files that preattentive processes deliver up for attentive checking in this condition are poorly adapted to the task of finding the blue circle target, because each pair creates a potential illusory conjunction. It has to be broken up perceptually before being rejected.

Components of binding

Once the candidate objects for attention are specified, how do we actually bind their features? The second experiment, done with Seiffert and Weber, is an attempt to analyze the binding process and to see what brain mechanisms are involved. We distinguish three different components to the binding task in visual search: shift, suppress, and bind.

1. We must *shift* the attention window in space to select one object after another.
2. We must exclude or *suppress* features of other objects, to prevent illusory conjunctions
3. Finally we must *bind* the selected features together

We used a difficult conjunction search task, initially tested by Wolfe and Bennett (1997), to try to separate the contribution of each of these components. The target was a plus with a blue vertical and a green horizontal bar. It appeared among either conjunction distractors (pluses with a green vertical and blue horizontal bar), or feature distractors with a unique feature not shared by the target (see Figure 15.5). In one experiment, the feature distractors differed from the target either in color or in orientation. They were a plus with a purple bar or a plus tilted 20 degrees left or right. In another experiment, they differed from the target either in color or in shape. They were a plus with a purple bar or a T with blue vertical and green horizontal bars. When the distractors have a purple bar or tilt, or when they differ from the target in a simple feature of shape, there should be no need to bind. They can be rejected on the basis of the unique nontarget feature. But when the target and distractors have the same colors and bars, the only way to determine whether they match the target is to bind the color, orientation, or T feature to the bars for each distractor in turn.

We presented sequences of eight displays (Figure 15.6), consisting of two components: a string of eight items in successive cued locations that could contain the target with 50% probability (we call this the target sequence), and a fixed set of five additional distractor items in other randomly selected uncued locations (we call this the surround). At the end of each string of eight displays, participants were asked whether a target (a plus with a blue vertical and green horizontal bar) was present anywhere in the sequence. It could only appear in one of the cued locations. We isolated the *binding* component by comparing detection rates when the target sequence consisted of conjunction distractors and when it consisted of feature distractors. We tested the *spatial shifting* component by presenting the items in the target sequence in different randomly selected locations, each one precued by

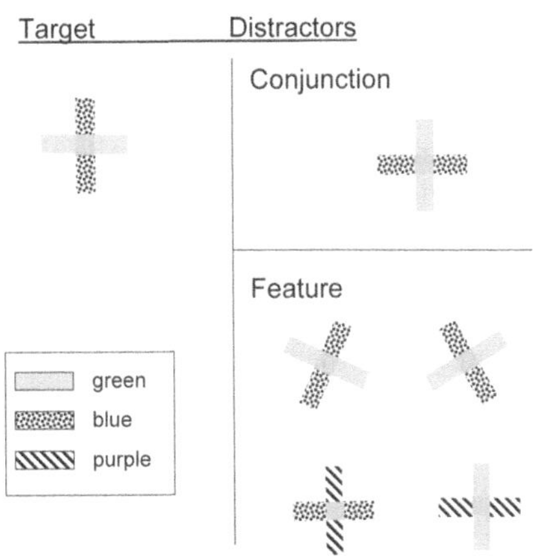

Figure 15.5 Stimuli used by Seiffert, Weber, and Treisman (unpublished) to test separate components of the binding process.

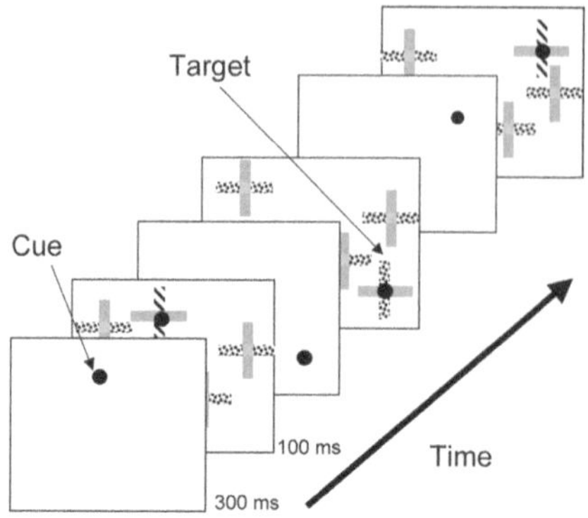

Figure 15.6 Example of a trial in the Components of Binding experiment. Each trial comprised a sequence of eight cued items, interleaved with a spatial cue (a black dot) preceding each display. If present (50% trials), the target always appeared at a cued location. The distractors differed from the target in either a Feature (color or tilt), or the Conjunction of features. Distractors were added in the surround to test suppression of non-target items. The figure shows the first three displays in a trial in which the shift-attention, and suppress-surround components are needed, but not the binding component for the cued sequence, since the cued items differ from the target in a simple feature (color).

a black dot, and comparing this shifting sequence with a sequence that appeared in a single cued location. We tested the *distractor suppression* component by varying the nature of the items in the surround. The five additional distractors could be conjunction distractors or feature distractors. The conjunction distractors should need active suppression to prevent their features from forming illusory conjunctions with those in the cued location.

Figure 15.7 shows the error rates (false alarms plus omissions) in each condition. There was a large effect of shifting attention around in the display. There was also a large effect of conjunction versus feature distractors in the sequence of cued locations. This is the component that reflects the need to bind the colors and bars. There was also an interaction between the effects of shifting and binding. When the relevant location was fixed, there was little effect of the cued distractors. They interfere mostly when attention must be reset for each item. Finally there was no overall effect of having conjunction versus feature distractors in the surround. Looking in more detail at the data for the Shifting sequence only, we found that there was a significant effect contrasting conjunction with *color* distractors in the surround (Figure 15.8a), and there was also an effect in the second experiment contrasting conjunction with color or with shape distractors (see Figure 15.8b). Thus there may be something special that makes orientation feature distractors in the surround harder to suppress than color or shape feature distractors and as hard as conjunction distractors. Finally in both experiments, when there were conjunction distractors in the cued sequence there was no additional decrement

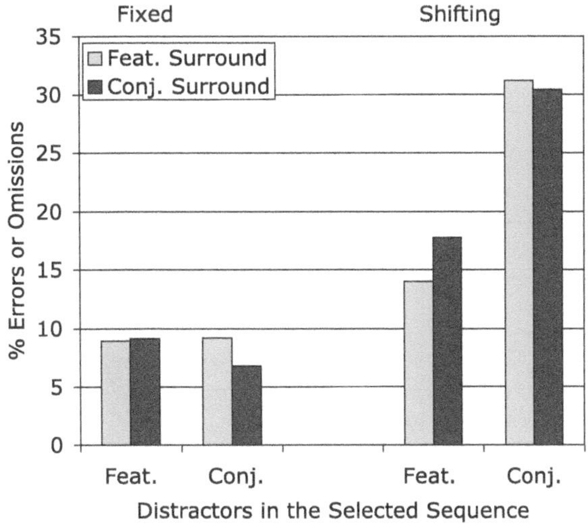

Figure 15.7 Percent errors and omissions made in the different conditions of experiment testing components of binding. Trials requiring shifts of attention are slower than those with fixed attention. When attention must be reset for each item, trials with conjunction distractors in the cued sequence are slower than those with feature distractors, suggesting that binding increases the difficulty. However there is no overall effect of conjunction distractors relative to feature distractors in the surround.

from replacing feature distractors in the surround with conjunction distractors. A possible reason could be the greater heterogeneity in the display with two different distractor types (feature and conjunction) compared to one (all conjunction distractors). We are currently testing with two kinds of feature distractors (e.g., color distractors in the cued locations and orientation distractors in the surround), and we find that, with heterogeneity controlled in this way, there is clearly more interference when conjunction distractors are present.

Brain imaging offers a new tool for dissecting separate operations. We were interested in testing the reality of these separate components of binding by relating them to different brain areas as well as to separate behavioral effects (Seiffert, Weber, & Treisman, 2003). We tested eight participants doing the Color-Orientation tasks in the Princeton Siemens fMRI brain scanner. To increase the sensitivity in the Shifting attention conditions, we tested only one of the Fixed Sequence conditions (conjunction distractors in both Sequence and Surround). Previous studies (e.g., Corbetta et al., 1995) have shown parietal activity in conjunction search, but most did not distinguish shifting from suppression or from binding. Comparing the activation in the corresponding Shifting and Fixed Sequence conditions, we found the expected parietal activation, and also plenty of occipital activation, probably due to the presence of motion. More interesting, we found two separate areas that were activated

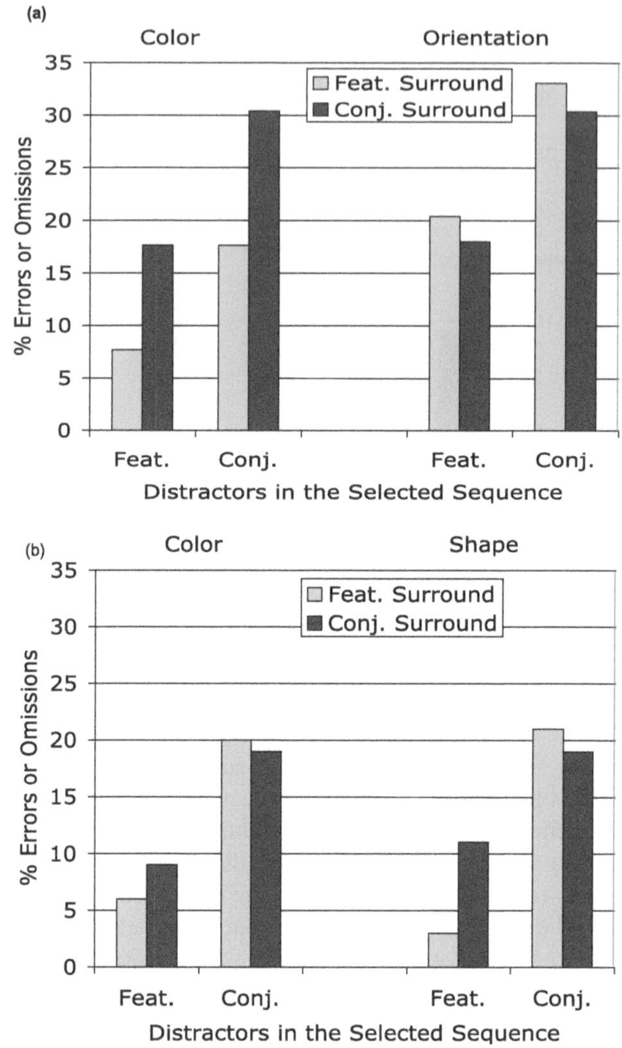

Figure 15.8 (a) Separating trials with color feature and trials with orientation feature distractors shows that tilt distractors are as difficult as conjunction distractors to suppress, but color feature distractors are easier. (b). Separate analysis of shape and color distractors (in shifting attention trials only) shows that both feature types are easier than conjunction distractors to suppress. However, neither of the experiments shows increased difficulty when conjunction distractors in the surround are added to conjunction distractors in the cued sequence. This may be because display heterogeneity is greater with feature distractors in the surround and conjunction distractors in the sequence. Two different distractor types must be excluded rather than a single type.

selectively in the *binding* comparison – Conjunction versus Feature distractors in the cued sequence. One was a medial frontal area, close to or in the anterior cingulate. This tends to be activated when there is some form of conflict present. In binding, there may be competition between relevant and irrelevant features to be integrated into the currently selected object. The other area showing activity selective to binding was the left anterior insula. We also found this area in another conjunction search experiment, so we think it may be a real effect. But its function is more mysterious. The anterior insula appears to be activated in a wide variety of rather specific but diverse situations, ranging from disgust (Critchley, Wiens, Rotshtein, Öhman, & Dolan, 2004), to imitation of facial expressions (Carr, Iacoboni, Dubeau, Mazziotta, & Lenzi, 2003), to articulation in speech (Dronkers, 1996; Wise, Greene, Buchel, & Scott, 1999), as well as to several other equally disparate situations. It seems unlikely that what they all have in common is binding! Of course there may well be different specialized sub-areas *within* the insula involved in these different tasks, one of which may be concerned with binding. Further research will be needed to explore that possibility.

There is no complete story yet on the neural instantiation of binding. My speculation is that it reflects a process of re-entry after the first initial pass through the sensory hierarchy, returning to the early visual areas where fine localization and detailed features can be retrieved. The idea of re-entry (first proposed in the context of memory by Damasio, 1989), is very much in the air these days. For example it is used in the Reverse Hierarchy Theory proposed by Hochstein and Ahissar (2002) and in the model of visual masking by object substitution proposed by Di Lollo, Enns, and Rensink (2000). I suggested that it may also play a role in binding, as follows (Treisman, 1996). The first response to visual stimulation may activate feature detectors that connect automatically to the object nodes with which they are compatible, and perhaps inhibit those with which they conflict. To check whether the conjunctions are real, the features must be retraced to the early visual areas V1 or V2 where localization is more precise. The features of any particular object may then be bound through focused attention to its location. Binding would depend on parietal areas controlling a serial re-entry scan through these areas to retrieve the features present in each. The binding itself might involve the area we found in the anterior insula combining the selected features to form an integrated object representation.

Distributed attention

The second part of the chapter explores the effects of deploying attention more globally over several objects at once or over the display as a whole. The hypothesis is that this provides different information from that available in the focused binding mode. Figure 15.9 shows the attention window encompassing three objects instead of one, making all their features available to potential object files. A separate choice can then be made of whether to open

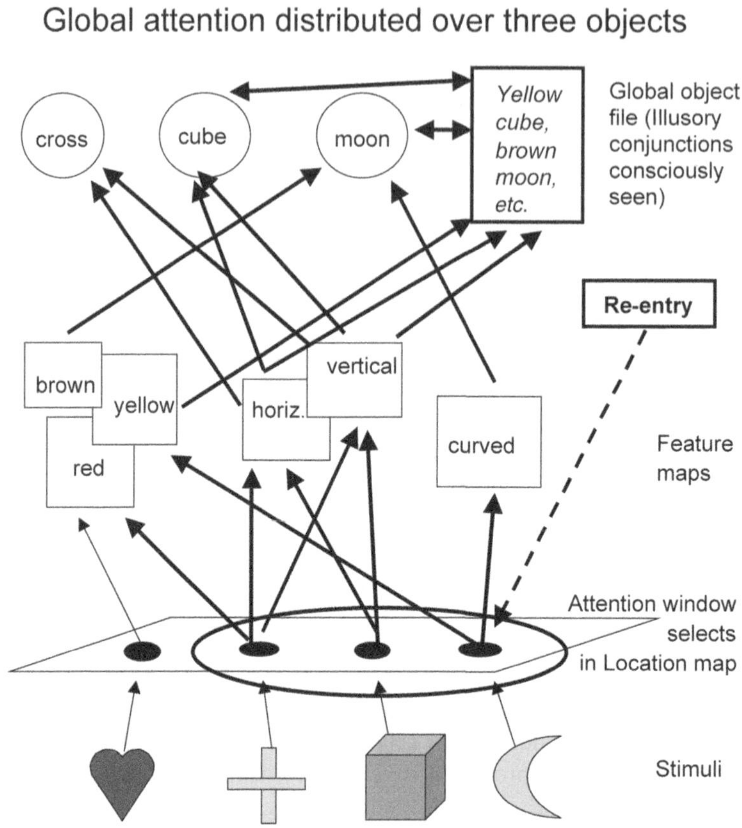

Figure 15.9 Sketch of model with attention spread over three items rather than focused on one. The hypothesis is that this produces binding failures within the attention window.

separate object files for the individual elements, running the risk that a random selection of features may result in illusory conjunctions. The yellow cube in the figure is an illusory conjunction of two attended features that actually belong to different objects. Because it is in an object file, it could become consciously available. Alternatively one could choose to open a single object file for the attended group as a whole, making a different set of properties available, including the global shape, global boundaries, and global relations between elements. The "whole bunch of dots" reported by our Balint's patient may reflect processing of a global patch as a unitary object.

What useful information might this global deployment provide? Table 15.2 lists a number of possibilities

1 First, it could be an efficient way of revealing the presence of a target feature anywhere in the display. If we are looking for something "red"

Table 15.2 Information potentially available with distributed or global attention

1.	Target with unique feature (popout effect in search)
2.	Global boundaries defined by features (not conjunctions)
3.	Global shape
4.	Global illumination and 3D orientation
5.	Gist of the scene (e.g., mountain landscape, or kitchen)
6.	Statistical properties

and red appears in the global object file, we can detect its presence, and then rapidly home in on it in the location map with more narrowly focused attention.

2 It might define global boundaries between groups of objects where the groups differ in some feature that is shared by elements within each group and differs for elements between groups. Groups defined only by conjunctions of features do not create boundaries that are perceptually available (Treisman & Gelade, 1980).

3 It should give the global shape of the objects, at some expense to the local objects that compose them (Navon, 1977).

4 It should provide some general parameters like the global illumination of the elements, allowing us to detect an odd object that is lit from a different direction or oriented differently in three-dimensional space, even though the unique object seems to be distinguished only by a conjunction of shape and contrast (Enns & Rensink, 1996)

5 With more complex natural scenes, global attention may also give us the gist of the scene – for example a mountain landscape, or a kitchen, perhaps through priming from disjunctive sets of features (see below).

6 Finally, our current hypothesis is that it may offer some simple statistical properties of sets of similar objects.

Statistical processing with distributed attention

The world is full of sets that vary on a range of different dimensions, for example the cars in a parking lot, or the apples on a tree. It would be wasteful and probably beyond our attentional capacity to specify each element in the representation we form. Instead we may generate a statistical description, including the frequencies of different element types, the mean, the range, and the variance of sizes, colors, orientations that they encompass, facilitating rapid decisions based, for example, on the quality of the fruit, the density of the traffic, or the rockiness of the terrain (see Figure 15.10).

One important proviso is that this statistical information should be restricted to features, since it comes from pooled feature maps rather than from individuated objects. I recently tested this prediction by asking participants to judge the frequencies either of features or of conjunctions. I presented brief displays of colored shapes – the letters, O, X, and T in red, green, and blue – and asked people to estimate proportions, for example what proportion were

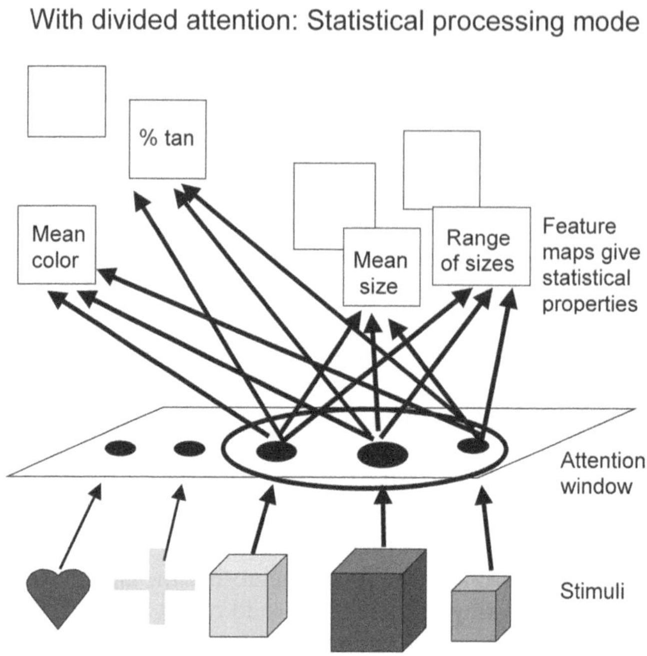

Figure 15.10 Statistical properties may be automatically computed at the feature level when attention is distributed over sets of similar items.

green, or were Ts, or were green Ts. I post-cued which feature or conjunction was relevant (Figure 15.11). On each trial participants saw the display for 500 ms, then 500 ms blank screen, and then a single color patch or a single white letter or a single colored letter as a probe. The task was to say what proportion of the display that particular feature or conjunction represented. Participants were good at judging the proportions of the separate features that were present, but very poor at judging the proportions of conjunctions. For example, they gave similar estimates for the proportion of blue Xs in the two displays of Figure 15.12a and 15.12b. The two displays contain exactly the same proportions of the different features (half blue letters, half Xs, a quarter each red letters, green letters, Ts, and Os), but the features are differently bound in the two conditions. The first display actually has 36% blue Xs and the second has none. Yet the mean estimates hardly differed: they were 15% and 11%. Global attention gives us good estimates of feature proportions, but it does not yield proportions for bound objects.

Also exploring this framework of statistical perception, my student Chong and I have done some research on judgments of mean size with heterogenous arrays of circles. Our starting point was a paper by Ariely (2001) in which he showed that the mean size of a set of circles is recognized better than any individual size in the set, and that extraction of the mean is not

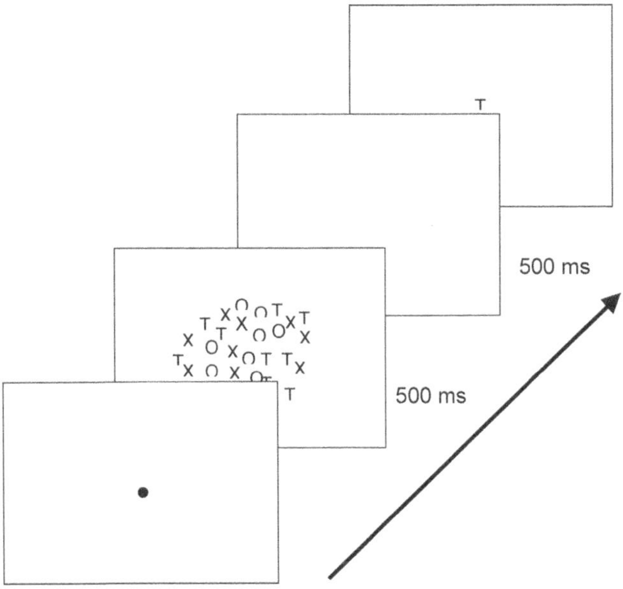

Figure 15.11 Experiment testing participants' ability to estimate the proportions of different features or of different conjunctions. The set of relevant targets to be reported (e.g., red items, Ts, or red Ts) was specified immediately after the display was presented.

impaired by increasing the number of items in the display. We found this result quite surprising and it piqued our curiosity. First we compared the threshold for judging mean sizes with the threshold for judging the size of an individual circle presented alone, to see just how good the statistical judgment is (Chong & Treisman, 2003). With a single item, we can focus attention and give it our full resources, so we might expect to get much more accurate discriminations. We used forced choice judgments of which side of a display had the larger size, or the larger mean size, and we added a third condition in which people judged the sizes of circles in two homogenous sets (Figure 15.13). We found very little difference between the three conditions. Computing the mean size in heterogenous arrays was about as accurate as judging the presented size of single circles or of homogenous arrays. Next we tried varying the exposure duration. If the mean is computed by serially adding each individual size and dividing by N, we would expect a clear deterioration as the available time was reduced. But we found very little. Moreover, the decrement was no larger for the mean than for the homogenous displays (Figure 15.14). The measure is the size threshold, expressed as a percentage of the difference in diameter required to give 75% correct discrimination.

Do the displays have to be simultaneously available? Or can we hold onto one in memory? We compared simultaneous with successive presentations of the two displays (Figure 15.15), and used two delays in the successive condi-

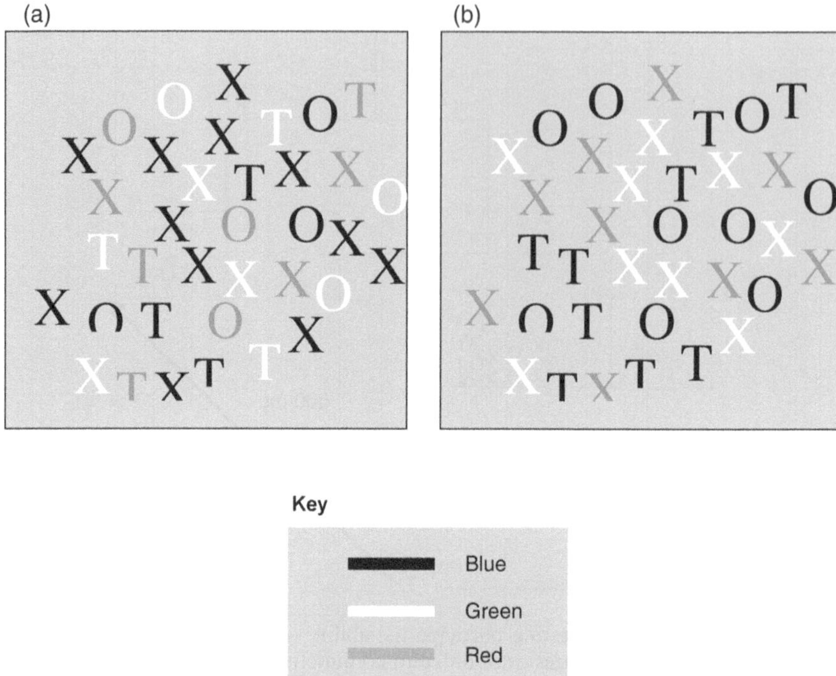

Figure 15.12 Examples of two displays with equal numbers of each feature type but different numbers of various conjunctions. Black represents blue letters. The display in (a) has 36% blue Xs and the display in (b) has none. The mean estimates were 15% and 11% respectively.

tion (100 ms and 2 s) to see whether performance depended on perceptual availability or whether the first display could be briefly retained in visual memory. Again there was surprisingly little difference between any of these conditions (Figure 15.16). The mean judgment showed a small decrement with the 2-second ISI but so did the single circles. Either we compute the mean and hold that in memory, or we store the display as such and make the comparison when the second display appears.

Were participants really computing the mean? Or might they be, for example, looking just at the largest size? To find out, we tested them on displays with 12 items to the left and 12 to the right of the center. The task was to say which side of the display had the larger mean size. The two sides of the display could either be drawn from the same distribution (one of the four shown in Figure 15.17) or from any possible pair of these different distributions (see Figure 15.17). Again people were surprisingly good at making these statistical judgments (Figure 15.18). They were only slightly worse at comparing across two different distributions than comparing two samples from the same distributions. See, for example, the threshold for Normal versus Normal and for Normal versus Homogenous – they are about the same, although the sizes

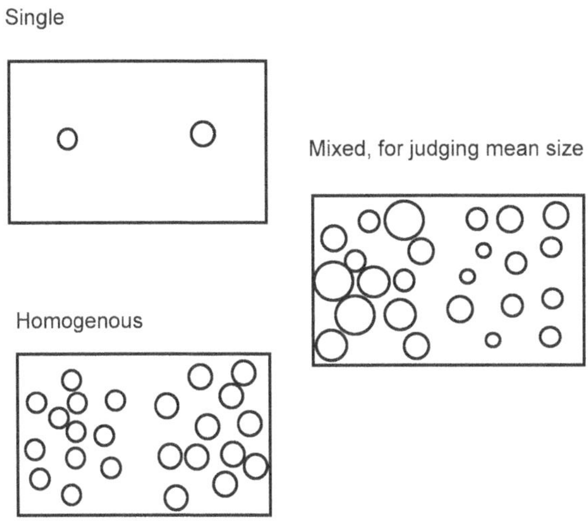

Figure 15.13 Examples of stimuli for size judgments. Participants decided which side had the larger size or the larger mean size.

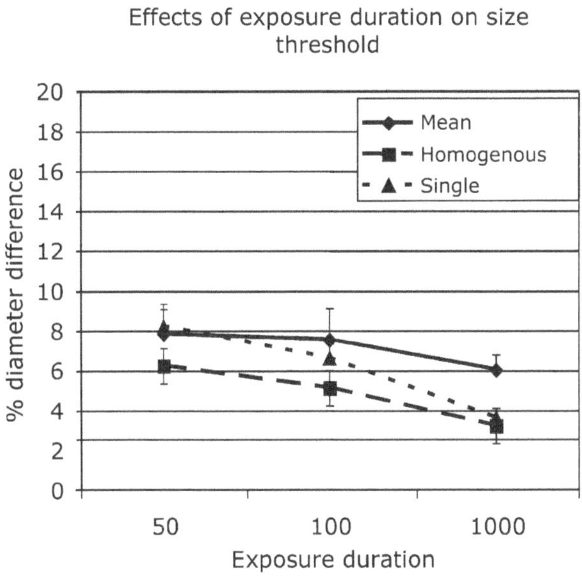

Figure 15.14 Effects of exposure duration on mean thresholds for size judgment with single circles, homogenous sets, or mixed sets. The measure is the % diameter difference giving 75% accuracy in the forced choice judgment.

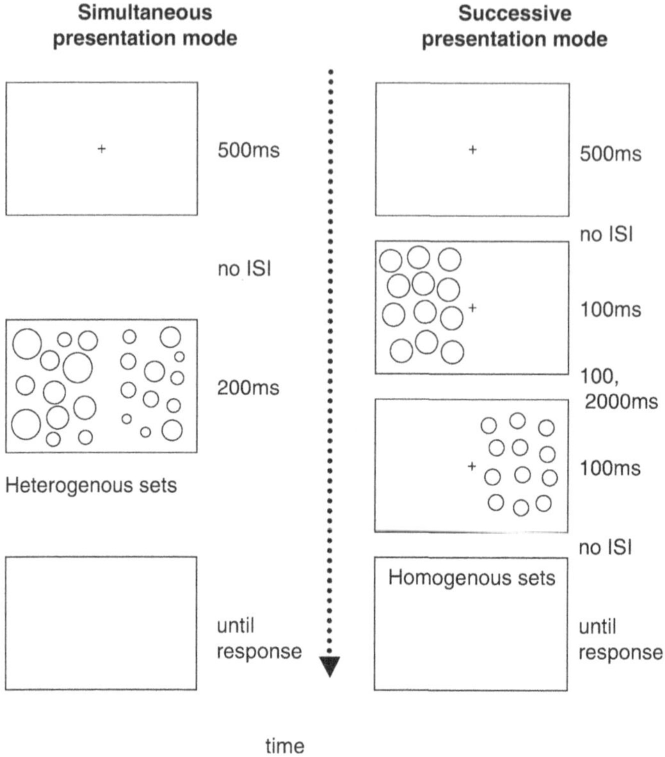

Figure 15.15 Procedure for comparing simultaneous presentation with successive presentation of two displays.

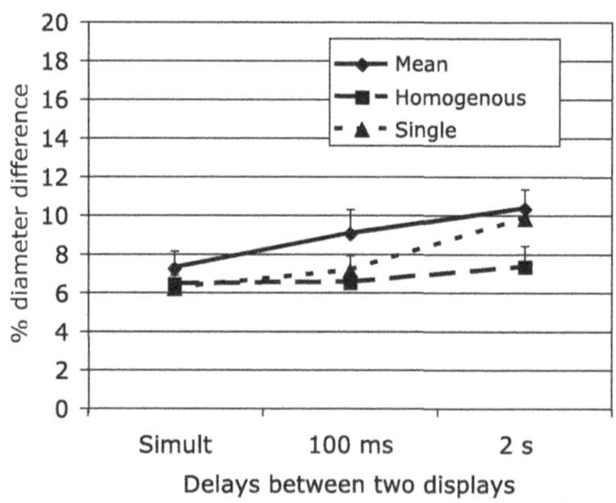

Figure 15.16 Effects of delay between the two sets of stimuli on thresholds for judging size or mean size.

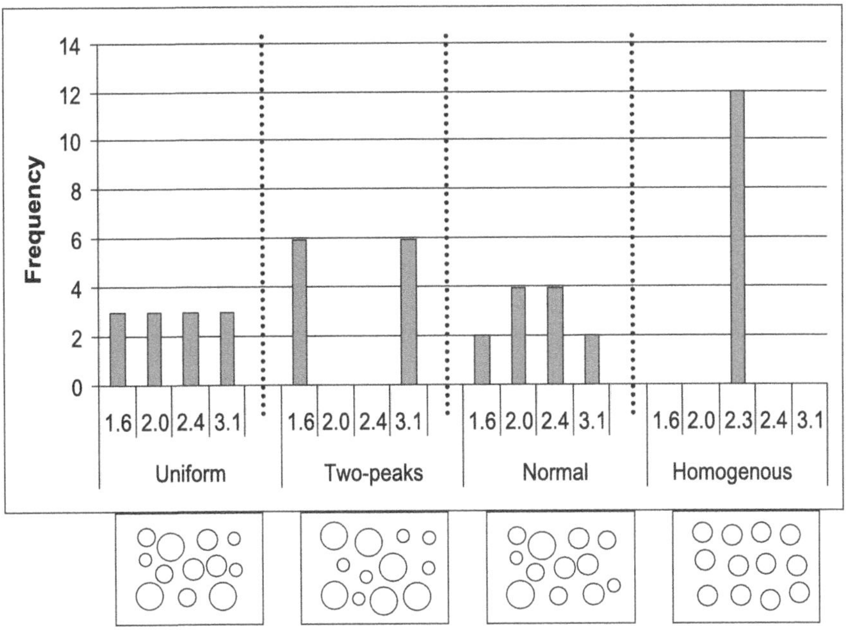

Figure 15.17 Different distributions tested in mean size judgments. Comparisons were made both within and across distributions. The numbers indicate the mean diameter size in degrees of visual angle.

are identical in the Normal versus Normal and have no overlap in the Normal versus Homogenous. This suggests that participants really were computing the mean.

Our hypothesis is that statistical processing occurs automatically when attention is globally distributed over a set of similar items. To test this we tried a couple of dual task paradigms, both using the same displays of 12 circles of four different sizes (Chong & Treisman, 2004). We combined tests of statistical judgments of the mean size with two visual search tasks: one that seems to require focused attention to each item in turn and one that gives popout or parallel processing and which, according to our hypothesis, is done with global attention to the display as a whole. The focused attention task was search for a closed circle among circles with gaps, and the parallel processing version was search for a circle with a gap among closed circles (Figure 15.19). Participants saw the display and did the search task as quickly as they could. As soon as they pressed a key to signal target present or absent, two probe circles appeared and participants made a forced choice judgment of which matched either the mean size or the size of an individual circle sampled at random from the display. The location of the relevant circle was post-cued by a small location marker presented at the same time as the two

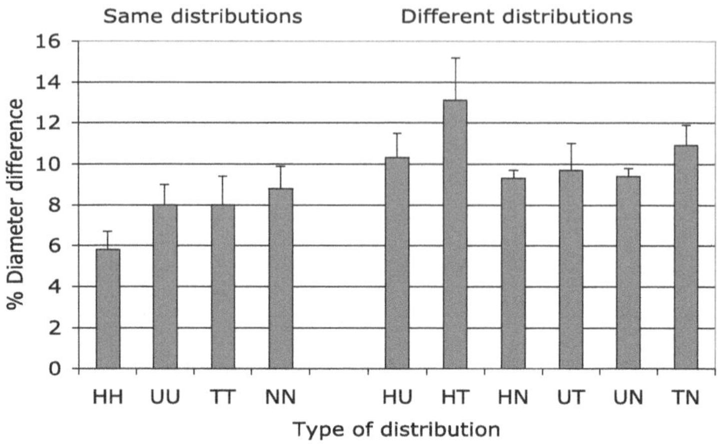

Figure 15.18 Mean thresholds within and across distributions. H = Homogenous, U = Uniform, T = Two peaks, N = Normal.

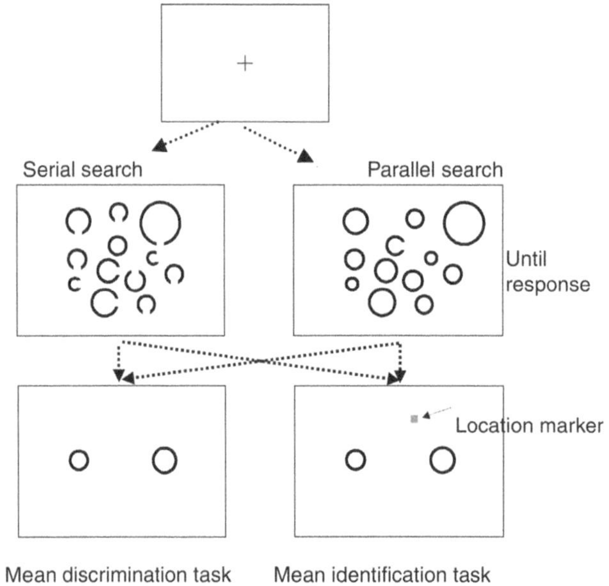

Figure 15.19 Design of experiment testing the effect of a concurrent task requiring either focused attention (search for a closed circle among circles with gaps) or distributed attention (search for a circle with a gap among closed circles) on two size judgment tasks – judgment of the mean size and judgment of the size of an individual post-cued circle.

probe circles. Figure 15.20 shows the results, with the predicted interaction. Performance was better on the mean judgment when the concurrent task was the popout task using global attention, and slightly but not significantly better on the individual item judgment when the concurrent task required focused attention.

Does the extra task impair the statistical processing at all, or is the mean size computed automatically? We compared performance in the dual task with attention globally deployed and performance when the statistical task was the only one required. There was no decrement with the global attention version of the dual task, relative to single task thresholds. It seems that when attention is spread over the display as a whole, the mean size is automatically extracted with no demand for additional resources.

We tested the automaticity idea in a different way as well, by seeing whether the extraction of the mean size is automatic in the sense of producing implicit priming. We presented an array of 12 circles of just two sizes, large and small, followed by a speeded same–different matching task on two new circles (Figure 15.21). One or both of the target circles would match either the mean of the previous set, or one of the two presented sizes, or some other size, either within the range or outside the range. If observers automatically form a representation of the mean size when they see a heterogenous display, we might expect priming for subsequent perception of an individual circle at the mean size. And that is what we found (Figure 15.22). The latency to respond same or different was shorter for circles primed by the mean size than for any other size, including the ones that were physically presented.

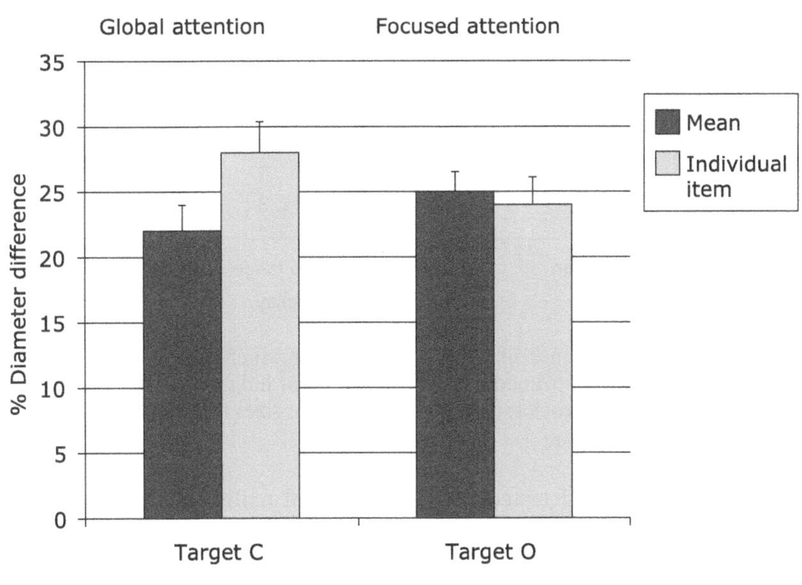

Figure 15.20 Effects of different deployments of attention in concurrent visual search tasks on accuracy of statistical judgments of mean size.

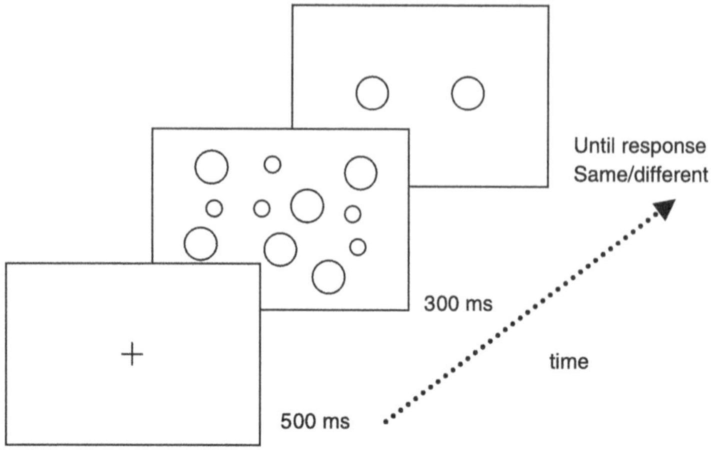

Figure 15.21 Design of experiment testing whether perception of the mean size of the preceding display is favored in a subsequent same–different judgment task.

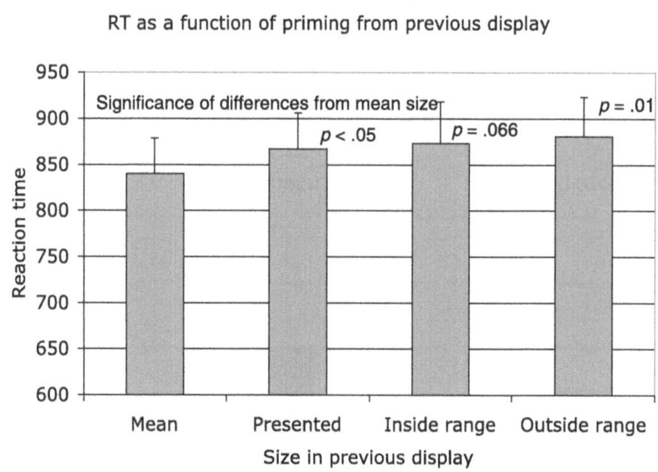

Figure 15.22 Mean response times as a function of which size from the preceding display was primed in the same–different judgment. The mean gives the shortest latencies, even compared to the sizes that were actually present in the display.

Finally Chong and I tested the psychological reality of the mean size by seeing whether it would generate false positive responses in a visual search task. Would people see illusory targets when the real target matched the mean size of the search display? We controlled for discriminability by matching the difference between the target and the nearest distractor size. The stimuli were selected from six possible sizes, two distractor sizes that were always present (fixed), a third optional distractor size that was either the largest or the smallest size (extreme), and a fourth size that was either the target size or another distractor size (critical). The choice of which extreme distractor size was included determined which critical size matched the mean size of the display (see Figure 15.23). The displays contained 12 circles, including three each of the two fixed distractor sizes, three of one extreme size, and three of one of the critical sizes. By adding either the large or the small extreme distractor size, we could shift the mean size of the display to one or other of the two possible critical sizes (see Figure 15.23). There were four conditions: Target present with targets at the mean size, target present with targets at the other critical size, target absent with additional distractors at the mean size, and target absent with additional distractors at the other critical size. Note that each of the two critical sizes played all four roles across different conditions. All that differed was the size of the extreme set of distractors. The conditions were randomly mixed across trials, and participants were shown the relevant target circle before each display. As predicted, participants made more false alarms on target absent trials when the target matched the mean size of the search display (mean 34% compared to 28% when the target was not the mean size), suggesting that seeing a set of similar stimuli does indeed automatically generate a mental representation of the mean size (and perhaps of other statistical parameters as well).

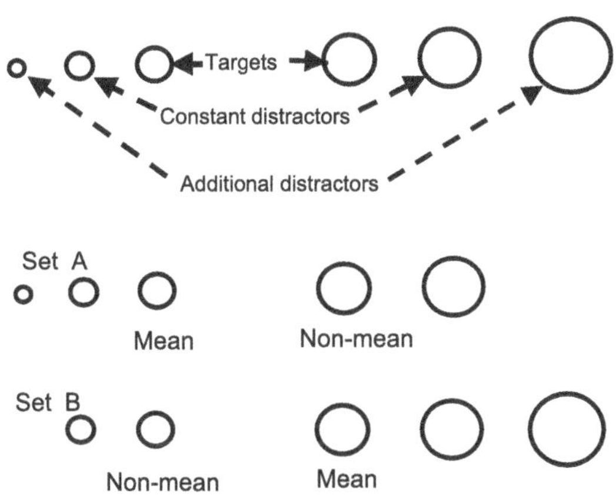

Figure 15.23 Schematic representation of stimuli to test the effect of target size in relation to the mean of the display in a visual search task. The Fixed distractor sizes appeared in all displays and one of the two Extreme distractor sizes was added. Depending on which was added, one or other of the Critical sizes became the mean size and the other the control size. One of these was designated the target size and could be either present or absent. When it was absent the other critical size was present as a fourth distractor size. Each display had three instances of each of the four relevant sizes. The target size was cued in advance of each display.

So what conclusions emerge from these experiments on statistical processing? Discrimination of the mean size of a set of objects seems to occur very rapidly and about as accurately as discrimination of the size of a single individual object. It seems to be automatic, provided that attention is globally deployed. Even when the display contains just two sizes, a representation is formed of the mean size, which primes subsequent perception more strongly than do either of the sizes that were actually presented. We plan to look at other dimensions and other statistical measures, but we think we have some evidence for a separate mode of processing visual information using distributed or global attention, which contrasts with the focused mode used in binding and individuating separate objects.

Perception of meaning and gist

Returning again to the general framework: Is this enough to get us seeing the everyday world? I am not sure. There are some puzzling results in the literature. So far I have discussed results obtained with simple displays, designed to tease apart particular mechanisms underlying performance. However, the world we deal with is normally rich, complex, full of meaning and emotional associations. I will contrast some research findings that deal with this richer world and ask what implications they have for a more complete understanding. One recent paradigm studying change blindness fits well, suggesting that we deal with the complexity quite simply by ignoring it. Rensink, Simons, and others showed that, if simple low-level cues to change (like apparent motion and visual transients) are removed or masked, we are very slow to detect quite salient changes in natural scenes (O'Regan, Rensink, & Clark, 1999; Rensink, 2000, 2004; Simons, 1996; Simons & Levin, 1998). If we happen to attend to the changing object, we are likely to become aware of the change, but otherwise it may take us several seconds to find it. O'Regan et al. suggest that we briefly summarize the scene and rely on the world itself to store the information in case we need to refer to any part of it in detail. Note, however, that the change detection task requires us not only to form representations of all the objects in the scene, but also to store and compare them across successive frames. It does not rule out more complex perception, which is instantly lost or erased by the next display (Wolfe, 1998).

The other contrasting line of research probes immediate perception rather than memory and suggests a much larger capacity and the possibility of attention-free semantic processing. It goes back to Potter's demonstrations in the 1970s (Potter, 1975), in which she showed strings of natural scenes at high speed, successively in the same location, and asked people to find semantic targets, for example, a clown, or an airplane, or a donkey. She found that they could do this pretty well at presentation rates of up to 10 pictures/s, although memory for the nontarget pictures was very poor. More recently, Li, VanRullen, Koch, and Perona (2002) have looked at the attention demands of this task and found a surprising result. They occupied attention at a central foveal location by asking people to decide whether five small letters – Ts and/or Ls in random orientations – were all the same or contained one odd letter. This is a very demanding task and leaves people badly impaired in discriminating a single target letter in the periphery. However, when Li et al. briefly flashed a picture of a natural scene in the periphery, and asked people to determine whether it contained an animal, performance was just as good when attention was focused on the foveal T/L task as when the scene classification task was the only one required.

So we have an apparently paradoxical pair of findings. You cannot even see a salient object like an airplane engine coming and going in the change blindness picture, but you can detect the presence of an unknown animal in a 50 ms exposure while focused on a completely different set of stimuli. Can we reconcile those findings? How would they fit the framework I proposed? The animal detection task clearly is not using the binding mode with focused attention, since that is devoted to the foveal letter task. But without attention, we can still detect disjunctive sets of features. So participants may be set to sense, in parallel, a highly overlearned vocabulary of features that characterize a particular semantic category. For example animals might be signaled by the presence of a compact curvilinear figure against the background, a set of legs, a head, an eye, wings, or fur. If present, these animal features would prime the general, semantic category and could perhaps distinguish a slide with an animal from one without (see Levin, Takarae, Miner, & Keil, 2001). Evans and I have shown that detecting an animal in RSVP strings of natural scenes is much harder when the scenes also contain humans than when they do not (66% vs 78% hits), presumably because shared features required observers to raise their criteria. On the other hand, detecting a vehicle is not affected by whether or not humans are present in the distractor slides. Participants were also quite bad at locating the target animal (to the left, center, or right of the scene) suggesting a failure to bind the features to their locations. Of the 73% correct detections, only 53% were also correctly located (where chance was 33%). The target animal was correctly identified on only 43% of the hit trials (e.g., as a bear, a butterfly, or a goldfish), although observers had at least some information about the superordinate category (e.g., mammal, insect, or fish) correct on 78% of those trials. The categories should be available from one or more distinctive features (wings, fur, etc.).

In our second experiment, we tested attention limits by putting two successive targets in a single string of pictures – essentially an Attentional Blink paradigm – and looked at people's ability to detect a second target as a function of their temporal separation. Here we found very large interference effects on detecting the second target when participants also had to identify the first. Figure 15.24a shows the results. We found a huge blink for the same-category targets and an even bigger one for different categories. It takes about 880 ms to recover and be ready to detect a second target from the same category and more than that to reset sufficiently to detect a target from a different category. So when we forced participants to bind the features of the

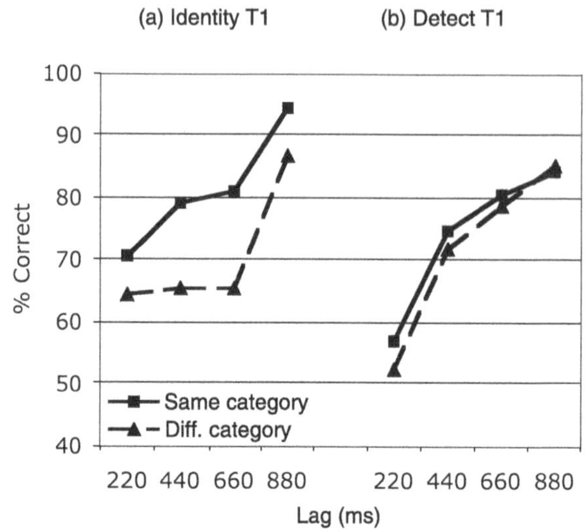

Figure 15.24 Accuracy in identifying T2 after either identifying or detecting T1 in rapid serial visual presentation of pictures of natural scenes. The two targets could either be from the same category (both animals or both vehicles), or they could be from different categories (one of each).

first target in order to identify it correctly, attention limits were striking and lasted longer than in the usual AB paradigm with letters.

Is this really due to the need for binding? We changed the task slightly to see if simply detecting the first target – a task that we thought could be based on sets of unbound features – would interfere equally. We asked participants to identify only the second animal in the string, which meant they had to detect the first, since there were 20% catch trials with only one target. But they did not need to identify which animal it was. The blink in this condition was greatly reduced and lasted only 200 ms instead of nearly 1 s (Figure 24b). It seems, then, that attention is required when the animal must be identified, but that parallel detection of unbound features may occur with little need for focused attention. These results do not prove our account, but they do make it clear that there are attention limits to high-level visual perception, and they would be compatible with the idea of global feature-based detection of gist rather than detailed feature binding.

One objection that might be raised is that these animal features are *physically* more complex than the colors, shapes, and orientations used in my earlier research. They do not sound like features in the usual sense of the term. In reply, first, I do not claim in the theory to have identified any a priori set of features. They cannot be defined independently of the contrast set from which they are to be discriminated in any given setting. The set of feature detectors used in any task is an empirical question, to be tested with a set of converging operations such as those shown in Table 15.3. This is a boot-strapping

Table 15.3 Diagnostics for separable feature detectors (see Treisman, 1986)

Mediate parallel search
Support perceptual grouping and segregation
Can migrate independently in illusory conjunctions
Can be separately attended
Show selective adaptation and selective masking
Neural evidence – separate populations of single units

account, but if the tests do converge, we have learned something. Second, the animal features may not be more complex for the visual system than the "simple" colors, line orientations, directions of motion, and so on tested in psychophysical experiments. We have evolved to detect the natural components of real-world objects and their natural textures and colors. Gross, Rocha-Miranda, and Bender (1972) showed that single units in area IT respond to monkey hands or faces, and Tanaka (1993) found many units in IT that respond to what look like elementary components of natural objects.

Animals are a natural category with which we have evolved, so it might make sense to have fur and eye detectors. However another possible objection arises when we consider that Li et al. got similar results using the category of vehicles. Admittedly, it is harder to tell an evolutionary story about the features of man-made objects like cars and airplanes. I would not expect wheel and engine detectors to be part of our innate repertoire. However, there is a great deal of plasticity in the brain, and feature detectors may be created to carry out any discrimination that proves useful. Evolution would provide the plasticity at the feature level to enable whatever elements prove useful to be detected automatically. Freedman and his colleagues (Freedman, Riesenhuber, Poggio & Miller, 2001, 2002) recorded from single units in prefrontal cortex of monkeys, discriminating members of the cat family from various breeds of dogs, together with many intermediate morphs. When the reward contingencies were changed from distinguishing cats and dogs to distinguishing creatures that varied on the orthogonal dimension – dog/catness versus cat/dogness – the same units learned to respond selectively to one of the new categories.

Given the possibility of flexible feature sets, we may be able to account for visual category detection within the framework I am using, as shown in Figure 15.25. Once the category is primed, if the target animal or vehicle is still present and attention is available we can form an object file to make it consciously accessible. If not, we may be able to tell simply from its features which animal it is likely to be – cats seldom have wings and beaks. But we might make mistakes.

Why would this framework not also predict easy change detection? There are a number of differences that would make change detection harder than category detection: First, change detection depends on comparing successive displays, thus involving both visual memory and a matching process between a current display and a stored one; second, participants are not cued in

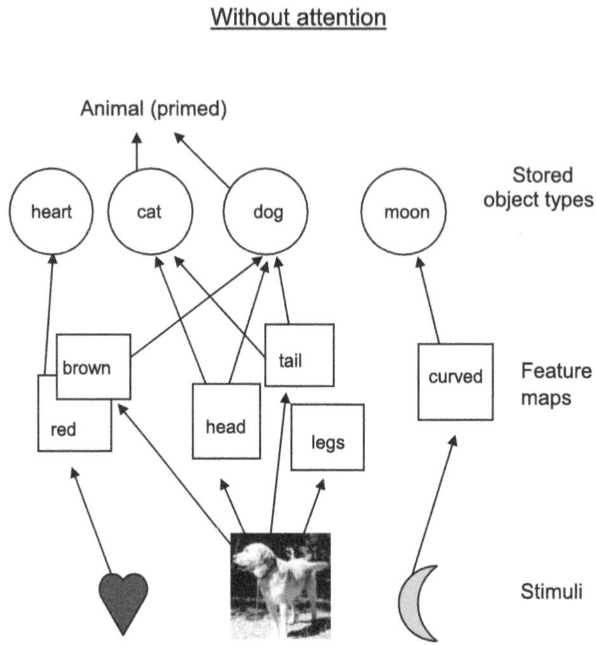

Figure 15.25 Sketch of model to account for detection of high-level perceptual categories. The suggestion is that sets of learned features may be detected in parallel and prime their category without being bound through focused attention.

advance with the relevant category (or the relevant sets of features) to look for. Primed detection of a prespecified category could potentially be mediated by unbound features, whereas the change detection task imposes a much heavier load, involving binding, and also non-selective memory, and a non-selective comparison process.

This chapter has specified three ways of deploying attention and three types of information that they may provide: (1) Focused attention, offering conscious access to individuated objects with bound features in their current locations, viewpoints, and configurations; (2) at the other end of what is actually a continuum, global or distributed attention, offering global and statistical properties of groups of objects or the general layout of a scene; (3) rapid preattention, or more prolonged inattention, offering parallel and automatic access to sets of unbound features which can also prime semantic categories in a recognition network. Perhaps in combination, the parallel feature detectors, flexibly evolved through learning, the attention-controlled construction of a small set of explicit object files, and the statistical descriptions of sets of similar elements, may approach the outlines of an explanation for our amazing ability to see and interact with the world around us, even with the limited resources set by visual attention.

Notes

1 Note however that some physical conjunctions may create emergent features, which could also play a part in activating only recognition units with which they are compatible.
2 While conscious perception depends on object files, the converse may not be the case. Binding can sometimes occur without the bound objects becoming consciously accessible. For example in the negative priming paradigm, because only two objects are present, accurate binding can happen without attention. The attended object is consciously and correctly bound, and the remaining features belonging to the unattended object are bound by default, with the resulting object tokens surviving sometimes for several days or weeks (Treisman & DeSchepper, 1996). But this unattended shape may fail to be consciously registered.

Acknowledgments

The research was supported by grants from the NIH Conte Center # P50 MH62196, from the Israeli Binational Science Foundation, # 1000274, and from NIH grant 2004 2RO1 MH 05838304A1 Visual coding and the deployment of attention.

References

Ariely, D. (2001). Seeing sets: Representation by statistical properties. *Psychological Science*, *12*, 157–162.

Balint, R. (1909). Seelenlahmung des "Schauens", optische Ataxie, raumliche Storung der Aufmerksamkeit. *Monatschrift für Psychiatrie und Neurologie*, *25*, 5–81.

Carr, L., Iacoboni, M., Dubeau, M.J., Mazziotta, J., & Lenzi, G. (2003). Neural mechanisms of empathy in humans: A relay from neural systems for imitation to limbic areas. *Proceedings of the National Academy of Sciences*, *100*, 5497–5502.

Chong, S., & Treisman, A. (2003). Representation of statistical properties. *Vision Research*, *43*, 393–404.

Chong, S.-C., & Treisman, A. (2004). Attentional spread in the statistical processing of visual displays. *Perception and Psychophysics*, *66*, 1282–1294.

Corbetta, M., Shulman, G.L., Miezin, F.M., & Petersen, S.E. (1995). Superior parietal cortex activation during spatial attention shifts and visual feature conjunction. *Science*, *270*, 802–805.

Critchley, H., Wiens, S., Rotshtein, P., Öhman, A., & Dolan, R. (2004). Neural systems supporting interoceptive awareness. *Nature Neuroscience*, *7*(2), 189–195.

Damasio, A.R. (1989). Time-locked multiregional retroactivation: A systems-level proposal for the neural substrates of recall and recognition. *Cognition*, *33*, 25–62.

Di Lollo, V., Enns, J.T., & Rensink, R. (2000). Competition for consciousness among visual events: The psychophysics of reentrant visual processes. *Journal of Experimental Psychology: General*, *129*, 481–507.

Dronkers, N.F. (1996). A new brain region for coordinating speech articulation. *Nature*, *384*, 159–161.

Egly, R., Driver, J., & Rafal, R. (1994). Shifting visual attention between objects and locations: Evidence from normal and parietal lesion subjects. *Journal of Experimental Psychology: General*, *123*(2), 161–177.

Enns, J.T., & Rensink, R.A. (1996). An object completion process in early vision. In A. Gale (Ed.), *Visual search III*. London: Taylor & Francis.

Freedman, D., Riesenhuber, M., Poggio, T., & Miller, E. (2002). Visual categorization and the primate prefrontal cortex: Neurophysiology and behavior. *Journal of Neurophysiology*, *88*(2), 929–941.

Freedman, D.J., Riesenhuber, M., Poggio, T., & Miller, E.K. (2001). Categorical representation of visual stimuli in the primate prefrontal cortex. *Science*, *291*, 312–316.

Gross, C., Rocha-Miranda, C.E., & Bender, D.B. (1972). Visual properties of neurons in inferotemporal cortex of the macaque. *Journal of Neurophysiology*, *35*, 96–111.

Hochstein, S., & Ahissar, M. (2002). View from the top: Hierarchies and reverse hierarchies in the visual system. *Neuron*, *36*, 791–804.

Houck, M.R., & Hoffman, J.E. (1986). Conjunction of color and form without attention: Evidence from an orientation-contingent color aftereffect. *Journal of Experimental Psychology: Human Perception and Performance*, *12*, 186–199.

Humphreys, G.W., Cinel, C., Wolfe, J.M., Olson, A., & Klempen, N. (2000). Fractionating the binding process: Neuropsychological evidence distinguishing binding of form from binding of surface features. *Vision Research*, *40*(10–12), 1569–1596.

Humphreys, G.W., & Riddoch, M.J. (1993). Interactions between object and space systems revealed through neuropsychology. In S. Kornblum (Ed.), *Attention and Performance XIV* (pp. 183–218). Cambridge, MA: MIT Press.

Kahneman, D., Treisman, A., & Gibbs, B. (1992). The reviewing of object files: Object-specific integration of information. *Cognitive Psychology*, *24*, 175–219.

Levin, D.T., Takarae, Y., Miner, A.G., & Keil, F. (2001). Efficient visual search by category: Specifying the features that mark the difference between artifacts and animals in preattentive vision. *Perception and Psychophysics*, *63*, 676–697.

Li, F., VanRullen, R., Koch, C., & Perona, P. (2002). Rapid natural scene categorization in the near absence of attention. *Proceedings of the National Academy of Sciences, USA*, *99*(14), 9596–9601.

Luck, S.J., & Vogel, E.K. (1997). The capacity of visual working memory for features and conjunctions. *Nature*, *390*, 279–281.

McCollough, C. (1965). Color adaptation of edge-detectors in the human visual system. *Science*, *149*, 1115–1116.

Navon, D. (1977). Forest before trees: The precedence of global features in visual perception. *Cognitive Psychology*, *9*, 353–383.

O'Regan, J.K., Rensink, R.A., & Clark, J.J. (1999). Change-blindness as a result of "mudsplashes". *Nature*, *398*, 34.

Potter, M. (1975). Short-term conceptual memory for pictures. *Science*, *187*, 965–966.

Rensink, R.A. (2000). Visual search for change: A probe into the nature of attentional processing. *Visual Cognition*, *7*, 345–376.

Rensink, R.A. (2004). Visual sensing without seeing. *Psychological Science*, *15*(1), 27–32.

Robertson, L., Treisman, A., Friedman-Hill, S., & Grabowecky, M. (1997). The interaction of spatial and object pathways: Evidence from Balint's syndrome. *Journal of Cognitive Neuroscience*, *9*, 254–276.

Seiffert, A.E., Weber, M., & Treisman, A. (2003). *Isolating feature binding in visual search*. Society for Neuroscience meeting in New Orleans (Nov. 8–12).

Simons, D., & Levin, D. (1998). Change blindness. *Trends in Cognitive Science*, *1*, 261–267.

Simons, D.J. (1996). In sight, out of mind. *Psychological Science*, *7*, 301–305.

Tanaka, K. (1993). Neuronal mechanisms of object recognition. *Science, 262*, 685–688.
Thorpe, S., Fize, D., & Marlot, C. (1996). Speed of processing in the human visual system. *Nature, 381*, 520–522.
Treisman, A. (1986). Properties, parts and objects. In J. Thomas (Ed.), *Handbook of perception and human performance* (pp. 1–70). New York: Wiley.
Treisman, A. (1988). Features and objects: The Fourteenth Bartlett Memorial Lecture. *Quarterly Journal of Experimental Psychology, 40*A, 201–237.
Treisman, A. (1996). The binding problem. *Current Opinion in Neurobiology, 6*, 171–178.
Treisman, A., & DeSchepper, B. (1996). Object tokens, attention, and visual memory. In T. Inui & J. McClelland (Eds.), *Attention and performance XVI: Information integration in perception and communication* (pp. 15–46). Cambridge, MA: MIT Press.
Treisman, A., & Gelade, G. (1980). A feature integration theory of attention. *Cognitive Psychology, 12*, 97–136.
Treisman, A., & Sato, S. (1990). Conjunction search revisited. *Journal of Experimental Psychology: Human Perception and Performance, 16*, 459–478.
Treisman, A., & Schmidt, H. (1982). Illusory conjunctions in the perception of objects. *Cognitive Psychology, 14*, 107–141.
Wise, R., Greene, J., Buchel, C., & Scott, S. (1999). Brain regions involved in articulation. *The Lancet, 353*, 1057–61.
Wolfe, J.M. (1998). Inattentional amnesia. In V. Coltheart (Ed.), *Fleeting memories* (pp. 71–94). Cambridge, MA: MIT Press.
Wolfe, J.M., & Bennett, S.C. (1997). Preattentive object files: Shapeless bundles of basic features. *Vision Research, 37*, 25–44.
Wolfe, J.M., Cave, K.R., & Franzel, S.L. (1989). Guided search: An alternative to the feature integration model for visual search. *Journal of Experimental Psychology: Human Perception and Performance, 15*, 419–433.

16 Models of attention

Claus Bundesen and
Thomas Habekost

Modern research on attention dates back to the early 1950s, when Colin Cherry and others conducted studies on selective listening. Cherry (1953) investigated the ability to attend to one speaker in the presence of other voices (the *cocktail party problem*). Subjects were asked to repeat a prose message while they heard it, rather than waiting until it finished. When the message to be repeated was presented to one ear while a message to be ignored was presented to the other ear, subjects were unable to recall the content of the unattended message. If the message to be ignored consisted of normal human speech, the subjects could identify the message as speech, but they were unable to identify any word or phrase heard in the rejected ear. Except for simple physical characteristics, the message to be ignored appeared to be "filtered out".

The studies on selective listening in the early 1950s formed the basis of the first modern theory of attention, the *filter* theory of Donald Broadbent (1958) (see Figure 16.1). In this theory, information flows from the senses through many parallel input channels into a short-term memory store. The short-term store can hold the information for a brief period (a few seconds). Later in the system there is a *limited-capacity channel*, which can transmit

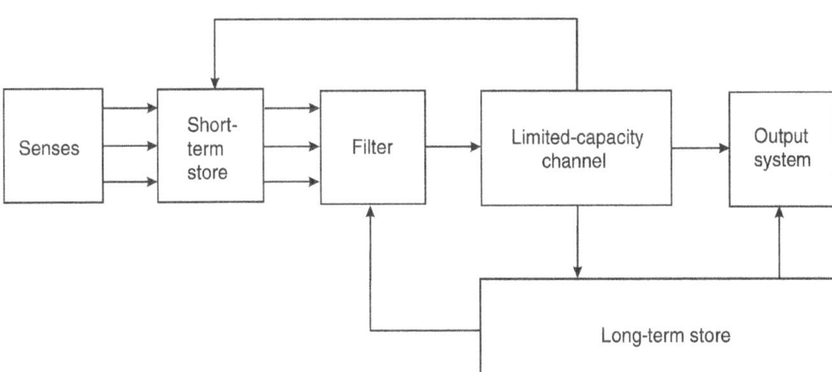

Figure 16.1 Flow diagram illustrating the filter theory of Broadbent (1958).

much less information than is available in the parallel input channels. This creates a need for a selective filter between the short-term memory and the limited-capacity channel. In Broadbent's model the filter acts as an all-or-none switch that selects information from just a single input channel at a time.

Broadbent (1958) defined an input channel as a class of sensory events sharing a simple physical feature (e.g., a position in auditory space). Except for such features, information on unattended channels should not be analyzed. This simple model accounted for the main results of the early studies on selective listening.

The question of selection turned out to be more complex. Studies by Neville Moray (1959) and others showed that subjectively important words such as the listener's own name could be perceived even if presented on the unattended channel. To explain such findings, Anne Treisman (1964a, 1964b) proposed a variation of filter theory in which the filter operates in a graded instead of an all-or-none fashion. In Treisman's *attenuation* theory, unattended messages are weakened instead of blocked from further analyses. Both selected and attenuated messages are transmitted to a system with word recognition units. With the additional assumption that thresholds of recognition units for important words are lowered, Treisman could explain why important words tend to be recognized even when appearing in attenuated messages.

In the filter theories of Broadbent and Treisman attentional selection can occur at an early stage of processing; that is, before pattern recognition. This is the defining characteristic of *early-selection* theories. These theories were challenged by *late-selection* theories, in which attentional selection can only occur later in processing than pattern recognition.

The first late-selection theory was presented by J. Anthony Deutsch and Diana Deutsch in 1963. Deutsch and Deutsch argued that the early filtering mechanism in Treisman's theory was redundant. It seemed simpler to assume that there was only one locus of selection. Deutsch and Deutsch proposed that attended and unattended messages receive the same amount of analysis by the pattern recognition system. Only after a stimulus has been recognized is the *importance* of the stimulus retrieved, and the stimulus with the greatest importance is selected for further processing, including conscious awareness.

The general theories of Broadbent, Treisman, and Deutsch and Deutsch set the stage for the development of more specific models of attention. Most of these models were based on experimental findings on visual processing: data on our ability to *divide* attention between multiple, simultaneous targets and data on our ability to *focus* attention on targets rather than distractors (see Bundesen, 1996; Logan, 2004).

Serial models

In serial models of attention only one stimulus is attended at a time. Within this framework there has been a theoretical evolution from simple serial models to selective serial models. The following sections present the highlights of this development.

Simple serial models

In the 1960s and the following decades, visual search became the dominant experimental paradigm for attention research. In most experiments on visual search, the subject is instructed to indicate "as quickly as possible" whether or not a certain type of target is present in a display. Latencies of target-present responses (*positive* reaction times) and target-absent responses (*negative* reaction times) are analyzed as functions of the number of items in the display (the *display set size*). Serial models of attention were developed mainly to account for data from this type of task. The first simple serial models of visual search were proposed in the 1960s by William K. Estes, Saul Sternberg, and others (Estes & Taylor, 1964; Sternberg, 1967).

According to these simple serial models, items are scanned one by one, and the order in which items are scanned does not depend on their status as targets versus distractors. In other words, selection is random. As each item is scanned, it is classified as a target or as a distractor. A negative response is initiated if all items have been scanned and classified as distractors. Thus the number of items processed before a negative response is made equals the display set size, N. This implies that mean negative reaction time is a linear function of display set size, with a slope equal to the mean time taken to process one item.

In simple *self-terminating* search, a positive response is made as soon as a target is found, so the number of items processed before a positive response is made varies randomly between 1 and N and averages $(1 + N)/2$. Thus the rate of increase in mean positive reaction time as a function of display set size equals only one half of the mean time taken to process one item. A representative pair of search reaction time functions with a positive-to-negative slope ratio of about 1:2 is illustrated in Figure 16.2.

In *feature search*, the target is distinguished by a simple physical feature not shared by any of the distractors (see, e.g., Treisman & Gelade, 1980). For example, the target can be a green T among brown Ts. In *conjunction search*, the target differs from the distractors by possessing a predefined combination of physical features, but the target is not unique in any of the component features of the conjunction. For example the target can be a green T among brown Ts and green Xs.

Many experiments on conjunction search have yielded results conforming to the predictions from simple self-terminating serial models: positive and negative mean reaction times that are approximately linear functions of display set size with substantial slopes and positive-to-negative slope ratios of about 1:2. Experiments on feature search with high similarity between targets and distractors have yielded a similar pattern of results.

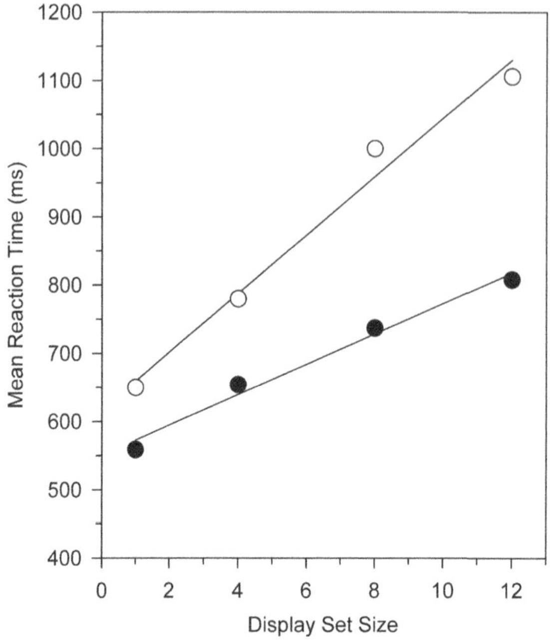

Figure 16.2 Positive and negative mean reaction times as functions of display set size in visual search for a T in one of four possible orientations among similarly rotated Ls. (The observed reaction times were read from Wolfe, 1994, Figure 1B, p. 204.) The slopes of the fitted least squares lines are 22 ms/item and 43 ms/item, respectively.

Selective serial models

In selective serial models, items in the stimulus display are attended one at a time, but the serial order in which items are attended depends on their status as targets versus distractors: targets gain attention early on.

The first selective serial model of visual search was published in 1978 by James Hoffman. The model was based on findings from Charles Eriksen's laboratory on the time taken to shift attention in response to a visual cue (e.g., Colegate, Hoffman, & Eriksen, 1973). The findings went against the assumption that attention can be shifted from item to item at the high rates required by simple (nonselective) serial models of processing.

In Hoffman's model, visual search is a two-stage process. At the first stage, the entire stimulus display is evaluated in parallel. The evaluation is preattentive and quick but rough. For each item in the display, it yields a measure of the likelihood that the item is a target. The parallel evaluation guides a slow serial mechanism that transfers items one by one (about one item per 100 ms) to the second stage of processing. Although the serial transfer mechanism is slow, it makes search efficient by transferring items in order of decreasing likelihood that the items are targets. Hence, if there is a target in the display, the target is likely to be among the first items that are transferred to the second stage of processing.

Jeremy Wolfe and his collaborators have proposed an influential selective serial model called Guided Search (Wolfe, 1994; Wolfe, Cave, & Franzel, 1989). Guided Search combines elements of the two-stage model of Hoffman with elements of the *feature integration* theory of Treisman and her associates (Treisman, 1988; Treisman & Gelade, 1980). Like feature integration theory, Guided Search assumes that simple stimulus features such as color, size, and orientation are registered automatically, without attention, and in parallel across the visual field. Registration of objects (i.e., items defined by conjunctions of features) requires a further stage of processing at which attention is directed serially to each object. Like Hoffman's model, Guided Search assumes the outcome of the first, parallel stage of processing guides the serial processing at the second stage. The guidance works as follows.

For each feature dimension (e.g., color, size, or orientation), the parallel stage generates an array of activation values (attention values) forming a map of the visual field. Each value is a sum of a bottom-up and a top-down component. In a map for a given feature dimension, the bottom-up component for a particular location is a measure of differences between the value of the feature at that location and values of the same feature at neighboring locations. The top-down component for the location is a measure of the difference between the value of the feature at the given location and the target value for the feature dimension. When activations have been calculated in separate maps for each feature dimension, they are summed across feature dimensions to produce a single overall activation map. In computer simulations, a certain level of gaussian noise is also added at each location. The final overall activation values represent the evaluation given by the parallel stage of how likely the stimulus at each location is to be the target.

The serial stage processes the items in order of decreasing activation in the overall activation map. When an item is processed, it is classified as a target or as a distractor. The processing continues until a target is found or until all items with activations above a certain value have been processed.

Guided Search accounts for many findings from experiments on visual search. The model was motivated, in part, by demonstrations of fast conjunction search. Guided Search explains some demonstrations of fast conjunction search (e.g., Nakayama & Silverman, 1986) by assuming that for some feature dimensions, top-down control is very effective. Other demonstrations (e.g., Wolfe et al., 1989) are explained by assuming that in some subjects, the level of gaussian noise is very low.

Parallel models

In parallel models of attention, several stimuli can be attended at the same time. Like serial models, parallel models have progressed towards more complex and powerful accounts. This section examines the development from simple parallel (independent channels) models to limited-capacity parallel models and race-based models of selection.

Independent channels model

The first detailed parallel model of visual processing of multi-element displays was the independent channels model developed by Eriksen and his associates in the 1960s (e.g., Eriksen & Lappin, 1967; Eriksen & Spencer, 1969). It was based on the assumption that spatially separated display items are processed in parallel and independently up to and including the stage of pattern recognition. The assumption implies that the way in which a display item is processed is independent of display set size and independent of random variations in the way other display items are processed.

The principle of independent channels (*unlimited-capacity parallel processing*) has mainly been used in explaining cases in which visual search is highly efficient (small effects of display set size). The prime example is feature search with low similarity between targets and distractors. In a theory proposed by Richard Shiffrin and Walter Schneider in 1977, the principle of independent channels is also applied to cases of search for more complex targets (e.g., particular alphanumeric characters) when subjects have been trained consistently in detecting those particular targets.

In the theory of Shiffrin and Schneider, slow, serial, *controlled search* for particular targets can develop into fast, parallel, *automatic detection* of the targets. Automatic detection occurs involuntarily and without stressing the capacity limitations of the system. However, automatic detection only develops if the mapping of stimuli to responses is *consistent* rather than *varied* over trials (Schneider & Shiffrin, 1977; Shiffrin & Schneider, 1977).

Limited-capacity models

The linear relations between mean reaction time and display set size that are predicted by simple serial models are difficult to explain by parallel models with independent channels (unlimited-capacity parallel models). However, the linear relations can be explained by parallel models with *limited processing capacity*. The following example was published independently by James Townsend and by Richard C. Atkinson and his associates in 1969.

Consider a display of N items that are processed in parallel. Assume the processing speed for an item (specifically, the hazard function for the processing time of the item; see Townsend & Ashby, 1983) equals the amount of processing capacity devoted to the item, and assume the total processing capacity spread across items in the display is a constant C. The assumptions imply that the time taken to complete processing of the first item is exponentially distributed with rate parameter C. Further, assume that when the first completion occurs, the processing capacity is instantaneously redistributed among the remaining $N - 1$ items. Then the time from the first to the second completion is exponentially distributed with the same rate parameter C. If the process repeats until all N items have been completed, then the mean time taken to complete processing of the N items increases linearly with display set size N. Thus parallel models can also explain this basic finding in visual search experiments.

Race models of selection

In race models of selection from multi-element displays, display items are processed in parallel, and attentional selection is made of those items that first finish processing (the winners of the race). Accordingly, selection of targets rather than distractors is based on processing of targets being faster than processing of distractors (Bundesen, 1987).

Race models of selection can be either limited or unlimited in processing capacity (see Bundesen, 1987, 1993). In race models with unlimited processing capacity, the processing time of an item is independent of the display set size. In race models with limited processing capacity, the processing time of an item decreases as the display set size is increased.

In 1988, Hitomi Shibuya and Claus Bundesen proposed the following two-stage fixed-capacity independent race model (FIRM). At the first stage of processing, an *attentional weight* is computed for each item in the stimulus display. The weight is a measure of the strength of the sensory evidence that the item is a target. When the attentional weights have been computed, the fixed processing capacity (a total amount of C items/s) is distributed across the items in proportion to their weights. The amount of processing capacity allocated to an item determines the speed of processing at the second stage: encoding into visual short-term memory (VSTM). Specifically, the time taken to encode an item into VSTM is exponentially distributed with a rate parameter equal to the amount of processing capacity allocated to the item. The items that are selected (i.e., stored in VSTM) are those items whose encoding processes complete before the stimulus presentation terminates and before VSTM has been filled up.

Detailed tests of FIRM have been made in *partial-report* experiments in which subjects report as many targets as possible from a briefly exposed display showing a mixture of targets (e.g., digits) and distractors (e.g., letters). FIRM has provided precise quantitative accounts of the effects of selection criterion, exposure duration, and numbers of targets and distractors in the display (see Figure 16.3).

Theory of visual attention (TVA)

The theory of visual attention (TVA) proposed by Bundesen (1990) is a generalization of FIRM. In TVA, both visual recognition and selection of items in the visual field consist in making *perceptual categorizations* (i.e., encoding

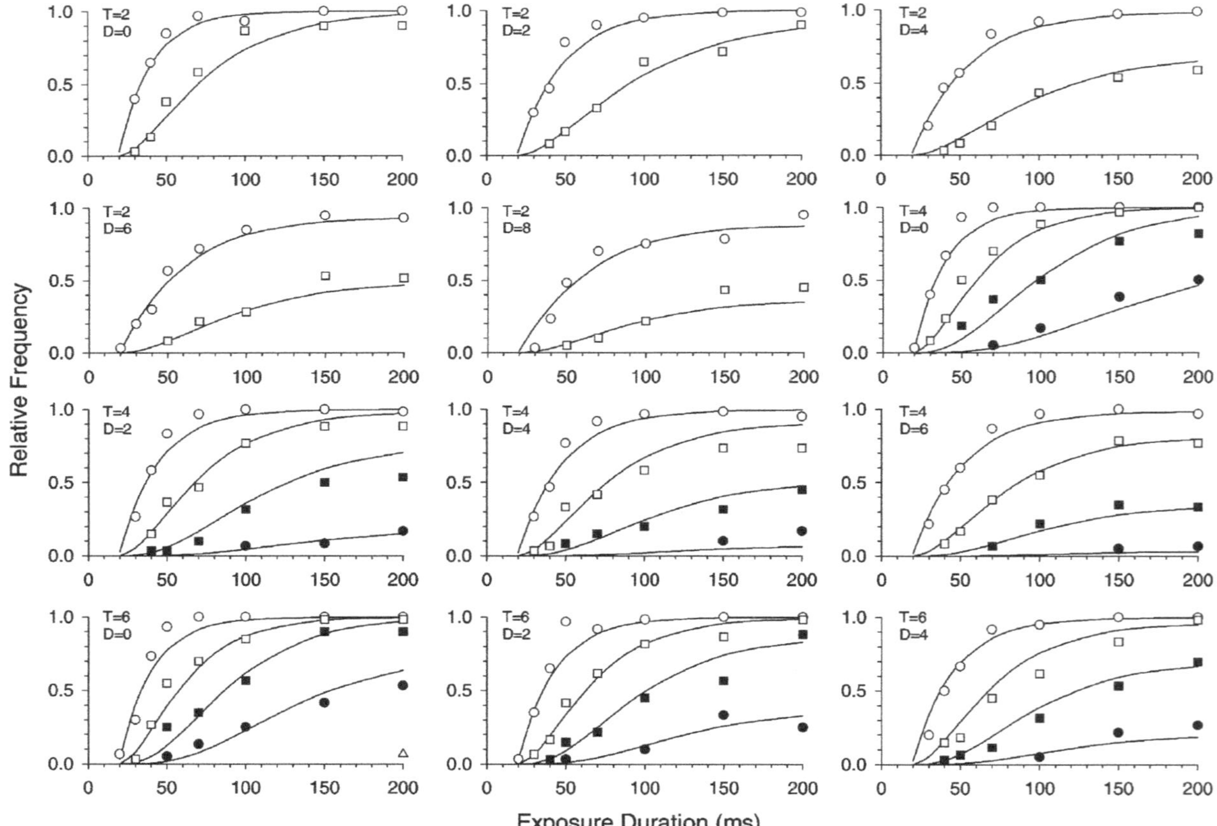

Figure 16.3 Relative frequency of scores of *j* or more (correctly reported targets) as a function of exposure duration with *j*, number of targets *T*, and number of distractors *D* as parameters in partial report of digits among letters. Parameters *T* and *D* vary between panels. Parameter *j* is 1 (open circles), 2 (open squares), 3 (solid squares), 4 (solid circles), or 5 (triangle). Smooth curves represent a theoretical fit to the data by the fixed-capacity independent race model (FIRM). For clarity, observed frequencies less than 0.02 were omitted from the figure. From "Visual selection from multielement displays: Measuring and modeling effects of exposure duration" by H. Shibuya and C. Bundesen, 1988, *Journal of Experimental Psychology: Human Perception and Performance*, p. 595. Copyright 1988 by the American Psychological Association.

categorizations into VSTM). When one makes the perceptual categorization that a given item belongs to a certain category, the item is said (a) to be selected and (b) to be recognized as a member of the category. Thus, attentional selection is neither early (i.e., occurring before stimulus recognition) nor late (after recognition). Attentional selection and initial stimulus recognition occur at the same time (*simultaneous selection*; Logan, 2002).

Recognition and selection depend on the outcome of a biased race between possible perceptual categorizations. Consider a possible perceptual categorization of the form "object x belongs to category i" or, equivalently, "object x has feature i". The rate at which the categorization is processed increases with (a) the strength of the sensory evidence that supports the categorization, (b) the subject's bias for assigning objects to category i, and (c) the attentional weight of item x. Specifically,

$$v(x, i) = \eta(x, i)\, \beta_i \frac{w_x}{\sum_{z \in S} w_z}, \tag{16.1}$$

where $v(x, i)$ is the rate of processing of the categorization that object x belongs to category i, $\eta(x, i)$ is the strength of the sensory evidence that supports the categorization, β_i is the subject's bias for assigning objects to category i, w_x is the attentional weight of object x, and the denominator is the sum of the attentional weights of all objects in the visual field. When a categorization completes processing, it enters VSTM if memory space is available there. The span of VSTM is limited to about four items (Luck & Vogel, 1997; Sperling, 1960). Competition between mutually incompatible categorizations of the same item is resolved in favor of the first-completing categorization.

TVA accounts for many findings on single-stimulus recognition, whole report, partial report, search, and detection (see Bundesen, 1990). Besides attentional processes, the scope of the theory has been extended by Gordon Logan to encompass aspects of perception, memory, and executive control (Logan, 1996, 2002; Logan & Gordon, 2001; also see Logan & Bundesen, 1996, 2003, 2004).

Connectionist models

Mathematical models like TVA are highly abstract. Connectionist models are attempts to theorize at a level closer to neurobiology (see McClelland & Rumelhart, 1986; O'Reilly & Munakata, 2000; Rumelhart & McClelland, 1986). In connectionist models, information processing consists in a flow of activation through a network of neuron-like units linked together by facilitatory and inhibitory connections. A fairly simple and representative example of a connectionist model of attention is the *neurodynamical* model of

Gustavo Deco and Josef Zihl (2001), which is described below. Other important examples are the selective attention model (SLAM) of Hans Phaf, Lex van der Heijden, and Patrick Hudson (1990; see also van der Heijden, 1992, 2004), the multiple object recognition and attentional selection (MORSEL) model of Michael Mozer (1991), the search via recursive rejection (SERR) model of Glyn Humphreys and Hermann Müller (1993), and the selective attention for identification model (SAIM) of Dietmar Heinke and Glyn Humphreys (2003).

Neurodynamical model

The architecture of the neurodynamical model of Deco and Zihl (2001) is shown in Figure 16.4. The basic units of the model are populations of neurons. The input to the system is represented in a *retina map*, which has excitatory connections to a set of retinotopic *feature maps* (representing

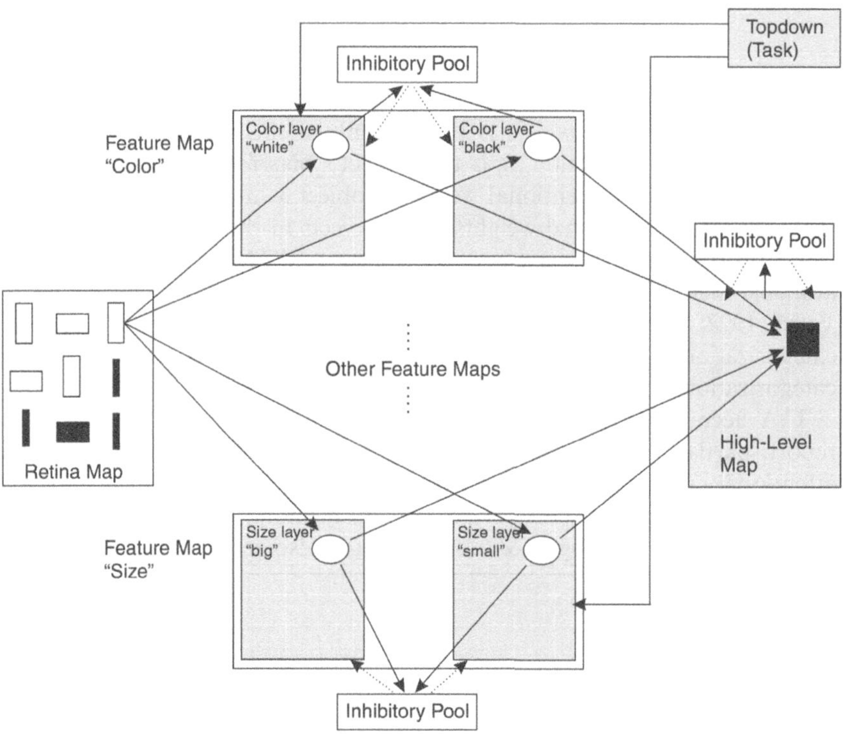

Figure 16.4 Architecture of the neurodynamical model of Deco and Zihl (2001). Solid arrows represent excitatory connections between modules, dotted arrows represent inhibitory connections. From "Top-down selective visual attention: A neurodynamical approach" by G. Deco and J. Zihl, 2001, *Visual Cognition, 8*, p. 123. Copyright 2001 by kind permission of Psychology Press, www.psypress.co.uk/journals.asp, 2005.

color, size, etc.) with separate layers for each value of the feature (e.g., white, big). Thus, activity in the feature maps represent values of features at specific locations on the retina. For each feature map there is a pool of inhibitory neurons. Each layer of the feature map sends excitatory connections to this pool, which inhibits activity in other layers of the feature map. In this way feature values compete for activation in a winner-take-all fashion. Conjunctions of features are represented in a retinotopic *high-level map*. A unit representing a conjunction of features at a certain location in the high-level map receives excitatory inputs from representations of the components of the conjunction at corresponding locations in the feature maps. The high-level map is connected to a separate pool of inhibitory neurons, which produces competition among conjunctions at different locations. A *top-down module* provides task-related information about the target. This information is transmitted by excitatory inputs to the relevant feature layers. For example, if the target is "small" and "white", all activations in these layers of the feature maps are enhanced.

The neurodynamical model works as follows. In a visual search task the system is given sensory input and a specification of the search target. The parallel competition mechanisms in the feature and conjunction maps eventually yield convergence of activity levels throughout the system: Only the neuron populations receiving both bottom-up and top-down excitatory inputs (i.e., units with sensory inputs matching the target features) will be able to develop and sustain high activity levels. This convergence of activity corresponds to focusing of attention at the target object. One critical variable is the reaction time of the system; that is, how long time convergence takes to develop. Deco and Zihl found that simulated reaction times of the system were qualitatively similar to human performance in various feature and conjunction search tasks. Thus, the linear relations between mean reaction time and display set size predicted by simple serial models of conjunction search could be generated by the parallel dynamics of the system.

Neurophysiological models

In recent years the study of attention has been strongly influenced by findings and models of neuroscience. Neural aspects of attention have been investigated by a wide range of methods including patient and brain-imaging studies (for overviews, see Humphreys, Duncan, & Treisman, 1999; Parasuraman, 1998). A particularly interesting development is that models of attention have been closely related to selective processes at the single-cell level, establishing direct links between psychological and neurophysiological theories of attention.

The *classical receptive fields* (RFs) of individual neurons (i.e., those parts of the visual field in which individual neurons are responsive to stimuli) increase greatly in size along the pathways from low- to high-level visual areas in the brain. Whereas RFs in primary visual cortex typically subtend less than one degree by one degree of visual angle, many neurons in inferior temporal cortex (IT) can be driven by stimuli from most of the visual field. To protect these high-level neurons from information overload by concurrent stimuli, some sort of selective mechanism seems necessary. In a sense the individual nerve cell is confronted with the same selection problem as the whole organism; the problem that has motivated models of attention from Broadbent's filter theory to present-day accounts.

In a seminal study using single-cell recordings, Jeffrey Moran and Robert Desimone (1985) demonstrated attentional filtering of visual stimuli in brain areas V4 and IT of macaque monkeys. When both a target and a distractor were located within the recorded neuron's RF, the firing rate was nearly the same as when the target was presented alone. The distractor seemed to be "filtered out", as if the neuron's RF had been contracted around the target. In an influential series of experiments in the 1990s Desimone and colleagues further investigated the neurophysiological correlates of attention (Chelazzi, Duncan, Miller, & Desimone, 1998; Chelazzi, Miller, Duncan, & Desimone, 1993; Luck, Chelazzi, Hillyard, & Desimone, 1997), eventually replacing the notion of absolute filtering with a weighting-based model (Reynolds, Chelazzi, & Desimone, 1999).

Biased competition model

Robert Desimone and John Duncan (1995) proposed a *biased competition* model of attention (see also Desimone, 1999; Duncan, 1996, 1999). In this model, multiple objects in the visual field initially activate many brain systems in parallel. The activations interact so that activations representing features of the same object reinforce each other whereas activations representing different objects are mutually suppressive. Eventually the brain tends to reach a relatively stable state in which activations of the same object dominate throughout (see Deco & Zihl, 2001; Phaf et al., 1990), making its different features available together for consciousness and control of behavior.

In the biased competition model, attentional selection emerges from competitive interactions between neural representations in multiple brain systems. Consistent with psychophysical findings on attentional dwell times, resolution of the competition is assumed to take hundreds of milliseconds. The competition is *biased* in favor of objects with particular features. Top-down priming of target-selective neurons gives a competitive advantage to currently relevant objects (see Chelazzi et al., 1998), and bottom-up mechanisms also affect the probability of selecting a given object (see Wolfe, 1994). Spatial location is just one among many dimensions of selection, and biasing works on numerous attributes including color, shape, and complex conjunctions of features.

Neural TVA

Claus Bundesen, Thomas Habekost, and Søren Kyllingsbæk (2005) proposed a neurophysiological interpretation of TVA: Neural TVA (NTVA). The interpretation links attentional processes at the psychological level to selective processes at the level of single cells. In TVA, categorizations of the form "object x has feature i" compete for entrance into VSTM, each with a processing rate parameter of $v(x, i)$ (see Equation 16.1). In NTVA, $v(x, i)$ is interpreted as the expected value of the *total rate of activation* of the population of neurons that represent the categorization "object x has feature i" at the level of processing where objects compete for entrance into VSTM. At this level in the visual system, it is assumed that the classical RFs of neurons are so large that each RF covers the entire visual field. However, the *effective* RF of each neuron is thought to contract so that the neuron represents the properties of only one of the objects in the visual field (Moran & Desimone, 1985). The probability that a given neuron selects object x is determined by the attentional weight of object x, w_x. Thus the expected number of neurons with RFs contracted around object x equals a certain proportion of all the neurons at this stage of processing, and this proportion is given by $w_x/\Sigma_{z \in S} w_z$ (see Equation 16.1). In this way *dynamic remapping* of RFs accounts for the selective mechanism of filtering (determining *which* objects are selected).

Pigeonholing (determining *how* the selected objects are categorized) depends on a different mechanism. Whereas filtering changes the number of neurons in which an object x is represented, pigeonholing changes the way the object is responded to in each of the neurons allocated to the object. Specifically, pigeonholing is assumed to be done by a *feature-based* mechanism of attention which scales the rates of activation in feature-i selective neurons by multiplication with a certain factor, β_i (see Equation 16.1). Suggestive evidence for a feature-based mechanism of attention that selects groups of neurons with similar stimulus preferences for a multiplicative change in response strength has been provided by Stefan Treue and Julio Martinez Trujillo (1999; also see McAdams & Maunsell, 1999a, 1999b). Apparently, attention research has reached a point at which integration of quantitative psychological and neurophysiological models has become feasible.

Conclusion

Modern research on attention sprang from the theoretical framework developed by Broadbent, Treisman, and other pioneers. Since the early work most research has concerned visual attention. Fundamental issues like the question of serial versus parallel processing continue to give rise to debate. Although no consensus has been reached, some convergence between theories is discernible. For example, contemporary parallel models allow for serial processing by reallocation of attentional resources, whereas serial models include (preattentive) parallel processing as an essential component.

Two developments seem particularly promising for future research. First, formal models of attention have increased in power and scope, and the time seems ripe for general formal theories that integrate attention with related functions such as memory, object recognition, and executive control. Second, the involvement of neuroscience has come to stay, and neural models can be expected to shed further light on the basic issues in the study of attention.

References

Atkinson, R.C., Holmgren, J.E., & Juola, J.F. (1969). Processing time as influenced by the number of elements in a visual display. *Perception & Psychophysics*, *6*, 321–326.

Broadbent, D.E. (1958). *Perception and communication*. London: Pergamon Press.

Bundesen, C. (1987). Visual attention: Race models for selection from multielement displays. *Psychological Research*, *49*, 113–121.

Bundesen, C. (1990). A theory of visual attention. *Psychological Review*, *97*, 523–547.

Bundesen, C. (1993). The relationship between independent race models and Luce's choice axiom. *Journal of Mathematical Psychology*, *37*, 446–471.

Bundesen, C. (1996). Formal models of visual attention: A tutorial review. In A.F. Kramer, M.G.H. Coles, & G.D. Logan (Eds.), *Converging operations in the study of visual selective attention* (pp. 1–43). Washington, DC: American Psychological Association.

Bundesen, C., Habekost, T., & Kyllingsbæk, S. (2005). A neural theory of visual attention: Bridging cognition and neurophysiology. *Psychological Review*, *112*, 291–328.

Chelazzi, L., Duncan, J., Miller, E.K., & Desimone, R. (1998). Responses of neurons in inferior temporal cortex during memory guided visual search. *Journal of Neurophysiology*, *80*, 2918–2940.

Chelazzi, L., Miller, E.K., Duncan, J., & Desimone, R. (1993). A neural basis for visual search in inferior temporal cortex. *Nature*, *363*, 345–347.

Cherry, E.C. (1953). Some experiments on the recognition of speech, with one and with two ears. *Journal of the Acoustical Society of America*, *25*, 975–979.

Colegate, R.L., Hoffman, J.E., & Eriksen, C.W. (1973). Selective encoding from multielement visual displays. *Perception & Psychophysics*, *14*, 217–224.

Deco, G., & Zihl, J. (2001). Top-down selective visual attention: A neurodynamical approach. *Visual Cognition*, *8*, 119–141.

Desimone, R. (1999). Visual attention mediated by biased competition in extrastriate visual cortex. In G.W. Humphreys, J. Duncan, & A.M. Treisman (Eds.), *Attention, space, and action* (pp. 13–30). Oxford: Oxford University Press.

Desimone, R., & Duncan, J. (1995). Neural mechanisms of selective visual attention. *Annual Review of Neuroscience*, *18*, 193–222.

Deutsch, J.A., & Deutsch, D. (1963). Attention: Some theoretical considerations. *Psychological Review*, *70*, 80–90.

Duncan, J. (1996). Cooperating brain systems in selective perception and action. In T. Inui & J.L. McClelland (Eds.), *Attention and performance XVI: Information integration in perception and communication* (pp. 549–578). Cambridge, MA: MIT Press.

Duncan, J. (1999). Converging levels of analysis in the cognitive neuroscience of visual attention. In G.W. Humphreys, J. Duncan, & A.M. Treisman (Eds.), *Attention, space, and action* (pp. 112–129). Oxford: Oxford University Press.

Eriksen, C.W., & Lappin, J.S. (1967). Independence in the perception of simultaneously presented forms at brief durations. *Journal of Experimental Psychology, 73*, 468–472.

Eriksen, C.W., & Spencer, T. (1969). Rate of information processing in visual perception: Some results and methodological considerations. *Journal of Experimental Psychology Monograph, 79*(2, Pt. 2).

Estes, W.K., & Taylor, H.A. (1964). A detection method and probabilistic models for assessing information processing from brief visual displays. *Proceedings of the National Academy of Sciences, USA, 52*, 446–454.

Heinke, D., & Humphreys, G.W. (2003). Attention, spatial representation, and visual neglect: Simulating emergent attention and spatial memory in the selective attention for identification model (SAIM). *Psychological Review, 110*, 29–87.

Hoffman, J.E. (1978). Search through a sequentially presented visual display. *Perception & Psychophysics, 23*, 1–11.

Humphreys, G.W., Duncan, J., & Treisman, A.M. (Eds.). (1999). *Attention, space, and action*. Oxford: Oxford University Press.

Humphreys, G.W., & Müller, H.J. (1993). SEarch via Recursive Rejection (SERR): A connectionist model of visual search. *Cognitive Psychology, 25*, 43–110.

Logan, G.D. (1996). The CODE theory of visual attention: An integration of space-based and object-based attention. *Psychological Review, 103*, 603–649.

Logan, G.D. (2002). An instance theory of attention and memory. *Psychological Review, 109*, 376–400.

Logan, G.D. (2004). Cumulative progress in formal theories of attention. *Annual Review of Psychology, 55*, 207–234.

Logan, G.D., & Bundesen, C. (1996). Spatial effects in the partial report paradigm: A challenge for theories of visual spatial attention. In D.L. Medin (Ed.), *The psychology of learning and motivation* (Vol. 35, pp. 243–282). San Diego, CA: Academic Press.

Logan, G.D., & Bundesen, C. (2003). Clever homunculus: Is there an endogenous act of control in the explicit task cuing procedure? *Journal of Experimental Psychology: Human Perception and Performance, 29*, 575–599.

Logan, G.D., & Bundesen, C. (2004). Very clever homunculus: Compound stimulus strategies for the explicit task-cuing procedure. *Psychonomic Bulletin & Review, 11*, 832–840.

Logan, G.D., & Gordon, R.D. (2001). Executive control of visual attention in dual-task situations. *Psychological Review, 108*, 393–434.

Luck, S.J., Chelazzi, L., Hillyard, S.A., & Desimone, R. (1997). Neural mechanisms of spatial selective attention in areas V1, V2 and V4 of macaque visual cortex. *Journal of Neurophysiology, 77*, 24–42.

Luck, S.J., & Vogel, E.K. (1997). The capacity of visual working memory for features and conjunctions. *Nature, 390*, 279–281.

McAdams, C.J., & Maunsell, J.H.R. (1999a). Effects of attention on orientation-tuning functions of single neurons in macaque cortical area V4. *Journal of Neuroscience, 19*, 431–441.

McAdams, C.J., & Maunsell, J.H.R. (1999b). Effects of attention on the reliability of individual neurons in monkey visual cortex. *Neuron, 23*, 765–773.

McClelland, J.L., & Rumelhart, D.E. (Eds.). (1986). *Parallel distributed processing, Vol. 2*. Cambridge, MA: MIT Press.

Moran, J., & Desimone, R. (1985). Selective attention gates visual processing in the extrastriate cortex. *Science, 229*, 782–784.

Moray, N. (1959). Attention in dichotic listening: Affective cues and the influence of instructions. *Quarterly Journal of Experimental Psychology*, *11*, 56–60.

Mozer, M.C. (1991). *The perception of multiple objects: A connectionist approach*. Cambridge, MA: MIT Press.

Nakayama, K., & Silverman, G.H. (1986). Serial and parallel processing of visual feature conjunctions. *Nature*, *320*, 264–265.

O'Reilly, R.C., & Munakata, Y. (2000). *Computational explorations in cognitive neuroscience: Understanding the mind by simulating the brain*. Cambridge, MA: MIT Press.

Parasuraman, R. (Ed.). (1998). *The attentive brain*. Cambridge, MA: MIT Press.

Phaf, R.H., van der Heijden, A.H.C., & Hudson, P.T.W. (1990). SLAM: A connectionist model for attention in visual selection tasks. *Cognitive Psychology*, *22*, 273–341.

Reynolds, J.H., Chelazzi, L., & Desimone, R. (1999). Competitive mechanisms subserve attention in macaque areas V2 and V4. *Journal of Neuroscience*, *19*, 1736–1753.

Rumelhart, D.E., & McClelland, J.L. (Eds.). (1986). *Parallel distributed processing, Vol. 1*. Cambridge, MA: MIT Press.

Schneider, W., & Shiffrin, R.M. (1977). Controlled and automatic human information processing: I. Detection, search, and attention. *Psychological Review*, *84*, 1–66.

Shibuya, H., & Bundesen, C. (1988). Visual selection from multielement displays: Measuring and modeling effects of exposure duration. *Journal of Experimental Psychology: Human Perception and Performance*, *14*, 591–600.

Shiffrin, R.M., & Schneider, W. (1977). Controlled and automatic human information processing: II. Perceptual learning, automatic attending, and a general theory. *Psychological Review*, *84*, 127–190.

Sperling, G. (1960). The information available in brief visual presentations. *Psychological Monographs*, *74*(11, Whole No. 498).

Sternberg, S. (1967, April). *Scanning a persisting visual image versus a memorized list*. Paper presented at the Annual Meeting of the Eastern Psychological Association.

Townsend, J.T. (1969). Mock parallel and serial models and experimental detection of these. In *Purdue Centennial Symposium on Information Processing* (pp. 617–628). Purdue University, Indiana, USA.

Townsend, J.T., & Ashby, F.G. (1983). *The stochastic modeling of elementary psychological processes*. Cambridge: Cambridge University Press.

Treisman, A.M. (1964a). The effect of irrelevant material on the efficiency of selective listening. *American Journal of Psychology*, *77*, 533–546.

Treisman, A.M. (1964b). Verbal cues, language, and meaning in selective attention. *American Journal of Psychology*, *77*, 206–219.

Treisman, A.M. (1988). Features and objects: The fourteenth Bartlett memorial lecture. *Quarterly Journal of Experimental Psychology*, *40A*, 201–237.

Treisman, A.M., & Gelade, G. (1980). A feature-integration theory of attention. *Cognitive Psychology*, *12*, 97–136.

Treue, S., & Trujillo, J.C.M. (1999). Feature-based attention influences motion processing gain in macaque visual cortex. *Nature*, *399*, 575–579.

van der Heijden, A.H.C. (1992). *Selective attention in vision*. London: Routledge.

van der Heijden, A.H.C. (2004). *Attention in vision: Perception, communication and action*. London: Routledge and Psychology Press.

Wolfe, J.M. (1994). Guided search 2.0: A revised model of visual search. *Psychonomic Bulletin & Review*, *1*, 202–238.

Wolfe, J.M., Cave, K.R., & Franzel, S.L. (1989). Guided search: An alternative to the feature integration model for visual search. *Journal of Experimental Psychology: Human Perception and Performance*, *15*, 419–433.

17 Automatic processes in emotion: Capture of attention and emotion activation

Arne Öhman

Humans strive for happiness and for avoiding misery in a capricious world that all too often fails to conform to their plans and wishes. Thus emotion is at the core of human existence. However, rather than having been afforded the center stage position that it deserves in psychology, it has been viewed with skepticism. From the ancient Greeks and onwards, a recurrent theme in Western philosophy has been the need to domesticate emotion by the reason that has been taken as the necessary premise for virtue.

When psychology broke off from philosophy some 150 years ago some of the founding fathers of the new discipline, such as Wundt, Darwin, James, and Freud, pioneered important contributions to the psychology of emotion, but their insights had limited impact for most of the twentieth century. Partly this lack of interest can be attributed to the common conceptualization of emotion in terms of feelings, which placed them among the conscious experience that fell from grace about a hundred years ago when psychology moved across the Atlantic. This move changed psychology from a science of conscious content to a functional science of behavior. With the mid-century cognitive revolution, the behavioral orthodoxy was overthrown, and eventually the way was paved for reintroducing concepts with a mentalistic flavor into psychology. Yet for many years the focus remained on cold cognition such as perception, attention, and memory rather than on hot cognitions spiced by emotion.

However, in the early twenty-first century, we can look back to a couple of decades of expanding inquiry into the nature of emotion in psychology, as well as in related disciplines such as philosophy, anthropology, and neuroscience. Indeed, we are beginning to understand at least some emotion in neural terms, and this emergent understanding is the theme for this chapter.

What is emotion: A functional perspective

Current research on emotion typically views feelings as one of several components of emotion, rather than as the necessary defining feature. Emotions are viewed as complex responses that are manifested in several relatively independent response systems, such as verbal reports (on feelings), psychophysiological responses, and behavior (e.g., Lang, 1993). One consequence of this conceptual change is that what used to be a contradiction in terms in the feeling-focused perspective, nonconscious emotion, becomes a possible object of study. In operational terms it simply means compelling evidence of emotion in terms of psychophysiological and behavioral responses that are not accessible to consciousness (as manifested in verbal reports). Such a definition comes close to Freud's notion of "repressed emotion", but without taking a stand on the reason for the inaccessibility of the emotion to consciousness.

The role of the response systems becomes apparent when emotion is viewed in a functional perspective (e.g., Öhman & Wiens, 2003). Evolution has imbued us with emotion in order to promote our primary task as biological creatures: the furthering of genes across generations. In short, emotion makes us want to do what our forefathers had to do in order to fulfill this task. Thus, emotions give precedence to stimuli that we need to attend to and cope with in order to survive and breed. They typically intervene to break up rigid stimulus–response relationships in order to provide a flexible organization of behavior in relation to valued goals (e.g., Scherer, 1984). An essential role of emotion is to give value to stimuli (Dolan, 2002). Consequently, the liking of stimuli (or their valence) is a central dimension of emotion, and the feeling of liking functions to reinforce and articulate our goal orientation and assist flexible, long-range plans and action in order to reach goals.

Many emotional stimuli must be more or less urgently dealt with. Hence, they make demands on the behavioral capacity of organisms. For example, cues signaling the presence of a potentially deadly predator activate metabolically taxing defenses such as flight or fight. Activating these defenses requires recruitment of metabolic support from the autonomic nervous system to prepare for action. The activation of the body can, but need not, be felt. Therefore, measuring psychophysiological responses is a main avenue to investigate nonconscious emotion. However, when felt, psychophysiological responses are also main determinants of self-reported emotional arousal, which is another important dimension of emotion.

To cope with potentially disastrous stimuli, action alternatives must be evaluated. An important factor in assessing the situation is one's power in relation to the stimulus. For example, if challenged by a conspecific, are the strength relations such that one should face the challenge or yield to the challenger? Dominance or power, therefore, is the third basic dimension of emotion (see Lang, Bradley, & Cuthbert, 1997, for further discussions of dimensions of emotion).

Another factor when assessing the need to cope with emotional stimuli is their imminence, temporally or spatially. Fanselow (1994) launched the concept of a predatory imminence continuum (subsequently developed by Lang et al., 1997; and Öhman & Wiens, 2003) to account for the type of fear behavior that a more or less distant predator elicits. Depending on the imminence of the threat, the fear response may range from mere attentiveness to fullblown fight and flight responses, with supporting autonomic psychophysiology.

An evolutionary analysis of the emotion of fear

Fear and its varieties

There are several reasons to give fear a privileged position among emotions. First, it is one of a handful of basic or primary emotions that are familiar to all humans. Second, in itself and because of its close relation to anxiety it is often taken as a key for understanding anxiety disorder (e.g., Öhman & Mineka, 2001). Third, because we are starting to understand a good deal about fear and its neural underpinning (e.g., LeDoux, 1996; Rosen & Schulkin, 1998), it may serve as a model for understanding other emotions as well.

Fear is an activated, aversive emotional state that serves to motivate the organism to cope with threatening events (Öhman, 2000). The coping attempts are more or less clearly focused on defensive behaviors such as immobility (freezing), escape, or attack. The origin of fear goes far back in evolution and defense behaviors that may be seen as precursors of fear behavior, such as escape and avoidance, can be identified even in organisms lacking a nervous system.

Öhman, Dimberg, and Öst (1985) distinguished between social fears and animal fears. They argued that the former resulted from a dominance–submissiveness system, the adaptive function of which was to promote social order by means of facilitating the establishment of dominance hierarchies within groups. Animal fears, on the other hand, were attributed to a predatory defense system, originating in the fear of reptiles by early mammals, and prompting rapid escape from potential predators. The social submissiveness and predatory fears can be viewed as alternative routes to the common final path to activate fear; that is, the fear module that is presented below. These basically adaptive systems provide the basis for fear-related anxiety disorders, such as panic disorder, phobias, and post-traumatic stress disorder (see Krueger, 1999). In particular, Öhman et al. (1985) tied social and animal phobias to the social submissiveness and the predatory fear systems, respectively.

The concept of a fear module

Öhman and Mineka (2001) developed the concept of an evolved fear module as a final common pathway for the social submissiveness and predatory fear systems. Briefly, the fear module reflects an evolutionarily shaped neural circuit centered on the amygdala in the anterior medial temporal lobe. It is the characteristics of this circuit that determine the behavioral characteristics of the module. These characteristics include selectivity with regard to effective stimuli for activating the module, automaticity of activation, and encapsulation with regard to cognitive input.

The fear module is controlled by a specific neural circuit that has been evolutionarily shaped to mediate functional relationships between ecological threats and defensive behavior. Because the module reflects a common mammalian heritage, it is primarily located in subcortical and brainstem areas of the brain. Thus, it served animals with primitive brains long before more recent biological families with well-developed cortices emerged. In particular, this circuit was firmly established at the base of the brain that eventually, during relatively recent hominid evolution, became the site of cortical neural networks serving language and advanced cognition. Its ancient origin and location in the brain make it automatic and relatively impenetrable to cognition (LeDoux, 1996). Indeed, "although the experience of fear can be conscious, the brain mechanisms generating fear and the appraisal of stimuli as fearful are unconscious and automatic, similar to the workings of any other body organ" (Rosen & Schulkin, 1998, p. 326).

Evolutionarily shaped behavioral systems are likely to be selective with regard to the input they respond to. In case of the fear module, it is assumed to be sensitive to stimuli that have been correlated with threatening encounters in the evolutionary past. By limiting the set of effective stimuli, ready-made neural mechanisms could be devised for identifying critical events after only minimal neural processing, to promote rapid defense activation. One effect of this sensitivity is that stimuli activating the fear module are likely automatically to capture attention if presented in arrays of similar stimuli (e.g., Öhman, Flykt, & Lundqvist, 2000). The range of stimuli that can activate the fear module can be vastly expanded through Pavlovian conditioning, which may give stimuli that happen to coincide with the activation of the module power to activate the module by themselves. This conditioning effect occurs with particular ease, and results in fear responses highly resistant to extinction, if the conditioned stimulus (CS) is evolutionarily fear relevant (Öhman et al., 1985; Öhman & Mineka, 2001; Seligman, 1971). Thus, the selectivity of fear-eliciting stimuli has its origin in biases to selectively associate fear with recurrent survival threats rather than in innate fear stimuli.

Because of its origin in brains with little cortex, the fear module is, for evolutionary reasons, independent of cognition. The first aspect of this independence is automaticity. Because of its deep evolutionary origin, the fear module is not under voluntary control but is directly activated by stimuli that are evolutionarily primed for becoming associated with fear. In other words, it is independent of intentions. Thus, for effective stimuli the fear module is activated whether we want it or not and whether or not the stimulus has been represented in consciousness.

A second aspect of the fear module's independence of cognition is encapsulation, i.e., it is relatively impenetrable to other modules with which it lacks direct connections. Thus, once activated, the fear module tends to run its course with few possibilities for other processes to interfere with or stop it. In particular, it is resistant to conscious cognitive influences because its origin preceded recent evolutionary events such as the emergence of conscious thought and language. Encapsulation may appear closely related to automaticity. However, automaticity is primarily related to the *initiating of activity* whereas encapsulation refers more to the *maintaining of activity* over time.

The automaticity and encapsulation of the fear module help to explain the dissociation between rational thought and fear activation, which is at the core of anxiety disorders such as phobias. Even though people with specific phobias rate the phobic object as more dangerous than people in general do (e.g., Thorpe & Salkovskis, 1997), they typically realize that their fear when encountering the phobic object is far more intense than is motivated by the objective danger involved.

The purpose of the present chapter is to review different sets of data that are congruent with the concept of a fear module.

Behavioral data

Emotion and attention: Fear-relevant stimuli guide attention

The fear module includes "attentional control settings" (Folk, Remington, & Johnston, 1992) that orient attention towards threatening events (Öhman, Flykt, & Esteves, 2001a). Accordingly, Öhman et al. (2001a) demonstrated an enhanced bias to detect evolutionarily fear-relevant stimuli (snakes and spiders) in a complex array of stimuli (different flowers and mushrooms) in research participants selected to be specifically fearful of snakes or spiders. They used a visual search paradigm in which the participants were instructed to detect a discrepant target stimulus among different exemplars of a background category of stimuli. For example, the target could be a snake picture presented among distractor pictures of flowers. Normal non-fearful subjects were faster to locate snakes and spiders among flowers and mushrooms than vice versa, and this fear-relevance advantage was independent of the number of distractors in the display. This suggests that fear-relevant stimuli automatically captured attention in a processes were the targets "popped out" from the background. Snake-fearful participants were as quick as the controls in detecting spiders, but they were still faster in detecting snakes. Participants specifically fearful of spiders were faster to detect spiders than snakes, and they detected snakes faster than fear-irrelevant stimuli. Thus, people in general appeared to be sensitive to fear stimuli for which an evolutionary basis for their emotional effectiveness appears plausible (Öhman et al., 1985), and this sensitivity was further enhanced if the stimuli actually elicited fear.

The basic observation of faster detection of fear-relevant stimuli (snakes and spiders) among fear-irrelevant ones (flowers and mushrooms) were replicated by Lipp, Derakshan, Waters, and Logies (2004) and Tipples, Young, Quinlan, Broks, and Ellis (2002). In addition Lipp et al. (2004) extended the findings by showing faster search for fear-relevant targets (e.g., snakes) among fear-relevant distractors (e.g., spiders) than for fear-irrelevant targets (e.g., mushrooms) among fear-irrelevant distractors (e.g., flowers). The results reported by Lipp et al. (2004), similar to our data, also suggested that search for fear-relevant targets, in contrast to search for fear-irrelevant ones, was not slowed by increasing the number of distractors from three to eight. However, contrary to our results, Lipp et al. (2004) did not find that the threat advantage was enhanced in fearful subjects, which possibly could be attributed to their use of less fearful participants. However, Miltner, Krieschel, Hecht, Trippe, and Weiss (2004), in an interesting modification of the visual search paradigm, reported that spider phobics were significantly slowed by occasional spider pictures among flower distractors when they were instructed to search for a neutral (mushroom) target. Because the feared stimulus interfered with the top-down controlled search for a neutral target, this result suggests that fearful subjects are prone to have their attention captured by fear stimuli in an automatic, stimulus-driven, bottom-up process that is independent of intentions.

Lundqvist, Öhman, and colleagues (see review by Lundqvist & Öhman, 2005a) have provided further data supporting a threat advantage for biologically fear-relevant stimuli in visual search paradigms with stimuli from the social submissiveness system. In primates, facial expressions of threat and submissiveness provide an important channel of communication in dominance contests, which make facial threat a powerful fear stimulus that elicits strong psychophysiological responses (Dimberg & Öhman, 1996; Öhman & Dimberg, 1984).

Öhman, Lundqvist, and Esteves (2001b) used schematic faces in a visual search task similar to the one developed for animal stimuli by Öhman et al. (2001a) in order to examine whether threatening faces guided attention more efficiently than friendly faces. They reported that normal non-anxious participants were quicker to detect a discrepant threatening face among neutral and friendly distractors than a friendly face against neutral or threatening distractors (see also Fox, Lester, Russo, Bowles, Pichler, & Dutton, 2000). Furthermore, both Fox et al. (2000) and Eastwood, Smilek, and Merikle (2001) found less effect of crowd size on detection latency for finding negative than positive schematic targets among neutral distractors. Thus, schematic facial stimuli appear to show a threat advantage, similar to what was reported for snakes and spiders by Öhman et al. (2001a). Lundqvist and Öhman (2005b) reported an attempt to delineate what components were critical for obtaining the threat advantage to angry schematic faces by systematically varying the number of components (eyebrows, eyes, and mouth) that expressed anger or happiness. These emotional faces were then used as target stimuli among both emotional and neutral distractors. Their results suggested that eyebrows, eyes, and mouth all contributed to the threat advantage, and that none of them was necessary or sufficient for the effect. However, similar to Tipples, Atkinson, and Young (2002), Lundqvist and Öhman (2005b) reported that the eyebrows were particularly important. Furthermore, Lundqvist and Öhman reported a reliable relationship between rated emotion (particularly negative valence) and visual search for threatening target faces. Thus, the contrast in ratings of negative valence between angry and happy faces closely predicted the anger advantage in visual search across schematic faces that differed in how many features that expressed the threat. Juth, Lundqvist, Karlsson, and Öhman (2005) showed that socially anxious individuals, particularly when their anxiety was activated by a critical observer, showed an enhanced threat advantage compared to controls.

Automaticity: Autonomic responses to nonconsciously presented fear stimuli

When individuals who are fearful of snakes and spiders are exposed to a set of pictures that includes the feared animal, they show a strong psychophysiological response specifically to this picture (see e.g., Öhman, Hamm, & Hugdahl, 2000, for review). For example, Globisch, Hamm, Esteves, and Öhman (1999) reported enhanced skin conductance responses, a marked heart rate and blood pressure increase, and potentiation of the startle reflex in selected fearful students when they viewed their feared animal. This response, and particularly the startle potentiation component (see Davis & Whalen, 2001), points to the amygdala in the medial temporal lobe as a likely neural origin. The amygdala is one of the limbic structures that date back more than 100 million years in evolutionary time, to the juncture of reptiles and mammals. Thus its evolutionary origin rests with animal brains with little or no cortex. Still the amygdala has remained an important control station of fear as the neocortex expanded in mammals. Interestingly, it has become larger in primates, and this expansion is correlated with the growth of the frontal lobes (Barton & Aggleton, 2000), which suggests that the amygdala may have become an important structure for social cognition (Adolphs, 2003; Adolphs, Tranel, & Damasio, 1998; Öhman, 2002). Nevertheless, the amygdala has retained its role as a major nub in the general fear network of the human brain (e.g., LeDoux, 1996), and as such it has been assumed to remain relatively inaccessible to cortical control (e.g., Rosen & Schulkin, 1998).

From this scenario, it could be predicted that fear responses can be elicited after minimal cognitive processing. Öhman and Soares (1994) tested this hypothesis using a technique known as backward masking (see Wiens & Öhman, in press). Individuals with an intense fear of snakes but not spiders, or vice versa, were selected as research participants. Participants in the control group feared neither stimulus. Participants were exposed to series of pictures while skin conductance responses (SCRs) were measured. In one condition of the experiment, the content of the very briefly (30 ms) presented pictures was effectively masked from conscious recognition by immediately following similar pictures (presented for 100 ms) that had been randomly cut to pieces, randomly reassembled, and re-photographed. Pilot experiments ascertained that both fearful and non-fearful participants consistently failed to identify the target above chance with these masking parameters. Fearful participants showed larger SCRs to masked pictures of snakes than to masked pictures of spiders, and vice versa for the spider-fearful participants. The fearful participants did not respond more to the fear-relevant but non-feared stimulus (e.g., spiders for snake-fearful participants), and responses to the latter stimulus did not exceed those to neutral control stimuli (flowers and mushrooms), nor did their responses to non-feared stimuli exceed the levels of responses to any of the masked stimuli for the control group. These results show that conscious recognition of a fear stimulus is not necessary for activating fear responses. Given that backward masking of visual stimuli appears to disrupt processing at the level of the primary visual cortex (Rolls & Tovée, 1994; Rolls, Tovée, & Panzeri, 1999), and that the amygdala is critical in activating fear responses, they are consistent with LeDoux's (1996, 2000) "low road" notion that sensory information can access the amygdala without having to pass through the cortex.

The amygdala mediates human fear responses

Amygdala responses to masked facial stimuli

In order to test the hypothesis that masked fear elicitation is mediated by the amygdala, Morris, Öhman, and Dolan (1998) examined regional cerebral blood flow responses assessed by positron emission tomography (PET) to masked facial stimuli whose emotional impact had been enhanced by a conditioning procedure. The conditioning paradigm was developed by Esteves, Dimberg, and Öhman (1994) in order to demonstrate that responses that had been aversively conditioned to angry faces survived backward masking (see Dimberg & Öhman, 1996, for review). In the experiment reported by Morris et al. (1998), participants were presented with pictures of four different male faces, two of which were angry and two of which were neutral, immediately before PET scanning. One of the angry faces was paired with an aversive noise, and thus became a conditioned stimulus (a CS+). The second angry face was never paired with the noise and thus served as a CS–. Booster conditioning trials were presented in-between blocks of masked extinction trials with short intertrial (5 s) intervals that were presented during 60-s PET scans. There were four different conditions for extinction trials that were presented in different scans. Two of them involved the CS+ and the CS– as target stimuli, each presented for 30 ms, and each one immediately and consistently followed by one of the two neutral faces, presented for 45 ms as masks. In these conditions, therefore, the CSs were presented nonconsciously. Skin conductance response data confirmed reliably larger responses to the masked CS+ than to the masked CS– during the PET scans. By contrasting images of regional cerebral blood flow produced by the masked CS+ (conditioned angry face masked by a neutral face) and the masked CS– (a different angry face masked by a different neutral face), the difference would reveal locations in the brain of the fear response conditioned to the CS+ elicited by a masked fear stimulus.

Confirming the hypothesis of amygdala involvement, the contrast between the masked CS+s and the masked CS–s showed significant differential activations specifically (and exclusively) in the right amygdala region.

Amygdala activation to masked and nonmasked fear stimuli

To further elucidate the dynamics of fear activation in the human brain Carlsson, Petersson, Lundqvist, Karlsson, Ingvar, and Öhman (2004) recruited participants who were fearful of either snakes or spiders (but not of both, see Öhman & Soares, 1994) for a PET study with masked stimuli. In this way they could compare responses to a stimulus that was definitely feared (e.g., snakes) with responses to fear-relevant but not actually feared stimuli (e.g., spiders). During different scans participants were exposed to repeated 14 ms presentation of pictures of either snakes, spiders, or mushrooms that were effectively (14 ms masking interval, 56 ms mask) or ineffectively (294 ms masking interval, 56 ms mask) masked in different scans. Compared to the effectively masked mushroom control condition, the left amygdala was activated both to the feared (e.g., snakes) and the fear-relevant but non-feared (e.g., spiders) condition, with no difference between the two types of fear-relevant stimuli. There were no other significant activations in the effectively masked condition. This implies that the amygdala initially responded to the threat potential of stimuli rather than to a specifically defined fear stimulus.

However, as the processing time was extended to allow conscious perception of the stimuli, there was strong bilateral activation of the amygdala to the actually feared stimuli (e.g., snakes), but no significant amygdala activation on either side in the fear-relevant but non-feared condition (e.g., spiders for a snake-fearful participant). Furthermore, with time to consciously recognize the stimuli, the enhanced amygdala response (particularly on the right side) to the feared stimulus was associated with activation of a cortical affective processing network that included the anterior cingulated cortex (ACC), the anterior insula, the orbitofrontal cortex (OFC), as well as the midbrain periaqueductal gray (PAG), while neither the amygdala nor any other of the affective processing areas was significantly activated in the fear-relevant but non-feared condition. Thus, when the phobic stimulus became more completely processed, a fear network that included both subcortical and cortical nodes was recruited as fear accelerated. However, with time to decide that the fear-relevant (but non-feared) stimulus was in effect not dangerous, the initial amygdala response to the stimulus was relatively disengaged and the cortical areas were never recruited.

A subcortical route to amygdala activation?

A central point in the LeDoux (1996, 2000) model of fear activation is that the amgydala can be rapidly activated by a "low road" via the thalamus that does not require the cortex. This is the presumed neuroanatomical basis for the independence of fear from cognition. In further analyses of the data of Morris et al. (1998), Morris, Öhman, and Dolan (1999) examined whether the nonconscious activation of the amygdala by the conditioned angry face was occasioned through a subcortical route. Accordingly, they examined the neural connectivity between the amygdala and other brain regions when the amygdala was activated by masked stimuli. In support of the LeDoux (1996, 2000) hypothesis, Morris et al. (1999) reported that activation of the right amygdala by masked stimuli could be reliably predicted from activation of subcortical way-stations in the visual systems such as the superior colliculus and the right pulvinar, but not from any cortical regions. These effects are likely to be mediated by fast automatic perceptual pathways that are served by large rapidly conducting neurons working on low spatial frequency information (Leventhal, Rodieck, & Dreher, 1985). This is consistent with data reported by Vuilleumier, Armony, Driver, and Dolan (2003), who filtered the spatial frequency of pictures of faces to produce facial stimuli that retained only high- or low-frequency spatial information. Their results indicate that high spatial frequency face stimuli induced greater activation of the fusiform face area (an area specialized for face processing, e.g., Haxby, Hoffman, & Gobbini, 2000) than low spatial frequency stimuli, regardless of emotional expression. Amygdala responses, however, were larger for low-frequency faces provided that they showed expressions of fear. Moreover, they demonstrated activation of the pulvinar and superior colliculus specifically by low-frequency fearful faces. Thus, these results suggest that the superior colliculus–pulvinar pathway to the amygdala operates primarily on low-frequency information.

To supplement the correlational methodology used by Morris et al. (1999), Morris, DeGelder, Weiskrantz, and Dolan (2001) and Vuilleumier, Armony, Clarke, Husain, Driver, and Dolan (2002) examined patients with cortical lesions in order to test whether the amygdala can be activated independently of the cortex as postulated by the low road concept. Morris et al. (2001) examined a patient who reported blindness for objects presented in the damaged areas of the primary visual cortex. However, the reported blindness notwithstanding, he could guess stimuli characteristics (e.g., the location of stimuli and a screen) better than chance, i.e., he exhibited blindsight. Blindsight may be mediated by a parallel visual route through the superior colliculus and pulvinar nucleus of the thalamus (Weiskrantz, 1986), similar to the pathway delineated by Morris et al. (1999) and Vuilleumier et al. (2003). Indeed, the blindsight patient examined by Morris et al. (2001) showed reliable activation in the right amygdala to fearful faces presented in the cortically blind field, and a connectivity analysis suggested that this nonconsicous amygdala activation was mediated by the superior colliculus and the pulvinar.

In a further analysis of the role of cortex in amygdala activation, Vuilleumier et al. (2002) examined a patient with right inferior parietal lobe damage, who showed visual extinction to stimuli presented in the anatomically intact left visual field when another stimulus was simultaneously presented in the right visual field. For example, he failed to notice a picture of a face in the left visual field when a picture of a house was concurrently presented in the right visual field (even though he did perceive the face when it was presented alone in the left visual field). Nevertheless, recordings of functional magnetic resonance images (fMRI) showed amygdala activation to extinguished faces particularly when they were fearful. Thus, these lesion studies show amygdala activation by fear faces that remained nonperceived because they were presented in spatial locations corresponding to damaged areas of the primary sensory cortex (Morris et al., 2001), and in higher-order visual areas that failed to be attended because of spatial neglect and extinction (Vuilleumier et al., 2002), which supports the notion that amygdala activation does not require cortical processing.

Finally, even though this research suggests that the amygdala can be activated without the cortex, the amygdala may still have effects on the visual cortex (Armony & LeDoux, 2000; Emery & Amaral, 2000). In a study based on patients with focal amydala and hippocampal lesions, Vuilleumier, Richardson, Armony, Driver, and Dolan (2004) examined whether an intact amygdala influenced cortical processing of emotional stimuli. Previous studies (e.g., Vuilleumier, Armony, Driver, & Dolan, 2001) have shown enhanced activation of the fusiform facial area by fearful as compared to neutral faces (even though any face stimulus activates the fusiformis when the comparison stimulus consists of non-facial object, e.g, Haxby et al., 2000). Vuilleumier et al. (2004) replicated this emotional enhancement of the fusiform cortex to fearful faces in normal controls and patients with focal hippocampal lesions only. However, such emotional enhancement was not observed in the patients with focused amygdala lesions (with or without hippocampal lesions). Thus, these findings imply that the amygdala is rapidly activated by the colliculi–pulvinar pathway in order to prime the visual cortex for enhanced processing of emotional stimuli as suggested by LeDoux (1996, 2000).

Is amygdala activation independent of attention?

The low road concept and the supporting human data provided by Dolan's group (Morris et al., 1998, 1999, 2001; Vuilleumier et al., 2002, 2003, 2004), as well as by our group (Carlsson et al., 2004; Öhman et al., 2001a; Öhman & Mineka, 2001), strongly support that the amygdala can be automatically activated by emotional stimuli. This, in turn, implies that attention to the eliciting stimulus is not necessary. As reviewed above, strong behavioral data supporting this contention were presented by Miltner et al. (2004), who reported strong distraction effects of feared stimuli presented among the distractors in a visual search task. The role of attention in activating the amygdala was directly examined by Vuilleumier et al. (2001). They exposed their participants to pairs of faces and houses that were either horizontally or vertically arranged around a fixation cross. Attention was manipulated by requiring the participants to judge whether the pairs of faces or houses showed identical pictures. Activation of the fusiform facial area by faces was additively enhanced by attention (attending to faces vs attending to houses) and emotion (fearful vs neutral face). In contrast, activation of the amygdala was larger to fearful than to neutral faces with no effect of attention. Thus, these data concur with the conclusion that the amygdala may be automatically activated, independently of attention.

This, conclusion was further supported by Anderson, Christoff, Panitz, De Rosa, and Gabrieli (2003) in a similar paradigm in which participants attended to either faces (showing fear, disgust or a neutral expression) or houses in different colors that were superimposed on each other. However, Pessoa, McKenna, Gutierrez, and Ungerleider (2002b) reported strong effects of attention on the amygdala in a task where participants either attended to focally presented fearful, happy, and neutral faces by judging their gender, or to eccentrically presented bars in the upper left and right quadrants of the display by deciding whether their orientations were the same. Contrary to the other findings (Anderson et al., 2003; Vuillemier et al., 2001), Pessoa et al. (2002b) reported that none of the emotional faces differed from the neutral ones in amygdala activation in the unattended condition. The basis for this discrepant finding remains unclear. However, Bishop, Duncan, and Lawrence (2004) showed that the effect of attention on amygdala activation to fear faces interacted with the anxiety level of the participant, with an effect of attention only for low-anxious participants and vigilance for fearful faces independently of attention in high-anxious participants. Therefore, they argued that anxiety could be a confounding factor determining the effect of attention of amygdala activation.

Emotional modulation by the prefrontal cortex

The prefrontal cortex is often taken as the origin for regulating emotion (e.g., Davidson, Putnam, & Larson, 2000). Accordingly, in the study by Carlsson et al. (2004) the right dorsolateral prefrontal cortex (DLPFC) and the lateral OFC were *less* activated to the feared than to the fear-relevant but non-feared stimulus when the masking interval allowed conscious processing of the stimuli. This can be interpreted as emotional modulation of the amygdala activity from the prefrontal cortex when time was allowed to determine that the fear-relevant (but non-feared) stimulus in effect was harmless.

This interpretation can be supported by several arguments. First, there was an inverse relationship between activation of the OFC and the amygdala in this condition. Second, in an experiment in which the participants were instructed to try actively to attenuate their emotional response to negative visual stimuli, Ochsner, Bunge, Gross, and Gabrieli (2002) reported a similar inverse correlation between activation of the DLPFC and the amygdala. Third, as a primary site controlling working memory, the right DLPFC has been designated as involved in executive prefrontal control of cognitive processes such as, e.g., top-down control of attention (Corbetta & Shulman, 2002; Pessoa, Kastner, & Ungerleider, 2002a). Fourth, there is literature showing that the dopamine system normally activating the prefrontal cortex may be actively inhibited during intense fear states (Arnsten, 1998), in order to transfer control to the evolutionary time-proven subcortical defense systems (LeDoux, 1996). Thus, the normal prefrontal inhibitory control of amygdala activation seen in the fear-relevant condition may have been actively blocked in the feared stimulus condition. Indeed, such blocking could be an essential part of panic responses.

Finally, the findings of Carlsson et al. (2004) were constructively replicated by Cunningham, Johnson, Raye, Gatenby, Gore, and Banaji (2004). They examined brain activations to effectively masked and non-masked presentations of emotionally relevant stimuli, black and white faces for white participants, and reported larger amygdala activation to black than to white faces with effective but not with ineffective masking. With conscious recognition, there was larger activation to black than to white faces in the ACC, the right DLPFC, and OFC that was inversely related to changes in amygdala activation to black faces from the masked to the non-masked condition. Thus it appears that an automatic emotional response to individuals of a different race (which was associated with an implicit racial bias) was inhibited by a prefrontally controlled modulation of the automatically activated subcortical emotional network when more processing time was allowed.

Bishop, Duncan, Brett, and Lawrence (2004) showed reduced ACC activation to unexpected distractor stimuli as well as less recruitment of the lateral prefrontal cortex to these stimuli in people with high anxiety. These results suggest that anxiety is not only associated with increased amgydala activation to nonattended stimuli (Bishop, Duncan, & Lawrence, 2004), but also with less efficient prefrontal modulation of the amygdala response.

Conclusions

Research on emotion during the last few decades has made important headway in understanding, both at the level of psychology and neuroscience. If fear is taken as a case study, we have gained important knowledge about the factors that activate fear, including the role of nonconscious processes and the role of fear in guiding attention. Even more important, perhaps, is that we are beginning to come to grips with the neural mechanisms behind these behavioral effects. Fear stimuli engage a subcortical network of structures that is centered on the amygdala and that can activate fear responses via an automatic, subcortical, route. As a result of amygdala activation, the fear response is recruited and attention is drawn to the eliciting stimulus. The subcortical system interacts with the prefrontal cortex to modulate the emotional response to better conform to environmental and social circumstances. It remains to be seen whether this cortical–subcortial interaction is specific to fear or whether it illustrates a more general principle of the neural organization of emotion. Further psychological and neuroscientific elucidation of these systems, therefore, may not only offer new insights into fear-related disorders, but also assist in developing the more general understanding of emotion.

References

Adolphs, R. (2003). Is the human amygdala specialized for processing of social information? *Annals of the New York Academy of Sciences*, *985*, 326–340.

Adolphs, R., Tranel, D., & Damasio, A.R. (1998). The human amygdala in social judgment. *Nature*, *393*, 470–474.

Anderson, A.K., Christoff, K., Panitz, D., De Rosa, E., & Gabrieli, J.D.E. (2003). Neural correlates of the automatic processing of threat facial signals. *Journal of Neurosicence*, *23*, 5627–5633.

Armony, J.L., & LeDoux, J.E. (2000). How danger is encoded: Toward a systems, cellular, and computational understanding of cognitive–emotional interactions in fear. In M.S. Gazzaniga (Ed.), *The cognitive neurosciences* (pp. 1067–1079). Cambridge, MA: The MIT Press.

Arnsten, A.F.T. (1998). Catecholamine modulation of prefrontal cortical cognitive function. *Trends in Cognitive Sciences*, *11*, 436–447.

Barton, R.A., & Aggleton, J.P. (2000). Primate evolution and the amygdala. In J.P. Aggleton (Ed.), *The amygdala: A functional analysis* (2nd ed., pp. 479–508). New York: Oxford University Press.

Bishop, S.J., Duncan, J., Brett, M., & Lawrence, A. (2004). Prefrontal cortical function and anxiety: Controlling attention to threat related stimuli. *Nature Neuroscience*, *7*, 184–188.

Bishop, S.J., Duncan, J., & Lawrence, A.D. (2004). State anxiety modulation of the amygdala response to unattended threat-related stimuli. *Journal of Neuroscience*, *24*, 10364–10368.

Carlsson, K., Petersson, K.M., Lundqvist, D., Karlsson, A., Ingvar, M., & Öhman, A. (2004). Fear and the amygdala: Manipulation of awareness generates differential cerebral responses to phobic and fear-relevant (but non-feared) stimuli. *Emotion*, *4*, 340–353.

Corbetta, M., & Shulman, G.L. (2002). Control of goal-directed and stimulus-driven attention in the brain. *Nature Reviews. Neuroscience*, *3*, 201–215.

Cunningham, W.A., Johnson, M.K., Raye, C.L., Gatenby, J.C., Gore, J.C., & Banaji, M.R. (2004). Separable components in the processing of black and white faces. *Psychological Science*, *15*, 806–813.

Davidson, R.J., Putnam, K.M., & Larson, C.L. (2000). Dysfunction in the neural circuitry of emotion regulation – a possible prelude to violence. *Science*, *289*, 591–594.

Davis, M., & Whalen, P.J. (2001). The amygdala: Vigilance and emotion. *Molecular Psychiatry*, *6*, 13–34.

Dimberg, U., & Öhman, A. (1996). Behold the wrath: Psychophysiological responses to facial stimuli. *Motivation and Emotion, 20*, 149–182.

Dolan, R.J. (2002). Emotion, cognition, and behavior. *Science, 298*, 1191–1194.

Eastwood, J.D., Smilek, D., & Merikle, P.M. (2001). Differential attentional guidance by unattended faces expressing positive and negative emotion. *Perception and Psychophysics, 63*, 1004–1013.

Emery, N.J., & Amaral, D.G. (2000). The role of the amygdala in primate social cognition. In R. Lane & L. Nadel (Eds.), *The cognitive neuroscience of emotion* (pp. 156–191). New York: Oxford University Press.

Esteves, F., Dimberg, U., & Öhman, A. (1994). Automatically elicited fear: Conditioned skin conductance responses to masked facial expressions. *Cognition and Emotion, 8*, 393–413.

Fanselow, M.S. (1994). Neural organization of the defensive behavior system responsible for fear. *Psychonomic Bulletin and Review, 1*, 429–438.

Folk, C.L., Remington, R.W., & Johnston, J.C. (1992). Involuntary covert orienting is contingent on attentional control settings. *Journal of Experimental Psychology: Human Perception and Performance, 18*(4), 1030–1044.

Fox, E., Lester, V., Russo, R., Bowles, R.J., Pichler, A., & Dutton, K. (2000). Facial expressions of emotion: Are angry faces detected more efficiently? *Cognition and Emotion, 14*, 61–92.

Globisch, J., Hamm, A.O., Esteves, F., & Öhman, A. (1999). Fear appears fast: Temporal course of startle reflex potentiation in animal fearful subjects. *Psychophysiology, 36*, 66–75.

Haxby, J.V., Hoffman, E.A., & Gobbini, M.I. (2000). The distributed human neural system for face perception. *Trends in Cognitive Sciences, 4*, 223–233.

Juth, P., Lundqvist, D., Karlsson, A., & Öhman, A. (2005). Looking for foes and friends: Perceptual and emotional factors when finding a face in the crowd. *Emotion, 5*(4), 379–395.

Krueger, R.F. (1999). The structure of common mental disorders. *Archives of General Psychiatry, 56*, 921–926.

Lang, P.J. (1993). The three-system approach to emotion. In N. Birbaumer & A. Öhman (Eds.), *The structure of emotion: Psychophysiological, cognitive and clinical aspects* (pp. 18–30). Göttingen: Hogrefe & Huber.

Lang, P.J., Bradley, M.M., & Cuthbert, B.N. (1997). Motivated attention: Affect, activation, and action. In P.J. Lang, R.F. Simons, & M.T. Balaban (Eds.), *Attention and orienting: Sensory and motivational processes* (pp. 97–136). Hillsdale, NJ: Lawrence Erlbaum Associates Inc.

LeDoux, J.E. (1996). *The emotional brain*. New York: Simon & Schuster.

LeDoux, J.E. (2000). Emotion circuits in the brain. *Annual Review of Neuroscience, 23*, 155–184.

Leventhal, A.G., Rodieck, R.W., & Dreher, B. (1985). Central projection of cat retinal ganglion cells. *Journal of Comparative Neurology, 237*, 216–226.

Lipp, O.V., Derakshan, N., Waters, A., & Logies, S. (2004). Snakes and cats in the flower bed: Fast detection is not specific to pictures of fear-relevant stimuli. *Emotion, 4*, 233–250.

Lundqvist, D., & Öhman, A. (2005a). Caught by the evil eye: Nonconscious information processing, emotion, and attention to facial stimuli. In L. Feldman-Barett, P. Niedenthal, & P. Winkielman (Eds.), *Emotion: Unconscious and conscious* (pp. 97–122). New York: Guilford Press.

Lundqvist, D., & Öhman, A. (2005b). Emotion regulates attention: The relations between facial configurations, facial emotions, and visual attention. *Visual Cognition, 12*, 51–84.

Miltner, W.H.R., Krieschel, S., Hecht, H., Trippe, R., & Weiss, T. (2004). Eye movements and behavioral responses to threatening and nonthreatening stimuli during visual search in phobic and nonphobic subjects. *Emotion, 4*, 323–339.

Morris, J.S., DeGelder, B., Weiskrantz, L., & Dolan, R.J. (2001). Differential extra-geniculostriate and amygdala responses to presentation of emotional faces in a cortically blind field. *Brain, 124*, 1241–1252.

Morris, J.S., Öhman, A., & Dolan, R.J. (1998). Conscious and unconscious emotional learning in the human amygdala. *Nature, 393*, 467–470.

Morris, J.S., Öhman, A., & Dolan, R.J. (1999). A subcortical pathway to the right amygdala mediating "unseen" fear. *Proceedings of the National Academy of Sciences, USA, 96*, 1680–1685.

Ochsner, K.N., Bunge, S.A., Gross, J.J., & Gabrieli, J.D.E. (2002). Rethinking feelings: An fMRI study of the cognitive regulation of emotion. *Journal of Cognitive Neurosicence, 14*, 1215–1229.

Öhman, A. (2000). Fear. In G. Fink. (Ed.), *Encyclopedia of stress* (Vol. 2, pp. 111–116). San Diego, CA: Academic Press.

Öhman, A. (2002). Automaticity and the amygdala: Nonconscious responses to emotional faces. *Current Directions in Psychological Science, 11*, 62–66.

Öhman, A., & Dimberg, U. (1984). An evolutionary perspective on human social behavior. In W.M. Waid (Ed.), *Sociophysiology* (pp. 47–86). New York: Springer-Verlag.

Öhman, A., Dimberg, U., & Öst, L-G. (1985). Animal and social phobias: Biological constraints on learned fear responses. In S. Reiss & R.R. Bootzin (Eds.), *Theoretical issues in behavior therapy* (pp. 123–178). New York: Academic Press.

Öhman, A., Flykt, A., & Esteves, F. (2001a). Emotion drives attention: Detecting the snake in the grass. *Journal of Experimental Psychology: General, 130*, 466–478.

Öhman, A., Flykt, A., & Lundqvist, D. (2000). Unconscious emotion: Evolutionary perspectives, psychophysiological data, and neuropsychological mechanisms. In R. Lane & L. Nadel (Eds.), *The cognitive neuroscience of emotion* (pp. 296–327). New York: Oxford University Press.

Öhman, A., Hamm, A., & Hugdahl, K. (2000) Cognition and the autonomic nervous system: Orienting, anticipation, and conditioning. In J.T. Cacioppo, L.G. Tassinary, & G.G. Berntson (Eds.), *Handbook of psychophysiology* (pp. 522–575). New York: Cambridge University Press.

Öhman, A., Lundqvist, D., & Esteves, F. (2001b). The face in the crowd revisited. A threat advantage with schematic stimuli. *Journal of Personality and Social Psychology, 80*, 381–396.

Öhman, A., & Mineka, S. (2001). Fears, phobias, and preparedness: Toward an evolved module of fear and fear learning. *Psychological Review, 108*, 483–522.

Öhman, A., & Soares, J.J.F. (1994). "Unconscious anxiety": Phobic responses to masked stimuli. *Journal of Abnormal Psychology, 103*, 231–240.

Öhman, A., & Wiens, S. (2003). On the automaticity of autonomic responses in emotion: An evolutionary perspective. In R.J. Davidson, K.R. Scherer, & H.H. Goldsmith (Eds.), *Handbook of affective sciences* (pp. 256–275). New York: Oxford University Press.

Pessoa, L., Kastner, S., & Ungerleider, L.G. (2002a). Attentional control of the processing of neutral and emotional stimuli. *Cognitive Brain Research, 15*, 31–45.

Pessoa, L., McKenna, M., Gutierrez, E., & Ungerleider, L.G. (2002b). Neural processing of emotional faces requires attention. *Proceedings of the National Academy of Sciences, 99*, 11458–11463.

Rolls, E.T., & Tovée, M.J. (1994). Processing speed in the cerebral cortex and the neurophysiology of visual masking. *Proceedings of the Royal Society of London, Series B, 257*, 9–15.

Rolls, E.T., Tovée, M.J., & Panzeri, S. (1999). The neurophysiology of backward masking: Information analysis. *Journal of Cognitive Neuroscience, 11*, 300–311.

Rosen, J.B., & Schulkin, J. (1998). From normal fear to pathological anxiety. *Psychological Review, 105*, 325–350.

Scherer, K.R. (1984). Emotion serves to decouple stimulus and response. In P. Ekman & R.J. Davidson (Eds.), *The nature of emotion: Fundamental questions* (pp. 127–130). New York: Oxford University Press.

Seligman, M.E.P. (1971). Phobias and preparedness. *Behavior Therapy, 2*, 307–320.

Thorpe, S.J., & Salkovskis, P.M. (1997). Animal phobias. In G.C.L. Davey (Ed.), *Phobias: A handbook of theory, research and treatment* (pp. 81–105). Chichester, UK: Wiley.

Tipples, J., Atkinson, A.P., & Young, A.E. (2002). The eye-brow frown: A salient social signal. *Emotion, 2*, 288–296.

Tipples, J., Young A.W., Quinlan, P., Broks P., & Ellis A.W. (2002). Searching for threat. *The Quarterly Journal of Experimental Psychology, 55*A, 1007–1026.

Vuilleumier, P., Armony, J.L., Clarke, K., Husain, M., Driver, J., & Dolan, R.J. (2002). Neural response to emotional faces with and without awareness: Event-related fMRI in parietal patient with visual extinction and spatial neglect. *Neuropsychologia, 40*, 2156–2166.

Vuilleumier, P., Armony, J.L., Driver, J., & Dolan, R.J. (2001). Effects of attention and emotion on faces processing in the human brain: An event-related fMRI study. *Neuron, 30*, 829–841.

Vuilleumier, P., Armony, J.L., Driver, J., & Dolan, R.J. (2003). Distinct spatial frequency sensitivities for processing faces and emotional expressions. *Nature Neuroscience, 6*, 624–631.

Vuilleumier, P., Richardson, M.P., Armony, J.L., Driver, J., & Dolan, R.J. (2004). Distant influences of amygdala lesion on visual cortical activation during emotional face processing. *Nature Neuroscience, 7*, 1271–1278.

Weiskrantz, L. (1986). *Blindsight. A case study and implications.* Oxford: Oxford University Press.

Wiens, S., & Öhman, A. (in press). Probing unconscious emotional processes: On becoming a successful masketeer. In J. Allen & J. Coan (Eds.), *Handbook of emotion elicitation and assessment*. New York: Oxford University Press.

18 Neural circuitry involved in avoidance learning and memory: The amygdala and beyond

K. C. Liang

How the mind stores experience is an intensely studied issue in psychology and neuroscience. Students in both disciplines once entertained the idea of locating a brain region responsible for storing information of all sorts. Nowadays memory is no longer conceived as a monolithic mental faculty. Instead, it contains subsystems for encoding, storing, and operating information of different kinds. Two major types of memory have been proposed – declarative (explicit) and non-declarative (implicit); each of them is further divided into subcategories. Specific learning tasks have been designed to assess different forms of memory. Among them, memory of emotional events, often denoted as affective memory, attracts much attention in the mundane and scientific world due to its critical roles in adaptive and non-adaptive behavior as well as its rapid acquisition, long-lasting retention, and ready retrieval.

Intense endeavor has been taken to locate the neural substrate underlying each kind of memory. Despite some questions inherent in the current strategy of mapping a functional subsystem onto distinct neural entities (Gallistel, Chapter 3, this volume), studies have implicated various brain structures in subserving specific kinds of memory. A prevailing view is that the amygdala is the site for encoding, storage, and retrieval of emotional memory. This view gains much of its evidence from research on Pavlovian fear conditioning, namely compromised acquisition or expression of the conditioned response after suppression or lesions of the whole amygdala or certain nuclei of it, altered cellular electrophysiological or biochemical activities in response to the conditioned stimulus, and finally, presence of experience-driven synaptic plasticity such as long-term potentiation (LTP) in its input–output system (Davis, 2000).

However, when an organism encounters an aversive event, either in daily life or in a laboratory task designed for assessing fear memory, its reactions would be more than being afraid. It may learn to alter processing of the aversive event (Domjan, Chapter 4, this volume). It may try to cope with the situation or its consequence, either at the right moment or shortly afterwards. It may ponder how such a situation has come about, and how it can be avoided the next time. Such behavior or mental states may or may not be afforded by conditioned fear reflexes but are nonetheless activated in emotion-arousing incidents and included in the memory of them. Bearing this consideration in mind, I would like to entertain an alternative view in contemplating what memory for an emotional experience contains and how its underlying substrate works in the brain. It is proposed that when an emotional event occurs, it leaves in our brain memory traces more than association forged by classical conditioning. Formation of such memory engages widespread brain regions that include but extend beyond the amygdala. Further, the anatomical substrates involved in operating such memory undergo dynamic changes over the retention period. In the rest of this chapter I review data selectively accrued from my laboratory in support of this view.

The inhibitory avoidance task and memory of aversive experience

Evidence pertinent to the proposal is gathered mainly from studies on a one-trial step-through inhibitory avoidance task; in some cases we have generalized our effects to one-way active avoidance and the Morris water maze, which are also motivated by an aversive stimulus (Liang, Hon, Tyan, & Liao, 1994b; Liang, Lin, Chen, Hsieh, & Chen, 2001b; Liang, Tsui, Tyan, & Chiang, 1998). The task has been widely used in assessing memory of aversive experience. Briefly, a straight alley is divided into a lit chamber and a dark chamber. A rat is placed into the lit side; it has a strong tendency to go into the dark side where it encounters an inescapable footshock. Retention is tested at various times later by putting the rat back into the lit side and measuring how long it can resist going into the darkness. The longer it stays in the lit side, the better the memory. This response is easy to acquire, usually taking only a single trial. It creates a relatively robust memory and yet manipulating the footshock intensity can alter the memory strength such that both enhancing and impairing effects on memory can be readily studied for various treatments.

Application of the inhibitory avoidance task in assessing acquisition, consolidation, and retrieval processes

The task has also served as the most typical tool in assessing influences of various treatments on memory consolidation since its first deployment by Coons and Miller (1960) in studying retrograde amnesia caused by the electroconvulsive shock. The effect induced by a post-training treatment, being time dependent, has been argued convincingly as strong evidence for influences on memory formation per se (McGaugh, 2000). As a matter of fact, the single training trial and single test trial of this task offer tremendous advantages for experimental studies of memory, because each event in memory processing can be pinpointed precisely in a temporal dimension.

Treatments placed at various times relative to a training or test trial exert their influences specifically on acquisition, formation, or retrieval processes in memory.

For example, in a previous study we demonstrated that buspirone, an atypical anxiolytic drug working on 5-HT_{1A} receptors, given immediately after training, caused a retention deficit, and the effect was time dependent. Thus, activation of 5-HT_{1A} receptors impaired memory consolidation in the inhibitory avoidance task (Liang, 1999). Effects induced by this drug, or other treatments as well, given before the training or test trial could affect the acquisition or retrieval processes, but effects of these treatment regimens should be interpreted with caution unless influences on performance factors can be empirically ruled out. For example, we have shown that buspirone injected 30 minutes before a retention test had a profound effect on memory expression in a 1-day retention test, a weak effect in a 21-day test, and no effect in a 90-day test (Liang et al., 1998). General influences on performance cannot easily account for an effect that varies its magnitude along with the retention interval. This interval dependency may serve the same function in ruling out the confounding of performance factors in interpreting pretest treatment effects as does the time dependency in interpreting post-training treatment effects.

Multiple components of learning inherent in the inhibitory avoidance task

The inhibitory avoidance task has recently been viewed as equivalent to classical fear conditioning, in which the rat acquires freezing behavior in a context associated to electric shocks (Cammarota, Bevilaqua, Kerr, Medina, & Izquierdo, 2003). On the other hand, it has been shown that retention in this task is more susceptible to post-training treatments applied to the basolateral amygdala nuclei but impervious to those applied to the central amygdala nuclei (McGaugh, Ferry, Vazdarjanova, & Roozendaal, 2000). Evidence implicates the basolateral nuclei in voluntary or intentional choice responses to emotional events based on operant conditioning, and the central nuclei in reflexive, automatic responses evoked by salient stimuli acquired via classical conditioning (Killcross, Robbins, & Everitt, 1997). The latter two lines of evidence suggest that the inhibitory avoidance task may be operant conditioning in nature.

To directly address this issue by a behavioral experiment, the typical inhibitory avoidance task was modified into different versions to isolate individual components presumably involved in learning this task. In the operant conditioning version, the rat receives a shock as it steps from the lit compartment into the other side that is also lit, thus the shock is contingent only upon the rat's behavior. In the classical conditioning version, the rat is directly placed into a lit compartment and receives a shock shortly after the light's offset, thus the shock is contingent upon presence or absence of a specific cue. In a control condition, the rat is placed directly into a lit compartment and receives a shock with the light being on, thus the shock is contingent upon the context rather than on rat's behavior or a discrete cue. All rats were placed into the lit side of the apparatus identically 2 days after the training trial and tested for their latencies of entering the dark side.

Results indicated that at moderate training footshock, avoidance performance shaped by the operant conditioning version was better than that by the classical conditioning version, which in turn was better than that by the context conditioning (control) version. However, none of these modified training paradigms yielded the level of performance equivalent to that of the traditional one. Thus, memory acquired in a typical inhibitory avoidance task contains more than association forged by either operant conditioning or classical conditioning to a discrete cue or a context.

Involvement of the amygdala in formation and expression of inhibitory avoidance memory

Role of amygdala synaptic plasticity in the inhibitory avoidance learning

Long-term potentiation (LTP), a type of experience-driven neuronal plasticity, is viewed as a putative neural substrate of memory (Martin, Grimwood, & Morris, 2000). A form of LTP dependent on the N-methyl-D-aspartate (NMDA) receptors was detected in the amygdala (Gean, Chang, Huang, Lin, & Way, 1993). Researchers have conceived this neural plasticity as playing a role in strengthening transmission in the synapses mediating association between the conditioned stimulus and response. Evidence showed that the calcium/calmodulin-dependent protein kinase, an important enzyme to solidify synaptic changes in LTP, increased after inhibitory avoidance learning; blocking this enzyme shortly after training impaired later retention of the response (Tan & Liang, 1997). Induction of LTP activates the synthesis of nitric oxide (NO), which may serve as a retrograde signal to the presynaptic site acting on the guanylate cyclase that in turn stimulates protein kinase G (PKG), an enzyme implicated in LTP. A drug, 3-(5-hydroxymethyl-2-furyl)-1-benzyl-indazole (YC-1), potentiates sensitivity of the purified soluble guanylate cyclase to NO. My colleague Professor Fu and her student Chien at the department of pharmacology showed that in a slice preparation, three trains of tetanic stimuli to the external capsule induced a weak LTP in the lateral amygdala; however, perfusion of YC-1 transformed it into a more robust LTP (Chien, Liang, Teng, Kuo, Lee, & Fu, 2003).

Pretraining injection of the drug caused a memory enhancement in the inhibitory avoidance task. Enhancement in both neurophysiology and behavior showed similar susceptibility to drugs blocking the synthesis of NO or activation of PKG. One way to interpret the above data is that the drug enhanced the synaptic efficacy in the neural pathway mediating association between the task context and the inhibitory response. However, in a transfer test in which the rat was directly placed into the dark side, rats treated with an effective dose of this drug had the shortest latency of entering the lit side (Chien, Liang, Teng, Kuo, Lee, & Fu, 2005). These data suggest that what a rat acquires in an inhibitory avoidance task is not a fixed action pattern of freezing in response to the cues; instead it acquires some knowledge that can be used flexibly to avoid potential danger based on the situation. Flexibility in application is a defining feature of declarative memory (Eichenbaum, 1997); such memory has been attributed to the hippocampus instead of the amygdala. These data suggest that formation of inhibitory avoidance memory engages not only the amygdala but also the hippocampus; they both are influenced by YC-1 given systemically, and may subserve different functions, an issue to be addressed in a later section.

Neurophysiological correlates of memory expression in amygdala neurons

Recording of amygdala neuronal activity provides correlative clues for its role in learning and memory. In collaboration with Professor Yen and his student Chang at the department of zoology, a series of experiments were launched to study unit activity changes in different amygdala nuclei induced by inhibitory avoidance training (Chang, Liang & Yen, 2005). Rats bearing bundle-type electrodes made of eight micro-wires (50 μm) chronically implanted in the central or basolateral/lateral amygdala nuclei were subjected to a step-through inhibitory avoidance task. Rats in the experimental group were acclimatized to, trained, and tested in the task apparatus, while rats in the control group were acclimatized to and tested in the task apparatus but received footshock training in another environment. Behavioral assessment on both initial step-through latencies and total time spent in the lit side (for a period of 5 minutes) showed strong avoidance memory in the experimental group, but not in the control group. Such memory lasted for at least 10 days.

Unit activity was recorded in the amygdala of a behaving rat before, during, and after performing the task. Single units were isolated by principal component analyses and algorithm of template matching. Unit activity was correlated to behavior by comparing unit firing among the 5-minute periods before, during, and after the task. For individual neurons, activity was found to co-vary with behavior in various ways. When the ensemble activities were collapsed from all recorded neurons, both the experimental and control groups showed habituation of amygdala discharges during the acclimatization phase. One population of amygdala neurons increased their firing rates shortly after the training phase but not at a 1-day test session, another group of neurons showed increase of discharges at a 1-day retention test. These changes were specific to the learning experience because they appeared only in the experimental group, but not in the control group. In the experimental group, no hemispheric difference was detected in activity changes, despite previous evidence showing greater involvement of the right amygdala in acquisition, consolidation, or expression of inhibitory avoidance memory (Coleman-Mesches & McGaugh, 1995a, 1995b).

Consistent with the notion that inhibitory avoidance learning contains both classical and operant conditioning components, increased firing rate was detected in both the lateral/basolateral complex and central nuclei, and pretraining lesions applied to either site impaired retention (Chen, Chang, Yen, & Liang, 2002). However, up to this moment, we have not been able to detect any firing increase 10 days after the training, at which time the rat still showed very robust avoidance memory. While negative results as such are always hard to interpret, they nonetheless point out a possibility that sites other than the amygdala may mediate the long-term storage. The failure to detect apparent activity changes in amygdala neurons 10 days after training echoes the findings in an early study showing that amygdala lesions made 12 days after training failed to impair retention in comparison with the sham-operated controls, although the same lesions made shortly before training or within 5 days after training produced a marked retention deficit (Liang, McGaugh, Martinez, Jensen, Vasquez, & Messing, 1982).

Involvement of other brain regions in formation of inhibitory avoidance memory

The role of amygdala pathways in mediating influences of the amygdala on retention of the inhibitory avoidance response

Several lines of evidence hint at the involvement of other structures than the amygdala in inhibitory avoidance memory. In an early study, we found that infusion of norepinephrine (NE) into the amygdala immediately after training caused robust memory enhancement in this task (Liang, Juler, & McGaugh, 1986). Such an effect could have been interpreted as NE affecting formation of the trace residing in the region. Yet a subsequent study showed that this effect was abolished by transecting the stria terminalis, an input–output pathway of the amygdala (Liang, McGuagh, & Yao, 1990), suggesting that the effect of NE infused into the amygdala relies on the communication between the amygdala and its interconnected targets. Consistently, lesions of the stria terminalis which contains met-enkephalin fibers or infusion of naloxone into its target – the bed nucleus of the stria terminalis (BNST) – attenuated the amnesic effect of post-training electrical stimulation of the amygdala (Liang & McGaugh, 1983; Liang, Messing, & McGaugh, 1983).

Correlative evidence for involvement of other brain structures in inhibitory avoidance learning

Expression of the immediate early gene *c-fos* is a widely adopted marker for neural activation. Recently my collaborators Huang at the Mackay Junior

College of Nursing and Dr Tsai at the National Yang-Ming University examined Fos expression in the brain of rats. Influenced by the finding that human female victims of trauma have a higher incidence of post-traumatic stress disorder than males, we trained sham-operated or ovariectomized rats in the inhibitory avoidance task, and found that ovariectomy impaired memory in this task and the deficit was fully attenuated by a systemic injection of estradiol; this effect could be mimicked by estradiol infused immediately after training into not only the amygdala, but also the hippocampus (Huang, Tsai, Chen, Chen & Liang, 2004). Given these results, another group of ovariectomized rats was subjected to the same training and injection regimen and sacrificed at various times after training to stain for Fos expression. By contrasting the two groups subjected to treatments which should have yielded the best and worst retention performance, significant differences in Fos expression were detected not only in the amygdala, but also in many other regions of the brain, including the dentate gyrus, frontal cortex, nucleus accumbens, lateral septum, etc. These data provide us with clues to those brain regions that may be involved in the task in addition to the amygdala.

Multiple anatomical and neurochemical systems support memory formation in the inhibitory avoidance task

Subsequent studies indicate that other brain regions exert causal influences on formation or expression of inhibitory avoidance memory. Post-training infusion of 8-hydroxy-2-(di-n-propylamino)tetralin (8-OH-DPAT), a 5-HT_{1A} agonist, into the lateral septum, amygdala, dorsal hippocampus, ventral hippocampus, and medial prefrontal cortex (mPFC) all impaired retention of the inhibitory avoidance response (Lee, Chen, Lin, Shiu, & Liang, 1992; Liang, 2000). That infusion of NE into the amygdala exerts biphasic influences on inhibitory avoidance memory is well documented (Liang, 1998; Liang, Chen, & Huang, 1995). Similar effects were also reported after infusion of NE into the dorsal hippocampus, mPFC, or BNST (Chen, Chen, Chen, & Liang, 2004; Hu, 1996; Liang, Chen, & Chen, 2001a). Likewise, glutamate agonists or antagonists enhanced or impaired retention, respectively, when infused into the amygdala, dorsal hippocampus, nucleus accumbens, mPFC, or BNST (Jerusalinsky et al., 1992; Lee, Lee, Wang, & Lin, 1993; Liang, Hon, & Davis, 1994a; Liang, Hu, & Chang, 1996; Liang, Lin, & Tyan, 1993; Liang et al., 2001b; Liu, 2004).

The amnesia induced by blocking a specific neurotransmitter system implies that the intrinsic neurochemical may serve as an endogenous memory enhancer under normal conditions, and thus agonists given exogenously act to modulate the neurotransmission involved in coding the learned information. Two caveats should be brought forth in this regard. It is intriguing that glutamate, which presumably mediates excitatory transmission of sensory input, also enhanced retention when infused into certain brain areas. It is hard to conceive how a non-discriminatory excitation exogenously imposed could enhance rather than disrupt the intricate firing pattern activated endogenously in an organized circuit to code specific information, unless the glutamate exerts its effect by releasing neuromodulators. Further, we found that blocking 5-HT_{1A} receptors enhanced retention, suggesting that 5-HT may serve as an endogenous memory suppressor (Liang, 1999). The presence of an intrinsic memory-suppressing mechanism in the brain invites speculation on the function it serves. Nevertheless, these data indicate that formation of inhibitory avoidance memory relies on integrated functioning of interconnected regions that are widely distributed.

Interaction of the amygdala and other brain regions in formation of inhibitory avoidance memory

Interaction between the amygdala and mPFC in formation of inhibitory avoidance memory

It is of interest to know whether and how these regions may interact in affecting the memory formation processes. On the basis of a rationale that influences from a downstream site should override those from an upstream site, the issue was examined by giving an activating agent to one area and a suppressing agent to the other. We recently approached the relationship between the amygdala and mPFC with such a strategy (Liang, 2002). Results of the first experiment showed that suppressing the mPFC with lidocaine or 6-cyano-7-nitroquinoxaline-2,3-dione (CNQX), an antagonist to the glutamate α-amino-3-hydroxyl-5-methyl-4-isoxazole propionate (AMPA) receptor antagonist, abolished the memory-enhancing effect induced by intra-amygdala infusion of NE, suggesting an information flow from the amygdala to the mPFC. Yet results of the next experiment showed that suppressing the amygdala with lidocaine or CNQX also abolished memory-enhancing effects of NE infused into the mPFC, suggesting an information flow in the opposite direction. Further results showed that if either of these two structures was suppressed by lidocaine, activating the other by glutamate at a memory-enhancing dose could not attenuate the deficit. Two explanations can be offered to interpret these results: Either the amygdala and mPFC form a reverberating circuit that is activated during memory formation, or each structure provides indispensable inputs to a third site for memory formation. In each case, blocking either of the two regions will induce a devastating effect on retention.

Modulation of the nucleus accumbens by the amygdala in formation of avoidance memory

The same strategy was also applied to examine possible interactions between the amygdala and nucleus accumbens (Liang, Lin, Chen, Hsieh, & Chen, 2001c). The influences of these two structures are not likely to converge on a common target, because infusing a sub-amnesic dose of CNQX simultaneously into both structures yielded no additive effect. On the other hand, the memory-enhancing effect of intra-amygdala infusion of NE was totally blocked by suppressing the nucleus accumbens with a non-amnesic dose of CNQX, and infusing a non-enhancing dose of glutamate into the nucleus accumbens attenuated the amnesic effect of CNQX infused into the amygdala. Moreover, a higher dose of glutamate infused into the nucleus accumbens enhanced memory, which was impervious to suppression of the amygdala with CNQX. These data indicate an information flow from the amygdala to the nucleus accumbens during formation of inhibitory avoidance memory.

Modulation of the hippocampus by the amygdala in formation of avoidance memory

Recently, my laboratory examined possible interaction between the amygdala and the hippocampus in a latent learning paradigm of the task that relies on integrity of the hippocampus. Briefly, rats in the no, short, or long pre-exposure group on the first day explored the apparatus for 0, 1, or 3 minutes but received no footshock. On the second day, the rat was placed into the lit side and received a normal training trial with a mild footshock. Retention was tested on the third day as usual. Results showed that different pre-exposure times on the first day did not influence entrance latencies on the second day. However, on the third day the long pre-exposure group showed better avoidance than other two groups. These data were interpreted as showing that the long pre-exposure group gains better knowledge of the apparatus on the first day, which remains latent if the exploration results in no surprising consequences. Yet the better knowledge affords stronger association when a shock is encountered on the second day and thus improves memory on the third-day test. This latent learning involves the hippocampus: Infusion of lidocaine into the hippocampus, but not the amygdala, shortly after the pre-exposure trial abolished the pre-exposure effect.

Previous evidence has shown that epinephrine (E) given immediately after training enhances memory formation and this effect is mediated by NE acting on the amygdala β adrenergic receptors (Liang, 1998; Liang et al., 1986). This also holds for latent learning. Our findings showed that E at a dose of 0.01 or 0.1 mg/kg given after a short pre-exposure trial did not affect the entrance latency on the second day, but significantly enhanced avoidance behavior on the third day (Liang, 2001). This enhancing effect was durable: When the shock training trial was delayed for 3 to 21 days after the pre-exposure trial, avoidance behavior of the E group was still better than the saline group. These results suggest that memory for cues in the training context, once formed, can be held in a latent form for weeks before it is linked to any consequence and affects behavior explicitly.

Infusion of propranolol into the amygdala, but not the hippocampus, shortly after the pre-exposure trial attenuated the enhancing effect of E on latent memory, while intra-amygdala infusion of NE after the pre-exposure trial enhanced memory. Lidocaine suppression of the hippocampus in the pre-exposure trial blocked both the enhancing effects of E injected systemically and NE infused into the amygdala. These findings suggest that peripheral E exerts a memory-enhancing influence on memory acquired in latent learning. This effect is mediated through NE released in the amygdala, which in turn modulates hippocampal functioning involved in formation of a latent memory for the training context.

Differential roles of various structures in formation of inhibitory avoidance memory

A two-phase training paradigm in dissociation of contextual and affective learning

The involvement of multiple brain regions in formation of inhibitory avoidance memory invokes an interesting question; namely, do all the regions subserve the same or a different role? Findings described in the above section hint that the amygdala and hippocampus appear to have different roles: The former is involved in processing the affective valence, the latter in processing the spatial or contextual information. This issue has been addressed in a two-phase learning paradigm of the inhibitory avoidance task. In this paradigm on the first day denoted as context training, a rat is placed into the apparatus for exploration but receives no shock. On the second day denoted as shock training, the rat is directly placed into the dark end and receives a shock. Retention is tested as usual on the third day. A moderate footshock would generate retention performance in this two-phase training paradigm similar to that in the traditional paradigm (Liang, 1999). An advantage of this paradigm is that it permits independent manipulation of memory processing for the context cues and affective cues. For example, buspirone, an anxiolytic drug, impaired retention when given immediately after the shock-training phase but had no effect when given immediately after the context-training phase (Liang, 1999).

Dissociating roles of the amygdala, dorsal hippocampus, nucleus accumbens in processing different information in the inhibitory avoidance task

We applied this paradigm to dissociate the amygdala, dorsal hippocampus, and nucleus accumbens in memory formation (Liang et al., 2001c). Different groups of rats were trained on this two-phase paradigm, and CNQX, a drug known to induce amnesia, was infused into each of these structures after either context training or shock training. The results showed that CNQX impaired retention when infused into the hippocampus shortly after the context training, but had no effect if given after shock training. Conversely,

CNQX impaired retention when infused into the amygdala shortly after shock training, but had no effect if given after context training. For the nucleus accumbens, CNQX infused at either phase induced a marked retention deficit. The findings suggest that the hippocampus is involved in processing context/spatial information, the amygdala in processing shock information. The nucleus accumbens receiving convergent inputs from both structures is essential for processing both types of information.

Dissociating different modes of information processing in the amygdala, dorsal hippocampus, ventral hippocampus, and mPFC during memory formation

A similar strategy was also applied to study the effects of 8-OH-DPAT infused into the amygdala, dorsal hippocampus, ventral hippocampus, or mPFC after either phase of training (Liang, 2000). Results on the amygdala and dorsal hippocampus showed that 8-OH-DPAT impaired retention when given into the dorsal hippocampus shortly after the context-training phase. It impaired retention when given into the amygdala shortly after the shock-training phase. These findings essentially replicate those of the CNQX studies. Manipulation of the other two structures reveals quite interesting results. In the ventral hippocampus, a profound memory deficit was observed only when 8-OH-DPAT was infused at both the context- and shock-training phases. For the mPFC, poor memory resulted from infusion of 8-OH-DPAT at either the context- or shock-training phase. These findings indicate that the ventral hippocampus acts quite differently from its dorsal counterpart involved in spatial/contextual processing. Memory formation fails only when both context and shock cues are processed under compromised functioning of this region. In contrast, memory formation fails as long as one type of information is processed under compromised functioning of the mPFC. Thus, under normal conditions, the ventral hippocampus acts as an "OR" gate for associating spatial cues and emotional valence, while the mPFC acts as an "AND" gate in associating these two types of cues.

Roles of various structures in expression of inhibitory avoidance memory

Limbic regions involved in expressing the inhibitory avoidance response acquired recently

Whether emotional memory is permanently stored in the amygdala has been an issue under heated debate (LeDoux, 2000; Maren, 2001; McGaugh, 2004). To address this issue in the inhibitory avoidance task, various groups of rats were trained on the task and tested on 1, 2, 5, 12, or 21 days after training (Liang, 1991). The amygdala was suppressed during the retention test with infusion of lidocaine 5 minutes prior to the test, which exerted the best suppression effect during the retention period. The results showed that the impairing effect of lidocaine given before testing was significant only when retention was tested within 1, 2, 5 days after training. In the 12- and 21-day tests, pretest intra-amygdala infusion of lidocaine did not have an effect. Experiments using a between- or within-subjects design yielded the same pattern of results.

Further studies indicated that pretest infusion of lidocaine into the dorsal or ventral hippocampus also affected the 1-day but not 21-day retention. In contrast, the BNST was not involved in expression of either 1-day or 21-day memory (Liang, 2002). It is interesting to note that the lidocaine suppression of the nucleus accumbens during 1-day or 21-day test produced an incomplete retention deficit (Liang et al., 2001c). These findings suggest that functional integrity of the amygdala, dorsal or ventral hippocampus, and nucleus accumbens is required for expressing inhibitory avoidance memory acquired recently but not for expressing memory acquired at a remote time.

However, in conditioned-fear potentiation of startle, electrolytic lesions of the amygdala 6 or 30 days after training induced similar memory deficits (Kim & Davis, 1993b). In contextual fear conditioning, NMDA lesions of the basolateral amygdala impaired expression of memory formed 1 day or 16 months before (Gale et al., 2004). These studies differed from ours not only in the adopted tasks (classical conditioning versus avoidance learning) but also in the amygdala treatments used (irreversible lesions versus reversible suppression); and the discrepancy in results remains to be resolved. Nonetheless, it should be noted that the two studies observing retrograde amnesia without temporal gradient after post-training amygdala lesions found that the lesions did not prevent reacquisition of the abolished response (Gale et al., 2004; Kim & Davis, 1993a), suggesting that the trace for fear memory underlying reacquisition must be stored outside the destroyed amygdala.

Cortical regions involved in expressing inhibitory avoidance response acquired at a remote time

A subsequent question is what brain region is required for expressing a 21-day memory in the inhibitory avoidance task. Cortical regions have been implicated for long-term storage of information. Therefore we applied the same experimental design to study the role of some cortical regions implicated in emotion or memory function by previous evidence, namely the medial prefrontal, insular, and perirhinal cortices. Rats were trained on the inhibitory avoidance task and tested for retention either 1 and/or 21 days after training. Shortly prior to a retention test, lidocaine was infused into one of these cortical regions. The results on the mPFC or insular cortex were clear-cut: Suppressing either region during a retention test impaired the 21-day retention, but had no effect on the 1-day retention (Liang & Liao, 1995). These findings suggest that expression of 21-day memory, but not 1-day memory, requires integrity of the mPFC and insular cortex (and, possibly, nucleus accumbens also). The differential involvement of the amygdala and mPFC, respectively, in expressing recent and remote memories of an inhibitory avoidance response was further tested by infusing CNQX into these two regions (Liang et al., 1996).

Findings on the perirhinal cortex turned out to be more complicated: A between-subjects design experiment showed that pretest inactivation of the perirhinal cortex affected neither 1-day nor 21-day retention. Yet when rats were treated and tested repeatedly in a within-subject design experiment, lidocaine infused into this region did not impair retention in a 1-day test, but did so in the 21-day test, regardless of the treatment (vehicle or lidocaine) administered in the 1-day test. A further experiment showed that increased susceptibility of the 21-day memory trace to suppression of the perirhinal cortex developed only when the rat was tested for retention and received an infusion on the first day, neither the treatment nor the test experience by itself created this effect (Liang & Liao, 1995). These results suggest that a mild perturbation to the perirhinal cortex such as local infusion of vehicle under the activation of a recent memory trace leaves a latent deficit by increasing vulnerability of the trace to future challenge to perirhinal functioning. This suggestion instigates speculation and invites further examination into the exact role of the perirhinal cortex in operating inhibitory avoidance memory.

The dual roles of the medial prefrontal cortex in processing affective memory

An intriguing role of the mPFC emerges from the above findings. The structure appears to be critical for both memory formation and retrieval of remote memory, but has little role in retrieving a recent memory. Thus, training experience initiates dual memory processing in the mPFC. On the one hand, it interacts with the amygdala and other brain regions to form a reverberating circuit during memory formation; the trace thus formed may locate elsewhere. Meanwhile there are changes occurring in the mPFC, which takes time to mature and is critical for operating a late trace. Data pertinent to this view have accrued: Post-training intra-mPFC infusion of 2-amino-5-phosphonovaleric acid (APV), an NMDA antagonist presumably blocking experience-driven plasticity, caused a latent memory deficit, no effect in a 1-day test, but a pronounced impairment when tested 20 days later. Consistently, post-training intra-mPFC infusion of glutamate caused persistent memory enhancement in 1- and 21-day tests. Blocking the normal glutamate transmission with CNQX abolished memory-enhancing effects at both tests. In contrast, blocking NMDA receptors with APV did not interfere with memory enhancement at the 1-day test, but abolished it in the 21-day test (Liang et al., 1996), suggesting that plasticity inherent to the mPFC is important for remote memory. Thus, glutamatergic innervations to the mPFC subserve at least a dual role: They communicate with other brain regions via AMPA receptors to facilitate the formation of a new memory trace, and via NMDA receptors they forge local neural plasticity critical for operating a remote memory trace.

If memory trace of remote emotional experience is finally stored in the cortex, it would be interesting to investigate whether maturation of this trace requires sustaining amygdala input. If it turns out to be the case, then experience-driven plasticity, such as NMDA-dependent LTP, observed in the amygdala could have roles other than subserving formation of memory trace in situ. Synaptic changes in the amygdala may allow this structure, in the absence of further external driving, to exert prolonged modulation on a remote trace maturing long after training, just as the training experience drives it to exert immediate influences on formation of a trace for recent memory matured shortly after training. According to this view, presence of LTP in the amygdala should no longer be taken as evidence incompatible with a modulating role of this structure.

Conclusion

Findings reviewed above bring forth the following picture on how memory for an emotional event may operate: Experience activates not only sensory processing, but also hormonal responses. The various aspects of this experience engage a set of brain regions that include but extend beyond the amygdala, to code for affective values, context information or other facets (such as consequences of coping) and thus engrave multiple traces in the brain that last for different periods of time. To bind all these traces into an integrated neural representation, the amygdala activated by the emotional significance of the experience must interact with other regions, such as the mPFC, nucleus accumbens, hippocampus etc., either directly or through the BNST. The interactions include modulation, convergence, exchange, or even suppression of information being processed, and each mode of these actions may be activated at different moments and last for different periods of time. These interactions lead to a dynamic change of the integrated neural representation underlying emotional experience in storage: It relies more on the limbic system in its early operation, but more on cortical regions as time passes by. Maturation of the cortical trace for emotional experience may be responsible for disengagement of limbic regions from operating memory for that experience. It has been documented that mPFC exerts an inhibitory influence on the amygdala and is involved in extinction of conditioned fear (Morgan & LeDoux, 1995). Consistent with this notion is the scientific evidence that recollecting long-past fear experience caused no activation of the amygdala in normal subjects (Damasio et al., 2000), and our own awareness that recollection of a recent emotional event activates both vivid declarative memory and emotional agitation, but in recollecting a remote one, the former may persist but the latter often abates.

The neural circuitry underlying memory for emotional experience proposed above is different in terms of anatomical distribution and temporal operation from the prevailing view that emotional memory relies solely on plasticity within the amygdala. From an evolutionary point of view, brain structures and connections evolve to meet the survival demands. In view of the extensive influences of emotion on various behavioral functions supported by the massive connections between the amygdala and other regions, it should not be at all surprising that representing memory for emotional experience requires a widespread circuitry in the brain.

Acknowledgments

This project is supported in part by grants from the National Science Council of ROC including NSC-93–2752-H-002–006-PAE. The author would like to thank collaborators, particularly Dr C.T. Yen at the Institute of Zoology, Dr W.M. Fu at the Institute of Pharmacology, Ms H.-J. Huang at the Mackay Junior College of Nursing, and Dr S.-J. Tsai at the Taipei Veterans General Hospital, as well as students and staff members at the National Taiwan University for their contribution to experiments described in this article. The author would also like to express his gratitude to Dr McGaugh for his continual support and encouragement.

References

Cammarota, M., Bevilaqua, L.R.M., Kerr, D., Medina, J.H., & Izquierdo, I. (2003). Inhibition of mRNA and protein synthesis in the CA1 region of the dorsal hippocampus blocks reinstallment of an extinguished conditioned fear response. *Journal of Neuroscience*, *23*, 737–741.

Chang, C.-H., Liang, K.C., & Yen, C.T. (2005). Inhibitory avoidance learning altered ensemble activity of amygdaloid neurons in rats. *European Journal of Neuroscience*, *21*, 210–218.

Chen, C.C., Chang, C.H., Yen, C.T., & Liang, K.C. (2002). Involvement of amygdala nuclei in learning avoidance tasks [Abstract]. *Society for Neuroscience Abstract*, *28*, #284.19.

Chen, H.-C., Chen, D.-Y., Chen, C.-C., & Liang, K.C. (2004). Pre- and post-training infusion of prazosin into bed nucleus of stria terminalis impaired acquisition and retention in a Morris water maze task. *Chinese Journal of Physiology*, *47*, 51–60.

Chien, W.-L., Liang, K.-C., Teng, C.-M., Kuo, S.-C., Lee, F.Y., & Fu, W.-M. (2003). Enhancement of long-term potentiation by a potent nitric oxide-guanylyl cyclase activator 3-(5-hydroxymethyl-2-furyl).-1-benzyl-indazole. *Molecular Pharmacology*, *63*, 1322–1328.

Chien, W.-L., Liang, K.-C., Teng, C.-M., Kuo, S.-C., Lee, F.-Y., & Fu, W.-M. (2005). Enhancement of learning behavior by a potent nitric oxide-guanylate cyclase activator YC-1. *European Journal of Neuroscience*, *21*, 1679–1688.

Coleman-Mesches, K., & McGaugh, J.L. (1995a). Differential involvement of the right and left amygdala in expression of memory for aversively motivated training. *Brain Research*, *670*, 75–81.

Coleman-Mesches, K., & McGaugh, J.L. (1995b). Differential effects of pretraining inactivation of the right or left amygdala on retention of inhibitory avoidance training. *Behavioral Neuroscience*, *109*, 642–647.

Coons, E.E., & Miller, N.E. (1960). Conflict versus consolidation of memory traces to explain "retrograde amnesia" produced by ECS. *Journal of Comparative and Physiological Psychology*, *53*, 524–531.

Damasio, A.R., Grabowski, T.J., Bechara, A., Damasio, H., Ponto, L.L.B., Parvizi, J. et al. (2000). Subcortical and cortical brain activity during the feeling of self-generated emotions. *Nature Neuroscience*, *3*, 1049–1056.

Davis, M. (2000). The role of the amygdala in conditioned and unconditioned fear and anxiety. In J. Aggleton (Ed.), *The amygdala: A functional analysis* (pp. 213–287). New York: Oxford University Press.

Eichenbaum, H. (1997). Declarative memory insights from cognitive neurobiology. *Annual Review of Psychology*, *48*, 547–572.

Gale, G.D., Ananostaras, S.G., Godsil, B.P., Mitchell, S., Nozawa, T., Sage, J.R. et al. (2004). Role of the basolateral amygdala in the storage of fear memories across the adult lifetime of rats. *Journal of Neuroscience*, *24*, 3810–3815.

Gean, P.W., Chang, F.C., Huang, C.C., Lin, J.H., & Way, L.J. (1993). Long-term enhancement of EPSP and NMDA receptor mediated synaptic transmission in the amygdala. *Brain Research Bulletin*, *31*, 7–11.

Hu, S.J. (1996). *Involvement of the prefrontal cortex in formation and retrieval of inhibitory avoidance memory*. Unpublished Masters thesis, National Taiwan University, Taipei, Taiwan.

Huang, H.-J., Tsai, S.-J., Chen, C.-C., Chen, J.-G., & Liang, K.C. (2004). *Estrogen enhanced retention of an inhibitory avoidance response in ovariectomized rats – involvement of the hippocampus and amygdala*. Manuscript in preparation.

Jerusalinsky, D., Ferreira, M.B.C., Walz, R., Da Silva, R.C., Bianchin, M., Ruschel, A.C. et al. (1992). Amnesia by posttraining infusion of glutamate receptor antagonists into the amygdala, hippocampus and entorhinal cortex. *Behavioral & Neural Biology*, *58*, 76–80.

Killcross, S., Robbins, T.W., & Everitt, B.J. (1997). Different types of fear-conditioned behaviour mediated by separate nuclei within amygdala. *Nature*, *388*, 377–380.

Kim, M., & Davis, M. (1993a). Electrolytic lesions of the amygdala block acquisition and expression of fear-potentiated startle even with extensive training but do not prevent reacquisition. *Behavioral Neuroscience*, *107*, 580–595.

Kim, M., & Davis, M. (1993b). Lack of a temporal gradient of retrograde-amnesia in rats with amygdala lesions assessed with the fear-potentiated startle paradigm. *Behavioral Neuroscience*, *107*, 1088–1092.

LeDoux, J.E. (2000). Emotion circuits in the brain. *Annual Review of Neuroscience*, *23*, 155–184.

Lee, E.H.Y., Lee, C.P., Wang, H.L., & Lin, W.R. (1993). Hippocampal CRF, NE and NMDA system interactions in memory processing in the rat. *Synapse*, *14*, 144–153.

Lee, E.H.Y., Chen, H.Y., Lin, W.R., Shiu, W.H., & Liang, K.C. (1992). Retention of an inhibitory avoidance response in rats is enhanced by fluoxetine and impaired by 8-OH-DPAT injected into the lateral septum. *Physiology and Behavior*, *51*, 681–688.

Liang, K.C. (1991). Pretest intra-amygdala injection of lidocaine or glutamate antagonists impairs retention performance in an inhibitory avoidance task [Abstract]. *Society for Neuroscience. Abstract*, *17*, 486.

Liang, K.C. (1998). Intra-amygdala infusion of DSP-4 impaired retention in the inhibitory avoidance task: Involvement of norepinephrine but not serotonin in the memory enhancing effect. *Chinese Journal of Physiology*, *41*, 223–233.

Liang, K.C. (1999). Pre- or posttraining injection of buspirone impaired retention in the inhibitory avoidance task: Involvement of amygdala 5-HT1A receptors. *European Journal of Neuroscience*, *11*, 1491–1500.

Liang, K.C. (2000). Posttraining infusion of 8-OH-DPAT impaired inhibitory avoidance memory: Different roles of the amygdala and hippocampus [Abstract]. *Society for Neuroscience Abstract*, *26*, Abstract No. 72.20.

Liang, K.C. (2001). Epinephrine modulation of memory: Amygdala activation and regulation of long-term storage. In P.E. Gold & W.T. Greenough (Eds.), *Memory consolidation* (pp. 165–183). Washington, DC: American Psychological Association.

Liang, K.C. (2002). Neural circuitry involved in avoidance learning and memory revealed by pharmacological studies [Abstract]. *Biomedical Abstract*, *17*, 35.

Liang, K.C., Chen, H.-C., & Chen, D.-Y. (2001a). Posttraining infusion of norepinephrine and corticotropin releasing factor into the bed nucleus of the stria terminalis enhanced retention in an inhibitory avoidance task. *Chinese Journal of Physiology*, *44*, 35–47.

Liang, K.C., Chen, L.L., & Huang, T.-Z. (1995). The role of amygdala norepinephrine in memory formation: Involvement in the memory enhancing effect of peripheral epinephrine. *Chinese Journal of Physiology*, *38*, 77–87.

Liang, K.C., Hon., W., & Davis, M. (1994a). Pre- and post-training infusion of N-Methyl-D-aspartate receptor antagonists into the amygdala impair memory in an inhibitory avoidance task. *Behavioral Neuroscience*, *108*, 241–253.

Liang, K.C., Hon, W., Tyan, Y.-M., & Liao, W.-L. (1994b). Involvement of hippocampal NMDA and AMPA receptors in acquisition, formation and retrieval of spatial memory in the Morris water maze. *Chinese Journal of Physiology*, *37*, 201–212.

Liang, K.C., Hu, S.-J., & Chang, S.C. (1996). Formation and retrieval of inhibitory avoidance memory: Differential roles of glutamate receptors in the amygdala and medial prefrontal cortex. *Chinese Journal of Physiology*, *39*, 155–166.

Liang, K.C., Juler, R.G., & McGaugh, J.L. (1986). Modulating effects of posttraining epinephrine on memory: Involvement of the amygdala noradrenergic system. *Brain Research*, *368*, 125–133.

Liang, K.C., & Liao, W.-L. (1995). Pretest infusion of lidocaine into the insular or medial prefrontal cortex impairs retrieval of remote memory in an inhibitory avoidance task [Abstract]. *Society for Neuroscience Abstract*, *21*, 1448.

Liang, K.C., Lin, Y.-C., Chen, D.-Y., Hiseh, C.-C., & Chen, H.C. (2001b). *Intra-nucleus accumbens infusion of CNQX impaired memory formation or expression in avoidance tasks*. Poster presented at the 7th Conference on the Neurobiology of Learning and Memory, Irvine, CA.

Liang, K.C., Lin, Y.-C., Chen, D.-Y., Hsieh, C.-C., & Chen, H.C. (2001c). Infusion of AMPA antagonists into the nucleus accumbens impaired avoidance memory: Interaction with the amygdala [Abstract]. *Society for Neuroscience Abstract*, *27*, Abstract No. 84.12.

Liang, K.C., Lin, M.-H., & Tyan, Y.-M. (1993). Involvement of amygdala N-methyl-D-aspartate receptors in long-term retention of an inhibitory avoidance response in rats. *Chinese Journal of Physiology*, *36*, 47–56.

Liang, K.C., & McGaugh, J.L. (1983). Lesions of the stria terminalis attenuate the amnestic effect of amygdaloid stimulation on avoidance responses. *Brain Research*, *274*, 309–318.

Liang, K.C., McGaugh, J.L., Martinez, J.L. Jr., Jensen, R.A., Vasquez, B.J., & Messing, R.B. (1982). Posttraining amygdaloid lesions impair retention of an inhibitory avoidance response. *Behavioral Brain Research*, *4*, 237–249.

Liang, K.C., McGaugh, J.L., & Yao, H.-Y. (1990). Involvement of amygdala pathways in the influence of post-training intra-amygdala norepinephrine and peripheral epinephrine on memory storage. *Brain Research*, *508*, 225–233.

Liang, K.C., Messing, R.B., & McGaugh, J.L. (1983). Naloxone attenuates amnesia caused by amygdaloid stimulation: The involvement of a central opioid system. *Brain Research*, *271*, 41–49.

Liang, K.C., Tsui, K.-Y., Tyan, Y.-M., & Chiang, T.-C. (1998). Buspirone impaired acquisition and retention in avoidance tasks: Involvement of the hippocampus. *Chinese Journal of Physiology*, *41*, 33–44.

Liu, T.-L. (2004). *Role of the bed nucleus of the stria terminalis on memory formation processes: Interaction between norepinephrine and glutamate*. Unpublished Masters thesis, National Taiwan University, Taipei, Taiwan.

Maren, S. (2001). Neurobiology of Pavlovian fear conditioning. *Annual Review of Neuroscience*, *25*, 563–594.

Martin, S.J., Grimwood, P.D., & Morris, R.G.M. (2000). Synaptic plasticity and memory: An evaluation of the hypothesis. *Annual Review of Neuroscience*, *23*, 649–711.

McGaugh, J.L. (2000). Memory – a century of consolidation. *Science*, *287*, 248–251.

McGaugh, J.L. (2004). The amygdala modulates the consolidation of memories of emotionally arousing experiences. *Annual Review of Neuroscience*, 27, 1–29.

McGaugh, J.L., Ferry, B., Vazdarjanova, A., & Roozendaal, B. (2000). Amygdala: Role in modulation of memory storage. In J. Aggleton (Ed.), *The amygdala: A functional analysis* (pp. 391–423). New York: Oxford University Press.

Morgan, M.A., & LeDoux, J.E. (1995). Differential contribution of dorsal and ventral medial prefrontal cortex to the acquisition and extinction of conditioned fear in rats. *Behavioral Neuroscience*, *109*, 681–688.

Tan, S.-E., & Liang, K.C. (1997). Inhibitory avoidance learning alters amygdala calcium/calmodulin dependent protein kinase II activity in rats. *Brain Research*, *748*, 227–233.

19 Neural foundations of threat processing in phobic subjects

Wolfgang H.R. Miltner, Thomas Straube, and Thomas Weiss

Ancestral stimuli like snakes, spiders or rodents represent the core group of stimuli that humans are most frequently afraid of (Agras, Sylvester, & Oliveau, 1969; Marks, 1969). Phobic responses to these stimuli are almost equally prevalent among different populations (9–14%) with a significant dominance among females. Whether this prevalence and dominance is based on phylogenetic preparedness (Öhman, Esteves, & Soares, 1995; Seligman, 1971) or on other evolutionary-based information processing systems of the brain (LeDoux, 1996), or whether it is the result of acquired cognitive schemata (Beck & Emery, 1985) or specialized memory functions (Bower, 1981; Lang, Davis, & Öhman, 2000; Williams, Watts, MacLeod, & Mathews, 1997) is still a matter of debate. However, there is general agreement that the presence of these stimuli automatically captures subjects' attention. Simultaneously, subjects' arousal increases significantly and behavioral flight/fight responses and emotional feelings of threat are generated (Lang et al., 2000; Marks & Lader, 1973; Williams et al., 1997).

The salience of these and other fear-relevant stimuli was supported by a number of studies based on the emotional Stroop paradigm (see Logan & Goetsch, 1993; Williams, Mathews, & MacLeod, 1996), the dot-probe paradigm (see MacLeod, Mathews, & Tata, 1986), the dichotic listening paradigm (see Foa & McNally, 1986), and the Eriksen flanker paradigm (see Lavy, Van den Hout, & Arntz, 1993; Streblow, Hoffmann, & Kasielke, 1985), suggesting that the processing of such stimuli is significantly biased in phobic and non-phobic anxious subjects and subjects with high trait anxiety test scores (Williams et al., 1997). Researchers became particularly interested in disentangling individual differences in the attentional bias to threat, and demonstrated that the attention of anxious subjects is automatically drawn to threatening stimuli (Logan & Goetsch, 1993; MacLeod, 1991, 1999; MacLeod & Mathews, 1991) and threat is processed with high priority in anxious subjects (Williams et al., 1997). The biased and priority processing of threat was further supported by subliminal paradigms where neutral and threatening stimuli were presented very briefly so that subjects were unable to recognize them correctly. For example, Greenwald and coworkers (Greenwald, Klinger, & Liu, 1989; Greenwald, Klinger, & Schuh, 1995) reported significantly faster affective categorization of words, when these words were primed by items with similar emotional valence. Furthermore, affective pictograms seemed to become preferentially selected as compared to neutral ones when they were presented earlier as subliminal primes (Murphy & Zajonc, 1993; Niedenthal, 1990; Seamon, Marsh, & Brody, 1984; Winkielman, Zajonc, & Schwarz, 1997).

As a general result of these studies it was shown consistently that the attention of anxious or fearful subjects is automatically allocated to threatening stimuli, which are already rapidly processed and evaluated during early and pre-attentive stages of information processing, Furthermore, the allocation of attention was demonstrated to happen particularly when stimuli are strongly related to individual anxious concerns of subjects (Logan & Goetsch, 1993; Williams et al., 1997).

Attentional bias: Voluntary or involuntary bias of attention?

Although several studies have supported the attentional bias in anxious subjects, it is still not certain whether this bias likewise accounts for voluntary and involuntary forms of attention. In modern terms of cognitive psychology involuntary attention is characterized as a bottom-up, stimulus- or data-driven mode of attention (Eimer, Nattkemper, Schroeger, & Prinz, 1996) in relation to stimuli occurring automatically and/or non-intentionally and/or non-consciously (Egeth & Yantis, 1997). In this operation mode, stimuli processing occurs pre-attentively and this, as well as the allocation of attention, is passively controlled by latent memories or schemata or – less well understood – by internal drives, needs, or latent (sometimes pathological) behavioral dispositions (Eimer et al., 1996). In contrast, voluntary attention denotes a goal-directed mode of attention (Eimer et al., 1996) that is controlled top-down by sequential cognitive operations generated by personal interests, conscious intentions, or action plans (Egeth & Yantis, 1997).

Results on the attentional bias do not provide answers to the question of whether anxious as compared to non-anxious subjects still show this bias when they are instructed to voluntarily search for a predefined threatening stimulus in their environment. The main reason is that differences of this bias between anxious and non-anxious subjects in all of these paradigms are inferred indirectly from behavioral interference or priming effects of threat on responses to different features of neutral target stimuli (i.e., its color, its location of presentation, etc.).

Furthermore, the attentional bias was almost exclusively inferred from behavioral response measures that normally mark the end of a complete stream of processing steps between the initial sensory input and the final response. Whether the attentional bias thus reflects differences of the allocation of attention, or of stimulus selection, stimulus evaluation, or response selection and organization, can hardly be decided from such a highly integrative measure. It might well be that anxious and non-anxious subjects process threatening and non-threatening stimuli with equal attentional capacity and selectivity, and that the main difference between both groups is due to differences in subjects' response organization, i.e., to the fact that anxious subjects' response selection and execution occur significantly *faster* than that of non-anxious subjects.

While cognitive approaches mainly presume that the attentional bias is an unfortunate side effect of some negative personal experience with threat, evolutionary models have suggested this bias represents a consequence of natural selection, whereby this fast pre-attentive responding to threat has gradually evolved as a generic feature of our ancestors to successfully cope with dangerous animals. Some confirmation for this view can be derived from a recent visual search study (Öhman, Flykt, & Esteves, 2001) where phobic and non-phobic subjects were requested to decide whether small images composing a matrix of four or nine pictures were all from one category or whether a single stimulus was different from the remaining array. When a spider was presented as a single deviant stimulus in an array of flowers, phobics and non-phobics were significantly faster in detecting the deviant as compared to a condition where a neutral stimulus (a mushroom) was presented in an array of spiders (Öhman et al., 2001). Additionally, spider phobics were significantly faster than non-phobics. Thus, this study confirmed the faster processing of spiders by both groups with an additional potentiation of threat detection in phobics.

For further elaboration of this question we have recently conducted a number of studies with spider phobics and healthy controls where, in addition to reaction times, eye movements were recorded (Miltner, Krieschel, Hecht, Trippe, & Weiss, 2004). In two of these experiments a visual search paradigm was used that combined features of the emotional Stroop paradigm with those of visual search paradigms to investigate whether the attentional bias in phobics can be observed in conditions of voluntary and involuntary attention. In the voluntary attention condition, subjects were instructed to search for a single spider or mushroom target presented at random locations in a matrix of 15 neutral flower pictures, and to press a button as soon as the target was identified. In the involuntary attention condition again a single spider or a single mushroom was presented as target in the matrix of flowers, but either a single spider or a mushroom was added as additional distractor. When the spider was a target, a mushroom always served as distractor and vice versa. Before the matrix was presented, subjects were requested to fixate a small cross in the middle of the screen. Results revealed faster key-press responses of all subjects to the neutral mushroom than to feared targets (spiders) or fear-relevant targets (spiders for healthy subjects). However, when neutral targets were presented together with a feared distractor, phobic subjects showed significant delays of responses not observed in control subjects. The eye-movement data suggest that the eyes of spider-phobic subjects were automatically drawn to these feared distractors before fixating the neutral target. This effect was absent in control subjects. Results thus indicate that threat seems to capture the attention of phobic subjects only when it is part of the background to which subjects are not explicitly requested to attend.

Psychological and neurobiological basis of the attentional bias

Based on Beck's theory of anxiety (Beck & Emery, 1985) cognitive models of the attentional bias assume that the attentional bias towards threat is a function of acquired dysfunctional cognitive schemata or emotional memory network (Bower, 1981) by which the representation of a stimulus becomes associated with the memories of the emotional states present during the original encounter. When the stimulus reoccurs, it will ease the induction of the original emotional state. Furthermore, when the actual mood or emotional state of the subject matches with the original emotional state, the stimulus will be processed with enhanced selective attention. The schema concept and the emotional memory model share the assumption that the attentional bias represents an acquired function of stimulus processing that instantiates a vicious circle, where the experience of threat constitutes the enhanced processing sensitivity for future threat. Since the model could not explain why depressed subjects don't show an attentional bias towards negative information, Williams and coworkers have postulated an affective decision mechanism (ADM) (Williams et al., 1997) that pre-attentively and unconsciously evaluates whether a stimulus is threatening or not. If threatening, such a stimulus is tagged and subsequently processed with high selectivity by succeeding processing modules that organize behavioral resources (resource allocation mechanism, RAM) to cope with the threat. Mathews and Mackintosh (1998) suggested a similar concept.

Öhman (1993) has recently agued that priority processing of threat might be organized by a defense system that developed during hominid evolution, comprising five subsystems. The first component of this system consists of a feature detector that acts like Broadbent's stimulus-set filter (Broadbent, 1970) and provides preliminary stimulus segregation before the information is passed to succeeding processing components. In the case of life-threatening physical stimuli, this system sends signals to a downstream arousal system that quickly pushes the organism into arousal, and alerts succeeding processing systems that subserve conscious perception and memory-based response selection and coping. Additionally, this system may also be set genetically to discover biologically life-threatening stimuli or by conditioning to discover stimuli of threatening autobiographic relevance. Information on all other stimuli is passed on to a significance evaluation system that automatically and still pre-attentively assesses stimuli for relevance.

According to Öhman (1993), this system operates like a Broadbentian responses-set filter (Broadbent, 1970) with stimulus selection being controlled top-down by memory-based response schemata and situational emotional memories. It is primarily this system that constitutes the attentional bias to threat, since it primes succeeding processing systems to become oriented towards threat (often at the cost of other tasks). It can additionally be tuned by the arousal system. Then information becomes finally processed by different conscious high-level processing systems that extract more detailed aspects from stimuli and compare the new input with autobiographic and emotional non-declarative memory systems. This high-level cognitive system is also affected significantly by the arousal system and it continuously interacts with an additional high-level expectancy system. This system relies on the organization of emotion in memory and is able to bias the significance evaluation system and high-level processing units to respond optimally to further input that matches with the present emotional mood of an individual. This expectancy biasing of significance evaluation must not get to individuals' conscious awareness but may be expressed as hypervigilance of the whole processing system towards threat.

So far, only little is known of how the brains of phobic subjects organize the biased processing of stimuli and the attention towards threat differently than from those of non-phobic subjects. According to LeDoux (1996), evolution has developed a brain system for the reliable detection of threat in the environment and the generation of successful responses for coping with threat. A centerpiece of this system is composed of the amygdala, whose main task is to check the emotional significance of each incoming stimulus and to alert the brain to any threat or danger. The amygdala gets input from sensory thalamic nuclei and cortical sensory brain areas, perirhinal cortex, hippocampus, and medial prefrontal areas of both hemispheres. Its output projects to the central gray matter, hypothalamus, and the reticular pontine nucleus, and directly to sensory processing areas. Activity of the central gray matter, for example, leads to fear-induced freezing; the lateral hypothalamus increases blood pressure and heart rate. The hypothalamus and pineal gland induce the release of stress hormones from the adrenal gland while the caudal and pontine parts of the reticular nucleus modulate the startle response. Finally, projections from the amygdala to sensory processing networks ensure detailed stimulus analysis and memory consolidation for future encounters with threat (Amaral, 2000).

According to LeDoux (1996), this central role of the amygdala is enabled by two neural pathways, i.e., by a direct pathway from the sensory nuclei of the thalamus to the lateral nucleus of the amygdala (the "dirty" or fast pathway) and by a "higher" but slower pathway from the thalamus via the sensory and association cortices back to the amygdala. Information processing of the dirty pathway is blurred and does not allow detailed analysis of stimuli. However, it helps to quickly activate arousal and preparation of motor responses. Strong mutual connections of this pathway to the ventral and dorsal visual pathways seem to be relevant for the fast processing of emotional stimuli (Junghöfer, Bradley, Elbert, & Lang, 2001). In contrast, the slower cortical pathway processes information in detail involving all sensory cortical areas, association cortices, frontal brain areas and the anterior cingulate cortex, insula, and hippocampal system. Stimuli are compared with the subject's earlier experience, his/her temperament and actual mood, and expectancies about available coping skills. The higher pathway can correct, inhibit, or enhance the outcome of the dirty pathway and change the cognitive system from an automatic to a controlled mode of operation.

Neuroscientific observations of threat processing in phobics

Only a few studies have investigated neural correlates of the processing of threatening stimuli in phobic subjects by means of modern brain research methods like brain electrical event-related potentials (ERPs) or functional brain-imaging techniques such as positron emission tomography (PET) and functional magnetic resonance imaging (fMRI).

Imaging studies

Although the role of the amygdala in the processing of fear-related stimuli is widely recognized (LeDoux, 1996; Öhman & Mineka, 2001), previous neuroimaging studies did not uniformly find increased amygdala activation when animal phobics were exposed to phobia-related visual stimuli. For example, based on PET, Wik et al. (1993) showed increased regional cerebral blood flow (rCBF) in the secondary visual cortex but reduced rCBF in different temporal and frontal regions of the brain during processing of phobia-related as compared to neutral visual stimuli (see also Fredrikson, Wik, Annas, Ericson, & Stone-Elander, 1995; Fredrikson et al., 1993). A previous fMRI study found activation of the prefrontal, parahippocampal, and visual cortex but no evidence of amygdala activation when spider phobics were exposed to film clips of spiders (Paquette et al., 2003).

In contrast to these negative results, several fMRI studies have shown specific activation of the amygdala to conditioned fear-eliciting stimuli (for a review see Büchel & Dolan, 2000) and in social phobics in response to face pictures (Birbaumer et al., 1998; Breiter et al., 1996; Stein, Goldin, Sareen, Eyler, & Brown, 2002; Straube et al., 2004b). Using an event-related fMRI design, we (Dilger et al., 2003) recently re-examined the role of the amygdala in processing threatening stimuli by spider phobics and healthy controls when subjects were exposed to phobia-related stimuli. Besides the amygdala, we also investigated whether additional brain regions show significant phobia-specific blood oxygen level dependent (BOLD) signal increases. We found increased activation of the left amygdala to phobia-related pictures (spiders) relative to potentially fear-related (snakes) or neutral pictures (mushrooms) in spider phobics during free viewing conditions, while this effect was absent in control subjects. Between-group analyses revealed significant activation of the left amygdala for spider pictures in phobics compared to control subjects, whereas no differences in amygdala activation were found for the other stimulus categories. The activity of the left amygdala is consistent with previous demonstration of left-lateralized activation of the amygdala during negative emotion processing (e.g., see Breiter et al., 1996; Phelps et al., 2001; but for opposite results see Canli, Zhao, Desmond, Glover, & Gabrieli, 1999; Zalla et al., 2000).

Interestingly, Morris, Öhman, and Dolan (1998) showed that left amygdala activation was specifically associated with the processing of unmasked, consciously perceived fear-conditioned stimuli, while the right amygdala was activated only during subliminal presentation of these stimuli. Our data thus suggested that conscious processing of briefly presented phobic stimuli involves the left amygdala. Besides amygdala activation, we found evidence for an involvement of further brain regions, such as the right and left insula or areas in visual cortex, in the processing of phobia-related stimuli. The effects for the insula are in accordance with other studies indicating a role of this brain region in the evaluation of threatening stimuli in phobics. For example, we described activation of the insula in animal phobics in response to phobia-related words (Straube et al., 2004a) and in social phobics during the processing of angry faces (Straube et al., 2004b). Higher activation of visual areas in response to emotional pictures, including spiders and angry faces, as compared to neutral pictures was shown in several studies in healthy subjects and phobics (e.g., see Lang et al., 1998; Wik et al., 1993; Straube et al., 2004b).

In another recent fMRI study (Straube, Mentzel, & Miltner, in press), we investigated the brain activation of 12 female spider-phobic and 12 non-phobic subjects while the subjects' attention was involuntarily or voluntarily focused on the processing of phobogenic or neutral stimuli. The study aimed to test the hypothesis of a specific hyper-responsitivity of the amygdala in subjects with specific phobia during pre-attentive processing of threat. Brain activation to phobia-related and neutral pictures (spiders and mushrooms) was measured by means of event-related fMRI, while subjects' attentional focus was varied by task instruction. In the direct voluntary attention task, subjects were asked to identify the object (spider or mushroom). In the involuntary attention task, subjects had to match geometric figures displayed in the foreground of the pictures and to ignore the objects in the background of pictures, some of which presented threat. In control subjects, we did not obtain any increase of brain activation to spider vs mushroom pictures under any task conditions. In contrast, phobics showed greater responses in the left amygdala, left insula, left anterior cingulate gyrus (ACC), and left dorsomedial prefrontal cortex (DMPFC) to spider than to mushroom pictures when subjects were directly and voluntarily attending to the stimuli. However, when phobic subjects' attention was focused on the geometrical figure and thus distracted from the phobic stimuli being displayed in the background, there was only activation in the left and right amygdala but not in the other regions. These results confirm the crucial role of the amygdala in processing threatening stimuli with different activation of the left and right amygdala as a function of attention. When the threatening stimuli were voluntarily attended, the left amygdala and other brain regions were activated, whereas activation of the right amygdala only was observed when phobics involuntarily and pre-attentively processed the phobogenic threat. Furthermore, the absence of responses in areas such as the insula, ACC, and DMPFC during the latter condition indicates that activation of these areas requires sufficient attentional resources. Thus, our findings propose specific neural correlates of automatic vs more detailed evaluation of phobia-relevant threat.

Studies based on event-related potentials (ERPs)

Only a few studies have tested the salience of threatening stimuli and the biased processing of threat by means of brain electrical event-related potentials. Although fMRI methods provide excellent spatial resolution of brain electrical activity, they only yield blurred information about the timing of neural activity associated with stimulus processing. In contrast, ERPs provide high temporal resolution but only small spatial resolution of stimulus processing. While the amplitude, latency, and topographic distribution of the P1 and N1 component of the ERP in response to visual stimuli were demonstrated to represent signatures of different early selective attentional operations (Hansen & Hillyard, 1980; Hillyard & Picton, 1979), late components like the P3 and the positive slow wave (late positive complex, LPC) were demonstrated to be affected by the probability of an event's occurrence and its relevance to the observer's task (see Johnson, 1986). Additionally, P3 amplitude is considered as a cortical correlate of the amount of attention being paid to discrete stimuli at later stages of information processing and as a significant index of different memory encoding operations. Further relationships were reported between P3 amplitude/latency and the amount of subjects' intentional engagement towards a stimulus, its demand characteristics, its arousal-inducing qualities, and salience (Johnson, 1986). Finally, it was shown that P3 amplitude and its latency is systematically affected by the emotional valence of a stimulus (Begleiter, Gross, & Kissin, 1967; Begleiter, Porjesz, Chou, & Aunon, 1983; Farwell & Donchin, 1991; Hömberg, Grünewald, & Grünewald-Zuberbier, 1981; Hömberg, Grünewald, & Netz, 1984; Johnson, 1986; Johnston, Miller, & Burleson, 1986; Naumann, Maier, Diedrich, Becker, & Bartussek, 1997; Oliver Rodriguez, Guan, & Johnston, 1999; Palomba, Angrilli, & Mini, 1997; Pauli et al., 1997; Wang, Johnston, & Oliver, 1992). The majority of these studies revealed that the processing of emotional stimuli results in larger P3 amplitudes than the processing of non-emotional stimuli with neutral valence and low arousing qualities.

Furthermore, in a recent study by Pauli et al. (1997), P300 (P3b) amplitude was used to investigate whether brain electrical activities of subjects with psychopathological disorders are affected differently by stimuli whose meaning reflects critical concerns associated with emotional stress as compared to emotional neutral stimuli. Using body-related and non-somatic words, presented tachistoscopically to 15 panic patients and 15 healthy controls at each subject's perceptual threshold for correctly identifying 50% of neutral words, it was demonstrated that panic patients recognized more body-related words than non-body-related words. Furthermore, compared to words not related to individual concerns, body-related words were associated with larger P3 amplitudes than non-body-related words. In healthy controls, no equivalent difference in word identification or in P3 amplitude was observed. When LPC activities to body-related and non-body-related words were compared, panic patients additionally showed larger positive slow waves than healthy controls.

With reference to the study by Pauli and coworkers (Pauli et al., 1997), we recently examined (Miltner et al., 2005) which ERP amplitude (N1, P2, N2, P3, LPC) is significantly increased when phobic subjects as compared to control subjects are processing visual stimuli related to their own specific phobic fear (i.e., spider images in spider phobics and snake images in snake phobics) as compared to fear-relevant stimuli depicting objects of non-personal meaning (snake images for spider phobics and spider images for snake phobics) or to objects with emotionally neutral (ornamental fish and birds) or positive meaning (images of young animals). In a second study, heart-rate measures were recorded in addition to ERP recordings, while phobic and control subjects were processing feared and non-feared stimuli, in order to obtain additional information on how feared stimuli as compared to the other types of stimuli affect the autonomous nervous system. Physiological recordings were measured in response to slides depicting feared and fear-relevant objects and to visual stimuli with neutral and positive emotional valence. According to the Pauli et al. (1997) study and the other P3 studies mentioned above, we expected the following outcome: When P3 amplitude and the magnitude of LPC are correlates of stimulus salience we should obtain significant larger P3 and LPC amplitudes when phobic subjects are processing images related to their personal phobic concerns than to stimuli evaluated as fearful by others or to neutral or positive stimuli. Control subjects, being selected to be free of any phobia, should not show this enhancement of P3 amplitude in response to spider or snake stimuli. Responses to these stimuli should be like those observed for neutral or positive slides. Furthermore, similar results were expected for the late positive complex.

Results on valence and arousal ratings of spider/snake phobics and control subjects in response to neutral and positive stimuli confirmed earlier observations in a German population (Hamm & Vaitl, 1993) that images of young animals are commonly judged to be of positive valence while ornamental fish and birds are rated as emotionally neutral. As in the earlier studies (Hamm & Vaitl, 1993; Lang, Bradley, & Cuthbert, 1999), subjects of our study also judged these stimuli to be of only minimally arousing quality. A similar correspondence to these earlier findings was observed in control subjects for spider and snake images. As in the Hamm and Vaitl (1993) and the Lang et al. (1999) studies, control subjects considered spider and snake stimuli to be significantly more negative and more arousing than neutral and positive stimuli. However, compared to phobic subjects, they were judged by control subjects to be significantly less negative and arousing. When spider phobics were processing spider images and snake phobics were processing snake images, i.e., when phobic subjects were processing feared stimuli, valence and arousal ratings of these stimuli significantly reflected the threatening quality of these stimuli for these individuals and confirmed their fear of spiders and snakes assessed by the Snake Phobia and Spider Phobia Questionnaires (Fredrikson, 1983; Klorman, Weerts, Hastings, Melamed, & Lang, 1974). Although results of both phobia questionnaires indicated that spider phobics considered themselves not to be anxious of snakes and snake phobics reported not being fearful of spiders, arousal and valence ratings to these stimuli indicate that both subgroups of phobic subjects were also more negatively affected by these fear-relevant stimuli than control subjects. Rating values on arousal and valence in response to these fear-relevant stimuli were in between responses to neutral/positive and feared stimuli. Finally, across blocks of stimuli, results demonstrate that these patterns of ratings were fairly consistent in both groups of subjects for all stimulus categories throughout the course of stimulation.

Furthermore, results of this study demonstrate large P3 amplitudes and large magnitudes of LPC of visual ERPs when snake- and spider-phobic subjects were processing feared stimuli associated with their individual phobic fear, as compared to neutral or positive stimuli or to stimuli fearful for others. Whereas large P3 and LPC magnitudes were obtained when spider phobics saw images of spiders, these subjects did not show large amplitudes when exposed to images of snakes. Conversely, snake phobics only exhibited large P3 and LPC amplitudes when processing images of snakes but not when processing images of spiders. Thus P3 and LPC amplitudes were not affected when phobics attended to stimuli that were phobic for others or neutral. When non-phobic subjects processed images of spiders or snakes, the magnitudes of P3 and LPC did not differ significantly from each other and from magnitudes observed for neutral and positive objects. It is important to note that the increased magnitudes of the P3 and LPC did not purely reflect negative valence and/or increased arousal induced by stimuli rated as emotionally negative. While spider stimuli were rated significantly more negatively and arousing by snake phobics, and snake objects were rated more negatively and arousing by spider phobics, the magnitudes of phobic subjects' late components in response to these fear-relevant stimuli did not differ significantly from those observed to neutral and positive stimuli. Furthermore, P3 and LPC amplitudes of phobic subjects to neutral, positive, and fear-relevant stimuli were similar to those observed in control subjects. Phobic subjects only showed increased magnitudes of the P3 and LPC when they were processing fearful stimuli of personal concern.

Earlier components, i.e., the N1, P2, and N2 components, did not show this close relationship to threat. Magnitudes of the N1, P2, and N2 components in response to any of the four stimulus categories did not differ significantly between groups and there was no general significant difference between categories. If the N1 component is interpreted as an index of attention to external stimuli (Hansen & Hillyard, 1980; Hillyard & Picton, 1979), then data of the present study further suggest that the four stimulus categories did not induce different early attention sets in phobic and non-phobic subjects. This observation does not confirm results based on a rapid serial visual presentation paradigm (RSVP) observed recently by Junghöfer et al. (2001). These authors presented arousing and less arousing emotional stimuli composed of images from the international affective picture series (Lang et al., 1999) to healthy subjects at a very high presentation rate with the duration of each single stimulus varying between 200 ms and 333 ms. Results showed that emotional as compared to neutral stimuli were accompanied by stronger cortical activity in occipital areas starting around 80 ms and reaching its maximum at around 260 ms post-stimulus.

In our second study, the results of ratings and ERPs were mainly replicated. Furthermore, results on heart rate confirmed marked and significant differences between spider phobics and healthy controls. Processing of stimuli associated with individual fears was accompanied by systematic heart rate accelerations of more than four beats per minute as compared to a pre-stimulus baseline period. This acceleration held on for about 3.5 s following the onset of feared stimuli and then started to decelerate again. Based on earlier observations indicating that such accelerations of heart rate represent psychophysiological correlates of defense responses (Sokolov & Cacioppo, 1997; Sokolov & Vinogradova, 1975), data supported on-line observations with a number of phobic subjects that images of spiders induced threat and defense responses in spider phobics whereas snake images induced threat and defense responses in snake phobics. This acceleration underpins the significantly threatening quality of spider stimuli for spider-phobic subjects and of snake stimuli for snake-phobic subjects. In contrast to this acceleration during the processing of fearful stimuli, phobic subjects showed a slight deceleration of heart rate when processing neutral, positive, and fear-relevant stimuli, indicating that these stimuli induced orienting and threat-free elaboration of images. Heart rate of controls became slightly decelerated in response to stimuli feared by phobics or to stimuli being defined as fear-relevant, whereas neutral and positive stimuli hardly induced any change of heart rate as compared to the pre-stimulus baseline period.

In summary, results from our studies on the P3 amplitude and heart rate during processing of threat confirm that the personal emotional meaning and the high arousal are significant constituents of the P3 amplitude and one major source of variation of the LPC magnitude. Therefore, results suggest that late brain electrical components are useful psychophysiological tools to investigate the personal relevancy, arousal function, and threatening meaning of fearful stimuli. Furthermore, our and others' ERP and fMRI studies support observations that the brains of phobic subjects respond rather selectively and with strong activation when exposed to threatening stimuli of personal concern.

Summary

Experimental studies on the processing of threatening stimuli have demonstrated consistently that threatening stimuli are processed pre-attentively and phobic subjects' attention is drawn automatically towards threat. This biased attention was supported by supraliminal, subliminal, and several priming paradigms. When threatening stimuli were presented subliminally and outside of subjects' conscious recognition, some authors have even shown that succeeding behavioral responses to threat become improved. Subjects showed faster behavioral responses following subliminal presentation than to stimuli presented at conscious levels (Fox, 1996; MacLeod & Rutherford, 1992).

Following results from our visual search and fMRI studies, the attentional bias does not seem to reflect biased attention in general (i.e., during voluntary and involuntary attention). It primarily represents a biased form of involuntary attention. In this data-driven mode, attention is especially drawn to threat when the threatening event occurs suddenly and outside of subjects' attentional focus. In this case, very rapid sensory pathways become activated, with information being transferred to the amygdala and other limbic and autonomous structures to prioritize stimulus processing and the preparation of neural and hormonal conditions that ease succeeding flight/fight responses. Succeeding, more detailed, analysis of stimuli in sensory, associative, and memory networks of the brain secures the selection and organization of more elaborate coping behaviors and the formation of autobiographic and emotional memories for future threat encounters. This cascade of neural activation is especially tuned towards threat of personal concern in phobic subjects. It represents the neural basis of their phobic disorder.

Acknowledgements

Preparation of this manuscript was supported by a grant from the Deutsche Forschungsgemeinschaft (German Research Council) (Mi-165/6-1/2). We also thank Ralf Trippe PhD, Silke Krieschel PhD, Ingmar Gutberlet PhD, and Holger Hecht, for help during data acquisition and analysis, and for very helpful discussions of earlier versions of the paper.

References

Agras, W.S., Sylvester, D., & Oliveau, D. (1969). The epidemiology of common fear and phobia. *Comprehensive Psychiatry, 10*, 151–156.

Amaral, D.G. (2000). Organization of connections of the basal and accessory basal nuclei in the monkey amygdala. *European Journal of Neuroscience, 12*, 4153–4153.

Beck, A.T., & Emery, G. (1985). *Anxiety disorders and phobias: A cognitive perspective*. New York: Basic Books.

Begleiter, H., Gross, M.M., & Kissin, B. (1967). Evoked cortical responses to affective visual stimuli. *Psychophysiology, 3*, 336–344.

Begleiter, H., Porjesz, B., Chou, C.L., & Aunon, J.I. (1983). P3 and stimulus incentive value. *Psychophysiology*, *20*, 95–101.

Birbaumer, N., Grodd, W., Diedrich, O., Klose, U., Erb, M., Lotze, M., et al. (1998). fMRI reveals amygdala activation to human faces in social phobics. *Neuroreport*, *9*(6), 1223–1226.

Bower, G.H. (1981). Mood and memory. *American Psychologist*, *36*, 129–148.

Breiter, H.C., Etcoff, N.L., Whalen, P.J., Kennedy, W.A., Rauch, S.L., Buckner, R.L. et al. (1996). Response and habituation of the human amygdala during visual processing of facial expression. *Neuron*, *17*, 875–887.

Broadbent, D.E. (1970). Stimulus set and response set: Two kinds of selective attention. In D.J. Mostofsky (Ed.), *Attention: Contemporary theory and analysis*. New York: Appleton Century Crofts.

Büchel, C., & Dolan, R.J. (2000). Classical fear conditioning in functional neuroimaging. *Current Opinion in Neurobiology*, *10*, 219–223.

Canli, T., Zhao, Z., Desmond, J.E., Glover, G., & Gabrieli, J.E. (1999). fMRI identifies a network of structures correlated with retention of positive and negative emotional memory. *Psychobiology*, *27*, 441–452.

Dilger, S., Straube, T., Mentzel, H.J., Fitzek, C., Reichenbach, H.R., Hecht, H. et al. (2003). Brain activation to phobia-related pictures in spider phobic humans: An event-related functional magnetic resonance imaging study. *Neuroscience Letters*, *348*, 29–32.

Egeth, H.E., & Yantis, S. (1997). Visual attention: Control, representation, and time course. *Annual Review of Psychology*, *48*, 269–297.

Eimer, M., Nattkemper, D., Schroeger, E., & Prinz, W. (1996). Involuntary attention. In O. Neumann & A.F. Sanders (Eds.), *Handbook of perception and action: Attention* (Vol. 3, pp. 155–184). San Diego: Academic Press.

Farwell, L.A., & Donchin, E. (1991). The truth will out: Interrogative polygraphy ("lie detection") with event-related brain potentials. *Psychophysiology*, *28*, 531–547.

Foa, E.B., & McNally, R.J. (1986). Sensitivity to feared stimuli in obsessive-compulsives: A dichotic listening analysis. *Cognitive Therapy and Research*, *10*, 477–485.

Fox, E. (1996). Selective processing of threatening words in anxiety: The role of awareness. *Cognition and Emotion*, *10*, 449–480.

Fredrikson, M. (1983). Reliability and validity of some specific fear questionnaires. *Scandinavian Journal of Psychology*, *24*, 331–334.

Fredrikson, M., Wik, G., Annas, P., Ericson, K., & Stone-Elander, S. (1995). Functional neuroanatomy of visually elicited simple phobic fear: Additional data and theoretical analysis. *Psychophysiology*, *32*, 43–48.

Fredrikson, M., Wik, G., Greitz, T., Eriksson, L. et al. (1993). Regional cerebral blood flow during experimental phobic fear. *Psychophysiology*, *30*, 126–130.

Greenwald, A.G., Klinger, M.R., & Liu, T.J. (1989). Unconscious processing of dichotically masked words. *Memory and Cognition*, *17*, 35–47.

Greenwald, A.G., Klinger, M.R., & Schuh, E.S. (1995). Activation by marginally perceptible ("subliminal") stimuli: Dissociation of unconscious from conscious cognition. *Journal of Experimental Psychology General*, *124*, 22–42.

Hamm, A.O., & Vaitl, D. (1993). Emotionsinduktion durch visuelle Reize: Validierung einer Stimulationsmethode auf drei Reaktionsebenen. *Psychologische Rundschau*, *44*, 143–161.

Hansen, J.C., & Hillyard, S.A. (1980). Endogenous brain potentials associated with selective auditory attention. *Electroencephalography and Clinical Neurophysiology, 49*, 277–290.

Hillyard, S., & Picton, T.W. (1979). Conscious perception and cerebral event-related potentials. In J.E. Desmedt (Ed.), *Progress in Clinical Neurophysiology* (Vol. 6, pp. 1–52). Basel: Karger.

Hömberg, V., Grünewald, G., & Grünewald-Zuberbier, E. (1981). The variation of P300 amplitude in a money-winning paradigm in children. *Psychophysiology, 18*, 258–262.

Hömberg, V., Grünewald, G., & Netz, J. (1984). Category scaling of the interest value of complex visual stimuli and late positive components of the evoked potential. *Annals of the New York Academy of Science, 425*, 216–222.

Johnson, R. (1986). A triarchic model of P300 amplitude. *Psychophysiology, 23*, 367–384.

Johnston, V.S., Miller, D.R., & Burleson, M.H. (1986). Multiple P3s to emotional stimuli and their theoretical significance. *Psychophysiology, 23*, 684–694.

Junghöfer, M., Bradley, M.M., Elbert, T.R., & Lang, P.J. (2001). Fleeting images: A new look at early emotion discrimination. *Psychophysiology, 38*, 175–178.

Klorman, R., Weerts, T.C., Hastings, J.E., Melamed, B.G., & Lang, P.J. (1974). Psychometric description of some specific-fear questionnaires. *Behavior Therapy, 5*, 401–409.

Lang, P.J., Bradley, M.M., & Cuthbert, B.N. (1999). *International Affective Picture System (IAPS). Technical manual and affective ratings*. Gainsville, FL: The Center for Research in Psychophysiology, University of Florida.

Lang, P.J., Bradley, M.M., Fitzsimmons, J.R., Cuthbert, B.N., Scott, J.D., Moulder, B. et al. (1998). Emotional arousal and activation of the visual cortex: An fMRI analysis. *Psychophysiology, 35*, 199–210.

Lang, P.J., Davis, M., & Öhman, A. (2000). Fear and anxiety: Animal models and human cognitive psychophysiology. *Journal of Affective Disorders, 61*, 137–159.

Lavy, E.H., Van den Hout, M., & Arntz, A. (1993). Attentional bias and spider phobia: Conceptual and clinical issues. *Behaviour Research and Therapy, 31*, 17–24.

LeDoux, J. (1996). *The emotional brain: The mysterious underpinnings of emotional life*. New York: Simon & Schuster.

Logan, A.C., & Goetsch, V.L. (1993). Attention to external threat cues in anxiety states. *Clinical Psychology Review, 13*, 541–559.

MacLeod, C. (1991). Clinical anxiety and the selective enconding of threatening information. *International Review of Psychiatry, 3*, 279–292.

MacLeod, C. (1999). Anxiety and anxiety disorders. In T. Dalgleish & M.J. Power (Eds.), *Handbook of cognition and emotion* (pp. 447–477). Chichester, UK: John Wiley & Sons Ltd.

MacLeod, C., & Mathews, A. (1991). Biased cognitive operations in anxiety: Accessibility of information or assignment of processing priorities. *Behaviour Research and Therapy, 29*(6), 599–610.

MacLeod, C., Mathews, A., & Tata, P. (1986). Attentional bias in emotional disorders. *Journal of Abnormal Psychology, 95*, 15–20.

MacLeod, C., & Rutherford, E.M. (1992). Anxiety and the selective processing of emotional information: Mediating roles of awareness, trait and state variables, and personal relevance of stimulus materials. *Behaviour Research and Therapy, 30*, 479–491.

Marks, I., & Lader, M. (1973). Anxiety states (anxiety neurosis): A review. *Journal of Nervous & Mental Disease, 156*, 3–18.

Marks, J.M. (1969). *Fear and phobias*. New York: Oxford University Press.

Mathews, A., & Mackintosh, B. (1998). A cognitive model of selective processing in anxiety. *Cognitive Therapy and Research, 22*, 539–560.

Miltner, W.H.R., Krieschel, S., Hecht, H., Trippe, R., & Weiss, T. (2004). Eye-movements and behavioral responses to threatening and non-threatening stimuli during visual search in phobic and non-phobic subjects. *Emotion, 4*, 323–339.

Miltner, W.H.R., Trippe, R., Krieschel, S., Gutberlet, I., Hecht, H., & Weiss, T. (2005). Event-related brain potentials and affective responses to threat in spider-/snake-phobic and non-phobic subjects. *International Journal of Psychophysiology, 57*(1), 43–52.

Morris, J.S., Öhman, A., & Dolan, R.J. (1998). Conscious and unconscious emotional learning in the human amygdala. *Nature, 393*, 467–470.

Murphy, S.T., & Zajonc, R.B. (1993). Affect, cognition, and awareness: Affective priming with optimal and suboptimal stimulus exposures. *Journal of Personality and Social Psychology, 64*, 723–739.

Naumann, E., Maier, S., Diedrich, O., Becker, G., & Bartussek, D. (1997). Structural, semantic, and emotion-focused processing of neutral and negative nouns: Event-related potential correlates. *Journal of Psychophysiology, 11*, 158–172.

Niedenthal, P.M. (1990). Implicit perception of affective information. *Journal of Experimental Social Psychology, 26*, 505–527.

Öhman, A. (1993). Fear and anxiety as emotional phenomena: Clinical phenomenology, evolutionary perspectives and information-processing mechanisms. In M. Lewis & J.M. Haviland (Eds.), *Handbook of emotions* (pp. 511–536). New York/London: The Guilford Press.

Öhman, A., Esteves, F., & Soares, J.J.F. (1995). Preparedness and preattentive associative learning – electrodermal conditioning to masked stimuli. *Journal of Psychophysiology, 9*, 99–108.

Öhman, A., Flykt, A., & Esteves, F. (2001). Emotion drives attention: Detecting the snake in the grass. *Journal of Experimental Psychology: General, 130*, 466–478.

Öhman, A., & Mineka, S. (2001). Fears, phobias, and preparedness: Toward an evolved module of fear and fear learning. *Psychological Review, 108*, 483–522.

Oliver Rodriguez, J.C., Guan, Z.Q., & Johnston, V.S. (1999). Gender differences in late positive components evoked by human faces. *Psychophysiology, 36*, 176–185.

Palomba, D., Angrilli, A., & Mini, A. (1997). Visual evoked potentials, heart rate responses and memory to emotional pictorial stimuli. *International Journal of Psychophysiology, 27*, 55–67.

Paquette, V., Levesque, J., Mensour, B., Leroux, J.M., Beaudoin, G., Bourgouin, P. et al. (2003). "Change the mind and you change the brain": Effects of cognitive-behavioral therapy on the neural correlates of spider phobia. *Neuroimage, 18*, 401–409.

Pauli, P., Dengler, W., Wiedemann, G., Montoya, P., Birbaumer, N., Flor, H. et al. (1997). Behavioral and neurophysiological evidence for altered processing of anxiety-related words in panic disorder. *Journal of Abnormal Psychology, 106*, 213–220.

Phelps, E.A., O'Connor, K.J., Gatenby, J.C., Gore, J.C., Grillon, C., & Davis, M. (2001). Activation of the left amygdala to a cognitive representation of fear. *Nature Neuroscience, 4*, 437–441.

Seamon, J.G., Marsh, R.L., & Brody, N. (1984). Critical importance of exposure duration for affective discrimination of stimuli that are not recognized. *Journal of Experimental Psychology: Learning, Memory, and Cognition*, *10*, 465–469.

Seligman, M.E.P. (1971). Phobias and preparedness. *Behavior Therapy*, *2*, 307–320.

Sokolov, E.N., & Cacioppo, J.T. (1997). Orienting and defense reflexes: Vector coding the cardiac response. In P.J. Lang, R.F. Simons, & M. Balaban (Eds.), *Attention and orienting: Sensory and motivational processes* (pp. 1–22). Mahwah, NJ: Lawrence Erlbaum Associates Inc.

Sokolov, E.N., & Vinogradova, O.S. (Eds.). (1975). *Neural mechanisms of the orienting reflex*. New York: J. Wiley & Sons.

Stein, M.B., Goldin, P.R., Sareen, J., Eyler, L.T., & Brown, G.G. (2002). Increased amygdala activation to angry and contemptuous faces in generalized social phobia. *Archives of General Psychiatry*, *59*, 1027–1034.

Straube, T., Kolassa, I.T., Glauer, M., Mentzel, H.J., & Miltner, W.H. (2004b). Effect of task conditions on brain responses to threatening faces in social phobics: An event-related functional magnetic resonance imaging study. *Biological Psychiatry*, *56*, 921–30.

Straube, T., Mentzel, H.J., Glauer, M., & Miltner, W.H. (2004a). Brain activation to phobia-related words in phobic subjects. *Neuroscience Letters*, *372*, 204–208.

Straube, T., Mentzel, H.-J., & Miltner, W.H.R. (in press). Neural mechanisms of automatic and direct processing of phobogenic stimuli in specific phobia. *Biological Psychology*.

Streblow, H., Hoffmann, J., & Kasielke, E. (1985). Experimentalpsychologische Analyse von Gedaechtnisprozessen bei Phobikern [Experimental psychological analysis of memory processes in phobics]. *Zeitschrift fuer Psychologie*, *193*, 147–161.

Wang, X., Johnston, V.S., & Oliver, J.C. (1992). Evoked brain potential studies of emotional and cognitive processes: Emotional adaptation hypothesis. *Acta Psychologica Sinica*, *24*, 406–414.

Wik, G., Fredrikson, M., Ericson, K., Eriksson, L., Stone-Elander, T., & Greitz, A. (1993). A functional cerebral response to frightening visual stimulation. *Psychiatry Research Neuroimaging*, *50*, 15–24.

Williams, J.M.G., Mathews, A., & MacLeod, C. (1996). The emotional Stroop task and psychopathology. *Psychological Bulletin*, *120*, 3–24.

Williams, J.M.G., Watts, F.N., MacLeod, C., & Mathews, A. (1997). *Cognitive psychology and emotional disorders*. Chichester, UK: Wiley.

Winkielman, P., Zajonc, R.B., & Schwarz, N. (1997). Subliminal affective priming resists attributional interventions. *Cognition and Emotion*, *11*, 433–465.

Zalla, T., Koechlin, E., Pietrini, P., Basso, G., Aquino, P., Sirigu, A. et al. (2000). Differential amygdala responses to winning and losing: A functional magnetic resonance imaging study in humans. *European Journal of Neuroscience*, *12*, 1764–1770.

20 A double-structure structural equation model for the study of emotions and their components

Paul De Boeck and Dirk Smits

It is a common practice in psychology to explain observations from underlying concepts. The observations are considered to be expressions of the concept or caused by the concept, and in return the observations are considered to be a tool for the measurement or the identification (operational definition) of the concept. This way of thinking is at the basis of psychometric models, such as structural equation models and item response theory (Borsboom, Mellenbergh, & van Heerden, 2003).

For example, let us assume that respondents are asked to rate their anger in three different scenarios:

- You find out that a friend is spreading gossip about you.
- A friend lets you down on an appointment to go out.
- You find out that a friend of yours is in love with the same person as you are.

The responses may be seen as three indicators of the disposition to anger, and their sum can be used as a measure of the corresponding concept. Suppose the same three scenarios are presented again but now with the instruction to rate the degree of frustration. Again the responses may be seen as three indicators, but now of the disposition to frustration, and their sum can be used as a measure of the corresponding concept. The next step may be putting one concept into relation with the other, for example on the basis of the simple theory that frustration causes anger. Note that in this case, there is no basis for an inference on the direction of causality. A simple correlation between two concepts does not tell us anything about the direction of causality. It can only tell us whether, independent of the direction, a causal theory makes any chance.

Two disciplines

Thus far it was implicitly assumed that concepts are about individual differences. The concepts are therefore also called latent traits. Such an individual-difference approach is not uncommon in psychology. It is at the basis of the correlational paradigm, but this is only one of two possible paradigms (Cronbach, 1957; Underwood, 1975). In the so-called experimental paradigm, primarily differences between situations are investigated, and in particular between situations that are under the control of the experimenter. For example, an experimental paradigm would imply that the frustration level is manipulated from one condition to the other, and that in the resulting conditions the degree of anger is measured.

The independent variable of the experiment just described is a situation variable. On the other hand this variable is assumed to affect the experience of frustration. If not, it would not be possible to test the hypothesis that frustration increases anger. In fact, a check on the validity (effectiveness) of the experimental manipulation would imply that the degree of frustration is actually assessed to see whether it depends on the condition. The experimental effect may therefore be interpreted as a covariation over situations (conditions) between frustration and anger. When viewed from this perspective, the experimental method is as correlational as the correlational method. The former is based on covariation over situations and the latter on covariation over persons. A crucial difference is that in the experimental paradigm the variation in one variable is under the control of the experimenter, whereas the variation between people is not.

Two possibly different structures

The structure of individual differences is not necessarily the same as the structure of situational differences, whereas they both seem relevant for the study of relations between concepts such as anger and frustration. To give an example of how the correlation over persons can differ from the correlation over situations, we refer to a study by Fontaine et al. (in press) on the differentiation between shame and guilt.

The study was set up in three different countries (Peru, Hungary, Belgium), and a scenario-based method was used, with the kind of situations as in the example given earlier. Respondents had to indicate for 14 scenarios whether they felt shame and guilt. Questions regarding the components of shame and guilt were also asked. For shame, ratings were made of how much one felt gazed at (situational interpretation), how much one's reputation was felt to be in danger (appraisal of consequence), and how strong the tendency to disappear would be (action tendency). For guilt, analogous questions related to norm violation (situational interpretation), self-reproach (appraisal of consequence), and tendency to repair (action tendency). The design of this study allows for an analysis of the two structures, based on correlations over persons, and correlations over situations, respectively.

The findings were very similar for the three cultures, so that one may conclude in line with the literature that the emotions' concepts and expressions are universal (Ekman, 1992). On the other hand, clear differences were found between the two kinds of structures:

1. Guilt and shame are much less differentiated in the person-based structure than in the situation-based structure. The conclusion that guilt proneness and shame proneness are strongly related does not contradict that some situations make people feel shame but not guilt and vice versa. For example, when at an official reception one turns out not to be appropriately dressed (e.g., without a tie whereas all the other men are formally dressed), one would feel shame rather than guilt. The degree to which guilt is felt in such situations might still be highly correlated with feelings of shame (correlation over persons).
2. The emotion components are generally better differentiated in the person structure than in the situation structure. In the situational structure, a rather tight shame cluster is found with shame, gazed at, reputation in danger, and tendency to disappear, and also a rather tight guilt cluster, with guilt, norm violation, self-reproach, and tendency to repair. In the structure of individual differences, no such clusters appear. It makes sense from a personality point of view that norm violation, self-reproach, and the tendency to repair are not so highly correlated, because they refer to different dimensions of the big five personality structure: conscientiousness (feeling that one has violated a norm), neuroticism (self-reproach), and altruism (tendency to repair). On the other hand it makes sense that they are all three closely connect to guilt when looked at over situations. Situations may rather be structured into discrete categories, and these categories may capture the main structure in the variability of situations, just as the basic categories do in a structure of psychological categories for objects (Rosch, 1975).

The difference between individual differences and situational difference structure is also relevant for the structure of emotions. One of the remarkable findings is that from a dispositional point of view, negative affect (NA) and positive affect (PA) are found to be independent traits (Larsen & Ketelaar, 1989; Watson, Clark, & Tellegen, 1988), whereas they have clearly opposite meanings. This discrepancy can possibly be explained as a discrepancy between correlations over persons and correlations over situations (Vansteelandt, Van Mechelen & Nezlek, 2005). When studying emotions from a situational perspective, it seems quite plausible that one does not feel happy and unhappy at the same time (Ekman, 1992; Frijda, 1986). It is possible that positive and negative emotions are mutually exclusive and therefore do not tend to co-occur in the same situation (especially not if the situations are clear situations from a emotional point of view) (Izard, 1992; Stein & Oatley, 1992), whereas the persons who experience these feelings may combine the corresponding dispositions. This line of thinking is at the basis of studies by Zelenski and Larsen (2000), and Vansteelandt et al. (2005), and in both studies some support was found for it.

To give another example, there might be situations in which one would tend to help another person and other situations where one tends to leave the person alone out of respect. These two behaviors would not co-occur over situations, but they may both rely on the common trait of agreeableness, which implies both a willingness to help and respect for other people.

We believe it is important to study the relation between psychological variables not just from an individual-difference perspective, but also from a situational-difference perspective. For the two structures to be comparable, it is better that they are derived from the same set of data than from two different data sets, and that the common data are analyzed with a model that includes both aspects and allows for a simultaneous estimation.

For the data gathering, this implies that three-mode data are gathered, the three modes being persons, situations, and responses. In the examples we have discussed thus far, the responses were emotional responses related to anger, guilt, and shame. Three-mode data are not a novelty in psychology, as will be described in the following. For the data analysis, this implies that a model for the data is used which includes a latent structure for the individual differences and for the situational differences at the same time. Such a model has not been described yet. It would be a structural equation model (SEM) with a double structure: with latent person variables, and with latent situation variables at the same time. Structural equation models thus far contain only latent person variables.

Three-mode data and designs

Three-mode data have a long history in psychology. For example, Cattell (1946, 1952) has given an extensive description of the different types. In most cases these data have persons and responses (behaviors) as two of the three modes. The third mode is either defined by time points or by situations. Examples of the former are multivariate longitudinal data or panel data, and multivariate time series data. An example of the latter is when the data stem from so-called SR inventories; these are inventories with a design of situations by reactions, for example, for anxiety (Endler & Hunt, 1966), and for hostility (Endler & Hunt, 1969). We will concentrate here on situations as the third mode.

If one wants to study the situational-difference structure, it is important to use a *fully crossed design*, with all three modes crossed: persons by situations by variables (responses). Data from such a design are perfectly appropriate for the double-structure structural equation model we have in mind, but the design also has serious drawbacks, which can make it less attractive: (1) long and repetitive inventories, because a rather large set of situations is needed and all response variables need to be crossed with all situations; (2) less natural observations, because it is highly unlikely that all situations are equally relevant for all the persons, and because the respondents are not actually experiencing the situations while they give their responses.

Two alternative designs may be considered: categorical situations, and experience sampling. The *categorical situation design* means that one presents categories of situations, such as: "frustrating, unexpected, not under control", and asks the respondent to remember or to imagine such a situation from her or his personal life, and to keep it in mind while responding. This design still allows for a full crossing, whereas it is also personalized. A practical problem is that the categories are necessarily rather abstract and therefore not very appealing, and a methodological problem is that the actual situations may largely differ depending on the respondent.

The *experience sampling design* requires the respondent to answer questions for a set of sampled situations she or he is experiencing. The sampling is time-based (Delespaul, 1995; Schwartz & Stone, 1998), with signals sent following a time schedule (random or fixed), or event-based; see Bolger, Davis, and Rafaeli (2003) for a discussion. The experience sampling method guarantees that the sampled situations are natural for the person who receives the signal, because she or he is experiencing the situations or has just experienced them when responding to the questions. However, as a result the situations are different depending on the persons, even more than in the format with categorical situations. In fact the situations are nested within the persons. As a consequence, inferences about the specific situations become impossible. It is still possible to study the covariation of the variables over situations within persons, but the design has some serious drawbacks. A first drawback is that when the covariation over persons is studied, each person may represent a different set of situations, so that individual differences would be confounded with situational differences. A second drawback is that the variation within persons may be much smaller and different depending on the person, in comparison with a fully crossed design.

The three designs differ on two important dimensions. The first dimension is the quality of the form of the design. The crossed design is clearly the most complete form with theoretically the best potentiality for inferences, because everything is crossed with everything. The experience sampling design is a nested design and it does not yield a basis for all the kinds of inferences one can make with a fully crossed design, for example regarding situations. The second dimension is the quality of the data one obtains with the design. On this second dimension the experience sampling design does best, because the data relate to natural situations, and because the responses are given when experiencing the situations in question. The categorical situation design has a middle position between the two extremes, on both dimensions.

Note that the experience sampling design may also be considered a design with time as a third mode (if time based), with moments in time being nested within persons. The nestedness is no problem for studying the covariation between variables within persons, but it is definitely a problem for the study of variation over situations/time points, and it may be a problem for the study of covariation between variables over persons, because persons may be confounded with situations/time points, as mentioned earlier.

The double-structure structural equation model

The model we will use is one for categorical data and belongs to the class of item response models. All variables are binary. However, we will first explain some general principles that can be followed for the analysis of continuous data, and afterwards these principles will be generalized to the way binary data can be modeled.

Two parts in each observation

Each observation may be considered as consisting of two parts: a systematic part that can be explained on the basis of variation in terms of the modes of the data (persons, situations, behaviors) and features characterizing the elements of these modes, and a random part with unexplained variation.

$$Y_{psr} = \eta_{psr} + \varepsilon_{psr} \tag{20.1}$$

Y_{psr} is the observation variable for person p ($p = 1, \ldots, P$), situation s ($s = 1, \ldots, S$), and response r ($r = 1, \ldots, R$). The two parts are the systematic part, η_{psr}, and the unexplained random part, ε_{psr}. The latter may be considered as drawn from a distribution with mean zero that is equal for all triples (p,s,r) (i.e., homoscedasticity). As mentioned, the systematic part is a term that is determined by the modes.

Decomposition of the systematic part

A simple way for determining η_{psr} is that each mode has an element-specific contribution:

$$\eta_{psr} = \theta_p + \beta_s + \tau_r \tag{20.2}$$

with θ_p, β_s, and τ_r being the contributions of person p, situation s, and response r (the elements). The resulting model is a main-effects model. The three effects may be defined as fixed effects, inherent to the specific person, situation, or response; or they may be considered random effects drawn from a distribution for persons, situations, and responses. The two combinations we will consider here are: (1) random person effects, random situation effects, and fixed response effects, (2) random person effects, fixed situation effects, and fixed response effects. The reason for this choice is that commonly persons are considered as drawn from a given distribution, whereas the situation can be sampled (in experience sampling) or not (as possibly in the categorical situation design and in the fully crossed design), and the responses are always chosen based on the research issue at hand and are thus not randomly chosen.

We will continue the explanation for the first option, with random situation effects, and will come back to the second later. Let us further assume that θ_p is normally distributed with mean 0 and variance σ^2_θ: $\theta_p \sim N(0, \sigma^2_\theta)$ and that β_s is also normally distributed, with mean 0 and variance σ^2_β: $\beta_s \sim N(0, \sigma^2_\beta)$. Normality is a common assumption, and the restriction of the mean to zero is only a convention, given that τ_r is a free parameter.

Latent person variables and latent situation variables

A more complicated way of decomposing η_{psr} is in terms of multiple latent person variables and multiple latent situation variables. In Equation 20.2 there is one latent person variable, θ_p, and one latent situation variable, β_s (and one latent response variable, τ_r). We can expand the equation, so that more than one latent person variable and more than one latent situation variable play a role. For example, a different latent person variable and a different latent situation may play for each response:

$$\eta_{psr} = \theta_{pr} + \beta_{sr} + \tau_r, \qquad (20.3)$$

so that there are R latent person variables and also R latent situation variables. Equation 20.3 can be rewritten as follows:

$$\eta_{psr^*} = \Sigma_r \alpha_{r^*r} \theta_{pr} + \Sigma_r \gamma_{r^*r} \beta_{sr} + \tau_{r^*}, \qquad (20.4)$$

so that $\alpha_{r^*r} = \gamma_{r^*r} = 1$ if $r = r^*$, and $\alpha_{r^*r} = \gamma_{r^*r} = 0$ otherwise. Because there are now multiple latent variables, one also needs to specify their multivariate distribution, which is commonly a multivariate normal distribution with means equal to zero and covariance matrix Σ.

A double-structure factor model

The model as expressed in Equations 20.3 and 20.4 is a confirmatory factor model, with one latent person variable and one latent situation variable per response. The loadings equal 1 if response r is involved, and 0 if not. The indicators for latent person variable r are the S observations per person (S is the number of situations), and the indicators for the latent situation variable are the P observations per situation (P is the number of persons). This is the model we will illustrate in the application.

It is also possible that there are fewer latent variables than there are types of responses (fewer than R), that the latent variables differ in number and kind depending on whether the covariation is looked at over persons or over situations, and that the loadings are not fixed. Therefore, we present a more general equation:

$$\eta_{psr} = \Sigma_{i=1} \alpha_{ri} \theta_{pi} + \Sigma_{j=1} \gamma_{rj} \beta_{sj} + \tau_r, \qquad (20.5)$$

with i ($i = 1, \ldots, I$) as an index for latent person variables, and j ($j = 1, \ldots, J$) as an index for latent situation variables, and $I, J < R$. The factor loadings are the elements of the $R \times I$ matrix **A**, and of the $R \times J$ matrix Γ.

The models of Equations 20.4 and 20.5 are double-structure factor models. They are based on two kinds of factors: one to explain the individual-difference structure and the other to explain the situational-difference structure. The model of Equation 20.5 is exploratory, but when some of the αs and γs are fixed, the model becomes confirmatory, as in Equation 20.4. Further, it should be noted that because of the first term in Equation 20.5, the model is one with person-by-response interactions (see the products of α and θ), and that because of the second term in Equation 20.5, it is also one with situation-by-response interactions (see the products of γ and β), in contrast with the model of Equation 20.2 which allows only for person and situation main effects.

A double-structure structural equation model

The kind of model as defined thus far is considered a *measurement model* in the literature, because it connects observable variables (*Y*s) to latent variables (θs, βs), so that these latent variables can be measured, but without specifying the structural relations between the latent variables. Specifications of these structural relations are made in the *structural model.*

In the structural model, one or more θ-variables are made a function of one or more other θ-variables, and in a similar way, one or more β-variables are made a function of one or more other β-variables. For example, in Equations 20.6 and 20.7

$$\theta_{p1} = \omega_{12}\theta_{p2} + \omega_{13}\theta_{p3} + \theta^*_{p1}, \tag{20.6}$$

$$\beta_{s1} = \lambda_{12}\beta_{s2} + \lambda_{13}\beta_{s3} + \beta^*_{s1}, \tag{20.7}$$

θ_{p1} is made a linear function of two other θ-variables, θ_{p2} and θ_{p3}, and β_{s1} is made a function of two other β-variables, β_{s2} and β_{s3}, weighted with ω_{12} and ω_{13}, and with λ_{12} and λ_{13}, respectively. The unexplained parts, or residual terms, are denoted as θ^*_{p1} and β^*_{s1}, respectively. In a general model formulation, a $\mathrm{I} \times \mathrm{I}$ matrix Ω can be used to connect the various θ-variables, and a $\mathrm{J} \times \mathrm{J}$ matrix Λ to connect the various β-variables. It must be possible to reorder the two matrices so that all ω-values and λ-values in the upper diagonal part are zero. In this way feedback loops are avoided. The issue of whether the individual-differences structure is the same as the situational-difference structure can now be reformulated in two questions: (1) $\mathbf{A} = \Gamma$? (2) $\Omega = \Lambda$?

Binary data and the logistic model formulation

The data we will analyze are binary data. The equations we have formulated thus far are equations for continuous variables and they do not apply as such to dichotomous data. For binary data, it common practice to use logistic models (De Boeck & Wilson, 2004). The model as formulated in Equation 20.5 then becomes a model for the conditional probability of $Y_{psr}=1$ given the values of θ_{psr} and β_{sr}, and is expressed in:

$$\pi_{psr} = \exp(\Sigma_i \alpha_{ri}\theta_{pi} + \Sigma_j \gamma_{rj}\beta_{sj} + \tau_r)/(1 + \exp(\Sigma_i \alpha_{ri}\theta_{pi} + \Sigma_j \gamma_{rj}\beta_{sj} + \tau_r)) \quad (20.8)$$

with exp(x) indicating e to the power of x. For a presentation and discussion of SEMs for binary and categorical data (including multilevel modeling), see Skrondal and Rabe-Hesketh (2004).

Fixed situation effects

Using random latent person variables and random latent situation variables at the same time means that the random effects of two modes of the data are crossed. Such models are not easy to estimate. One can either opt for an approximate method based on multilevel modeling as explained by Van den Noortgate, De Boeck, and Meulders (2003), or for more exact methods which imply the calculation of a P × S-dimensional integral or the use of a Markov chain Monte Carlo approach (Janssen, Schepers, & Peres, 2004).

The problem can be avoided when the situation parameters β are fixed effects. The structural equation formulation then leads to a MIRID, an acronym for Model with Internal Restrictions on Item Difficulty (Butter, De Boeck, & Verhelst, 1998). The model described by Butter et al. (1998) is a structural equation model with fixed situation effects and only one latent person variable, but it can easily be extended to a model with multiple latent person variables. The consequence of using fixed effects for the situation is that there is no residual term included when the βs are decomposed into a weighted sum of other βs. For example, when β_1 is a function of β_2 and β_3, as in Equation 20.7, then the β^*_{s1} term is omitted:

$$\beta_{s1} = \lambda_{12}\beta_{s2} + \lambda_{13}\beta_{s3} \quad (20.9)$$

Because there are no longer random latent situation variables, it is no longer possible to specify a multivariate distribution for these variables, so that the correlation between the variables also cannot be estimated. Remember that fixed situation effects were presented earlier as an alternative.

Application

The topic of the application is a comparison of anger and irritation. The distinction between anger and irritation is an intriguing and difficult issue that is best formulated by Averill (1983), when he states that "even when anger and annoyance are indistinguishable in terms of object or response, people typically have little difficulty identifying the state they are in, although they may have a great deal of difficulty stating the basis for their judgment" (p. 1152). Several authors conceptualize irritation as a rather mild form of anger (Averill, 1982, 1983; Gidron, Stewart, Ben-Zur, & Breznitz, 1998; Johnson-Laird & Oatley, 1989; Spielberger, Jacobs, Russell, & Crane, 1983), whereas other authors conceptualize irritation as a related, but qualitatively different emotion (Frijda, Kuipers, & ter Schure, 1989; Russell, 1980; Scherer, 1993, 2001). We will argue in favor of the latter and explain why the former can also be correct when viewed from a certain perspective.

Two hypotheses will be tested. First, both, anger and irritation are related to frustration and an antagonistic action tendency. Frustration is generally accepted as an important determinant of anger and irritation (e.g., Averill, 1982; Ellsworth & Smith, 1988; Izard, 1977; Kuppens, Van Mechelen, Smits, & De Boeck, 2003; Ortony, Clore, & Collins, 1988; Scherer, 1993; Smith & Lazarus, 1993). In appraisal theory (e.g., Ellsworth & Smith, 1988; Frijda, 1986; Scherer, 1993; Smith & Lazarus, 1993) and in the theories of Wierzbicka (1992) and Smedslund (1997), frustration is conceptualized as basically an appreciation of the situation, which can clearly be differentiated from anger/irritation because it doesn't comprise an action-related component. Following Wierzbicka (1992), and Smedslund (1997) and numerous other theories, the antagonistic action tendency is associated with anger-like emotions under various forms, like the tendency to do something against the unpleasant situation, to remove the obstacle of frustration, to blame a perceived wrongdoer, etc. (Ellsworth & Smith, 1988; Frijda, 1986; Frijda et al., 1989; Skiffington, Fernandez, & McFarland, 1998; Smedslund, 1997).

Second, irritation is hypothesized to be primarily related to frustration, whereas anger is hypothesized to be more related to the action tendency. For example, Frijda et al. (1989) found that anger, in contrast to annoyance, which is similar to irritation, was associated with a reactant "move against" action tendency. An analogous differentiation is made by Scherer (1993, 2001) between irritation/cold anger and hot anger. Hot anger is characterized by a higher perceived power to cope with the event than irritation/cold anger, and therefore it may be expected to be more action oriented.

The second hypothesis is based on the more general assumption that there are two kinds of components for emotions: feelings and action tendencies. Feelings reflect the receptive mode of affect, and thus how a situation is received. An important aspect of the reception is an evaluation, and an additional aspect is an explanation for why the situation occurred and why it is experienced as pleasant or unpleasant. With the term "feeling" we refer to evaluative affective responses to situations as well as to associated appraisals of the situation. For example, the feeling of frustration implies a negative evaluation because the situation does not agree with one's desire, wish, plan, expectation, etc. Goal blocking is common term to explain the source of displeasure. Action tendencies reflect the action mode; what one tends to do about the situation. The antagonistic action in the case of anger is a clear example. Other examples of action tendencies are fleeing in the case of fear, and restitution in the case of guilt. The distinction between feelings and action tendencies resembles the distinction Frijda et al. (1989) made between appraisals and action readiness, but we also include the evaluative affective response and not just the appraisals in the concept of feelings. In general, emotions may differ in how much they are feeling based, and how much they are action oriented. Some might be mainly feeling based, such as frustration, and joy, whereas others, such as anger, and love, may have a much stronger action component.

The two hypotheses at the basis of the study can be simply summarized as follows:

1 Both anger and irritation are based on frustration and on an antagonistic action tendency.
2 Anger is primarily action based (based on an antagonistic action tendency), whereas irritation is primarily feeling based (based on the feeling of frustration). The hypotheses will be tested with a double-structure SEM, and we expect that they hold for both structures.

The data concern the responses of 679 Dutch-speaking respondents in the last year in high school, to four questions regarding 11 situations of the type described in the introduction, and varying on the features that are considered important for anger and irritation in the literature (Kuppens et al., 2003). The situations were presented with the instruction to indicate whether one would be frustrated, whether one would be inclined to take antagonistic action, whether one would be irritated, and whether one would be angry in the situation in question.

The model we will use contains four double latent variables: frustration, antagonistic action tendency, irritation, and anger. The measurement model is the model from Equations 20.3 and 20.4, but with the latent situation variables modeled as fixed effects, so that each situation is assumed to have a fixed value on each of the latent situation variables. The latent person variables are modeled as random effects with a multivariate normal distribution. For the structural model, three different assumptions are made regarding the θs and βs, yielding three different models:

(a) No restrictions are imposed on the relations between the four latent person variables and between the four latent situation variables (no assumptions are made regarding the covariance of the latent person variables and the four kinds of βs are free parameters).

(b) Frustration and the antagonistic action tendency are assumed to have an effect on irritation and anger (whereas irritation is assumed to have no effect on anger and vice versa):

$$\theta_{p,irr} = \omega_{irr,frus}\theta_{p,frus} + \omega_{irr,anta}\theta_{p,anta} + \theta^*_{p,irr}$$

$$\beta_{s,irr} = \lambda_{irr,frus}\beta_{s,frus} + \lambda_{irr,anta}\beta_{s,anta}$$

$$\theta_{p,anger} = \omega_{anger,frus}\theta_{p,frus} + \omega_{anger,anta}\theta_{p,anta} + \theta^*_{p,anger}$$

$$\beta_{s,anger} = \lambda_{anger,frus}\beta_{s,frus} + \lambda_{anger,anta}\beta_{s,anta}$$

As for the distribution of the input θs ($\theta^*_{p,irr}$, $\theta^*_{p,ang}$, $\theta_{p,frus}$, $\theta_{p,anta}$), the means are set equal to zero, the variances are free parameters, and the covariance between $\theta^*_{p,irr}$ and $\theta_{p,frus}$, $\theta_{p,anta}$, and between $\theta^*_{p,anger}$ and $\theta_{p,frus}$, $\theta_{p,anta}$ are fixed to zero, whereas the other covariances are free parameters.

(c) The model is the same as Model b, except for the restriction that the effects of frustration and the antagonistic action tendency on irritation and anger are the same in the two structures:

$$\omega_{irr,frus} = \lambda_{irr,frus}, \omega_{anger,frus} = \lambda_{anger,frus}, \omega_{irr,anta} = \lambda_{irr,anta}, \omega_{anger,anta} = \lambda_{anger,anta},$$

or in matrix terms, $\Omega = \Lambda$. A preliminary condition is that the two measurement models are equivalent, or $A = \Gamma$. This condition is imposed in all three models by defining four latent person variables so that $\alpha_{r^*r} = 1$ if $r^* = r$, and $\alpha_{r^*r} = 0$ otherwise, and by similarly setting $\gamma_{r^*r} = 1$ if $r^* = r$, and $\gamma_{r^*r} = 0$ otherwise.

In Models b and c, frustration and the antagonistic action tendency are the exogenous latent variables, and irritation and anger are the endogenous latent variables. The former two are each expected to have an effect on irritation and anger, but in such a way that the weight of frustration is higher than that of the antagonistic action tendency for irritation, and vice versa for anger. We expect this inequality to hold for the two structures. Note that, because we allow for a correlation between the unexplained parts of the endogenous latent variables, we cannot differentiate between the models we use and the corresponding alternative models with effects in the opposite direction (with the roles of endogenous and exogenous variables interchanged).

Results

Models a, b, and c were estimated using the SAS PROC NLMIXED procedure (SAS Institute, 1999). It was found that Model b was the best in terms of the Bayesian information criterion (BIC).

The effects for the latent person variables were as follows (see Figure 20.1). Frustration and the antagonistic action tendency had an effect on irritation, of .51 and .47 respectively, and both effects were highly significant ($p < .001$). Frustration and the antagonistic action tendency had an effect on anger, of .29 and .52 respectively, and these two effects were also highly significant ($p < .001$). The fact that frustration *and* the antagonistic action tendency had an effect on both irritation and anger, means that the first hypothesis is confirmed for the structure with latent person variables. The second hypothesis is also supported, because frustration seems more important than an

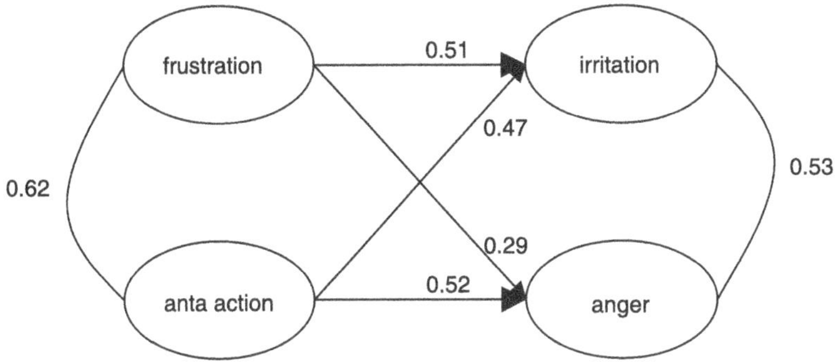

Figure 20.1 The latent person structure of anger and irritation and the corresponding feeling and action tendency.

antagonistic action tendency for irritation, whereas the action tendency is more important than frustration for anger. The dominance of frustration for irritation is not very strong, but the dominance of the antagonistic action tendency for anger is strong indeed.

In a similar way, the two hypotheses were supported for the structure with latent situation variables (see Figure 20.2). Frustration and the antagonistic action tendency had an effect on irritation, of .52 and .39 respectively, and both effects were highly significant ($p < .001$). Frustration and antagonistic action tendency had an effect on anger, of .54 and .87 respectively, and these two effects were also highly significant ($p < .001$). The dominance of frustration for irritation is slightly stronger in this second structure, and the dominance of the antagonistic action tendency for anger is again very strong. Because the goodness of fit was better for Model b than for Model c, it may be concluded that the two structures are different, although they both are in line with the hypothesis. In sum, anger and irritation can be differentiated in both structures, but slightly better in the situation-based structure.

It is worth mentioning that the correlation between frustration and the antagonistic action tendency in the person-based structure is .62, and that the correlation in the same structure between the residuals of frustration and anger is .53. This latter correlation is still rather high, which means that the relation between irritation and anger is far from totally explained by the effect of the latent frustration and antagonistic person variables. Similar correlations cannot be estimated for the latent situation variables because they are modeled with fixed effects.

Discussion

The results of the application are in line with the hypotheses. Clearly, irritation and anger share the components of frustration and an antagonistic action tendency, so that it makes sense that they have been considered as

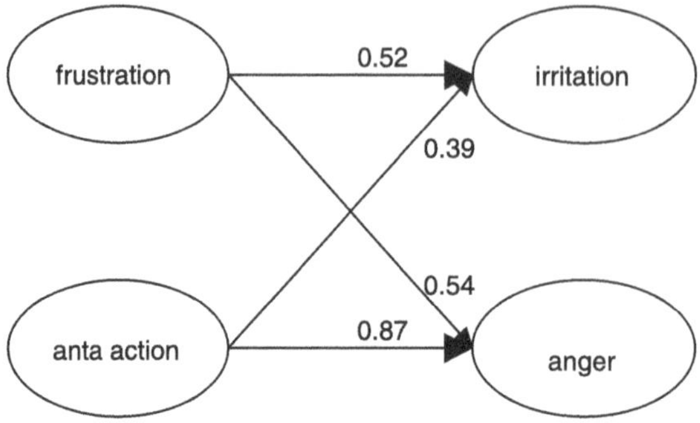

Figure 20.2 The latent situation structure of anger and irritation and the corresponding feeling and action tendency (because fixed effects were used, there are no correlation parameters as in Figure 20.1).

closely similar if not equivalent emotions. On the other hand, the two shared components are also a basis for a meaningful qualitative difference. As expected, irritation seems to be more feeling based, whereas anger seems more action based. It would be interesting to study more of such pairs of emotions, or to find out for a broader set of emotions how much they are feeling based and action based.

The finding that the situational structure differentiates emotions slightly better than the personal structure is not surprising, given the results reported by Fontaine et al. (in press) and by Vansteelandt et al. (2005), and given our general conjectures concerning the structure of individual differences and situational differences.

General discussion

Although it is common practice in psychology to approach psychological concepts and theories with a correlational method or with an experimental method, it is interesting to combine the two, as is done by Sternberg (1977) for example, for the study of intelligence, and more in general, to have an eye for both individual and situational differences. We have shown how the structure of both types of differences can be separated in one common model, a double-structure structural equation model.

The specific variant we have used does not allow for person by situation interactions, whereas this kind of interaction may seem quite plausible. Note that Equation 20.5 does leave room for such an interaction, and that it is a natural extension of the model we used. An investigation of this extension is planned, especially with respect to estimation, because for high-dimensional structures, the extension implies a lot of parameters

We have not paid much attention thus far to a third possible structure, which is the within-person structure. The model we have formulated implies that the within-person structure is the same as the situation-based structure. In the case of a design with the situations nested within persons, as in the experience sampling design, it is also assumed that the within-person structure is the same for all persons (Vansteelandt et al., 2005). However, it is possible that individual persons differ as to how the variables are structured. This kind of individual differences would require a very complex modeling, for example with the parameters of the structural model (the ωs and the λs) as latent person variables. This would be a nice extension, but unfortunately there would be no solid basis for the estimation of the parameters, unless some strong restrictions were imposed or a very large set of situations used.

Although it is certainly of interest to study the person-based structure and the situation-based structure simultaneously, the appropriate data for a fully crossed design are not without drawbacks, and the data analysis is complex. Perhaps the most serious problem is the ecological validity of the situations. A possible solution is to work with a group of persons who all share a set of situations in their daily life. It would require a thorough preliminary study to obtain such a list, but it is perhaps worth pursuing this line of investigation, or looking for alternatives to improve the fully crossed design. The motivation for such an endeavor could be that with an integration of the two disciplines of psychology one can avoid one-sided conclusions and prevent confusions in research findings stemming from different approaches.

References

Averill, J.R. (1982). *Anger and aggression: An essay on emotion.* New York: Springer-Verlag.

Averill, J.R. (1983). Studies on anger and aggression: Implications for theories of emotion. *American Psychologist, 38*, 1145–1160.

Bolger, N., Davis, A., & Rafaeli, E. (2003). Diary methods: Capturing life as it is lived. *Annual Review of Psychology, 54*, 579–616.

Borsboom, D., Mellenbergh, G., & van Heerden, J. (2003). The theoretical status of latent variables. *Psychological Review, 110*, 203–219.

Butter, R., De Boeck, P., & Verhelst, N.D. (1998). An item response model with internal restrictions on item difficulty. *Psychometrika, 63*, 1–17.

Cattell, R.B. (1946). *Description and measurement of personality.* New York: World Book Co.

Cattell, R.B. (1952). *Factor analysis: An introduction and manual for the psychologist and social scientist.* New York: Harper.

Cronbach, L.J. (1957). The two disciplines of scientific psychology. *American Psychologist, 12*, 672–684.

De Boeck, P., & Wilson, M. (2004). A framework for item response models. In P. De Boeck & M. Wilson (Eds.), *Explanatory item response models. A generalized linear and nonlinear approach* (pp. 3–41). New York: Springer.

Delespaul, P.A.E.G. (1995). *Assessing schizophrenia in daily life. The experience sampling method.* Maastricht: Universitaire Pers Maastricht.

Ekman, P. (1992). An argument for basic emotions. *Cognition and Emotion, 6*, 169–200.

Ellsworth, P.C., & Smith, C.A. (1988). From appraisal to emotion: Differences among unpleasant feelings. *Motivation and Emotion, 12*, 271–303.

Endler, N.S., & Hunt, J.McV. (1966). Sources of behavioral variance as measured by the S-R inventory of anxiousness. *Psychological Bulletin, 65*, 336–346.

Endler, N.S., & Hunt, J.McV. (1969). S-R inventories of hostility and comparisons of the proportions of variance from persons, responses and situations for hostility and anxiousness. *Journal of Personality and Social Psychology, 37*, 1–24.

Fontaine, J.R.J., Luyten, P., De Boeck, P., Corveleyn, J., Fernandez, M., Herrera, D. et al. (in press). Untying the gordian knot of guilt and shame: The structure of guilt and shame reactions based on situation and person variation in Belgium, Hungary, and Peru. *Journal of Cross-Cultural Psychology*.

Frijda, N.H. (1986). *The emotions*. Cambridge: University Press.

Frijda, N.H., Kuipers, P., & ter Schure, E. (1989). Relations among emotion, appraisal, and emotional action readiness. *Journal of Personality and Social Psychology, 57*, 212–228.

Gidron, Y., Stewart, S.H., Ben-Zur, H., & Breznitz, S. (1998). Situational and individual-difference correlates of annoyance extent and variability in daily provocations. *British Journal of Health Psychology, 3*, 123–135.

Izard, C.E. (1977). *Human emotions*. New York: Plenum Press.

Izard, C.E. (1992). Basic emotions, relations among emotions, and emotion–cognition relations. *Psychological Review, 99*, 561–565.

Janssen, R., Schepers, J., & Peres, D. (2004). Models with item and item group predictors. In P. De Boeck & M. Wilson (Eds.), *Explanatory item response models. A generalized linear and nonlinear approach* (pp. 189–212). New York: Springer.

Johnson-Laird, P.N., & Oatley, K. (1989). The language of emotions: An analysis of a semantic field. *Cognition and Emotion, 3*, 81–123.

Kuppens, P., Van Mechelen, I., Smits, D.J.M., & De Boeck, P. (2003). The appraisal basis of anger: Specificity, necessity and sufficiency of components. *Emotion, 3*, 254–269.

Larsen, R.J., & Ketelaar, T. (1989). Extraversion, neuroticism and susceptibility to positive and negative mood induction procedures. *Personality and Individual Differences, 10*, 1221–1228.

Ortony, A., Clore, G.L., & Collins, A. (1988). *The cognitive structure of emotions*. New York: Cambridge University Press.

Rosch, E. (1975). Cognitive representations of semantic categories. *Journal of Experimental Psychology: General, 104*, 192–233.

Russell, J.A. (1980). A circumplex model of affect. *Journal of Personality and Social Psychology, 39*, 1161–1178.

SAS Institute. (1999). *SAS online Doc (Version 8)* [software manual on CD-ROM]. Cary, NC: SAS Institute Inc.

Scherer, K.R. (1993). Studying the emotion-antecedent appraisal process: An expert system approach. *Cognition and Emotion, 7*, 325–355.

Scherer, K.R. (2001). Appraisal considered as a process of multilevel sequential checking. In K.R. Scherer, A. Schorr, & T. Johnstone (Eds.), *Appraisal processes in emotion: Theory, methods, research* (pp. 92–120). New York: Oxford University Press.

Schwartz, J.E., & Stone, A.A. (1998). Strategies for analyzing ecological momentary assessment data. *Health Psychology, 17*, 6–16.

Skiffington, S., Fernandez, E., & McFarland, K. (1998). Towards a validation of multiple features in the assessment of emotions. *European Journal of Psychological Assessment*, *14*, 202–210.

Skrondal, A., & Rabe-Hesketh, S. (2004). *Generalized latent variable modeling: Multilevel, longitudinal and structural equation models*. Boca Raton, FL: Chapman & Hall/CRC.

Smedslund, J. (1997). *The structure of psychological common sense*. Mahwah, NJ: Lawrence Erlbaum Associates Inc.

Smith, C.A., & Lazarus, R.S. (1993). Appraisal components, core relational themes, and the emotions. *Cognition and Emotion*, *7*, 233–269.

Spielberger, C.D., Jacobs, G.H., Russell, S.F., & Crane, R.S. (1983). Assessment of anger: the state-trait anger scale. In J.N. Butcher & C.D. Spielberger (Eds.), *Advances in personality assessment* (Vol. 2, pp. 20–36). Hillsdale, NJ: Lawrence Erlbaum Associates Inc.

Stein, N.L., & Oatley, K. (1992). Basic emotions: Theory and measurement. *Cognition and Emotion*, *6*, 161–168.

Sternberg, R.J. (1977). Component processes in analogical reasoning. *Psychological Review*, *84*, 353–378.

Underwood, B.J. (1975). Individual differences as a crucible in theory construction. *American Psychologist*, *30*, 128–134.

Van den Noortgate, W., De Boeck, P., & Meulders, M. (2003). Cross-classification multilevel logistic models in psychometrics. *Journal of Educational and Behavioral Statistics*, *28*, 369–386.

Vansteelandt, K., Van Mechelen, I., & Nezlek, J.B. (2005). The co-occurence of emotions in daily life: A multilevel approach. *Journal of Research in Personality*, *39*, 325–335.

Watson, D., Clark, L.A., & Tellegen, A. (1988). Development and validation of brief Measures of positive and negative affect: The PANAS scales. *Journal of Personality and Social Psychology*, *54*(6), 1063–1070.

Wierzbicka, A. (1992). Defining emotion concepts. *Cognitive Science*, *16*, 539–581.

Zelenski, J.M., & Larsen, R.J. (2000). The distribution of basic emotions in everyday life: A state and trait perspective from experience sampling data. *Journal of Research in Personality*, *34*, 178–197.

21 Language processing: Implications from the study of Chinese

Hsuan-Chih Chen

Language processing has concerned psychologists and cognitive researchers for a long time, not only because it reflects one of the most complex mental activities and has the potential to reveal the nature and uniqueness of human intelligence, but also because the ability to use language well is critical for academic and job success. This topic is also fundamental for scholars and specialists in other fields, such as educators concerned with language acquisition and teaching, computer scientists trying to use natural human language as a medium for both computer processing and human–machine interface, as well as neuroscientists and language therapists tackling different kinds of language disorders and their neurological causes.

There has been considerable progress over the past several decades in understanding the mental processes and representations involved in language use. However, it is important to note that most research on language and cognition has been conducted in English or other European languages, and only a very small amount has been addressed to non-European languages. This bias puts serious and unnecessary constraints on the development of a general theory of language processing for two obvious reasons (Chen, 1992, 1996).

Foremost, because there are remarkable differences between European and non-European languages, it is by no means self-evident that the same cognitive processes underlie both language groups (for relevant discussions and evidence see, e.g., Chen, 1996; Chen & Juola, 1982; Cheung, Chen, Lai, Wong, & Hills, 2001; Otake, Hatano, Cutler, & Mehler, 1993). Take written language as an example. Most European languages adopt an alphabetic writing system in which the main idea is to make the visual symbols (i.e., letters) correspond to basic units in speech (i.e., phonemes). There are, however, other scripts (e.g., Chinese) that have been developed following a logographic principle in which the individual symbols (i.e., characters) are made to represent basic units of meaning (i.e., morphemes). Given that various scripts are constructed on distinct principles and present linguistic information in diverse forms, it is not obvious whether the same mechanisms and conclusions relating to reading comprehension that have been drawn through studies with the alphabetic script can readily be generalized to the logographic script.

Furthermore, a theory of human language processing developed from a small set of similar languages cannot account for the processing roles played by linguistic properties not existing in that specific set of languages. For example, lexical tone is not used in European languages to distinguish utterances, but is used in some non-European languages such as Chinese and Thai. Hence, in order to gain knowledge about how tone is used in language processing, one has no choice but to study those tone languages.

Thus, to build a genuinely comprehensive theory of language processing, it is important and useful to carry out cross-language research. Among various non-European languages, Chinese is perhaps the most enduring and widely used. More importantly, the Chinese language, due to its salient differences in structure from European languages, provides challenging opportunities to explore both language-specific processes involved in comprehension and communication, and the universality of theories developed from the study of European languages. Hence, selected recent studies on processing Chinese are reviewed in this chapter, and their implications for the general understanding of human language processing are discussed. Note, however, that not all aspects of processing Chinese are covered in this chapter. Rather, the focus is on lexical processing because this topic is fundamental in the study of psycholinguistics, and is also the most extensively studied.

There are five main parts to this chapter. The first one presents a short review of the main properties of the Chinese language, focusing specifically on those related to lexical processing. The second part describes some recent studies on how a peculiar characteristic of spoken Chinese (i.e., lexical tone) is processed. The third turns to visual encoding in reading. The succeeding section is on the processes involved in semantic access. The final section discusses the roles of words in language processing.

Some general properties of the Chinese language

Spoken Chinese actually consists of a family of different dialects, including, for example, those used in the northern part of China (e.g., Mandarin), in the southern area (e.g., Cantonese or Yue, Min, and Hakka), and in the central part (e.g., Wu, Xiang, and Gan). Although these dialects may differ from one another to a dramatic extent (i.e., being mutually unintelligible), they share certain common properties (e.g., lexical tone) and can be represented using the same logographic writing system.

The most well-known property of Chinese dialects is lexical tone (i.e., a contrastive pitch pattern realized on a syllable). While some European languages (e.g., English) use such prosodic features as stress to distinguish utterances, Chinese dialects typically use tone for the same purpose. It is important to note, however, that stress is usually not lexically distinctive. Even when stress is used to distinguish lexical items as in Dutch or English, it is hardly the case that stress alone accomplishes the task of lexical distinction. A very different picture can be seen in Chinese – a lexically distinctive function can be served by the tone itself without involving any aspect of segmental difference.

Note that monosyllables are distinct phonological units of spoken Chinese because they almost always represent morphemes and can therefore be written down with individual logographic characters. In addition, the shape of Chinese syllables generally exemplifies a relatively simple structure (Chen, 2001; Cheung et al., 2001). Two factors contribute to the overall simple syllable structure relative to many European languages. First, there are severe restrictions with respect to how individual sounds can possibly be combined in a Chinese syllable. For example, consecutive consonants may not appear in a syllable. Second, there is a large proportion of consonant–vowel open syllables in Chinese speech.

Similar to spoken Chinese, the Chinese script also has a number of notable properties. To begin, let us look at the layout of a Chinese text. Written Chinese is formed by arrays of little square symbols of equal size called characters. Each character is made up of single or multiple strokes, radicals (i.e., certain combinations of strokes), simple characters, or a certain combination of these components in a constant box-form region. Because different characters can vary in number of strokes, in number of radicals, or in manner of construction, the complexity of the characters can be very high.

Apart from being the fundamental building blocks of Chinese text, characters have the following peculiar properties (Chen, 1992, 1996). First, as mentioned above, Chinese characters are logographic in nature. However, the meaning of a character may not be transparent by itself and can be highly context dependent. This is because words in modern Chinese often comprise more than one single character, and the majority of characters can join others to form multiple-character words with distinctively different meanings. Second, many Chinese characters (over 80%) are actually compounds in the sense that they are formed by two components, namely the radical and the phonetic. The radical provides a categorical cue to the meaning of the character, whereas the phonetic may cue in an all-or-none fashion the pronunciation of the character as a whole. Note that the phonetic components in those compound characters are themselves characters having their own pronunciation (thus providing phonetic cues) and distinct meanings, but the radicals usually are not. Third, characters are monosyllabic in general. As there are many more characters that are commonly used (about 4500) than there are possible syllables (about 400, or 1300 including tones, in the most commonly used dialect, Mandarin), the degree of homophony in the language is very high. Finally, characters are distinct orthographic units in Chinese well known to and widely used by the users of the language. In fact, individual characters are the primary objects of learning when users of the Chinese script start learning how to read and write.

Lexical tone in speech processing

Thus far we have reviewed some striking properties of the Chinese language. The question to consider now is: How are the peculiar properties of the language such as lexical tone processed in speech perception?

Languages use two types of prosodic information (i.e., stress and tone) to distinguish utterances. The experimental evidence available in stress languages such as English suggests that while stress information contributes to lexical segmentation in processing continuous speech (e.g., Cutler & Butterfield, 1992), it is not crucial in lexical access (Cutler, 1986; Cutler & Clifton, 1984). For instance, Cutler (1986) reported that hearing either one of two words differing only in stress (e.g., *FORebear* or *forBEAR*) facilitates the recognition of words related to either of them (e.g., *ancestor* or *tolerate*). It is then not too surprising to find that prosodic information is usually ignored and only segmental information is considered in modeling spoken-word recognition dealing with European languages (e.g., Marslen-Wilson, Moss, & van Halen, 1996; McClelland & Elman, 1986; Norris, 1994).

Note that in stress languages like English, there are very few words where prosodic information is crucial in identification. Thus, English listeners can afford to rely solely on segmental information in lexical access simply because the cost involved in ignoring prosodic information is negligible. However, the situation is very different in tone languages such as Mandarin and Cantonese, where words differing only in tone are not uncommon at all. Thus, it is interesting and important to examine how prosodic information (i.e., lexical tone in this case), relative to segmental information, is processed in tone languages.

To probe the role of tone in Cantonese spoken-word processing, Cutler and Chen (1997) conducted a series of experiments using both lexical decision and syllable comparison tasks. They found that Cantonese listeners often made errors in lexical decision when the only difference between nonwords and real words was in tone, and they relied more heavily on segmental than tonal information in making same–different judgments on two consecutively presented syllables. In addition, the disadvantage for tone on syllable comparison was more pronounced for both Cantonese and non-Cantonese (Dutch) listeners when the difference in the onset of fundamental frequency between correct and incorrect tone was relatively small. These results led Cutler and Chen to conclude that (a) although tonal information participates fully in lexical access for Cantonese listeners, it seems to become available later than does the corresponding segmental information (the vowel) upon which the tone is realized, and (b) the observed disadvantage for tone is probably determined by the acoustic, rather than linguistic, properties of stimuli and the requirement of speeded responses in the tasks adopted.

A similar advantage for segmental information over tone in processing Chinese has been reported by Ye and Connine (1999) using a target (syllable, vowel, or tone) monitoring task with Mandarin listeners. These researchers further demonstrated that the disadvantage for tone disappears with the presence of strong contextual information as in idioms, indicating that when dealing with stimuli resembling more closely those used in daily life situations, tone and vowel contribute equally to speech processing.

There are, however, two points in the studies described above (i.e., Cutler & Chen, 1997; Ye & Connine, 1999) that deserve attention. First, semantic processing is an essential component in natural language processing, but the tasks adopted in the reviewed studies do not require the use of semantic information. Second, the behavioral data collected in those studies may not be sensitive enough to reveal the time course of tone and segmental processing. Thus, it is not clear whether their findings can be generalized to speech comprehension in more natural situations. Fortunately, a recent event related potential (ERP) study conducted and reported by Schirmer, Tang, Penney, Gunter, and Chen (2005) is free from these limitations. Specifically, their subjects listened to sentences and were asked to decide whether each sentence was semantically congruous or not. Semantically incongruous sentences contained a word (the target word) that did not fit into the sentence context because its tone, rime, or both differed from the congruous word. The results showed that semantic violations induced by tonal and segmental mismatches produced highly comparable results. These results indicate that the two types of information play an equivalent role and have a similar time course during Cantonese speech comprehension.

In contrast to the finding in European languages that the role of prosodic information such as stress is restricted to segmentation and is insignificant for lexical activation, the reviewed studies on processing of lexical tone clearly reveal that prosodic information can play a crucial role and contributes fully to lexical access in tone languages. Thus, it appears that the role of prosodic information in speech processing is language specific and should not be overlooked in theorizing about spoken word processing.

Visual encoding in reading

After seeing the processing of tonal information in speech, we now turn to look at the way in which visual information is extracted from the text. Given that the physical layout of logographic Chinese is strikingly different from that of alphabetic systems such as English, it is interesting to know how visual encoding is done in reading Chinese.

Text written in an alphabetic system is typically formed by strings of words of various lengths and shapes. Since the alphabetic words separated by spaces differ greatly along the horizontal dimension, even for people who are naïve to the alphabetic system, it is obvious that the text is arranged horizontally. In other words, the layout of an alphabetic text provides many visual-spatial cues along the horizontal dimension to its readers. In contrast, Chinese text is constructed by arrays of little square symbols of equal size called characters. For each character, there are many visual details packed in a constant, square-shaped area. An obvious consequence of characters with relatively high construction complexity is that recognizing characters may need to be done in the center of vision, because visual acuity rapidly drops off from the fixation points. Given that all Chinese characters take a constant space in print, they can be freely arranged either horizontally or vertically, and the characters themselves provide no clue to indicate the overall organization of the print.

A main issue in the study of visual encoding in reading concerns the size and shape of the effective visual field (also called "perceptual span") in which useful information can be obtained during a single fixation. Past research on this topic (e.g., Rayner, Well, Pollatsek, & Bertera, 1982) indicates that in reading English, the effective visual field is skewed in the direction of scanning, and extends about 15 letter spaces to the right of the current fixation and about 4 letter spaces to the left. A similar pattern can also be seen in reading Chinese text printed in a horizontal format from left to right. Indeed, recent studies on reading Chinese have shown that the effective visual field is also asymmetrical, though it is very limited in size, composing the fixated character and about two to three characters to its right (Chen & Tang, 1998; Inhoff & Liu, 1997).

Note, however, that the size of the right-side perceptual span is very similar to the average size of forward saccades in reading Chinese (i.e., about 2.6 character spaces, according to Chen, Song, Lau, Wong, & Tang, 2003). In other words, each successive fixation brings in the maximum amount of new information in reading Chinese. This stands in sharp contrast to the situation in reading English. According to McConkie and Rayner (1975), the average forward saccade in reading English is about seven to eight letter spaces, but the perceptual span extends to about 15 letter spaces to the right of a fixation. Thus, there is substantial overlap (up to about 50%) between the to-be-fixated-side areas of successive spans in reading English.

Another point that is worth mentioning here concerns the developmental pattern of visual encoding in reading. In general, a typical finding on this topic is that children tend to make shorter saccades, longer fixations, and more regressions than skilled adult readers. However, there are notable differences between the patterns of eye movements in reading text printed in different scripts. For instance, the length of forward saccades and the regression rate continue to change from primary school to college in reading English (Rayner, 1978; Taylor, 1965). However, these two aspects of eye movements do not show much change as children become more proficient in reading Chinese, and indeed have stabilized by the end of primary school (Chen et al., 2003). Thus, it appears that there is more room for improvement in mastering the control of eye movements in reading alphabetic text than in reading logographic Chinese where the layout is extremely symmetrical.

The finding that both the perceptual span and the size of overlap in successive spans in Chinese are smaller than those in English is striking but not really very surprising. This is because the visual encoding pattern in reading

Chinese can be related in meaningful ways to the layout properties of written Chinese discussed above. These properties include: (1) that the visual complexity of Chinese characters is relatively high, and (2) that there is very limited parafoveal information available in written Chinese. In addition to the layout factors, another factor responsible for the specific pattern of visual encoding in Chinese is informational density. It is known that informational density is related to the reader's saccade length in reading, because saccade length decreases as the text becomes more difficult (Rayner & Pollatsek, 1989). The informational density in Chinese is relatively high, compared to that in English and other European languages. This is because, unlike in many alphabetic scripts, various forms of syntactic information such as inflectional markings and intrasentential concordance rules are usually absent in the Chinese text itself, and need instead to be inferred from the meanings of individual words and the sequence of words in text. Hence, Chinese sentences are relatively less redundant and often comprise fewer words than do their English equivalents.

In sum, the evidence available suggests that although there are common patterns of eye movements across scripts, readers of Chinese are capable of displaying unique patterns of eye movements. The pattern of visual encoding in Chinese appears to have its basis in the important differences of the layout of written Chinese from that of alphabetic scripts. This clearly suggests that how information is extracted from a printed page can indeed be affected by language-specific factors of the written language.

Phonological and orthographic processing in semantic access

In the literature, several different hypotheses have been proposed to account for how a visually presented word is processed for comprehension. For example, the phonological mediation hypothesis postulates that a printed word is first transformed to phonology and then the meaning of the word is accessed by the phonological representation (Frost, 1998; Lukatela & Turvey, 1991; Rubenstein, Lewis, & Rubenstein, 1971; Van Orden, 1987). In contrast, the direct access hypothesis argues that comprehension is accomplished mainly by a direct connection between orthography and semantics, and the mediation of phonology is not required in this process (Baron, 1973; Daneman & Reingold, 1993). Alternatively, the dual-route hypothesis proposes that both phonological mediation and direct visual path are possible ways of semantic access (Coltheart, 1980).

However, although a great deal of effort has been devoted to investigating the issue of semantic access in visual word recognition, past research using English or other alphabetic scripts as stimuli has failed to produce a consistent pattern of results. For instance, using a semantic categorization task, Van Orden (1987) demonstrated that homophonic distractors (e.g., *rows*, which is a homophone of a real exemplar of the category *flower*) were more likely to be misclassified as correct exemplars, compared to unrelated controls.

Given that the semantic categorization task presumably does not require any use of phonology, Van Orden's result thus seems to suggest that phonology is automatically activated in the recognition of visually presented English words. Yet there is evidence to show that phonological properties such as regularity affect performance in a naming task, which clearly requires the use of phonology, but not in the semantic categorization task (Taft & van Graan, 1998).

A similar picture can also be seen in studies investigating word recognition in context. For example, it has been shown that reading either a homophonic distractor (e.g., *hare*, which is homophonic to a contextually appropriate word *hair*) or a non-homophonic control distractor (*hire*) in a passage is equally disruptive, as reflected by the pattern of gaze durations (Daneman, Reingold, & Davidson, 1995). However, there are also findings that reading homophonic distractors is less disruptive than reading non-homophonic controls (Rayner, Pollatsek, & Binder, 1998).

It is not clear why the results in alphabetic scripts concerning the role of phonology in semantic access are so inconsistent. One possible reason is that orthography and phonology in most alphabetic scripts are closely related and thus cannot be totally unconfounded. However, a similar confounding between orthography and phonology is absent in those languages such as Chinese in which a logographic script is used. Therefore, written Chinese provides a unique opportunity to examine the role of orthography and phonology in semantic access and the existence of the direct access from orthography to meaning.

To probe lexical activation during the recognition of Chinese characters, a number of studies have been conducted. Interestingly, although Chinese characters are logographic in nature and the Chinese language has a highly opaque symbol-to-sound correspondence and a high degree of homophony, there are findings to indicate that phonological activation can be associated with the recognition of Chinese characters. However, it has been shown that some of the phonological effects found in Chinese are due to task demand (i.e., such tasks as naming characters aloud or making homophony decisions demand the use of phonological information; see, e.g., Shen & Forster, 1999, for relevant findings and discussions). In addition, some of the other findings of phonological effects (e.g., Perfetti & Tan, 1998; Tan & Perfetti, 1997) have proven difficult to replicate (e.g., Chen & Shu, 2001; Wu & Chou, 2000; Zhou & Marslen-Wilson, 1999). Furthermore, there is good evidence to indicate that for skilled adult readers, although phonology can possibly be activated in the course of character identification, orthography rather than phonology plays a more crucial role in recognizing Chinese characters either in isolation (e.g., Chen, Flores d'Arcais, & Cheung, 1995; Chen & Shu, 2001; Chen & Zhou, 1999; Leck, Weekes, & Chen, 1995; Shen & Forster, 1999; Zhou & Marslen-Wilson, 1999) or in text (Feng, Miller, Shu, & Zhang, 2001; Wong & Chen, 1999).

For example, Chen et al. (1995) adopted the semantic categorization task, similar to the one in English used by Van Orden (1987), to study semantic processing in Chinese. Their participants made more errors and longer categorization latencies on orthographically similar foils than on the corresponding controls, whereas no reliable phonological effect was found with homophonic foils. A similar pattern of results has also been reported in reading Chinese text. For instance, using the error disruption task of Daneman et al. (1995), Feng et al. (2001) investigated the activation and use of phonological information in reading passages written in Chinese and English. They found that early phonology could sometimes be shown in English, but not in Chinese. Apart from this, they also discovered that homophonic distractors produced facilitation in those measures (e.g., total reading time on the target word) that reflect later post-lexical stages of operations in both languages. These results are in line with the findings and suggestions of Wong and Chen (1999) that orthography plays an early and dominant role in semantic access of Chinese characters, whereas phonology contributes to the later stages of processing in reading (e.g., error recovery).

On the basis of the findings in Chinese, it seems reasonable to conclude that the direct visual route to lexical access does exist, and that phonological mediation is unlikely to be a universal principle for semantic access especially in logographic scripts such as Chinese.

The role of words in language processing

Contemporary theories of language processing unexceptionally consider words as the basis of complex comprehension processes. Indeed, a common assumption, shared by both reading researchers (e.g., Rayner & Pollatsek, 1989) and those who study speech (e.g., Marslen-Wilson & Tyler, 1980), is that the process of language comprehension is basically word-by-word. This is hardly surprising because, after all, words are units that are widely used in daily life and are transparent units for users of European languages. For example, individual words are listed as basic entries in dictionaries and word boundaries are explicitly marked by spaces in writing. It is therefore no wonder that, among various topics in language processing, how words are processed is by far the most extensively investigated.

It is worthwhile to note, however, that words are not transparent units in other languages such as Chinese. In fact, users of the Chinese language have only very vague ideas about what a word is (Chao, 1968). This is in line with the finding that there is considerable disagreement concerning what are word boundaries in simple sentences, even among skilled readers of Chinese (Hoosain, 1992). To understand why this is the case, we need to look at the basic properties of Chinese words.

Words in Chinese can be made up of one or more characters (or syllables in the case of spoken Chinese). In other words, the size of a Chinese word is not constant. In addition, even for highly skilled adult readers, identifying individual words in written Chinese may not be a simple and straightforward matter, because word boundaries are not explicitly marked by extra spacing in writing. Take the sentence 他喜歡打高爾夫球, meaning *he likes playing golf*, as an example. It is not possible to know, on the basis of spacing, that the sentence is formed by two single-character words (他 and 打, *he* and *playing*), a two-character word (喜歡, *likes*), and a four-character word (高爾夫球). Furthermore, Chinese words generally have neither explicit markers nor inflectional indicators to specify various kinds of information such as grammatical categories, number, gender, case, tense, and aspect. Thus, words in Chinese are not as salient and obvious as those in European languages.

Given the properties of Chinese words mentioned above, it is sensible to consider the role of words in Chinese. To this end, let us examine some studies on how words are processed in Chinese.

Chen (1987) reported an experiment in which participants were asked to read Chinese sentences and to perform a character detection task (i.e., to respond to the occurrence of a given character while reading a sentence for comprehension). The results showed a clear word superiority effect, in the sense that response latencies were significantly longer and detection errors were larger when a target character was part of a two-character nonword than when it was part of a two-character word. This striking result stands in strong contrast to both the word inferiority effect in English (e.g., Healy & Drewnowski, 1983) and the character inferiority effect in Chinese (Chen, 1984).

In the study of Healy and Drewnowski (1983), they asked people to read a prose passage and to detect every instance of a target letter (e.g., *t*), and found that many more letter detection errors were made on words (e.g., *the*) than on misspelled, and consequently meaningless words (e.g., *thd*). These results indicate that words can be better perceived than letters and the basic encoding unit in processing written English is the word, and not the letter. Similarly, Chen (1984) reported a character inferiority effect in reading Chinese text using a component detection task, by which more detection errors were found when a target component was embedded in genuine characters than in pseudo-characters. Following the logic of Healy and Drewnowski, characters are important encoding units in Chinese, but not character components.

In the context of Healy and Drewnowski (1983) and Chen (1984), we can now consider the implications of the word superiority effect in Chinese mentioned above (Chen, 1987). If the word were the most prominent unit of Chinese reading, one would expect to find a word inferiority effect similar to that in English rather than a word superiority effect. This is because the word-level processing should enjoy a higher priority than the character-level processing, and the word context should create an effect disruptive to the character detection task. However, what was found in the literature of reading Chinese text was the word superiority (and character inferiority) effect, rather than the word inferiority effect. The findings in reading Chinese (Chen, 1984, 1987), therefore, imply that Chinese words are not likely to serve as important encoding units, as is the case for alphabetic words or Chinese characters in reading.

Further evidence for the view that the Chinese character rather than the Chinese word plays a more distinctive role in Chinese reading was provided by Chen et al. (2003). In this study, eye-movement patterns in reading Chinese text were collected from both skilled adult readers and three groups of children (second-, fourth-, and sixth-graders). A multiple-regression approach was adopted to relate different measures of eye movements (e.g., fixation durations, regression rates, and skipping rates) to properties of the individual character at various levels of linguistic structure (i.e., character, word, sentence, and text). The basic idea behind this approach is that readers perform a wide variety of analyses at different levels during reading for comprehension. Consequently, variables at each of the different levels work as a whole to affect the reader's cognitive load and are manifested at various measures of eye movements.

Using the multiple-regression approach, a common finding in studies of English is that both word- and sentence-level variables (e.g., word frequency and length) show robust effects on fixation times on words (Haberlandt & Graesser, 1985; Just & Carpenter, 1980). However, a different picture is seen in the Chinese data (Chen et al., 2003). Specifically, for the skilled adult readers, the basic properties of words do not generally produce significant effects on various eye-movement measures. In contrast, character-level variables have consistently shown a reliable impact on the data. The most striking result for the children, however, is that there is a developmental shift from a word-dominant pattern to a character-dominant pattern. For the second-graders, the word-level variables produced some reliable effects on various indices, whereas the effects of character-level variables were negligible in general. The sixth-graders, on the other hand, showed a pattern similar to the adults, while the pattern for the fourth-graders was in between the two extremes. These results clearly suggest that Chinese characters, rather than words, are prominent units of encoding during reading for comprehension. The results further suggest that although characters are orthographically distinctive, noticing their prominence in the Chinese script and being able to extract the various sorts of information provided by individual characters are not easy and obvious at all for beginners, but are skills that take time to build up in learning to read Chinese.

In summary, we have seen that without being explicitly marked in text, Chinese words themselves are not notable units in visual encoding, as with Chinese characters or alphabetic words in reading. In addition to visual encoding, Chinese characters can also contribute to overall comprehension in the sense that when the characters serve as part of a multiple-character word, they promote the identification of that word especially if their meaning relates to the overall concept of the word, whereas when they themselves are words (i.e., single-character words), they serve as basic processing units in syntactic and semantic analyses (see, e.g., Chen, 1999; Chen, Cheung, Tang,

& Wong, 2000). However, characters are typically morphemes, but not words. In fact, some Chinese studies on issues related to reading comprehension have shown that character-based eye-movement data were not as sensitive to certain linguistic manipulations as word-based measures were (Feng et al., 2001; Wong & Chen, 1999). It appears that, though not serving as the major unit of perception, Chinese words do play an important role in comprehension processes, especially in higher-level analyses such as syntactic parsing and integration, just as words in alphabetic systems are used. Thus, the idea that all processes of language comprehension are essentially word-by-word is called into question. The research in Chinese indicates clearly that at least in visual encoding, characters (morphemes), rather than words, are more prominent units of processing.

Conclusions

The results obtained from the cognitive studies of the Chinese language complement the studies that have proved the perceptual and cognitive mechanisms that are involved in the use of European languages. Together these studies on distinctively different languages provide valuable insights into the formation of a genuinely comprehensive theory of human language processing.

Given that there is good evidence to show that language-specific properties can indeed affect various kinds of comprehension processes, some revision of the theory of language processing developed on the basis of English and/or a small group of European languages is in order. However, although there has been an upsurge of interest in recent years in conducting cognitive research across different languages, systematic study of languages with distinctive structures has only just begun. Much work remains to be done. Hence, identifying universal principles and language-specific processes should continue to be a challenge to researchers in the twenty-first century and beyond.

Acknowledgements

This work was supported by direct grants for research from the Social Science and Education Panel of the Chinese University of Hong Kong (2020718 & 2020767) and a grant from the Research Grants Council of the Hong Kong Special Administrative Region, China (Project No. CUHK4142/04H).

References

Baron, J. (1973). Phonemic stage not necessary for reading: Lexical access and/or production? *Quarterly Journal of Experimental Psychology*, *25*, 241–246.

Chao, Y.R. (1968). *A grammar of spoken Chinese*. Berkeley, CA: University of California Press.

Chen, H.-C. (1984). Detecting radical components of Chinese characters in visual reading. *Chinese Journal of Psychology*, *26*, 29–34.

Chen, H.-C. (1987). Character detection in reading Chinese: Effects of context and display format. *Chinese Journal of Psychology*, *29*, 45–50.

Chen, H.-C. (1992). Reading comprehension in Chinese: Some implications from character reading times. In H.-C. Chen & O. Tzeng (Eds.), *Language processing in Chinese* (pp. 175–205). Amsterdam: North-Holland (Elsevier).

Chen, H.-C. (1996). Chinese reading and comprehension: A cognitive psychology perspective. In M.H. Bond (Ed.), *Handbook of Chinese psychology* (pp. 43–62). Hong Kong: Oxford University Press.

Chen, H.-C. (1999). How do readers of Chinese process words during reading for comprehension? In J. Wang, A.W. Inhoff, & H.-C. Chen (Eds.), *Reading Chinese script: A cognitive analysis* (pp. 257–278). Mahwah, NJ: Lawrence Erlbaum Associates Inc.

Chen, H.-C. (2001). Speech processing in Chinese: An introduction. *Journal of Psychology in Chinese Societies*, *2*, 155–158.

Chen, H.-C., Cheung, H., Tang, S.L., & Wong, Y.T. (2000). Effects of antecedent order and semantic context on Chinese pronoun resolution. *Memory & Cognition*, *28*, 427–438.

Chen, H.-C., Flores d'Arcais, G.B., & Cheung, S.L. (1995). Orthographic and phonological activation in recognizing Chinese characters. *Psychological Research*, *58*, 144–153.

Chen, H.-C. & Juola, J.F. (1982). Dimensions of lexical coding in Chinese and English. *Memory and Cognition*, *10*, 216–224.

Chen, H.-C. & Shu, H. (2001). Lexical activation during the recognition of Chinese characters: Evidence against early phonological activation. *Psychonomic Bulletin and Review*, *8*, 511–8.

Chen, H.-C., Song, H., Lau, W.Y., Wong, K.F.E., & Tang, S.L. (2003). Developmental characteristics of eye movements in reading Chinese. In C. McBride-Chang & H.-C. Chen (Eds.), *Reading development in Chinese children* (pp. 157–169). Westport, CT: Praeger.

Chen, H.-C., & Tang, C.K. (1998). The effective visual field in reading Chinese. *Reading and Writing*, *10*, 245–254.

Chen, H.-C., & Zhou, X. (1999). Processing East Asian languages. *Language and Cognitive Processes*, *14*, 425–428.

Cheung, H., Chen, H.-C., Lai, C.Y., Wong, O.C., & Hills, M. (2001). The development of phonological awareness: Effects of speech experience, orthography, and literacy. *Cognition*, *81*, 227–241.

Coltheart, M. (1980). Reading phonological recoding and deep dyslexia. In M. Coltheart, K. Patterson, & J.C. Marshal (Eds.), *Deep dyslexia* (pp. 197–226). London: Routledge & Kegan Paul.

Cutler, A. (1986). Forbear is a homophone: Lexical prosody does not constrain lexical access. *Language and Speech*, *29*, 201–220.

Cutler, A., & Butterfield, S. (1992). Rhythmic cues to speech segmentation: Evidence from juncture misperception. *Journal of Memory and Language*, *31*, 218–236.

Cutler, A., & Chen, H.-C. (1997). Lexical tone in Cantonese spoken-word processing. *Perception and Psychophysics*, *59*, 165–179.

Cutler, A., & Clifton, C.E. (1984). The use of prosodic inforamtion in word recognition. In H. Bouma & D.G. Bouwhuis (Eds.), *Attention and performance X: Control of language processes* (pp. 183–196), Hillsdale, NJ: Lawrence Erlbaum Associates Inc.

Daneman, M., & Reingold, E.M. (1993). What eye fixations tell us about phonological recoding during reading. *Canadian Journal of Experimental Psychology, 47*, 153–178.

Daneman, M., Reingold, E.M., & Davidson, M. (1995). Time course of phonological activation during reading: Evidence from eye fixations. *Journal of Experimental Psychology, 21*, 884–898.

Feng, G., Miller, K., Shu, H., & Zhang, H. (2001). Rowed to recovery: The use of phonological and orthographic information in reading Chinese and English. *Journal of Experimental Psychology: Learning, Memory, and Cognition, 27*, 1079–1100.

Frost, R. (1998). Toward a strong phonological theory of visual recognition: True issues and false trials. *Psychological Bulletin, 123*, 71–99.

Haberlandt, K.F., & Graesser, A.C. (1985). Component processes in text comprehension and some of their interactions. *Journal of Experimental Psychology: General, 114*, 357–374.

Healy, A.F., & Drewnowski, A. (1983). Investigating the boundaries of reading units. *Journal of Experimental Psychology: Human Perception and Performance, 9*, 413–426.

Hoosain, R. (1992). Psychological reality of the word in Chinese. In H.-C. Chen & O.J.L. Tzeng (Eds.), *Language processing in Chinese* (pp. 111–130). Amsterdam: Elsevier.

Inhoff, A.W., & Liu, W. (1997). The range of effective vision during the reading of Chinese sentences. In H.-C. Chen (Ed.), *Cognitive processing of Chinese and related Asian languages* (pp. 243–265). Hong Kong: Chinese University Press.

Just, M.A., & Carpenter, P.A. (1980). A theory of reading: From eye fixation to comprehension. *Psychological Review, 87*, 329–354.

Leck, K.J., Weekes, B.S., & Chen, M.-J. (1995). Visual and phonological pathways to the lexicon: Evidence from Chinese readers. *Memory, and Cognition, 23*, 468–476.

Lukatela, G., & Turvey, M.T. (1991). Phonological access of the lexicon: Evidence from associative priming with pseudohomophones. *Journal of Experimental Psychology: Human Perception and Performance, 17*, 951–966.

Marslen-Wilson, W.D., Moss, H.E., & van Halen, S. (1996). Perceptual distance and competition in lexical access. *Journal of Experimental Psychology: Human Perception and Performance, 22*, 1376–1392.

Marslen-Wilson, W.D., & Tyler, L.K. (1980). The temporal structure of spoken language understanding. *Cognition, 8*, 1–71.

McClelland, J.L., & Elman, J.L. (1986). The TRACE model of speech perception. *Cognitive Psychology, 18*, 1–86.

McConkie, G.W., & Rayner, K. (1975). The span of the effective stimulus during a fixation in reading. *Perception and Psychophysics, 17*, 578–586.

Norris, D. (1994). Shortlist: A connectionist model of continuous speech recognition. *Cognition, 52*, 189–234.

Otake, T., Hatano, G., Cutler, A., & Mehler, J. (1993). Mora or syllable? Speech segmentation in Japanese. *Journal of Memory and Language, 32*, 258–278.

Perfetti, C.A., & Tan, L.H. (1998). The time course of graphic, phonological, and semantic activation in Chinese character identification. *Journal of Experimental Psychology: Learning, Memory, and Cognition, 24*, 101–118.

Rayner, K. (1978). Eye movements in reading and information processing. *Psychological Bulletin, 85*, 618–660.

Rayner, K., & Pollatsek, A. (1989). *The psychology of reading*. Englewood Cliffs, NJ: Prentice Hall.

Rayner, K., Pollatsek, A., & Binder, K.S. (1998). Phonological codes and eye movements in reading. *Journal of Experimental Psychology: Learning, Memory, and Cognition*, *24*, 476–497.

Rayner, K., Well, A.D., Pollatsek, A., & Bertera, J.H. (1982). The availability of useful information to the right of fixation in reading. *Perception and Psychophysics*, *31*, 537–550.

Rubenstein, H., Lewis, S.S., & Rubenstein, M.A. (1971). Evidence for phonemic recording in visual word recognition. *Journal of Verbal Learning and Verbal Behavior*, *10*, 645–657.

Schirmer, A., Tang, S.-L., Penney, T.B., Gunter, T.C., & Chen, H.-C. (2005). Brain responses to segmentally and tonally induced semantic violations in Cantonese. *Journal of Cognitive Neuroscience*, *17*, 1–12.

Shen, D., & Forster, K.I. (1999). Masked phonological priming in reading Chinese words depends on the task. *Language and Cognitive Processes*, *14*, 429–459.

Taft, M., & van Graan, F. (1998). Lack of phonological mediation in a semantic categorization task. *Journal of Memory and Language*, *38*, 203–224.

Tan, L.H., & Perfetti, C.A. (1997). Visual Chinese character recognition: Does phonological information mediate access to meaning? *Journal of Memory and Language*, *37*, 41–57.

Taylor, S.E. (1965). Eye movements in reading: Facts and fallacies. *American Educational Research Journal*, *2*, 187–202.

Van Orden, G.C. (1987). A ROWS is a ROSE: Spelling, sound and reading. *Memory & Cognition*, *15*, 181–198.

Wong, K.F.E., & Chen, H.-C. (1999). Orthographic and phonological processing in reading Chinese. *Language and Cognitive Processes*, *14*, 461–480.

Wu, J.T., & Chou, T.L. (2000). The comparison of relative effects of semantic, homophonic, and graphic priming on Chinese character recognition and naming. *Acta Psychologica Sinica*, *32* (Suppl.), 34–41.

Ye, Y., & Connine, C.M. (1999). Processing spoken Chinese: The role of tone information. *Language and Cognitive Processes*, *14*, 609–630.

Zhou, X., & Marslen-Wilson, W. (1999). Phonology, orthography, and lexical semantic activation in reading Chinese. *Journal of Memory and Language*, *41*, 579–606.

22 Cognitive and neuroscience perspectives on speech and sign processing: Evidence from persons with deafness, hearing impairment, and normal hearing

Jerker Rönnberg

Introduction

The review assumes a broad perspective on working memory and working memory related cognitive functions primarily involved in visual communication. The purpose of this chapter is to use a comparative and contrastive approach to point to similarities and differences in the ways that working memory processes in particular are engaged in different modes of visual speech and sign understanding. As a result, a framework is proposed that focuses on the role of *sensory* and *language modality* in the formulation of a working memory system for processing of language, and the ease with which language understanding can be accomplished.

Terminology

Speech understanding

In this chapter, the term "speech understanding" refers to the process of unlocking the meaning of poorly specified or distorted auditory speech signals – whether they are provided through cochlear implants, tactile aids, or hearing aids, in conditions of speech understanding in noise, or as visual speech only – and implies that this process involves cognitive operations that facilitate inference making (Lidestam, 2003; Lyxell et al., 1998; Rönnberg et al., 1998a). Understanding speech implies extracting the meaning of a message, and sometimes also co-constructing meaning in an ongoing dialogue (Markova & Linell, 1996). On the whole, the general appraisal is that speech-understanding tests are more cognitively loaded than traditional speech-perception tests, which typically focus on tests to assess the phonetic level of speech (e.g., Bernstein, Demorest, & Tucker, 2000).

Speech-understanding tests typically involve the use of sentence materials and have the listener/speech-reader orally repeat the test items. When the test involves connected speech, the listener may be asked to rate the speech understanding (Cox & McDaniel, 1989), to adjust the speech-to-noise ratio to allow a certain degree of speech understanding (Gustafsson & Arlinger, 1994; Hawkins, Montgomery, Mueller, & Sedge, 1998; Hygge, Rönnberg, Larsby, & Arlinger, 1992), or even to engage in dialogues in laboratory format (Erber, 1998), and in more naturalistic procedures involving complex materials (Borg, 2003; Gagné, 2003; Rönnberg, Samuelsson, & Borg, 2000a). Thus, it becomes important to view speech understanding as an activity that capitalizes on a multitude of sources of information: sensory signals, linguistic and contextual factors, the acoustic environment in general, as well as the nonverbal gestures accompanying the dialogue (see Arnold, 1997).

Ease of language understanding (ELU)

"Ease" refers to how smoothly processing stages necessary for language understanding, signed or spoken, are conducted, without undue processing costs, delays, or misunderstandings. Ease is generally connected to performance in language-understanding tasks, but not always – processing costs can be compensated for if the individual is equipped with, e.g., a high working memory capacity (Rönnberg, 2003; see Lyxell, Andersson, Borg, & Ohlsson, 2003).

Deafness

When the term deafness is used throughout this article, it refers to persons with a congenital hearing loss (or a loss acquired before the development of language) that exceeds 90 dB hearing loss, who may or may not communicate using signed language. Visual speech understanding typically does not apply to individuals who are deaf. Rather, it applies to persons who have acquired a hearing loss postlingually, and we use the term persons with adventitious hearing impairment, or simply persons with hearing impairment to refer to these persons. Sign language users may be hearing or deaf native users, or just hearing signers.

Sensory modality and ease of speech understanding

Visual speech understanding

Spontaneous improvement of visual speech understanding in normal or adventitiously hearing-impaired persons is in general small or non-existent, even after many years of exposure to visual speech (Rönnberg, 1990). In other words, compensatory improvements in visual speech understanding in persons with hearing impairment – compared to a matched control group – are generally lacking (Boothroyd, 1988; Mogford, 1987). In fact, this general result can be observed regardless of type of presentation (video vs real-life; Rönnberg, Öhngren, & Nilsson, 1983), type of materials (digits vs discourse; Rönnberg et al., 1983), for just-follow conversation tasks (Hygge et al., 1992), and for different durations and magnitudes of hearing loss (e.g., Lyxell & Rönnberg, 1989; Rönnberg, 1990; Rönnberg, Öhngren, & Nilsson, 1982; Rönnberg et al., 1983). Therefore, putative compensatory improvement in visual speech understanding for persons with hearing impairment seems to be a cherished myth rather than a definite reality (Rönnberg, 1995b). However, the generalization is limited to adventitiously hearing-impaired persons and does not hold true for deaf individuals (Rönnberg, 2003), who may show compensatory visual phonetic perception abilities (Bernstein et al., 2000).

Cognitive predictors

Although later studies on deaf persons have demonstrated compensatory improvements (e.g.,Tillberg et al., 1996), a significant portion of the variance in speech understanding can be predicted by cognitive factors for both deaf and adventitiously hearing-impaired persons. However, most of these studies have focused on adventitiously hearing-impaired persons and the initial studies were simple single-factor attempts to explain visual speech understanding skill (see Jeffers & Barley, 1971). Current research supports the notion of multi-factor conceptualizations related to visual feature extraction/decoding and problem solving/guessing (Gailey, 1987; Lyxell, 1989). It has been shown that sentence-based visual speech understanding is related to skill at word-decoding tests (i.e., when the task demands meaning analysis as opposed to mere discrimination of visual patterns of lip movements; Lyxell & Rönnberg, 1991), and to speed of information processing, again when the task is targeted to lexical meaning extraction (i.e., lexical and semantic decisions; Rönnberg, 1990). When verbal inference making is assessed by a time-constrained sentence-completion test rather than a word-completion test, it represents a significant predictor (Lyxell & Rönnberg, 1989). In general, visual decoding and processing speed – as opposed to inference making – account for twice as much of the variance in a typical sentence-based speech-understanding task (Rönnberg, 1990).

Other cognitive functions that support sentence-based visual speech understanding are (a) the amplitude measure in the visual evoked potential (Rönnberg, Arlinger, Lyxell, & Kinnefors, 1989) – the cognitive interpretation being that of a short-lived memory trace crucial for lexical access (Näätänen, 1986) – (b) complex information-processing and storage tasks, measured by the reading or listening span tasks (Daneman & Carpenter, 1980; Daneman & Merikle, 1996; Lyxell & Rönnberg, 1989; see DeFilippo, 1982), and (c) verbal ability, measured by synonym–antonym tests (Lyxell & Rönnberg, 1992).

Thus, in general it may be claimed that several kinds of cognitive abilities together contribute to visual speech understanding skill. Some predictors tap bottom-up processes (visual evoked potentials, lexical access speed, and phonology), whereas, e.g., inference making in combination with complex working memory functions are typically construed as top-down processes.

Visual speech understanding with supplementary information

Bernstein, Tucker, and Auer (1998) have found signs of compensatory improvements in visual speech understanding for early deaf hearing-aid users in vibro-tactilely mediated speech perception tasks. Bernstein et al. (1998) propose that the long-term vibrotactile stimulation was accomplished by the previous use of high-powered hearing aids (see also Bernstein, Demorest, Coulter, & O'Connell, 1991). One implication of the Bernstein et al. (1998) results is that efficient lexical access can be established by early and intense visual-tactile information processing, without relying on the auditory modality. The visual-tactile percept can presumably be recoded into nonsound phonological representations, without relying on sound. Such representations (assessed by text-based rhyme tests) have also been shown to be an important predictor of visual-tactile speech-tracking skill (Öhngren, 1992; Rönnberg, Andersson, Lyxell, & Spens, 1998b).

Studies on cochlear implants (CI), using different levels of complexity of speech material, reveal both higher and lower activation patterns compared to persons with normal hearing, with increased phonological processing and decreased semantic processing, as well as memory compensations to keep stimuli in mind during on-line comprehension (Giraud et al., 2000). Also, extra recruitment of visual areas, immediately after implantation, has recently been observed by Giraud, Price, Graham, Truy, and Frackowiak (2001). A preliminary appraisal of these data suggests not only that cognitive resources are taken into account to a larger extent with post-lingual CI-patients, but also that there is a need for a strategic system for maintaining several modality-specific sources of information while ambiguous information is being decoded: This system is working memory. This is compatible with the data on CI patients by Lyxell et al. (1996, 1998) where cognitive predictions of visual speech understanding are tapped by phonological tasks as well as by individual capacity for simultaneous processing and storage of information in working memory. Exactly these cognitive functions are prerequisites for information processing with a CI (see Pisoni, 2000), and the amodal, integrative working memory functions seem especially important (Lachs, Pisoni, & Kirk, 2001).

Finally, early use of cued speech (i.e., before the age of 3) is facilitative of several verbal and cognitive functions. In cued speech, supplementary visual cues augment speech to aid understanding, such that easily lip-read phonemes share a hand shape or hand position, whereas those phonemes that are hard to discriminate are accompanied by cues that belong to distinctly different groups. Leybaert (1998) argues that early practice in phonological cued-speech distinctions in children who are deaf has been empirically demonstrated to augment lip-reading, spelling, rhyme judgements, and reading (e.g., Leybaert & Lechat, 2001a), left-hemisphere specialisation (Leybaert & D'Hondt, 2003), as well as short-term memory (Leybaert & Charlier, 1996). There is no doubt that cued speech is effective in establishing non-sound phonological representations important for working memory and visual language perception and production.

Toward a working memory model for ease of spoken language understanding (ELU)

In the area of spoken language understanding in adventitiously hearing-impaired persons, there is a need for formulating a working memory model that relates working memory capacities to the ease of understanding ongoing spoken discourse. Such a model must take into account the time pressures of on-line comprehension, as well as the interaction of insufficiently specific input with stored lexical (i.e., phonological and semantic) knowledge in long-term memory. Existing working memory models are not developed primarily for such communicative purposes (e.g., Baddeley, 2000). Rönnberg (2003) proposed a model that accounts for the bottom-up and top-down influences on speech understanding by introducing the terms implicit and explicit language processing, and describing how they relate to ELU. The model builds on existing data patterns and results, but some of the *interactions* among the parameters remain to be tested *in extenso*. In that sense, the model should be viewed as a conceptual model.

Implicit processing

The implicit part of the model is viewed as a process where perceived spoken tokens (unimodally or multimodally) directly map on to a distributed lexical representation including phonological and semantic information (e.g., Gaskell & Marslen-Wilson, 1997), where efficiency in accessing lexical representations of meaning is assumed to be mediated by the quality and precision of phonological representations as they (as part of the distributed representation) help retrieve the lexical identity (Rönnberg, 1990). Less precise representations, derived from the perceptual input, evoke a larger number of potentially correct lexical neighbours. Lexical retrieval will therefore suffer unless constrained by appropriate context. The quality of phonological input to the system is assumed to be determined by the sensory features of the hearing impairment, the signal-to-noise ratio, by nonsound, supplementary visual (Leybaert & D'Hondt, 2003) and tactile (Öhngren,1992) information, or by CI-mediated information about speech (Lyxell et al., 1996). Furthermore, it is assumed that the phonological information represented in the lexical unit is located at the "syllable" level, or at least related to a linguistic unit larger than the phoneme: This assumption was deemed appropriate on general neurophysiological, cognitive, and linguistic grounds.

"Auditory" cortical activations may be generated by other nonauditory visual and tactile simple speech stimuli (e.g., Calvert et al., 1997; Levänen, 1998), demonstrating important neural flexibility in speech processing. Cognitively, performance in rhyme tests that draw on syllabic representations in long-term memory predicts performance in many speech-understanding tests (Andersson, 2001). Linguistically, it is quite plausible that the syllable assumption holds true for natural languages (see Höien, Lundberg, Stanovich, & Bjaalid, 1995, for the importance of the "phoneme" in artefactual languages), where co-articulation and prosodic effects are easier to "catch" by means of the syllable, and where information about speech sometimes comes in combinations of visual, tactile, and/or auditory streams. These streams of information – should they be integrated into one percept – are by their very nature (e.g., for tactile speech and visual speech) not very precise at the phoneme level, but carry important syllable-based information which can be effectively combined (Öhngren, 1992), Thus, syllable-like phonological representations of speech will typically allow for efficient lexical access [parameter fp(P)].

We know from many studies that cognitive speed [parameter fs(S)] is an important determinant of speech processing in various circumstances (Rönnberg, 1990; Rönnberg et al., 1998a). This means that long-term memory tests that assess lexical and semantic access speed are critical indicators of smooth ongoing speech understanding, and in line with the claim of a temporally early lexical access system (Rönnberg, 1990). As long as fs(S) and fp(P) are reasonably intact, processing – and hence ELU in the dialogue – is assumed to proceed implicitly, and with ease. If on the other hand the fs(S) by fp(P) interaction is insufficiently precise to "unlock" the lexicon at a rate that matches the dialogue and supports further encoding of semantic information to make sense of the dialogue (see Watson, 2003), then there will be an instant need for explicit processes to be invoked.

Explicit processing

If the phonological, contextual, or semantic factors lead the lexical access mechanism astray (Samuelsson & Rönnberg, 1993), the cognitive system is assumed to produce a mismatch signal (see Näätänen & Escera, 2002; Pettigrew, Murdoch, Chenery, & Kei, 2004). As long as no mismatch occurs, the system is conservative and does not use explicit resources. When a mismatch occurs, for example when the spoken input is unexpected, parameter fe(E) is set accordingly. Parameter fe(E) determines the degree to which individual working memory storage and processing capacity, parameter fc(C), is needed, for example to resolve anaphoric references, to make inferences, and to make predictions of future speech input (Lidestam, 2003). Parameter fe(E) can be manipulated experimentally by using typical vs less typical items, more or less semantically constrained sentence materials, or by introducing noise to the point where explicit processing is necessary. Individuals who possess a high capacity for simultaneous processing and storage operations in working memory may be expected to compensate even when the fs(S) by fp(P) interaction is less favourable – within certain signal detection thresholds (for mathematical formulations see Rönnberg, 2003).

In dialogical situations, there are presumably always fluctuations of the ratio between implicit processing on the one hand [I = fs(S)fp(P)], and demands on explicit processing on the other [E = fe(E)]. The ratio, I/E and its interaction with fc(C) depend on individual, dialogical, and contextual factors.

Extreme case studies reveal invariance of implicit and explicit capacities

Invariance of high working memory capacity [fc(C)] has been demonstrated in a set of case studies of extremely communicatively skilled individuals, with different communication modes: tactile-visual speech understanding (Case GS, see Rönnberg, 1993), bilingual communication (i.e., spoken and signed) (Case MM, see Rönnberg et al., 1999), and pure visual speech understanding (Case SJ, see Lyxell, 1994), and with different onsets of impairment (prelingual and postlingual, see Rönnberg, 1995a). Across these cases, two aspects of the data are especially important to note.

First, implicit processing (i.e., phonological processing and speed of lexical access) is critical up to a certain *threshold* only, comparable to normal hearing controls (Rönnberg, Samuelsson, & Lyxell, 1998c), and is generalisable to both children (e.g., Lyxell & Holmberg, 2000) and adults (Rönnberg et al., 2000a). The existence of such a threshold is presumed to be constrained by visual-neural and lexical-access speed, and by the quality (Andersson, 2001) and speed (Pichora-Fuller, 2003; Pichora-Fuller, Schneider, & Daneman, 1995) with which phonological representations are activated.

Second, top-down, explicit resources (e.g., verbal inference making and complex information storage and processing capacity) are crucial for expert speech understanding. Without highly developed explicit resources, expertise is not likely to develop (Lyxell, 1994; Plant, Gnosspelius, & Levitt, 2000; Rönnberg, 1993; Rönnberg et al., 1999; but see Andersson & Lidestam, 2005).

Language modality and ease of understanding

While alternative speech communication through the use of tactile aids, cochlear implants, and cued speech has been an important tool for furthering our understanding of the role of cognitive components in speech understanding, a significant breakthrough has come about with the rise of behavioural and neuroscience work on sign language (for recent reviews, see Bavelier, Corina, & Neville, 1998; Emmorey, 2003; Rönnberg, Söderfeldt & Risberg, 2000b; Wilson, 2001). Already at a preliminary stage, it seems as if the case studies of communicatively skilled individuals referred to may lay the foundation of a possible generalisation of the ELU model across forms of speech to signed language, implying a relatively modality-free working memory system.

A common working memory system for sign and speech?

From a working memory perspective, it is thus possible that speed of image generation, image maintenance, and image manipulation capacity, as well as mental rotation abilities, represent inherent aspects of a visuo-spatial working memory system specific to signed language (Emmorey et al., 2002; Emmorey, Klima, & Hickok, 1998; Newman, Bavelier, Corina, Jezzard, & Neville, 2002). The question is whether the cognitive representations of such a system are modality specific or modality free.

Phonology

There are some recent data to suggest that at the neurophysiological level there are striking *phonological similarities* in the activation of planum temporale in syllable-based processing that compared speech and sign in a long-term memory-based rhyme task (Petitto et al., 2000). The syllable assumption is also compatible with the idea that syllables represent an important perceptual–cognitive bridge for natural languages, but not necessarily for artifacts, like script. Interestingly, "inner signing" of sentences also engages functional networks in the brain similar to those associated with the activation of the phonological loop: left inferior frontal cortex, rather than visuospatial areas (McGuire et al., 1997). In a recent study on verb generation in response to nouns, signs produced almost identical lexical-semantic processing patterns in the left inferior frontal lobe and the right cerebellum as speech (Corina et al., 2003).

In addition, behavioural data suggest that there are similarities across signed and spoken languages with respect to "phonological similarity" effects in working memory (Wilson & Emmorey, 1997), and with respect to the capacity of the "phonological" loop (Marschark & Mayer, 1998). Phonological loop effects have also been observed with cued speech (Leybaert & Lechat, 2001b) and hence seem to be a rather general operating characteristic of working memory for visual language as well. On the whole, many classical working memory effects are analoguous for sign and speech (i.e., similarity, length, and suppression effects; Wilson, 2001).

Long-term memory access speed

Temporal processing skill is not something which can be ascribed to compensatory effects of sign language; it rather represents a common individual difference variable that cuts across hearing status of participants (Poizner & Tallal, 1987). When articulation rate is controlled for in speech and sign, "phonological loop" capacities may also be the same (Marschark & Mayer, 1998). Finally, there may also be a linguistic basis for speed of image generation in the experienced signer (Emmorey & Kosslyn, 1996), which, again, may be secondary to implicit processing skills in signed language.

Explicit storage and processing capacity

We have seen that implicit processes (i.e., speed of lexical/semantic access via multimodally specified phonology and visuo-spatial representations) may represent an important part of the perceptual platform on the basis of which explicit working memory capacities may contribute to ELU. We expect that contextual and semantic constraints inherent in the mismatch function and parameter fe(E) typically are language modality free in terms of neural mechanisms (Corina et al., 2003; Price, 1998). However, one of several critical issues that remain is whether fc(C) has a similar representation for sign compared to speech.

In a PET study of eight bilingual, native sign language users (Rönnberg, Rudner, & Ingvar, 2004), we have found that working memory for unrelated signed words engages bilateral parietal (dorsal stream), middle temporal (ventral stream), and left premotor cortical areas, whereas working memory for spoken items specifically engages superior temporal areas. The results are not due to task difficulty, differences in recoding operations, or to production differences; they seem to reflect genuine, language modality specific explicit storage and processing differences [parameter fc(c)]. In a re-analysis of the data on five of the bilinguals who had started using both languages in infancy, it could be observed that the bilateral parietal activation shifted over to a more focal, left-sided, parietal activation, suggesting that although all eight participants were fluent in sign language, implicit competence may be reserved for either deaf users or for bilinguals who start language acquisition in infancy.

In a recent study of working memory for visually and auditorily presented verbal materials, modality specificity was found in the left intraparietal sulcus and the left inferior parietal area such that visual items activated these areas more intensively than auditory stimuli (Crottaz-Herbette, Anagnoson, & Menon, 2004). This implies that visual to auditory recoding operations in verbal working memory tasks engage qualitatively similar parietal areas used for phonological storage, but that the intensity of activity is different. For rehearsal processes as such, no differential activity was found (i.e., in Broca's, the premotor, and supplementary motor cortex areas), as was generally the case for the comparison between sign and speech (Rönnberg et al., 2004). Chinese-English nonfluent bilinguals also demonstrate very similar left-hemisphere fronto-parietal working memory activations for Chinese and English, and the volume of activity was larger in English, suggesting a less automatic recruitment of resources (Xue, Dong, Jin, & Chen, 2004; see Crottaz-Herbette et al., 2004). Thus, a qualitatively similar network is suggested but with varying intensity of neural involvement.

As the data in Rönnberg et al. (2004) suggested a lack of recoding operations – but still a language modality specific effect in the left parietal lobes (sign – speech) – it was suggested that the activity corresponded to generation of a visual-spatial array to support working memory processing.

Recent data by Capek et al. (2004) suggest that audiovisual processing of sentences typically engages left-hemisphere cortical areas in English-speaking subjects, but with the same design we also know from another study of deaf participants that understanding of ASL sentences in addition activates specific right-hemisphere areas that are not simply a function of prosody, facial expression, and early acquisition (see Neville et al., 1998).

We cannot be certain as to the ratio between implicit and explicit processing in sign language understanding or production tasks used so far in the literature, but the neurofunctional picture seems to be one of sign specificity in findings even for more semantically and conceptually driven activity: story comprehension tasks (e.g., in the visual ventral processing stream; Neville et al., 1998; Söderfeldt et al., 1997; Söderfeldt, Rönnberg & Risberg, 1994) or discourse production tasks (e.g., in the dorsal stream; Braun, Guillemin, Hosey, & Varga, 2001).

General discussion

The framework and working memory model by Rönnberg (2003) points out amodal cognitive features that bind together the competencies of speech readers who use different sensory modality information about speech. The model seems generalisable to implicit aspects of sign language use as well, but in terms of brain activity the explicit fc(C) parameter remains language-modality specific. Moreover, research on working memory predictions of sign language understanding in difficult circumstances (e.g., in elderly users, sign dyslexia, or for poor signal-to-noise ratios) is still lacking. Whereas we are starting to know about the implicit and explicit working memory components involved in sign language processing, we know very little about their relation to an ELU model.

Generally, then, the emerging picture is compatible with working memory conceptualizations that posit a mixture of amodal and language modality specific components (Wilson, 2001). It is especially compatible with Wilson and Emmorey's (2003) proposal that both visual and visuo-spatial components are represented in working memory for sign, and it also fits well with our data on both ventral and dorsal processing components (Rönnberg et al., 2004). It is potentially compatible with a more classic model of the visuo-spatial sketch-pad, given that previous assumptions about the sketch-pad are relaxed to include a linguistic dimension, or that the episodic buffer can be supposed to integrate the linguistically relevant multidimensional stimuli needed in working memory for sign (e.g., Baddeley, 2000).

The implicit/explicit processing modes assumption constrains the concept of working memory. Current working memory models have not relied on the processing economy inherent in such an assumption; for example, Logie (1996) and Baddeley (2000) seem to assume that for a given input, long-term memory representations, as well as the corresponding modality-specific "slave-systems", are active during task performance – and by implication always involve an explicit executive capacity. Non-constrained activity in working memory seems appropriate for memory and cognitive tasks as such, but less so when cognition is put to action in time-pressed language-understanding tasks. For language processing in general, it therefore seems important to develop better methods for estimating the ratio of implicit to explicit processing. In general, the degree of effort invested in a comprehension task and the ease with which comprehension can actually occur are necessarily functions of this ratio.

Early sign language use is associated with certain communicatively relevant cognitive benefits: Compensatory functions have been observed for, for example, visuo-spatial cognition (Parasnis, Samar, Bettger, & Sathe, 1996), higher speed in generating mental images (Emmorey, Kosslyn & Bellugi, 1993), mental rotation of non-linguistic objects (Emmorey et al., 1998), and for deaf ASL-signers in episodic memory for faces (Bettger, Emmorey, McCullough, & Bellugi, 1997; McCullough & Emmorey, 1997).

Thus, there is a possibility that the sign language modality specificity observed in terms of the proposed framework and model is a result of compensatory effects for persons with deafness, and when compensation is not reached – as is the case for adventitiously hearing-impaired persons – then amodal working memory constructs are better predictors of ELU. When we do observe compensations inherent in the fc(C) parameter of the model, the current hypothesis is that predictions of ELU are better accomplished with a sign language specific model.

Acknowledgement

This research is supported by a grant from the Swedish Council for Social Research (30305108).

References

Andersson, U. (2001). Cognitive deafness: The deterioration of phonological representations in adults with an acquired severe hearing loss and its implications for speech understanding. Dissertation. *Studies from the Swedish Institute for Disability Research No 3*. Linköping University, Sweden.

Andersson, U., & Lidestam, B. (2005). Bottom-up driven speechreading in a speechreading expert: The case of AA (JK023). *Ear and Hearing*, *26*(2), 214–224.

Arnold, P. (1997). The structure and optimisation of speechreading. *Journal of Deaf Studies and Deaf Education*, *2*, 199–221.

Baddeley, A.D. (2000). The episodic buffer: A new component of working memory? *Trends in Cognitive Science*, *4*, 417–423.

Bavelier, D., Corina, D., & Neville, H.J. (1998). Brain and language: A perspective from sign language. *Neuron*, *21*, 275–278.

Bernstein, L.E., Demorest, M.E., Coulter, D.C., & O'Connell, M.P. (1991). Lipreading sentences with vibrotactile vocoders: Performance of normal-hearing and hearing-impaired subjects. *Journal of the Acoustical Society of America*, *95*, 2971–2984.

Bernstein, L.E., Demorest, M.E., & Tucker, P.E. (2000). Speech perception without hearing. *Perception & Psychophysics*, *62*, 233–252.

Bernstein, L.E., Tucker P.E., & Auer E.T. (1998). Potential perceptual bases for successful use of a vibrotactile speech perception aid. *Scandinavian Journal of Psychology*, *39*, 181–186.

Bettger, J.G., Emmorey, K., McCullough, S.H., & Bellugi, U. (1997). Enhanced facial discrimination: Effects of experience with American Sign Language. *Journal of Deaf Studies and Deaf Education*, *2*, 223–233.

Boothroyd, A. (1988). Linguistic factors in speechreading. *Volta Review*, *90*, 77–87.

Borg, E. (2003). Application of an ecological framework in audiological assessment. *International Journal of Audiology*, *42*, S23–S33.

Braun, A.R., Guillemin, A., Hosey, L., & Varga, M. (2001). The neural organization of discourse. An $H_2{}^{15}O$-PET study of narrative production in English and American sign language. *Brain*, *124*, 2028–2044.

Calvert, G., Bullmore, E., Brammer, M., Campbell, R., Woodruff, P., McGuire, P. et al. (1997). Activation of auditory cortex during silent speechreading. *Science*, *276*, 593–596.

Capek, C.M., Bavelier, D., Corina, D., Newman, A.J., Jezzard, P., & Neville, H.J. (2004). The cortical organization of audio-visual sentence comprehension: An fMRI study at 4 Tesla. *Cognitive Brain Research*, *20*(2), 111–119.

Corina, D.P., San Jose-Robertson, L., Guillemin, A., High, J., & Braun A.R. (2003). Language lateralization in a bimanual language. *Journal of Cognitive Neuroscience*, *15*, 718–730.

Cox, R., & McDaniel, D.M. (1989). Development of the speech intelligibility rating (SIR) test for hearing aid comparisons. *Journal of Speech and Hearing Research*, *32*, 347–52.

Crottaz-Herbette, S., Anagnoson, R.T., & Menon, V. (2004). Modality effects in verbal working memory: Differential prefrontal and parietal responses to auditory and visual stimuli. *Neuroimage*, *21*, 340–351.

Daneman, M., & Carpenter, P.A. (1980). Individual differences in integrating information between and within sentences. *Journal of Experimental Psychology: Learning, Memory and Cognition*, *9*, 561–584.

Daneman, M., & Merikle, P.M. (1996). Working memory and language comprehension: A meta-analysis. *Psychonomic Bulletin & Review*, *3*, 422–433.

DeFilippo, C.L. (1982). Memory for articulated sentences and lipreading performance of hearing-impaired observers. *Volta Review*, *April*, 134–146.

Emmorey, K. (2003). The neural systems underlying sign language. In M. Marschark & P. Spencer (Eds.), *Oxford handbook of deaf studies, language and education* (pp. 361–378). New York: Oxford University Press.

Emmorey, K., Damasio, H., McCullough, S., Grabowski, T., Ponto, L., Hichwa, R. et al. (2002). Neural systems underlying spatial language in American Sign Language. *Neuroimage*, *17*, 812–824.

Emmorey, K., Klima, E., & Hickok, G. (1998). Mental rotation within linguistic and non-linguistic domains in users of American sign language. *Cognition*, *68*, 221–246.

Emmorey, K., & Kosslyn, S.M. (1996). Enhanced image generation abilities in deaf signers: A right hemisphere effect. *Brain & Cognition*, *32*, 28–44.

Emmorey, K., Kosslyn, S.M., & Bellugi, U. (1993). Visual imagery and visual-spatial language. Enhanced imagery abilities in deaf and hearing ASL signers. *Cognition*, *46*, 139–181.

Erber, N.P. (1998). DYALOG: A computer-based measure of conversational performance. *Journal of the Academy of Rehabilitative Audiology*, *31*, 69–76.

Gagné, J.-P. (2003). Treatment effectiveness research in audiological rehabilitation: Fundamental issues related to dependent variables. *International Journal of Audiology*, *42*, S104–S112.

Gailey, L. (1987). Psychological parameters of lipreading skill. In B. Dodd & R. Campbell (Eds.), *Hearing by eye: The psychology of lipreading* (pp. 115–141). Hove, UK: Lawrence Erlbaum Associates Ltd.

Gaskell, M.G., & Marslen-Wilson, W.D. (1997). Integrating form and meaning: A distributed model of speech perception. *Language and Cognitive Processes*, *12*, 613–656.

Giraud, A.-L., Price, C.J., Graham, J.M., Truy, E., & Frackowiak, R.S.J. (2001). Cross-modal plasticity underpins language recovery after cochlear implantation. *Neuron*, *30*, 657–663.

Giraud, A.-L., Truy, E., Frackowiak, R.S.J., Grégoire, M.-C., Pujol, J.-F., & Collet, L. (2000). Differential recruitment of the speech processing system in healthy subjects and rehabilitated cochlear implant patients. *Brain*, *123*, 1391–1402.

Gustafsson, H.Å. & Arlinger, S.D. (1994). Masking of speech by amplitude-modulated noise. *Journal of the Acoustical Society of America*, *95*, 518–29.

Hawkins, D.B., Montgomery, A.A., Mueller, H.G., & Sedge, R.K. (1998). Assessment of speech intelligibility by hearing-impaired listeners. In B. Berglund, J. Karlsson, & T. Lindvall (Eds.), *Noise as a public health problem* (pp. 241–246). Stockholm: Swedish Council for Building Research.

Höien, T., Lundberg, I., Stanovich, K.E., & Bjaalid, I.-K. (1995). Components of phonological awareness. *Reading and Writing*, *7*, 171–188.

Hygge, S., Rönnberg, J., Larsby, B., & Arlinger, S.D. (1992). Normal and hearing-impaired subjects' ability to just follow conversation in competing speech, reversed speech, and noise backgrounds. *Journal of Speech and Hearing Research*, *35*, 208–215.

Jeffers, J., & Barley, M. (1971). *Speechreading*. Springfield, IL: Ch. C. Thomas Publ.

Lachs, L., Pisoni, D.B., & Kirk, K.I. (2001). Use of audiovisual information in speech perception by prelingually deaf children with cochlear implants: A first report. *Ear and Hearing*, *22*, 236–251.

Levänen, S. (1998). Neuromagnetic studies of human auditory cortex function and reorganization. *Scandinavian Audiology*, *27* (Suppl 49), 1–6.

Leybaert, J. (1998). Phonological representations in deaf children: The importance of early linguistic experience. *Scandinavian Journal of Psychology*, *39*, 169–173.

Leybaert, J., & Charlier, B.L. (1996). Visual speech in the head: The effect of cued speech on rhyming, remembering and spelling. *Journal of Deaf Studies and Deaf Education*, *1*, 234–248.

Leybaert, J., & D'Hondt, M. (2003). Neurolinguistic development in deaf children: The effect of early language experience. *International Journal of Audiology*, *42*, S34–S40

Leybaert, J., & Lechat, J. (2001a). Variability in deaf children's spelling: The effect of language experience. *Journal of Educational Psychology*, *93*, 554–562.

Leybaert, J., & Lechat, J. (2001b). Phonological similarity effects in memory for serial order of cued speech. *Journal of Speech, Language, and Hearing Research*, *44*, 949–963.

Lidestam, B. (2003). Semantic framing of speech: Emotional and topical cues in perception of poorly specified speech. Doctoral thesis. *Linköping Studies in Education and Psychology no. 94*. Department of Behavioural Sciences, Linköping University, Sweden.

Logie, R.H. (1996). The seven ages of working memory. In J.T.E. Richardson et al. (Eds.), *Working memory and human cognition* (pp. 31–59). Oxford: Oxford University Press.

Lyxell, B. (1989). *Beyond lips: Components of speechreading skill*. PhD thesis, Department of Psychology, University of Umeå, Sweden.

Lyxell, B. (1994). Skilled speechreading – a single case study. *Scandinavian Journal of Psychology, 35*, 212–219.

Lyxell, B., Andersson, U., Borg, E., & Ohlsson, I.S. (2003). Working-memory capacity and phonological processing in deafened adults and individuals with a severe hearing impairment. *International Journal of Audiology, 42*, S86–S89.

Lyxell, B., Arlinger, S., Andersson, J., Bredberg, G., Harder, H., & Rönnberg, J. (1998). Phonological representation and speech understanding with cochlear implants in deafened adults. *Scandinavian Journal of Psychology, 39*, 175–179.

Lyxell, B., Arlinger, S., Andersson, J., Harder, H., Näsström, E., Svensson, H. et al. (1996). Information-processing capabilities and cochlear implants: Pre-operative predictors for speech understanding. *Journal of Deaf Studies & Deaf Education, 1*, 190–201.

Lyxell, B., & Holmberg, I. (2000). Visual speechreading and cognitive performance in hearing-impaired and normal hearing children (11–14 years). *British Journal of Educational Psychology, 70*, 505–518.

Lyxell, B., & Rönnberg, J. (1989). Information-processing skills and speechreading. *British Journal of Audiology, 23*, 339–347.

Lyxell, B., & Rönnberg, J. (1991). Visual speech processing: Word decoding and word discrimination related to sentence-based speechreading and hearing-impairment. *Scandinavian Journal of Psychology, 32*, 9–17.

Lyxell, B., & Rönnberg, J. (1992). The relationship between verbal ability and sentence-based speechreading. *Scandinavian Audiology, 21*, 67–72.

Markova, I., & Linell P. (1996). Coding elementary contributions to dialogue: Individual acts versus dialogical interactions. *Journal for the Theory of Social Behavior, 26*, 353–373.

Marschark, M., & Mayer, T.S. (1998). Interactions of language and memory in deaf children and adults. *Scandinavian Journal of Psychology, 39*, 145–148.

McCullough, S., & Emmorey, K. (1997). Face processing by deaf ASL signers: Evidence for expertise in distinguishing local features. *Journal of Deaf Studies and Deaf Education, 2*, 212–222.

McGuire, P.K., Robertson, D., Thacker, A., David, A.S., Kitson, N., Frackowiak, R.S.J. et al. (1997). Neural correlates of thinking in sign language. *Neuroreport, 8*, 695–698.

Mogford, K. (1987). Lip-reading in the pre-lingually deaf. In B. Dodd & R. Campbell (Eds.), *Hearing by eye: The psychology of lip-reading* (pp. 191–211). Hove, UK: Lawrence Erlbaum Associates Ltd.

Näätänen, R. (1986). Neurophysiological basis of the echoic memory as suggested by event-related potentials and magnetoencephalogram. In F. Klix & H. Hagendorf (Eds.), *Human memory and cognitive capabilities* (pp. 615–628). Amsterdam: North Holland.

Näätänen, R., & Escera, C. (2002). Mismatch negativity: Clinical and other applications. *Audiology and Neuro-otology*, *5*, 105–110.
Newman, A.J., Bavelier, D., Corina, D., Jezzard, P., & Neville, H.J. (2002). A critical period for right hemisphere recruitment in American Sign Language processing. *Nature Neuroscience*, *5*, 76–80.
Neville, H.J., Bavelier, D., Corina, D., Rauschecker, J., Karni, A., Lawani, A. et al. (1998). Cerebral organization for language in deaf and hearing subjects: Biological constraints and effects of experience. *Proceedings of the National Academy of Science*, *95*, 922–929.
Öhngren, G. (1992). *Components of tactually mediated speechreading*. Unpublished PhD Thesis, Uppsala University, Sweden.
Parasnis, I., Samar, V., Bettger, J., & Sathe, K. (1996). Does deafness lead to enhancement of visual spatial cognition in children? Negative evidence from deaf nonsigners. *Journal of Deaf Studies and Deaf Education*, *1*, 145–152.
Petitto, L.A., Zatorre, R.J., Gauna, K., Nikelski, E.J., Dostie, D., & Evans, A.C. (2000). Speech-like cerebral activity in profoundly deaf people processing signed languages: Implications for the neural basis of human language. *Proceedings of the National Academy of Sciences of the United States of America*, *97*, 13961–13966.
Pettigrew, C., Murdoch, B.E., Chenery, H.J., & Kei, J. (2004). The relationship between mismatch negativity (MMN) and psycholinguistic models of spoken word processing. *Aphasiology*, *18*, 3–38.
Pichora-Fuller, K. (2003). Processing speed: Psychoacoustics, speech perception, and comprehension. *International Journal of Audiology*, *42*, S59–S67.
Pichora-Fuller, M.K., Schneider, B.A., & Daneman, M. (1995). How young and old adults listen to and remember speech in noise. *Journal of Acoustical Society of America*, *97*, 593–608.
Pisoni, D.B. (2000). Cognitive factors and cochlear implants: Some thoughts on perception, learning, and memory in speech perception. *Ear & Hearing*, *21*, 70–78.
Plant, G., Gnosspelius, J., & Levitt, H. (2000). The use of tactile supplements in lipreading Swedish and English: A single-subject study. *Journal of Speech, Language and Hearing Research*, *43*, 178–183.
Poizner, H., & Tallal, P. (1987). Temporal processing in deaf signers. *Brain and Language*, *30*, 52–62.
Price, C. (1998). The functional anatomy of word comprehension and production. *Trends in Cognitive Science*, *2*, 281–288.
Rönnberg, J. (1990). Cognitive and communicative function: The effects of chronological age and "handicap age". *European Journal of Cognitive Psychology*, *2*, 253–273.
Rönnberg, J. (1993). Cognitive characteristics of skilled tactiling: The case of GS. *European Journal of Cognitive Psychology*, *5*, 19–33.
Rönnberg, J. (1995a). What makes a skilled speechreader? In G. Plant & K. Spens (Eds.), *Profound deafness and speech communication* (pp. 393–416). London: Whurr Publishers.
Rönnberg, J. (1995b). Perceptual compensation in the deaf and blind: Myth or reality? In R.A. Dixon & L. Bäckman (Eds.), *Compensating for psychological deficits and declines: Managing losses and promoting gains* (pp. 251–274). Mahwah, NJ: Lawrence Erlbaum Associates Inc.
Rönnberg, J. (2003). Cognition in the hearing impaired and deaf as a bridge between

signal and dialogue: A framework and a model. *International Journal of Audiology, 42*, S68–S76.

Rönnberg, J., Andersson, J., Andersson, U., Johansson, K., Lyxell, B., & Samuelsson, S. (1998a). Cognition as a bridge between signal and dialogue: Communication in the hearing impaired and deaf. *Scandinavian Audiology, 27*(suppl. 49), 101–108.

Rönnberg, J., Andersson, U., Lyxell, B., & Spens, K. (1998b). Vibrotactile speechreading support: Cognitive prerequisites for training. *Journal of Deaf Studies & Deaf Education, 3*, 143–156.

Rönnberg, J., Andersson, J., Samuelsson, S., Söderfeldt, B., Lyxell, B., & Risberg, J. (1999). A speechreading expert: The case of MM. *Journal of Speech, Language and Hearing Research, 42*, 5–20.

Rönnberg, J., Arlinger, S., Lyxell, B., & Kinnefors, C. (1989). Visual evoked potentials: Relation to adult speechreading and cognitive function. *Journal of Speech and Hearing Research, 32*, 725–735.

Rönnberg, J., Öhngren, G., & Nilsson, L-G. (1982). Hearing deficiency, speechreading and memory functions. *Scandinavian Audiology, 11*, 261–268.

Rönnberg, J., Öhngren, G., & Nilsson, L-G. (1983). Speechreading performance evaluated by means of TV and real-life presentation: A comparison between a normally hearing, moderately impaired and profoundly hearing-impaired group. *Scandinavian Audiology, 12*, 71–77.

Rönnberg, J., Rudner, M., & Ingvar, M. (2004). Neural correlates of working memory for sign language. *Cognitive Brain Research, 20*, 165–182.

Rönnberg, J., Samuelsson, E., & Borg, E. (2000a). Visual cognitive tests, central auditory function and auditory communication. *Scandinavian Audiology, 29*, 196–206.

Rönnberg, J., Samuelsson, S., & Lyxell, B. (1998c). Conceptual constraints in sentence-based lipreading in the hearing impaired. In R. Campbell, B. Dodd, & D. Burnham (Eds.), *Hearing by eye: Part II. Advances in the psychology of speechreading and audiovisual speech* (pp. 143–153). London: Lawrence Erlbaum Associates Ltd.

Rönnberg, J., Söderfeldt, B., & Risberg, J. (2000b). The cognitive neuroscience of signed language. *Acta Psychologica, 105*, 237–254.

Samuelsson, S., & Rönnberg, J. (1993). Implicit and explicit use of scripted constraints in lipreading. *European Journal of Cognitive Psychology, 5*, 201–233.

Söderfeldt, B., Ingvar, M., Rönnberg, J., Eriksson, L., Serrander, M., & Stone-Elander, S. (1997). Signed and spoken language perception studied by positron emission tomography. *Neurology, 49*, 82–87.

Söderfeldt, B., Rönnberg, J., & Risberg, J. (1994). Regional cerebral blood flow in sign-language users. *Brain and Language, 46*, 59–68.

Tillberg, I., Rönnberg, J., Svärd, I., & Ahlner, B. (1996). Audio-visual tests in a group of hearing-aid users: The effects of onset age, handicap age, and degree of hearing loss. *Scandinavian Audiology, 25*, 267–272.

Watson, D.R. (2003). *Cognitive effects of impaired auditory abilities and use of visual speech to supplement perception.* Unpublished doctoral thesis: Faculty of Science, Queen's University of Belfast.

Wilson, M. (2001). The case for sensorimotor coding in working memory. *Psychonomic Bulletin & Review, 8*, 44–57.

Wilson, M., & Emmorey, K. (1997). Working memory for sign language: A window into the architecture of the working memory system. *Journal of Deaf Studies and Deaf Education, 2*, 121–130.

Wilson, M., & Emmorey, K. (2003). The effect of irrelevant visual input on working memory for sign language. *Journal of Deaf Studies and Deaf Education*, *8*, 97–103.
Xue, G., Dong, Q., Jin, Z., & Chen, C. (2004). Mapping of verbal working memory in nonfluent Chinese-English bilinguals with functional MRI. *Neuroimage*, *22*, 1–10.

23 Conscious and unconscious cognition: A graded, dynamic perspective

Axel Cleeremans

Consider the following three situations: learning to perform a complex skill such as gymastics (a stunning demonstration of which participants to ICP 2004 experienced during the opening ceremony), learning a complex game such as the ancient Chinese game of Weichi (more widely known as Go), or learning natural language. What these situations have in common, beyond the sheer complexity of the required skills, is the fact that most of what we learn about each appears to proceed in a manner that does not depend so much on the acquisition of explicit, declarative information or on the deployment of intentional strategies, but instead critically depends on repeated practice: Developing the skills needed to execute complex movements in gymnastics, to "see" the correct move in a game of Go, or to fluently produce natural language all involve what Zhu and Simon (1987) dubbed "learning by doing".

Interestingly, in all such cases, it is also often found that people have limited conscious knowledge of what it is they have learned. Thus, people may be, to some degree at least, unaware *that* they have learned anything, unaware of *what* it is that they have learned, or unaware that their behaviour is influenced by something they have previously learned about. Hence we obtain changes in performance that are not accompanied by correlated changes in subjective experience or in people's ability to verbalize knowledge about what was learned. These observations, replicated numerous times over the years (see below for several illustrations) in different domains, have generated and continue to generate controversy. Authors disagree on two apparent implications of such dissociation findings.

First, such findings suggest that *unconscious knowledge can be causally efficacious*. However, many authors would disagree with the notion that the sorts of representations one would want to call "cognitive" can also be unconscious (Perruchet & Vinter, 2002; Shanks & St. John, 1994). Second, such dissociation findings also suggest that there may be exist *separable conscious and unconscious processing systems*. In this chapter I attempt to show that both implications are in fact unwarranted. First, the notion of unconscious representation is only problematic under certain assumptions of what one means by representation. Second, dissociation findings do not necessarily imply the existence of distinct systems whose function it is to subserve implicit or explicit learning. I instead suggest that traditional accounts of the differences between cognition with and without consciousness need to be replaced by subsymbolic accounts, which characterize both representation and processing in a profoundly different manner.

This analysis is rooted in a novel conceptual framework (Cleeremans, forthcoming; Cleeremans & Jiménez, 2002) that takes as its starting points (1) that the main function of consciousness is to make flexible, adaptive control over behaviour possible; (2) that consciousness is best viewed as involving a graded continuum expressed over representations; and (3) that learning is a mandatory process that always accompanies information processing, and through which our conscious representations of the world are made to reflect those contents which are most in need of control at some point in time. The central claim of the framework is that implicit and explicit learning do not depend on separable, distinct learning and memory systems (although the framework is not wholly incompatible with this perspective either, but not in the specific sense that there exist separable implicit and explicit memory systems), but rather that they are different manifestations of a single set of interacting learning mechanisms and representational systems dedicated to serve specific, and sometimes incompatible, computational, objectives.

In the following, I begin with an overview of some recent findings about the ubiquity of learning. Next, I illustrate through several examples how changes in behaviour can fail to be accompanied by changes in subjective experience, and briefly discuss how these findings of dissociation have tended to be interpreted by traditional models in cognitive psychology. I then present the sketch of an alternative framework through which to link learning and consciousness.

Learning and consciousness

The recent years have brought forward a staggering amount of evidence suggesting not only that the brain is far more plastic than previously thought, but also that the effects of learning can be tracked all the way down to the organization of local connectivity. For instance, expert players of stringed instruments exhibit larger-than-normal areas of the somatosensory cortex dedicated to representing input from the fingering digits (Elbert, Pantey, Wienbruch, Rockstroh, & Taub, 1995). Likewise, not only is posterior hippocampus – a region of the brain involved in episodic and spatial memory – enlarged in experienced taxi drivers compared to subjects who do not have extensive experience in memorizing complex maps, but the observed size differences further depend on the amount of driving experience (Maguire et al., 2000). There is also considerable evidence that the brain can recover in various flexible ways after trauma, and even suggestions that the very organization of the somatosensory cortex (the famous Penfield homunculus) depends on pre-natal sensory experience (Farah, 1998). These spectacular findings all reassert that adaptation plays a fundamental role in cognition and, just as importantly, that learning actually modifies the very structure of the "machine" – the brain – in which information processing takes place.

What, then, can we say about the relationships between learning and consciousness? Is it the case, as some authors contend (Perruchet & Vinter, 2002; Shanks & St. John, 1994) that learning is always accompanied by conscious awareness, or is change possible without concomitant changes in subjective experience? More generally, is information processing in general accompanied by conscious experience, or can one find cases where action seems to be dissociated from introspective accounts?

If learning often fails to produce changes in subjective experience, examples of dissociation between action and consciousness should be abundant. As it turns out, they are. Indeed, everyday experience suggests that we often seem to know more than we can tell. Riding a bicycle, playing tennis, or driving a car, for instance, all involve mastering complex sets of motor skills, yet we are at a loss when it comes to explaining exactly how we perform such physical feats. These dissociations between our ability to report on cognitive processes and the behaviours that involve these processes are not limited to action but extend to higher-level cognition as well. Most native speakers of a language are unable to articulate the grammatical rules they nevertheless follow when speaking natural language. Likewise, expertise in domains such as medical diagnosis or chess, as well as social or aesthetic judgements, all involve intuitive knowledge that one seems to have little introspective access to.

We also often seem to tell more than we can know. In a classic article, social psychologists Nisbett and Wilson (1977) reported on many experimental demonstrations of the fact that accounts of our own behaviour frequently reflect reconstructive and interpretative processes rather than genuine introspection.

Demonstrations of dissociations between conscious awareness and stimulation and/or behaviour have now been reported in many domains of psychology, and in fact date back to the very beginnings of scientific psychology in the nineteenth century (e.g., Pierce & Jastrow, 1880).

One of the most convincing demonstrations of dissociations between conscious knowledge and behaviour was obtained in a eye-blink conditioning situation (Perruchet, 1985). In this experiment, people were exposed to a series of identical tones, 50% of which could be followed after a short interval by an air puff directed to the left cornea. Immediately after each tone was presented (and before the puff occurred in reinforced trials), people were asked to indicate the extent to which they expected the tone to be followed by an air puff on a 0–7-point scale. A trial-by-trial analysis of the results indicated that eye-blink responses were increasingly likely to occur after presentation of a tone if the corresponding trial had been preceded by a series of reinforced trials (i.e., trials during which the tone had indeed been followed by an air puff). In stark contrast, however, people's subjective expectancy of the occurrence of an air puff tended to *decrease* with the number of reinforced trials that preceded the trial under consideration. In other words, people's eye-blink responses were completely dissociated from their conscious expectations about when each tone would be followed by an air puff.

Dissociations of a somewhat different kind can also be observed in situations that do not involve the motor system (see Cleeremans, Destrebecqz, & Boyer, 1998, for a review). Arthur Reber, in a classic series of studies conducted in 1967, first suggested that learning might be "implicit", to the extent that people appear to be able to learn new information without intending to do so and in such a way that the resulting knowledge is difficult to express. In Reber's seminal study of *artificial grammar learning* (Reber, 1967), subjects were asked to memorize a set of meaningless letter strings generated by a simple set of rules embodied in a finite-state grammar. After this memorization phase, they were told that the strings followed the rules of a grammar, and were asked to classify novel strings as grammatical or not. In this experiment and in many subsequent replications, subjects were able to perform this classification task better than chance would predict, despite remaining unable to describe the rules of the grammar in verbal reports. This dissociation between classification performance and verbal report is the finding that prompted Reber to describe learning as implicit, for subjects appeared sensitive to and could apply knowledge (the rules of the grammar) that they remained unable to describe and had had no intention to learn.

Today, another paradigm – sequence learning – has become dominant in the investigation of implicit learning. Nissen and Bullemer (1987) first demonstrated that subjects asked to respond as fast and as accurately as possible to a series of visual events progressively learned about the sequential structure of the stimulus sequence, in spite of showing little evidence of being aware that the material contained structure. Numerous subsequent studies of this effect have indicated that subjects can learn about complex sequential relationships despite remaining unable to fully express this knowledge in corresponding direct, explicit tasks (e.g., Cleeremans & McClelland, 1991), thus once again suggesting that learning can occur without corresponding changes in our ability to express the acquired knowledge explicitly.

Examples of dissociations between action, memory, and perception on the one hand, and subjective experience on the other, are thus commonplace in many different domains. How can we account for these dissociations? How should we conceptualize the relationships between conscious and unconscious cognition? In the next section, I briefly overview traditional perspectives on these issues.

The function of consciousness: Commander Data meets the Zombies

In a recent overview article, Dehaene and Naccache (2001) conclude that "The present view associates consciousness with a unified neural workspace through which many processes can communicate. The evolutionary advantages that this system confers to the organism may be related to the increased independence that it affords" (p. 31). Dehaene and Naccache thus suggest that consciousness allows organisms to free themselves from acting out their intentions in the real world, relying instead on less hazardous simulation made possible by the neural workspace. While I certainly agree with this conclusion, it begs the question of how consciousness came to play these functions in the first place. How can conscious states of the system come to reflect the most adaptive representation of the current situation, given that "what is most adaptive" continuously changes?

This complex, dynamical relationship between consciousness and learning, however, often tends to be overlooked in classical models of cognition. As argued in Cleeremans (1997) and also in Cleeremans and Jiménez (2002), this is most likely due to the fact that classical models of cognition (the "Computational Theory of Mind", see Fodor, 1975) take it as a starting point that *cognition is symbol manipulation*. If, however, one takes cognition to be exclusively and exhaustively about symbol manipulation, the only way to separate conscious from unconscious cognition is either (1) to assume that unconscious cognition is just like conscious cognition, only minus consciousness (Searle, 1992), or (2) to deny unconscious cognition altogether. Jiménez and I have dubbed these two (admittedly caricatural) perspectives "Zombie" and "Commander Data" models respectively.

Star Trek: The Next Generation's character Data is an android whose bodily and cognitive innards are fully transparent to himself. Except in rare circumstances, Data thus exhibits perfect episodic memory and perfect introspection. Commander Data theorists likewise assume that cognition is fully transparent – that is, (1) that whatever knowledge is expressed through behaviour is also transparently available to introspection, and (2) that consciousness allows access, with sufficient effort or attention, to all aspects of our inner lives.

In contrast, philosophical zombies (Chalmers, 1996) are perfectly opaque, and in this sense instantiate absolutely implicit beings: Whatever internal knowledge currently influences their behaviour can neither be explicit nor conscious because, by definition, they lack conscious experience. Zombie theorists thus take it as a starting point that consciousness has an epiphenomenal character: There is a zombie within you and, while you may not be aware of its existence, it could in fact be responsible for most of your actions. It is capable of processing all the information you can process in the same way that you do, with one crucial difference: "All is dark inside" (Chalmers, 1996, p. 96); your zombie is unconscious.

Needless to say, both of these perspectives are profoundly unsatisfactory. On the one hand, zombie perspectives (ZP) ascribe no role whatsoever to consciousness in information processing and – because it is absurd to deny consciousness altogether – are ultimately forced to assume the existence of equally powerful conscious and unconscious systems. On the other hand, Commander Data perspectives (CDP), by assuming that all of cognition is conscious, paradoxically likewise depict consciousness as epiphenomenal. Crucially, both perspectives assume that consciousness does not change cognition in any principled way, and hence that *consciousness plays no functional role* beyond that of a epiphenomenon that accompanies either a functionally redundant subset of (ZP) or all (CDP) cognitive events.

In the face of the deeply counterintuitive flavour of both perspectives, it seems surprising to see that the past few years have witnessed the appearance of several broad theoretical proposals that intentionally or inadvertently endorse either of these perspectives. Thus for instance, Holender (1986), based on an extensive review of the subliminal perception literature, found no evidence for the existence of unconscious priming. Likewise, Shanks and St. John (1994) conclude their target article dedicated to implicit learning with the statement that "Human learning is almost invariably accompanied by conscious awareness" (p. 394). O'Brien and Opie (1999) propose that the contents of phenomenal consciousness include all stable neural states, and that it is only those stable states that are causally efficacious, that is, susceptible to influence further processing and, ultimately, behaviour. Perruchet and Vinter (2002), consider that unconscious influences on behaviour should be ascribed exclusively to noncognitive, neural processes and state that "Mental life is posited as co-extensive with consciousness" (p. 299, see also Dulany, 1997).

The debate is rooted not so much in equivocal empirical findings but rather in the deep conceptual problems associated with the notion of unconscious representation. Hence, defenders of the claim that cognition can be unconscious often succumb to some version of the ZP, while defenders of the opposite view can often be taken to endorse some variant of the CDP.

In the next section, I sketch out an alternative, subsymbolic, framework through which to think about the relationship between learning and consciousness – one that I believe offers a clear function to consciousness by linking it with adaptability in cognitive systems.

The framework

If the central assumption that the function of consciousness is to offer adaptive control over behaviour is correct, then consciousness is necessarily closely related to processes of learning, because one of the central consequences of successful adaptation is that conscious control is no longer required over the corresponding behaviour. Indeed, it might seem particularly adaptive for complex organisms to be capable of behaviour that does not require conscious control, for instance because behaviour that does not require monitoring of any kind can be executed faster or more efficiently than behaviour that does require such control. Like Perruchet and Vinter (2002), I assume that there is a dynamic relationship between consciousness and learning such that (1) awareness of a particular state of affairs triggers learning and (2) this learning in turn changes the contents of subjective experience so as to make these contents more adapted.

I would now like to introduce the set of assumptions that together form the core of the framework (see Cleeremans, forthcoming; Cleeremans & Jiménez, 2002, for more detailed accounts). It is important to keep in mind that the framework is based on the connectionist framework (e.g., Rumelhart & McClelland, 1986). It is therefore based on many central ideas that characterize the connectionist approach, such as the fact that information processing is graded and continuous, and that it takes place over many interconnected modules consisting of processing units. In such systems, long-term knowledge is embodied in the pattern of connectivity between the processing units of each module and between the modules themselves, while the transient patterns of activation over the units of each module capture the temporary results of information processing.

This being said, a first important assumption is that *representations are graded, dynamic, active, and constantly causally efficacious*. Patterns of activation in neural networks and in the brain are typically distributed and can therefore vary on a number of dimensions, such as their stability in time, their strength, or their distinctiveness. *Stability* in time refers to how long a representation can be maintained active during processing. There are many indications that different neural systems involve representations that differ along this dimension. For instance, prefrontal cortex, which plays a central role in working memory, is widely assumed to involve circuits specialized in the formation of the enduring representations needed for the active maintenance of task-relevant information. *Strength* of representation simply refers to how many processing units are involved in the representation, and to how strongly activated these units are. As a rule, strong activation patterns will exert more influence on ongoing processing than weak patterns. Finally, *distinctiveness* of representation is inversely related to the extent of overlap that exists between representations of similar instances. Distinctiveness has been hypothesized as the main dimension through which cortical and hippocampal representations differ (McClelland, McNaughton, & O'Reilly, 1995; O'Reilly & Munakata, 2000), with the latter becoming active only when the specific conjunctions of features that they code for are active themselves.

In the following, I will collectively refer to these different dimensions as "quality of representation" (see also Farah, 1994). The most important notion that underpins these different dimensions is that representations, in contrast to the all-or-none propositional representations typically used in classical theories, instead have a *graded* character that enables any particular representation to convey the extent to which what it refers to is indeed present.

Another important aspect of this characterization of representational systems in the brain is that, far from being static propositions waiting to be accessed by some process, representations instead continuously influence processing regardless of their quality. This assumption takes its roots in McClelland's (1979) analysis of cascaded processing which, by showing how modules interacting with each other need not "wait" for other modules to have completed their processing before starting their own, demonstrated how stage-like performance could emerge out of such continuous, non-linear systems. Thus, even weak, poor-quality traces are capable of influencing processing, for instance through associative priming mechanisms – that is, in *conjunction* with other sources of stimulation. Strong, high-quality traces, in contrast have *generative capacity*, in the sense that they can influence performance independently of the influence of other constraints – that is, whenever their preferred stimulus is present.

A second important assumption is that *learning is a mandatory consequence of information processing*. Indeed, every form of neural information processing produces adaptive changes in the connectivity of the system, through mechanisms such as Long Term Potentiation (LTP) or Long Term Depression (LTD) in neural systems, or hebbian learning in connectionist systems. An important aspect of these mechanisms is that they are mandatory in the sense that they take place whenever the sending and receiving units or processing modules are co-active. O'Reilly and Munakata (2000) have described hebbian learning as instantiating what they call *model learning*. The fundamental computational objective of such unsupervised learning mechanisms is to enable the cognitive system to develop useful, informative models of the world by capturing its correlational structure. As such, they stand in contrast with *task learning* mechanisms, which instantiate the different computational objective of mastering specific input–output mappings (i.e., achieving specific goals) in the context of specific tasks through error-correcting learning procedures.

Having put in place assumptions about representations and learning, the central ideas that I would now like to explore are (1) that the extent to which a particular representation is available to consciousness depends on its quality, (2) that learning produces, over time, higher-quality (and therefore adapted) representations, and (3) that the function of consciousness is to offer necessary control over those representations that are strong enough to influence behaviour, yet not sufficiently adapted that their influence does not require control any more.

Figure 23.1 aims to capture these ideas by representing the relationships between quality of representation (x-axis) on the one hand and (1) potency, or the extent to which a representation can influence behaviour, (2) availability to control, (3) availability to subjective experience. I discuss the figure at length in the following section. Let us simply note here that the x-axis represents a continuum between weak, poor-quality representations on the left and very strong, high-quality representations on the right.

Two further points are important to keep in mind with respect to Figure 23.1. First, the relationships depicted in the figure are intended to represent *availability* to some dimension of behaviour or consciousness independently of other considerations. Many potentially important modulatory influences on the state of any particular module are thus simply not meant to be captured, neither by Figure 23.1, nor by the framework presented here. Second, the

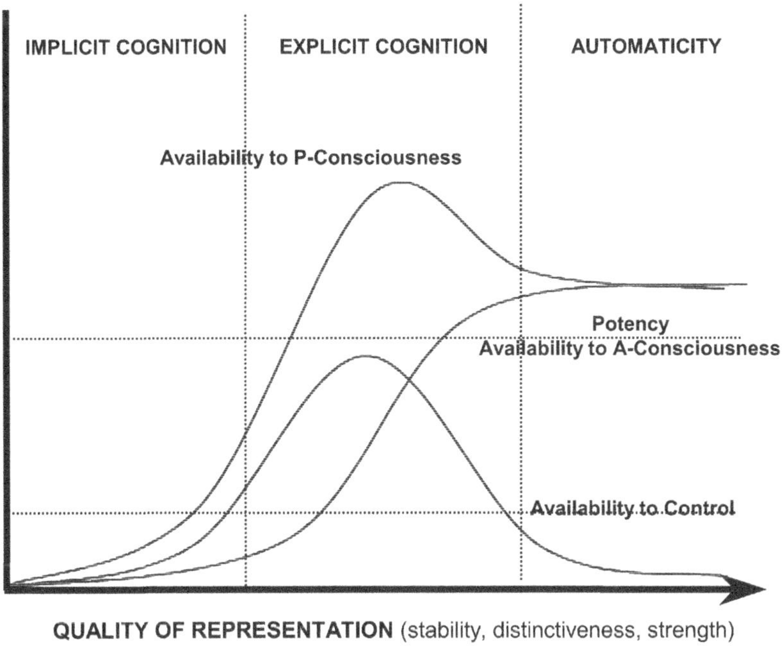

Figure 23.1 Graphical representation of the relationships between quality of representation (x-axis) and (1) potency, (2) availability to control, (3) availability to subjective experience. See text for further details.

figure is intended to represent what happens in *each* of many processing modules involved in any particular cognitive task. Thus, at any point in time, there will be many such modules active, each contributing to some extent to behaviour and to conscious experience; each modulating the activity of other modules. With these caveats in mind, let me now turn to four assumptions about consciousness and its relationship with learning.

C1. Consciousness involves two dimensions: Subjective experience and control

As argued by Ned Block (1995, 2005) and even though there is continuing debate about this issue, consciousness involves at least two separable aspects, namely access consciousness (A-consciousness) and phenomenal consciousness (P-consciousness). According to Block (1995), "A perceptual state is access-conscious roughly speaking if its content – what is represented by the perceptual state – is processed via that information processing function, that is, if its content gets to the Executive system, whereby it can be used to control reasoning and behavior" (p. 234). In other words, whether a state is A-conscious is defined essentially by the causal efficacy of that state; the extent to which it is available for global control of action. Control refers to the ability of an agent to control, to modulate, and to inhibit the influence of particular representations on processing. In this framework, control is simply a function of potency, as described in assumption C3. In contrast, P-consciousness refers to the phenomenal aspects of subjective experience. A state is P-conscious to the extent that there is something it is like to be in that state: I am currently experiencing a pain, hearing a beautiful piece of music, entertaining the memory of a joyful event. While the extent to which potency (i.e., availability to access consciousness) and control on the one hand, and subjective experience (i.e., availability to phenomenal consciousness) on the other, are dissociable is debatable, the framework suggests that potency, control and phenomenal experience are closely related to each other.

C2. Availability to consciousness correlates with quality of representation

This assumption is also a central one in this framework. It states that explicit, conscious knowledge involves higher-quality memory traces than implicit knowledge. "Quality of representation" designates several properties of memory traces, such as their relative strength in the relevant information-processing pathways, their distinctiveness, or their stability in time. The assumption is consistent with the theoretical positions expressed by several different authors over the last few years. O'Brien and Opie (1999) have perhaps been the most direct in endorsing a characterization of phenomenal consciousness in terms of the properties of mental representations in defending the idea that "consciousness equals stability of representation", that is, that the particular mental contents that one is aware of at some point in time correspond to those representations that are sufficiently stable in time. Mathis and Mozer (1996) have also suggested that consciousness involves stable representations, specifically by offering a computational model of priming phenomena in which stability literally corresponds to the state that a dynamic "attractor" network reaches when the activations of a subset of its units stop changing and settle into a stable, unchanging state.

A slightly different perspective on the notion of "quality of representation" is offered by authors who emphasize not stability, but strength of representation as the important feature through which to characterize availability to consciousness. One finds echoes of this position in the writings of Kinsbourne (1997), for whom availability to consciousness depends on properties of representations such as duration, activation, or congruence.

In Figure 23.1, I have represented the extent to which a given representation is available to the different components of consciousness (phenomenal consciousness, access-consciousness/potency, and control) as functions of a single underlying dimension expressed in terms of the quality of this representation. Availability to access-consciousness is represented by the curve labelled "potency", which expresses the extent to which representations can influence behaviour as a function of their quality: High-quality, strong, distinctive representations, by definition, are more potent than weaker representations and hence more likely to influence behaviour. "Availability to control processes" is represented by a second curve, so labelled. We simply assume that both weak and very strong representations are difficult to control, and that maximal control can be achieved on representations that are strong enough that they can begin to influence behaviour in significant ways, yet not so strong that they have become utterly dominant in processing. Finally, availability to phenomenal experience is represented by the third curve, obtained simply by adding the other two. The underlying intuition, discussed in the context of assumption C4, is that which contents enter subjective experience is a function both of availability to control and of potency.

C3. Developing high-quality representations takes time

This assumption states that the emergence of high-quality representations in a given processing module takes time, both over training or development, as well as during processing of a single event. Figure 23.1 can thus be viewed as representing not only the relationships between quality of representation and their availability to the different components of consciousness, but also as a depiction of the dynamics of how a particular representation will change over the different time scales corresponding to development, learning, or within-trial processing.

Both skill acquisition and development, for instance, involve the long-term progressive emergence of high-quality, strong memory traces based on early availability of weaker traces. Likewise, the extent to which memory traces can influence performance at any moment (e.g., during a single trial) depends both on available processing time, as well as on overall trace strength. These processes of change operate on the connection weights between units, and can involve either task-dependent, error-correcting procedures, or unsupervised procedures such as hebbian learning. In either case, continued exposure to exemplars of the domain will result in the development of increasingly congruent and strong internal representations that capture more and more of the relevant variance. Although I think of this process as essentially continuous, three stages in the formation of such internal representations (each depicted as separate regions in Figure 23.1 can be distinguished: Implicit representations, explicit representations, and automatic representations.

The first region, labelled "Implicit Cognition" in Figure 23.1, is meant to correspond to the point at which processing starts in the context of a single trial, or to some early stage of development or skill acquisition. In either case, this stage is characterized by weak, poor-quality representations. A first important point is that representations at this stage are already capable of influencing performance, as long as they can be brought to bear on processing together with other sources of constraints, that is, essentially through mechanisms of associative priming and constraint satisfaction. A second important point is that this influence is best described as "implicit", because the relevant representations are too weak (i.e., not distinctive enough) for the system as a whole to be capable of exerting control over them: You cannot control what you cannot identify as distinct from something else.

The second region of Figure 23.1 corresponds to the emergence of explicit representations, defined as representations over which one can exert control. In the terminology of attractor networks, this would correspond to a stage during learning at which attractors become better defined – deeper, wider, and more distinctive. It is also at this point that the relevant representations acquire generative capacity, in the sense that they now have accrued sufficient strength to have the potential to determine appropriate responses when their preferred stimulus is presented to the system alone. Because awareness is partially tied to control in this framework, one would thus also be aware both of these internal representations and of their influence on our behaviour. Because one is aware of these representations, one can then also possess metaknowledge about them, and recode them in various different ways, for instance, as linguistic propositions.

The third region involves what I call automatic representations, that is, representations that have become so strong that their influence on behaviour can no longer be controlled (i.e., inhibited). Such representations exert a mandatory influence on processing. Importantly, however, one is aware both of possessing them (that is, one has relevant metaknowledge) and of their influence on processing (see also Tzelgov, 1997), because availability to conscious awareness depends on the quality of internal representations, and that strong representations are of high quality. In this perspective then, one can always be conscious of automatic behaviour, but not necessarily with the possibility of control over these behaviours.

In this framework, skill acquisition and development therefore involve a continuum at both ends of which control over representations is impossible or difficult, but for very different reasons: Implicit representations influence performance but cannot be controlled because they are not yet sufficiently distinctive and strong for the system to even know it possesses them. This might in turn be related to the fact that, precisely because of their weakness, implicit representations cannot influence behaviour on their own, but only in conjunction with other sources of constraints. Automatic representations, on the other hand, cannot be controlled because they are too strong, but the system is aware both of their presence and of their influence on performance.

C4. The function of consciousness is to offer flexible, adaptive control over behaviour

The framework gives consciousness a central place in information processing, in the sense that its function is to enable flexible control over behaviour. Crucially, however, consciousness is not necessary for information processing, or for adaptation in general, thus giving a place for implicit learning in cognition. I believe this perspective to be congruent with theories of adaptation and optimality in general.

Indeed, another way to think about the role of learning in consciousness is to ask: "When does one *need* control over behaviour?" Control is perhaps not necessary for implicit representations, for their influence on behaviour is necessarily weak (in virtue of the fact that precisely because they are weak, such representations are unlikely to be detrimental to the organism even if they are not particularly well adapted). Likewise, control is not necessary for automatic representations, because presumably, those representations that have become automatic after extensive training should be *adapted* (optimal) as long as the processes of learning that have produced them can themselves be assumed to be adaptive. Automatic behaviour is thus necessarily optimal behaviour in this framework, except, precisely, in cases such as addiction, obsessive-compulsive behaviour, or laboratory situations where the automatic response is manipulated to be non-optimal, such as in the Stroop situation. Referring again to Figure 23.1, my analysis therefore suggests that the representations that most require control are the explicit representations that correspond to the central region of Figure 23.1: Representations that are strong enough that they have the potential to influence behaviour in and of themselves (and hence that one should really care about, in contrast to implicit representations), but not sufficiently strong that they can be assumed to be already adapted, as is the case for automatic representations. It is for those representations that control is needed, and, for this reason, it is these representations that one is most aware of.

Likewise, this analysis also predicts that the dominant contents of subjective experience at any point in time consist precisely of those representations that are both strong enough that they can influence behaviour, yet weak enough that they still require control. Figure 23.1 reflects these ideas by suggesting that the contents of phenomenal experience depend on the potency of currently active representations as well as on their availability to control. Since availability to control is inversely related to potency for representations associated with automatic behaviour, this indeed predicts weaker availability to phenomenal experience of "very strong" representations as compared to "merely strong" representations. In other words, such representations can become conscious if appropriate attention is directed towards their contents – as in cases where normally automatic behaviour (such as walking) suddenly becomes conscious because the normal unfolding of the behaviour has been interrupted (e.g., because I've stumbled upon something) – but they are not normally part of the central focus of awareness nor do they require conscious control.

The framework thus leaves open four distinct possibilities for knowledge to be implicit. First, knowledge that is embedded in the connection weights within and between processing modules can never be directly available to conscious awareness and control. This is simply a consequence of the fact that I assume that consciousness necessarily involves representations (patterns of activation over processing units). The knowledge embedded in connection weights will, however, shape the representations that depend on it, and its effects will therefore be detectable – but only indirectly, and only to the extent that these effects are sufficiently marked in the corresponding representations.

Second, to enter conscious awareness, a representation needs to be of sufficiently high quality in terms of strength, stability in time, or distinctiveness. Weak representations are therefore poor candidates to enter conscious awareness. This, however, does not necessarily imply that they remain causally inert, for they can influence further processing in other modules, even if only weakly so.

Third, a representation can be strong enough to enter conscious awareness, but fail to be recognized as relevant to the particular situation that is currently unfolding. Conscious contents, indeed, have to be linked together in a coherent manner before they can be made available globally for conscious report and for the control of action. There are thus many opportunities for a particular conscious content to remain implicit, not because its representational vehicle does not have the appropriate properties, but because it fails to be integrated with other conscious contents. Dienes and Perner (2002) offer an insightful analysis of the different ways in which what I have called high-quality representations can remain implicit.

Finally, a representation can be so strong that its influence can be no longer be controlled. In these cases, it is debatable whether the knowledge should be taken as genuinely unconscious, because it can certainly become fully conscious as long as appropriate attention is directed to it, but the point is that such very strong representations can trigger and support behaviour without conscious intention and without the need for conscious monitoring of the unfolding behaviour.

Conclusions

In this article I have attempted to outline a framework that offers a clear functional role to consciousness by linking conscious awareness with adaptation in general, and with learning in particular. I have argued that if we take consciousness as the only mechanism through which flexible control can be achieved over action, then it follows that learning should be the most important factor that determines the contents of conscious experience. Learning thus shapes consciousness, and consciousness, in turn, reflects the adapted appreciation of the dynamics of the current situation that is necessary to make flexible control over action possible (Perruchet & Vinter, 2002).

The framework does not assume that there exists a strong distinction between conscious and non-conscious aspects of cognition. Rather, it assumes that conscious and unconscious aspects of cognition are simply that – *aspects* of a single ensemble of learning mechanisms and of representational systems.

The analysis presented above resonates well with recent computational models of overall cerebral function. O'Reilly and colleagues (Atallah, Frank, & O'Reilly, 2004; McClelland et al., 1995; O'Reilly & Munakata, 2000), for instance, have recently proposed that different regions of the brain have evolved to solve different – and incompatible – computational problems by using different representational formats and different learning regimes (McClelland et al., 1995). In their "tripartite" proposal, the brain is organized in three broad interacting systems: the hippocampus (HC), prefrontal cortex/basal ganglia (FC), and posterior cortex (PC). In this framework, each system uses similar, but not identical, learning mechanisms and representational formats. The main function of the hippocampus is to rapidly learn about specific novel facts (episodic memory). Posterior cortex's function, in contrast, is to learn about the statistical regularities shared by many exemplars of a given domain (semantic memory). Finally, the main function of frontal cortex is to maintain information in an active state (active maintenance, subtending working memory) and to rapidly switch between active representations. Achieving each of these functions requires different (but germane) learning mechanisms and different representational formats. Thus, the hippocampus uses the sparse, conjunctive representations necessary to avoid catastrophic interference, and a high learning rate that makes it possible to rapidly bind together the various elements of the current percept. Posterior cortex, in contrast, slowly accumulates information over largely overlapping, distributed representations, so that broad semantic knowledge can progressively emerge over learning and development. Finally, frontal cortex is characterized by self-sustaining representational systems involving the recurrent connectivity necessary for active maintenance as well as the gating mechanisms necessary for rapid switching.

The three systems also differ from each other in terms of processing and learning mechanisms. Thus, O'Reilly and Munakata (2000) argue that the functions typically attributed to frontal cortex (i.e., working memory, inhibition, executive control, and monitoring) require "activation-based processing", characterized by mechanisms of active maintenance through which representations can remain strongly activated for long periods of time as well as rapidly updated so as to make it possible for these representations to modulate processing elsewhere in the brain. Note how this is consistent with Crick and Koch's (2003) notion that the front of the brain is looking at the back. Because of these properties, frontal representations are thus more accessible to verbalization and other reporting systems. To do this, they oppose "weight-based processing", characteristic of posterior cortex, in which knowledge is encoded directly by the pattern of connectivity between processing units and hence tends to remain tacit to the extent that this knowledge only manifests itself through the effects it exerts on ongoing processing rather than through the form of representations themselves.

Finally, one might wonder about an essential aspect of consciousness that I have not discussed at all in the context of this chapter: Who, or what, is doing the controlling? How are we to conceptualize the self in this framework? I believe that the framework makes it possible to cast that story without resorting to a homunculus, but explaining how is clearly beyond the goals of this article. Suffice it to say here that while the framework indeed involves something of a homunculus, this homunculus need not be a real one but can instead itself be viewed as emergent.

Acknowledgements

Axel Cleeremans is a Senior Research Associate with the National Fund for Scientific Research (FNRS, Belgium). This work was supported by an institutional grant from the Université Libre de Bruxelles to Axel Cleeremans and by grant HPRN-CT-1999-00065 from the European Commission. The FNRS and the Ministère de la Communauté Française de Belgique both contributed to make my participation to the congress possible. Significant portions of this article were adapted from the following publications: (1) Cleeremans, A. & Jiménez, L. (2002). Implicit learning and consciousness: A graded, dynamic perspective. In R.M. French & A. Cleeremans (Eds.), *Implicit learning and consciousness: An empirical, computational and philosophical consensus in the making?* Hove, UK: Psychology Press. (2) Cleeremans, A. (2002). Handlung und Bewusstsein: Ein Rahmenkonzept für den Fertigkeitserwerb. *Psychologie und Sport*, *9*, 2–19. (3) Cleeremans, A. (2005). Computational correlates of consciousness. In S. Laureys (Ed.), *Progress in brain research* (Vol. 150, pp. 81–98). Amsterdam: Elsevier.

References

Atallah, H., Frank, M.J., & O'Reilly, R.C. (2004). Hippocampus, cortex, and basal ganglia: Insights from computational models of complementary learning systems. *Neurobiology of Learning and Memory*, *82*, 253–267.

Block, N. (1995). On a confusion about a function of consciousness. *Behavioral and Brain Sciences*, *18*, 227–287.

Block, N. (2005). Two neural correlates of consciousness. *Trends in Cognitive Science*, *9*(2), 46–52.

Chalmers, D.J. (1996). *The conscious mind: In search of a fundamental theory*. Oxford: Oxford University Press.

Cleeremans, A. (1997). Principles for implicit learning. In D.C. Berry (Ed.), *How implicit is implicit learning?* (pp. 195–234). Oxford: Oxford University Press.

Cleeremans, A. (forthcoming). *Being virtual*. Oxford: Oxford University Press.

Cleeremans, A., Destrebecqz, A., & Boyer, M. (1998). Implicit learning: News from the front. *Trends in Cognitive Sciences*, *2*, 406–416.

Cleeremans, A., & Jiménez, L. (2002). Implicit learning and consciousness: A graded, dynamic perspective. In R.M. French & A. Cleeremans (Eds.), *Implicit learning and consciousness: An empirical, computational and philosophical consensus in the making?* (pp. 1–40). Hove, UK: Psychology Press.

Cleeremans, A., & McClelland, J.L. (1991). Learning the structure of event sequences, *Journal of Experimental Psychology: General*, *120*, 235–253.

Crick, F.H.C., & Koch, C. (2003). A framework for consciousness. *Nature Neuroscience*, *6*(2), 119–126.

Dehaene, S., & Naccache, L. (2001). Towards a cognitive neuroscience of consciousness: Basic evidence and a workspace framework. *Cognition*, *79*, 1–37.

Dienes, Z., & Perner, J. (2002). A theory of the implicit nature of implicit learning. In R.M. French & A. Cleeremans (Eds.), *Implicit learning and consciousness: An empirical, computational and philosophical consensus in the making?* (pp. 68–92). Hove, UK: Psychology Press.

Dulany, D.E. (1997). Consciousness in the explicit (deliberative) and implicit (evocative). In J.D. Cohen & J.W. Schooler (Eds.), *Scientific approaches to consciousness* (pp. 179–212). Mahwah, NJ: Lawrence Erlbaum Associates Inc.

Elbert, T., Pantey, C., Wienbruch, C., Rockstroh, B., & Taub, E. (1995). Increased cortical representation of the fingers of the left hand in string players. *Science*, *270*, 305–307.

Farah, M.J. (1994). Visual perception and visual awareness after brain damage: A tutorial overview. In C. Umiltà & M. Moscovitch (Eds.), *Attention and Performance XV: Conscious and nonconscious information processing* (pp. 37–76). Cambridge, MA: MIT Press.

Farah, M.J. (1998). Why does the somatosensory homunculus have hands next to face and feet next to genitals: A hypothesis. *Neural Computation*, *10*(8), 1983–1985.

Fodor, J.A. (1975). *The language of thought*. New York: Harper & Row.

Holender, D. (1986). Semantic activation without conscious activation in dichotic listening, parafoveal vision, and visual masking: A survey and appraisal. *Behavioral and Brain Sciences*, *9*, 1–23.

Kinsbourne, M. (1997). What qualifies a representation for a role in consciousness? In J.D. Cohen & J.W. Schooler (Eds.), *Scientific approaches to consciousness* (pp. 335–355). Mahwah, NJ: Lawrence Erlbaum Associates Inc.

Maguire, E.A., Gadian, D.G., Johnsrude, I.S., Good, C.D., Ashburner, J., Frackowiak, R.S. et al. (2000). Navigation-related structural change in the hippocampi of taxi drivers. *Proceedings of the National Academy of Sciences of the USA*, *10*, 1073.

Mathis, W.D., & Mozer, M.C. (1996). Conscious and unconscious perception: A computational theory. In *Proceedings of the Eighteenth Annual Conference of the Cognitive Science Society* (pp. 324–328). Hillsdale, NJ: Lawrence Erlbaum Associates Inc.

McClelland, J.L. (1979). On the time-relations of mental processes: An examination of systems in cascade. *Psychological Review*, *86*, 287–330.

McClelland, J.L., McNaughton, B.L., & O'Reilly, R.C. (1995). Why there are complementary learning systems in the hippocampus and neocortex: Insights from the successes and failures of connectionist models of learning and memory. *Psychological Review*, *102*, 419–457.

Nisbett, R.E., & Wilson, T.D. (1977). Telling more than we can do: Verbal reports on mental processes. *Psychological Review*, *84*, 231–259.

Nissen, M.J., & Bullemer, P. (1987). Attentional requirement of learning: Evidence from performance measures. *Cognitive Psychology*, *19*, 1–32.

O'Brien, G., & Opie, J. (1999). A connectionist theory of phenomenal experience. *Behavioral and Brain Sciences*, *22*, 175–196.

O'Reilly, R.C., & Munakata, Y. (2000). *Computational explorations in cognitive neuroscience: Understanding the mind by simulating the brain*. Cambridge, MA: MIT Press.

Perruchet, P. (1985). A pitfall for the expectancy theory of human eyelid conditioning. *Pavlovian Journal of Biological Science*, *20*, 163–170.

Perruchet, P., & Vinter, A. (2002). The self-organizing consciousness. *Behavioral and Brain Sciences*, *25*(3), 297–330.

Pierce, C.S., & Jastrow, J. (1880). On small differences in sensation. *Memoirs of the National Academy of Sciences*, *3*, 75–83.

Reber, A.S. (1967). Implicit learning of artificial grammars. *Journal of Verbal Learning and Verbal Behavior*, *5*, 855–863.

Rumelhart, D.E., & McClelland, J.L. (1986). *Parallel distributed processing: Explorations in the microstructure of cognition. Volume 1: Foundations*. Cambridge, MA: MIT Press.

Searle, J.R. (1992). *The rediscovery of the mind*. Cambridge, MA: MIT Press.

Shanks, D.R., & St. John, M.F. (1994). Characteristics of dissociable human learning systems. *Behavioral and Brain Sciences*, *17*, 367–447.

Tzelgov, J. (1997). Automatic but conscious: That is how we act most of the time. In R.S. Wyer (Ed.), *The automaticity of everyday life* (Vol. X, pp. 217–230). Mahwah, NJ: Lawrence Erlbaum Associates Inc.

Zhu, X., & Simon, H.A. (1987). Learning mathematics by examples and by doing. *Cognition and Instruction*, *4*, 137–166.

Section IV

Life-span developmental psychology

24 Cognitive aging: Some recent developments

Patrick Lemaire

The main goal of research in cognitive aging is to understand how cognition changes with age. This first entails determining what changes and what remains stable with age (which cognitive processes are affected and which are not affected during aging). It also requires investigating who is aging fast and who is aging more slowly so as to determine individual characteristics (e.g., lifestyle, cognitive profiles) underlying individual differences during aging. The third general goal of research in cognitive aging is to determine the mechanisms by which age exerts its effects on human cognition. It is not enough to describe age-related differences or similarities in human cognition. It is also necessary to understand the mechanisms responsible for these changes. Finally, research on cognitive aging is conducted with the hope that some means will be discovered to more effectively help older people to have a better life and stay autonomous as long as possible.

This chapter reviews some recent findings in cognitive aging that speak to two of these fundamental issues. First, we shall see that a great deal of research has been carried out to discover what changes and what does not change with age in human cognition. The findings that are used to illustrate how psychologists have been pursuing this goal show that we are still trying to find out what characterizes processes spared during aging. In particular, we see that what are thought to be the main characteristics (i.e., automaticity of cognitive processes) may not be the crucial dimension. Next, I argue that one of the most important recent conceptual developments in research on cognitive aging lies in the goal of trying to understand how changes occur during aging. In particular, I consider some examples of my research (and that of others) which suggest that looking at strategic variations is fruitful to pursue this goal. I then give a few words of conclusion recapitulating why it is important to look at strategic variations to understanding cognitive aging.

What does or does not change with age in human cognition?

How do our intellectual abilities change with age? What are the abilities that decline and what are those that remain stable (or even improve)? At what age do we start to see age-related decline in human cognition? Is age-related decreased cognitive performance seen in all individuals or are there individual differences? If there are individual differences, what are the causal factors? What is the speed of age-related decline in human cognition? Is age-related decline in human cognition smooth and gradual or abrupt and stage-wise? Is such decline reversible? Are the path, speed, and breadth of age-related changes predictable from a restricted set of factors? In other words, the main issue is whether all cognitive processes decline with age or whether only some processes are negatively affected by age. Answering this fundamental question is very important because it speaks to whether aging is the result of one or more change mechanisms. Global negative effects would suggest that a single, or a restricted set of, cognitive processes may be responsible for aging. Alternatively, differential effects on cognitive processes may suggest several causes of cognitive aging.

A number of results reported by different labs coming from all over the world where research on cognitive aging is carried out first suggested that aging has deleterious effects on most if not all cognitive activities (see Craik & Salthouse, 2000; Perfect & Maylor, 2000; Salthouse, 1991, for reviews). A good example is the findings reported by Schaie and colleagues in their sequential studies. Schaie and colleagues tested more than 2800 participants between 1956 and 1991. These participants' cognitive performance on the Primary Mental Ability test was collected either longitudinally or cross-sectionally. Performance on each of the verbal meaning, space, reasoning, numerical processing, and word fluency tests was plotted for each decade between 20 and more than 70 years old (see Schaie, 1996), and all showed age-related decline. Some abilities decreased faster and more than others. For example, number processing decreased the least and reasoning decreased the most.

However, research outside the psychometric tradition, carried out with the information-processing perspective, suggests that some cognitive processes are much less affected than others by aging. To take an example of research from my lab, I can cite the data on arithmetic processing that Sandrine Duverne and I published in 2004. Three groups of young, middle-age, and older adults had to solve three-digit addition problems like 112+324. All problems varied on the basis of their correct sums, with some problems having small sums (e.g., 112+124) and others having large sums (e.g., 517+429). When we ran regression analyses predicting mean solution times from correct sums in each age group, we found that so-called peripheral processes (such as encoding or responding) declined with age, whereas so-called central processes (such as retrieval of partial sums or basic arithmetic facts from long-term memory) were equally efficient in both age groups (see Allen et al., 1992, 1997; Allen et al., 2005, for similar findings).

There are some instances of activities that show overall equal young and older adults' performance. To illustrate with some findings from my research, we can look at an ongoing project on age-related differences and similarities in numerosity estimation. Numerosity estimation is the ability to determine the approximate number of items in a collection. Illustrated in Figure 24.1 is the collection of dots the numerosity of which our participants had to estimate in less than 6 s (Gandini, Lemaire, & Dufau, 2004). What we found is that under- and over-estimation biases are not different in young and older adults. For example, on small numerosities (i.e., smaller than 200), young and older adults provided estimates that were 12% and 13% away from the correct answer (e.g., they said 112 when 100 dots were shown to them). On large numerosities (i.e., larger than 200), young and older adults provided estimates that were 10% away from correct estimates.

Finding no age-related differences always contains the risk of similar performance being the result of different sets of cognitive processes or different approaches to the task. To have more information regarding participants' approach to this numerosity estimation task, we collected eye movements. What was most interesting in the data was the fact that young and older adults' eye-movement data were very similar. On average, both young and older adults needed 12 eye fixations (each of which had an average duration of 232 ms), respectively. These data suggest that there are some cognitive activities showing no age-related differences. As a consequence, psychologists wish to determine the characteristics of cognitive processes that are spared versus impaired during aging.

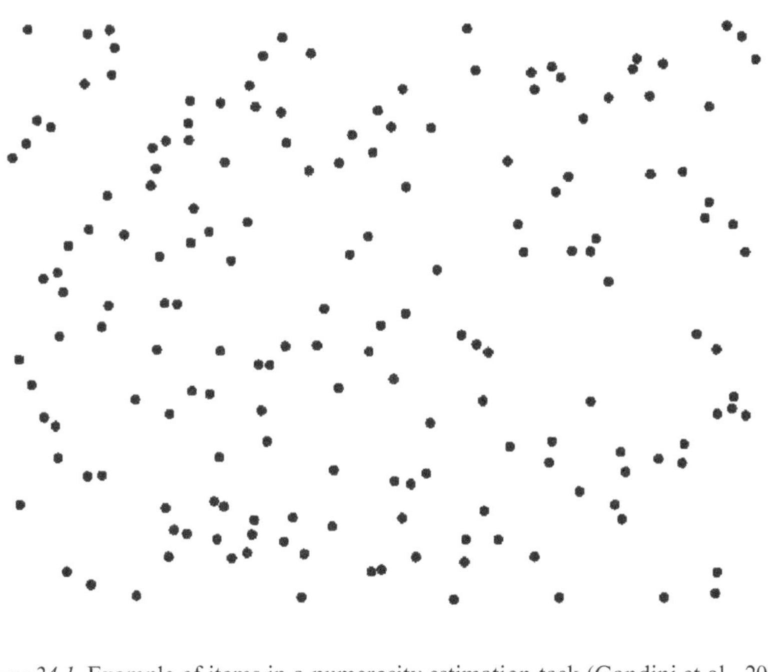

Figure 24.1 Example of items in a numerosity estimation task (Gandini et al., 2004). Participants have to determine the number of dots in less than 6 seconds.

One hypothesis is that automatic processes would be spared during aging while controlled processes would decline. There have been some variants of this hypothesis but all variants have in common that the most effortful processes are the most affected by aging and the less effortful processes are either less or not affected. Consistent with this hypothesis are most robust age-related differences in episodic memory tasks (which involved effortful encoding and retrieval processes) compared to no or smaller age effects on priming effects (e.g., Balota, Black, & Cheney, 1992; Duchek & Balota, 1993). Priming effects are shown in studies where participants see a target stimulus (like a series of letters) and have to process this target stimulus to say whether this target stimulus is a word (e.g., *doctor*) or a nonword (e.g., *crotdo*). Immediately preceding the target stimulus, participants see a prime stimulus which can be a word or a nonword. Some of the prime words are related to target words (e.g., *nurse*); others are not (e.g., *apple*). Priming effects are seen when participants are significantly faster on related prime–target pairs than on unrelated prime–target pairs. Aging studies on priming have shown comparable priming effects in young and older adults (Balota et al., 1992; Duchek & Balota, 1993). Priming effects arise from activation of primes in long-term memory that spread automatically in the long-term memory network of associates. When a target is presented, if it is an associate of primes, as it has received some activation from primes its processing is facilitated. Such priming effects are consistent with the automaticity hypothesis stating that automatic processes (like automatic retrieval and spreading activation) are spared with age.

In a recent study, a PhD student of mine and I reported data that challenged the hypothesis that the automatic–control distinction is the appropriate one to distinguish among impaired and spared processes during aging. We tested subliminal priming effects in young and older adults (Fabre & Lemaire, in press). Subliminal priming experiments are like priming experiments, except that primes are presented much more briefly (for 50 ms or less). Such a brief presentation is enough for the cognitive system to perceive the prime, although unconsciously (participants are unaware that a prime was presented to them and are unable to say what the primes are when informed that primes preceded targets). Such subliminal priming effects result from automatic spreading activation from primes to targets. In the Fabre and Lemaire (in press) study, we presented participants with digits as targets. Participants had to press one button to say if the target digit was an even digit, or another button if the target digit was an odd digit. Unknown to them, a prime digit was presented for 43 ms before the target digits. These prime digits could be either odd or even, so that there were congruent (odd–odd, even–even) and incongruent (odd–even, even–odd) pairs of prime–target digits. We collected latencies, percent errors, and event-related potentials (or brain electrical activity) on 32 electrodes at the surface of the scalp. The data are shown in Figure 24.2. As can be seen from Figure 24.2, the solution times show subliminal priming effects in both young and older adults. However, what is

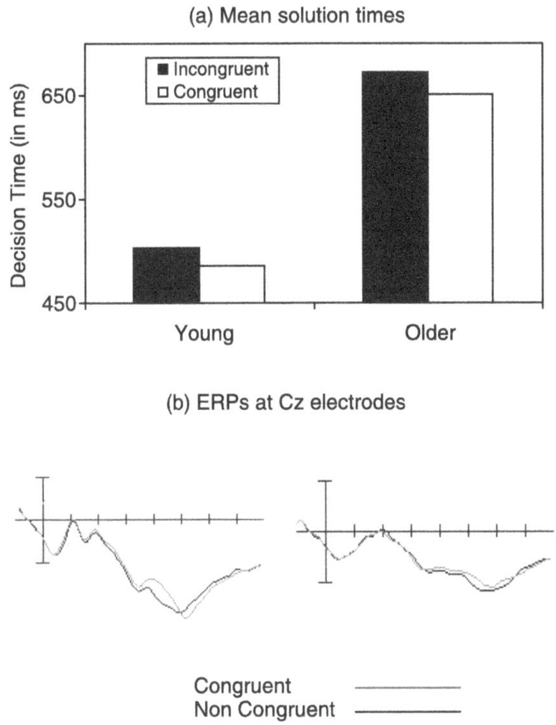

Figure 24.2 Mean reaction times (a) and ERPs at Cz electrodes (b) in young and older adults of the Fabre and Lemaire (in press) subliminal priming experiment.

most interesting is that event-related potentials (ERPs) were more sensitive to aging effects. As can be seen from Figure 24.2b, congruent and incongruent waves diverged 370 ms after target display in younger adults and 495 ms in older adults. Such a difference was absorbed in reaction times because reaction times are the end-product of the chain of processes going from stimulus encoding to response. ERPs were more sensitive to aging research. At a more general level, this suggests that researchers in aging always try to use the most sensitive measure that will most likely reveal age-related differences. It is indeed always possible that a lack of age-related differences may be caused by insufficiently sensitive measures or poor research design. All in all, findings like Fabre and Lemaire's suggest that the automatic–control distinction may not be the appropriate one to characterize processes that are impaired versus spared during aging.

Of course, it is always possible to argue that there are actually no processes that are not affected by aging, if we are to believe that a lack of age-related differences stems from insensitive measures. No age-related differences today may become age-related differences tomorrow when more sensitive measures are used. However, the example of numerosity estimation above may suggest that some of the cognitive processes remain stable in older adults. Although this may be disconfirmed in future research, it makes sense that processes like numerosity estimation may be spared during aging. Such processes may have had high adaptive and survival values during evolution, as it has always been important to be able to determine the numerosity of potential predators and prey in order to survive. Consistent with this are the findings of such numerosity processing in babies (e.g., Barth, Kanwisher, & Spelke, 2003) as well as in non-human primates (Nieder, Freedman, & Miller, 2002). Although quite speculative at this stage, it is possible that skills that were built during evolution, or the premises of which were built, may also be those that are the least affected by aging, whereas skills that have recently appeared during evolution may be those that decline with age (see Geary & Lin, 1998, for a similar hypothesis).

To conclude, psychologists working on aging effects on human cognition have asked whether all processes or intellectual abilities decline with age. Although early evidence suggested massive and general decline in cognitive skills, some recent developments suggest that this may not be the case. Some cognitive processes are spared, others are impaired during aging. What distinguishes impaired versus spared processes is not a settled issue. The first hypothesis, according to which only automatic processes are spared, is disconfirmed by some recent findings on subliminal priming. Such recent findings, if replicated, would suggest that spared processes have characteristics other than automaticity. One possibility that remains to be tested is the evolutionary bases of spared processes, with processes that arose early during evolution being more spared than processes that emerged later.

How changes occur with age: Strategic variations approach to cognitive aging

It is one thing to describe age-related changes in human cognition. It is another one to understand how such changes occur. Observing that not all processes are affected by aging suggests the adoption of two research strategies to understand cognitive aging. First, it is important to assess a wide variety of cognitive activities and processes to assess generality of age-related differences. Second, it is important to try to understand how people accomplish cognitive tasks. This latter is a necessary step to determine if age-related differences stem from people's approaches to the tasks. It is possible that young and older adults do not use the same approaches and that these approaches lead to different performance. One way to look at how people of varying ages approach cognitive tasks is to try to understand which strategies they use.

Several research projects have already tried to look at strategic variations during aging. However, results are mixed. In cognitive domains as diverse as memory (e.g., Parkinson, Lindholm, & Inman, 1982), language processing (e.g., Cohen & Faulkner, 1983), problem solving or reasoning (Salthouse et al., 1990), people have found no strategic variations associated with aging. However, in these same domains, age-related differences in strategic variations were found, sometimes by the same authors, whether in memory (e.g., Dunlosky & Hertzog, 1998), language processing (e.g., Reder et al., 1986), or problem solving and reasoning (e.g., Siegler & Lemaire, 1997).

I would like to argue here that there are at least two kinds of reasons for this inconsistency, namely the lack of an appropriate conceptual framework and of a set of adequate research methods. All previous research on age-related differences in strategic variations has not had a common appropriate conceptual framework that would guide research projects regarding which strategy dimensions to look at. What I want to propose here is to use the conceptual framework that Siegler and I (Lemaire & Siegler, 1995) have proposed to investigate cognitive development in children. In this framework, we make the distinction between four strategy dimensions: strategy repertoire, strategy distribution, strategy execution, and strategy selection. Strategy repertoire refers to the type of strategies that people use (or how they accomplish the task). Several definitions of strategy have been given in cognitive psychology. They all have in common a view of strategy as "a procedure or a set of procedures used to accomplish a goal" (Lemaire & Reder, 1999, p. 365). Strategy distribution refers to the relative percentages of use of each strategy (which strategy is used most often?). Strategy execution, the third dimension of our framework, refers to how fast and accurate each strategy is when applied. Finally, and most originally, the last dimension, strategy selection, concerns how people choose each strategy on a trial-by-trial basis, or what are the choice mechanisms and which factors affect strategy use.

The lack of appropriate research methods has also probably contributed to inconsistent results regarding aging effects on strategic variations. It is not always easy to know how to determine the type of strategies people use to accomplish a task. Indeed, for some tasks, people provide no external behavioural evidence of strategy use. In this case, we have to infer their strategies from variations in performance as a function of task characteristics, such as stimulus features, at the risk of circularity (i.e., performance varies as a function of stimulus features because people use different strategies for different types of stimulus, and using different strategies leads them to have different performance). When people show external behavioural evidence, which is always what should be preferred, the problem is to investigate each strategy dimension independently so that strategy performance is not contaminated by artifactual strategy choices. Siegler and Lemaire (1997) proposed the choice/no-choice method to achieve this end. In this method, participants were first tested under a choice condition in which they chose whichever strategy was available to them to solve each problem. Next, they solved matched problems and were asked to use a single strategy on all problems. Next, they again solved matched problems and were asked to use another single strategy on all problems, and so on until all available strategies had been used in each no-choice condition. This has the advantage of assessing strategy execution (speed, accuracy) independently of strategies being used unequally often, on different sets of problems, and by different types of people. Next, let me illustrate assessments of strategic variations in different types of tasks, where strategies can be assessed either directly or not, so as to know whether there are age-related differences in strategic variations.

To illustrate findings on age effects in strategic variations, let us look at the data that I published with one of my PhD students, Radouane El Yagoubi, and a colleague in Marseille, Mireille Besson (El Yagoubi, Lemaire, & Besson, 2003, 2005). In this study, young and older adults were asked to solve arithmetic problems, while their performance (solution latencies and percent errors) and ERPs were collected. On a computer screen participants saw first a two-digit operand (e.g., 48) for 500 ms, then a second two-digit operand (e.g., 51), and had to decide whether the sum of the two operands was smaller or larger than 100. People had two kinds of problems, so-called small- versus large-split problems. Small-split problems had correct sums that were close (e.g., 43+56) to correct sums, whereas large-split problems had correct sums that were far from correct sums (e.g., 43+42). Solution times and ERPs results, displayed in Figure 24.3, showed an Age × Problem interaction. In young adults, small-split problems produced slower solution times than large-split problems, whereas older adults needed the same amount of time to solve both types of problems. These data suggest that young adults used two different strategies, one for each type of problems, while older adults used the same single strategy for both types of problems. Young adults were slower in solving small-split problems because they had to run all verification processes (i.e., encoding the problem, finding the solution, deciding whether it was smaller or larger than 100, and responding). In large-split problems, because the correct answer was so far away from the target 100, participants could easily and quickly make their smaller/larger decision from operands without calculating the correct answer. Older adults seemed to have calculated the correct answer for both small- and large-split problems. Such a strategy interpretation is reinforced with ERP data. Indeed, brain electric waves (shown in Figure 24.3) display quite different profiles in young and older adults. Waves for small- and large-split problems diverged at about 250 ms after second-operand presentation in young adults, but they did not diverge in older adults. The wave divergence in young adults suggests that each type of problem was solved with a different set of processes. In older adults, waves for small- and large-split problems had exactly the same temporal (and topographical) distribution, as if older adults used the same processes for the two types of problems. In sum, this study on arithmetic problem verification in which no external behavioural evidence can be collected has shown that young and older adults can differ in the type of strategies they use to accomplish a cognitive task. ERP data provided different sources yet converging evidence for such a strategy interpretation. Future studies may test the

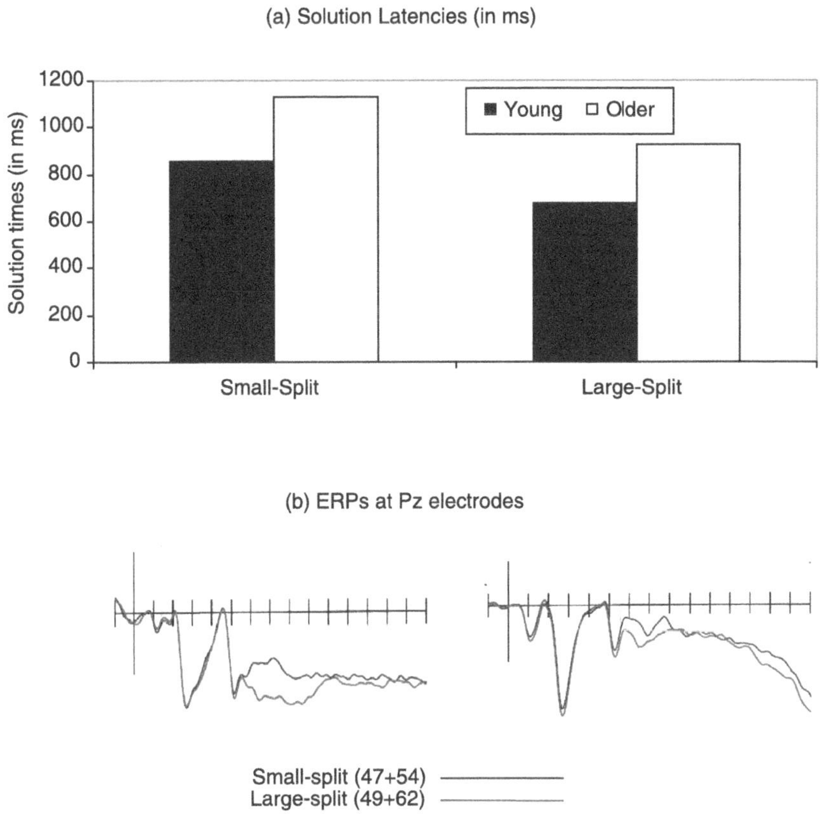

Figure 24.3 Mean reaction times (a) and ERPs at Pz electrodes (b) in young and older adults of the El Yagoubi et al. (2005) experiment.

generality of the conclusion that young and older adults may differ in their strategy repertoire to accomplish some cognitive tasks.

Even if many cognitive tasks do not show external behavioural evidence of strategies, if our goal is to investigate age-related differences in strategic variations it is much better to try to concentrate on tasks that show such evidence. Arithmetic is a nice domain for this, as strategies are often easily seen in many arithmetic tasks. This is perfect to investigate age-related differences in strategy execution. In a paper that Mireille Lecacheur and I published in 2001, we investigated age-related differences in between-currency conversion tasks. In these tasks, people are given an amount in one currency and have to convert it into another currency. In a series of studies, run just before the advent of the Euro in Euroland, we asked participants to convert amounts given in French Francs into Euros (or the reverse). After uncovering the set of strategies that young and old people use in these tasks (Lemaire, Lecacheur, & Ferréol-Barbey, 2000), we focused on two strategies, so-called divide-by-three and multiply-by-six strategies to convert from Euros to French Francs. In the divide-by-three strategy, participants first divide the amount by three (e.g., 150 Euros = 150/3 = 50), then multiply the result by two (50 × 2 = 100), and then multiply that product by ten (100 × 10 = 1000). In the multiply-by-six strategy, participants first multiply the amount by six (150 = 900) and add 10% to this product (900 + 90 = 990). Participants were tested with the choice/no-choice method, in which they first converted a series of amounts with whichever of the two strategies they wanted to use on each problem. Then, they converted matched problems first with divide-by-three and finally with multiply-by-six (half participants saw the reverse order). The data (shown in Figure 24.4) display age-related differences in strategy execution. It is very interesting to see that age-related differences are larger on the most difficult strategy, the multiply-by-six strategy. Recall that these data come from the no-choice condition and are, as a consequence, not the result of strategy choices; they are pure estimates of strategy latencies. This suggests that, even when we control for age-related differences in strategy use, age-related differences in performance are still observed, because young and older participants differ in strategy execution.

Do young and older participants differ in strategy selection? To answer this question, colleagues in Marseille and I collected data on computational estimation (Lemaire, Arnaud, & Lecacheur, 2004). Computational estimation tasks consist in finding an approximate solution to an arithmetic problem without calculating the exact answer (e.g., 32 × 48 = 30 × 50 = 1500). Examples of daily life situations in which computational estimation tasks are accomplished include finding out approximate prices of groceries or between-currency conversion tasks. In a laboratory version of such computational

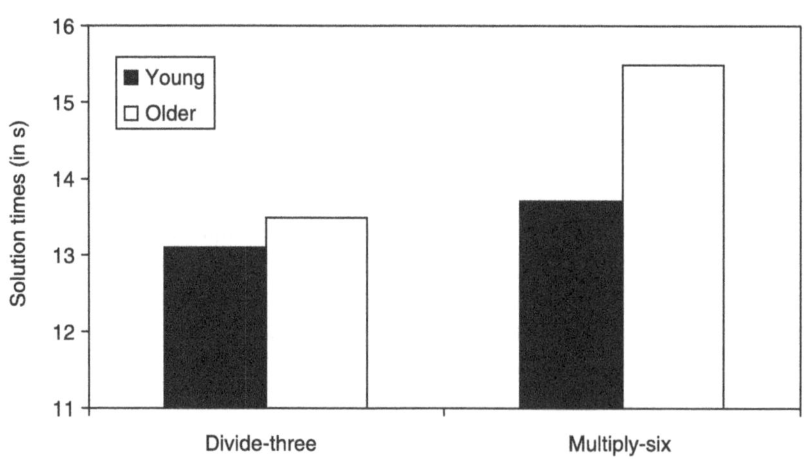

Figure 24.4 Mean solution latencies (in s) in young and older adults while using the multiply-by-six and divide-by-three conversion strategies in the Lemaire and Lecacheur (2001) experiment.

estimation tasks, we asked participants to find approximate products of two-digit multiplication tasks. Participants could use two strategies on each problem: rounding-down both operands (i.e., rounding both operands down to the closest smaller decades like doing 40 × 50 to find an estimate for 42 × 57) or rounding-up both operands (i.e., rounding both operands up to the closest larger decades like doing 50 × 60). The problems were selected so that for each problem one of the two strategies yielded an estimate that was closest to the correct product. For example, rounding-down yielded a better estimate on 26 × 43 and a poorest estimate on 29 × 34. The question was: Are young and older adults equally able to choose the best strategy on each problem so as to increase their overall performance? Data were collected under two accuracy pressure conditions, one in which instructions emphasized speed and accuracy equally, and one in which emphasis was put on accuracy. As can be seen from the data summarized in Figure 24.5, older adults chose the best strategy on each problem less often than young adults, and adjusted their strategy selection less systematically to accuracy pressure than young adults. Not, though, that accuracy pressure did result in changes in mean percent use of best strategy in older adults, suggesting that they are not rigid and not influenced by task constraints. They are just less flexible and less adaptive.

To summarize, looking at strategic variations with a conceptual framework that makes a distinction between different strategy dimensions, and using appropriate methods to independently assess each of these dimensions, proved useful to look at aging effects on strategic variations. In some tasks, young and older adults do not use the same strategy. In other tasks, they use the same strategy repertoire, but use strategies with different relative frequencies or execute each strategy with different levels of efficiency. Finally,

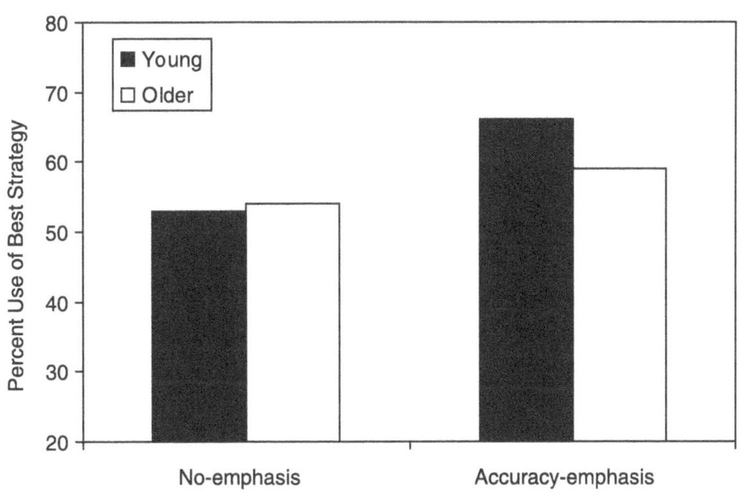

Figure 24.5 Mean percent use of best strategy under each accuracy pressure condition in young and older adults (from Lemaire et al., 2004).

another source of age-related differences lies in strategy selection: Older adults may not be as systematic as young adults in strategy choices and not as good in selecting strategies when they work the best.

Conclusions

The field of cognitive aging is extremely exciting. It addresses some fundamental and important issues both at the theoretical and at the practical levels. Previous research has revealed age-related differences and similarities in human cognition, with some cognitive aging having deleterious effects on some activities or processes and having no such effects in other cognitive areas. Future research in cognitive aging will continue to address issues already tackled such as determining the nature of those processes that remain fully functional during the lifespan. Future research will also address new issues, such as determining the exact nature of age-related differences in terms of how people accomplish cognitive tasks. I have illustrated here the usefulness of a conceptual framework that makes a distinction among several strategy dimensions. I have also illustrated how an appropriate conceptual framework could make possible independent assessments of each of these strategy dimensions.

As the field makes great advances, asking the strategy question may be most important whatever the theoretical or methodological approach one adopts to understand sources of adults' age-related differences in human cognition. Investigating cognitive strategies is important (a) because of the ubiquity of multiple strategy use by young and older adults (in many cognitive tasks, people are not using a single strategy); (b) because it will help to understand previous empirical inconsistencies; (c) because strategies provide a great window on the series of cognitive processes by which young and older adults accomplish cognitive tasks; (d) because it provides a mechanistic account of both behavioural and neuroimaging findings in cognitive aging (e.g., to what extent the hemispheric asymmetry reduction often found in neuroimaging is due to older adults using different strategies compared to young adults); (e) because it enables the discovery of compensatory mechanisms to cope with age-related decrease in cognitive performance and to unravel the nature of these compensatory mechanisms. Finally, asking the question of strategies in aging research opens up new avenues for research. No doubt the field will continue to be an exciting adventure for a while!

References

Allen, P.A., Ashcraft, M.H. et al. (1992). On mental multiplication and age. *Psychology and Aging*, *7*, 536–545.

Allen, P.A., Bucur, B., Lemaire, P., Duverne, S., Ogrocki, P.K., & Sanders, R.E. (2005). Influence of probable Alzheimer's disease on multiplication verification and production. *Aging, Neuropsychology, and Cognition*, *12*(1), 1–31.

Allen, P.A., Smith, A.F. et al. (1997). Age differences in mental multiplication: Evidence for peripheral but not central decrements. *Journal of Gerontology: Psychological Sciences*, *52b*(2), 81–90.

Balota, D.A., Black, S.R., & Cheney, M. (1992). Automatic and attentional priming in young and older adults: Reevaluation of the two-process model. *Journal of Experimental Psychology: Human Perception & Performance*, *18*, 485–502.

Barth, H., Kanwisher, N., & Spelke, E. (2003). The construction of large number representations in adults. *Cognition*, *86*, 201–221.

Cohen, G., & Faulkner, D. (1983). Age differences in performance on two information-processing tasks: Strategy selection and processing efficiency. *Journal of Gerontology*, *38*, 447–454.

Craik, F.I.M., & Salthouse, T.A. (2000). *The handbook of aging and cognition* (2nd ed.). Mahwah, NJ: Lawrence Erlbaum Associates Inc.

Duchek, J.M., & Balota, D.A. (1993). Sparing activation processes in older adults. In J.R.J. Cerella, W. Hoyer, & M.L. Commons (Eds.), *Adult information processing: Limits on loss* (pp. 384–403). New York: Academic Press.

Dunlosky, J., & Hertzog, C. (1998). Aging and deficits in associative memory: What is the role of strategy production? *Psychology and Aging*, *13*, 597–607.

Duverne, S., & Lemaire, P. (2004). Age-related differences in arithmetic problem verification strategies. *Journal of Gerontology: Psychological Sciences*, *59*, 135–142.

El Yagoubi, R., Lemaire, P., & Besson, M. (2003). Different brain mechanisms mediate two strategies in arithmetic: Evidence from event-related brain potentials. *Neuropsychologia*, *41*, 855–862.

El Yagoubi, R., Lemaire, P., & Besson, M. (2005). Effects of aging on arithmetic problem-solving: An event-related brain potential study. *Journal of Cognitive Neuroscience*, *17*(1), 37–50.

Fabre, L., & Lemaire, P. (in press). Age-related differences in automatic stimulus–response associations: Insights from young and older adults' parity judgment. *Psychonomic Bulletin & Review*.

Gandini, D., Lemaire, P., & Dufau, J. (2004). *Age-related differences for approximate quantification*. Paper presented at the 46th Annual Meeting of the Psychonomic Society, Toronto, November.

Geary, D., & Lin, J. (1998). Numerical cognition: Age-related differences in the speed of executing biologically primary and biologically secondary processes. *Experimental Aging Research*, *24*(2), 101–138.

Lemaire, P., Arnaud, L., & Lecacheur, M. (2004). Adults' age-related differences in adaptivity of strategy choices: Evidence from computational estimation. *Psychology and Aging*, *10*(3), 467–481.

Lemaire, P., & Lecacheur, M. (2001). Older and younger adults' strategy use and execution in currency conversion tasks: Insights from French Franc to Euro and Euro to French Franc conversions. *Journal of Experimental Psychology: Applied*, *3*, 195–206.

Lemaire, P., Lecacheur, M., & Ferréol-Barbey, M. (2001). Strategy choices in conversion tasks: The examples of French Franc to Euro and Euro to French Franc conversions. *Current Psychology Letters*, *4*, 39–50.

Lemaire, P., & Reder, L. (1999). What affects strategy selection in arithmetic? An example of parity and five effects on product verification. *Memory & Cognition*, *22*, 364–382.

Lemaire, P., & Siegler, R.S. (1995). Four aspects of strategic change: Contributions to children's learning of multiplication. *Journal of Experimental Psychology: General, 124*(1), 83–97.

Nieder, A., Freedman, D.J., & Miller, E.K. (2002). Representation of quantity of visual items in the primate prefrontal cortex. *Science, 297*, 1708–711.

Parkinson, S.R., Lindholm, J.M., & Inman, V.W. (1982). An analysis of age differences in immediate recall. *Journal of Gerontology, 37*, 425–431.

Perfect, T.J., & Maylor, E.A. (2000). *Models of cognitive aging*. New York: Oxford University Press.

Reder, L.M., Wible, C. et al. (1986). Differential memory changes with age: Exact retrieval versus plausible inference. *Journal of Experimental psychology: Learning, Memory, and Cognition, 12*(1), 72–81.

Salthouse, T.A. (1991). *Theoretical perspectives on cognitive aging*. Hillsdale, NJ, Lawrence Erlbaum Associates Inc.

Salthouse, T.A., Legg, S.E. et al. (1990). Memory factors in age-related differences in simple reasoning. *Psychology and Aging, 5*, 9–15.

Schaie, W.K. (1996). *Intellectual development in adulthood*. Cambridge: Cambridge University Press.

Siegler, R.S., & Lemaire, P. (1997). Older and younger adults' strategy choices in multiplication: Testing predictions of ASCM using the choice/no-choice method. *Journal of Experimental Psychology: General, 126*(1), 71–92.

25 An overview of the cognitive neuroscience of aging

Denise C. Park and Eric D. Leshikar

Aging, cognition and behavior: An overview

There is a wealth of evidence suggesting that older adults have more trouble learning new information, exhibit less efficient reasoning skills, are slower to respond on all types of cognitive tasks, and are more susceptible to disruption from interfering information than younger adults (see reviews on these topics in edited volumes by Craik & Salthouse, 2000; Park & Schwarz, 2000). Here we review some of the major findings.

The nature of decline

There are a variety of mechanisms that have been suggested as fundamental causes for the decreased memory and information-processing abilities of older adults, and they fall into two general categories. One is a global, undifferentiated, single-mechanism view. For example, Salthouse (1991, 1996) has suggested that age-related declines in the speed at which information is processed account for age differences on essentially all cognitive tasks. Speed of processing is measured by how rapidly young and old adults can make simple same–different judgments when presented with two figures or strings of letters or digits side by side. This simple task shows consistent declines across the lifespan (see Digit Symbol, Letter Comparison, and Pattern Comparison in Figure 25.1) and predicts most if not all age-related variance on a broad array of cognitive tasks. In a related vein, Baltes and Lindenberger (1997) have suggested that crude measures of sensory function (visual and auditory acuity) are even more fundamental than speed of processing in explaining age differences. They found that these sensory measures explained 49% of overall task variance on 14 different tasks in a sample of adults aged 70–103. They argue that this relationship is so strong because sensory function provides a crude overall measure of declining neuronal integrity in the older adult. The view that all types of cognitive decline with age are caused by a single mechanism has been labeled the "common cause" hypothesis (Lindenberger & Baltes, 1994).

An alternative approach assumes that age-related declines are due to

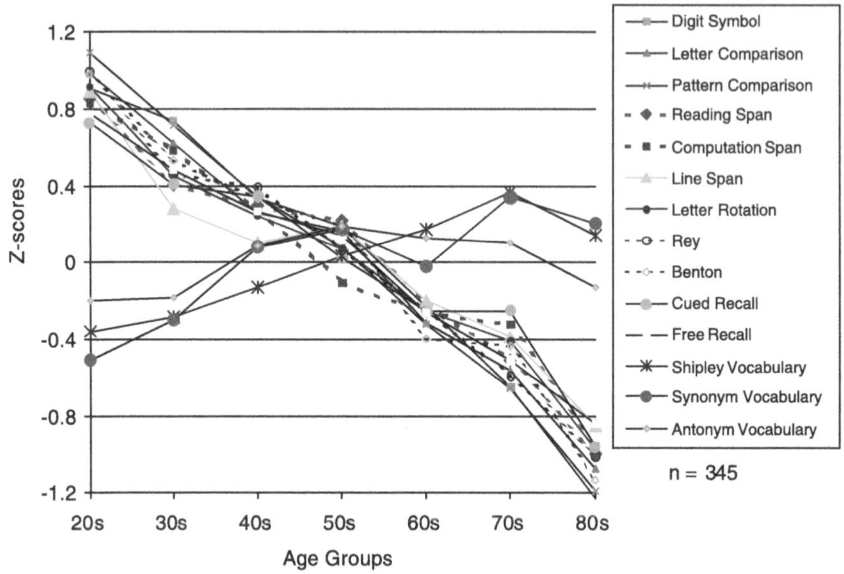

Figure 25.1 Performance on speed, working memory and long-term memory across the lifespan.

problems with specific cognitive mechanisms. For example, there is evidence that executive functions (e.g., working memory processes, inhibitory function, and the ability to switch among tasks) decline with age (see Park, 2000, and Zacks, Hasher, & Li, 2000, for reviews). Executive functions are used in service of many cognitive tasks including reasoning, strategic encoding, and retrieval of information in long-term memory, and many everyday or work-related tasks that require learning or responding to novel information.

We will consider working memory first, as it is the best understood of the executive functions. Working memory deficits can be thought of as decreased on-line capacity, or limited ability to store, process, and manipulate information. Working memory is typically assumed to consist of a central executive system that processes information drawn from two passive storage subsystems that are domain specific – verbal and visuo-spatial stores (Baddeley, 1986). Virtually all cognitive tasks that require effortful processing are thought to require working memory. There is a range of models of working memory (Engle, Tuholski, Laughlin, & Conway, 1999; Shah & Miyake, 1996), but most are variants of the Baddeley model. Regardless of the view one adopts, there is no question that working memory declines with age, particularly the processing or central executive component, as evidenced by the Reading Span and Computation Span scores presented in Figure 25.1 (Park, Davidson, Lautenschlager, Smith, Smith, & Hedden, 2002; Park et al., 1996).

Hasher and Zacks (1988) have emphasized the role of inhibition, rather than working memory, in age-related cognitive declines. They proposed that older adults are less effective at inhibiting irrelevant information than young adults. They argue that working memory capacity is not limited with age, but rather is filled with "mental clutter" so that capacity appears to be diminished. Older adults are assumed to be particularly deficient in a deletion operation in working memory whereby irrelevant information is efficiently discarded when it is no longer needed. There is considerable evidence that older adults have difficulty inhibiting irrelevant information in working memory (Hedden & Park, 2001; May, Hasher, & Kane, 1999; Zacks & Hasher, 1994, 1997).

There is also evidence that older adults have difficulty in flexibly deploying mental resources and/or switching among different tasks. Two good everyday examples that require task switching are day-trading stocks and piloting an airplane. Both the day trader and airline pilot must constantly shift attention among various indicators and adjust their behavior accordingly (e.g., trade a stock; adjust altitude). There is considerable evidence that older adults have difficulty switching from one operation to another, relative to young adults (Kramer, Hahn, & Gopher, 1999; Kray & Lindenberger, 2000; Mayr, 2001), with older adults showing larger time costs for switching between tasks (or metaphorically, reloading mental software) than young adults; the age difference was smaller when subjects made repeated trials on the same task.

Another process that is important for many cognitive tasks, but particularly long-term memory tasks, is the ability to connect a memory event to a context. For example, an older adult may remember that he was told to take shark cartilage to improve his/her arthritis. What the older adult may not remember is whether they were instructed to do this by a personal physician or were told to do this by a friend who had just read the *National Enquirer*. Thus, the older adults may find they remember a fact, but not the source of the information (Johnson, DeLeonardis, Hashtroudi, & Ferguson, 1995; Spencer & Raz, 1994). This decreased ability to bind target information to source or context is a problem for older adults in long-term memory tasks (Chalfonte & Johnson, 1996; Park & Puglisi, 1985; Park Puglisi & Lutz, 1982) as well as working memory tasks (Hedden & Park, 2001).

Finally, there is no question that long-term memory declines with age (see Cued Recall and Free Recall tasks in Figure 25.1). Problems with decreases in speed, working memory, switching, inhibition, and binding could all contribute to poor long-term memory. One problem with the behavioral literature in cognitive aging is that hypotheses about the mechanisms of age-related decline on cognitive tasks have frequently been presented as though evidence for age-sensitivity in one mechanism is evidence against another. This type of thinking is naïve. It is likely that all of the different executive processes as well as speed of processing decline with age and collectively contribute to difficulties in reasoning, memory, and other higher-order cognitive functions. Park et al. (1996) examined the joint contributions of speed and working memory to long-term memory function across the lifespan using structural equation models, and showed that both were important in explaining long-term memory function. This study thus verifies that global mechanisms like speed as well as specific mechanisms like working memory, as specified by the structural equation modeling, are both fundamental in explaining variance in higher-order cognitive function. In a later study, Park et al. (2002) reiterated this finding for both visuo-spatial and verbal working and long-term memory.

It is also important to recognize that these mechanisms may not all decline at the same rate within subjects and that deterioration of different mechanisms might be controlling similar levels of decline in different individuals. Cognitive aging researchers have devoted relatively little attention to understanding how the different mechanisms work separately or together in specific individuals to explain declines in cognitive function, and this is an important direction for future research.

Other important behavioral issues

Three other important issues with respect to behavioral changes in cognitive performance with age relate to rates of change across the lifespan, spared cognitive processes, and the potential to improve cognitive function.

Decline is continuous across the lifespan

Besides demonstrating that, with age, knowledge (vocabulary tests) may increase while performance on processing-intensive tasks decreases, Figure 25.1 also illustrates one poorly understood and little-recognized phenomenon of some importance: Both cross-sectional and longitudinal data suggest that decline is relatively continuous across the lifespan, beginning in young adulthood. We believe that symptoms of cognitive decline that begin occurring in the second decade of life become more noticeable in late adulthood only because they have accrued to the point where they result in noticeable declines in function (Park & Hedden, 2001). As a crude metaphor, consider that an individual with a million dollars probably would not be very concerned initially about the loss of $2,000 per year, but would be much more likely to notice and worry 50 years later when $100,000 in losses had accrued. So it seems to be with cognitive aging. It is also important to consider that losses of executive function and long-term memory in middle-aged adults may not be too apparent to the individual because they are offset by increases in expertise and skill. Little is understood about the interplay among increasing knowledge and declining executive function and memory across the lifespan. This is a tremendously important issue that we will have more to say about later.

Spared processes and growth of knowledge

We should also note that memory decline does not occur on tasks that are low in their requirements for executive processes – that is tasks where little effortful and strategic processing is required. Memory tasks where age invariance has been demonstrated include picture recognition (Park, Puglisi & Smith, 1986) and implicit memory (LaVoie & Light, 1994; Light & LaVoie, 1993; Park & Shaw, 1992) – both are passive, non-strategic tasks. Also, there is some evidence that age differences are more pronounced for encoding new material, compared to retrieving information (Anderson, Craik, Naveh-Benjamin, 1998; Park, Smith, Dudley, & Lafronza, 1989) due to the obligatory or automatic nature of retrieval (Craik, Govoni, Naveh-Benjamin, & Anderson, 1996). Finally, knowledge organization and semantic memory remain relatively unchanged with age (Howard, McAndrews, & Lasaga, 1981; Light, 1992). Figure 25.1 demonstrates that world knowledge, as measured by vocabulary, is not subjected to age-related declines, and may even show growth across the lifespan. As Figure 25.1 illustrates, it is only tasks that require considerable mental effort or deliberate recollection that show age declines (Light, 1991).

Repairing declining cognition

The primary view among cognitive psychologists of how to "repair" declining cognition has been to provide older adults with memory supports that bypass the need to encode items actively or deliberately, thus lessening the executive processing requirements of the tasks (Craik, 1986). Specific examples in which environmental supports have effectively repaired the memory of older adults include (a) using matching pictures to support memory for sentences, resulting in dramatically better memory in older adults (probably due to dual coding of the material which provides two routes to recall; Cherry, Park, Frieske, & Smith, 1996), and (b) providing older adults with memory cues that are conceptually related to target words, resulting in larger memory improvements for the words in the old compared to the young (Park, Smith, Morrell, Puglisi, & Dudley, 1990). The conceptually related cues built upon existing world knowledge possessed by older adults, and relied on activation of existing information rather than only on engagement of executive processes (primarily working memory). In a recent study, Hedden, Lautenschlager, and Park (2005) provided evidence that older adults use world knowledge (vocabulary) to compensate for decreases in speed and working memory when performing a paired-associate memory task, a direct demonstration of the compensatory role that world knowledge plays as cognitive resources decline with age.

Neural underpinnings of cognitive aging

Recently, the fields of neuroscience and cognitive aging have begun to merge, and already we have learned a number of things that were not previously considered in a systematic way in the cognitive aging literature. In the following sections, we discuss what is known about neural decline and reorganization as it relates to aging, with a primary emphasis on work conducted in the Park laboratory at the University of Illinois at Urbana-Champaign.

Brain atrophy

Structural imaging of brains indicates that although the brain shrinks or shows volumetric changes with age, these changes are not equal across brain structures. There is more shrinkage with age in the frontal cortex, intermediate shrinkage in mediotemporal areas, and little decrease in volume in the occipital cortex (Raz, 2000; Raz et al., 2004). There is also some evidence that suggests age-related shrinkage of the parietal cortex (Resnick, Pham, Kraut, Zonderman, & Davatzikos, 2003). There are decreases in both grey matter and white matter, and evidence for demyelination (Kemper, 1994; Raz, 2000). Increases in white matter hyperintensities occur with age (Gunning-Dixon & Raz, 2000). These are small decreases in white matter tissue irregularly distributed across regions. These lesions are viewed as pathological, but their cause is poorly understood and may be related to transient cerebral ischemia or hypertension. At the cellular level, dopamine receptors (Seeman et al., 1987; Volkow et al., 1996), transporters (Volkow et al., 1996) and storage vesicles (Frey et al., 1998) all decline with aging, with rate estimates at 2–8% per decade. Volkow et al. (2000) found that this loss correlated with decreased activity in frontal and cingulate metabolism.

Functional imaging of the aging brain

Functional imaging of the brain allows us to examine neural activity in specific brain structures while a cognitive task is being performed and has provided surprising findings about neural activity in the aging brain. Given the declines in cognitive performance portrayed in Figure 25.1, one might intuitively expect that these declines are accompanied by decreased activation in the aging brain. The most common finding from the cognitive neuroscience literature on aging, however, is that older adults show activation across more neural structures than young adults. In particular, there is evidence that when young adults perform a cognitive task that shows activations that are highly lateralized in one hemisphere of the dorsolateral prefrontal cortex, older adults will tend to show activation in both hemispheres. This finding has been reported for both working memory (Reuter-Lorenz et al., 2000) and long-term memory (Cabeza et al., 1997), and has been replicated reliably in many other laboratories beyond this initial report (Bäckman et al., 1997; Grady,

Bernstein, Beig, & Siegenthaler, 2002; Madden et al., 1999; Morcom, Good, Frackowiak, & Rugg, 2003; Rosen et al., 2002). Both Reuter-Lorenz et al. (2000) and Cabeza (2002) argue that this bilateral distribution of frontal activation in old adults represents a compensatory activation that occurs in the aging brain to accommodate in response to the decreased volume of neural tissue and declining efficiency of neural circuitry.

In addition to speculation about the compensatory aspects of the bilateral activation in frontal cortex, this has also often been cited as an example of "dedifferentiation", that is, the engagement of a more distributed and less specific set of neural structures by old adults on tasks where young adults show a highly specialized pattern of neural activations. The term "dedifferentiation" comes from cognitive/behavioral work on aging, as this term has been frequently used to describe a behavioral phenomenon where performance on an array of tasks that is uncorrelated in young adults, is highly intercorrelated for older adults. Lindenberger and Baltes (1994) argue that dedifferentiation is a fundamental aspect of cognitive aging, and they reported an important finding in an influential paper. Lindenberger and Baltes (1994) collected a large array of cognitive measures from a sample of adults aged 70 to 103 and noted that sensory function (auditory and visual function after correction with lens and hearing aids) was highly intercorrelated with measures of cognition. Upon further analysis, they determined that sensory function mediated nearly all of the age-related variance in this elderly sample, and speculated that this occurred because decline in sensory and cognitive measures jointly represent a measure of central nervous system integrity. Older adults experiencing considerable neural degradation would experience declines in visual and auditory function mediated at the cortical level, and hence sensory function provided a crude window into the overall neural health of an individual. Moreover, due to declining neural integrity with age, measures of performance that were not strongly related in young adults, became intercorrelated with age, as neural function became less focal and more "dedifferentiated". These studies (Baltes & Lindenberger, 1997; Lindenberger & Baltes, 1994) were conducted before functional neuroimaging work had begun on older adults, but the speculations about brain structure and function in these articles proved to be prescient. In the research program that we describe in these next few pages, we will show how this important behavioral work of Baltes and Lindenberger (1997) became an important theoretical guide to a program of neuroimaging in the Park laboratory that spanned multiple brain structures and used paradigms that examined attention, working memory, and long-term memory processes in young and old adults.

Much of the initial work in the field of the cognitive neuroscience of aging focused on the frontal cortex. In our laboratory, we adopted a "whole brain" approach, examining paradigms that focused primarily on sensory, on medial temporal, or on frontal cortex in an effort to develop a comprehensive view of neurocognitive function with age. We discuss our initial work on attentional processes in ventral visual cortex, followed by a working memory paradigm where frontal-hippocampal relationships are predominant, and close with work on long-term memory. Two themes predominate in this work. One is the role that dedifferentiation and decreased neural specialization play in patterns of neural activation associated with age. The other is a systematic investigation of the hypothesis that increased frontal activation in the old compensates for decreased hippocampal activation and decreased neural specialization in the ventral stream.

Visuo-attentional processes

There is clear evidence for highly specialized sites in the ventral visual cortex that are uniquely tuned to processing faces (fusiform face area, FFA; Kanwisher, McDermott, & Chun, 1997), locations and places (the parahipp-pocampal place area, PPA; Epstein & Kanwisher, 1998), and even letters (left fusiform word form area) and words (Polk & Farah, 1998; Puce, Allison, Asgari, Gore, & McCarthy, 1996). We reasoned that if sensory dedifferentiation was a fundamental cause of age-related decline in cognition as suggested by Baltes and Lindenberger (1997), we would expect that older adults would not have such well-defined neurosensory sites for processing the unique visual information available in faces, places, and words. To test this hypothesis, we presented young and old adults with blocks of pictures of faces, blocks of houses, blocks of pseudo words, and blocks of phase-scrambled pictures (abstract images that contain visual detail but no meaningful information) while conducting a functional imaging scan in an MRI machine. Using subtraction methods, we isolated the top 15 voxels in young adults that were uniquely activated by faces. We were not surprised to find that these "face voxels" showed little activation to the other categories of stimuli (houses and words). In contrast, when we isolated the voxels for the old adults that responded most strongly to faces, these "face voxels" turned out not to be so specialized, and responded quite strongly to other categories of stimuli, including houses and words (Park, Polk, Park, Minear, Savage, & Smith, 2004). We found the same results when we examined how specialized the top voxels were for houses and words. The voxels that responded most strongly to each category in the young did not respond very strongly to the other categories. In the old, however, there was much less specialization of voxels. As shown in Figure 25.2, voxels that responded to one category frequently responded to other categories as well. The results held, whether we isolated the top 10, 15, or 20 voxels for each category. Figure 25.3 shows how many shared voxels there were across categories in young compared to old adults, and the numbers are significantly higher for the old. This pattern of decreased specificity of activations to categories where young show highly specialized activation seemed to us to represent clear evidence for dedifferentiation of neural function with age, verifying the theorizing of Baltes and Lindenberger that with age, the brain becomes dedifferentiated. Nevertheless, it remains to be

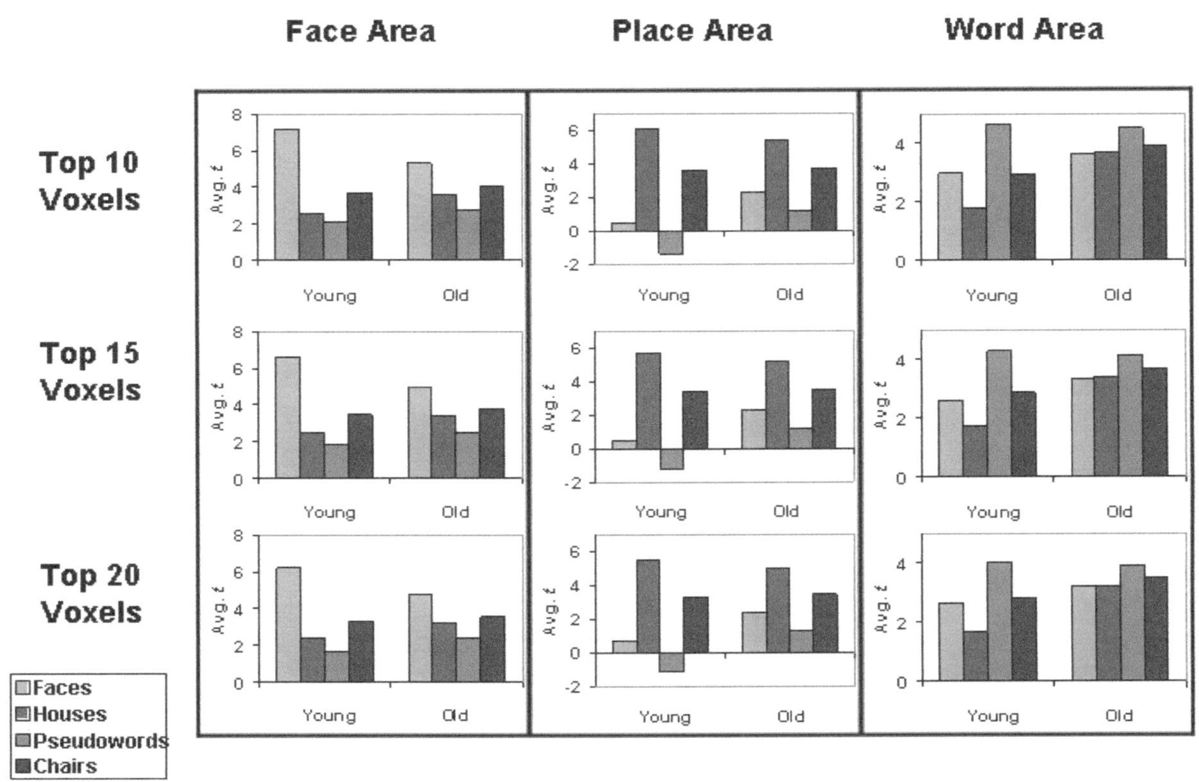

Figure 25.2 Mean t-values for the most active voxels for faces (left column), places (middle), and words (right), for the young and old groups in the top 10 (top), top 15 (middle), and top 20 voxels (bottom). Copyright 2004 National Academy of Sciences, USA.

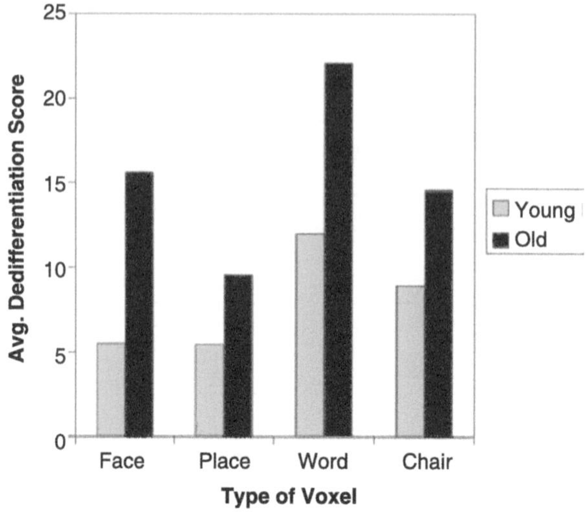

Figure 25.3 The number of shared voxels for each category type. A higher number represents greater dedifferentiation, or number of shared voxels, for each category. Copyright 2004 National Academy of Sciences, USA.

demonstrated that dedifferentiation of neural sites plays an important role in declining cognition with age. One would expect that individuals who have the most overlapping voxels across categories would also show the poorest cognition. Additionally, it is tempting to speculate that increased frontal activation is compensatory for the decreased specialization of the ventral visual cortex, a position advanced by Park et al. (2004) and supported by recent work by Cabeza, Daselaar, Dolcos, Prince, Budde, and Nyberg (2004).

Working memory

In other work, we have investigated the relationship between frontal and hippocampal activation. Park and Gutchess (2005) have argued that increased frontal activation with age may be in response to age-related decrease in hippocampal activation. Pictures are an ideal stimulus medium for understanding the relationship between frontal and hippocampal activations because the requirement that the various elements of pictures be bound into a unitary whole (relational processing) is highly demanding of hippocampal resources (Cohen, Ryan, Hunt, Romine, Wszalek, & Nash, 1999). To assess the relationship between frontal and hippocampal activations, we used an event-related fMRI design with two conditions for studying pictures in a working memory task (Park et al., 2003). As shown in Figure 25.4, subjects received two types of trials. In the Extended Visual condition, subjects studied a picture for 6 seconds and then saw a fragment of the picture. They

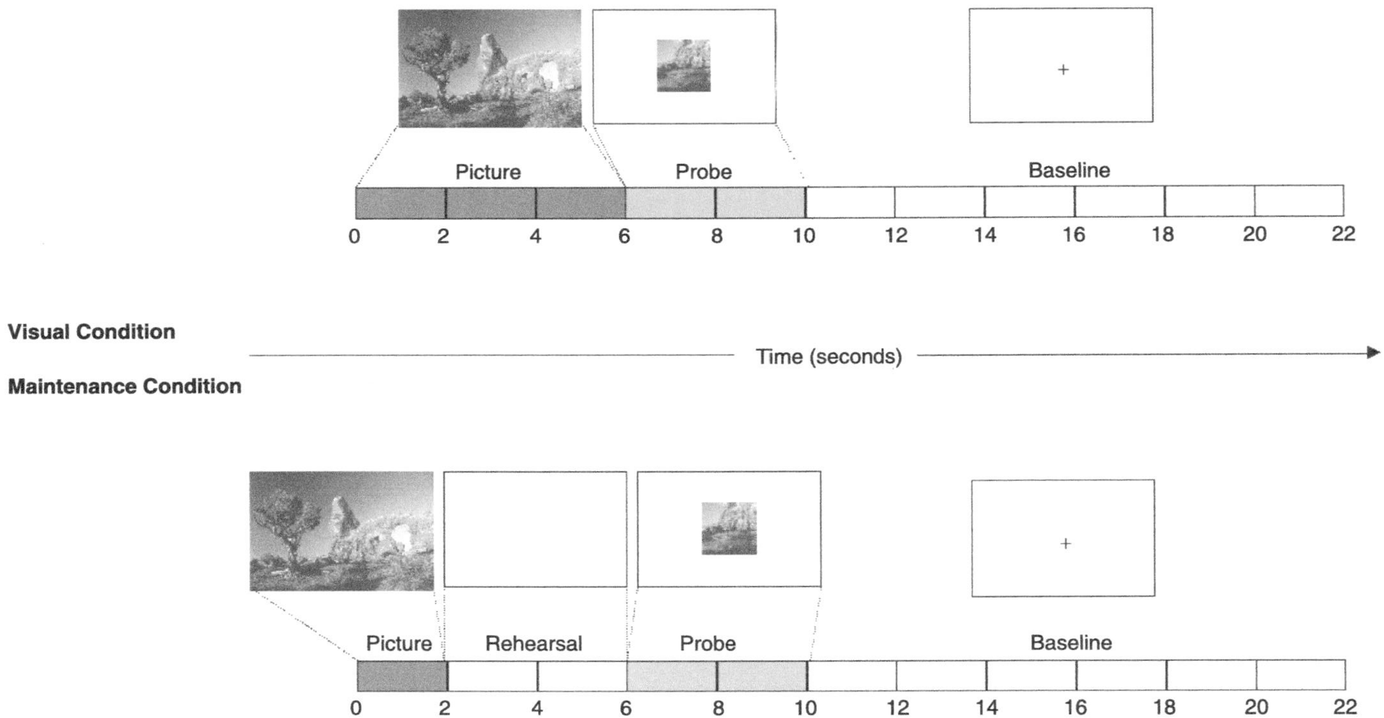

Figure 25.4 Representation of the trial sequence for the Visual and Maintenance conditions.

judged whether that fragment was part of the picture they had just seen by responding "yes" or "no" with a button press. In the Maintenance condition, subjects studied a picture of a complex scene for only 2 seconds and then maintained it in their working memory for an additional 4 seconds before seeing the fragment. The results indicated that there was significant activation in the left anterior hippocampus (Figure 25.5). As shown in the time course analyses in Figure 25.5, it is clear that in young subjects the hippocampus activated more in the Extended Visual condition than in the Maintenance condition. In contrast, the old showed much less systematicity in their hippocampal activations and little differentiation between the Extended Visual

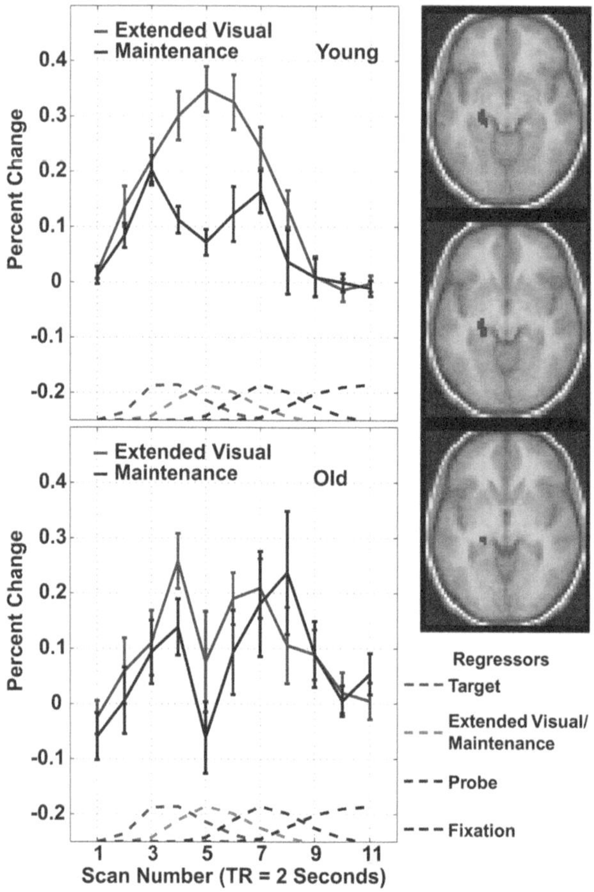

Figure 25.5 Averaged time course for the Extended Visual and Maintenance trials for the young (top) and old groups (bottom) in the left hippocampus. Four model regressors are shown as dashed lines from left to right (initial 2-second target; Extended Visual and Maintenance; Probe; and Baseline), which were convolved with a standard HRF.

and Maintenance conditions, again providing evidence for dedifferentiation. Despite the deficient hippocampal activations, older adults performed as well as young on the working memory task, with about an 82% accuracy rate across all four conditions for both old and young adults. An analysis of the neural activations during probe provided a potential reason for the good behavioral performance. An analysis of the proportional increase of activation showed that the older adults had significantly more activation in left and right inferior frontal cortex (see Figure 25.6) during the probe and maintenance intervals, seemingly activating these important strategic/semantic areas to compensate for the decreased hippocampal activations relative to young adults. Unfortunately, the design did not provide direct evidence that the increased frontal activation at probe was compensatory. Perhaps the activation was related to some other aspect of the task or strategy differences between old and young. To assess the hypothesis that frontal activation directly compensates in old adults for deficient hippocampal activation, as proposed by Park and Gutchess (2005), we conducted another study on long-term memory, using a subsequent memory paradigm.

Long-term memory

In a subsequent memory paradigm, an event-related design is used at encoding, permitting the experimenter to back-sort the neural activations associated with items that are remembered versus forgotten. We used such a technique with complex pictures of outdoor scenes (Gutchess et al., 2005) where

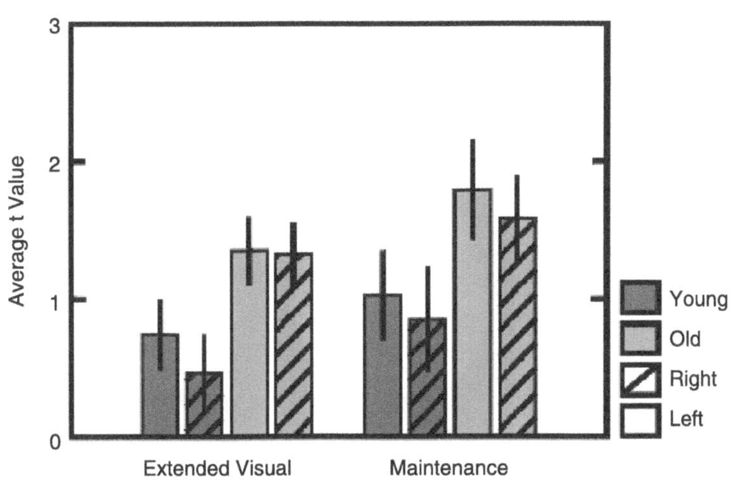

Figure 25.6 Activation in probe and maintenance intervals for the Extended Visual and Maintenance conditions in left and right inferior frontal regions.

subjects were presented with a series of pictures about which to make semantic judgments, and then their memory for the pictures was tested. We were able to subtract neural activations associated with forgotten pictures from remembered pictures, providing us with activations uniquely associated with remembered items. We found evidence that young adults, in contrast to old, showed more activation in the bilateral parahippocampus for remembered pictures (Figure 25.7). In contrast, old adults showed more activation than young in the frontal cortex in the middle frontal gyrus (Figure 25.8). It is virtually certain that the frontal activations were compensatory, because they were uniquely associated with remembered but not forgotten pictures. Moreover, there was a strong inverse relationship in old but not young adults between hippocampal and frontal activations. In other words, when hippocampal engagement was low, frontal engagement was high for old adults,

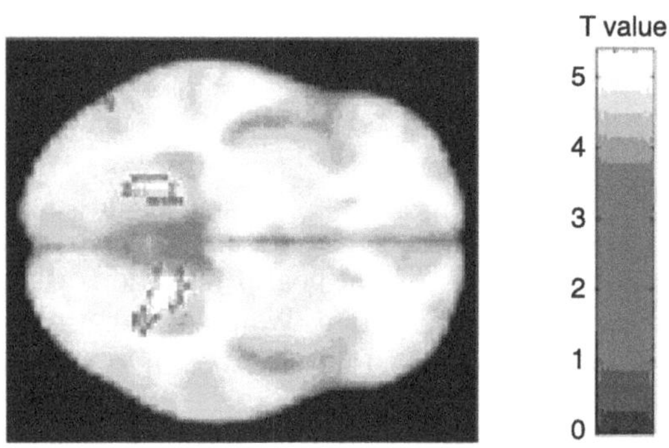

Figure 25.7 Age differences in subsequent memory (Remembered minus Forgotten contrast) with younger adults activating more bilateral parahippocampus than old.

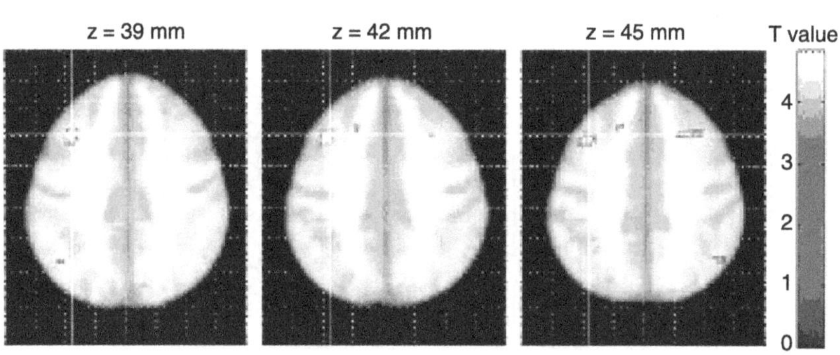

Figure 25.8 Age differences in subsequent memory (Remembered minus Forgotten contrast) with older adults activating more middle frontal cortex than young.

providing strong evidence for the compensatory nature of the frontal activations.

Summary

The new field of the cognitive neuroscience of aging provides us with an unprecedented opportunity to link behavioral phenomenon to underlying neurophysiology (Cabeza, Nyberg, & Park, 2005). The present chapter is an attempt to detail the linkage between theoretical accounts of cognitive aging in the behavioral literature with more recent work on neuroimaging. The field of neuroimaging is particularly exciting with respect to aging because it provides clear evidence that the brain, even in late adulthood, is plastic and can reorganize. We now have compelling evidence that the brain does not just reflect passive decline, but is a dynamic structure that is reactive to experience, evidencing both gains and losses with age. Indeed, Kempermann, Kuhn, and Gage (1998) have demonstrated growth of new neurons in response to complex environments in aged rats, suggesting that stimulating experiences may enhance the organization and function of the brain. At this point, the neuroimaging literature on aging has just begun to uncover some of the activation patterns which characterize aging. This issue is a most exciting and challenging area of research – to understand how a process such as dedifferentiation, a term descriptively applied to imaging results, might reflect changes in neuronal plasticity.

References

Anderson, N.D., Craik, F.I.M., & Naveh-Benjamin, M. (1998). The attentional demands of encoding and retrieval in younger and older adults: I. Evidence from divided attention costs. *Psychology and Aging*, *13*, 405–423.

Bäckman, L., Almkvist, O., Andersson, J., Nordberg, A., Winblad, B., Reineck, R. et al. (1997). Brain activation in young and older adults during implicit and explicit retrieval. *Journal of Cognitive Neuroscience*, *9*, 378–391.

Baddeley, A. (1986). *Working memory*. Oxford: Clarendon Press.

Baltes, P.B., & Lindenberger, U. (1997). Emergence of a powerful connection between sensory and cognitive functions across the adult life span: A new window to the study of cognitive aging? *Psychology and Aging*, *12*(1), 12–21.

Cabeza, R. (2002). Hemispheric asymmetry reduction in older adults: The HAROLD model. *Psychology and Aging*, *17*, 85–100.

Cabeza, R., Daselaar, S.M., Dolcos, F., Prince, S.E., Budde, M., & Nyberg, L. (2004). Task-independent and task-specific age effects on brain activity during working memory, visual attention, and episodic retrieval. *Cerebral Cortex*, *14*(4), 364–375.

Cabeza, R., McIntosh, A.R., Tulving, E., Nyberg, L., & Grady, C.L. (1997). Age-related differences in effective neural connectivity during encoding and recall. *Neuroreport*, *8*, 3479–3483.

Cabeza, R., Nyberg, L., & Park, D.C. (Eds.). (2005). *Cognitive neuroscience of aging*. New York: Oxford University Press.

Chalfonte, B.L., & Johnson, M.K. (1996). Feature memory and binding in young and older adults. *Memory and Cognition*, *24*, 403–416.

Cherry, K.E., Park, D.C., Frieske, D.A., & Smith A.D. (1996). Verbal and pictorial elaborations enhance memory in young and older adults. *Aging, Neuropsychology, and Cognition*, *3*, 15–29.

Cohen, N.J., Ryan, J., Hunt, C., Romine, L., Wszalek, T., & Nash, C., (1999). Hippocampal systems and declarative (relational) memory: Summarizing the data from functional neuroimaging studies. *Hippocampus*, *9*, 83–98.

Craik, F.I.M. (1986). A functional account of age differences in memory. In F. Klix & H. Hagendorf (Eds.), *Human memory and cognitive capabilities, mechanisms, and performances* (pp. 409–422). North Holland: Elsevier.

Craik, F.I.M., Govoni, R., Naveh-Benjamin, M., & Anderson, N.D. (1996). The effects of divided attention on encoding and retrieval processes in human memory. *Journal of Experimental Psychology: General*, *125*, 159–180.

Craik, F.I.M., & Salthouse, T.A. (2000). *The handbook of aging and cognition* (2nd ed.). Mahwah, NJ: Lawrence Erlbaum Associates Inc.

Engle, R.W., Tuholski, S.W., Laughlin, J.E., & Conway, A.R.A. (1999). Working memory, short-term memory, and general fluid intelligence: A latent-variable approach. *Journal of Experimental Psychology: General*, *128*, 309–331.

Epstein, R., & Kanwisher, N. (1998). A cortical representation of the local visual environment. *Nature*, *392*, 598–601.

Frey, K.A., Bohnen, N.I., Meyer P. et al. (1998). Presynaptic monoaminergic vesicles in normal aging studied by (+)-[C-11]DTBZ PET. *Journal of Nuclear Medicine*, 39S:15.

Grady, C.L., Bernstein, L.J., Beig, S., & Siegenthaler, A.L. (2002). The effects of encoding strategy on age-related changes in the functional neuroanatomy of face memory. *Psychology and Aging*, *17*, 7–23.

Gunning-Dixon, F.M., & Raz, N. (2000). The cognitive correlates of white matter abnormalities in normal aging: A quantitative review. *Neuropsychology*, *14*, 224–232.

Gutchess, A.H., Welsh, R.C., Hedden, T., Bangert, A., Minear, M., Liu, L.L. et al. (2005). Aging and the neural correlates of successful picture encoding: Frontal activations compensate for deactivations. *Journal of Cognitive Neuroscience*, *17*, 84–96.

Hasher, L., & Zacks, R.T. (1988). Working memory, comprehension, and aging: A review and a new view. In G.H. Bower (Ed.), *The psychology of learning and motivation* (pp. 193–225). New York: Academic Press.

Hedden, T., Lautenschlager, G., & Park, D.C. (2005). Contributions of processing ability and knowledge to verbal memory tasks across the adult lifespan. *Quarterly Journal of Experimental Psychology*, *58*A, 169–190.

Hedden, T., & Park, D.C. (2001). Aging and interference in verbal working memory. *Psychology and Aging*, *16*, 666–681.

Howard, D.V., McAndrews, M.P., & Lasaga, M.I. (1981). Semantic priming of lexical decisions in young and old adults. *Journal of Gerontology*, *36*, 707–714.

Johnson, M.K., DeLeonardis, D.M., Hashtroudi, S., & Ferguson, S.A. (1995). Aging and single versus multiple cues in source monitoring. *Psychology and Aging*, *10*, 507–517.

Kanwisher, N., McDermott, J., & Chun, M.M. (1997). The fusiform face area: A module in human extrastriate cortex specialized for face perception. *Journal of Neuroscience*, *17*(11), 4302–4311.

Kemper, T.L. (1994). Neuroanatomical and neuropathogical changes during aging and in dementia. In M.L. Albert & E.J.E. Knoepfel (Eds.), *Clinical neurology of aging* (2nd ed., pp. 3–67). New York: Oxford University Press.

Kempermann, G., Kuhn, H.G., & Gage, F.H. (1998). Experience-induced neurogenesis in the senescent dentate gyrus. *Journal of Neuroscience*, *18*, 3206–3212.

Kramer, A.F., Hahn, S., & Gopher, D. (1999). Task coordination and aging: Explorations of executive control processes in the task switching paradigm. *Acta Psychologica*, *101*, 339–378.

Kray, J., & Lindenberger, U. (2000). Adult age differences in task switching. *Psychology and Aging*, *15*, 126–147.

LaVoie, D., & Light, L.L. (1994). Adult age differences in repetition priming. A meta-analysis. *Psychology and Aging*, *4*, 539–553.

Light, L. (1992). The organization of memory in old age. In F.I.M. Craik & T.A. Salthouse (Eds.), *The handbook of aging and cognition* (pp. 111–165). Hillsdale, NJ: Lawrence Erlbaum Associates Inc.

Light, L.L. (1991). Memory and aging: Four hypothesis in search of data. In M.R. Rosenweig (Ed.), *Annual Review of Psychology*, *42*, 333–376.

Light, L.L., & LaVoie, D. (1993). Direct and indirect measures of memory in old age. In P. Graf & M.E.J. Masson (Eds.), *Implicit memory: New directions in cognition, development, and neuropsychology* (pp. 207–230). Hillsdale, NJ: Lawrence Erlbaum Associates Inc.

Lindenberger, U., & Baltes, P.B. (1994). Sensory functioning and intelligence in old age: A strong connection. *Psychology and Aging*, *9*, 339–355.

Madden, D.J., Turkington, T.G., Provenzale, J.M., Denny, L.L., Hawk, T.C., Gottlob, L.R. et al. (1999). Adult age differences in the functional neuroanatomy of verbal recognition memory. *Human Brain Mapping*, *7*, 115–135.

May, C.P., Hasher, L., & Kane, M.J. (1999). The role of interference in memory span. *Memory and Cognition*, *27*, 759–767.

Mayr, U. (2001). Age differences in the selection of mental sets: The role of inhibition, stimulus ambiguity, and response-set overlap. *Psychology and Aging*, *16*, 96–109.

Morcom, A.M., Good, C.D., Frackowiak, R.S., & Rugg, M.D. (2003). Age effects on the neural correlates of successful memory encoding. *Brain*, *126*, 213–229.

Park, D.C. (2000). The basic mechanisms accounting for age-related decline in cognitive function. In D.C. Park & N. Schwarz (Eds.), *Cognitive aging: A primer* (pp. 3–22). Philadelphia, PA: Psychology Press.

Park, D.C., Davidson, N.S., Lautenschlager, G., Smith, A.D., Smith, P.K., & Hedden, T. (2002). Models of visuo-spatial and verbal working memory across the adult life span. *Psychology and Aging*, *17*(2), 299–320.

Park, D.C., & Gutchess, A.H. (2005). Long-term memory and aging: A cognitive neuroscience perspective. In R. Cabeza, L. Nyberg, & D.C. Park (Eds.), *Cognitive neuroscience of aging: Linking cognitive and cerebral aging*. New York: Oxford University Press.

Park, D.C., & Hedden, T. (2001). Working memory and aging. In M. Naveh-Benjamin, M. Moscovitch, & H.L. Roediger III (Eds.), *Perspectives on human memory and cognitive aging: Essays in honour of Fergus Craik*. Hove, UK: Psychology Press.

Park, D.C., Polk, T.A., Park, R., Minear, M., Savage, A., & Smith, M.R. (2004). Aging reduces neural specialization in ventral visual cortex. *Proceedings of the National Academy of Sciences USA*, *101*(35), 13091–13095.

Park, D.C., & Puglisi, J.T. (1985). Older adults' memory for the color of matched pictures and words. *Journal of Gerontology*, *40*, 198–204.

Park, D.C., Puglisi, J.T., & Lutz, R. (1982). Spatial memory in older adults: Effects of intentionality. *Journal of Gerontology*, *37*, 330–335.

Park, D.C., Puglisi, J.T., & Smith, A.D. (1986). Memory for pictures: Does an age-related decline exist? *Psychology and Aging*, *1*(1), 11–17.

Park, D.C., & Schwarz, N. (2000). *Cognitive aging: A primer*. Philadelphia, PA: Psychology Press.

Park, D.C., & Shaw, R.J. (1992). Effect of environmental support on implicit and explicit memory in younger and older adults. *Psychology and Aging*, *7*, 632–642.

Park, D.C., Smith, A.D., Dudley, W.N., & Lafronza V. (1989). The effects of age and a divided attention task presented during encoding and retrieval on memory. *Journal of Experimental Psychology: Learning, Memory, and Cognition*, *15*, 1185–1191.

Park, D.C., Smith, A.D., Lautenschlager, G., Earles, J., Frieske, D., Zwahr, M. et al. (1996). Mediators of long-term memory performance across the life span. *Psychology and Aging*, *11*, 621–637.

Park, D.C., Smith, A.D., Morrell, R.W., Puglisi, J.T., & Dudley, W.N. (1990). Effects of contextual integration on recall of pictures by older adults. *Journal of Gerontology: Pyschological Sciences*, *45*(2), 52–57.

Park, D.C., Welsh, R.C., Marshuetz, C., Gutchess, A.H., Mikels, J., Polk, T.A. et al. (2003). Working memory for complex scenes: Age differences in frontal and hippocampal activations. *Journal of Cognitive Neuroscience*, *15*(8), 1122–1134.

Polk, T.A., & Farah, M.J. (1998). The neural development and organization of letter recognition: Evidence from functional neuroimaging, computational modeling, and behavioral studies. *Proceedings of the National Academy of Sciences USA*, *95*, 847–852.

Puce, A., Allison, T., Asgari, M., Gore, J.C., & McCarthy, G. (1996). Differential sensitivity of human visual cortex to faces, letter strings, and textures: A functional magnetic resonance imaging study. *Journal of Neuroscience*, *16*(16), 5205–5215.

Raz, N. (2000). Aging of the brain and its impact on cognitive performance: Integration of structural and functional findings. In F.I.M. Craik & T.A. Salthouse (Eds.), *Handbook of aging and cognition*. Mahwah, NJ: Lawrence Erlbaum Associates Inc.

Raz, N., Gunning-Dixon F., Head, D., Rodrigue, K.M., Williamson, A., & Acker, J.D. (2004). Aging, sexual dimorphism, and hemispheric asymmetry of the cerebral cortex: Replicability of regional differences in volume. *Neurobiology of Aging*, *25*(3), 377–96.

Resnick, S.M., Pham, D.L., Kraut, M.A., Zonderman, A.B., & Davatzikos, C. (2003). Longitudinal magnetic resonance imaging studies of older adults: A shrinking brain. *Journal of Neuroscience*, *8*, 3295–3301.

Reuter-Lorenz, P., Jonides, J., Smith, E.E., Hartley, A., Miller, A., Marshuetz, C. et al. (2000). Age differences in the frontal lateralization of verbal and spatial working memory revealed by PET. *Journal of Cognitive Neuroscience*, *12*(1), 174–187.

Rosen, A.C., Prull, M.W., O'Hara, R., Race, E.A., Desmond, J.E., Glover, G.H. et al. (2002). Variable effects of aging on frontal lobe contributions to memory. *Neuroreport*, *13*, 2425–2428.

Salthouse, T.A. (1991). *Theoretical perspectives on cognitive aging*. Hillsdale, NJ: Lawrence Erlbaum Associates Inc.

Salthouse, T.A. (1996). The processing-speed theory of adult age differences in cognition. *Psychological Review*, *103*, 403–428.

Seeman, P., Bzowej, N.H., Guan, H.C., Bergeron C., Becker L.E., Reynolds G.P. et al. (1987). Human brain dopamine receptors in children and aging adults. *Synapse, 1*, 399–404.

Shah, P., & Miyake, A. (1996). The separability of working memory resources for spatial thinking and language processing: An individual differences approach. *Journal of Experimental Psychology: General, 125*, 4–27.

Spencer, W.D., & Raz, N. (1994). Memory for facts, source, and context: Can frontal lobe dysfunction explain age-related differences? *Psychology and Aging, 9*, 149–159.

Volkow, N.D., Logan, J., Fowler, J.S., Wang, G.J., Gur, R.C., Wong, C. et al. (2000). Association between age-related decline in brain dopamine activity and impairment in frontal and cingulate metabolism. *American Journal of Psychiatry, 157*, 75–80.

Volkow, N.D., Wang, G.J., Fowler, J.S. et al. (1996). Measuring age-related changes in dopamine D2 receptors with 11C-raclopride and 18F-N-methylspiroperidol. *Psychiatry Research, 67*, 11–16.

Zacks, R., & Hasher, L. (1994). Directed ignoring: Inhibitory regulation of working memory. In D. Dagenback & T.H. Carr (Eds.), *Inhibitory processes in attention, memory, and language* (pp. 241–264). San Diego, CA: Academic Press.

Zacks, R., & Hasher, L. (1997). Cognitive gerontology and attentional inhibition: A reply to Burke and McDowd. *Journal of Gerontology: Psychological Sciences*, 274–285.

Zacks, R.T., Hasher, L., & Li, K.Z.H. (2000). Human memory. In F.I.M. Craik & T.A. Salthouse (Eds.), *The handbook of aging and cognition* (2nd ed., pp. 293–358). Mahwah, NJ: Lawrence Erlbaum Associates Inc.

26 Dopamine and cognitive aging: A strong relationship

Lars Bäckman, Lars Nyberg, and Lars Farde

This chapter addresses the extent to which age-related deficits in various cognitive functions are linked to age-related changes in dopaminergic neurotransmission. The chapter is organized into four subsections. We begin with a brief review of some major trends in behavioral research on cognitive aging. We then discuss in some detail in vitro and molecular-imaging findings demonstrating strong negative linkages between adult age and different dopamine (DA) markers. Following this, we present converging evidence that DA is critically implicated in multiple cognitive functions. Finally, these three sections are synthesized into a review of research on the correlative triad among adult age, DA markers, and cognitive performance.

Aging and cognition

Despite substantial individual differences in onset, rate, and scope, there is pervasive evidence that several cognitive functions decline during the course of the normal aging process (for an overview, see Bäckman, Small, Wahlin, & Larsson, 1999). For example, within the domain of memory, tasks assessing the ability to maintain and manipulate information (i.e., working memory) and tasks assessing the ability to consciously recollect information acquired in a certain place at a certain time (i.e., episodic memory), exhibit a marked performance deterioration from early to late adulthood (for an overview, see Bäckman, Small, & Wahlin, 2001). Similarly, psychometric tests reflecting fluid aspects of intelligence (e.g., Digit Symbol, Block Design) as well as related experimental tasks tapping, for example, perceptual closure and syllogistic reasoning abilities reveal robust decline across the adult life span (e.g., Kausler, 1991; Salthouse, 1992). Such tests involve relatively unfamiliar materials and require fast and efficient solutions to new problems.

Along with findings from research targeting other cognitive domains demonstrating age-related deficits (e.g., executive functioning; for an overview, see West, 1996), the pattern of results emerging from this brief review suggests that older adults are especially disadvantaged when fast and efficient processing in novel task situations is required. Although it is debated whether the decline in these cognitive domains begins in early (e.g., Park et al., 2002) or middle (e.g., Rönnlund, Nyberg, Bäckman, & Nilsson, 2005) adulthood, most available evidence indicates that the decline process proceeds in a continuous rather than in a discrete fashion after its onset. The relationship of age-related deficits in cognitive abilities such as perceptual speed, executive functioning, and episodic memory to age-related DA losses is at the heart of this chapter.

Aging and dopamine

Much of the work on aging and DA has focused on the caudate and the putamen, two structures in the striatal complex in which the dopaminergic innervation is particularly dense. There is unequivocal evidence for age-related losses of pre- and postsynaptic biochemical markers of the nigrostriatal DA system. Postsynaptically, autopsy studies indicate losses of both D_1 (e.g., Cortes, Gueye, Pazos, & Palacios, 1989; Rinne, Lönnberg, & Marjamäki, 1990) and D_2 (e.g., Seeman et al., 1987; Severson, Marcusson, Winblad, & Finch, 1982) receptor binding from early to later adulthood, the rate of decline being just below 10% per decade. Similar findings for D_1 (Suhara et al., 1991; Wang et al., 1998) and D_2 (e.g., Antonini et al., 1993; Ichise et al., 1998; Nordström et al., 1992) receptor densities have been documented in vivo, using positron emission tomography (PET) and single-photon emission computed tomography (SPECT).

The DA transporter (DAT) is a commonly used marker of the presynaptic neuron. As with D_1 and D_2 binding, post-mortem studies (e.g., Allard & Marcusson, 1989; Bannon et al., 1992; Bannon & Whitty, 1997; Ma et al., 1999) as well as PET and SPECT studies (e.g., Rinne et al., 1998; Van Dyck et al., 1995) indicate clear age-related losses of the DAT, the average age-related decrease mimicking that observed for postsynaptic markers.

Consistent with these parallel patterns, Volkow et al. (1998b) found a sizable relationship between D_2 receptor binding and DAT binding in the striatum. Importantly, this association remained after partialing out age. This suggests that the expression of receptors and transporters may reflect functional demands on dopaminergic pathways. Indeed, work on DAT knock-out mice shows a reduction of D_2 receptor mRNA in postsynaptic medium spiny neurons (Gainetdinov, Jones, & Caron, 1999). Given that loss of DAT may initially result in increased DA (Shinkai, Zhang, Mathias, & Roth, 1997), one possibility is that increased DA levels lead to functional down-regulation of these neurons, contributing to the age-related postsynaptic losses (e.g., Sakata, Farooqui, & Prasad, 1992; Zhang, Ravipati, Joseph, & Roth, 1995).

As noted, the bulk of research on the relationship between aging and DA has focused on striatal DA markers. Studies on extrastriatal DA markers are rare because suitable radioligands for imaging of the sparse dopaminergic innervation of extrastriatal regions have been lacking. However, an early PET study focusing on D_1 receptor binding found comparable rates of age-related loss in the striatum and the frontal cortex (Suhara et al., 1991). Post-mortem evidence also demonstrates an age-related decrease of frontal D_1 receptor densities (De Keyser, De Backer, Vauquelin, & Ebinger, 1990). These findings were extended to the D_2 receptor subtype in PET studies using a highly selective ligand for extrastriatal D_2 binding (Inoue et al., 2001; Kaasinen et al., 2000). These studies revealed clear age-related losses in D_2 binding not only in the frontal cortex, but also in the temporal, parietal, and occipital cortices as well as in hippocampus, amygdala, and thalamus. The magnitude of these age differences in extrastriatal DA functions resembles closely those observed for the striatum. Thus, an age-related decrease of DA markers in a wide variety of brain regions appears to be part of the normal aging process.

Similar to the behavioral literature on cognitive aging, there is some controversy as to whether the age-related DA loss is linear across the adult span. Although most studies have reported evidence for a linear age–DA relationship (for an overview, see Reeves, Bench, & Howard, 2002), an exponential age trajectory with exacerbated loss after middle adulthood has been observed for both D_2 receptor densities (e.g., Antonini et al., 1993; Rinne et al., 1990) and DAT binding potential (e.g., Bannon & Whitty, 1997; Ma et al., 1999). The latter trajectory concurs with observations of a later onset of age-related cognitive decline (Rönnlund et al., 2005).

The age-related DA loss may have multiple loci. First, there is an age-related reduction of DA-producing neurons in substantia nigra, with the average loss estimated to be around 3% per decade (Fearnley & Lees, 1991). In a unique study, post-mortem cell counts in the substantia nigra were highly related to ante-mortem indicators of DA levels (Snow et al., 1993). This suggests that neuronal number influences the total synthesis rate of DA. Second, there is a loss of synapses that progresses from childhood and continues in adulthood and old age through a process termed synaptic pruning (Gopnik, Meltzoff, & Kuhl, 1999). Third, there is also evidence suggesting an age-related decrease in the number of proteins per cell. Specifically, work with rodents has demonstrated substantial age-related losses in steady-state levels and synthesis of D_2 receptor messenger ribonucleic acid (mRNA; e.g., Mesco, Carlsson, Joseph, & Roth, 1993). Relatedly, human work shows that the age-related decrease in DAT mRNA may exceed the extent of neuronal loss (De Keyser et al., 1990). Thus, the bottom line is that age-related alterations in neuronal number, synapses, and protein concentrations may all contribute to the general down-regulation of the DA system with advancing adult age.

With regard to putative causative factors behind this down-regulation, the age-independent relationship between DAT and receptor densities, and the parallel age-related loss of pre- and postsynaptic markers, have been interpreted to mean that (a) a common mechanism regulating both pre- and postsynaptic maturation of the DA systems during neurodevelopment may determine their concentrations, and (b) an age-related decrease in the functional demands on dopaminergic pathways may occur during adulthood (Bäckman & Farde, 2004). As to the latter, it has been suggested that age-related DA losses may reflect failure in responding to oxidative stress and cell damage (e.g., Joseph, Denisova, & Villalobos-Molina, 1996). Supportive evidence comes from animal research indicating a relationship among striatal DA levels, markers of oxidative damage, and motor function (Cardozo-Pelaez et al., 1999). It has also been suggested that the expression of DA itself may contribute to degenerative processes through the production of neurotoxins during auto-oxidation (Fornstedt, Pileblad, & Carlsson, 1990; Luo & Roth, 2000).

Dopamine and cognition

In addition to its well-established role in efficient motor functioning (e.g., Freed & Yamamoto, 1985; McEntee, Mair, & Langlais, 1987), several lines of evidence suggest that DA is also critically implicated in many higher-order cognitive abilities.

Patient evidence

Studies on patient populations with severe alterations to the DA system, such as patients with Huntington's disease (HD) and Parkinson's disease (PD), indicate deficits across multiple cognitive domains including executive functions, visuospatial skill, episodic memory, verbal fluency, perceptual speed, and reasoning (e.g., Brandt & Butters, 1986; Brown & Marsden, 1990). Note that these patterns of impairment resemble those observed in aging (Prull, Gabrieli, & Bunge, 1999). Further, PET studies have demonstrated a sizable relationship of D_1 and D_2 receptor binding as well as DAT binding to performance in the aforementioned task domains in groups of mildly to moderately ill HD patients (Bäckman et al., 1997; Lawrence et al., 1998). A similarly strong relationship between PET-derived measures of presynaptic kinetics of [^{18}F]DOPA and executive functioning has been documented in PD (Remy et al., 2000).

Animal evidence

There is substantial evidence from experimental animal work that depletion of dopaminergic pathways results in cognitive deficits. For example, destructions of dopaminergic nerve terminals at different sites (e.g., septum, nucleus accumbens, prefrontal cortex) produce impairment across multiple cognitive domains in rodents and monkeys alike, including memory (Simon, Taghzouti, & Le Moal, 1986), inhibitory functions (Jones & Robbins, 1992), set-shifting (Roberts et al., 1994), and spatial attention (Boussaoud & Kermadi, 1997). In a similar vein, lesioning dopaminergic pathways at the level of the subthalamic nucleus, which leads to deprivation of nigral DA input, results in deficits in tasks assessing attentional as well as executive functioning and motor sequencing (Baunez, Nieoullon, & Amalric, 1995;

Baunez & Robbins, 1999). Thus, lesion data indicate an important role of DA in regulating performance across a variety of higher-order cognitive domains.

Genetic evidence

Recent research on the cognitive effects of allelic variations in the gene coding for Catechol-O-methyltransferase (COMT) provides further support for the DA–cognition link. COMT inactivates released DA through enzymatic conversion to 3-methoxythyramine (Weinshilboum, Otterness, & Szumlanski, 1999). The role of COMT in regulating DA levels appears to be unique to the prefrontal cortex (Gogos, et al., 1998; Karoum, Chrapusta, & Egan, 1994). A common polymorphism (Val108/158Met) in the COMT gene has been associated with most of the human variation in enzyme activity (Mannisto & Kaakkola, 1999). Of chief importance, the enzymatic activity is three to four times as high for the Val than for the Met variant at normal body temperatures (Lotta et al., 1995). The alleles are codominant with heterozygous persons (Val/Met) having intermediate enzyme activity between homozygotic persons (i.e., Val/Val > Val/Met > Met/Met; Weinshilboum et al., 1999). As a result of the allelic differences in enzymatic activity, Val carriers have less DA signaling in the synaptic cleft compared to Met carriers, leading to reduced signal-to-noise ratio in prefrontal neurons (Egan et al., 2001).

Basic evidence of an influence of COMT on cognition comes from studies on COMT knock-out mice (Kneavel, Gogos, Karayiorgou, & Luine, 2000) as well as animal (Liljequist et al., 1997) and human (Gasparini et al., 1997) research demonstrating performance enhancement from COMT inhibitors in working-memory tasks. Cognitive studies comparing the different allelic variants indicate an advantage of Met over Val carriers in executive functioning (i.e., fewer perseverative errors in the Wisconsin Card Sorting Test; Egan et al., 2001; Joober et al., 2002; Malhotra et al., 2002; Mattay et al., 2003) as well as in tasks assessing processing speed and attention (Bilder et al., 2002). Some of these studies on young and middle-aged adults involve schizophrenic patients, others involve normal subjects, and still others have a mixture of patients and controls. In general, the results are similar for the different subject groups. These findings have been recently extended to children and older adults. Diamond, Briand, Fossella, and Gehlbach (2004) showed a selective superiority in 10-year old Met/Met children for a task taxing working memory and inhibitory functions; no genotype group differences were seen in a working memory task with low inhibitory demands, or in episodic recall and mental rotation tasks. A similar Met/Met advantage in middle-aged, young-old, and old-old adults was reported by de Frias et al. (2004) for episodic and semantic memory and by de Frias et al. (2005) for executive functioning and visuospatial skill.

Although there may be differential sensitivity of COMT genotype to different cognitive domains within individual studies, the pattern emerging across studies is one of a rather broad influence on performance in many different kinds of cognitive tests. A final point to note is that some studies (Egan et al., 2001) suggest a dose–response effect of genotype on cognitive performance (i.e., Met/Met > Val/Met > Val/Val), others (de Frias et al., 2004; Diamond et al., 2004) suggest that the major effect lies between homozygotic Met carriers and the other groups, and still others (Mattay et al., 2003) show that the most pronounced difference is between the homyzygotic Val carriers and the other genotype groups.

Pharmacological evidence

There is evidence from both animals and humans that pharmacological manipulations of DA transmission are related to cognitive performance. Administration of D-amphetamine (D-AMP) elevates the synaptic concentration of DA and may serve as a model for DA hyperactivity. Several studies have reported D-AMP-related performance gains in tasks assessing information-processing speed (e.g., Halliday et al., 1994), discrimination (e.g., Kelly, Foltin, & Fischman, 1991), and vigilance (Spiegel, 1978). In a series of studies, Luciana and colleagues (Luciana & Collins, 1997; Luciana, Collins, & Depue, 1998; Luciana, Depue, Arbisi, & Leon, 1992) found that bromocriptine, a D_2 receptor agonist, facilitates delayed spatial working-memory performance in healthy volunteers. The pattern of findings in these studies suggests that the effects were not secondary to changes in basic sensorimotor, attentional, or global arousal processes. Rather, they seemed to reflect changes in the temporal integration between a sensory cue and the requested response.

Conversely, Luciana and Collins (1997) demonstrated that administration of haloperidol, a D_2 receptor antagonist, worsened performance in a working-memory task in which beneficial effects were seen from a D_2 agonist. In a related study, Ramaekers et al. (1999) reported that a rather low dose of haloperidol impaired performance in tasks assessing psychomotor speed and working memory. Likewise, several studies with monkeys (e.g., Sawaguchi & Goldman-Rakic, 1991) indicate that blockade of DA receptors results in reversible impairment in motor and cognitive tasks.

However, there are inconsistencies in the extant pharmacological literature. Inconsistent observations may depend on doses, pre-experimental cognitive skill, or drug affinities for different DA receptor subtypes. Luciana and Collins (1997) reported a facilitative effect of bromocriptine on spatial working memory at lower doses, but not at the same doses as initially reported by Luciana et al. (1992). Kimberg, D'Esposito, and Farah (1997) found that persons with low working-memory capacity showed positive bromocriptine-related effects on working-memory performance, whereas those with high working-memory capacity showed negative effects (see also Mehta et al., 2000). By contrast, Kimberg and D'Esposito (2003) documented larger effects of pergolide, an agonist for both the D_1 and the D_2 receptor subtypes, on delayed working-memory performance for persons with greater working memory capacity than for those with lower capacity.

Although the reasons for the mixed findings remain unclear, they may reflect interactions between subject-related and drug-related factors that vary between receptor subtypes. Interestingly, similar inconsistencies have been observed at a neurophysiological level. There is evidence of an inverted U-shaped dose–response function with administration of DA agonists in monkeys (Cai & Arnsten, 1997). Thus, a DA agonist may promote or inhibit firing in the same neural circuitry depending on both dosage and initial endogenous DA levels.

In a recent pharmacogenomic imaging study on brain activation during working memory (n-back) performance, Mattay et al. (2003) obtained evidence of direct relevance to the inverted U-shaped function hypothesized to characterize the relationship of DA signaling to brain and cognitive functioning. The key finding was a triple interaction among COMT genotype, D-AMP, and cognitive demand. In line with the notion that DA levels (and demand-induced shift in DA levels) are affected by all three factors (Met/Met > Val/Val; drug > placebo; higher cognitive demand > lower cognitive demand), the Val/Val carriers improved working memory and showed a more efficient left-frontal response under the influence of D-AMP when n-back conditions were most demanding. By contrast, the Met/Met carriers exhibited worse performance and a less efficient frontal response under these conditions. This pattern is entirely consistent with the U-shaped DA-brain/cognition relationship. Specifically, administration of D-AMP and increasing cognitive demands should move the Val/Val carriers from a lower-than-optimal toward an optimal DA level. By contrast, given that the Met/Met carriers are closer to an optimal DA level under baseline conditions, the experimentally induced DA increases may have shifted their DA level to the decline portion of the inverted U function.

Neurocomputational evidence

Some of the empirical observations discussed in this chapter have been integrated into neurocomputational models. In these models, DA is commonly hypothesized to facilitate the responsivity of neural networks in activity transmission both within and between neural networks (e.g., Oades, 1985). By enhancing the neural signal relative to background noise (Sawaguchi, Matsamura, & Kubota, 1988), DA is assumed to promote the firing frequency of innervated neurons (Daniel et al., 1991).

Servan-Schreiber, Bruno, Carter, and Cohen (1998a) proposed a model specifically developed to accomodate the effects of D-AMP on selective attention. In this model, DA effects are simulated as a change in gain of neural assemblies in the area of release. Interestingly, effects on motor performance are thought to result from gains over the response layer, resulting in increased speed, but impaired accuracy. By contrast, effects on attention are simulated as a change in gains over the attention layer, resulting in improved speed and accuracy, particularly under demanding conditions. Results from a study (Servan-Schreiber, Carter, Bruno, & Cohen, 1998b) investigating the effects of D-AMP on motor and cognitive performance in a selective attention task were in excellent agreement with the proposed model.

Li, Lindenberger, and Sikström (2001) modeled age-related cognitive deficits as a function of deficient dopaminergic modulation that leads to reduced neuronal responsivity, which, in turn, increases neural noise and results in less distinctive activation patterns. These less distinctive activation patterns are hypothesized to be a key determinant of cognitive aging. The model also accounts for the inverted U-shaped dose–performance function by demonstrating that, at extremely high DA levels, neuronal activity in response to different inputs saturates, resulting in less discriminative activation patterns and poorer cognitive performance (Li & Sikström, 2002).

Aging, dopamine, and cognition

Given that (a) adult age is negatively related to cognitive performance and DA markers; and (b) DA markers are positively related to cognitive performance, a logical next step is to relate all these variables that form a correlative triad. Although relatively few studies have examined the relationship of age-related DA changes to age-related cognitive changes, the pattern of findings is strikingly consistent, and supportive of an important role of DA in cognitive aging (Bäckman & Farde, 2004). A common feature of these studies is that they involve adult life-span samples with a rectangular age distribution from early to late adulthood.

Using PET, Wang et al. (1998) found strong relationships among age, striatal D_1 receptor binding, and performance in a psychomotor test. Similar results were obtained in a recent SPECT study examining the association among age, striatal D_2 receptor binding, and finger-tapping performance (Yang et al., 2003). Although these studies reported bivariate correlations only, the results are important in that they document the correlative triad within specific samples.

In another PET study, Volkow et al. (1998a) determined striatal D_2 binding and administered a cognitive battery including tests of executive and motor functioning as well as perceptual speed; all these domains are known to be sensitive to both aging and striatal dysfunction. In line with earlier studies, D_2 receptor binding decreased with advancing age and there were negative relationships between age and performance in the cognitive tests.

The most interesting finding was that partial correlations also revealed moderate to strong relationships of D_2 binding to motor and cognitive performance after controlling for age. These results indicate that age-related decreases in DA function are associated with decline in both cognitive and motor functioning, and suggest that DA activity may influence performance irrespective of age.

These findings were corroborated in a related PET study by Bäckman et al. (2000), which examined striatal D_2 binding and cognitive performance using a somewhat different constellation of tasks. Here, two age-sensitive cognitive domains were targeted: episodic memory and perceptual speed. As expected, increasing age was negatively associated with performance in the episodic memory and speed tasks, and there was a marked decrease in striatal D_2 binding across age. The key finding was that statistical control of D_2 binding effectively eliminated the influence of age on cognitive performance, whereas D_2 binding contributed to the cognitive variation independent of age. These results provide further evidence for the view that DA is implicated in age-related cognitive deficits as well as in cognitive functioning in general.

In these studies, postsynaptic DA markers were assessed. It has been suggested that the density of the DAT is more sensitive than postsynaptic receptor densities as a marker of the activity of the dopaminergic system (Mozley et al., 1999). Specifically, because DAT activity indirectly regulates the occupancy of DA on D_1 and D_2 receptor-containing neurons, this protein may serve as a more general marker of the DA system. In a SPECT study, Mozley, Gur, Mozley, and Gur (2001) reported age-related reductions of the DAT in the striatum along with age-related deficits in verbal episodic memory. Importantly, DAT binding in the striatum was strongly associated with memory performance in both younger and older adults.

Using PET, Erixon-Lindroth et al. (2005) also found an age-related decrease of DAT density in caudate and putamen. Further, age-related deficits were found in tests of episodic memory, working memory, and word fluency, but not in tests of general knowledge. Similar to the Bäckman et al. (2000) data on D_2 binding, the age-related cognitive deficits were completely mediated by DAT density, although DAT density contributed to the performance variation in memory and fluency over and above age. The latter finding was substantiated by the result that DAT density was also related to performance variability in the age-insensitive knowledge test.

Thus, the available evidence suggests that pre- and postsynaptic markers of the nigrostriatal DA system are powerful mediators of the cognitive changes that occur across adulthood and old age, as well as strong general correlates of cognitive performance. With regard to the apparent similarity in patterns of data for pre- and postsynaptic DA markers, note that Volkow et al. (1998b) demonstrated a sizable relationship between losses in DAT and D_2 receptors across adulthood. The DAT–D_2 association was independent of age, suggesting that common genetic or adaptive mechanisms may regulate the expression of DA receptors and transporters irrespective of age. Support for a genetic regulation of DA markers is provided in research demonstrating an association between polymorphisms of the D_2 gene and the density of D_2 receptors (e.g., Jönsson et al., 1999). Thus, changes in pre- and postsynaptic DA function may be an interdependent and generalized phenomenon in human aging (Morgan & Finch, 1998).

Acknowledgements

Preparation of this chapter was supported by grants from the Swedish Research Council and the Bank of Sweden Tercentenary Foundation to Lars Bäckman, and from the Swedish Research Council to Lars Nyberg and Lars Farde.

References

Allard, P., & Marcusson, J. (1989). Age-correlated loss of dopamine uptake sites labeled with [3H]GBR-12935 in human putamen. *Neurobiology of Aging, 10*, 661–664.

Antonini, A., Leenders, K.L., Reist, H., Thomann, R., Beer, H.-F., & Locher, J. (1993). Effect of age on D_2 dopamine receptors in normal human brain measured by positron emission tomography and [^{11}C] raclopride. *Archives of Neurology, 50*, 474–480.

Bäckman, L., & Farde, L. (2004). The role of dopamine functions in cognitive aging. In R.L. Nyberg & D.C. Park (Eds.), *Cognitive neuroscience of aging: Linking cognitive and cerebral aging* (pp. 58–84). New York: Oxford University Press.

Bäckman, L., Ginovart, N., Dixon, R.A. et al. (2000). Age-related cognitive deficits mediated by changes in the striatal dopamine system. *American Journal of Psychiatry, 157*, 635–637.

Bäckman, L., Robins-Wahlin, T.-B., Lundin, A., Ginovart, N., & Farde, L. (1997). Cognitive deficits in Huntington's disease are predicted by dopaminergic PET markers and brain volumes. *Brain, 120*, 2207–2217.

Bäckman, L., Small, B.J., & Wahlin, Å. (2001). Aging and memory: Cognitive and biological perspectives. In J.E. Birren & K.W. Schaie (Eds.), *Handbook of the psychology of aging* (5th ed., pp. 349–377). San Diego, CA: Academic Press.

Bäckman, L., Small, B.J., Wahlin. Å., & Larsson, M. (1999). Cognitive functioning in very old age. In F.I.M. Craik & T.A. Salthouse (Eds.), *Handbook of aging and cognition* (Vol. 2., pp. 499–558). Mahwah, NJ: Lawrence Erlbaum Associates Inc.

Bannon, M.J., Poosch, M.S., Xia, Y., Goebel, D.J., Cassin, B., & Kapatos, G. (1992). Dopamine transporter mRNA content in human substantia nigra decreases precipitously with age. *Proceedings of the National Academy of Sciences, USA, 89*, 7095–7099.

Bannon, M.J., & Whitty, C.J. (1997). Age-related and regional differences in dopamine mRNA expression in human midbrain. *Neurology, 48*, 969–977.

Baunez, C., Nieoullon, A., & Amalric, M. (1995). Dopamine and complex sensorimotor integration: Further studies in a conditioned motor task in the rat. *Neuroscience, 65*, 375–384.

Baunez, C., & Robbins, T.W. (1999). Effects of dopamine depletion of the dorsal striatum and further interaction with subthalamic nucleus lesions in an attentional task in the rat. *Neuroscience, 92*, 1343–1356.

Bilder, R.M., Volavka, J., Czobor, P. et al. (2002). Neurocognitive correlates of the COMT Val^{158}Met polymorphism in chronic schizophrenia. *Biological Psychiatry, 52*, 701–707.

Boussaoud, D., & Kermadi, I. (1997). The primate striatum: Neuronal activity in relation to spatial attention versus motor preparation. *European Journal of Neuroscience*, *9*, 2152–2162.

Brandt, J., & Butters, N. (1986). The neuropsychology of Huntington's disease. *Trends in Neuroscience*, *9*, 118–120.

Brown, R.G., & Marsden, C.D. (1990). Cognitive function in Parkinson's disease: From description to theory. *Trends in Neuroscience*, *13*, 21–29.

Cai, J.X., & Arnsten, A.F. (1997). Dose-dependent effects of the dopamine receptor agonists A77636 and SKF81297 on spatial working memory in aged monkeys. *Journal of Pharmacology and Experimental Therapeutics*, *283*, 183–189.

Cardozo-Pelaez, F., Song, S., Partasarathy, A. et al. (1999). Oxidative damage in the aging mouse brain. *Movement Disorders*, *14*, 972–980.

Cortes, R., Gueye, B., Pazos, A., & Palacios, J.M. (1989). Dopamine receptors in human brain: Autoradiographic distribution of D_1 sites. *Neuroscience*, *28*, 262–273.

Daniel, D.G., Weinberger, D.R., Jones, D.W. et al. (1991). The effect of amphetamine on regional cerebral blood flow during cognitive activation in schizophrenia. *Journal of Neuroscience*, *11*, 1907–1917.

de Frias, C.M., Annerbrink, K., Westberg, L. et al. (2004). COMT gene polymorphism is associated with declarative memory in adulthood and old age. *Behavior Genetics*, *34*, 533–539.

de Frias, C.M., Annerbrink, K., Westberg, L., Eriksson, E., Adolfsson, R., & Nilsson, L.-G. (2005). Catechol O-methyltransferase Val^{158}Met polymorphism is associated with cognitive performance in nondemented adults. *Journal of Cognitive Neuroscience*, *17*, 1018–1025.

De Keyser, J., De Backer, J.P., Vauquelin, G., & Ebinger, G. (1990). The effect of aging on the D_1 dopamine receptors in human frontal cortex. *Brain Research*, *528*, 308–310.

Diamond, A., Briand, L., Fossella, J., & Gehlbach, L. (2004). Genetic and neurochemical modulation of prefrontal cognitive functions in children. *American Journal of Psychiatry*, *161*, 125–132.

Egan, M.F., Goldberg, T.E., Kolachana, B.S. et al. (2001). Effect of COMT Val108/158Met genotype on frontal lobe function and risk for schizophrenia. *Proceedings of the National Academy of Sciences, USA*, *98*, 6917–6922.

Erixon-Lindroth, N., Farde, L., Halldin, C. et al. (2005). The role of the striatal dopamine transporter in cognitive aging. *Psychiatry Research: Neuroimaging*, *138*, 1–12.

Fearnley, J.M., & Lees, A.J. (1991). Aging and Parkinson's disease: Substantia nigra regional selectivity. *Brain*, *114*, 2283–2301.

Fornstedt, B., Pileblad, E., & Carlsson, A. (1990). In vivo autooxidation of dopamine in guinea pig striatum increases with age. *Journal of Neurochemistry*, *55*, 655–659.

Freed, C.R., & Yamamoto, B.K. (1985). Regional brain dopamine metabolism: A marker for the speed, direction, and posture of moving animals. *Science*, *229*, 62–65.

Gainetdinov, R.R., Jones, S.R., & Caron, M.G. (1999). Functional hyperdopaminerga in dopamine transporter knock-out mice. *Biological Psychiatry*, *46*, 303–311.

Gasparini, M., Fabrizio, E., Bonifati, E. et al. (1997). Cognitive improvement during Tolcapone treatment in Parkinson's disease. *Journal of Neural Transmission*, *104*, 887–894.

Gogos, J.A., Morgan, M., Luine, V. et al. (1998). Catechol-O-methyltransferase-deficient mice exhibit sexually dimorphic changes in catecholamine levels and behavior. *Proceedings of the National Academy of Sciences, USA*, *95*, 9991–9996.

Gopnik, A., Meltzoff, A., & Kuhl, P. (1999). *The scientist in the crib: What early learning tells us about the mind.* New York: HarperCollins.

Halliday, R., Naylor, H., Brandeis, D., Callaway, E., Yano, L., & Herzig, K. (1994). The effect of d-amphetamine, clonidine, and yohimbine on human information processing. *Psychophysiology, 31*, 331–337.

Ichise, M., Ballinger, J.R., Tanaka, F. et al. (1998). Age-related changes in D_2 receptor binding with iodine-123-iodobenzofuran SPECT. *Journal of Nuclear Medicine, 39*, 1511–1518.

Inoue, M., Suhara, T., Sudo, Y. et al. (2001). Age-related reduction of extrastriatal dopamine D_2 receptor measured by PET. *Life Sciences, 69*, 1079–1084.

Jones, G.H., & Robbins, T.W. (1992). Differential effects of mesocortical, mesolimbic, and mesostriatal dopamine depletion on spontaneous, conditioned, and drug-induced locomotor activity. *Pharmacology, Biochemistry, and Behavior, 43*, 883–895.

Jönsson, E.G., Nothen, M.M., Grunhage, F. et al. (1999) Polymorphisms in the dopamine D_2 receptor gene and their relationships to striatal dopamine receptor density of healthy volunteers. *Molecular Psychiatry, 4*, 290–296.

Joober, R., Gauthier, J., Lal, S. et al. (2002). Catechol-O-methyltransferase Val-108/158-Met gene variants associated with performance on the Wisconsin Card Sorting Test. *Archives of General Psychiatry, 59*, 662–663.

Joseph, J.A., Denisova, N., & Villalobos-Molina, R. (1996). Oxidative stress and age-related neuronal deficits. *Molecular Chemistry and Neuropathology, 28*, 35–40.

Kaasinen, V., Vilkman, H., Hietala, J. et al. (2000). Age-related D_2/D_3 receptor loss in extrastriatal regions of the human brain. *Neurobiology of Aging, 21*, 683–688.

Karoum, F., Chrapusta, S.J., & Egan, M.F. (1994). 3-methoxtyramine is the major metabolite of released dopamine in the rat frontal cortex: Reassessment of the effects of antipsychotics on the dynamics of dopamine release and metabolism in the frontal cortex, nucleus accumbens, and striatum by a simple two pool model. *Journal of Neurochemistry, 63*, 972–979.

Kausler, D.H. (1991). *Experimental psychology, cognition, and human aging* (2nd ed.). New York: Springer-Verlag.

Kelly, T.H., Foltin, R.W., & Fischman, M.W. (1991). The effects of repeated amphetamine exposure on multiple measures of human behavior. *Pharmacology, Biochemistry, and Behavior, 38*, 417–426.

Kimberg, D.Y., & D'Esposito, M. (2003). Cognitive effects of the dopamine receptor agonist pergolide. *Neuropsychologia, 41*, 1020–1027.

Kimberg, D.Y., D'Esposito, M., & Farah, M.J. (1997). Effects of bromocriptine on human subjects depend on working memory capacity. *NeuroReport, 8*, 3581–3585.

Kneavel, M., Gogos, J., Karayiorgou, K., & Luine, V. (2000). Interactions of COMT gene deletion and environment on cognition. *Society for Neuroscience Abstracts, 26*, 1–2.

Lawrence, A.D., Weeks, R.A., Brooks, D.J. et al. (1998). The relationship between dopamine receptor binding and cognitive performance in Huntington's disease. *Brain, 121*, 1343–1355.

Li, S.-C., Lindenberger, U., & Sikström, S. (2001). Aging cognition: From neuromodulation to representation to cognition. *Trends in Cognitive Sciences, 5*, 479–486.

Li, S.-C., & Sikström, S. (2002). Integrative neurocomputational perspectives on cognitive aging, neuromodulation, and representation. *Neuroscience and Biobehavioral Reviews, 26*, 795–808.

Liljequist, R., Haapalinna, H., Ahlander, M. et al. (1997). Catechol-O-methyltransferase inhibitor tolcapone has minor influences on performance in experimental memory models in rats. *Behavioral Brain Research*, *82*, 195–202.

Lotta, T., Vidgren, J., Tilgmann, C. et al. (1995). Kinetics of human soluble and membrane-bound catechol-O-methyltransferase: A revised mechanism and description of the termolabile variant of the enzyme. *Biochemistry*, *34*, 4202–4210.

Luciana, M., & Collins, P.F. (1997). Dopamine modulates working memory for spatial but not object cues in normal humans. *Journal of Cognitive Neuroscience*, *9*, 330–347.

Luciana, M., Collins, P.F., & Depue, R.A. (1998). Opposing roles for dopamine and serotonin in the modulation of human spatial working memory functions. *Cerebral Cortex*, *8*, 218–226.

Luciana, M., Depue, R.A., Arbisi, P., & Leon, A. (1992). Facilitation of working memory in humans by a D_2 dopamine receptor agonist. *Journal of Cognitive Neuroscience*, *4*, 58–68.

Luo, Y., & Roth, G.S. (2000). The roles of dopamine oxidative stress and dopamine receptor signaling in aging and age-related neurodegeneration. *Antioxidants & Redox Signaling*, *2*, 449–460.

Ma, S.Y., Ciliax, B.J., Stebbins, G. et al. (1999). Dopamine transporter-immunoreactive neurons decrease with age in the human substantia nigra. *Journal of Comparative Neurology*, *409*, 25–37.

Malhotra, A.K., Kestler, L.J., Mazzanti, C. et al. (2002). A functional polymorphism in the COMT gene and performance on a test of prefrontal cognition. *American Journal of Psychiatry*, *159*, 652–654.

Mannisto, P.T., & Kaakkola, S. (1999). Catechol-O-methyltransferase (COMT): Biochemistry, molecular biology, and clinical efficacy of the new selective COMT inhibitors. *Pharmacological Reviews*, *51*, 593–628.

Mattay, V.S., Goldberg, T.E., Fera, F. et al. (2003). Catechol O-methyltransferase val^{158}-met genotype and individual variation in the brain response to amphetamine. *Proceedings of the National Academy of Sciences, USA*, *100*, 6186–6191.

McEntee, W.J., Mair, R.G., & Langlais, P.J. (1987). Neurochemical specificity of learning: Dopamine and motor learning. *Yale Journal of Biology and Medicine*, *60*, 187–193.

Mehta, M.A., Owen, A.M., Sahaikan, B.J. et al. (2000). Methylphenidate enhances working memory by modulating discrete frontal and parietal lobe regions in the human brain. *Journal of Neuroscience Online*, *20*, RC 65.

Mesco, E.R., Carlsson, S.G., Joseph, J.A., & Roth, G.S. (1993). Decreased striatal D_2 dopamine receptor mRNA synthesis during aging. *Molecular Brain Research*, *17*, 160–162.

Morgan, D.G., & Finch, C.E. (1998). Dopaminergic changes in the basal ganglia: A generalized phenomenon of aging in mammals. *Annals of the New York Academy of Sciences*, *515*, 145–160.

Mozley, P.D., Acton, P.D., Barraclough, E.D. et al. (1999). Effects of age on dopamine transporters in healthy humans. *Journal of Nuclear Medicine*, *40*, 1812–1817.

Mozley, L.H., Gur, R.C., Mozley, P.D., & Gur, R.E. (2001). Striatal dopamine transporters and cognitive functioning in healthy men and women. *American Journal of Psychiatry*, *158*, 1492–1499.

Nordström, A.L., Farde, L., Pauli, S., Litton, J.E., & Halldin, C. (1992). PET analysis of [11C] raclopride binding in healthy young adults and schiziphrenic patients: Reliability and age effects. *Human Psychopharmacology*, *7*, 157–165.

Oades, R.D. (1985). The role of noradrenaline in tuning and dopamine in switching between signals in the CNS. *Neuroscience and Biobehavioral Reviews*, *9*, 261–282.

Park, D.C., Lautenschlager, G., Hedden, T., Davidson, N.S., Smith, A.D., & Smith, P.K. (2002). Models of visuospatial and verbal memory across the adult life span. *Psychology and Aging*, *17*, 299–320.

Prull, M.W., Gabrieli, J.D.E., & Bunge, S.A. (1999). Age-related changes in memory: A cognitive neuroscience perspective. In F.I.M. Craik & T.A. Salthouse (Eds.), *The handbook of aging and cognition* (pp. 91–153). Mahwah, NJ: Lawrence Erlbaum Associates Inc.

Ramaekers, J.G., Louwerens, J.W., Muntjewerff, N.D. et al. (1999). Psychomotor, cognitive, extrapyramidal and affective functions of healthy volunteers during treatment with an atypical (amisulpiride) and a classic (haloperidol) antipsychotic. *Journal of Clinical Psychopharmacology*, *19*, 209–221.

Reeves, S., Bench, C., & Howard, R. (2002). Aging and the nigrostriatal dopamine system. *International Journal of Geriatric Psychiatry*, *17*, 359–370.

Remy, P., Jackson, P.L., Ribeiro, M.J. et al. (2000). Relationships between cognitive deficits and dopaminergic function in the striatum of Parkinson's disease patients. *Neurology*, *54* (Suppl.), 372.

Rinne, J.O., Lönnberg, P., & Marjamäki, P. (1990). Age-dependent decline of dopamine- D_1 and dopamine- D_2 receptor. *Brain Research*, *508*, 349–352.

Rinne, J.O., Sahlberg, N., Ruottinen, H., Nagren, K., & Lehikoinen, P (1998). Striatal uptake of the dopamine reuptake ligand [^{11}C]β-CFT is reduced in Alzheimer's disease assessed by positron emission tomography. *Neurology*, *50*, 152–156.

Roberts, A.C., De Salvia, M.A., Wilkinson, L.S. et al. (1994). 6-hydroxydopamine lesions of the prefrontal cortex in monkeys enhance performance on an analog of the Wisconsin Card Sort Test: Possible interactions with subcortical dopamine. *Journal of Neuroscience*, *14*, 2531–2544.

Rönnlund, M., Nyberg, L., Bäckman, L., & Nilsson, L.-G. (2005). Stability, growth, and decline in adult life-span development of declarative memory: Cross-sectional and longitudinal data from a population-based study. *Psychology and Aging*, *20*(1), 3–18.

Sakata, M., Farooqui, S.M., & Prasad, C. (1992). Post-transcriptional regulation of loss of rat striatal D_2 dopamine receptor during aging. *Brain Research*, *575*, 309–314.

Salthouse, T.A. (1992). Reasoning and spatial abilities. In F.I.M. Craik & T.A. Salthouse (Eds.), *Handbook of aging and cognition* (pp. 167–211). Hillsdale, NJ: Lawrence Erlbaum Associates Inc.

Sawaguchi, T., & Goldman-Rakic, P.S. (1991). D_1 dopamine receptors in prefrontal cortex: Involvement in working memory. *Science*, *251*, 947–950.

Sawaguchi, T., Matsamura, M., & Kubota, K. (1988). Dopamine enhances the neuronal activity of spatial short-term memory in the primate prefrontal cortex. *Neuroscience Research*, *5*, 465–473.

Seeman, P., Bzowej, N.H., Guan, H.C. et al. (1987). Human brain dopamine receptors in children and aging adults. *Synapse*, *1*, 399–404.

Servan-Schreiber, D., Bruno, R.M., Carter, C.S., & Cohen, J.D. (1998a). Dopamine and the mechanisms of cognition: Part I. A neural network model predicting dopamine effects on selective attention. *Biological Psychiatry*, *43*, 713–722.

Servan-Schreiber, D., Carter, C.S., Bruno, R.M., & Cohen, J.D. (1998b). Dopamine and the mechanisms of cognition: Part II. D-amphetamine effects in human subjects performing a selective attention task. *Biological Psychiatry*, *43*, 723–729.

Severson, J.A., Marcusson, J., Winblad, B., & Finch, C.E. (1982). Age-correlated loss of dopaminergic binding sites in human basal ganglia. *Journal of Neurochemistry*, *39*, 1623–1631.

Shinkai, T., Zhang, L., Mathias, S.A., & Roth, G.S. (1997). Dopamine induces apoptosis in cultured rat striatal neurons: Possible mechanism of D_2-dopamine receptor neuron loss during aging. *Journal of Neuroscience Research*, *47*, 393–399.

Simon, H., Taghzouti, K., & Le Moal, M. (1986). Deficits in spatial-memory tasks following lesions of septal dopaminergic terminals in the rat. *Behavioral and Brain Research*, *19*, 7–16.

Snow, B.J., Tooyama, I., McGeer E.G. et al. (1993). Human positron emission tomographic [18F]fluorodopa studies correlate with dopamine cell counts and levels. *Annals of Neurology*, *34*, 324–330.

Spiegel, R. (1978). Effects of amphetamines on performance and on polygraphic sleep parameters in man. *Advances in Bioscience*, *21*, 189–201.

Suhara, T., Fukuda, H., Inoue, O., Itoh, T., Suzuki, K., Yamasaki, T. et al. (1991). Age-related changes in human D_1 dopamine receptors measured by positron emission tomography. *Psychopharmacology*, *103*, 41–45.

Van Dyck, C.H., Seibyl, J.P., Malison, R.T. et al. (1995). Age-related decline in striatal dopamine transporter binding with iodine-123-β-CIT. *Journal of Nuclear Medicine*, *36*, 1175–1181.

Volkow, N.D., Gur, R.C., Wang, G.-J. et al. (1998a). Association between decline in brain dopamine activity with age and cognitive and motor impairment in healthy individuals. *American Journal of Psychiatry*, *155*, 344–349.

Volkow, N.D., Wang, G.-J., Fowler, J.S. et al. (1998b). Parallel loss of presynaptic and postsynaptic dopamine markers in normal aging. *Annals of Neurology*, *44*, 143–147.

Wang, Y., Chan G.L.Y., Holden, J.E. et al. (1998). Age-dependent decline of dopamine D_1 receptors in human brain: A PET study. *Synapse*, *30*, 56–61.

Weinshilboum, R.M., Otterness, D.M., & Szumlanski, C.L. (1999). Methylation pharmacogenetics: Catechol-O-methyltransferase, thiopurine methyltransferase, and histamine N-methyltransferase. *Annual Review of Pharmacology and Toxicology*, *39*, 19–52.

West, R.L. (1996). An application of prefrontal cortex function theory to cognitive aging. *Psychological Bulletin*, *120*, 272–292.

Yang, Y.K., Chiu, N.T., Chen, C.C. et al. (2003). Correlation between fine motor activity and striatal dopamine D_2 receptor density in patients with schizophrenia and healthy controls. *Psychiatry Research: Neuroimaging*, *123*, 191–197.

Zhang, L., Ravipati, A., Joseph, J., & Roth, G.S. (1995). Aging-related changes in rat striatal D_2 dopamine receptor mRNA-containing neurons: A quantitative nonradioactive in situ hybridization study. *Journal of Neuroscience*, *15*, 1735–1740.

27 Touch in infancy: The development of haptic abilities in very young infants

Arlette Streri

Touch and cognition

Is it possible to know something just by touching it? Touch differs from vision and hearing in that it depends on contact and on the quality of proximal reception. Because of this property, the tactual perceptual field is limited to the zone of contact with objects. In passive tactile perception (cutaneous perception), the perceptual field is limited and has the exact dimensions of the surface of the skin in contact with the stimulus. In most cases, in order to apprehend the whole object, voluntary movements must be made to compensate for the smallness of the tactile perceptual field. The kinaesthetic perception resulting from these movements is closely linked to cutaneous perception and they form *active touch* or *haptic perception*. As a result, object perception in the haptic mode is highly sequential. This latter property increases the load on working memory and requires a mental recognition and synthesis to obtain a unified representation of the object (J.J. Gibson, 1966; Revesz, 1950; see Hatwell, Streri, & Gentaz, 2003).

The hands are also the motor organs used to reach, hold, transport, and transform objects in our everyday life. In consequence, the hands are a complex system involving two functions: a perceptual function ("knowing") and an instrumental function ("doing"). More than in all the other modalities, perception and action are closely linked. Klatzky and Lederman (1993) defined two types of object properties: material properties such as texture, substance and temperature, and geometric properties such as shape and size. Our studies focused on object shape because shape allows the object identification and is the basis of object categorization. Lederman and Klatzky (1987) also defined exploratory procedures (Eps) in the adult's haptic mode that allow detection and identification of each object property with precision. For example, *lateral motion* allows detection of texture, *unsupported holding* is a suitable procedure for evaluating weight, etc. The two exploratory procedures that are interesting for our research are *enclosure* because we can detect global shape and volume, and *contour following* because it allows detection of precise shape.

How can babies know by touch? To answer this fundamental question, we consider three aspects of knowledge: perceptual aspects, intermodal transfer between touch and vision, and haptic cognition.

Perceiving with the hands

In contrast to adults, babies possess several means to perceive the environment by touching: the mouth and the hands. In the oral mode, young infants spontaneously display numerous behaviors with their mouth. From the beginning of life, the mouth plays a salient role in feeding and need gratification. Numerous studies have focused on neonatal facial imitation (e.g., Meltzoff & Moore, 1977). These studies show the infant's early abilities especially with tongue protrusion or mouth opening. Studies have also focused on cross-modal transfer from mouth to eyes (Gibson & Walker, 1984; Meltzoff & Borton, 1979). Based on this work, the baby's mouth was considered by researchers as an exploratory tool and an important part of the haptic system playing a major role in the infant's acquisition of information about objects. Researchers agree that the mouth predominates initial exploration in very young infants.

Our research focused mainly on the infant's hands, because the human hands are a major tool used for feeding, stroking, etc. Hands are essential for human beings. Anthropological studies have established a link between the development of human intelligence and the conquest of bipedal walking which freed the hands. In consequence, in research about the evolution of our species, brain and hands are always closely linked. Moreover, researchers have also suggested that in our species, language emerged from manual gestures (Corballis, 2003).

For numerous years, newborns and older infants were described as displaying only reflex actions and clumsy arm movements; For example, Twitchell (1965) described two main types of manual reflexes, avoiding reflex and grasping reflex. However, grasping reflex looks like an adult's *enclosure* procedure. Newborns strongly close their fingers on the object or the experimenter's finger. Just as a reminder, *enclosure* allows detection of global shape and volume. However, beyond hand reflexes, infants at birth are able to handle a small object. To reveal such an ability, we applied a habituation and dishabituation procedure to the manual mode, just as it is used in the visual mode (Streri, Lhote, & Dutilleul, 2000). Infants were seated in a rigid seat and an experimenter put a small object in their right or left palm. Newborns rarely tried to look at an object that they held. When it was necessary, the experimenter hid the object with her hands to prevent the baby from looking at it. But older infants often did try to look, and therefore we used a cloth screen to prevent looking. The screen separated the visual field from the tactile field, but infants could explore the objects freely. As a result, infants touched objects, but never saw them. So, all information was gained haptically.

The habituation/dishabituation procedure involved two phases. The habituation phase included a series of trials: The infants received a small object in their hand. A trial began when the infant held the object and ended when the infant dropped the object or after a duration defined by the experimenter. This was repeated several times. Over the course of these trials, we observed a decrease in holding times. Then, in the dishabituation phase, a novel object was put in the infant's hand. If we saw an increase in holding time or a novelty reaction, we inferred that the baby noticed the difference between the two objects. This procedure, controlled by the infant, is effective for revealing the early discriminatory capacities of young babies. Moreover, it is now well established that habituation process and memory are closely linked, revealing a form of mental representation of stimuli. In consequence, haptic memory in its manual mode is present from birth.

Streri et al. (2000) showed that newborns (the youngest was 16 hours old) were able to detect differences in the contours of two small objects (a prism and a cylinder) with both the right and left hands (see Figure 27.1). After

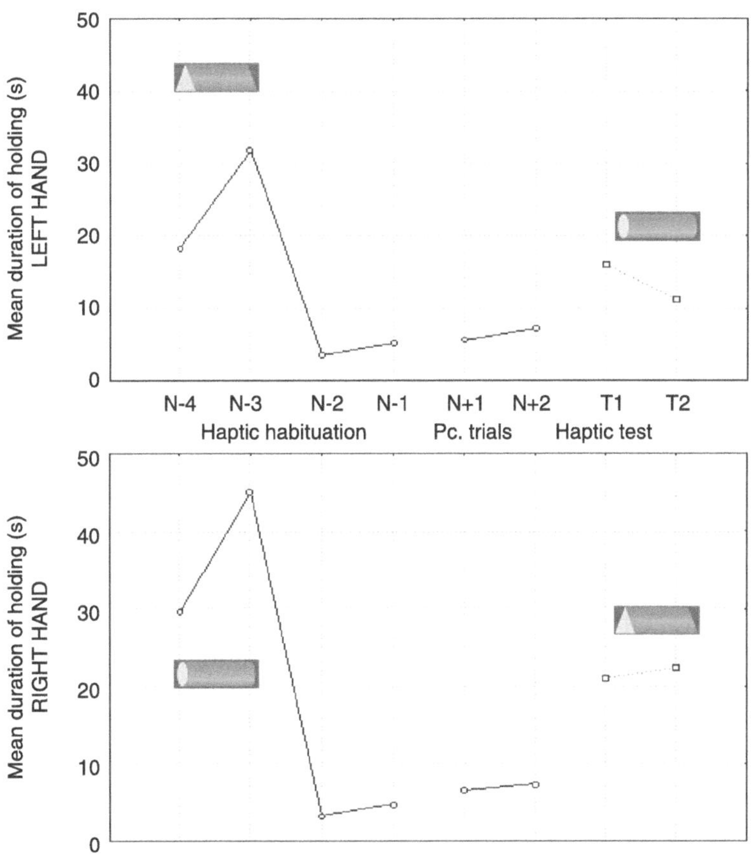

Figure 27.1 Habituation and discrimination of object shape in newborns. (Streri et al., 2000.)

habituation with an object, confirmed by two more trials, a novelty reaction was observed when a new object was put in the newborn's hand. So, this was the first evidence of habituation and reaction to novelty that was observed with the left as well as the right hand in newborns.

To sum up, from birth infants are able to take in, process, and memorize information about shape without visual control and discriminate between different shapes. In consequence, the grasping reflex is sufficient to detect similarities and differences among objects. The process appears to be similar in the manual and visual modes. This last conclusion is important. Because the process appears to be similar in the two modalities, we can ask about how infants transfer information across the haptic and the visual modes.

Seeing with the hands

Stein and Wallace (2001, p. 107) wrote:

> . . . it is important to note that the ability to integrate cues from different sensory modalities did not arise with the appearance of humans. Rather, it is an ancient scheme that antedates mammals and even the evolution of the nervous system. . . . In fact, it would be unprecedented to find an animal in which there exists a complete segregation of sensory cortex.

Neuropsychological studies in animals determined the brain centers of intersensory integration. Stein and Meredith (1993) suggested the cat's superior colliculus as a model of multisensory integration. The superior colliculus is a midbrain structure in which visual, auditory, and somatosensory inputs converge. There is not much human research. Instead, the monkey is used to explore multimodal areas in the brain. Precentral gyrus (area 6), ventral intraparietal (area 7b), and putamen (subcortical structure) are involved in adult monkeys according to Graziano and Gross (1995). These areas are approximatively the same in human beings. However, these structures correspond more to the integration of visual and haptic inputs in prehension of objects in near space than in integration of inputs from the different modalities.

Experimental studies concerning the relations between sensory modes use the cross-modal transfer paradigm. This is a cognitive task in which adults, children, or infants have to process and retain information in one modality, and then recognize this information in another modality. In human adults, the right claustrum is a center involved in cross-modal transfer of information between the haptic and visual modes (Hadjikhani & Roland, 1998).

Therefore, the old problem of the relations between sensory modes has been captured in the philosophical question asked in the seventeenth century. Molyneux asked his friend Locke (1689, p. 186) the following question. It corresponds precisely to the cross-modal transfer task.

> Suppose a man born blind, and now adult, and taught by his touch to distinguish between a cube and a sphere of the same metal, and nearly of the same bigness, so as to tell, when he felt one and the other, which is the cube, which the sphere. Suppose then the cube and sphere placed on a table, and the blind man be made to see: whether by his sight, before he touched them, he could now distinguish and tell which is the globe which the cube?

The philosopher Diderot (1749) was the first to compare the blind person to a neonate, and argued that vision must be very imperfect in an infant that opens its eyes for the first time, or in a blind person just after his or her operation. Diderot was right when he said that the newborn's vision is very imperfect. However, many experiments have since provided evidence that neonates perceive several properties of the world, such as shape, face, color, movement, etc. (see Slater, 1998).

For a long time, the answer to the Molyneux's question was negative. According to the empiricist model, three arguments have been proposed: (1) The neonate's experience is confused; (2) The sensory modalities do not naturally communicate; (3) Molyneux's problem receives a negative answer because experience in the manual mode is not sufficient for learning to perceive in the visual mode. This third argument is also taken up by some infant researchers. For example, in their cross-modal study of transfer from the mouth to the eyes in 1-month-old infants, Meltzoff and Borton (1979) thought that young infants were not able to explore objects manually. In consequence, for the tactile exploration phase, the authors put a pacifier in the baby's mouth and not an object in the infant's hand. The same argument and methodology were proposed by Gibson and Walker (1984) in a similar cross-modal study.

At the present time, infant studies give several positive answers to Molyneux's question. One-month-old infants visually recognize an object that they have previously explored orally through its substance (Gibson & Walker, 1984) or texture (Meltzoff & Borton, 1979). Two-month-old infants are able to recognize the shape of an object that they have previously manipulated with their right hand (Streri, 1987). However, several questions regarding intermodal transfer remain: (1) In these experiments, the subjects were not newborns. Today, we know that in the first 2 months after birth infants are able to establish links between visual, auditory, and haptic inputs; (2) Sometimes infants prefer the familiar object (see Meltzoff & Borton, 1979) but sometimes they prefer the novel object (see Gibson & Walker, 1984); (3) Meltzoff and Borton's results have not been replicated (Maurer, Stager, & Mondloch, 1999); (4) Mouthing involves different exploratory procedures from handling and may involve different processes; (5) Finally, texture and substance are material properties and not geometric properties like shape.

A genuine answer to Molyneux's problem would be to investigate whether newborns can coordinate information between both modalities in a cross-modal transfer task from hand to eyes with objects varying in shape. Haptic discrimination between shapes by newborns is a prerequisite if we refer to Molyneux's question. We know that newborns are able to discriminate between a curvilinear (a cylinder) vs a rectilinear (a prism) shape with both their right and left hands (see Streri et al., 2000).

Recently, Streri and Gentaz (2003) conducted an experiment on cross-modal recognition of shape from the right hand to eyes in human newborns. They used an intersensory paired-preference procedure that included two phases: a haptic familiarization phase in which newborns were given an object to explore manually without seeing it, followed by a visual test phase in which infants were shown the familiar object paired with a novel one for 60 s. Subjects were 24 newborns (mean age: 62 h, range from 16 h to 110 h). Tactile objects were a small cylinder (10 mm in diameter) and a small prism (10 mm triangle base). Visual objects were the same 3D objects, but ten times larger. An experimental group (12 subjects) received the two phases (haptic + visual) whereas a baseline group received only the visual phase. The comparison of looking times between the two groups allowed us to provide evidence of cross-modal recognition of shape from hand to eyes in the experimental group. Results showed that the newborns in the experimental group looked longer at the novel object than at the familiar one. In contrast, the newborns in the baseline group looked equally at the two objects. Moreover, the number of gaze shifts was important in both groups. This suggests that the newborns were not attracted visually by one object only. However, in the experimental group, the mean number of looks at the novel object was significantly higher than at the familiar object. In the baseline group it was not the case. The results suggest that newborns recognized the familiar object through a visual comparison process.

In conclusion, newborns are able to transfer shape information from right hand to eyes before they have had the opportunity to learn the pairing of visual and tactual experience. These results challenge the empiricist philosophical conception and modern connectionist models that sensory modalities cannot communicate in newborns. The results reveal an early developing ability, largely independent of common experience, to detect abstract amodal higher-order properties of objects. It is a prerequisite schema of perceptual loops necessary to the development of knowledge in infancy.

How should we interpret this result? Several explanations have been proposed:

1. Maurer (1993) suggested that newborns cannot yet distinguish among the various senses. On this view, early cross-modal transfer is based on a lack of distinction rather than on a cross-modal recognition of objects. A *synesthesia* phenomenon would be more appropriate to understand the relations between sensory modes.
2. Meltzoff and Moore (1997) proposed the *Active Intermodal Matching hypothesis*. Infants match what they see and what they explore orally.

They use a supramodal code that allows them to unify information processed from different sensory modes in one common framework. The same mechanism would explain neonatal imitations, such as tongue protrusion or mouth opening.

3 E.J. Gibson (1969) suggests that infants are able to abstract *amodal* or common information. Abstraction of common information involves equivalence between modalities with regard to amodal properties such as location, texture, movement, shape, duration, etc. Since Gibson's suggestion, the concept of amodal perception is often used to describe the link between modalities. A common percept independent from any one sense is created.

To distinguish among these three explanations, it is necessary to examine whether cross-modal transfer is a general property of the newborn human brain or whether it is modality specific, evidenced only in certain directions of transfer. In a first experiment, Streri and Gentaz (2004) tested for cross-modal transfer from the left hand to eyes as well as transfer from the right hand. They observed 60 newborns and used another methodology, in which 24 newborns had the tactile habituation phase with the left hand, 24 other newborns had it with the right hand, and 12 newborns did not receive a tactual habituation phase. In the visual phase, all newborns looked at the familiar object and at the novel object in four sequential trials (one object per trial). Cross-modal recognition was again evidenced from the right hand: Newborns looked longer at the novel object. No visual recognition was evidenced from infants in the left-hand group. In the control group, newborns looked equally at the two objects.

In a second experiment, Sann and Streri (2005) tested the reverse transfer from eyes to hands. If this is the case, then a complete primitive unity of senses would be shown. After a visual habituation to an object, we put a familiar and a novel object in the infant's right hand. The tactile objects were presented sequentially in an alternating manner. Twelve newborns participated in the experiment. Following visual habituation, no haptic recognition was found.

The results have to be discussed according to the three models described earlier. First, an account that relies on confusion of senses is not supported. Haptic inputs are diffused to the visual mode but the reverse is not true. Second, intermodal matching is not possible because the transfer is not reversible. A felt object is matched with a seen object, but a seen object is not matched with a felt object. Plausibly, a common framework may exist, but the matching process is not reversible as regards the object properties. Facial imitation and cross-modal transfer do not rely on the same mechanisms.

Third, detection of amodal information seems to be the most plausible hypothesis because habituation and dishabituation are observed in both modalities. Newborns detect invariants whatever the modality that receives information. But this hypothesis must be made more precise. How is amodal information perceptually linked, since transfer is not reversible? We suggest that information processed by vision is, from birth, immediately global, whereas information processed by touch is partial and limited. This discrepancy between exploratory strategies could be the cause of non-reversible transfer between vision and touch. A seen object is processed as a whole and the newborn does not manually recognize this totality from a felt feature. In contrast, an infant can visually recognize a part of an object that he or she previously felt. Because the perception always goes from simpler to more complex level and not the reverse (see Streri, 1993), amodal perception obtained is the result from the simplest processed information, that is, information processed by the haptic modality. In consequence, the amodal percept is partial because the newborn's hand is not able to gain a complete percept of the object. After all, *contour following*, an exploratory procedure that allows detection of precise shape, is not yet available.

And after birth? Previous experiments have investigated reversible cross-modal transfer of object shape from hand to eyes and from eyes to hand in 2-month-old infants when they exhibit low levels of prehensile activity (Streri, 1987), and in 5-month-old infants when visually guided prehension is developing rapidly (Streri & Pêcheux, 1986).

In 2-month-old infants, we used different methodologies and various shapes. The findings provided evidence of cross-modal recognition of shape from touch to vision but not from vision to touch (Streri, 1987; Streri & Millet, 1988; Streri & Molina, 1993; see Table 27.1). Streri and Molina (1993)

Table 27.1 Cross-modal recognition of object shape

Ages	*Objects*	*Touch/vision*	*Vision/touch*
Newborns			
Streri & Gentaz (2003) *Somatosensory and Motor Research*		+	
Streri & Gentaz (2004) *Neurosychologia*	Right hand Left hand	+ –	
Sann & Streri (2005) *(submitted)*			–
2-month-olds			
Streri (1987) *British Jour. Developmental Psychology*		+	–
Streri & Millet (1988) *L'Année Psychologique*		+	–
Streri & Molina (1993) *Perception*		+	+ if pictures – if objects
5-month-olds			
Streri & Pêcheux (1986) *British Jour. Developmental Psychology*		–	+

examined whether degraded visual information could give a blurred percept that would match the manual percept. In this condition, we observed a transfer from vision to touch and both representations are matched.

In 5-month-old infants, we observed cross-modal recognition of shape from vision to touch but not from touch to vision (Streri & Pêcheux, 1986). How should we interpret the change of transfer from neonates to 5-month-old infants? Just as a reminder, there are two functions of the hand: a perceptual function that is shown at birth (Streri et al., 2000) and an instrumental function. This second function appears later, at about 5 months old, when babies catch the seen object or transport the held object through space. We suggest that the instrumental function temporarily disturbs the perceptual function. Indeed, cross-modal transfer from touch to vision is again found in infants aged 6 months and older (see Rose, 1994). However, at 5 months, the link between the two modalities is supported thanks to the visual mode.

In short, coordination between touch and vision exists at birth. The links between the two modalities are fragile because they depend on the efficiency of information processing of each modality (vision or touch). The relations between modes are mainly supported by the haptic mode in the first months after birth as in children and adults (see Hatwell, 2003). Transfer is rarely reversible because the exploratory strategies in the visual and haptic modes are quite different, but coordination is always present either from the hands or from the eyes. At about 6 months of age, bimodal exploration of an object is possible. Coordination between senses is reinforced.

Thinking with the hands

In the cross-modal transfer tasks, the objects were small and infants could see and feel them in their totality. What happens when infants manually explore objects partially because they are too large? Are they able to recognize them visually? To understand how the infants think with their hands, we again used the cross-modal transfer task paradigm. Two examples will be presented; perception of object unity and discrimination of small numbers in the haptic mode.

Perception of object unity in infancy

To study infants' perception of unity under occlusion, Kellman and Spelke (1983) developed a method using habituation and recovery of visual attention. This method included two phases. In the habituation phase, infants saw a display containing a rod behind an occluder. The rod moved in translation behind the occluder. In the test phase, infants were presented with two visual displays: A complete rod or two separate pieces corresponding to the visible areas present in the occlusion display. The logic was the following: If, in the habituation phase, infants thought they saw a complete rod, they should look less at the complete rod than at the separate pieces. The reverse is also true. If, in the habituation phase, infants thought they saw two visible pieces, they should look longer at the complete rod than at the separate pieces in the visual test.

We present the conditions in which babies consider that a partially occluded object is seen as one unity, or two separate units (see Table 27.2).

All the experiments provided evidence that 4-month-old infants consider the occluded rod as complete in the condition where it is in translation behind a stable occluder. When the occluder moved in a contingent manner with the rod, or when the occluder moved and the rod was stable, or when the whole display was stable, then perception of the complete rod was not clear. When the visible edges of these two parts were not relatable nor were linked according to similarity or any other Gestalt principle, but they were moved back and forth with a common lateral translation, unity was perceived (see Kellman & Arterberry, 1998, for a review). As a result, common motion of the rod alone specifies object unity. Subsequent research (Kellman, Spelke, & Short, 1986) sought out the motion relationships that underlie unit perception. They found that rigid translations along any axis, including translations in depth, led to infants' perception of unity. In contrast, rotary motion did not lead to infants' perception of unity, until they were at least 6 months old (see Eizenman & Berthental, 1998). All the results provided evidence that

Table 27.2 Perception of object unity in 4-month-old infants (visual mode)

Translating condition	*Vision habituation displays*	*Test displays*	*Results*
Rod movement			One unit
Rod and block movement			–
Block movement			–
No movement			–
No relatable edges			One unit
Rotating condition			–

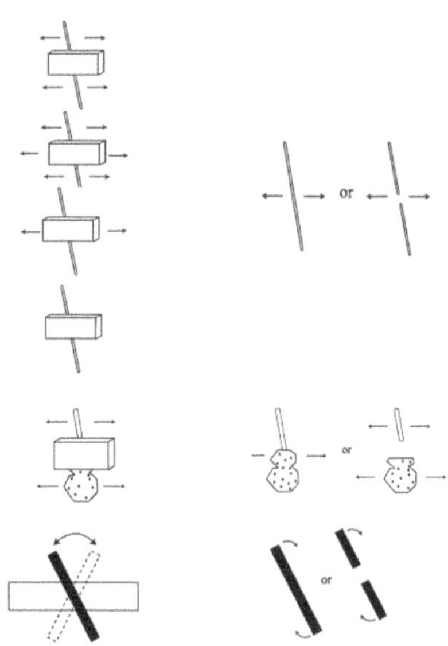

beyond perception, infants are able to conceive a partially seen object in its totality.

In a series of experiments, we adapted the designs to examine haptic perception. We used the cross-modal paradigm to discover whether perception of unity is amodal and involves a thinking process in the haptic mode under the same conditions as the visual mode (see Table 27.3).

Infants aged 4–5 months held two rings, one in each hand, under a cloth that blocked their view of the rings and the space between them. In one condition the rings were rigidly connected and moved together, whereas in the other condition the rings could be moved independently. After exploring the rings haptically, infants received a visual test with pairs of rings that were connected or separated. Across all experiments, infants explored the rings bimanually during habituation, producing patterns of rigid or independent motion. The experiments provided evidence that infants perceive the unity and boundaries of objects by detecting the motion patterns they themselves produced. Infants who explored the independently moveable rings perceived two distinct objects; infants who explored the rigidly moveable rings perceived a single object (Streri & Spelke, 1988).

In the other experiments, Streri and Spelke (1989) wanted to test whether figural goodness or motion relationships predominate in the haptic modality. Either the rings moved rigidly together and had the same substance, texture,

Table 27.3 Perception of object unity in the haptic mode

Ages	*Haptic displays*	*Visual displays*	*Results*
4-month-olds Streri & Spelke (1988) *Cognitive Psychology*	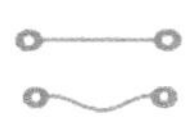 Rigid connection Flexible connection		1 unit 2 units
Streri & Spelke (1989) *Child development*	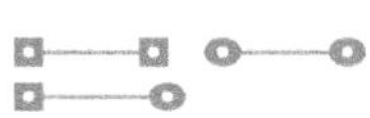		1 unit
Streri, Spelke & Rameix (1993) *Cognition* Active condition Passive condition	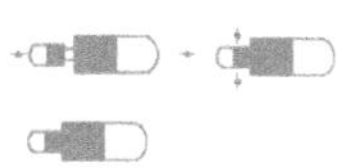	 or 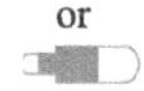	2 units 1 unit Ambiguous
4/5-month-olds Streri, Gentaz, Spelke & Van de Walle (2004) *Quarterly Journal of Experimental Psychology*	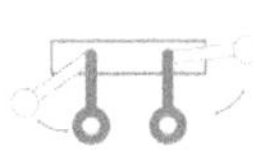 Unconnected Independent movement		2 units
	 Connected Rigid movement		1 unit
	 Connected Independent movement	or	Ambiguous
	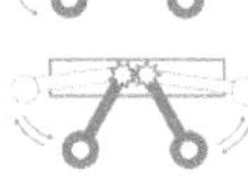 Connected Opposite movement		Ambiguous

weight, etc., or the rings differed in all these characteristics. In the haptic modality as in the visual modality, infants appear to perceive object unity by analyzing motion relationships but not by analyzing figural goodness.

Streri, Spelke, and Rameix (1993) sought out the kind of motion relationships that underlie unity perception in the haptic mode. In five experiments, 4- to 5-month-old infants manipulated a device made up of a small and a large surface that they could hold in each hand by a handle. In one condition, the surfaces were rigidly connected. In the second condition, the handles could be moved by sliding the small surface vertically along the large surface. In the final condition, the small surface could be pulled away from the large surface and pushed towards it. In a passive condition, the experimenter held and moved the device. The findings revealed that infants who explored the rigidly connected device visually perceived the display as a single unit. When infants explore the device either by sliding or by moving apart the two elements, they perceived it as two units. When the experimenter moved the display, the infants' responses were indeterminate.

Finally, Streri, Gentaz, Spelke, and Van de Walle (2004) investigated infants' perception of unity in relation to two properties of the assemblies. First, we varied whether the two rings were connected to the same pivot point or to two spatially separated pivot points. Second, we varied whether the two rings underwent a single rigid, rotary motion, opposite rotary motions (like scissors), or independent rotary motions. We asked whether infants perceive object unity in the haptic mode on the basis of patterns of rotary motion, and whether their perception is affected by specific spatial and temporal properties of the motion patterns. When the infants explored the unconnected independent movement display, they visually perceived two units. When the infants explored the connected rigid movement display, they visually perceived one unit. When the infants explored the connected independent movement display or the connected opposite movement display, their perception was ambiguous. The findings suggest that all rigid rotations are potentially informative to infants. The perception of object unity is influenced by three spatio-temporal properties of rotary motion: the presence or absence of a common fixed point of rotation, the presence or absence of a common pattern of rigid displacement, and the presence or absence of a contingent motion.

In short, with their hands and without visual control, infants are able to detect some physical laws that constrain the movement of simple or composite objects. They are able to think about physical events with their hands and possess representational capacities that are identical in the visual and haptic modes.

Can babies count on their fingers?

Previous research provided evidence that newborns and young infants are able to discriminate different small numerosities presented in the visual mode

(Starkey & Cooper, 1980). We asked the question whether infants have an abstract and amodal mechanism for numerical representation. Féron, Gentaz, and Streri (2005) studied numerical correspondences between sets of haptic and visible items.

Twelve infants received two objects (a cube and a ring) successively in their right hand (2-haptic-object group) for 30 s each. In a second group, 12 other infants received three objects (a cube, a sphere, a ring) successively for 30 s each (3-haptic-object group). Then, they were presented with two visual displays containing two or three objects. To avoid a cross-modal transfer task of object shape, the visual objects did not look like the haptic objects but were composed of some topological and metric characteristics of the three haptic objects. Visual targets displayed a square with a hole in the center and a circle placed against one of the sides (see Table 27.4). The two-object-display and the three-object display were visually presented in alternation (one by one) three times. If infants were able to perceive the number of held objects and transfer the numerical information to the visual mode, then a reaction to novelty was to be expected, that is, a longer looking time for the non-numerical corresponding display. The results revealed that infants prefer to look at the non-corresponding display to the felt number of objects. In the 2-haptic-object group, infants looked longer at the three-object display than the two-object display, and infants in the 3-haptic-object group looked longer at the two-object display than the three-object display.

The results suggest that 5-month-olds detect the number of distinct entities in spite of variations in object features (shape), memorize this number, and recognize it in the visual mode. They possess a detector of numerosities that operates in an amodal and cognitive way.

General conclusion

In short, our research provided evidence for amodal mechanisms in the two modalities to gain information from the world (habituation/dishabituation). But substitutions are partial in transfer tasks because modal specificities such

Table 27.4 Haptic perception of small numbers

Age	*Haptic displays*	*Visual displays*
5-month-old infants Feron, Gentaz & Steri (2005) *Cognitive Development*		

as exploratory strategies and different functions of the haptic mode constrain the links between the modes. However, despite these discrepancies, conceiving the world is possible with hands as with eyes.

Just before closing, we would like to point out some ways in which our research on normal infants may tell us about impaired infants' abilities.

Of course, the young infants in the experiments who were working without visual input, are not comparable to blind infants. Still, our results suggest that the haptic mode is the best candidate to substitute for their visual deficits. We suggest that when blind infants contact and explore objects with their hands, they come to perceive and understand the world.

We know that infants with autism have some problem integrating information among the sensory modes. This deficit in sensory integration is probably related to their well-documented difficulty in body schema. We suggest that research on intermodal transfer tasks in normal infants may provide a model for this population.

References

Corballis, M.C. (2003). From hand to mouth: Gesture, speech, and the evolution of right-handedness. *Behavioral and Brain Sciences*, *26*, 199–208.

Diderot, D. (1749/1972). *La lettre sur les aveugles à l'usage de ceux qui voient*. Paris: Garnier-Flammarion.

Eizenman, D.R., & Berthenthal, B.I. (1998). Infant's perception of unity in translating and rotating displays. *Developmental Psychology*, *34*, 426–434.

Féron, J., Gentaz, E., & Streri, A. (2005). Evidence of amodal representation of small numbers across visuo-tactile modalities in 5-month-old infants. *Cognitive Development* (in press).

Gibson, E.J. (1969). *Principles of perceptual learning and development*. New York: Academic Press.

Gibson, E.J., & Walker, A. (1984). Development of knowledge of visual-tactual affordances of substance, *Child Development*, *55*, 453–460.

Gibson, J.J. (1966). *The senses considered as perceptual systems*. Boston, MA: Houghton Mifflin.

Graziano, M., & Gross, C. (1995). The representation of extrapersonal space: A possible role for bimodal, visual-tactile neurons. In M. Gazzaniga (Ed.), *The cognitive neurosciences* (pp. 1021–1034). Cambridge, MA: MIT Press.

Hadjikhani, N., & Roland, P.E. (1998). Cross-modal transfer of information between the tactile and the visual representations in the human brain: A positron emission tomographic study. *Journal of Neurosciences*, *18*, 1072–1084.

Hatwell, Y. (2003). Intermodal coordination in children and adults. In Y. Hatwell, A. Streri, & E. Gentaz (Eds.), *Touching for knowing. Cognitive psychology of tactile manual perception* (pp. 207–219). Amsterdam: Johns Benjamins Publishing Company.

Hatwell, Y., Streri, A., & Gentaz, E. (2003). *Touching for knowing. Cognitive psychology of tactile manual perception*. Amsterdam: Johns Benjamins Publishing Company.

Kellman, P., & Arterberry, M. (1998). *The cradle of knowledge. Development of perception in infancy*. Cambrige, MA. MIT Press.

Kellman, P.J., & Spelke, E.S. (1983). Perception of partly occluded objects in infancy. *Cognitive Psychology*, *15*, 483–524.

Kellman, P.J., Spelke, E.S., & Short, K.R. (1986). Infant perception of object unity from translatory motion in depth and vertical translation. *Child Development*, *57*, 72–86.

Klatzky, R.L., & Lederman, S.J. (1993). Toward a computational model of constraint-driven exploration and haptic object identification. *Perception*, *22*, 597–621.

Lederman, S.J., & Klatzky, R.L. (1987). Hand movements: A window into haptic object recognition. *Cognitive Psychology*, *19*, 342–368.

Locke, J. (1689/1975). *An essay concerning human understanding*. P.H. Nidditch, Oxford: University Press.

Maurer, D. (1993). Neonatal synesthesia: Implications for the processing of speech and faces. In B. de Boysson-Bardies et al. (Eds.), *Developmental neurocognition: Speech and face processing in the first year of life* (pp. 109–124). The Netherlands: Kluwer Academic Publishers.

Maurer, D., Stager, C., & Mondloch, C. (1999). Cross-modal transfer of shape is difficult to demonstrate in one-month-olds. *Child Development*, *70*, 1047–1057.

Meltzoff, A.N., & Borton, R.W. (1979). Intermodal matching by human neonates. *Nature*, *282*, 403–404.

Meltzoff, A.N., & Moore, M.K. (1977). Imitation of facial and manual gestures by human neonates, *Science*, *198*, 75–78.

Meltzoff, A.N., & Moore, M.K. (1997). Explaining facial imitation. A theoretical model. *Early Development and Parenting*, *6*, 179–192.

Revesz, G. (1950). *Psychology and art of the blind*. London: Longmans Green.

Rose, S.A. (1994). From hand to eye: Findings and issues in infant cross-modal transfer. In D. J. Lewkowicz & R. Lickliter (Eds.), *The development of intersensory perception. Comparative perspectives* (pp 265–284). Hillsdale, NJ: Lawrence Erlbaum Associates Inc.

Sann, C., & Streri, A. (2005). *Perception of object shape and texture in human newborns: Evidence from cross-modal transfer tasks*. Manuscript submitted for publication.

Slater, A. (1998). *Perceptual development. Visual, auditory and speech perception in infancy*. Hove, UK: Psychology Press.

Starkey, P., & Cooper, R.G. (1980). Perception of number by human infants. *Science*, *210*, 1033–1035.

Stein, B.E., & Meredith, M.A. (1993). *The merging of the senses*. Cambridge, MA: MIT Press.

Stein, B.E., & Wallace, M.T. (2001). Intersensory Integration. Underlying neural mechanisms. In P.G. Grossenbacher (Ed.), *Finding consciousness in the brain. A neurocognitive approach* (pp. 105–131). Amsterdam: John Benjamins Publishing Company.

Streri, A. (1987). Tactile discrimination of shape and intermodal transfer in 2- to 3- month-old infants. *British Journal of Developmental Psychology*, *5*, 213–220.

Streri, A. (1993). *Seeing, reaching, touching. The relations between vision and touch in infancy*. London: Harvester Wheatsheaf.

Streri, A., & Gentaz, E. (2003). Cross-modal recognition of shape from hand to eyes in human newborns. *Somatosensory & Motor Research*, *20*, 11–16.

Streri, A., & Gentaz, E. (2004). Cross-modal recognition of shape from hand to eyes and handedness in human newborns. *Neuropsychologia*, *42*, 1365–1369.

Streri, A., Gentaz, E., Spelke, E.S., & Van de Walle, G. (2004). Haptic perception of object unity in rotating displays. *The Quarterly Journal of Experimental Psychology*, *57*, 523–538.

Streri, A., Lhote, M., & Dutilleul, S. (2000). Haptic perception in newborns. *Developmental Science*, *3*, 319–327.

Streri, A., & Millet, S. (1988). Equivalences intermodales de la forme des objets entre la vision et le toucher chez les bébés de 2 mois. *L'Année Psychologique*, *88*, 329–341.

Streri, A., & Molina, M. (1993). Visual-tactual and tactual-visual transfer between objects and pictures in 2-month-old infants. *Perception*, *22*, 1299–1318.

Streri, A., & Pêcheux, M.G. (1986). Vision to touch and touch to vision transfer of form in 5-month-old infants. *British Journal of Developmental Psychology*, *4*, 161–167.

Streri, A., & Spelke, E.S. (1988). Haptic perception of objects. *Cognitive Psychology*, *20*, 1–23.

Streri, A., & Spelke, E.S. (1989). Effects of motion and figural goodness on haptic object perception in infancy. *Child Development*, *60*, 1111–1125.

Streri, A., Spelke, E.S., & Rameix, E. (1993). Specific and amodal mechanisms of object perception and exploration in infancy: The case of active touch. *Cognition*, *47*, 251–279.

Twitchell, T.E. (1965). The automatic grasping responses of infants, *Neuropsychologia*, *3*, 47–259.

28 How children grasp the causal structure of the world

Frank C. Keil

Over the past decade, one of the most powerful themes in both cognitive science in general and cognitive development in particular has been the idea that intuitive theories are essential to understanding our mental lives (Carey, 1985; Gopnik & Wellman, 1994; Keil, 1989; Murphy & Medin, 1985). It has become commonplace to talk about adults, children, and sometimes even infants having naïve or intuitive theories about various facets of the world (Gelman & Koenig, 2003). The words "naïve" and "intuitive" have somewhat varying senses but there are several features that tend to reappear in their use with theories. Usually these theories are not taught to their owners in any pedagogical manner; instead they are acquired through encounters with the world. The role of culture varies across accounts. Sometimes the child developing an intuitive theory seems to be presented as an intellectual hermit on an isolated desert island of themselves and the environment they are trying to explain or understand. Other times, culture is seen as biasing the child, or adult, towards one intuitive theory versus another even if it isn't explicitly presenting the theory as such. For example, traditional rural dwellers in parts of Central America can develop quite different biological theories, such as taxonomic versus ecological ones, as a result of the culture in which they are embedded (Medin & Atran, 2004). The culture may not explicitly provide the theory as such, but nonetheless can convey a particular kind of causal schema as central to the study of living things.

A second theme often found in discussions of intuitive theories is the idea that the theories themselves are implicit. Although an individual might eventually come to be able to articulate a theory, such an awareness is not needed for a person to have an intuitive theory. At the same time, there is a strong sense that intuitive theories are more than simply automatically executed modules such as those involved in object perception, language use, and face recognition (Fodor, 1983). Intuitive theories are thought to be more revisable as a function of experience than modules. Moreover, in many cases, the presence of an intuitive theory is often justified through explicit articulation of its elements by those who have the theory.

A third theme is that intuitive theories are domain specific. Theories of everything (e.g., Weinberg, 1993) are not normally considered compatible with notions of intuitive theories which seem to cover bounded sets of phenomena such as biology, psychology, and mechanics, or sub-areas of these such as disease.

Related to the notion of domain specificity is the fourth theme of coherence. In a coherent theory, the laws and/or principles of a theory work together in a manner where each reinforces the presence of the other and each tends to follow from combinations of other elements (Thagard, 1989, 2000). Theories are thought to contain several elements that mutually strengthen each other and provide boundaries relative to other theories, boundaries that may also be linked to their domain specificity. Coherence is an appealing notion. We routinely talk about sets of ideas that "hang together" or provide an integrated understanding. In practice, however, it is much more difficult to formally describe and measure the coherence of a theory (Amini, 2003; Thagard, 2000). If the underlying principles for explaining a seemingly bounded set of phenomena (such as the seasons of our planet) internally contradict each other, such contradictions would work against notions of coherence. One can also ask how many elements a theory must have to be coherent. Consider two examples, a primitive folk biology (Inagaki & Hatano, 2002) and a primitive folk psychology (Wellman, 1992). Coherence in such systems may not mean much if there are only two or three elements in the earliest versions of these theories.

Coherence also remains an important issue in cognitive science because of its links to the philosophical problem of foundationalism, namely the idea that all science must ultimately be grounded in a set of primitives, usually those of physics. This form of reductionism has both in-principle difficulties as well as practical difficulties in terms of everyday cognition. Coherentist approaches are often posed as an alternative to foundationalism (Thagard, 2000) with the assumption that coherence offers a way give a kind of local completeness to a theory while not requiring it to be reducible to a bedrock of physics. In that way, an intuitive theory might be thought of as meeting some level of adequacy without requiring it to be fully reductionistic.

A fifth theme sees intuitive theories as more universal across cultures than those that are explicitly taught. Universal patterns in the world that all children encounter are thought to form a common data set for the generation of intuitive theories. For certain classes of phenomena this assumption seems correct. Basic notions of the physical mechanics of simple bounded objects and of human social interactions may be shared across all cultures. Similarly, notions of living kinds as having essences and as being arrayed in unique taxonomies may be universal (e.g., Atran, 1998). Not all aspects of untutored explanatory understanding are universal, however. Particular cultures offer unique experiences that provide distinct sets of data for the building of theories. Moreover, the culture, in both explicit and implicit ways, may set up biases to construct explanations of certain forms and not others. Thus, it has been repeatedly argued that some Eastern cultures make causal interpretations that pay more attention to embedding environments than do some

Western cultures (Nisbett, 2003). Similarly, as noted earlier, the agricultural practices of cultures can bias whether they explain biological systems in more or less ecological terms.

Finally, a sixth theme places causal relations as central to intuitive theories. Certainly, theories in principle can avoid use of causal arguments, either by exploiting the formalisms of mathematics or by simply making statements about spatial and temporal contingencies without any mention of cause. In the formal sciences, theories of this acausal sort are common and indeed have been argued by some to be the only correct way of doing a science (Russell, 1913). In practice, however, even scientists rarely escape invoking causally rich arguments. In everyday language and cognition, causal accounts are even more ubiquitous, as are appeals to causal mechanisms (Ahn & Kalish, 2000). Whatever form most intuitive theories ultimately take, causal notions may be essential in characterizing their structure.

It is clear as we go through each of these different aspects of intuitive theories that there is not a perfect consensus on what they are. The purpose of this chapter is to explore some ways in which children grasp the causal structure of the world and to ask how those ways of grasping causal structure fit with various notions of intuitive theories. To develop this account, however, it is useful to consider more closely some of limitations of theories as they are normally characterized.

Trouble with traditional views of theories

Consider, first, some limitations of theories in formal science when such theories are examined in the minds of individual scientists. It is reasonable to assume that lay people are likely to have at least those limitations as well. One critical drawback of theories in the minds of individual scientists is their necessary incompleteness. Each scientist in a community, especially in the present day, often only fully grasps a small part of a full theoretical account of the phenomena they study. In addition, the fragments of theory that a scientist knows may not all fit together into a coherent whole without the collaboration of other scientists who know other essential components.

A second limitation of scientists is the extent to which they depart from classical models of nomological-deductive reasoning in which they purportedly propose laws that act as axioms and then explore their deductive consequences as one does a proof in logic (Hempel, 1965). In reality, sciences almost never proceed in such a manner. They are far more messy enterprises in which hypotheses do not simply follow the laws of logic (Salmon, 1989). This has been particularly evident in studies conducted "in vivo" by having psychologists embedded in working laboratories and watching how scientific progress advances in real time (e.g. Dunbar, 2000). In such cases, there is considerable serendipity, analogies at various levels of abstraction and looseness, and a number of false starts and retracing of steps. The theories that emerge in these cases are often patched together in ways that still have large holes and even contradictions.

It has been suggested that the incompleteness of theories is so serious that they may be nothing more than a large set of unintegrated primitive and highly local causal notions, some times called "p-prims" (di Sessa, 1993; di Sessa, Gillespie, & Esterly, 2004; Nakhleh & Samarapungavan, 1999). In this view, any pattern of overarching conceptual interpretations is largely illusory. People notice local patterns, often on the basis of perceptually salient scenarios, and show little in the way of general principles that apply widely across situations. This may be true for precise mechanistic principles or for consistent use of various laws of Newtonian mechanics, such as those governing forces and trajectories; but as will be seen later in this chapter, at a more implicit and abstract level, there may be a sense of patterns that hold across very large domains of phenomena.

The degree of implicitness of intuitive theories also needs further analysis, as it is not clear how to cleanly characterize theories as implicit, nor whether any sense of "implicit" neatly captures intuitive theories. Certainly not all intuitive theories need be implicit. One can on at least some occasions verbalize quite easily beliefs about the world that were not explicitly taught. In addition, there varying degrees of explicitness. Consider three such levels for what it means to have an explicit theory: (1) A person could explicitly provide a complete explanation of how something works; (2) A person could explicitly know a theory but not be able to put it in words, perhaps instead showing their knowledge by making a diagram; (3) A person might not be able to create an explanation in any form but could explicitly, recognize the correct one when presented explicitly, and reject incorrect ones. All of these senses of explicitness are different from simply being able to make predictions but not able to explain why those predictions come to mind, which can include cases that would never count as "having an intuitive theory". Thus, one might be able to predict the occluded contours of some objects but one may do so on the basis of an object perception module that is far removed from having a theory. Similarly, one might be able to predict that an elevator is about to stop at a floor, based on vestibular input of information about deceleration, while being completely unable to explain the basis for such a prediction. The ability to make predictions without explicit justifications may therefore cover a wide range of mental activities, only some of which are normally seen as intuitive theories. As seen shortly, there may be several other implicit levels of processing that enable predictions about causal relations in the world but which also do not conform with typical notions of theories. In the end, these levels of processing of causal information may be critical to understanding how we make sense of the world, especially if we are mistaken in the extent to which we have intuitive theories as they are normally understood. These mistaken impressions are considered next.

The false fidelity of our intuitions about our explanatory understandings

We have seen that there are clear conceptual problems in attempting to have deep and complete and fully mechanistic understandings of the world around us. It simply isn't possible for any individual to do so, even the practicing scientist. This limitation might be substantially mitigated by simply being aware of explanatory gaps and shortcomings. That sort of meta-cognitive awareness of the shallowness of our understandings would enable us to know precisely when to seek out additional information or to reduce confidence in our own explanations. It turns out, however, that we do not seem to have a good grasp of how well we understand the world around us, and in fact, we labor under an "illusion of explanatory depth" (Rozenblit & Keil, 2002). This illusion has been documented primarily through a procedure in which participants go through eight steps:

1 They are taught a rating scale on how well they understand how something works.
2 They are asked to initially rate their understanding of a large set of phenomena ranging from artifacts such as helicopters to natural phenomena such as thunderstorms.
3 They are asked to then provide the most comprehensive explanations they can of how a subset of those items work.
4 They are asked to re-rate their initial knowledge in light of that explanation.
5 They are asked to answer a critical diagnostic question about the object or phenomenon.
6 They are asked to again re-rate their initial knowledge in light of their answer to that diagnostic question.
7 They are asked to read an expert explanation of the artifact or phenomenon.
8 Finally, they are asked to again re-rate their initial knowledge in light of reading that expert explanation. In some studies, participants made additional ratings that checked whether their self assessments would rise as a function of what they thought they had learned from reading the expert explanations.

Over several studies a reliable pattern appears (Mills & Keil, 2004; Rozenblit & Keil, 2002). Adults and children alike show substantial drops in ratings from their initial self-ratings to later re-ratings after being confronted with questions about how well things actually work. Thus, they labor under an illusion that they are able to explain the structure of the world in far greater depth than they really are. In many cases subjects are distinctly surprised at just how inadequate their understandings are relative to their initial estimates. Moreover, just the event of trying to give a full explanation without any experimenter probes is enough to cause a substantial drop.

Several other findings of relevance have also emerged (Mills & Keil, 2004; Rozenblit & Keil, 2002). The illusion is specific to explanatory forms of understanding. People are much better calibrated for estimates of how well they know facts, procedures, or narratives. There seem to be distinct properties of explanatory understandings that provide an especially powerful feeling of knowing. Our studies suggest that several factors converge to create an especially strong illusion for explanations as opposed to other forms of knowledge. One factor involves confusions of higher-level functional understandings with lower-level more mechanistic ones. A second influential factor is a tendency to underestimate the degree to which one figures out causal relations "on the fly" when an entity is available for inspection as opposed to having all the information represented in one's head.

The illusion of explanatory depth raises a critical problem for the idea that young children grasp the causal structure of the world by means of intuitive theories. If those theories are far sparser and more incomplete than intuition and introspection suggest in adults, what reason is there to believe that children have anything more than the most tenuous grasp on causal relations that govern various regularities in the world? The rest of the research described in this chapter starts to provide an answer to that question.

Different ways of tracking causal structure

The illusion of explanatory depth studies might be taken as implying that all people, and especially children, are so bad at tracking causal structure that there is little they can grasp concerning the causal structure of the world. That conclusion would be warranted if the only way of demonstrating a grasp of such structure were to show the presence of detailed, mechanistic theories of the world. Such theories are rarely seen even in sophisticated scientists. To the extent that intuitive theories share some features with those of more traditional explicit ones, children barely have them in most cases, if at all. It is not uncommon to draw parallels between intuitive theories and those of a science (e.g., Gopnik, Meltzoff, & Kuhl, 2000). Properties such as coherence and domain specificity have frequently been mentioned. But coherence loses much of its bite if the theory only has one or two elements. Thus, if a theory of mind in a young child is little more than that beliefs cause desires that cause actions, coherence between those elements doesn't amount to much. Similarly, if a young child's folk biology is roughly that living things have vital forces that cause them to move and grow (Inagaki & Hatano, 2002), there is not much involved in having those beliefs be interconnected. If intuitive theories have to honor some level of explicitness as described earlier, then young children often fail as well. Children often cannot provide reasons for their judgments.

There are, however, other ways of tracking causal structures that, while not conforming to traditional notions of either explicit or intuitive theories, might provide powerful support for making sense of the world, guiding concept acquisition and change, and evaluating explanations offered by others. Moreover, these other ways of tracking causal structure can also provide alternative ways of thinking about phenomena related to domain specificity, coherence, and universality among others. One can envision levels of tracking causal structure, with the very bottom level corresponding to the usually unattainable level having full mechanistic detailed theories of the world. Consider one characterization of those levels, starting at the top (see Keil, 2003). At least four distinct levels that are above that of full mechanistic theories are apparent: causal relevance, causal powers, functional relations among stable subassemblies, and causal fragments.

Causal relevance is one of the most fundamental and universal ways of tracking causal structure, one that appears to even exist across species. It is a level devoid of notions of mechanism, function, or even of disposition. It is merely a way of noting what kinds of properties tend to be most causally relevant, or important, in a domain. For example, color tends to be considered causally more relevant to natural kinds than to artifacts (Keil et al., 1998). By contrast, overall shape or silhouette may be considered more important, in general, for most artifacts. These are general tendencies for high-level categories and may not hold for all instances. For intuitions about novel members of artifact and natural-kind categories, however, there are clear and reliable patterns of differences that hold at all ages (Keil et al., 1998). Thus, it is possible to construct a "causal relevancy profile" across large sets of property types such as color, shape, surface markings, fragility, number of discrete parts, and size. When these profiles are constructed, the degree of causal relevance for each of these types has a characteristic profile that is surprisingly similar across a wide range of artifacts. The artifact profiles, however, are strikingly different from the profiles for the same property types across a set of living kinds, and different yet again for non-living natural kinds. In addition, there are indications that other species apprehend some versions of such causal patterns as well. For example, rhesus macaque monkeys see color as important to generalizations about novel foods and not shape, while seeing shape but not color as important to generalizations about novel tools that they have been taught to use (Santos et al., 2002a). Similar demonstrations are now emerging with human infants (Santos, Hauser, & Spelke, 2002b).

The critical point to the ability to track causal relevance is that it is different from tracking how often a feature occurs with members of a category. For example, perhaps all the tires one has seen are black; yet color is still seen as largely causally irrelevant to being a tire. By contrast, even if members of a species are found in several different colors, it is hardly assumed that color is causally arbitrary for members of those species. The causal connections can also work in different ways. In some cases, a property such as shape might be seen as causally central to tools, in that changes in shape will change the tool's utility. In other cases, changes in color, such as in an animal, may not immediately change its utility but is assumed nonetheless to be causally related to the kind of thing it is, in ways not found in artifacts where it is less closely linked to a kind's essential nature.

Important questions remain concerning how causal relevance is extracted from observations of the world. How does one rise above mere patterns of correlation and association between feature types and category members to infer those links that are specifically causal in nature? There has been a surge of interest in this question in recent years from several different perspectives (e.g., Gopnik et al., 2004; Rogers & McClelland, 2004; Tenenbaum & Griffiths, 2001). A fascinating area of future research is to better understand how such patterns are uncovered and can stand distinct against other, more frequency-based measures, using a method of learning that would be found not just in children and adults but also in infants and some other species.

The second level of tracking causal powers refers to the ability to know that certain classes of things have dispositions to cause certain effects, even as one may not have a good sense of how the properties cause those effects, what function they serve, or why they should be present. Thus, a young child may observe that connecting a seatbelt causes a ringing sound in the car to cease, but may have no idea of why the belt has that effect. The function of the ringing as a warning that the belt is unconnected may not yet be apprehended. Children and adult alike frequently form strong impressions that one type of thing causes an effect in another, but have no understanding of why. Adults, for example, may know that a common cold may cause a fever, but have no understanding of why common colds have that effect or what function, if any, a fever may serve. Moreover, the causal notions may be fleshed out beyond the general notion of cause. One type of thing might be understood as preventing another, enabling another, or hurting another, with little understanding of why or how it has that effect. Critical questions remain here as to whether even infants have a primitive vocabulary of several distinct causal notions, such as prevent, support, hurt, and contain, or whether their earliest and most primitive notions are simply of x causing y with different kinds of causation emerging later. There are some indications that a primitive causal vocabulary of several different kinds of cause may be present at least in the first half-year of life (Mandler, 2004). Moreover, such notions seem to be associated with broad domains. For example, animate entities may be seen as capable of distinctive causal powers not found in other sorts of things (Bloom, 2004; Gergely et al., 1995; Newman et al., 2005). One example that has been uncovered in our laboratory concerns the apparent ability of preverbal infants to know that animate and/or intentional agents can create order out of disorder in ways non-intentional agents cannot.

It is at this level that we start to see how an alternative sense of coherence might emerge in the tracking of causal relations in the world. While one level of coherence in theories might require consistent and non-contradictory relations among propositions in a theory, a much cruder sense can be found at the level of causal powers and is more properly thought of as causal connectedness. Certain kinds of causal powers may cluster among each other, providing a form of mutual support that maintains a stable set of properties. One version of this effect is known as "causal homeostasis" in which natural kinds are thought to exist because several distinct properties co-occur to causally reinforce the presence of others in ways that create a causally homeostatic property cluster (Boyd, 1999; Keil, 1989). There may, therefore, be distinctive interconnected patterns of kinds of causes that are associated with specific domains. For example, entities capable of reacting contingently with another at a distance may be inferred as more likely to have causal powers associated with goals (Gergely et al., 1995). If a child develops the impression that a particular set of causal powers are tightly clustered together in an organism, that impression may be the grounds for loftier claims of coherence. This, in turn, may be related to intuitions about sets of features that create strong impressions of causal centrality (Sloman et al., 1998).

The next level of functional relations among stable subassemblies is where people may have strong intuitions about the reason for a causal relation between two entities but be unable to break down those causal relations in more detailed and more mechanistic terms. Thus, one may believe that a car key has the unique function of causing a car to start running, yet one may have no idea of how turning the key in a car's steering column causes the engine to start and the steering wheel to unlock. A boat operator may know the tiller of a boat has the function of steering the boat, but may have no idea of why or how pushing a tiller to starboard causes the boat to steer to port. It is useful here to invoke the notion of "stable subassemblies" (Simon, 1996), which are units in both artificial and natural systems that are highly stable on their own and which can act as functional units in a larger system. Stable subassemblies can be found at the cellular and organ level in a body, in both mechanical machines such as traditional watches, and in electronic ones such as GPS receivers, and even in the non-physical realm such as in large computer software programs. It would be impossible, for example, to develop the millions of lines of code of an application suite of software if there were not highly stable subassemblies. Indeed, that stability is a sacred rule of any open-source software community.

One major reason for the illusion of explanatory depth is a confusion between genuine insight gained of functional relations between very large subassemblies in a system and an understanding of causal mechanisms within those subassemblies. Take for example the working knowledge of an average computer user. One may know that the function of the computer mouse is to move a cursor on the screen and to open and close windows and initiate operations through clicks on the mouse. One might know that the function of the screen is to display images, and the CD slot is to load in or store data. One may have vaguer notions about memory, processing power, and hard drives; and that knowledge may pretty much exhaust an average user's understanding of how a computer works. There may be no understanding of how the movement of a mouse on a surface results in changes in an image on a screen, or how a CD stores or reads data. The computer is understood as a set of "black boxes" with functions such as storing, displaying, and manipulating information.

However, a computer user may, in the rush of gaining functional insights, confuse those genuine insights with having some portion of deeper mechanistic insights or even of more coherence of how all the functions fit together. The tendency to think about things in functional terms appears to be very basic and early emerging (e.g., Keleman, 1999), and may be part of a "design stance" that explains the fundamental manner of thought (Dennett, 1998). It is much less obvious, however, whether other species also think about objects and systems in functional terms, or whether they do so with anywhere near the natural proclivity of humans of all ages. The classic debates on tool use in non-humans are just one facet of the more general cognitive ability to understand entities in terms of their functions.

One example of an early appreciation of causal functional relations can be seen in a study in our laboratory in which children are introduced to novel artifacts and animals, and are invited to ask questions about them (Greif, Guitterez, Keil, & Kemler-Nelson, in press). Although both artifacts and animals have many aspects that have functions, for adults at least, it is odd to ask about the function of an animal as a whole. To ask what a tiger is "for" seems anomalous, while such a question is highly appropriate for most artifacts. When 3- and 4-year-olds are encouraged to ask questions about novel animals and tools, they employ very different question-asking strategies, almost never asking about the function of the animal as a whole, while doing so freely for tools. Hence different patterns of functional construals for high-level categories can have strong domain specificity and are present at least by toddlerhood.

The next level of causal understanding involves highly specific mechanisms but often only fragments of such mechanisms rather than a full-fledged and interconnected system. This sort of understanding was often revealed in the illusion of explanatory depth studies, where participants might reveal an understanding of one or two fragments but could not see how they worked together in an integrated functioning system.

In short, there are several levels at which causal information might be apprehended but which do not seem to accord nicely with any normal sense of theory, either explicit or intuitive. Moreover, several of these senses seem highly implicit and may normally function far outside of awareness, and may only be revealed in tasks that specifically look for them, even as their users may be largely unaware of having that kind of knowledge. If we use too narrow a sense of intuitive theories, we may grossly underestimate the powerful ways in which we do track causal structures as well as the ways in which such tracking helps us make sense of the world around us.

Using causal impressions to leverage understanding

I have suggested that causal impressions above the level of well worked out mechanisms can nonetheless provide powerful support for making sense of the world while not having detailed, coherent theories in any traditional sense. There are several ways in which these causal impressions further understanding: by helping to evaluate novel theories, by helping to guide construction of ad hoc temporary theory segments on the fly with situational support, and by enabling us to better navigate the division of cognitive labor. Each of these influences is under active investigation in our laboratory. To illustrate such effects better, consider in a bit more detail how tracking of causal patterns might foster the ability to use knowledge in other minds.

Part of the very meaning of culture is the idea that different groups in a culture develop different skills that mutually support each other. A division of labor emerges as people become specialists in bounded areas of work, such as agriculture, healing, animal husbandry, and the building of shelter. With these specializations of work there must also arise specializations of cognitive expertise that enable higher levels of skill in each area. As cultures become more elaborate, these areas of expertise can proliferate to enormous extents and come to include the extraordinary diversity and depth of the sciences. As a consequence, members of most cultures today believe that there are groups of experts who can greatly expand on their understanding in many different domains, ranging from biology and medicine to economics and finance. To be able to exploit these areas of expertise, however, an individual must be able to know which experts are relevant for providing additional insight into a problem. This ability to know whom to consult and whom to defer to may well draw on common causal impressions that we all share.

It might seem that it is easy to find the relevant experts. If a problem is described as one of biology, simply ask people who proclaim themselves to be biologists; and so on for other domains of inquiry. In reality, however, problems often don't provide such clear clues to areas of expertise and experts may not easily provide labels. For example, if one wanted to know why salt melts ice in people's driveways, one would want to consult an expert in chemistry; but if one wanted to know why one's arms ache after shoveling snow in a driveway, one would want to consult an expert in biology. In one sense both problems are about clearing a driveway in winter and neither obviously advertises the real domain involved.

Through an extensive series of studies we have been able to explore how a sense of the division of cognitive labor emerges in childhood. The dominant method that we have used is a triad task in which a person is described as fully understanding one phenomenon. The participant is then asked which of two other phenomena that person might understand by virtue of understanding that first phenomenon. For example, a person might be said to know all about why wood burns but rocks don't. By virtue of having that full understanding, is that person more likely to know why some glues stick better to wood than to glass, or why it is more difficult to recognize faces that are upside down than right-side up? There is a strong intuition among adults that the glue and wood-burning cases are more likely to be known by the same person because they are in the realm of chemistry while the faces case is in the realm of psychology. When such tasks are given to young children, along with various mnemonic supports, they too often sense the appropriate clusters of knowledge. By second grade they largely mirror adult intuitions, and show some such intuitions above chance levels in kindergarten-age groups. Even preschoolers show some sense of clusters of knowledge on grounds that distinguish, say, biology from mechanics (Lutz & Keil, 2002).

There is a great deal more to children's understanding of the division of cognitive labor. For example, thinking of knowledge as organized in terms of disciplines roughly like academic departments becomes much more robust during the elementary school years. Compared to other possible ways of clustering knowledge, the discipline-based way becomes privileged in late elementary school (Danovitch & Keil, 2004). The key point here, however, concerns how the young children seem to be solving these tasks. When children do cluster knowledge in a manner that corresponds roughly with the major divisions of the natural sciences, they seem to be relying on causal impressions of the sort described earlier while often being completely ignorant of more specific mechanisms. For, example, a child who put the wood-burning and the glue-sticking forms of understanding together might have no idea of how glue works or why wood burns, but might still think that an understanding of both involves some sort of understanding of the stuff they are made of at micro-structural level, and of how those micro-structural properties influence surface ones. They could be wrong on all the details, just as adult alchemists were for centuries; but the general orientation may have some gist that is correct. Children who reliably sorted explanations usually did so without any ability to explicitly say why two phenomena were known by the same expert.

Tracking causal structure

There is a tendency to assume that the ability to grasp the causal structure of the world and use those apprehensions to guide cognition is evidence for having a theory. By allowing for such theories to be intuitive and perhaps even implicit, it may seem that a much broader range of knowledge structures might still be thought of as theories. This may be an unfortunate extension of the sense of theory to the point where the notion does little work. If we understand theories to be detailed, coherent, and mechanistic accounts of how the world works, then they are highly uncommon in both adults and children. Even if they are less mechanistic, it is not clear how often there are several interconnected beliefs about causal processes that are coherent and consistent. Theories in these more traditional senses may be quite uncommon at all points in development. Moreover, by labeling children's ways of making sense of the world as theories, we may look for these more traditional senses, and in doing so underestimate other powerful ways in which children do track causal structure. In other senses that are not so clearly labeled as theories there is a rich cognitive apparatus that tracks causal structures at all those levels above what we would normally think of as constituting a well-structured theory. Children grasp the causal structure of the world at all those levels, and use that information to evaluate explanations and theories, to construct more detailed explanations, and to know what experts to rely on.

There remains the troubling question of how to explain some highly systematic and interconnected sets of behaviors shown by human infants. Should the ways in which an infant has expectations about the mechanics of objects be seen as an intuitive theory of physics, and the ways in which an infant has expectations about the actions of animate creatures be seen as an intuitive theory of psychology? Some of the principles that infants seem to respect, such as "no action at a distance" and "solids can't interpenetrate" are interrelated in larger systems of cognitive expectations (Spelke et al., 1992). Moreover, those expectations show a degree of coherence and consistency. At the same time, these early abilities may often be heavily compartmentalized into relatively automatic modules with strong perceptually driven components – modules that are keyed for particular causal and visual patterns but which are cognitively impenetrable (Carey & Xu, 2001; Leslie, 2000; Scholl & Leslie, 1999). The ways in which infants move beyond such "core domains" into penetrable ones is an area of active debate (Scholl & Leslie, 1999) but one major factor concerns a certain degree of learning and flexibility. In this context, it is important to stress that all the levels of tracking causal structure just mentioned have important learning components and differentiate considerably during development. They may also be constrained heavily by ways in which information is delivered to them by modules, but they go beyond the modules in important ways as well.

The most typical meaning of "intuitive theory" seems to be of relatively detailed mental models of the world that are acquired without explicit instruction. These are seen as modestly degenerate cases of scientific theories and are usually considered to be a relatively rich set of interconnected and coherent propositions. Infant expectations are less clearly in this set because they are more heavily modularized and less flexible. Other ways of tracking causal structure also are not normally thought of as intuitive theories. I have suggested that, in this typical sense of intuitive theory, there may be far fewer cases in development and in adults than there seem to be at first.

It does not matter much what different ways of grasping causal structure are called. More critical are the implications of recognizing that adults and children alike grasp that structure in coarse but surprisingly powerful and effective ways, and of acknowledging that these ways are far different from neatly interconnected sets of propositions about the world. A critical question for the future is how to better characterize this "slice" through the causal complexity of the world, and how and why people of all ages seem to use it so easily and effectively.

Acknowledgment

Preparation of this paper and much of the research described therein was supported by NIH Grant R37-HD23922 to Frank Keil.

References

Ahn, W., & Kalish, C.W. (2000). The role of mechanism beliefs in causal reasoning. In F. Keil & R. Wilson (Eds.), *Explanation and cognition*. Cambridge, MA: MIT Press.

Amini, M. (2003). Has foundationalism failed? A critical review of coherence in thought and action by Paul Thagard. *Human Nature Review*, *3*, 119–123.

Atran, S. (1998). Folk biology and the anthropology of science: Cognitive universals and cultural particulars. *Behavioral and Brain Sciences*, *21*, 547–611.

Bloom, P. (2004). *Descartes' baby: How the science of child development explains what makes us human*. New York: Basic Books.

Boyd, R. (1999). Homeostasis, species, and higher taxa. In R. Wilson (Ed.), *Species: New interdisciplinary studies* (pp. 141–185). Cambridge, MA: MIT Press.

Carey, S. (1985). *Conceptual change in childhood*. Cambridge, MA: Bradford Books/MIT Press.

Carey, S., & Xu, F. (2001). Infants' knowledge of objects: Beyond object files and object tracking. *Cognition*, *80*, 179–213.

Danovitch, J.H., & Keil, F.C. (2004). Should you ask a fisherman or a biologist?: Developmental shifts in ways of clustering knowledge. *Child Development*, *5*, 918–931.

Dennett, D. (1998). The intentional stance. In R. Wilson & F. Keil (Eds.), *The MIT encyclopedia of cognitive sciences*. Cambridge, MA: MIT Press.

di Sessa, A. (1993). Towards an epistemology of physics. *Cognition and Instruction*, *10*, 105–225.

di Sessa, A., Gillespie, N.M., & Esterly, J.B. (2004). Coherence versus fragmentation in the development of the concept of force. *Cognitive Science*, *28*, 843–900.

Dunbar, K. (2000). How scientists think in the real world: Implications for science education. *Journal of Applied Developmental Psychology*, *21*, 49–58.

Fodor, J. (1983). *Modularity of mind*. Cambridge, MA: MIT Press.

Gelman, S.A., & Koenig, M.A. (2003). Theory based categorization in early childhood. In D.H. Rakison & L.M. Oakes (Eds.), *Early category and concept development: Making sense of the blooming buzzing confusion* (pp. 330–339). New York: Oxford University Press.

Gergely, G., Nadasdy, Z., Csibra, G., & Biro, S. (1995). Taking the intentional stance at 12 months of age. *Cognition*, *56*(2), 165–193.

Gopnik, A., Glymour, C. et al. (2004). Causal maps and Bayes nets: A theory of causal inference in young children. *Psychological Review*, *111*(1), 1–30.

Gopnik, A., Meltzoff, A.N., & Kuhl, P.K. (2000). *The scientist in the crib: What early learning tells us about the mind*. New York: Harper Collins.

Gopnik, A., & Wellman, H.M. (1994). The theory theory. In L.A. Hirschfeld & S.A. Gelman (Eds.), *Mapping the mind: Domain specificity in cognition and culture*. New York: Cambridge University Press.

Greif, M. Guitterez, F., Keil, F., & Kemler-Nelson, D. (in press). What do children want to know about animals and artifacts?: Domain-specific requests for information. *Psychological Science*.

Hempel, C.G. (1965). *Aspects of scientific explanation*. New York: The Free Press.

Inagaki, K., & Hatano, G. (2002). *Young children's naive thinking about the biological world*. New York: Psychology Press.

Keil, F.C. (1989). *Concepts, kinds and cognitive development*. Cambridge, MA: MIT Press.

Keil, F.C. (2003). Categorization, causation and the limits of understanding. *Language and Cognitive Processes*, *18*, 663–692.

Keil, F.C., Smith, C., Simons, D.J., & Levin, D.T. (1998). Two dogmas of conceptual empiricism: Implications for hybrid models of the structure of knowledge. *Cognition*, *65*, 103–135.

Keleman, D. (1999). Function, goals, and intention: Children's teleological reasoning about objects. *Trends in Cognitive Sciences*, *3*, 461–468.

Leslie, A.M. (2000). "Theory of mind" as a mechanism of selective attention. In M. Gazzaniga (Ed.), *The new cognitive neurosciences* (2nd ed., pp. 1235–1247). Cambridge, MA: MIT Press.

Lutz, D.R., & Keil, F.C. (2002). Early understanding of the division of cognitive labor. *Child Development*, *73*, 1073–1084.

Mandler, J.M. (2004). *The foundations of mind: Origins of conceptual thought*. New York: Oxford University Press.

Medin, D.L., & Atran. S. (2004). The native mind: Biological categorization, reasoning and decision making in development across cultures. *Psychological Review*, *111*(4), 960–983.

Mills, C., & Keil, F.C. (2004). Knowing the limits of one's understanding: The development of an awareness of an illusion of explanatory depth. *Journal of Experimental Child Psychology*, *87*, 1–32.

Murphy, G.L., & Medin, D.L. (1985). The role of theories in conceptual coherence. *Psychological Review*, *92*, 289–316.

Nakhleh, M.B., & Samarapungavan, A. (1999). Elementary school children's beliefs about matter. *Journal of Research on Science Teaching*, *36*, 777–805.

Newman, G., Keil, F.C., Kulhmeir, V., & Wynn, K. (2005). Infants contrastively apply the principle of entropy to intentional agents and inanimate objects.

Nisbett, R. (2003). *The geography of thought*. New York: The Free Press.

Rogers, T.T., & McClelland, J.L. (2004). *Semantic cognition: A parallel distributed processing approach*. Cambridge, MA: MIT Press.

Rozenblit, L.R., & Keil, F.C. (2002). The misunderstood limits of folk science: An illusion of explanatory depth. *Cognitive Science*, *26*, 521–562.

Russell, B. (1913). On the notion of cause. *Proceedings of the Aristotelian Society*, *13*, 1–26.

Salmon, W. (1989). Four decades of scientific explanation. In P. Kitcher & W. Salmon (Eds.), *Scientific explanation*. Minneapolis: University of Minnesota Press.

Santos, L.R., Hauser, M.D., & Spelke, E.S. (2002b). Domain-specific knowledge in human children and non-human primates: Artifact and food kinds. In M. Bekoff (Ed.), *The cognitive animal*. Cambridge, MA: MIT Press.

Santos, L.R., Sulkowski, G.M., Spaepen, G.M., & Hauser, M.D. (2002a). Object individuation using property/kind information in rhesus macaques (*Macaca mulatta*). *Cognition*, *83*, 241–264.

Scholl, B.J., & Leslie, A.M. (1999). Explaining the infant's object concept: Beyond the perception/cognition dichotomy. In E. Lepore & Z. Pylyshyn (Eds.), *What is cognitive science?* Oxford, UK: Blackwell Publishers.

Simon, H.A. (1996). *Science of the artificial* (3rd ed.). Cambridge, MA: MIT Press.

Sloman, S.A. et al. (1998). Feature centrality and conceptual coherence. *Cognitive Science*, *22*, 189–228.

Spelke, E.S., Breinlinger, K., Macomber, J., & Jacobson, K. (1992). Origins of knowledge. *Psychological Review*, *99*, 605–632.

Tenenbaum, J.B., & Griffiths, T.L. (2001). Generalization, similarity, and Bayesian inference. *Behavioral and Brain Sciences*, *24*, 629–64.

Thagard, P. (1989). Explanatory coherence. *Behavioral and Brain Sciences*, *12*, 435–502.

Thagard, P. (2000). *Coherence in thought and action*. Cambridge, MA: MIT Press.

Weinberg, S. (1993). *Dreams of an ultimate theory*. New York: Basic Books.

Wellman, H.M. (1992). *The child's theory of mind*. Cambridge, MA: MIT Press.

29 Theory of mind: A core human cognition

Henry M. Wellman

For almost 20 years there has been an increasing interest in and research on theory of mind. By now there are hundreds of papers from psychologists around the world – developmental psychologists, comparative psychologists, clinical psychologists, evolutionary psychologists, and more. In these papers, theory of mind has been increasingly construed as something like a core human cognition.

First a brief introduction to theory of mind: The focal topic is actually social cognition or folk psychology. Humans live our lives, raised by parents, in familial communities constantly interacting with, cooperating with and competing with other people. As a consequence we develop extensive knowledge about the social world: concepts of social entities (people, schools, nations), concepts of social interactions (aggression, sharing), concepts of social rules (obligations, moral edicts), and roles (doctors, teachers, speaker–audience). Given this welter of everyday social cognition, a key question arises: Are there core understandings that are crucial to and organize this commonplace but remarkable knowledge?

The claim behind the phrase "theory of mind" is that there are. In particular, social cognition is founded on an understanding of ourselves and others in terms of our inner mental, psychological states.

Consider this passage from the Chinese classic *The Dream of the Red Chamber*:

> On the night of the Festival of the Harvest Moon Yu-tsun found himself alone in his quarters in the Temple of the Gourd. He had not *forgotten* the maid, and on this festive occasion his *thoughts* again turned to her. The bright moon stimulated his *desires* and he composed a poem on their meeting. Then he sighed as he *thought* how far he was from realizing his *ambitions*. (Emphasis added)

This is classic literature. But understanding persons as thinking, forgetful, desiring, ambition-seeking beings is not only the stuff of great literature, it is the stuff of everyday life, conversation, musing, and gossip. It is the basis of our folk psychology.

What about the phrase "core human cognition"? The following quote (among many) refers to something like core human cognitions (Atran, 1996, p. 217):

> People from a very early age and through all their adult lives seem to think differently about different domains . . . So, a central issue in recent cognitive and developmental psychology concerns the scope and limits of conceptual modules such as folk mechanics, folk psychology, folk biology.

Many of these discussions consider core human cognition as divided into distinct modules. The philosopher Peter Carruthers develops this view (2002, p. 663):

> According to this account, besides a variety of input and output modules (including, e.g., early vision, face-recognition, and language), the mind also contains a number of innately channeled conceptual modules, designed to process conceptual information concerning particular domains . . . [such as] a naïve physics system, a naïve psychology or "mind-reading" system, a folk-biology system, an intuitive number system, a geometrical system for re-orienting and navigating in unusual environments.

I am not in favor of describing core human cognition as modules – a point I return to at the end of this chapter. But I am in favor of considering distinctive, separable, cognitive systems that each elaborate and process specific information, in certain characteristic ways. If there were such systems, this would be important. Such distinctive systems could help to specify the architecture of the human mind. They could specify cognitions that humans find easy and "natural" to make or to acquire. That is, core human cognition could provide a framework for thinking about intuitive and counterintuitive understandings; about "natural concepts" versus exotic ones. They could help to identify basic cognitive perspectives common to all humans, amid the numerous cognitive differences we develop over our lives in our different societies and local environments. They could also provide the building blocks for other analyses of human cognition, such as discussions about massive modularity (Carruthers, 2002), or domain specificity, or the naturalness of religion (Barrett, 2000), and more.

As is clear in these quotes, a frequent exemplar for a core cognitive domain is folk psychology or theory of mind. The proposal of core human cognitions is an empirical one – there may *not* be core human cognition or cognitive domains. And the proposal that theory of mind constitutes a core human domain is also an empirical one. Certainly, 15 years ago the notion of theory of mind as a core cognitive system was novel, and when mentioned was nothing but an intriguing promissory note.

In part what I want to do in this chapter is to cash that promissory note by reviewing some of the empirical data. I do this egocentrically by relying mostly on data collected by me and my collaborators. Regardless, the data are important, and for two reasons: (a) They help to address the general question of whether there are core human cognitions, and whether theory of mind counts as one. But (b) they also help to address the question of just what a core human cognition might look like. Here I think the data are particularly revealing – they suggest that core human cognitive systems are different from some of the claims made for them.

As background for the empirical data, how might we know a core human cognition when we saw one? I do not aim to be definitive, but here are a variety of features proposed at one place or another by one writer or another.

1 To begin with, core human cognitive systems should be *conceptually* basic – conceptual analyses should be available to argue that and how the system is a key part of, or a foundation for, numerous other conceptions.
2 Different core cognitive systems should be distinguishable one from another, such as: folk psychology, folk physics, folk biology (Wellman & Gelman, 1998).
3 Core human cognitions might be *developmentally* basic in the sense of rapidly acquired in normal development.
4 They might also be developmentally basic in the additional sense of undergoing change that then influences other cognitions.
5 Core human cognitions might be acquired by all humans and so should be universal – at some proper level of analysis.
6 They might be specially supported by and localized in the brain (if not early then later in development).
7 If a core system does have special neural substrates then that substrate could, potentially, be impaired in certain persons. Individuals with autism are the example often claimed for theory of mind (Baron-Cohen, 1995).
8 Core *human* cognition might also not be apparent (or much more minimally apparent) in nonhuman species, even other (nonhuman) primates.

I think there are good reasons to believe theory of mind has many (though not all) of the features just listed. Note that there are other features that might have been on the list above. A core cognitive system might be relatively *unrevisable* by human individual experiences in development. Indeed, several people claim core knowledge is set or fixed by evolution and unchanging from infancy to adulthood (e.g., Spelke, 1994). Core cognitive systems might also be those we *share* with other primates or even all mammals (Spelke, 2003). These features are not on my list, however. Indeed, I think such claims are problematic, at least for theory of mind. Instead, notice that my list talks about developmental change (number 4), and about uniqueness to humans (number 8). Theory of mind, I believe, stands alongside language as a distinctively human core capacity, and one that develops.

The development story of theory of mind is complex, but at its simplest it is a story of two parts: First, there is early competence – of an intriguingly abstract, nonperceptual sort. But beyond early competence there is conceptual change over the course of human development. So core human cognitions, at least theory of mind, are not static but importantly dynamic.

Theory of mind framework

To consider some of the data now available on these issues for theory of mind it is useful to briefly describe the general nature of theory of mind, at least as it has been increasingly described by philosophers (e.g., Stitch, 1983) and psychologists (e.g., Wellman, 1990).

To repeat, the essential claim behind the phrase "theory of mind" is that central to our conceptions of the social world is a construal of persons in terms of internal mental states and entities – the beliefs, desires, emotions, goals, and ideations of self and other. Conceptually, the theory picks out mental contents, states, and processes as a domain of things to consider, and distinguishes that mental world from the real world of physical objects, material states, and mechanical or behavioral processes. But mental states are not just distinguishable from behavioral or physical entities and acts, they constitute a system we use to explain and predict persons' actions and lives. This systems includes three important, basic constructs: beliefs–desires–actions. Because an actor has certain *beliefs* and *desires*, he or she engages in certain intentional *actions*. Or, people engage in acts they *think* will get them what they *want*. Take Romeo and Juliet. Because Romeo and Juliet want to be together, but believe their families will violently disprove, they see each other in secret.

In more detail, theory of mind reasoning probably encompasses something like the constructs and connections shown in Figure 29.1. So a bit more completely: Because Romeo *loves* Juliet he *wants* to be with her. Because

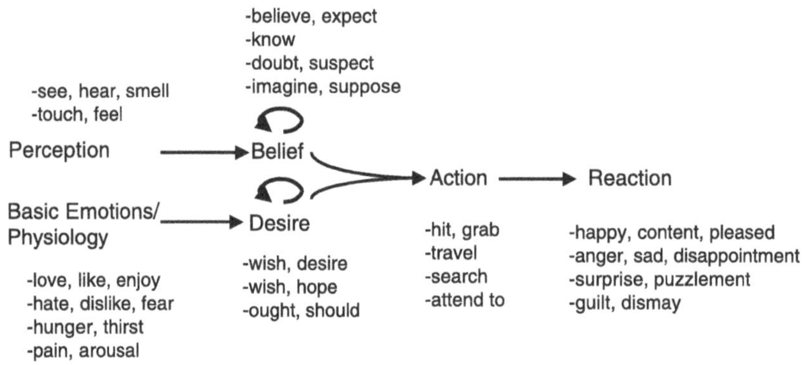

Figure 29.1 A scheme for depicting the connected constructs used in belief–desire reasoning. (Originally presented in Wellman, 1990.)

he *knows* his family's objections they proceed in secret. When he is successful and can be with her he is *happy* (indeed lovestruck and ecstatic). When unsuccessful and they are apart he is *sad* (indeed starkly disappointed and crestfallen).

Note that according to anything like the framework outlined in Figure 29.1, an understanding of beliefs is a core feature of our everyday theory of mind. People engage in acts they *think* will get them what they want. Of course they can be wrong – in which case they think and act mistakenly, often thwarting their own desires. Mistakes, errors, ignorance, and wrong ideas, are the very stuff of our everyday psychology and thus the very stuff of our everyday lives.

False belief

This centrality of beliefs, and mistaken beliefs, is why there has been so much research on children's understanding of false belief. A false-belief task: Maxi puts his chocolate in the drawer and goes away. While he can't see, the chocolate gets switched to the cupboard. Maxi comes back and he wants his chocolate: Where will Maxi look for his chocolate – the cupboard or the drawer?

Note that correct answers require reasoning about desires and beliefs: Maxi *wants* his chocolate, he *thinks* it is in the drawer. Where will he look? Correct answers – saying that Maxi will look in the drawer – show an understanding that people live their lives not so much in the world itself, but in the world as they mentally represent it.

Children who are 4 or 5 years of age typically solve this problem, as do adults. And, of course, to do so they say Maxi will thwart his own desires. Really the chocolate he wants is in the cupboard, but Maxi will look in the drawer – because beliefs, as well as desires, determine action.

Another sort of false-belief task focuses on unexpected contents of typical containers (rather than unexpected changes of location). For example, a child sees a crayon box, states that it has crayons inside, but sees (when it is opened) that there are candles inside instead. Then he is told of someone else, who has never seen inside: "We'll show Jill this box all closed up; what will she think is in there?"

Children of age 4 and older also often pass unexpected-contents false-belief tasks, but children younger than 4 years often fail all sorts of false-belief tasks. In failing, young children do not just answer randomly, they make a consistent false-belief error. They say Maxi will look in the cupboard, where the chocolate really is – even though he never saw the chocolate being moved. They say Jill will think there are candles in the box.

It is worth looking at these false-belief data in some detail, so we conducted a meta-analysis of the many and varied false-belief studies (Wellman, Cross, & Watson, 2001). In this analysis we included 176 studies encompassing almost 600 false-belief conditions and task variations. The tasks were verbal and nonverbal, and asked children to judge behavior or thoughts (where will Maxi look? what will Jill think?), to judge real live humans, video-taped humans, toy figurines, story characters.

The key initial finding is shown in Figure 29.2 which shows a plot of proportions correct from all conditions arrayed against mean age of the children in a condition. The data have been transformed so that the basic developmental trajectory becomes a linear one (allowing employment of linear regression analyses). With this transformation, chance performance is 0.

Notice the data seem to show robust childhood competence, as well as conceptual change. The competence is clear by 4 and 5 years when children are largely correct; on a vast array of false-belief situations they judge and explain correctly. The change is clear if one looks back to 2 and 3 years, where there is clear below-chance performance, that is, consistent false-belief errors.

But perhaps the story is not one of conceptual change but one of early competence. Perhaps typical false-belief tasks are just too difficult for children to reveal an early understanding of beliefs that they in fact possess. If so, then if we designed easier false-belief tasks, even young children should perform well. Accordingly, numerous researchers have attempted to modify and simplify false-belief tasks to make them easier. Part of the point of our meta-analysis was to address this crucial issue. Do the data suggest competence at understanding belief as well as desire from the start, or rather conceptual change?

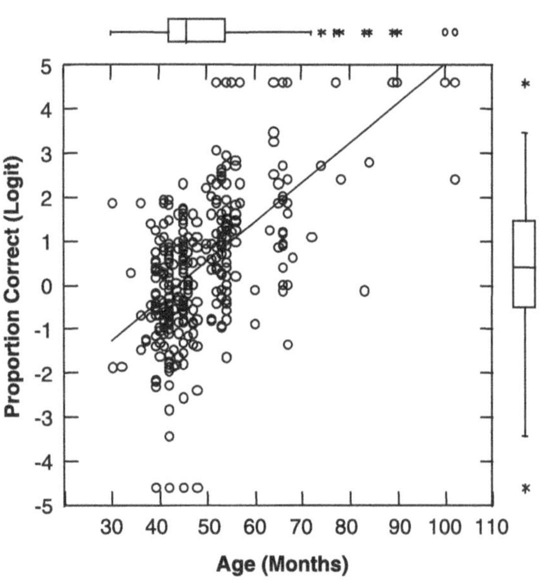

Figure 29.2 Scatterplot of false-belief conditions in the meta-analysis with a best-fit line showing the developmental trajectory from below- to above-chance responding. (Originally presented in Wellman et al., 2001.)

The way we proceeded was to examine the influence of various task modifications and simplifications on false-belief performance. For example, variations on a change-of-locations task can be essentially nonverbal. Just show the events and ensure that the protagonist does not see the crucial change of location. Then simply ask the child about behavior, without any use of terms like *think* or *know*. Where will Maxi look for his chocolate?

It is possible to vary unexpected-contents tasks too. For example, what if the child is asked about her *own* false beliefs. First the child actually experiences a false belief – she says, "I think it has crayons," and then finds "Hey, there's candles in here." Then the child is asked, "Before you looked inside what did you think was in here, candles or crayons?" Perhaps, being primed with experiencing a false belief *and* being asked about yourself would clarify for children the real nature of the questions, allowing even young children to reveal an understanding of false belief – an early competence otherwise masked.

Before examining the data, consider that any task variation could potentially influence the basic developmental trajectory in one of three ways shown in Figure 29.3: (1) No effect – that task modification or simplification has no influence on performance; (2) Main effect – it has an effect, but the differences affect performance similarly at all ages *and* the youngest children still fail; (3) Interaction effect – differences on the variable interact with age. The specific interaction depicted in Figure 29.3 is especially relevant for discriminating *conceptual change* accounts versus exclusively *early competence* accounts. To confirm early competence accounts, some task version(s) should increase even young children's responding to above-chance levels.

Non-effects

To make a long story short, most of the many task variations investigators have tried (and that we examined in our meta-analysis) make no reliable

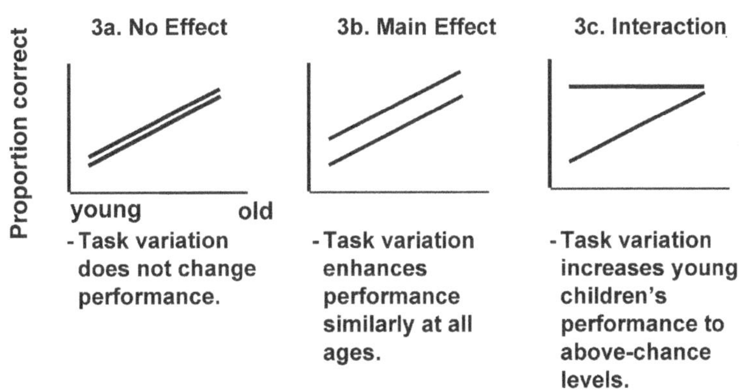

Figure 29.3 Three hypothetical patterns of results for tasks modifications designed to simplify false-belief tasks. (Originally presented in Wellman et al., 2001.)

difference to performance (Wellman et al., 2001). They look like Figure 29.3a. For example it makes no difference whether children are tested verbally or nonverbally; whether tested in change-of-location tasks or unexpected-contents tasks; whether the main character is a real person, a picture of a person, a puppet, or doll; whether the false-belief question asks about behavior ("Where will Maxi look?"), thoughts ("Where will Maxi think his X is?"), or speech ("Where will Maxi say his X is?").

As one example, consider whether the false-belief question is asked about someone else or the child himself. As can be seen in Figure 29.4, asking about self or other yields virtually identical results.

Main effects

Four task variables did affect performance; these variations make performance on false-belief tasks easier. They looked like Figure 29.3b. These are: (1) framing the task in terms of explicit deception; (2) decreasing the salience of the real-world state of affairs by having no contradictory real object present (e.g., Maxi's chocolate is eaten and gone, rather than moved to another location); (3) having the child actively participate in the key transformation (e.g., child herself moves Maxi's chocolate from the drawer to the cupboard); (4) increasing the salience of the character's mental state (e.g., by stating what Maxi thinks or depicting Maxi's initial impression in a picture). To illustrate, framing a false-belief task in terms of deception aids children, but aids

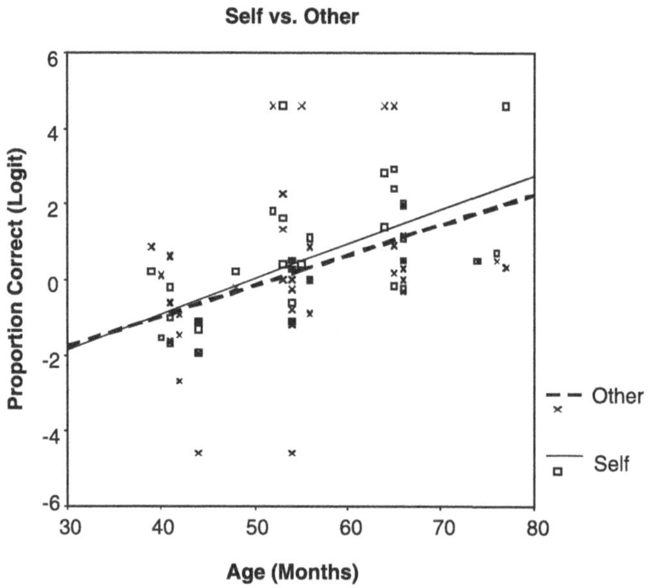

Figure 29.4 Meta-analytic results for false-belief judgments for self versus other. (Originally presented in Wellman et al., 2001.)

children at all ages, and even with deception young children remain at or below chance. That is, while these task variables affect performance, they do so without an interaction with age. In each case the essential developmental trajectory remains unchanged, and performance of the youngest children remains at chance or below chance.

Interaction effects

Finally, *no* task variation resulted in the early competence sort of interaction; no task variation gave a result like that in Figure 29.3c. Furthermore, a theoretical model predicting an early competence sort of pattern did not fit the data, whereas one predicting a pattern of genuine failure followed by genuine correct conception did fit the data (Wellman et al., 2001).

Thus, the meta-analysis provides substantial evidence that children's conceptions of beliefs do change importantly in the preschool years. Young children go from consistent error to consistently correct across all task variations. Even the simplest, most child-friendly tasks show this basic developmental trajectory.

Country

The meta-analysis also allowed us to address the extent to which basic theory of mind understandings are or are not *universal*, because the meta-analysis encompassed studies done in a great many different countries. Figure 29.5 shows the data arranged by country. Notice that the basic pattern is always the same. In all countries tested, the youngest children were significantly incorrect; and always, early failures were followed by later correct understanding.

This original meta-analysis included studies from various countries (the largest samples are labelled in Figure 29.5). But those data were decidedly skewed toward children growing up in Western-European style communities – USA, England, Austria, Australia – and speaking Indo-European language (English, German, Spanish). Of the 176 studies in that meta-analysis only one article came from China, only two from Japan, only two from Korea.

China

We have recently conducted an additional meta-analysis of false-belief reasoning in children from Chinese communities and languages. Chinese children grow up in non-Western families. Chinese languages are certainly not Indo-European. More than half of the world's children live in East Asia with the largest number of those being Chinese. If we want to know about the nature of theory of mind, including Chinese children seems essential.

Fortunately, over the last several years researchers have conducted numerous studies in China and many of these have included one or more false-belief

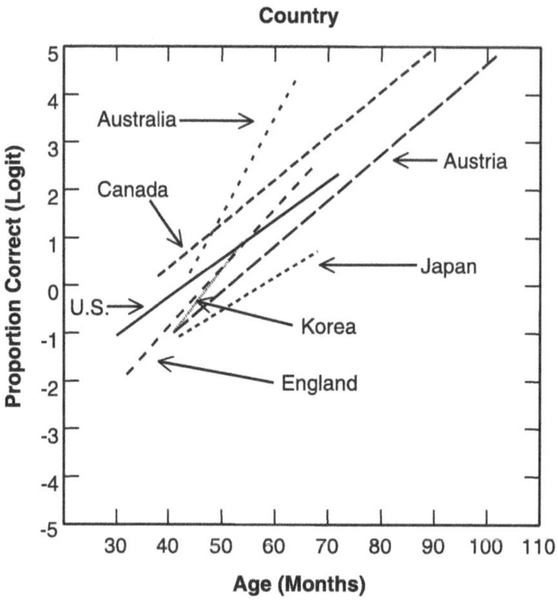

Figure 29.5 Meta-analytic results for false-belief judgments made by children in different countries. (Originally presented in Wellman et al., 2001.)

tasks. For this new meta-analysis (Liu, Wellman, Tardif, & Sabbagh, 2004) we assembled 196 conditions from Hong Kong and mainland China. These new data confirm those from our original meta-analysis. Figure 29.6 shows the Chinese data along with those from the USA and Canada for comparison. Again, children go from significantly incorrect performance to significantly correct during the preschool years. And in the Chinese data this pattern was robust for self, for other, and for a variety of task variations.

In sum, analyses of many false-belief studies show clear conceptual change, worldwide. This leads to the question, what is changing from 2 to 5? There are several possibilities. But I will concentrate on what I believe is the predominant and correct story first, and then briefly consider other possibilities. The correct story is one of a still earlier competence, coupled with conceptual change.

Desires to beliefs

How should we characterize the conceptual change demonstrated in our meta-analyses? Figure 29.7 shows a depiction that I like, to help capture the nature of this change.

A child who has a simple understanding of desires and certain emotions (as shown at the top of Figure 29.7) could understand people as subjectively connected to real objects or states of affairs: "I want that." "I hate that." But

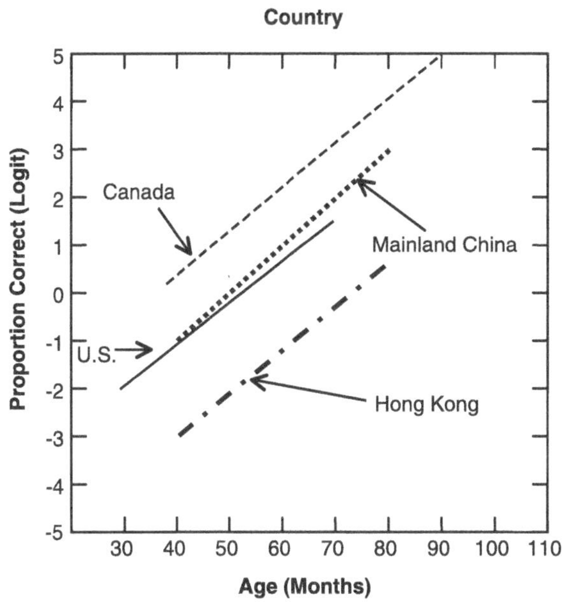

Figure 29.6 Meta-analytic results for false-belief judgments made by children in China versus North America. (Originally presented in Liu et al., 2004.)

an understanding of belief anything like our ordinary adult one (as shown at the bottom), requires understanding people as having something like representations of the world. For desires there are internal states directed toward external happenings. In some sense, then, there is only one realm of content for consideration, the contents of the world. But for belief and other such representational states, there are two realms of content to deal with – contents of the world and contents of the mind – and these might be different, as in false beliefs.

This analysis helps to capture why it would constitute a major conceptual change to move from a conception like the top one to the bottom one. Consider Romeo and Juliet again. Romeo not only loves Juliet, and wants her, but in the last act of the play he thinks Juliet is dead and so he kills himself. Imagine viewing Romeo and Juliet only in terms of their attraction for one another, with no understanding of the deceptions, lies, and false beliefs involved. Only with the conception at the bottom of Figure 29.7 are understandings such as false belief, lies, deception, surprise, and so on possible. Only with a conception of belief is *belief*–desire reasoning avaliable.

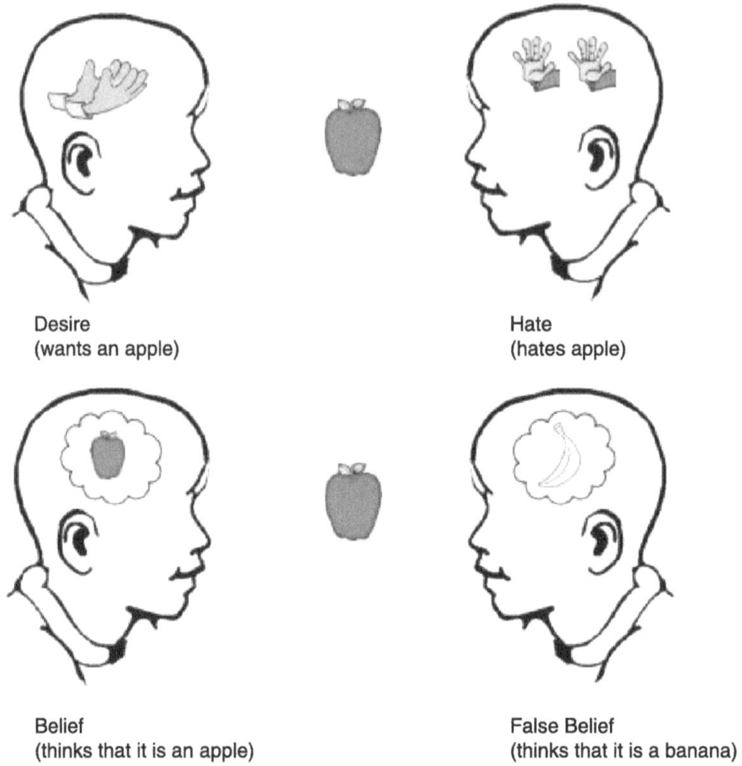

Figure 29.7 Graphic depiction of how someone might construe a person's desires (top) and beliefs (bottom). (Originally presented in Wellman, 1990.)

Conversation

A direct implication of this analysis is that the sort of change young children undergo is a conceptual one, from understanding persons in terms of actions and simple desires, to only later acquiring a representational understanding of mind. If so, then children's understanding of desires and emotions – at least simple desires and simple emotions – should appear earlier in development and ground a later understanding of belief. There is now substantial evidence for this transition.

To shift gear from experimental, false-belief tasks, consider children's everyday conversations: Children produce words such as *happy*, *sad*, *want*, and *think* beginning late in the second year of life (e.g., Bretherton & Beeghly, 1982; Shatz, Wellman, & Silber, 1983). These everyday conversations provide an important window into children's thinking. In Bartsch and Wellman (1995) we used the longitudinal corpora available in the CHILDES database to analyze children's conversations and conceptions. This database includes conversations from children at home with their parents recorded for about an hour every two weeks of their lives, from the time they were 2 years old or a bit younger until they were about 5 or 6 years old. More than 200,000 child utterances are included in our analyses.

In one set of analyses (Bartsch & Wellman, 1995), we searched these conversations for children's use of desire and belief terms such as, *want*, *like*, *hope*, *wish*, *think*, *know*, and *remember*. Approximately 8% of children's utterances included one or the other of these terms, so the sample of utterances we considered most focally includes more than 12,000 child conversations.

To be clear, at issue here is not when children begin to use these terms at all; our concern is when children begin to use these terms to talk of their own or others' internal, subjective states, as distinct from external, objective aspects of behavior and events. Beginning as soon as we have transcripts, children do use these terms to refer to inner mental states distinct from overt behavior. These conceptual distinctions are clearest when young children explicitly contrast beliefs and reality or desires and action, in utterances like this: "You have pockets to keep your hands warm. I didn't know that." In such utterances the child contrasts a mental state – knowledge or in this case ignorance – with reality. Or: "You don't want water; I want some." Here a child contrasts one person's mental state with another – you don't want any, but I do.

These examples show some of the ways in which children make genuine references to beliefs and desires in everyday talk. Figure 29.8 shows the occurrence of genuine reference to beliefs or desires. Note two things: genuine reference to a character's desire via terms like *want* begins quite early and seems well established by the second birthday. Reference to belief, however,

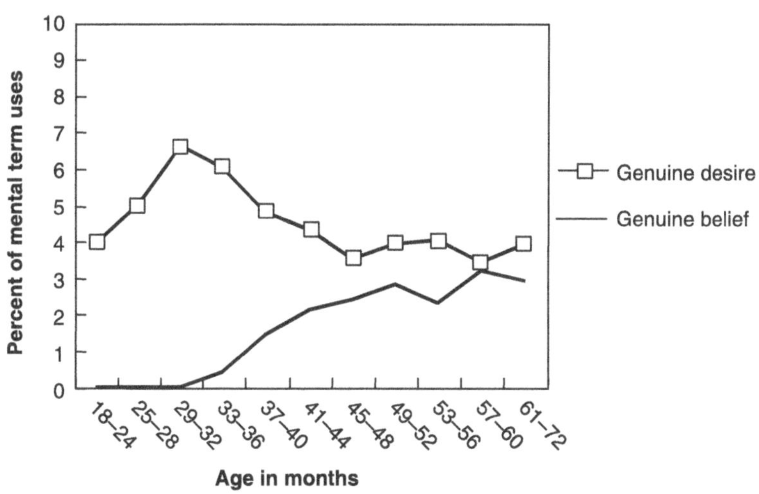

Figure 29.8 Children's conversational reference to persons' desires and beliefs. (Originally presented in Bartsch & Wellman, 1995.)

via terms like *think* and *know* begins much later. This absence of references to thinking and knowing in very young preschoolers is all the more striking, and convincing, considering that their parents talk to them about beliefs and thoughts as well as desires and emotions (Bartsch & Wellman, 1995).

Such data were initially available just for English-speaking children. However, Tardif and Wellman (2000) showed that just as English-speaking children talk about persons' desires well before later mention of beliefs, so too do Beijing and Hong Kong children acquiring Mandarin and Cantonese. Indeed, so too do deaf children learning sign language (Anderson & Reilly, 2002).

Sequence of theory of mind understandings

Early childhood conversations, therefore, seem to reveal a very early, genuine mentalistic construal of persons, albeit one bereft of an understanding of thoughts and beliefs. In fact, I believe there are a series of understandings that characterize preschool theory of mind. Consider the array of mental concepts and tasks listed in Table 29.1. Each of these tasks is different (e.g., in focusing on desires versus knowledge versus belief). But all address children's understanding of the subjectivity of various mental states in one form or another (e.g., that two people could have different states about the exact same item, or subjectively believe something at odds with objective reality, or overtly show one thing while subjectively feeling something else).

In Wellman and Liu (2004) we took 3-, 4-, and 5-year-old preschool

Table 29.1 Differing theory of mind tasks

Conceptual distinction	*Task content*
Diverse desires	Child judges that two persons (the child vs someone else) have different desires about the same objects.
Diverse beliefs	Child judges that two persons (the child vs someone else) have different beliefs about the same object, when the child does not know which belief is true or false.
Knowledge access	Child sees what's in a box and judges (yes – no) the knowledge of another person who does not see what is in a box.
Contents false belief	Child judges another person's false belief about what is in a distinctive container when child knows what it is in the container.
Explicit false belief	Child judges how someone will search, given that person's mistaken belief.
Real–apparent emotion	Child judges that a person can feel one thing but display a different emotion.

children and tested them on all these concepts using tasks that were very similar in format, materials, vocabulary, and so on. We found a very clear progression of development, as shown in Table 29.2. The results revealed a clear order of difficulty, indicating a consistent developmental progression among these five tasks. The consistency and significance of the sequence were confirmed by both Guttman and Rasch scaling analyses.

Note in Table 29.2 that children clearly understand desires before beliefs, even for very closely comparable tasks such as Diverse desires versus Diverse beliefs. More generally, children evidence a progression of understandings. Indeed, this progression begins still earlier, before the preschool years, in infancy.

Infants

Infants' understanding of persons is a classic question, but also a new topic addressed with new methods such as preferential looking and imitation paradigms. Infants cannot talk about mental states, so contemporary research investigates infants' perception of and reaction to observable intentional actions, actions that adults see as manifesting goals, desires, and knowledge.

Consider this study by Phillips and Wellman (in press). Using a habituation–dishabituation paradigm, infants saw a person reach over a barrier and grasp an object, as shown in Figure 29.9. Once the infants were habituated, the barrier was removed and they were shown two test events. One test event showed a *direct* reach for the object; the other showed an *indirect* reach. These test events contrast two different construals of the person's actions, one in terms of goal directedness and one in terms of physical motions of the arm. If in habituation the infant interpreted the actor's action as goal directed (as the actor going as directly as possible to get the goal object), then when the barrier is removed the direct reach is the expected action and the indirect reach would be more attention-worthy. In the indirect-reach test event, although the actor's arm movement remains the same as during habituation, the actor is no longer going directly to get the object.

Table 29.2 Theory of mind scale performance as obtained in Wellman and Liu (2004)

	0	*1*	*2*	*3*	*4*	*5*	
Diverse desire	–	+	+	+	+	+	
Diverse belief	–	–	+	+	+	+	
Knowledge–ignorance	–	–	–	+	+	+	
False-belief	–	–	–	–	+	+	Other 26
Hidden emotion	–	–	–	–	–	+	patterns
Total (these 6 patterns)	80% of children						20% of children

Figure 29.9 A depiction of the reaching events presented to infants in the study of Phillips and Wellman (in press).

In fact, during test, 12-month-olds look longer at the indirect reach. They dishabituate to the indirect reach (even though it is showing the exact same arm movement as in habituation) and do not dishabituate to the direct reach (even though it actually shows a different physical arm movement). This pattern supports the hypothesis that infants construe the reach as goal directed. (See Gergely et al., 1995 and Sodian, Schoeppner, & Metz, 2004 for similar data.)

Several control conditions indicate that the infant actually construes human action in terms of goal directedness. The most critical, we believe, appears in our research and involves showing the infant the same actions as in Figure 29.9 but with *no* goal object. In part, this controls for the possibility that infants might just prefer to look at a curving arm motion. But more crucially, if infants see the actions in Figure 29.9 as goal directed they should react differently if there is no goal object. So, for infants in the control condition, habituation and test were identical to those for infants in the experimental condition except that *no* object was ever present. In this case, since there was no object, there was no presentation of a goal-directed action in habituation. And in this case, appropriately, 12-month-old infants do *not* prefer the indirect-reach test event. So the experimental data do not just show a preference for looking at the curved arm motion. Infants do not prefer that in the control condition. And the data show appropriate differentiation between actions with and without goal objects. In sum, infant looking is sensitive to the goal-directedness of the action, and 9-month-olds (but not 6-month-olds) evidence the same pattern of findings (Csibra et al., 1999; Wellman & LaLonde, 2004).

Beyond assessing infants' understanding of *goal-directed* movement, recent studies employing similar methods also focus on infants' understanding of emotion and perception as *referential* (as signaling the focus of persons' attention and interests; Barna & Legerstee, 2005; Phillips, Wellman, & Spelke, 2002), and infants' ability to *parse* the continuous stream of human movement into intentional-action units or chunks (Baldwin & Baird, 2001).

One assumption of these studies is that early intention-understanding sets the stage for later theory of mind achievements. We (Wellman, Phillips, Dunphy-Lelii & LaLonde, 2004) provided initial validation of this assumption; we show significant connections between infants' attention to intentional action and the same children's theory of mind achievements as 4-year-olds (as measured on the Theory of Mind Scale shown in Table 29.2).

In total, therefore, I think the full developmental story for theory of mind looks something like this:

- 0 to 9 months: Special attention to human faces, voices.
- 9 to 15 months: Initial understanding of goal-directed (intentional) acts and states.
- 1.5 to 3 years: Simple desire psychology.
- 3.5 to 7 years: Belief–desire psychology.
- 7 years on: "Advanced" theory of mind understandings.

Conclusions

Rather than present any more findings, I want to conclude by briefly addressing two other issues: Is Theory of Mind, as a core human cognition, best thought of as a module? And what about culture? This [ICP, Beijing 2004] is an *International Congress*, so some discussion of culture and cultural differences in our folk psychologies seems mandatory.

Modules?

Let us say that a full look at the data, of which I have provided only a small sample, convinces you, as it convinces me, that theory of mind, mentalistic understanding of persons, is a core human cognition. What do the same data tell us about what core human cognitions are like? For example, ought we to think of them as mental modules? Or as something else? Some of us believe that the phrase Theory of Mind is not just a catchy phrase. It's apt. Children develop a *theory* of mind, an everyday theory of human action. I will not argue here for this theory-theory position (see Gopnik & Wellman, 1994), but I do want to argue against thinking about core human cognition as modules, in any hardnosed sense of that term.

Generally a mental module is defined as a genetically specified computational device in the mind/brain that works on its own inputs, and from those inputs then outputs some conceptual representation, computation, or new information. Modules, back to Fodor (1983), have some special properties. In particular, they are encapsulated and mandatory. In being encapsulated, the computations that transform inputs into outputs within the module, "work on their own". They are impervious to other information in the system, generating information in accord with algorithms not accessible to other systems. In being mandatory, given a module and given certain inputs, then the module's outputs mandatorily, necessarily follow.

In the literature on theory of mind Alan Leslie has argued most strongly for a theory of mind module – ToMM (Leslie, 1994; Scholl & Leslie, 2001). Leslie argues that ToMM accounts for the "fact" that "theory of mind has a specific innate basis, in that the essential character of theory of mind – including the concepts of belief, desire and pretense – is part of our genetic endowment, which are triggered by appropriate environmental factors" (Scholl & Leslie, 2001, p. 697). This triggering produces a universal, consistent developmental timetable, indeed ToMM comes on-line at about 2 years. When on-line, ToMM necessarily, "irresistibly", computes both beliefs and desires. The modular, innate neurological basis of theory of mind, according to this position, means that the module can be selectively impaired, as in autism.

Very briefly, here are three sorts of data *against* modular proposals (and more in line with theory-like ones).

1 *Universal, consistent timetables*? Universal consistent timetables would certainly be consistent with innately specified modules coming on-line. But remember the meta-analysis; the data do *not* show consistent timetables, they show a consistent trajectory but very different timetables in different countries and contexts (e.g., Figures 29.5 and 29.6). Unlike modules, a theory characterization predicts that different timetables would result from differences in individuals' experiences across their varied lives and societies, and hence differences in accumulating the type of evidence that would lead to theory change.
2 *Beliefs and desires*. What about the claim that a theory of mind module necessarily, mandatorily, outputs attributions of both beliefs and desires. Many of the data presented in this chapter show that rather than understanding (computing) beliefs and desires on the same timetable, children understand desires well before beliefs. Indeed as shown in Table 29.2, theory of mind understandings unfold in an extended progression.
3 *Autism*. One implication of positing theory of mind modules is that they might be impaired. And increasingly people have argued that individuals with autism are especially impaired in theory-of-mind understandings, arguably reflecting neurological impairment of a dedicated theory of mind module.

   Impaired theory-of-mind understandings certainly do appear in individuals with autism – such individuals, for example, are notoriously bad at false-belief tasks. However, another implication of positing theory of mind modules is that individuals who are not impaired in the relevant modules – for example, who do not have autism – should achieve mental-state understandings on a roughly standard timetable. Yet in recent studies, deaf preschool children raised by hearing parents show delays and deficiencies on theory of mind tasks comparable to those of children with autism (Gale et al. 1997; Peterson & Siegal, 1995, 2000). These deaf children have not suffered the same sort of neurological damage that children with autism have, as evident by the fact that deaf children raised by deaf parents do not show theory of mind delays.

Findings such as these challenge accounts of theory of mind development relying solely on neurological–maturational–modular mechanisms. Regardless of what one thinks about modules versus theories, the extant data underscore my main point about the *developmental* nature of theory of mind understandings. Theory of mind has, at a very general level of analysis, a basic shape. And theory of mind is in one sense early developing. But at the same time, theory of mind has an extended developmental course, exhibiting common trajectories in part, but also profound developmental change and important differences across societies and individuals.

These are features of importance, I contend, not just for thinking about theory of mind but for characterizing and properly understanding core human cognition more generally. These are features also necessary for properly understanding the interplay between core human cognition and culture.

Culture

Adult folk worldwide seem to have widely varying ideas about persons, actions, and the explanation of social life. Here are some nonrandom examples:

1 According to LeVine (1979, p. 358), the Gusii prefer to discuss overt behavior, and avoid talking about intentions and other aspects of mind: "Their habitual mode of expression was to describe actions and events . . . leaving out their own or the actors' personal reactions, opinions, judgments."

2 More radically, Fajans (1985, p. 367) claims: "The most challenging and interesting thing about the Baining (of Papua New Guinea) from the point of view of ethnopsychological studies is that they appear not to have a folk psychology. . . . If we understand the latter to be a domain of culture which includes a concern with affect and emotions, concepts of person and self, theories of deviance, interpretations of behavior, and ideas about cognition and personality development, the Baining manifest very little interest in these areas."

3 Less radically, Jin Li (2003, pp. 146–147) describes Chinese-Confucian versus Western-Socrates conceptions of knowledge and learning as follows: ". . . Confucius was rarely if at all concerned about the notion of 'truth' as defined in Western epistemology . . . Confucius' long-lasting influence resides in his fundamental teaching of the concept of *ren*, that is, a lifelong striving for any human being to become the most genuine, sincere, and humane person he or she can become.

The Socratic model may be about truth finding or even knowledge generation, but the Confucian model is about moral striving, which is very different from Western epistemology . . .

> These differences are apparent in contemporary conceptions of learning . . . [Comparing China and the US] What learning means to members of these two cultures is substantially different to the degree that there is little conceptual overlap between them."

At the very least, conceptions of persons, of essential social actors and agents, vary widely across cultures, encompassing people, cows, dead ancestors, rocks, carved images, and all manner of "counterintuitive" entities. I admit that it is not clear exactly what to make of all these claims and differences. But for my purposes I do not need to sensibly synthesize the evidence on adult folk psychologies. I only need to minimally agree that folk psychologies vary worldwide in some astonishing regards. Various ways of thinking about people exist – various folk psychologies exist – that are quite different one from another. That said, how does such diversity square with the notion of theory of mind, as I have been discussing it, as a core human cognition?

Consider the following scenario: Children worldwide, at some early age, share something like a framework psychological theory – a framework theory of mind. Accordingly, children tend to assume that people have subjective experiences, social intersubjectivity, and internal mental states. In this scenario, such assumptions are evident at ages 2 or 3 or so, but are themselves the products of earlier developments in infancy.

Note that such assumptions (the general background expectation that people possess thoughts, wants, perceptions, feelings) provide only a very general framework, and children must engage in much specific instantiation of the framework, prominently including much culture-specific learning. The framework constrains the sorts of hypotheses that children initially make about people, but such a framework does not specify any particular set of emotion categories, does not privilege thought over emotion or emotion over thought, does not confine personhood to live humans, and so on. Moreover, in theory-like ways, the framework is not developmentally static; it can revise and change to the extent of becoming in some parts and respects quite different from its initial assumptions.

This scenario yields several intriguing implications. On the one hand, the scenario predicts constraints on cultural variability in folk psychologies. After all, any specific folk psychology must be learnable by that "folk's" children. By definition, cultural communities cannot evolve a specially developed construal of *anything* that their members cannot learn. More intriguing, constrained variability should be especially notable in childhood. If you want to see the universal core of theory of mind, look at 3- and 4-year-olds. Complementarily, adults' conceptions of people might be much more dissimilar worldwide than childhood ones. Why? Because the initial framework is *enabling* as well as constraining, precisely in that it is a general framework *and* it works developmentally.

Initially, the framework provides a helpful ground for a community's members to communicate with their children. But, in part through this communication, community members will teach and socialize their children into their group's practices and beliefs. In terms of cultural development, cultural communities have centuries in which to develop unique understandings of persons, selves, psyches, and societies. In terms of individual development, those groups have many years, at the least from infancy to adulthood, in which to enculturate their children into their beliefs and worldviews. Resulting adult folk psychologies could be quite different from one another worldwide; each could be quite removed and advanced beyond, although grounded in, the initial framework assumptions of young children.

This scenario for how core human cognition and enculturation combine is one I favor. Something like it inspires my search for very basic understandings in young children that characterize their theory of mind. Note that this scenario is a developmental scenario; it is core human cognition, as an intrinsically developmental phenomenon. That is appropriate because I believe that the story of theory of mind as a core human cognition can only make sense, and only fits the data, as a *developmental* story.

References

Anderson, D., & Reilly, J. (2002). The McArthur developmental inventory: Data for American sign language. *Journal of Deaf Studies and Deaf Education*, *1*, 83–104.

Atran, S. (1996). Modes of thinking about living kinds: Science, symbolism and common sense. In D. Olson & N. Torrance (Eds.), *Modes of thought*. New York: Cambridge University Press.

Baldwin, D.A., & Baird, J.A. (2001). Discerning intentions in dynamic human action. *Trends in Cognitive Sciences*, *5*, 171–178.

Barna, J., & Legerstee, M. (2005). 9- and 12-month-old infants relate emotions to people's action. *Cognition and Emotion*, *19*, 53–67.

Baron-Cohen, S. (1995). *Mindblindness: An essay on autism and theory of mind*. Cambridge, MA: MIT Press.

Barrett, J.L. (2000). Exploring the natural foundations of religion. *Trends in Cognitive Science*, *4*, 29–34.

Bartsch, K., & Wellman, H.M. (1995). *Children talk about the mind*. New York: Oxford University Press.

Bretherton, I., & Beeghly, M. (1982). Talking about internal states: The acquisition of an explicit theory of mind. *Developmental Psychology*, *18*, 906–921.

Carruthers, P. (2002). The cognitive functions of language. *Behavioral and Brian Sciences*, *25*, 657–726.

Csibra, G., Gergely, G., Biro, S., Koos, O., & Brockbank, M. (1999). Goal attribution without agency cues: The perception of "pure reason" in infants. *Cognition*, *72*, 237–267.

Fajans, J. (1985). The person in social context: The social character of Baining "psychology". In G. White & J. Kirkpatrick (Eds.), *Person, self, and experience: Exploring pacific ethnopsychologies* (pp. 367–397). Los Angeles: University of California Press.

Fodor, J.A. (1983). *Modularity of mind*. Cambridge, MA: MIT Press.

Gale, E., DeVilliers, P.A., DeVilliers, J.G., & Pyers, J.E. (1997). *Language and theory of mind in deaf children*. Paper presented at the Proceedings of the 20th Boston Child Language Conference, Boston, MA.

Gergely, G., Nadasdy, Z., Csibra, G., & Biro, S. (1995). Taking the intentional stance at 12 months of age. *Cognition*, *56*, 165–193.

Gopnik, A., & Wellman, H.M. (1994). The theory theory. In L. Hirschfeld & S. Gelman (Eds.), *Domain specificity in cognition and culture* (pp. 257–293). New York: Cambridge University Press.

Leslie, A.M. (1994). ToMM, ToBy, and agency: Core architecture and domain specificity in cognition and culture. In L. Hirschfeld & S. Gelman (Eds.), *Domain specificity in cognition and culture* (pp. 119–148). New York: Cambridge University Press.

LeVine, S. (1979). *Mothers and wives*. Chicago: University of Chicago Press.

Li, J. (2003). The core of Confucian learning. *American Psychologist*, *58*, 146–147.

Liu, D., Wellman, H.M., Tardif, T., & Sabbagh, M.A. (2004). *A meta-analysis of Chinese theory of mind*. Paper presented at the International Congress of Psychology, Beijing, China.

Peterson, C.C., & Siegal, M. (1995). Deafness, conversation and theory of mind. *Journal of Child Psychology and Psychiatry*, *36*, 459–474.

Peterson, C.C., & Siegal, M. (2000). Insights into theory of mind from deafness and autism. *Mind & Language*, *15*, 123–145.

Phillips, A.T., & Wellman, H.M. (in press). Infants' understanding of object-directed action. *Cognition*.

Phillips, A.T., Wellman, H.M., & Spelke, E.S. (2002). Infants' ability to connect gaze and emotional expression to intentional action. *Cognition*, *85*, 53–78.

Scholl, B.J., & Leslie, A.M. (2001). Minds, modules, and meta-analysis. *Child Development*, *72*, 696–701.

Shatz, M., Wellman, H.M., & Silber, S. (1983). The acquisition of mental verbs: A systematic investigation of first references to mental state. *Cognition*, *14*, 301–321.

Sodian, B, Schoeppner, B., & Metz, U. (2004) Do infants apply the principle of rational action to human agents? *Infant Behavior & Development*, *27*, 31–41.

Spelke, E. (1994). Initial knowledge: Six suggestions. *Cognition*, *50*, 431–445.

Spelke, E. (2003). What makes us smart: Core knowledge and natural language. In D. Gentner & S. Goldin-Meadow (Eds.), *Language and mind*. Cambridge, MA: MIT Press.

Stitch, S. (1983). *From folk psychology to cognitive science*. Cambridge, MA: Bradford Books.

Tardif, T., & Wellman, H.M. (2000). Acquisition of mental state language in Mandarin- and Cantonese-speaking children. *Developmental Psychology*, *36*, 25–43.

Wellman, H.M. (1990). *The child's theory of mind*. Cambridge, MA: MIT Press.

Wellman, H.M., Cross, D., & Watson, J. (2001). Meta-analysis of theory of mind development: The truth about false belief. *Child Development*, *72*, 655–684.

Wellman, H.M., & Gelman, S.A. (1998). Knowledge acquisition in foundational domains. In D. Kuhn & R. Siegler (Eds.), *Cognition, perception and language. Volume 2 of the Handbook of child psychology* (5th ed., pp. 523–573). New York: Wiley.

Wellman, H.M. & LaLonde, N. (2004). *Six- and 9-month-olds' understanding of object-directed action.* Unpublished manuscript. University of Michigan, Ann Arbor, MI.

Wellman, H.M., & Liu, D. (2004). Scaling of theory of mind tasks. *Child Development*, *75*, 523–541.

Wellman, H.M., Phillips, A.T., Dunphy-Lelii, S., & LaLonde, N. (2004). Infant social attention predicts preschool social cognition. *Developmental Science*, *7*, 283–288.

30 Social change and transitions to adulthood

Rainer K. Silbereisen

Social change can be described as a change in the typical characteristics of a society, such as social structures and institutions, norms, values, cultural products, and symbols (Calhoun, 1992). A number of important distinctions can be made as to the nature of the change. It may be gradual, as in the case of the demographic changes in many countries, or it may occur abruptly, as in the breakdown of socialist countries in Europe in the 1990s. Further, social change may represent an overall improvement or worsening of conditions, and it can be comprehensive or relatively narrow in focus. In many cases, however, this is not a question of either/or but, at least in a longer time perspective, a mixture of basically all common aspects. Thus, the rapid and comprehensive change of all major social institutions in former East Germany was followed by a series of more gradual transformations that not only mirror the changed institutions but also reflect other effects of major societal trends, such as the change in the international distribution of labor due to globalization, or the challenges for intergenerational solidarity due to demographic change.

Obviously, unprecedented social change is not a new phenomenon, as witnessed by the rapid changes in industrialization of societies and their ramifications for the formation of societies and personal identities over the past few centuries. Consequently one could expect a long tradition of research efforts by psychologists into the effects of social change. However, comparatively little research has been conducted in psychology under the headings of social change or related topics. I deem this a sad state of affairs given the ubiquity of social change and its consequences.

Unwarranted assertions about implications for individual development

Under the pressure of the rapidly evolving political events, the first wave of studies on German unification was guided by hypotheses rooted less in specific scientific models than in popular presumptions. For instance, the tremendous increase in potentially distressing situations faced by many people, such as increasing unemployment rates and the loss of former frames of reference, were presumed to result in impaired levels of well-being and negative self-related attitudes. However, empirical studies that compared cohorts of East Germans with West Germans showed rather small and inconsistent differences (Pinquart & Silbereisen, 2004). Post hoc explanations were plentiful – lower stress levels than expected, unexpected buffering effects, successful coping efforts – but the reasons why such a theoretically underdeveloped set of hypotheses was formed in the first place are important to note.

First, at least concerning the German situation, a paradigm was prominent among scientists and politicians according to which the breakdown of the Eastern political system could be attributed to a lack of differentiation into well-coordinated and labor-divisive social institutions better suited to meet the new challenges of globalization than the top-down economic and political management in former East Germany. Based on this scenario, the concept of a "modernization catch-up" (Zapf, 1996) was suggested. This predicted that the introduction of West German legal, economic, and social institutions into the East would create a framework that, by virtue of its incentives and options, would result in a massive change of living conditions and subsequent adaptations by people within a short period of time following clearly predictable pathways.

In reality, however, the consequences of German unification turned out to be multidirectional and sometimes chaotic. This view led to a more differentiated perspective. According to a model promoted by a research consortium of social and behavioral scientists (Best, 2003), the study of unification and its transformations of the political and social fabric requires two dimensions to be distinguished. The first refers to the institutions established by the new political system and is located between the poles of rigidity versus flexibility of the new order and its expectations for individuals' behaviors and orientations. The second concerns the individuals and is defined by persistence versus readiness for change of behaviors rooted in the past. How "old" individuals and "new" institutions match defines different modes of adaptation to unification on the aggregate level that can be arranged as a four-fold table. Rapid and uniform adaptation could be predicted where a high individual readiness for change meets a system that is rather firm in its expectations for change. However, other modes possibly co-exist, thus establishing niches of opportunities that hold a particular ensemble of perceived challenges and threats, and which result in a particular pattern of reactions. Neither the niches nor the reactions are static, and this may be the primary reason why the course of social change and its effects often turned out to be less unidirectional and predictable than originally asserted.

Other unwarranted assertions also played a role in the expectation of a rapid convergence between the East and West. One was that differences were caused by the political division of Germany after WWII, when many were actually the result of long-lasting trends that had begun decades earlier. For example, the greater detachment from church and religion in former East

Germany had its roots in secularization that was already underway (Schühly & Müller, 1997). Likewise, the differences to be expected before unification were exaggerated, resulting in a tendency to attribute the diminished differences to converging societal developments. Values, for instance, were actually rather similar in the two political regions (Reitzle & Silbereisen, 2000a).

In conclusion, for the future one can only hope that we as behavioral and social scientists studying human development are better prepared with adequate heuristics and theories on the nature of social and political transformations and their consequences. We also need to look beyond rapid social change and to think of change that evolves over decades, such as demographic change. A major distinction may be that gradual change does not close down or open up opportunities immediately and often is not enforced by a powerful social institution. Consequently, individual differences in persistence versus readiness to change play a bigger role, thereby establishing better chances for innovative elites (Pinquart & Silbereisen, 2004).

The only safeguard against similar misconceptions and unwarranted assertions in the future is to make the systematic exploration (conceptually and empirically) of the current social changes and their role in human development a priority. And there are indications that the situation of research on social change will improve soon. In the USA as well as in other countries new programs of funding have been launched that will foster interdisciplinary research on the relationship between large-scale change in contexts and human development, such as the National Science Foundation program on "Human and Social Dynamics" (NSF 03–552).

Change in contexts and challenges to habits as source of adjustment

If one takes Bronfenbrenner's (1994) distinctions of a nested structure of macro-, exo-, meso-, and micro-systems and their time-related changes as a point of departure, German unification probably affected all contexts of human development. The social structures and institutions that were taken over from the West refer to the macro-system. A case in point is the removal of limitations (other than academic competence) for attending college-bound school tracks in East Germany that quickly led to a dramatic increase in the number of students attending this track, based on the belief among many parents that a high level of education will be crucial for successful adaptation (Kornadt, 1996). Besides profound changes in micro-, meso-, and exosystems, those of the chrono-system were particularly important: Some of the changes people in East Germany had to face following unification, such as the widespread unemployment, were unprecedented in their prior life, so that preparedness by past events was unlikely, making them especially vulnerable. Other changes, however, were closer to the previous life of many, such as the role of education and training for personal success and promotion, and thus individual differences in coping experiences were relevant and may have reduced the exposure to strains and stress (Rutter, 1994).

Concerning concepts that relate such changes in contexts to individual development, particularly in the macro- and chrono-systems referring to social structures, Glen Elder's seminal study *Children of the Great Depression* (1974) represents a landmark and was the inspiration for our research on German unification. Social change causes a disparity between claims and resources that does not allow individuals to maintain effectively habitual behaviors. This disparity leads to a sense of loss of control over one's life. In response, "control cycles" are undertaken with the aim of finding a new balance between claims and resources (Elder & Caspi, 1990). Against this conceptual backdrop, I now want to turn to a series of our studies on effects of German unification on the timing of psychosocial transitions.

Research by the Jena group on the timing of psychosocial transitions

According to the life-course approach to human development, social trajectories of education, work, and family offer individuals a framework for how to negotiate their life, and provide opportunities and constraints for individuals' agency. Social change may affect various properties of the transitions forming trajectories, such as the timing or the sequencing (Elder, 1998). Inspired by Elder's work, a large part of our research on German unification referred to the timing of important psychosocial transitions in adolescence and early adulthood. We studied more informal transitions, such as adolescent developmental tasks related to romantic involvement and family formation, and more formal ones, like the timing of social-institutional achievements or financial self-support. Our general view was that, first, prior to unification East/West differences should have existed in psychological domains affected by the differing social institutions that provided the "social clocks" for individuals' behavior. Second, we expected these differences to disappear gradually over time as a function of the changes in social institutions and in the developmental contexts influenced by these changes.

The design of the research followed the idea of a cohort comparison of otherwise equivalent samples. Large stratified samples were drawn in East and West in 1991 and again in 1996, and subsequently compared. They comprised a younger cohort of 13- to 19-year-old adolescents, and an older cohort of 20- to 29-year-old adults. In many regards, the year 1991, that is, shortly after unification, still represented the old circumstances, enriched by new opportunities but not yet tainted by the darker sides of unification, such as high unemployment. In 1996, however, 5 years into the process, the new social institutions had consolidated their influence, and people had experienced a multitude of challenges. To accommodate to the fact that not all participants had already made the transition in question, the timing of transitions was estimated by various forms of survival analysis techniques.

Group differences in the timing of education/work transitions

The timing of first occupational preferences in adolescence, a socio-institutional achievement, is a case in point. In the East a clear system of guidance by the school had been established, based on qualifications needed for the centrally planned work sector. Occupational choice was limited compared to the West. The unification-related change in the school system resulted in almost immediate changes in the curriculum and modes of instruction to resemble those of the West (Silbereisen & Wiesner, 2002). Consequently, among the 13- to 19-year-olds we expected an earlier timing of first occupational preferences in the East in 1991, followed by a diminished difference in 1996 due to a later timing in the East in response to the changes in schools and the mode of job training. Estimates of the transition ages in occupational preferences indeed confirmed these expectations (Vondracek, Reitzle, & Silbereisen, 1999). As these adolescents had experienced the former East German system of school and vocational guidance up to early adolescence, in 1993 we also looked at a younger group of 10- to 13-year-olds who were already attending school under the new Western system. No differences between East and West in the timing of occupational preferences were found, thus hinting at the possibility of a gradual adaptation over this short period of time (Silbereisen, 2000).

Among the older group of 20- to 29-year-olds, we studied the timing of financial self-support, again comparing 1991 and 1996. Depending on age at the time of unification, they were already settled in careers and committed to family roles when massive changes occurred in the labor market. Reitzle and Silbereisen (2000b) showed that in 1996 young adults from vocationally oriented school-tracks had achieved financial self-support later than those of the 1991 cohort. Under the economic conditions of the former East Germany, financial independence was automatically achieved upon completion of vocational training, whereas after unification the new conditions provided many obstacles, such as the need for renewed qualification and periods of unemployment.

Group differences in the timing of romance/family transitions

Compared to education and work, the domain of interpersonal relationships was less directly affected by the institutional changes, and this certainly applied to the timing of romantic involvement among the 13- to 19-year-olds. Consequently, we expected no period difference, and due to the shared cultural roots, also no differences between East and West. Analyzing the timing of three way-stations to romantic involvement – falling in love the first time, going steady with a boyfriend or girlfriend, and first sexual experience – Silbereisen and Wiesner (2002) confirmed these hypotheses.

Among 20- to 29-year-old young females, however, Juang and Silbereisen (2001) found a difference between the political regions in 1991 and 1996.

Women in the East traditionally married earlier, and this was also shown in the data. However, despite the persistence of differences between East and West, Easterners from vocationally oriented tracks showed a delayed timing of marriage in 1996 compared to 1991 (Silbereisen, Reitzle, & Haase, 2005). Thus, adaptation to Western timetables occurred, but it did not lead to a complete disappearance of East–West differences. At closer scrutiny, an even more differentiated picture emerged as a function of educational level (Juang & Silbereisen, 2001). In the West, education did not make a difference. The same applied to women from college-bound tracks in the East. Those from the vocationally oriented track, however, reported a later marriage age in 1996 as compared to 1991. The same pattern of results applied to the timing of first motherhood. We interpreted this result as reflecting the particularly insecure economic situation of Eastern women in the lower educational stratum.

What about another particularity of the East, namely the fact that a higher share than in the West had children before they married? In our understanding there was no element in the structural changes after unification that would have enforced a change in this pattern of family formation. The results showed that this difference between East and West, particularly among vocationally oriented school tracks, persisted between 1991 and 1996, and that the same applied to the temporal spacing between marriage and motherhood. Once more, the changes in living conditions seemed to have rather circumscribed effects. Delaying marriage and motherhood is a way to adjust to precarious material conditions, but this does not spill over to other aspects of family transitions. Beyond material security through full-time employment, the higher prevalence of non-traditional sequences of family formation in the East was rooted in other aspects relevant for parents and children, such as the easy availability and low costs of daycare, and this had not changed as rapidly by 1996.

Mediating mechanisms

We further investigated potential mediators of the effects of social change on individual transition ages. We found that the differences in timing pertaining to financial self-support were partly mediated by two factors: being in education and the experience of own unemployment (Reitzle & Silbereisen, 2000b). Thus, the relative delay in financial independence can in part be explained by individuals participating in the new options provided by unification or by their suffering from the new constraints.

Further analyses (Silbereisen et al., 2005) on the timing of marriage and parenthood in young adulthood revealed a similarity to the economic transition to financial independence. In both cases the later transition timing in the East 1996 versus 1991 could be fully explained by own or parental unemployment. This showed that the delayed timing of marriage among Easterners in 1996 could be attributed solely to social change related experiences that made particular individuals especially vulnerable. The need to be very specific when it comes to mediators was underscored when we attempted to explain the timing differences concerning other transitions. Indicators of educational involvement and unemployment showed no relationship to the transition of leaving the parental home (Juang, Silbereisen, & Wiesner, 1999). Thus, the earlier home leaving in the East 1996 compared to 1991 was not related to the activities undertaken in order to adjust to the changed labor market (Silbereisen, Reitzle, & Juang, 2002).

In sum, the relevance of unemployment experiences related to social and political transformation varies across psychosocial transitions, probably due to the relevance of career matters and their ramifications for the transitions under discussion.

As only a fraction of the differences between periods could be "explained away" by our predictors, other possibilities have to be considered. For example, the change in the timing of the psychosocial transitions may not require the individual experience of, for instance, difficulties in the apprenticeship market. As Silbereisen and Wiesner (2002) put it, it may be enough to be exposed to "collective molds", such as behaviors and attitudes held by neighbors and the public. According to the so-called dynamic social impact theory of Latané (1996), taking over such models and consequently changing one's behavior is more likely the more it is shared by the people with whom one interacts in the neighborhood.

The gist of the analyses and interpretations by the Jena group demonstrated a clear relationship between changed social structures and the timing of a number of important psychosocial transitions during adolescence and the period of "emerging adulthood" (Arnett, 2000). The further prediction that the changed social institutions would exert their influence on the individuals through a change in the necessities and opportunities with which individuals are confronted also found support. As the comparison between the timing of financial self-support and the timing of marriage and parenthood revealed, the new challenges do not exert a uniform effect, but seem to have a circumscribed and specific influence.

Compared to the proximal micro-mechanisms that researchers in the Elder tradition have been studying, our approach was restricted to very distant bridges between changed social institutions and individuals' behavior. When a new sweep of research on German unification was planned recently, closing this gap was an important issue. However, given the fact that there is a plethora of changes that affect family, school, work, and leisure, for pragmatic reasons it is not possible to identify and assess each proximal mechanism in detail. Thus, a better strategy may draw on more general models of how individuals control disparities between challenges and resources.

Resources and adjustment

The advantage of the model proposed by Elder is the differentiated view on the mediational role of micro-system resources between change on the structural level and individuals' behavior and development. It is rather abstract, however, with regard to the nature of the adjusting control cycles that individuals undertake. The Jena group was interested in a better understanding of personal resources accumulated before the structural changes took place, and in their role in moderating the adjustment process and developmental outcomes.

A behavioral model of developmental outcomes of social change

Our considerations departed from Elder's work, but also referred to other approaches that address how individuals treat and take advantage from disparities between challenges and resources. One is the transactional stress model by Lazarus (1998; Lazarus & Folkman, 1984). The other model we referred to is the life-span theory of control by Heckhausen and Schulz (1995). The principal constructs and processes of our "behavioral model of developmental outcomes of social change" are similar to stress and control models (Pinquart & Silbereisen, 2004). In contrast to other approaches, however, its main emphasis is on the change in the availability and functionality of developmental pathways affected by a large number of moderating and mediating variables. The changes in the pathways themselves are caused by the change in an individual's more proximal context that itself can be traced back to macro-system social change. The process is iterative. The changed developmental outcomes link back to the resources and options components of the model, thereby beginning a new cycle of adjustments with a re-evaluation of their functionality.

According to the model, social change not only affects available developmental opportunities, but also induces change in individual and social resources and vulnerabilities. A case in point is the devaluation of parental models and interpersonal linkages because social change made earlier experiences worthless. For instance, in our own studies conducted soon after unification, a high similarity between parents' current occupation and adolescents' occupational preferences was observed in the West, but quite a remarkable difference was prevalent in the East. The occupational preferences of those affected by unification already reflected the structural change and new priorities in the economy (Vondracek, Silbereisen, Reitzle, & Wiesner, 1999). This is indeed an indication of the loss of life-expertise for the parents, and illustrates a farther-reaching revision of intergenerational transfers (Kohli, Künemund, Motel, & Szydlik, 2000).

The evaluation of available options and the choice of behavior are the main mediating instances linking the changes induced by social change to consequences. According to Pinquart and Silbereisen (2004), surprisingly little research has been conducted on the specific ways of coping with the changes. One of the few exceptions is research that demonstrated how downward comparisons helped individuals to protect their well-being in spite of the fact that they had to face negative changes in their life (Schmitt, Maes,

& Schmal, 1998). Likewise, findings from our research group on economic hardship in East and West Germany soon after unification suggested that people in the East buffered themselves from economic hardship by self-protective interpretations of their situation. In the West, however, the model Elder and colleagues had confirmed did indeed apply (Forkel & Silbereisen, 2001). This result yielded striking similarity to findings from an earlier comparative study (Silbereisen, Walper, & Albrecht, 1990).

Most psychological research until now has been related to short-term effects of the unification experience. From research on the Great Depression, impressive long-term effects are known, such as the higher wisdom in old age among those who suffered from the economic declines but found a way to cope successfully, as indicated by better health trajectories following the times of hardship (Ardelt, 1998). As statistics conducted in a sociological-demographic framework revealed, there is good reason to believe that some of the changes that occurred soon after unification will have long-term effects possibly even over generations.

The bulk of studies conducted by researchers interested in human development referred to a few broad domains of competence and adjustment. In our research on developmental timetables we studied the influence of change in social structures and institutions on the socialization into major adult roles related to the spheres of work, career, and family formation. In other research the focus was on the role of social change on behavioral and psychological adjustment among individuals, and on intrafamilial relations, such as individuation processes during adolescence (Pinquart & Silbereisen, 2004).

The current status of research reveals some surprising lacunae. Foremost among them is the fact that until now researchers have not tapped behaviors that evince a clear proactive rather than reactive stance toward the challenges. By proactive I mean behaviors that aim beyond one's own individual situation and which also focus on an improvement for others, such as civic engagement. A point of departure could be the well-known perceived status inequalities between East and West Germans as social groups. This may initiate actions that in social psychology are referred to as "social change" (Wright, 2001). Attempts to improve one's own situation as member of a social group fall into a number of categories of behavior (Stangor, 2004). A particularly interesting strategy with regard to our model of development under conditions of social change is collective action to improve the actual status and standing of one's social group. This can be accomplished either by peaceful means such as heightened civic participation through lobbying or political protest, or by resorting to various forms of resistance and violence. The likelihood of collective action increases if group membership is seen as difficult to change, if the rival group reveals long-term instabilities, if one's own group identity is high, if status differences lack legitimacy, and if opportunities for communication with others and leadership are provided (Stangor, 2004).

The concepts from social psychology just mentioned are important because involving them would allow the question of how the developmental outcomes of social change at the individual level can feed back to the aggregate level of collective action. Such ideas were built into recent proposals by a research consortium for a new wave of studies on the ongoing social and political transformations in Germany and other European countries. The consortium received funding, but one has to wait for results to come (Sonderforschungbereich 580, 2004).

I want to turn now to the second piece of our own research. Whereas the studies on continuities and discontinuities of developmental timetables obviously referred to the role of institutional changes and their experience as mediators of adjustments to unification, we deal now with the role of resources in the entire process.

The Jena group research on self-efficacy as a resource

According to our model (Pinquart & Silbereisen, 2004), self-efficacy plays a prominent role among the individual resources that are likely to promote active coping with the new challenges brought by social change. Its development is fostered by the experience of contingencies between one's actions and the outcomes one perceives (Bandura, 1997). Being a highly controlling society, East Germany was seen as providing obstacles against such experiences. Hence many researchers assumed that the level of self-efficacy would be lower in former East Germany compared to the West (Little, Lopez, Oettingen, & Baltes, 2001).

This view was probably too pessimistic, because the East not only fostered heavily controlled public socialization environments, but because it also provided many alternative sources of self-efficacy in the private domain (Sydow, Wagner, Jülisch, & Kauf, 1999). In our analyses on school-related self-efficacy in 1993, we found even higher levels in the East, and discussed the possibility that the new school curricula and teaching methods may have led to an over-shooting effect known from acculturation research (Triandis, Kashima, Shimada, & Villareal, 1986).

An impressive example for the relevance of self-efficacy in mastering the challenges of social and political transformations was recently provided by Titma and Tuma (2005). They had at their disposal a longitudinally collected survey of young people who graduated in the early 1980s in various regions of the former USSR, and who were followed through the collapse of the political and economic system until the end of the 1990s. As a proxy for self-efficacy, the authors formed an index that represented a count of deliberately chosen activities outside of people's main job before the actual political changes had taken place, such as part-time and odd jobs, trading and producing, and growing things at home to sell. The results showed that under the new economic and political conditions this proxy to self-efficacy was a precursor of self-employment at the end of the 1990s. This relationship was moderated, however, by the national context and its traditions with regard to individual agency. The Baltic States, for instance, represented a more conducive environment as compared to many other successor states of the former USSR.

In our research on self-efficacy we had access to a prospective longitudinal sample of originally 12-year-old school students from Leipzig, a large city in East Germany. Data collection began several years before unification and was continued for several years afterwards. Self-efficacy referred to academic activities and school-related peer activities prior to unification. As predicted, we (Pinquart, Silbereisen, & Juang, 2004a) found a main effect of prior self-efficacy on better psychological adjustment at age 18, indicated by higher life satisfaction and future optimism. Note that this result was statistically controlled for parental warmth and school grades at age 12. The main interest, however, was in a potential buffering effect of self-efficacy in the face of adversities related to unification. More specifically, we expected that high levels of self-efficacy would buffer the effect of unification-related perceived deteriorations in the fields of family finances, occupational training, leisure opportunities, and life in general. Our findings confirmed this buffering effect. Utilizing the same data set with assessments of self-efficacy predating unification, Pinquart, Silbereisen, and Juang (2004b) showed that previous identification with the East German political system was not related to a change in psychological distress among those with average and high levels of self-efficacy. A high commitment to the old system corresponded to an increase in distress only among those with low self-efficacy pre-unification.

In sum, a picture emerges of self-efficacy as an important resource in mastering rapid change of the social and political system. It is also obvious that the studies thus far do not pay sufficient attention to the dynamic and iterative role as delineated in the model proposed (Pinquart & Silbereisen, 2004), but it is certainly a promising beginning. Other domains of self-efficacy should be investigated, including typical topics of social change, as well as other concepts of individual resources. Examples are individual differences in what Larson (2000) called initiative, the willingness to pick up new challenges and to pursue intrinsically motivated goals. Given the harmful effects of chronic stressors, such as unemployment – which even affects immune functions as evidenced by recent meta-analytic findings (Segerstrom & Miller, 2004) – empowering people by strengthening individual and social resources seems to be a promising and important way to a more productive negotiation of the challenges.

Conclusions

The concepts and results I have reported demonstrate some progress in our understanding of the effects of social change, but they also show the limitations of knowledge and the need for more adequate studies. Even by reducing the more general topic to the type of social and political transformations experienced in the Germany of the 1990s, the problems faced in conceptualizing the relationship between changes in the macro-system and human development on the individual level are highly complex. An important reduction of complexity can be achieved by focusing on particular characteristics. In the Jena group, for instance, we saw the unification experience in parallel to acculturation among immigrants (Crockett & Silbereisen, 2000). Whereas in an immigration situation people move to new contexts, here it was new social institutions that moved to people. The interest in developmental timetables was also induced by our previous research on immigration where we observed the long arm of traditional beliefs in the adaptation of timetables (Schmitt-Rodermund & Silbereisen, 2000). This led us to expect the gradual and inconsistent adjustment to the new circumstances from early on.

Today, more than a decade after German unification and other political and social transformations in Europe, evidence of the specificities of the linkage between social change and individual development is still scarce. From the new wave of studies on social change and individual development I have presented, it seems advisable to work with a combined strategy of comparative studies and intervention trials.

As the very nature of rapid social change limits replication, comparative research on similar phenomena of social change across national borders becomes important. As in cross-cultural research, this can be a way to become aware of commonalities and differences in the processes of social change. The Jena group, for example, has had joint discussions and conducted analyses with British researchers (Bynner & Silbereisen, 2000). Collaborations with colleagues from Eastern Europe also appear very attractive for researchers interested in social change (e.g., Titma & Tuma, 2005). Comparative studies seem particularly fruitful because many of the social and political transformations – for example, in Eastern Europe – constitute natural experiments that allow us to disentangle the effects of social change on human development.

Intervention trials, on the other hand, will allow us to corroborate evidence that now only comes from correlational studies by experimental control. Here, I want to address two issues. A first step would be an authoritative research synthesis with a view to intervention following the Campbell Collaboration protocol (www.campbellcollaboration.org). We need a clearer picture of what is known in general and of what effects can be expected from interventions into the likely mechanisms resulting in change of individual adjustments. A particular emphasis should be given to the mediating and moderating factors involved in the linkage between social change and individual development.

Some initial promising steps can already be noted. Among them, approaches that foster individual strengths and positive behaviors, rather than avoiding risks and problem behaviors, are particularly attractive. This is consonant with concepts put forward by Lerner and colleagues (Lerner, Anderson, Balsano, Dowling, & Bobek, 2003) on applied developmental science and positive youth development, and is reminiscent of other approaches to assess and improve so-called developmental assets (Benson, 2002). Some existing programs aiming at establishing prosocial bonds, fostering autonomous motivation, empowering individual and collective agency, or strengthening entrepreneurial orientation (Catalano, Hawkins, Berglund, Pollard, & Arthur, 2002; Schmitt-Rodermund & Schröder, 2004) may serve as blueprints for a type of intervention that provides positive experiences and social recognition in young people's dealing with issues related to social change. The idea is not to provide models of what is right, but to strengthen resources such as self-efficacy and initiative, and to develop a positive attitude towards change as an essential part of human life.

Acknowledgements

Obviously, this report rests on the shoulders of many in my research group, veterans and novices. Most of them are mentioned in the reference list. I want to mention especially Claudia M. Haase and Verona E. Christmas-Best who collaborated on this piece.

References

Ardelt, M. (1998). Social crisis and individual growth: The long-term effects of the Great Depression. *Journal of Aging Studies*, *12*, 291–314.

Arnett, J.J. (2000). Emerging adulthood: A theory of development from the late teens through the twenties. *American Psychologist*, *55*, 469–480.

Bandura, A. (1997). *Self-efficacy: The exercise of control*. New York: Freeman.

Benson, P.L. (2002). Adolescent development in social and community context: A program of research. *New Directions for Youth Development*, *95*, 123–147.

Best, H. (2003). Der langfristige Wandel politischer Eliten in Europa 1867–2000: Auf dem Weg der Konvergenz? [The long-term change of political elites in Europe 1867–2000: On the way of convergence?]. In S. Hradil & P. Imbusch (Eds.), *Oberschichten – Eliten – Herrschende Klassen* (pp. 369–399). Opladen, Germany: Leske & Budrich.

Bronfenbrenner, U. (1994). Ecological models of human development. In T. Husen & T.N. Postlethwaite (Eds.), *The international encyclopedia of education* (2nd ed., pp. 1643–1647). New York: Elsevier.

Bynner, J., & Silbereisen, R.K. (Eds.). (2000). *Adversity and challenge in life in the New Germany and England*. Hampshire, UK: Macmillan.

Calhoun, C. (1992). Social change. In E.F. Borgatta, & M.L. Borgatta (Eds.), *Encyclopedia of sociology* (Vol. 4, pp. 1807–1812). New York: Macmillan.

Catalano, R.F., Hawkins, J.D., Berglund, L., Pollard, J.A., & Arthur, M.W. (2002). Prevention science and positive youth development: Competitive or cooperative frameworks? *Journal of Adolescent Health*, *31*, 230–239.

Crockett, L.J., & Silbereisen, R.K. (Eds.). (2000). *Negotiating adolescence in times of social change*. Cambridge, MA: Cambridge University Press.

Elder, G.H. (1974). *Children of the Great Depression: Social change in life experience*. Chicago, IL: University of Chicago Press.

Elder, G.H. (1998). The life course as developmental theory. *Child Development*, *69*, 1–12.

Elder, G.H., & Caspi, A. (1990). Studying lives in a changing society: Sociological and personological explorations. In R.A. Zucker, A.I. Rabin, J. Aronoff, & S.J. Frank (Eds.), *Personality structure in the life course* (pp. 276–322). New York: Springer.

Forkel, I., & Silbereisen, R.K. (2001). Family economic hardship and depressed mood among young adolescents from former East and West Germany. [Special Issue on families and development in childhood and adolescence: Germany before and after reunification] *American Behavioral Scientist*, *44*, 1955–1971.

Heckhausen, J., & Schulz, R. (1995). A life-span theory of control. *Psychological Review*, *102*, 284–304.

Juang, L.P., & Silbereisen, R.K. (2001). Family transitions for young adult females in the context of a changed Germany: Timing, sequence, and duration. [Special Issue on families and development in childhood and adolescence: Germany before and after reunification] *American Behavioral Scientist*, *44*, 1899–1917.

Juang, L.P., Silbereisen, R.K., & Wiesner, M. (1999). Predictors for leaving the parental home in young adults raised in former East and West Germany in 1996: A replication and extension of a 1991 study. *Journal of Marriage and the Family*, *61*, 505–515.

Kohli, M., Künemund, H., Motel, A., & Szydlik, M. (2000). Families apart? Intergenerational transfers in East and West Germany. In S. Arber & C. Attias-Donfut (Eds.), *The myth of generational conflict* (pp. 88–99). London: Routledge.

Kornadt, H.-J. (1996). Erziehung und Bildung im Transformationsprozeß [Education in the process of transformation]. In S.H. Hormuth, W.R. Heinz, H.-J. Kornadt, H. Sydow, & G. Trommsdorff (Eds.), *Individuelle Entwicklung, Bildung und Berufsverläufe* (pp. 201–272). Opladen, Germany: Leske & Budrich.

Larson, R.W. (2000). Toward a psychology of positive youth development. *American Psychologist*, *55*, 170–183.

Latané, B. (1996). Strength from weakness: The fate of opinion minorities in spatially distributed groups. In E. Witte & J.H. Davis (Eds.), *Understanding group behavior: Consensual action by small groups* (Vol. 1, pp. 193–219). Mahwah, NJ: Lawrence Erlbaum Associates Inc.

Lazarus, R.S. (1998). *Fifty years of the research and theory of R.S. Lazarus: An analysis of historical and perennial issues*. Mahwah, NJ: Lawrence Erlbaum Associates Inc.

Lazarus, R.S., & Folkman, S. (1984). *Stress, appraisal, and coping*. New York: Springer.

Lerner, R.M., Anderson, P.M., Balsano, A.B., Dowling, E.M., & Bobek, D.L. (2003). Applied developmental science of positive human development. In I.B. Weiner (Series Ed.) & R.M. Lerner, M.A. Easterbrooks, & J. Mistry (Vol. Eds.), *Handbook of psychology: Vol. 6 Developmental psychology* (pp. 535–558). New York: Wiley.

Little, T.D., Lopez, D.F., Oettingen, G., & Baltes, P.B. (2001). A comparative-longitudinal study of action-control beliefs and school performance: On the role of context. *International Journal of Behavioral Development*, *25*, 237–245.

Pinquart, M., & Silbereisen, R.K. (2004). Human development in times of social change: Theoretical considerations and research needs. *International Journal of Behavioral Development*, *28*, 289–298.

Pinquart, M., Silbereisen, R.K., & Juang, L.P. (2004a). Moderating effects of adolescents' self-efficacy beliefs on psychological responses to social change. *Journal of Adolescent Research*, *19*, 340–359.

Pinquart, M., Silbereisen, R.K., & Juang, L.P. (2004b). Changes in psychological distress among East German adolescents facing German unification: The role of commitment to the old system and of self-efficacy beliefs. *Youth and Society*, *36*, 77–101.

Reitzle, M., & Silbereisen, R.K. (2000a). Adapting to social change: Adolescents' values in Eastern and Western Germany (pp. 123–152). In J. Bynner & R.K. Silbereisen (Eds.), *Adversity and challenge in life in the New Germany and England*. Hampshire, UK: Macmillan.

Reitzle, M., & Silbereisen, R.K. (2000b). The timing of adolescents' school-to-work transition in the course of social change: The example of German unification. *Swiss Journal of Psychology*, *59*, 240–255.

Rutter, M. (1994). Stress research: Accomplishments and tasks ahead. In R.J. Haggerty, L.R. Sherrod, N. Garmezy, & M. Rutter (Eds.), *Stress, risk, and resilience in children and adolescents* (pp. 354–385). Cambridge, MA: Cambridge University Press.

Schmitt, M., Maes, J., & Schmal, A. (1998). Ungerechtigkeitserleben im Vereinigungsprozeß: Folgen für das emotionale Befinden und die seelische Gesundheit [Perceived injustice in the process of unification: Consequences for well-being and mental health]. In M. Schmitt & L. Montada (Eds.), *Gerechtigkeitserleben im wiedervereinigten Deutschland* (pp. 169–212). Opladen, Germany: Leske & Budrich.

Schmitt-Rodermund, E., & Schröder, E. (2004). *Wer hat das Zeug zum Unternehmer? Training zur Förderung unternehmerischer Potenziale* [Who can be an entrepreneur? A training program to foster entrepreneurial potentials]. Göttingen, Germany: Hogrefe.

Schmitt-Rodermund, E., & Silbereisen, R.K. (2000). Adolescent immigrants' well-being: The case of ethnic German immigrants in Germany. *International Journal of Group Tensions*, *29*, 79–100.

Schühly, G.S.J., & Müller, U. (1997). *Secularization in Eastern and Western Europe: Results from the ISSP 1991 Survey on Religion in 10 West and East European Nations*. ZUMA-Arbeitsbericht 4.

Segerstrom, S.C., & Miller, G.E. (2004). Psychological stress and the human immune system: A meta-analytic study of 30 years of inquiry. *Psychological Bulletin*, *130*, 601–630.

Silbereisen, R.K. (2000). German unification and adolescents' developmental timetables: Continuities and discontinuities. In L.J. Crockett & R.K. Silbereisen (Eds.), *Negotiating adolescence in times of social change* (pp. 104–122). Cambridge, MA: Cambridge University Press.

Silbereisen, R.K., Reitzle, M., & Haase, C.M. (2005). *Transitions to marriage and first parenthood under conditions of social change*. Unpublished manuscript.

Silbereisen, R.K., Reitzle, M., & Juang, L. (2002). Time and change: Psychosocial transitions in German young adults 1991 and 1996. In L. Pulkkinen & A. Caspi (Eds.), *Paths to successful development: Personality in the life course* (pp. 227–254). Cambridge, MA: Cambridge University Press.

Silbereisen, R.K., Walper, S., & Albrecht. H.T. (1990). Families experiencing income loss and economic hardship: Antecedents of adolescents' problem behavior. In V. McLoyd & C. Flanagan (Eds.), *Risk and protective factors in children and adolescents' response to economic crises and deprivation. New Directions in Child Development* (pp. 27–47). San Francisco, CA: Jossey-Bass.

Silbereisen, R.K., & Wiesner, M. (2002). Lessons from research on the consequences of German unification: Continuity and discontinuity of self-efficacy and the timing of psychosocial transitions. *Applied Psychology: An International Review, 51*, 291–317.

Sonderforschungbereich 580. (Ed.). (2004). *Gesellschaftliche Entwicklungen nach dem Systemumbruch. Diskontinuität, Tradition, Strukturbildung* [Societal developments following the turnabout of the political system. Discontinuity, tradition, formation of new structures] Research consortium proposal re-funded by the German Research Foundation. University of Jena.

Stangor, C. (2004). *Social groups in action and interaction*. New York: Psychology Press.

Sydow, H., Wagner, C., Jülisch, B.-R., & Kauf, H. (1999). Future oriented control and subjective well-being of students in East- and West-Berlin. In R.K. Silbereisen & A. von Eye (Eds.), *Growing up in times of social change* (pp. 107–130). Berlin: de Gruyter.

Titma, M., & Tuma, N.B. (2005). Human agency in the transition from communism: Perspectives on the life course and aging. In K.W. Schaie & G.H. Elder (Eds.), *Historical influences on lives and aging* (pp. 108–143). New York: Springer.

Triandis, H.C., Kashima, Y., Shimada, E., & Villareal, M. (1986). Acculturation indices as a means of confirming cultural differences. *International Journal of Psychology, 21*, 43–70.

Vondracek, F.W., Reitzle, M., & Silbereisen, R.K. (1999). The influence of changing contexts and historical time on the timing of initial vocational choices. In R.K. Silbereisen & A. von Eye (Eds.), *Growing up in times of social change* (pp. 151–169). New York: de Gruyter.

Vondracek, F.W., Silbereisen, R.K., Reitzle, M., & Wiesner, M. (1999). Vocational preferences of early adolescents: Their development in social context. *Journal of Adolescent Research, 14*, 267–288.

Wright, S.C. (2001). Strategic collective action: Social psychology and social change. In R. Brown & S.L. Gaertner (Eds.), *Blackwell handbook of social psychology: Intergroup processes* (pp. 409–430). Oxford, UK: Blackwell.

Zapf, W. (1996). Zwei Geschwindigkeiten in Ost- und Westdeutschland. In M. Diewald & K.U. Mayer (Eds.), *Zwischenbilanz der Wiedervereinigung, Strukturwandel und Mobilität im Transformationsprozeß* (pp. 317–328). Opladen, Germany: Leske & Budrich.

Author index

Subject index

For Product Safety Concerns and Information please contact our EU representative GPSR@taylorandfrancis.com Taylor & Francis Verlag GmbH, Kaufingerstraße 24, 80331 München, Germany